DATE DUE

			PRINTED IN U.S.A.

SOMETHING ABOUT THE AUTHOR

ISSN 0276-816X

SOMETHING ABOUT THE AUTHOR

**Facts and Pictures about Authors
and Illustrators of Books for Young People**

EDITED BY
ANNE COMMIRE

VOLUME 55

Gale Research Inc.
**BOOK TOWER
DETROIT, MICHIGAN
48226**

Editor: Anne Commire

Associate Editors: Agnes Garrett, Helga P. McCue

Senior Assistant Editor: Dianne H. Anderson

Assistant Editors: Elisa Ann Ferraro, Eunice L. Petrini, Linda Shedd

Sketchwriters: Marguerite Feitlowitz, Mimi H. Hutson, Dieter Miller

Researcher: Catherine Ruello

Editorial Assistants: Catherine Coray, Joanne J. Ferraro, Marja T. Hiltunen,
Evelyn Johnson, June Lee, Karen Walker

Permissions Assistant: Susan Pfanner

Production Manager: Mary Beth Trimper

External Production Assistants: Linda Davis, Anthony J. Scolaro

Internal Production Associate: Louise Gagné

Art Director: Arthur Chartow

Special acknowledgment is due to the members of the *Something about the Author Autobiography Series* staff
who assisted in the preparation of this volume.

Computerized photocomposition by
Typographics, Incorporated
Kansas City, Missouri

Printed in the United States

Contents

Introduction   ix

Illustrations Index   183

Acknowledgments   xv

Author Index   203

A

Addams, Charles (Samuel)   1912-1988....................1

Atkinson, Allen G.   1953(?)-1987
   Obituary Notice................................... 10

Atticus
   see Davies, Hunter.............................. 21

B

Bachman, Richard
   see King, Stephen (Edwin)................. 61

Barnes, Michael   1934-   10

Benham, Mary Lile   1914-   11

Betancourt, Jeanne   1941-   12

Bridges, Laurie
   see Bruck, Lorraine 19

Bronowski, Jacob   1908-1974 15

Brothers Hildebrandt, The
   see Hildebrandt, Greg........................ 33
   see also Hildebrandt, Tim(othy) 43

Brown, Cassie   1919-1986 18

Bruck, Lorraine   1921-   19

Burleigh, Robert   1936-   20

C

Captain W. E. Johns
   see Johns, W(illiam) E(arl) 47

Carlyon, Richard 20

Carr, Mary Jane   1899-1988
   Obituary Notice................................... 21

Cermak, Martin
   see Duchacek, Ivo D(uka) 24

D

Davies, Hunter   1936-   21

Duchacek, Ivo D(uka)   1913-1988
   Obituary Notice................................... 24

Duka, Ivo
see Duchacek, Ivo D(uka) 24

Dumas, Jacqueline (Claudia)   1946-   24

E

Eager, Frances (Elisabeth Stuart)   1940-1978
   Obituary Notice................................... 25

Earle, William
   see Johns, W(illiam) E(arl) 47

Early, Jon
   see Johns, W(illiam) E(arl) 47

Elwood, Ann   1931-   25

Ernst, Lisa Campbell   1957-   25

F

Flesch, Yolande (Catarina)   1950-   26

Frank, Daniel B.   1956-   26

G

Goode, Stephen   1943-   28

Greene, Yvonne
   see Flesch, Yolande (Catarina) 26

H

Hamilton, Mary (E.)   1927-   28

Hanna, Nell(ie L.)   1908-   29

Harris, Steven Michael   1957-   29

Henbest, Nigel   1951-   30

Henderson, Kathy   1949-   31

Herriot, James
   see Wight, James Alfred 162

Hest, Amy 1950- 33

Hildebrandt, Greg 1939- 33

Hildebrandt, Tim(othy) 1939- 43

Hildebrandt, The Brothers
    see Hildebrandt, Greg......................... 33
    see Hildebrandt, Tim........................... 43

Hildebrandts, The
    see Hildebrandt, Greg......................... 33
    see also Hildebrandt, Tim(othy) 43

Hopf, Alice
    see Hopf, Alice (Martha) L(ightner) 47

Hopf, Alice (Martha) L(ightner) 1904-1988
    Obituary Notice...................................... 47

J

Johns, W(illiam) E(arl) 1893-1968 47

Judy, Stephen
    see Tchudi, Stephen N. 150

Judy, Stephen N.
    see Tchudi, Stephen N. 150

K

Kiddell-Monroe, Joan 1908- 58

King, Stephen (Edwin) 1947- 61

Klein, Robin 1936- 77

L

Laski, Marghanita 1915-1988 78

Laurie, Rona 1916- 80

Lawrence, R(onald) D(ouglas) 1921- 81

Lawson, Joan 1906- 82

Leaf, Margaret P. 1909(?)-1988
    Obituary Notice...................................... 83

LeVert, (William) John 1946- 83

Lightner, A. M.
    see Hopf, Alice (Martha) L(ightner) 47

Lightner, Alice
    see Hopf, Alice (Martha) L(ightner) 47

Lobel, Anita (Kempler) 1934- 84

Lobel, Arnold (Stark) 1933-1987 89

M

MacEwen, Gwendolyn (Margaret) 1941-1987
    Obituary Notice.................................... 107

Mayerson, Evelyn Wilde 1935- 108

McHugh, (Berit) Elisabet 1941- 108

McKendrick, Melveena (Christine) 1941- 109

Meadmore, Susan
    see Sallis, Susan (Diana)................... 145

Meier, Minta 1906- 109

Michael, Manfred
    see Winterfeld, Henry....................... 175

Miller, Mary
    see Northcott, (William) Cecil 123

Mowat, Farley (McGill) 1921- 109

N

Nakatani, Chiyoko 1930-1981............ 121

Nell
    see Hanna, Nell(ie L.)....................... 129

Northcott, (William) Cecil 1902-1987
    Obituary Notice.................................... 123

O

Ormerod, Jan(ette Louise) 1946- 123

Osborne, Mary Pope 1949- 125

P

Peck, Richard 1934- 126

Pollack, Merrill S. 1924-1988
    Obituary Notice.................................... 138

R

Rawding, F(rederick) W(illiam) 1930- 138

Rayner, William 1929- 139

Reigot, Betty Polisar 1924- 140

Rodd, Kathleen Tennant 1912-1988
    Obituary Notice.................................... 140

Rogers, Jean 1919- 140

Root, Phyllis 1949- 141

Rosenberg, Maxine B(erta) 1939- 143

Royds, Caroline 1953- 144

Russell, Sarah
  see Laski, Marghanita 78

S

Sallis, Susan (Diana) 1929- 145

Scott, Jane (Harrington) 1931- 146

Selman, LaRue W. 1927- 148

Smith, Betsy Covington 1937- 149

Stearns, Monroe (Mather) 1913-1987
  Obituary Notice.............................. 149

Stefanik, Alfred T. 1939- 150

T

Tchudi, Stephen N. 1942- 150

Temple, Arthur
  see Northcott, (William) Cecil 123

Tennant, Kylie
  see Rodd, Kathleen Tennant........................... 140

Thompson, Julian F(rancis) 1927- 152

Thomson, David (Robert Alexander) 1914-1988
  Obituary Notice............................ 153

Tolliver, Ruby C(hangos) 1922- 154

Torgersen, Don Arthur 1934- 155

Townsend, Sue 1946- 158

V

Vinton, Iris 1906(?)-1988
  Obituary Notice............................... 162

W

Wesley, Alison
  see Barnes, Michael 10

Wicker, Ireene 1905(?)-1987
  Obituary Notice............................... 162

Wight, James Alfred 1916- 162

William, Earle
  see Johns, W(illiam) E(arl) 47

Wilson, Budge 1927- 174

Wilson, Marjorie
  see Wilson, Budge.............................. 174

Winterfeld, Henry 1901- 175

Wittanen, Etolin 1907- 176

Y

Yadin, Yigael 1917-1984 177

Introduction

As the only ongoing reference series that deals with the lives and works of authors and illustrators of children's books, *Something about the Author (SATA)* is a unique source of information. The *SATA* series includes not only well-known authors and illustrators whose books are most widely read, but also those less prominent people whose works are just coming to be recognized. *SATA* is often the only readily available information source for less well-known writers or artists. You'll find *SATA* informative and entertaining whether you are:

—a student in junior high school (or perhaps one to two grades higher or lower) who needs information for a book report or some other assignment for an English class;

—a children's librarian who is searching for the answer to yet another question from a young reader or collecting background material to use for a story hour;

—an English teacher who is drawing up an assignment for your students or gathering information for a book talk;

—a student in a college of education or library science who is studying children's literature and reference sources in the field;

—a parent who is looking for a new way to interest your child in reading something more than the school curriculum prescribes;

—an adult who enjoys children's literature for its own sake, knowing that a good children's book has no age limits.

Scope

In *SATA* you will find detailed information about authors and illustrators who span the full time range of children's literature, from early figures like John Newbery and L. Frank Baum to contemporary figures like Judy Blume and Richard Peck. Authors in the series represent primarily English-speaking countries, particularly the United States, Canada, and the United Kingdom. Also included, however, are authors from around the world whose works are available in English translation, for example: from France, Jean and Laurent De Brunhoff; from Italy, Emanuele Luzzati; from the Netherlands, Jaap ter Haar; from Germany, James Krüss; from Norway, Babbis Friis-Baastad; from Japan, Toshiko Kanzawa; from the Soviet Union, Kornei Chukovsky; from Switzerland, Alois Carigiet, to name only a few. Also appearing in *SATA* are Newbery medalists from Hendrik Van Loon (1922) to Russell Freedman (1988). The writings represented in *SATA* include those created intentionally for children and young adults as well as those written for a general audience and known to interest younger readers. These writings cover the spectrum from picture books, humor, folk and fairy tales, animal stories, mystery and adventure, science fiction and fantasy, historical fiction, poetry and nonsense verse, to drama, biography, and nonfiction.

Information Features

In *SATA* you will find full-length entries that are being presented in the series for the first time. This volume, for example, marks the first full-length appearance of Charles Addams, Jeanne Betancourt, Robin Klein, Jan Ormerod, Maxine B. Rosenberg, Stephen N. Tchudi, and Sue Townsend.

Obituaries have been included in *SATA* since Volume 20. An Obituary is intended not only as a death notice but also as a concise view of a person's life and work. Obituaries may appear for persons who have entries in earlier *SATA* volumes, as well as for people who have not yet appeared in the series. In this volume Obituaries mark the recent deaths of Allen G. Atkinson, Mary Jane Carr, Ivo D. Duchacek, and Kathleen Tennant Rodd, among others.

Revised Entries

Since Volume 25, each *SATA* volume also includes newly revised and updated entries for a selection of *SATA* listees (usually four to six) who remain of interest to today's readers and who have been active enough to require extensive revision of their earlier biographies. For example, when Beverly Cleary first appeared in *SATA* Volume 2, she was the author of twenty-one books for children and young adults and the recipient of numerous awards. By the time her updated sketch appeared in Volume 43 (a span of fifteen years), this creator of the indefatigable Ramona Quimby and other memorable characters had produced a dozen new titles and garnered nearly fifty additional awards, including the 1984 Newbery Medal.

The entry for a given biographee may be revised as often as there is substantial new information to provide. In this volume, look for revised entries on Stephen King, Anita Lobel, Arnold Lobel, Farley Mowat, and Richard Peck.

Illustrations

While the textual information in *SATA* is its primary reason for existing, photographs and illustrations not only enliven the text but are an integral part of the information that *SATA* provides. Illustrations and text are wedded in such a special way in children's literature that artists and their works naturally occupy a prominent place among *SATA*'s listees. The illustrators that you'll find in the series include such past masters of children's book illustration as Randolph Caldecott, Walter Crane, Arthur Rackham, and Ernest H. Shepard, as well as such noted contemporary artists as Maurice Sendak, Edward Gorey, Tomie de Paola, and Margot Zemach. There are Caldecott medalists from Dorothy Lathrop (the first recipient in 1938) to John Schoenherr (the latest winner in 1988); cartoonists like Charles Schulz ("Peanuts"), Walt Kelly ("Pogo"), Hank Ketcham ("Dennis the Menace"), and Georges Rémi ("Tintin"); photographers like Jill Krementz, Tana Hoban, Bruce McMillan, and Bruce Curtis; and filmmakers like Walt Disney, Alfred Hitchcock, and Steven Spielberg.

In more than a dozen years of recording the metamorphosis of children's literature from the printed page to other media, *SATA* has become something of a repository of photographs that are unique in themselves and exist nowhere else as a group, particularly many of the classics of motion picture and stage history and photographs that have been specially loaned to us from private collections.

Indexes

Each *SATA* volume provides a cumulative index in two parts: first, the Illustrations Index, arranged by the name of the illustrator, gives the number of the volume and page where the illustrator's work appears in the current volume as well as all preceding volumes in the series; second, the Author Index gives the number of the volume in which a person's biographical sketch, Brief Entry, or Obituary appears in the current volume as well as all preceding volumes in the series. These indexes also include references to authors and illustrators who appear in *Yesterday's Authors of Books for Children* (described in detail below). Beginning with Volume 36, the *SATA* Author Index provides cross-references to authors who are included in *Children's Literature Review*.

Starting with Volume 42, you will also find cross-references to authors who are included in the *Something about the Author Autobiography Series* (described in detail below).

Character Index

If you're like many readers, the names of fictional characters may pop more easily into your mind than the names of the authors or illustrators who created them: Snow White, Charlotte the Spider, the Cat in the Hat, Peter Pan, Mary Poppins, Winnie-the-Pooh, Brer Rabbit, Little Toot, Charlie Bucket, Lassie, Rip Van Winkle, Bartholomew Cubbins—the list could go on and on. But who invented them? Now these characters, and several thousand others, can lead you to the *SATA* and *YABC* entries on the lives and works of their creators.

First published in Volume 50, the Character Index provides a broad selection of characters from books and other media—movies, plays, comic strips, cartoons, etc.—created by listees who have appeared in all the published volumes of *SATA* and *YABC*. This index gives the character name, followed by a *"See"* reference indicating the name of the creator and the number of the *SATA* or *YABC* volume in which the creator's bio-bibliographical entry can be found. As new *SATA* volumes are prepared, additional characters are included in the cumulative Character Index and published annually in *SATA*. (The cumulative Illustrations and Author Indexes still appear in each *SATA* volume.)

It would be impossible for the Character Index to include every important character created by *SATA* and *YABC* listees. (Several hundred important characters might be taken from Dickens alone, for example.) Therefore, the *SATA* editors have selected those characters that are best known and thus most likely to interest *SATA* users. Realizing that some of your favorite characters may not appear in this index, the editors invite you to suggest additional names. With your help, the editors hope to make the Character Index a uniquely useful reference tool for you.

What a *SATA* Entry Provides

Whether you're already familiar with the *SATA* series or just getting acquainted, you will want to be aware of the kind of information that an entry provides. In every *SATA* entry the editors attempt to give as complete a picture of the person's life and work as possible. In some cases that full range of information may simply be unavailable, or a biographee may choose not to reveal complete personal details. The information that the editors attempt to provide in every entry is arranged in the following categories:

1. The "head" of the entry gives

   —the most complete form of the name,
   —any part of the name not commonly used, included in parentheses,
   —birth and death dates, if known; a (?) indicates a discrepancy in published sources,
   —pseudonyms or name variants under which the person has had books published or is publicly known, in parentheses in the second line.

2. "Personal" section gives

   —date and place of birth and death,
   —parents' names and occupations,
   —name of spouse, date of marriage, and names of children,
   —educational institutions attended, degrees received, and dates,
   —religious and political affiliations,
   —agent's name and address,
   —home and/or office address.

3. "Career" section gives

   —name of employer, position, and dates for each career post,
   —military service,
   —memberships,
   —awards and honors.

4. "Writings" section gives

   —title, first publisher and date of publication, and illustration information for each book written; revised editions and other significant editions for books with particularly long publishing histories; genre, when known.

5. "Adaptations" section gives

   —title, major performers, producer, and date of all known reworkings of an author's material in another medium, like movies, filmstrips, television, recordings, plays, etc.

6. "Sidelights" section gives

> —commentary on the life or work of the biographee either directly from the person (and often written specifically for the *SATA* entry), or gathered from biographies, diaries, letters, interviews, or other published sources.

7. "For More Information See" section gives

> —books, feature articles, films, plays, and reviews in which the biographee's life or work has been treated.

How a *SATA* Entry Is Compiled

A *SATA* entry progresses through a series of steps. If the biographee is living, the *SATA* editors try to secure information directly from him or her through a questionnaire. From the information that the biographee supplies, the editors prepare an entry, filling in any essential missing details with research. The author or illustrator is then sent a copy of the entry to check for accuracy and completeness.

If the biographee is deceased or cannot be reached by questionnaire, the *SATA* editors examine a wide variety of published sources to gather information for an entry. Biographical sources are searched with the aid of Gale's *Biography and Genealogy Master Index*. Bibliographic sources like the *National Union Catalog*, the *Cumulative Book Index*, *American Book Publishing Record*, and the *British Museum Catalogue* are consulted, as are book reviews, feature articles, published interviews, and material sometimes obtained from the biographee's family, publishers, agent, or other associates.

For each entry presented in *SATA*, the editors also attempt to locate a photograph of the biographee as well as representative illustrations from his or her books. After surveying the available books which the biographee has written and/or illustrated, and then making a selection of appropriate photographs and illustrations, the editors request permission of the current copyright holders to reprint the material. In the case of older books for which the copyright may have passed through several hands, even locating the current copyright holder is often a long and involved process.

We invite you to examine the entire *SATA* series, starting with this volume. Described below are some of the people in Volume 55 that you may find particularly interesting.

Highlights of This Volume

GREG HILDEBRANDT......began drawing before he was two years old. "As far back as I can remember, I was involved with art of one kind or another." With his identical twin brother, he designed sets, made movies in high school, and spent several years in the commercial art field. In 1975, the Hildebrandts discovered an invitation, on the back of a J. R. R. Tolkien calendar, for artists to submit their drawings for next year's calendar. They were hired and thus began their careers as illustrators. Besides doing joint illustrations for books, Greg also illustrated such classics as *Dracula, Peter Pan,* and *Phantom of the Opera*. He is a diligent worker, averaging ten to twelve hours a day, six days a week, year round. "For me, art is my life. It is the center of my being....It is absolutely necessary to sustain my life. The act of living by itself is not enough."

TIM HILDEBRANDT......was born five minutes after his brother, Greg. Thereafter, Tim shared identical needs, interests, and a precocious artistic ability with his twin. They enjoyed the Disney films and science-fiction movies of the 1950s, even skipping high school graduation to attend a movie. "The outstanding influences on me," says Tim, "were the animated films of Walt Disney, such as 'Snow White and the Seven Dwarfs,' 'Pinocchio,' 'Fantasia,' and 'Bambi.' " Together the Hildebrandt brothers made animated and documentary films until they turned their attention to illustrations. "During the 1970s, my twin brother and I created hundreds of illustrations for books, magazines, and advertising." By the early 1980s, however, the brothers began to work independently. Tim's favorite medium is "acrylic. However, I do use watercolor and pen-and-ink. On very rare occasions I have used oils."

STEPHEN KING......went to every horror and science-fiction movie he could cram into a Saturday in his hometown of Portland, Maine. Always fascinated with the macabre, King's first novel, *Carrie,* "lives out a nightmare that all kids go through. Not being accepted....If I had any thesis to offer, it was that high school is a place of almost bottomless conservatism and bigotry." King's popularity has grown enormously since his first book; he is the only author ever to have three different books simultaneously on the *New York Times'* bestseller list: *Firestarter, The Dead Zone,* and *The Shining.* Known as the author of nightmares, King admits to having his own share of nocturnal fears: "At night, when I go to bed, I still am at pains to be sure that my legs are under the blankets...because if a cool hand ever reached out from under the bed...I might scream to wake the dead....The thing under my bed waiting to grab my ankle isn't real. I know that, and I also know that if I'm careful to keep my foot under the covers, it will never be able to grab my ankle."

ARNOLD LOBEL......lived "through a rather unhappy and neurotic childhood," until he "finally escaped to college." As a young art student at Pratt Institute, Lobel discovered that book illustration was his specialty. His first children's book was published by Harper & Row. "Reading my first contract, I discovered that if I wrote my own stories I would not have to share the royalty with another, which was a very good incentive to become a writer." Of the numerous books that Lobel wrote and illustrated, many were given awards, including the prestigious Caldecott Medal for *Fables.* "The creation of most picture books is a matter of daily, patient, simple-minded effort. To see a book appearing in front of one's eyes where before there was nothing is a pleasure and a joy."

FARLEY MOWAT......grew up "an outcast....I had no interest in sports whatsoever....I was a passionate bird watcher and, to cap it all off, a writer. My teachers thought this was great, but the other kids were pretty suspicious of a boy who spent most of his time on poetry." Writing also sustained him through World War II. *The Dog That Wouldn't Be,* a book about his childhood, was written "amid the bombs, grenades, strafing, death and dying." Years later, a book about his wartime experiences, *And No Birds Sang,* recounted the horrors he had seen. Immediately after the war, he "sought out solitude" in Saskatchewan and the Arctic. After living for two years with the Eskimos, Mowat wrote *People of the Deer,* which earned him the reputation of a crusader. His next book, *Never Cry Wolf,* was the result of a two-year study of a family of wolves. Mowat, devoted to preserving our environment, documents the horrors routinely inflicted on wildlife. "We must develop a new ethos whereby we apply the same morality to other forms of life that we apply to our own. There is no difference in my mind that animals feel everything we feel."

RICHARD PECK......was born "in *middle* Middle America." There he learned the art of storytelling from "old truckers and farmers and railroaders" who hung out at his father's Phillips 66 gas station. As a teenager in the 1950s, Peck "grubbed for grades, yearned for the scholarship, dreaded Korea, and feared the formless future." He won the college scholarship, and graduated from DePauw University four years later, just in time to serve his mandatory two-year army stint in Germany instead of Korea. There he was "a ghost writer for chaplains (all denominations)." His army career over, Peck found employment as a teacher, "got terribly involved with the kids, and that led on to writing for them." Today Peck is a popular writer of novels for young adults who are "the most important people in my life. In every one of my novels, somebody has to grow up. That isn't true of my readers. Growing up is optional for them. They can go along with the gang.... they ought to know that, if you are going to do anything in this world, you will be doing it on your own, just as I have to write a novel alone."

JAMES ALFRED WIGHT......was born "an only child, but I had the good luck to be born into a household which was full of books so I was never lonely....At an early age three things were implanted in my character: a love of animals, reading and the countryside. It is small wonder I am a happy man." Wight's love of animals led to a career as a veterinarian, "driving from farm to farm across the roof of England with a growing conviction that I was a privileged person." After twenty-five years as a dedicated country vet, fifty-year-old Wight sat down and wrote a book about his experiences, *If Only They Could Talk,* under the pseudonym James Herriot. In America his first two books collected under one title, *All Creatures Great and Small* was an instant success, both as a book and as a movie. Despite success, Wight is still a working vet, "in this beautiful district, having the great pleasure of being associated with animals. Oh, aye, it's been a marvelous life."

These are only a few of the authors and illustrators that you'll find in this volume. We hope you find all the entries in *SATA* both interesting and useful.

Yesterday's Authors of Books for Children

In a two-volume companion set to *SATA, Yesterday's Authors of Books for Children (YABC)* focuses on early authors and illustrators, from the beginnings of children's literature through 1960, whose books are still being read by children today. Here you will find "old favorites" like Hans Christian Andersen, J. M. Barrie, Kenneth Grahame, Betty MacDonald, A. A. Milne, Beatrix Potter, Samuel Clemens, Kate Greenaway, Rudyard Kipling, Robert Louis Stevenson, and many more.

Similar in format to *SATA, YABC* features bio-bibliographical entries that are divided into information categories such as Personal, Career, Writings, and Sidelights. The entries are further enhanced by book illustrations, author photos, movie stills, and many rare old photographs.

In Volume 2 you will find cumulative indexes to the authors and to the illustrations that appear in *YABC*. These listings can also be located in the *SATA* cumulative indexes.

By exploring both volumes of *YABC,* you will discover a special group of more than seventy authors and illustrators who represent some of the best in children's literature—individuals whose timeless works continue to delight children and adults of all ages. Other authors and illustrators from early children's literature are listed in *SATA,* starting with Volume 15.

Something about the Author Autobiography Series

You can complement the information in *SATA* with the *Something about the Author Autobiography Series (SAAS),* which provides autobiographical essays written by important current authors and illustrators of books for children and young adults. In every volume of *SAAS* you will find about twenty specially commissioned autobiographies, each accompanied by a selection of personal photographs supplied by the authors. The wide range of contemporary writers and artists who describe their lives and interests in the *Autobiography Series* includes Joan Aiken, Betsy Byars, Leonard Everett Fisher, Milton Meltzer, Maia Wojciechowska, and Jane Yolen, among others. Though the information presented in the autobiographies is as varied and unique as the authors, you can learn about the people and events that influenced these writers' early lives, how they began their careers, what problems they faced in becoming established in their professions, what prompted them to write or illustrate particular books, what they now find most challenging or rewarding in their lives, and what advice they may have for young people interested in following in their footsteps, among many other subjects.

Autobiographies included in the *SATA Autobiography Series* can be located through both the *SATA* cumulative index and the *SAAS* cumulative index, which lists not only the authors' names but also the subjects mentioned in their essays, such as titles of works and geographical and personal names.

The *SATA Autobiography Series* gives you the opportunity to view "close up" some of the fascinating people who are included in the *SATA* parent series. The combined *SATA* series makes available to you an unequaled range of comprehensive and in-depth information about the authors and illustrators of young people's literature.

Please write and tell us if we can make *SATA* even more helpful to you.

Acknowledgments

Grateful acknowledgment is made to the following publishers, authors, and artists for their kind permission to reproduce copyrighted material.

W. H. ALLEN & CO. LTD. Sidelight excerpts from *By Jove, Biggles! The Life of Captain W. E. Johns* by Peter Berresford Ellis and Piers Williams. Reprinted by permisson of W. H. Allen & Co. Ltd.

ATHENEUM PUBLISHERS. Jacket illustration by Tom Stoerrle from *To Keep an Island* by Jane Scott. Text copyright © 1983 by Jane Scott. Illustrations copyright © 1983 by Tom Stoerrle. Reprinted by permission of Atheneum Publishers.

BALLANTINE/DEL REY/FAWCETT BOOKS. Illustration by The Brothers Hildebrandt from the 1977 Tolkien calendar. Reprinted by permission of Ballantine/Del Rey/Fawcett Books.

BANTAM BOOKS, INC. Jacket illustration by Tom Galazinski from *Home Sweet Home* by Jeanne Betancourt. Illustrations copyright © 1988 by Tom Galazinski./ Cover illustration by Charles Geer from *Lost in the Barrens* by Farley Mowat. Copyright © 1956 by Farley Mowat. Copyright renewed © 1984 by Farley Mowat. Cover illustration copyright © 1982 by Bantam Books, Inc./ Cover illustration by Walt Disney Productions from *Never Cry Wolf* by Farley Mowat. Copyright © 1963, 1973 by Farley Mowat. Cover illustration copyright © 1983 by Walt Disney Productions./ Cover illustration by Paul Galdone from *The Dog Who Wouldn't Be* by Farley Mowat. Copyright © 1957 by The Curtis Publishing Co. Copyright © 1957 by Farley Mowat. Cover illustration copyright © 1980 by Bantam Books, Inc./ All reprinted by permission of Bantam Books, Inc.

THE BODLEY HEAD LTD. Illustration by Laurence Hutchins from *Flossie Teacake—Again!* by Hunter Davies. Text copyright © 1983 by Hunter Davies. Illustrations copyright © 1983 by Laurence Hutchins. Reprinted by permission of The Bodley Head Ltd.

THE BOSTON MILLS PRESS. Frontispiece photograph from Bob Atkinson's collection in *Killer in the Bush: The Great Fires of Northeastern Ontario* by Michael Barnes. Copyright © 1987 by Michael Barnes. Reprinted by permission of The Boston Mills Press.

CAEDMON. Illustration by Tim Hildebrandt from *Lilly, Willy and the Mail-Order Witch* by Othello Bach. Text copyright © 1983 by Othello Bach. Illustrations copyright © 1983 by Timothy Hildebrandt. Reprinted by permission of Caedmon.

CHILDRENS PRESS. Photograph by Lee Trail and Don Torgersen from *Elephant Herds and Rhino Horns* by Don Arthur Torgersen. Copyright © 1982 by Regensteiner Publishing Enterprises, Inc. Reprinted by permission of Childrens Press.

DELACORTE PRESS. Cover illustration by Frank Morris from *Princess Ashley* by Richard Peck. Text copyright © 1987 by Richard Peck. Illustrations copyright © 1987 by Frank Morris./ Jacket illustration by Joe Csatari from *The Burg-O-Rama Man* by Stephen Tchudi. Copyright © 1983 by Stephen Tchudi. Jacket illustration copyright © 1983 by Joe Csatari. Both reprinted by permission of Delacorte Press.

DELL PUBLISHING CO., INC. Cover illustration from *Ghosts I Have Been* by Richard Peck. Copyright © 1977 by Richard Peck./ Cover illustration from *Close Enough to Touch* by Richard Peck. Copyright © 1981 by Richard Peck./ Cover illustration from *Remembering the Good Times* by Richard Peck. Copyright © 1985 by Richard Peck./ Cover illustration from *Through a Brief Darkness* by Richard Peck. Copyright © 1973 by Richard Peck./ Cover illustration from *Father Figure* by Richard Peck. Copyright © 1978 by Richard Peck./ Cover illustration from *The Ghost Belonged to Me* by Richard Peck./ Cover illustration from *The Dreadful Future of Blossom Culp* by Richard Peck. Copyright © 1983 by Richard Peck./ Cover illustration from *Secrets of the Shopping Mall* by Richard Peck. All reprinted by permission of Dell Publishing Co., Inc.

J. M. DENT & SONS LTD. Illustration by Joan Kiddell-Monroe from *The Heroes* by Charles Kingsley. Illustrations copyright © 1963 by J. M. Dent & Sons Ltd. Reprinted by permission of J. M. Dent & Sons Ltd.

ANDRE DEUTSCH LTD. Illustration by Kathy Henderson from *Sam and the Box* by Kathy Henderson. Copyright © 1987 by Kathy Henderson. Reprinted by permission of Andre Deutsch Ltd.

DIAL BOOKS FOR YOUNG READERS. Illustration by Arnold Lobel from *More Tales of Oliver Pig* by Jean Van Leeuwen. Text copyright © 1981 by Jean Van Leeuwen. Illustration copyright by Arnold Lobel. Reprinted by permission of Dial Books for Young Readers.

FARRAR, STRAUS & GIROUX, INC. Illustration by Pauline Ellison from *The Dark Lord of Pengersick* by Richard Carlyon. Text copyright © 1976, 1980 by Richard Carlyon. Illustrations copyright © 1976 by Pauline Ellison. Reprinted by permission of Farrar, Straus & Giroux, Inc.

GREENWILLOW BOOKS. Illustration by Anita Lobel from *King Rooster, Queen Hen* by Anita Lobel. Copyright © 1975 by Anita Lobel./ Illustration by Anita Lobel from *On Market Street* by Arnold Lobel. Text copyright © 1981 by Arnold Lobel. Illustrations copyright © 1981 by Anita Lobel. Both reprinted by permission of Greenwillow Books.

HARPER & ROW, PUBLISHERS, INC. Jacket illustration by Weimer Pursell from *Biography of an Atom* by J. Bronowski and Millicent E. Selsam. Copyright © 1963 by J. Bronowski. Copyright © 1965 by J. Bronowski and Millicent E. Selsam./ Illustration by Anita Lobel from *Potatoes, Potatoes* by Anita Lobel. Copyright © 1967 by Anita Lobel./ Illustration by Anita Lobel from *Sven's Bridge* by Anita Lobel. Copyright © 1965 by Anita Lobel./ Illustration by Arnold Lobel from *The Devil and Mother Crump* by Valerie Scho Carey. Illustration copyright © 1987 by Valerie Scho Carey. Illustrations copyright © 1987 by Arnold Lobel./ Illustration by Arnold Lobel from *Frog and Toad Are Friends* by Arnold Lobel. Copyright © 1970 by Arnold Lobel./ Illustration by Arnold Lobel from *Mouse Tales* by Arnold Lobel. Copyright © 1972 by Arnold Lobel./ Illustration by Arnold Lobel from *On the Day Peter Stuyvesant Sailed into Town* by Arnold Lobel. Copyright © 1971 by Arnold Lobel./ Illustration by Arnold Lobel from "The Elephant and His Son" in *Fables* by Arnold Lobel. Copyright © 1980 by Arnold Lobel./ Illustration by Arnold Lobel from *Frog and Toad Together* by Arnold Lobel. Copyright © 1971, 1972 by Arnold Lobel./ Illustration by Arnold Lobel from *The Book of Pigericks: Pig Limericks* by Arnold Lobel. Copyright © 1983 by Arnold Lobel./ Illustration by Arnold Lobel from *Grasshopper on the Road* by Arnold Lobel. Copyright © 1978 by Arnold Lobel./ Illustration by Arnold Lobel from *Uncle Elephant* by Arnold Lobel. Copyright © 1981 by Arnold Lobel./ Illustration by Arnold Lobel from *Mouse Soup* by Arnold Lobel. Copyright © 1977 by Arnold Lobel./ Illustration by Sue Truesdell from *Soup for Supper* by Phyllis Root. Text copyright © 1986 by Phyllis Root. Illustrations copyright © 1986 by Susan G. Truesdell./ Jacket illustration by Bob Marstall from *Secret Places of the Stairs* by Susan Sallis. Copyright © 1984 by Susan Diana Sallis. Jacket illustration copyright © 1984 by Bob Marstall. Jacket copyright © 1984 by Harper & Row, Publishers, Inc. All reprinted by permission of Harper & Row, Publishers, Inc.

HODDER & STOUGHTON LTD. Cover illustration from *Biggles Learns to Fly* by Captain W. E. Johns. Copyright by the Estate of W. E. Johns./ Illustration by Leslie Stead from *Biggles Delivers the Goods* by Captain W. E. Johns./ Illustration by Leslie Stead from *Biggles Breaks the Silence* by Captain W. E. Johns. Copyright 1949 by Hodder & Stoughton Ltd. All reprinted by permission of Hodder & Stoughton Ltd.

HENRY HOLT & CO. Cover illustration by Norman Adams from *The North Runner* by R. D. Lawrence. Copyright © 1979 by R. D. Lawrence. Reprinted by permission of R. D. Lawrence.

THE HORN BOOK, INC. Sidelight excerpts from *Illustrators of Children's Books: 1957-1966*, compiled by Lee Kingman and others. Copyright © 1968 by The Horn Book, Inc./ Sidelight excerpts from an article "Caldecott Medal Acceptance Speech," by Arnold Lobel, August, 1981 in *Horn Book*./ Sidelight excerpts from an article "Young Adult Books," by Richard Peck, Sept./Oct., 1986 in *Horn Book*. All reprinted by permission of The Horn Book, Inc.

LITTLE, BROWN & CO. Photograph courtesy of Sir Hedley Atkins from *The Ascent of Man* by J. Bronowski. Copyright © 1973 by J. Bronowski./ Illustration by Charles Geer from *The Curse of the Viking Grave* by Farley Mowat. Copyright © 1966 by Farley Mowat./ Sidelight excerpts from *Never Cry Wolf* by Farley Mowat. Copyright © 1963 by Farley Mowat Ltd./ Jacket illustration by Paul Mock from *The Flight of the Cassowary* by John LeVert. Copyright © 1986 by John LeVert. All reprinted by permission of Little, Brown & Co.

LOTHROP, LEE & SHEPARD BOOKS. Illustration by Jan Ormerod from *Sunshine* by Jan Ormerod. Copyright © 1981 by Jan Ormerod./ Illustration by George Ancona from *Being a Twin/Having a Twin* by Maxine B. Rosenberg. Text copyright © 1985 by Maxine B.

Rosenberg. Illustrations copyright © 1985 by George Ancona. Both reprinted by permission of Lothrop, Lee & Shepard Books.

McGRAW-HILL BOOK CO. Photograph by Astrid Kirchherr from *The Beatles* by Hunter Davies. Copyright © 1968, 1978, 1985 by Hunter Davies. Reprinted by permission of McGraw-Hill Book Co.

METHUEN CHILDREN'S BOOKS LTD. Cover illustration by Caroline Holden from *The Secret Diary of Adrian Mole Aged 13¾* by Sue Townsend. Text copyright © 1982 by Sue Townsend. Illustrations copyright © 1982 by Caroline Holden. Reprinted by permission of Methuen Children's Books Ltd.

NEW AMERICAN LIBRARY. Illustration by Tim Hildebrandt from *Fang, the Gnome* by Michael Greatrex Coney. Text copyright © 1988 by Michael Coney. Illustrations copyright © 1988 by Tim Hildebrandt./ Cover illustration from *Misery* by Stephen King. Copyright © 1987 by Stephen King, Tabitha King, and Arthur B. Greene, Trustee. Both reprinted by permission of New American Library.

MAX PARRISH & CO. LTD. Illustration by William Randell from *The Biggles Book of Treasure Hunting* by Captain W. E. Johns. Copyright © 1962 by Captain W. E. Johns. Reprinted by permission of Max Parrish & Co. Ltd.

PUFFIN BOOKS. Cover illustration by Drew Aitken from *Hating Alison Ashley* by Robin Klein. Copyright © 1984 by Robin Klein. Reprinted by permission of Puffin Books.

RANDOM HOUSE, INC. Illustration by Arnold Lobel from *The Random House Book of Mother Goose,* selected by Arnold Lobel. Copyright © 1986 by Arnold Lobel./ Illustration from *The Story of Masada* by Yigael Yadin. Retold by Gerald Gottlieb. Copyright © 1969 by Random House, Inc. Both reprinted by permission of Random House, Inc.

RUNNING PRESS BOOK PUBLISHERS. Photograph by Scott Weiner from *Julian Lennon* by Yolande Flesch. Copyright © 1985 by Tern Enterprises. Reprinted by permission of Retna Ltd.

ST. MARTIN'S PRESS, INC. Photograph by Derry Brabbs and sidelight excerpts from *James Herriot's Yorkshire* by James Herriot. Copyright © 1979 by James Herriot./ Sidelight excerpts from *All Creatures Great and Small* by James Herriot./ Cover illustration and sidelight excerpts from *All Things Bright and Beautiful* by James Herriot. Copyright © 1973, 1974 by James Herriot./ Back cover photograph from *The Best of James Herriot* by James Herriot. Copyright © 1982 by The Reader's Digest Association, Inc./ Illustration by Ruth Brown from *Bonny's Big Day* by James Herriot. Text copyright © 1972, 1987 by James Herriot. Illustrations copyright © 1987 by Ruth Brown./ Illustration by Victor Ambrus from *The Best of James Herriot: Favourite Memories of a Country Vet* by James Herriot. Copyright © 1982 by The Reader's Digest Association, Inc./ Illustration by Peter Barrett from *Moses the Kitten* by James Herriot. Copyright © 1974, 1984 by James Herriot. Illustrations copyright 1984 by Peter Barrett. All reprinted by permission of St. Martin's Press, Inc.

SCHOLASTIC, INC. Illustration by Anita Lobel from *The Rose in My Garden* by Arnold Lobel. Text copyright © 1984 by Arnold Lobel. Illustrations copyright © 1984 by Anita Lobel./ Illustration by Arnold Lobel from *Ming Lo Moves the Mountain* by Arnold Lobel. Copyright © 1982 by Arnold Lobel./ Illustration by Anita Lobel from *A Treeful of Pigs* by Arnold Lobel. Text copyright © 1979 by Arnold Lobel. Illustration copyright © 1979 by Anita Lobel./ Illustration by Winslow Pinney Pels from *Beauty and the Beast,* retold by Mary Pope Osborne. Text copyright © 1987 by Mary Pope Osborne. Illustrations copyright © 1987 by Winslow Pinney Pels./ Jacket illustration by Jeff Walker from *Simon Pure* by Julian F. Thompson. Text copyright © 1987 by Julian F. Thompson. Jacket copyright © 1987 by Jeff Walker. All reprinted by permission of Scholastic, Inc.

SEAL PRESS. Cover illustration from *The Serpent's Coil* by Farley Mowat. Copyright © 1961 by Farley Mowat. Reprinted by permission of Seal Press.

SIMON & SCHUSTER, INC. Illustration by Charles Addams from *Creature Comforts* by Charles Addams. Copyright © 1981 by Charles Addams./ Illustration by Greg Hildebrandt from *A Christmas Carol* by Charles Dickens. Illustrations copyright © 1983 by Gregory J. Hildebrandt. Both reprinted by permission of Simon & Schuster, Inc.

THE SONCINO PRESS LTD. Illustration by Joan Kiddell-Monroe from "My Long Journey to Eisenhower: A Story of World War II" by Ernest W. Michel in *The Secret Weapon and Other Stories of Faith and Valor,* selected, translated and edited by Azriel Eisenberg and Leah Ain Globe. Copyright © 1966 by The Soncino Press Ltd. Reprinted by permission of The Soncino Press Ltd.

UNICORN PRESS, INC. Sidelight excerpts from *Tolkien to Oz: The Art of Greg Hildebrandt* by William McGuire./ Illustration by Greg Hildebrandt from *Peter Pan* by J. M. Barrie. Cover and interior graphics copyright © 1987 by The Unicorn Publishing House. Artwork copyright © 1987 by Greg Hildebrandt. Line art copyright © 1987 by Jean L. Scrocco./ Illustration by Greg Hildebrandt from *Pinocchio* by Carlo Collodi. Art work copyright © 1986 by Greg Hildebrandt. Cover and interior graphics copyright © 1986 by Unicorn Publishing House. Line art copyright © 1987 by Jean L. Scrocco./ Art work copyright © 1986 by Greg Hildebrandt from *The Wizard of Oz* by Frank L. Baum. Cover and interior graphics copyright © 1985 by The Unicorn Publishing House. Art work copyright © 1985 by Greg Hildebrandt./ Illustration by Greg Hildebrandt from *Peter Cottontail's Surprise* by Bonnie Worth. Copyright © 1985 by Unicorn Publishing House. Art work copyright © 1985 by Greg Hildebrandt./ Cover illustration by Greg Hildebrandt from *Dracula* by Bram Stoker. Cover and interior graphics copyright © 1985 by The Unicorn Publishing House. Art work copyright © 1985 by Greg Hildebrandt. Line art copyright © 1985 by Jean Scrocco. All reprinted by permission of Unicorn Press, Inc.

UNIVERSITY OF MINNESOTA PRESS. Sidelight excerpts from an article "A Quick Backward Glance," by Arnold Lobel in *New Books for Young Readers.* Reprinted by permission of University of Minnesota Press.

VIKING PENGUIN, INC. Jacket illustration by Bob Giusti from *It* by Stephen King. Copyright © 1986 by Stephen King./ Illustration by Don Freeman from *Monster Night at Grandma's House* by Richard Peck. Copyright © 1977 by Richard Peck and Don Freeman. Both reprinted by permission of Viking Penguin, Inc.

WARNER PRESS, INC. Jacket photograph by Robert Campbell from *Woman in the Mists: The Story of Dian Fossey and the Mountain Gorillas of Africa* by Farley Mowat. Copyright © 1987 by Farley Mowat Ltd. Reprinted by permission of Warner Press, Inc.

Sidelight excerpts from an article "A Father Praises His Progeny," by Charles Addams, October 30, 1965 in *TV Guide* magazine. Copyright © 1965 by Triangle Publishing, Inc. Reprinted by permission of Charles Addams./ Sidelight excerpts from *Books Are by People* by Lee Bennett Hopkins. Copyright © 1969 by Lee Bennett Hopkins. Reprinted by permission of Curtis Brown Ltd./ Sidelight excerpts from an article "Stephen King on *Carrie, The Shining,* Etc.," by Peter S. Perakos in *Cinefantastique,* Volume 8, number 1. Reprinted by permission of *Cinefantastique./* Sidelight excerpts from an article "Stephen King Takes a Vacation," by Edward Gross in *Fangoria,* number 58. Reprinted by permission of *Fangoria* magazine./ Sidelight excerpts from *Writer,* June, 1975. Copyright © 1975 by Stephen King. Reprinted by permission of Stephen King./ Sidelight excerpts from *And No Birds Sang* by Farley Mowat. Reprinted by permission of Farley Mowat Ltd./ Illustrations by Charles Addams from *The New Yorker Twenty-Fifth Anniversary Album 1925-1950* and from *Creature Comforts.* Reprinted by permission of The New Yorker Magazine, Inc./ Sidelight excerpts from an article by Arturof Gonzalez, May/June, 1986 in *Saturday Review.* Reprinted by permission of *Saturday Review./* Sidelight excerpts from an article "Growing Up Suburban: We Don't Use Slang, We're Gifted," by Richard Peck, October, 1985 in *School Library Journal.* Reprinted by permission of *School Library Journal./* Sidelight excerpts from an article "The Genteel Unshelving of a Book," by Richard Peck, May, 1986 in *School Library Journal.* Reprinted by permission of *School Library Journal./* Sidelight excerpts from an article "James Herriot Talking to William Foster," October 16, 1981 in *Scotsman* magazine. Reprinted by permission of *Scotsman* magazine./ Sidelight excerpts from an article "The Writing Life of Adrian Mole's Mum," by Nancy Smith, December, 1985 in *Writer's Monthly,* Volume 2, number 3. Reprinted by permission of Nancy Smith./ Sidelight excerpts from an article "A Father Praises His Progeny," by Charles Addams, October 30, 1965 in *TV Guide* magazine. Copyright © 1965 by Triangle Publishing, Inc. Reprinted by permission of Triangle Publishing, Inc./ Sidelight excerpts from an article "Stephen King: I Like to Go for the Jugular," by Charles L. Grant in *Twilight Zone* magazine, Volume 1, number 1. Copyright © 1986 by Stephen King. Reprinted by permission of *Twilight Zone* magazine./ Sidelight excerpts from an article "The Man Who Writes Nightmares," by Mel Allen, March, 1979 in *Yankee* magazine. Reprinted by permission of *Yankee* magazine.

PHOTOGRAPH CREDITS

Charles Addams: (van) Robert Levin/NYT Pictures; Charles Addams: Michael Tighe; Jacob Bronowski: Antony di Gesu; Cassie Brown: copyright © by Tooton's; R. D. Lawrence: Murray Palmer; Evelyn Wilde Mayerson: J. Rosenblatt; Farley Mowat: John de Visser; Jan Ormerod: copyright © by Carol Cutner; William Rayner: John Stock, Minehead; Maxine B. Rosenberg: copyright © 1986 by George Ancona; Budge Wilson: Murray Forbes; Jane Scott: Jim Graham; Sue Townsend: copyright © by Tessa Musgrave.

SOMETHING ABOUT THE AUTHOR

ADDAMS, Charles (Samuel) 1912-1988

PERSONAL: Born January 7, 1912, in Westfield, N.J.; died of a heart attack on September 29, 1988, in New York City; son of Charles Huey (manager for a piano company) and Grace M. (Spear) Addams; married Barbara Day, May 29, 1943 (divorced, October, 1951); married Barbara Barb (an attorney), December 1, 1954 (divorced, 1956); married Marilyn Matthews Miller, May 31, 1980. *Education:* Attended Colgate University, 1929-30, University of Pennsylvania, 1930-31, and Grand Central School of Art, New York, N.Y., 1931-32. *Home:* 25 West 54th St., New York, N.Y. 10020; and Sagaponack, N.Y.

CAREER: Macfadden Publications, New York, N.Y., in art department, 1932-33; free-lance cartoonist, beginning, 1933, work appearing regularly in *New Yorker,* beginning, 1936. Work exhibited at Fogg Art Museum, Rhode Island School of Design, Museum of the City of New York, University of Pennsylvania Museum, and Metropolitan Museum of Art. *Military service:* U.S. Army, Signal Corps, 1943-46. *Member:* Vintage Car Club of America, Armor and Arms Club, Century Association. *Awards, honors:* Humor Award, Yale University, 1954; special award of the Mystery Writers of America, 1961; honorary Doctor of Fine Arts, University of Pennsylvania, 1980.

WRITINGS:

CARTOONS

Drawn and Quartered (foreword by Boris Karloff), Random House, 1942, published as *D & Q: The Return of a Classic,* Simon & Schuster, 1962.
Addams and Evil (introduction by Wolcott Gibbs), Random House, 1947.
Monster Rally, Simon & Schuster, 1950.
Homebodies, Simon & Schuster, 1954.
Nightcrawlers, Simon & Schuster, 1957.

(Editor) *Dear Dead Days: A Family Album,* Putnam, 1959.
Black Maria, Simon & Schuster, 1960.
The Penguin Charles Addams, Penguin, 1962.
The Groaning Board, Simon & Schuster, 1964.
The Charles Addams Mother Goose, Windmill Books, 1967.
My Crowd, Simon & Schuster, 1970.
Charles Addams Favorite Haunts, Simon & Schuster, 1976 (published in England as *Favorite Haunts,* W. H. Allen, 1977).
Creature Comforts, Simon & Schuster, 1981.

Contributor to biennial *New Yorker Album, New Yorker War Album,* 1942, and *The New Yorker Album of Drawings,* Volume 1: *1925-1975,* Volume 2: *1975-1985.*

ILLUSTRATOR:

John Kobler, *Afternoon in the Attic,* Dodd, 1950.

Contributor of cartoons to periodicals, including *Life, Collier's,* and *Cosmopolitan.*

ADAPTATIONS:

"The Addams Family" (television series; based on characters created by Addams), ABC-TV, 1964-66.

SIDELIGHTS: **January 7, 1912.** Charles Addams was born in Westfield, New Jersey, the only son of Charles and Grace Addams. Growing up and attending school in a middle-class New Jersey suburb was uneventful. ". . .All in all, I had a normal healthy childhood."[1]

However, he was already attracted to the bizarre and spooky sides of life. "Actually, the idea of the bogeyman fascinated me."[2] "It probably helped that there were lots of scary old Victorian houses in my neighborhood. I'd stare at them for hours imagining the ghosts inside."[3]

CHARLES ADDAMS

"We had a dumbwaiter in our house. . .and I'd get inside on the ground floor, and then very quietly I'd haul myself up to grandmother's floor. . .and then I'd knock on the door. . .and when she came to open the door I'd jump out and scare the wits out of her. . . .

"But you know, I always wondered if maybe there wasn't something a little strange about my grandmother. . .who else would have opened a dumbwaiter door when somebody knocked from the INSIDE?"[1]

"Once I broke into a deserted house and drew skeletons all over the walls. The grounds were soggy with rain and there was a fine set of my footprints in the mud around the house for the detectives to see, so each day for a week I wore a different pair of shoes to throw them off the track. It worked out fine. I'm convinced I never would have been found out if the kid next door hadn't squealed. It took the cops a week to find me.

"It was the first time I had ever seen a policeman with his hat off."[4]

Early reading enthusiasms were Edgar Allan Poe, Grimms' *Fairy Tales* and the *Book of Knowledge*. Drawing and cartooning also held his interest. "It was during the First World War, and my first scrawlings were about the war. I was very

big on the Kaiser. I had him stabbed, shot, boiled in oil, and torpedoed at sea."[5]

"Father drew well himself, though his style, like most architects', was rather dry and sparse. He encouraged me to draw. But Mother always wanted me to get a regular job. I was making a lot in cartooning by the time she died, but she never thought it was actual money."[6]

1921. Entered an art contest sponsored by Rogers Peet Company and won first prize.

1929-1932. Attended Colgate University for one year, then switched to the University of Pennsylvania for their art program. "Only I found out later that it was not an art but an architectural course. Anyway, it didn't hurt me at all!"[4]

Addams eventually found his way to New York City where he studied at the Grand Central School of Arts for one year. He reportedly spent most of his time in the terminal watching people. "On one side of the Concourse was the art school, and on the other was a gallery. I think it still exists. It's called the Grand Central Gallery.

"The art school was discontinued during the war because of the danger in case the city was bombed, or something like that."[7]

1933. Sold his first cartoon to the *New Yorker*, beginning a long association with that magazine. "It was a picture of a hockey rink. All the players were there and one man was in his stocking feet. His toes were curled up on the ice. He says to one of the players, 'I forgot my skates.' Who would buy that cartoon now?"[2] "It was not very funny. . . ."[8]

Spent two years with a Macfadden publication, retouching photographs of murder victims in a detective magazine—what he considered his most valuable art education. "I did lettering, retouching of photographs and diagrams of the spot where the body was found. It paid me $15 a week, which was almost enough to pay for my sodas and my commutation ticket to Westfield. It was the last and only job I ever had."[8] "Some of those corpses were kind of interesting the way they were."[6]

1937. *New Yorker* published the first drawing of the Addams Family. During the next six years, he refined the family cartoon, and by 1944 its inner circle was completed. The Addams Family included a raven-haired vampirish wife, her Peter Lorre-like lover (Addams said he couldn't bear to think of them as married), a bald bug-eyed uncle, two innocently sinister children, a flabby, fungoid moral monster, and a Frankenstein-type butler. "They were the type of people I like—people I would be comfortable with."[2]

With the rise of black humor in America, the Addams Family and their cobwebby Victorian haunted house became very popular. And in 1947, *Addams and Evil,* featuring domestic vignettes of the goulish family, was published. Wolcott Gibbs wrote in the foreword of the book: "The thoughtful reader. . .will wonder about the inhabitants of that crumbling Gothic pile known, at least to me, as the 'Old Charles Addams Place.' What dark and shameful compulsion brought the proprietors together—the haggard ruined beauty and the ignoble half-breed? What unspeakable rites united them, if wed they are at all? We know their little girl has six toes on her left foot, that her younger brother likes to mix his childish poison brews, and that their only playmates are bats and spiders and probably The Thing that has no face but wails and drags his chains at night. And we know still less about the shambling giant who

(From the television series ''The Addams Family,'' starring Jackie Coogan, John Astin and Carolyn Jones. Premiered September 18, 1964 on ABC-TV.)

ministers their dreadful needs, except that he is apparently dumb and almost certainly a homicidal maniac.''[9]

Owing to his distinctive themes, the public soon equated Addams with the idea of the macabre. Hollow-cheeked women, cavernous-eyed-men, murderers, monsters and ghosts became his trademark. As his drawing style evolved, he began using a dark-gray wash which highlighted his sinister subject matter. ''I attribute my success with the macabre to children. I guess my cartooning is sort of in a state of arrested intellectual development.''[10]

Many of his ideas, he said, came from overheard conversations and observations. His work is also informed by the classic horror films of the late twenties and thirties. '''Frankenstein' is still the king of horror films. 'Nosferatu' was really good. It was only equaled by Lon Chaney in 'Phantom of the Opera,' when he takes off his mask and there's a wonderful skull-like face.''[2]

Of later Hollywood productions, however, Addams wrote: ''Though many of us will not find the perfection we seek, we cannot ignore some of the truly inspired efforts of the motion-picture industry. Their creators have perhaps leaned a little too heavily on hirsuteness and unclipped fingernails to achieve their effects. Speaking for myself only, I am inclined to favor the hairless, no-fingernail school, with burbling giggles, though there may be some who would jeer me as a pedant.

''Hollywood animals generally impress our audience as far too noble and four-legged, as witness 'The Beast from 20,000 Fathoms.' Nothing more than the old-fashioned dinosaur, or early Dark Age dragon at best. A casual evening stroll past Mott Street's bazaars will reward the student with a plethora of infinitely more sympathetic productions.

''There have been notable exceptions, of course, and we may recall with misty-eyed fondness the title character in the German film, 'The Cabinet of Doctor Caligari.' The Doctor, in the fancies of the hero, becomes a heavily shrouded figure, covered with a delightful growth of warts, together with a slack jaw and off-center eyes, staring out (as at the left) from behind a pair of the world's thickest spectacles. At the conclusion of the story, with his make-up removed, many of us were pleased, nay, transported, to see that he looked even worse, or better, than he did before.

''For these monsters, ghouls and vampires have chilled an adoring public for years and today are proving more popular than ever. Indeed, I think that few will deny that we have here a healthy escape from an almost hopeless tangle of psychoanalysts and freckle champs.''[11]

Addams' vocational interest with the grim, also included a fascination with death. ''I suppose it's cozy. I've done a lot of tombstone pictures, so I suppose you can have fun with it.''[1] ''My feet do begin to lead me if there's a churchyard in the neighborhood.''[12]

1942. First book, *Drawn and Quartered,* published. Boris Karloff, who acted the monster in the original American version of ''Frankenstein'' in 1931, and whom Addams immortalized in the person of the Addams Family's butler, was asked to write an introduction to the book. ''Why a collection of the drawings of Charles Addams should need any written introduction at all is as far beyond me as the writing of one! Addams seems to me to be the one comedic artist today whose drawings need no letterpress at all. Supremely he has achieved the primary and essential purpose of any drawing serious or comic, which is to tell a story graphically in one blinding flash without a single written word of explanation. While it is true that the general development has been consistently away from the style of the comic artists of *Punch* in the last century and even in the early part of this one, when every drawing was followed by five to ten lines of print containing an elaborate joke which often bore no relation to the drawing at all, few men have realized and practised the earliest and most eloquent of all forms of story-telling as has Addams.

''Perhaps Mr. Addams is happiest in his dealing with the macabre. His pre-occupation with hangman's nooses and lethal doses is always innocent and gay. He has the extraordinary faculty of making the normal appear idiotic when confronted by the abnormal, as in his scenes of cannibals, skiers and skaters. Somehow one never dreams of questioning his premise, but only the rather childish alarm of the onlookers. I am told that his priceless drawing of the fat lady who has left ski tracks on either side of a tree is used in a leading asylum for the mentally deficient as a text; the inmates receive some sort of rating that is based on the length of time it takes them to discover the point. One dear lady of my acquaintance, quite sane as far as I know, has never gotten it at all. She also takes exception to Mr. Addams' rather cynical approach to domestic bliss and old-fashioned chivalry. I have to admit that his methods of solving insupportable marital problems, while seemingly practical, are, shall we say, unusual. . . .''[13]

Millions of readers have smiled and chuckled over Addams' cartoons. They were not, however, well received everywhere. During World War II, Nazi Minister Josef Goebbels reprinted an Addams' cartoon from the *New Yorker,* in his own propaganda newspaper. The editorial distastefully commented that: ''Jokes of this sort often appear in magazines which are convinced of their mission in the American Century.''[6] Some years later, a newspaper in eastern Europe published some of Addams' work as evidence of the ''cannibalistic decadence'' of the West.

May 29, 1943. Married model Barbara Day. At the suggestion that he based the witch-like wife of the Addams Family on his own sleek, dark-haired wife, he said: ''I never used a model for her, although I must say that she has taken on weight and grows more attractive since I married Barbara.''[14] The marriage lasted eight years.

Served three years in U. S. Army Signal Corps on Long Island, New York, where he illustrated a manual for the troops in the art of barbershop harmony. His detachment was made up of professional artists, and he became close friends with cartoonist Sam Cobean. ''[Cobean's] drawings were beautiful—he drew more easily than anyone I ever knew. Oddly erect before the drawing board, he worked quickly, the pictures moving from his head to his hand to the paper—and they came out finished—the helpless but noncommital men, the predatory chippies, and the world's funniest dogs, bums, and peacocks. I own about a hundred Cobeans, many of them done when we were in the Army together. There was something about me, namely my nose, that amused, even amazed, Cobean, and he drew it endlessly. He was carried to great heights by my nose.''[15]

By the late forties, Addams was moving in the best artistic and literary circles. Some of his friends included playwright William Saroyan, writers John Cheever and John O'Hara, and cartoonist Saul Steinberg. He was regarded by his friends as a gentle sensitive man who liked to drink quietly, read Civil War stories, race foreign cars, and listen to rhumbas and dixieland jazz. According to John O'Hara, Addams ''is a big man, about six feet one inch, and around 195 pounds, a toxophilist who can handle a sixty-pound pull, but I don't think

(From *Creature Comforts* by Charles Addams. Illustrated by the author.)

he's hurt a fly. I never have seen him lose his temper, although that is not to say he doesn't get mad. He happens to be what is called easygoing, and has a decent contempt for the opinions of mankind. He speaks with a New Jersey twang plus a drawl of his own, and but for the grace of God, which gave him his enormous talent, his sense of humor, and his impatience with banality, he might have become a successful politician."[8]

Another friend added, "Charles is so popular he could get the Hamptons to secede from the Union, set up a monarchy, and appoint him king—just because he's a real person. He doesn't have a phony bone in his body and, of course, that makes him unique."[5]

1948. "[Barbara and I] spent the summer in Europe, for *Cosmopolitan* magazine. . .quite a trip. In England, we visited lots of castles. . .all equipped with big flapping crows. I never knew if they were expressly for my benefit or not.

"In Venice, we made a study of funerals. . .went to a cemetery and waited for them to show up. There were three kinds: the

first-class funeral comes in a black gondola, with a gondolier dressed in black, too. Actually there is one more expensive type—in speedboats. We didn't have time to wait for one of those to happen.

"In a theater [in Paris] converted from a church, we saw the Grand Guignol. . .better than the billboards! The best play was called 'Death in a Madhouse.' On stage, you see a nurse get an eye gouged out—and the blood spurts! Magnificent.

"And there was an old hag who held her face to a red hot stove and the steam sizzled to the ceiling. And for curtain calls, all the actors came back still bleeding or steaming!"[14]

1954. Married his second wife, attorney Barbara Barb. They were divorced two years later.

1964. When the Addams Family became the basis of a television series, the characters of the cartoon had to be named. The vampirish wife and her Peter Lorre-like lover were joined

Charles Addams adds creature comforts of a nineteenth-century home—stuffed birds, mirrors, cushions and stained glass—to his van.

in holy wedlock for the television version, and became Morticia and Gomez Addams. "The characters were not named before, when they were in the magazine. They were actually named for a series of dolls that were put out before the show, that had nothing to do with the show. . . .But when the dolls came out, I had to name them. I wanted to call the little boy Pubert, but they wouldn't do that. They thought it was somehow dirty. Which it wasn't. Then I said what about Irving? One of them said, 'What's so funny about Irving? My name's Irving.' So finally I thought of Pugsley: the name of a river up in the Bronx, which I saw on a map of New York."[7]

"It's almost like a typical suburban family. Not half as evil as my original characters. My people have that togetherness too—but in a different way."[16]

"Morticia, for example, was to be beautiful and aristocratic, the real head of the family and the critical and moving force behind it. Incisive and subtle, she is given to low-keyed rhapsodies about her garden of deadly nightshade, henbane and dwarf's hair. She indulges the mischievous activities of the children but feels that Uncle Fester must be held in check.

"Gomez is a crafty schemer but a jolly type in his own way. Sentimental and often puckish, he is full of enthusiasm, and a firm believer in the survival of the fittest. Wednesday, child of woe, is wan and delicate, with her mother's black hair and dead-white complexion. Quiet and sensitive, she loves picnics at the underground caverns. Pugsley is an energetic, pop-eyed boy and a dedicated troublemaker.

"As for Lurch, this towering butler has been a morose presence about the house forever. He is not a very good butler but a faithful one. The children are his favorites and he seems to guard them against good influences at all costs.

"Granny is foolishly good-natured, easily led, and some family troubles are due to her weak character.

"Uncle Fester is incorrigible and, except for the good nature of the family and the ignorance of the police, might be under lock and key. His complexion, like Morticia's, is dead white. The eyes are piglike and deeply imbedded and circled unhealthily in black. Without teeth and absolutely hairless, he has a peppery manner and a high-pitched voice.

"The casting has been superb, and Carolyn Jones and John Astin, as heads of the household, are beyond my reproach."[17]

Although Addams was dissatisfied with the show for being "too cute," it was very popular and ran as a prime-time comedy for two years.

After the show went on the air, the editor of the *New Yorker* felt that the characters were somehow sullied by being on television, and so they no longer appeared in the magazine. Addams continued to be represented in the magazine pages, as well as on occasional covers. He also did some advertisements, and designs for scarves, pottery and glassware.

Throughout his career, Addams' fans have sent him up to 200 ideas a week for cartoons. "All too horrible to be used," he said. And to keep up with his legend, he has been known to answer his mail using the letterhead of an imaginary mental institution.

"[Charles Adams is] still tops when it comes to projecting the nervous side of life," said John Gruen in his tribute to Addams' longevity and effectiveness as a cartoonist. "Thirty years on the *New Yorker* has not diminished his sting—nor, for that matter, his style, which is as unmistakable as a gabled and

(From the *New Yorker Twenty-Fifth Anniversary Album, 1925-1950.*)

turreted Victorian house, an architectural vintage he seems, in effect, to have invented.

"The Addams cartoon, singular, hilarious, and distinctly personal as it is, reflects a society that's only mildly off its rocker—at least by today's lunatic standards. It really doesn't claim to be anything more. The Addams cartoon engenders laughter by means of an outrageous juxtapositioning of several realities—none truly frightening or truly threatening.

"Its social comment doesn't really shake one up. It sticks to the lunatic fringe of human activity, and it sticks to it with something close to genius. Addams is not involved with violence—certainly not with butchery. The blood seldom flows in an Addams cartoon. Man is never put through a meat grinder, and man's follies have more to do with the rising of the moon than with the rising of that famous cloud."[18]

1971. Addams, a great lover of animals, acquired Alice B. Curr, "a dog of uncertain ancestry." "I found her at the Bide-a-Wee home. I picked Alice out where they have stray dogs out on Long Island, where I have the house. She was jumping higher than all the others. So I said, 'I like this dog,' and they said, 'We must warn you, this dog does not like children.' So I said, 'I'll take her.'

"My maid brings her child sometimes, and Alice goes right for it, right for the throat. She never really hurts them, just frightens them. Most of them are pretty good, but Alice mistrusts them. She settles down when they're about ten years old. It's the very young uncontrolled ones that she takes exception to. She's never bitten one, but she moves them along. She growls fiercely at them.

"Once I had a French midget up here, a famous movie actor, Andre Vilechaise. He's 3'8"—he came up here. He's also a painter, a very nice man, and Alice saw him and went for him. But after a while she calmed down and Andre said, 'That dog hasn't quite figured me out yet.'"[7]

Over the years, he has been the owner of five beloved dogs, including two poodles named Abraham and Strauss, one turtle and a canary named Birdie. A friend recalled that one day he received a card bordered in black stating: "This is to announce that Birdie has passed away.

"Charley was completely sincere in the gesture. He sent the cards only to the two people who really cared about the bird, no more."[1]

Alice B. Curr shares the life of Addams between his New York apartment near the Museum of Modern Art, and his house in Sagaponack, Long Island. The cartoonist carried his sense of the bizarre to his own daily surrounding, and his Manhattan apartment has been called "a museum of the macabre." In addition to the knick knacks his fans sent him—skulls, snake skins and pictures of bats—Addams built up his own collection of gruesome objects, including a stuffed piranna, a human thighbone, silver name plate from a casket, an entire suit of armor from 1520, a nineteenth-century model of a human body. "It's not exactly another human heart beating in the house, but it's close enough."[3]

Last, but not least, he owns an antique embalmer's table. "[There] is the handle to carry it in the region of the kidney, it has a rather sinister dark spot, I found. [There's] a little holder for the head, the neck. It folds up so it goes into a thing."[7] "I found it in the back of an antique shop in Gettysburgh, and the man told me it was an old embalmer's table.

I was looking for a coffee table at the time so I folded it up, put it in the car, and brought it home."[19]

The walls are lined with maces, swords, and late sixteenth-century crossbows he started collecting while in the army. "On the day after the atom bomb fell on Hiroshima, I began collecting crossbows—sort of symbolic."[14] "They are good defensive weapons. They go back to the 10th Century and before. They still use them for deer hunting."[7] "I have this fantasy. A robber breaks in and just as he comes through the door I get him—right through the neck! In my fantasy, it's *always* through the neck."[3]

1976. Drew the poster and titles sequence for Neil Simon's whodunit satire, "Murder by Death."

1980. Married his third wife, Marilyn Matthews Miller, in a pet cemetery. The bride wore a black velvet dress, and Alice B. Curr was in attendance, sporting a yellow ribbon.

1981. The Addams' purchased a van, affectionately dubbed "The Heap," and set out for a thousand-mile camping trip throughout America. "I've always thought of American cars as heaps, and this is just an old Dodge. I've had heaps before, but this is the only *true* heap. I had long wanted a van—something about the cosiness and the idea of the gypsy caravan. I think of it as my home away from home. Living in the Heap is like riding on a train in the great days of the first-class Pullman cars. The Heap is the poor man's Lucius Beebe railroad car. I'd love to take a trip to the Southwest. You know, Tombstone, Death Valley. We might pick up some nice mementoes there. One of the best things about the Heap is just the freedom of *having* it. You know—even if you never, ever travel in it."[12]

Published *Creature Comforts: A New Collection of Classic Cartoons.* On the cover, a man stands in pajamas and bathrobe facing his front door with five locks. A valentine has been pushed under the door. Addams commented: "I look at [the book cover] and I think maybe...of loneliness. Now that's not bizarre and it certainly isn't political. It used to be said that I was irreverent. I don't think I was.

"My cartoons don't have any political slant. I'm not trying to say anything. I'm just trying to be funny. I . . . saw 'An American Werewolf in London.' There was jugular blood all over the screen. I always hinted at that; I never showed it. Everything is more explicit now. I think it's better to hint."[2]

"I don't think much about why I do what I do. Probably better not to. If I found out why, I might lose it. Oh, I suppose it represents a kind of separate life, a dream thing."[1]

September 29, 1988. Died of a heart attack in New York City.

FOOTNOTE SOURCES

[1]Saul Pett, "As a Boy Artist Charles Addams Doodled Only Skulls and Bones," *San Francisco Chronicle,* November 1, 1953 (p. 29).

[2]Dolores Barclay, "Ghoulish Doodles," *Detroit News,* February 16, 1982.

[3]"Cartoonist Charles Addams Is the Master of the Macabre," *People,* September 13, 1976 (p. 89).

[4]Selma Robinson, "Arsenic and Old Racers," *New York Star Magazine,* September 19, 1948 (p.5).

[5]Virginia Sheward, "At Home with the Addams Family," *Holiday,* March/April, 1973 (p. 30).

"*George! George! Drop the keys!*"

(From the *New Yorker Twenty-Fifth Anniversary Album, 1925-1950.*)

[6]Dwight MacDonald, "Charles Addams, His Family, and His Friends," *Reporter,* July 21, 1953 (p. 37).
[7]Suzie Frankfurt, "At Home with the Charles Addams Family," *Interview,* Volume 8, number 5, 1978.
[8]*Current Biography 1954,* H. W. Wilson, 1955.
[9]Charles Addams, *Addams and Evil,* introduction by Wolcott Gibbs, Random House, 1947.
[10]*Contemporary Literary Criticism,* Volume 30, Gale, 1984.
[11]C. Addams, "Movie Monsters Rally," *New York Times Magazine,* August 9, 1953.
[12]Glenn Collins, "Charles Addams's Idosyncratic 'Heap,'" *New York Times,* June 11, 1981.
[13]C. Addams, *Drawn and Quartered,* foreword by Boris Karloff, Random House, 1942.
[14]Tex McCrary and Jinx Falkenburg, "New York Close-Up," *New York Herald Tribune,* October 5, 1949 (p.23).
[15]*The Cartoons of Cobean,* Harper, 1952.
[16]"The Sixteenth Man," *Newsweek,* July 5, 1965.
[17]C. Addams, "A Father Appraises His Progeny," *TV Guide,* October 30, 1965.

[18]John Gruen, *Close-Up,* Viking, 1968.
[19]Audrey Farolino, "Cartoonist Draws on the Macabre for Devilish Decor," *New York Post,* June 28, 1984 (p. 43).

FOR MORE INFORMATION SEE:

Time, November 9, 1942 (p. 48), October 23, 1950.
Look, December 15, 1942 (p. 60), May 19, 1953 (p. 98).
New York World-Telegram, January 30, 1943 (p. 1).
Times Literary Supplement, November 15, 1947 (p. 592), July 22, 1977, December 25, 1981.
New York Sun, August 31, 1948 (p. 14).
"May We Present. . .Addams' Rib," *Good Housekeeping,* July, 1957.
"Here Art Imitates Nature—or Is It Vice Versa?" *House Beautiful,* April, 1963 (p. 147).
Book World, November 5, 1967.
Dolores Barclay, "Behold Charles Addams, Guru of the Graveyard. . .," *Poughkeepsie Journal,* February 2, 1982 (p. 22).
Washington Post, November 17, 1982.

ATKINSON, Allen G. 1953(?)-1987

OBITUARY NOTICE: Born about 1953, in Norwalk, Conn.; died of a heart attack related to acquired immune deficiency syndrome (AIDS), June 22, 1987, in Danbury, Conn. Artist, author, and illustrator. Atkinson, who lived his entire life in rural Connecticut, graduated from the Prairie School of Art in Hamden, Conn. During his brief career as an illustrator, he produced over thirty children's books, including editions of such classics as Beatrix Potter's *The Tale of Peter Rabbit and Other Stories* (Knopf, 1982), *Grimm's Fairy Tales* (Wanderer Books, 1982), Margery Williams' *The Velveteen Rabbit* (Knopf, 1983), and *Mother Goose's Nursery Rhymes* (Knopf, 1984). His favorite subjects were the well-known stories which he read as a child. He also preferred using animals to represent characters normally portrayed as humans: in *Mother Goose's Nursery Rhymes,* for instance, the "Old Woman Who Lived in a Shoe" is a rabbit, and Jack Sprat and his wife appear as a giraffe and an elephant.

In addition to his children's book illustration, Atkinson also designed greeting cards and created toys. He designed four stuffed bean bag toys: Humpty Dumpty, Little Miss Muffet, Simple Simon, and a mouse from "The Three Blind Mice," which were all based on his illustrations in *Mother Goose's Nursery Rhymes.* At the time of his death at the age of thirty-four, he had just completed writing and illustrating his first original book, *Jack in the Green,* which was published by Crown in 1987.

FOR MORE INFORMATION SEE:

OBITUARIES

New York Times Biographical Service, June 24, 1987.
Publishers Weekly, September 11, 1987.

BARNES, Michael 1934-
(Alison Wesley)

PERSONAL: Born September 26, 1934, in London, England; emigrated to Canada in 1956; became naturalized Canadian citizen in 1960; son of George (a foreman) and Elsie (a homemaker; maiden name, Dicketts) Barnes; married Joan Wyatt (a teacher), January 31, 1959; children: Stephen, Alison, Wesley. *Education:* Institute of Education, London, teacher's certificate, 1955; University of Western Ontario, B.A., 1964; University of Toronto, M.Ed., 1971. *Home and office:* P.O. Box 243, Kirkland Lake, Ontario, Canada P2N 2G0.

CAREER: Teacher in elementary schools in England and Ontario, Canada, 1955-65; elementary school principal in Canada, 1965—; free-lance writer, 1967—. Conducts writers' workshops. *Member:* Writers Union of Canada.

WRITINGS:

JUVENILE

The Nelson Boys and Their Cobalt Adventure: The Mystery of the Old Mine (fiction), Highway Book Shop (Canada), 1973.
In the Public Service: The Ontario Provincial Police (nonfiction; illustrated by Stephen Wlad; photographs by Gary Stevens and others), Highway Book Shop, 1974.
The Nelson Boys and Their Wawa Adventure: The Lake Superior Diamond Mystery (nonfiction; illustrated by Michael Roberts), Highway Book Shop, 1975.
Night Search and Other Short Stories for Teens (nonfiction; illustrated by Elsa Stortroen), Highway Book Shop, 1975.

MICHAEL BARNES

Police Story (nonfiction), Scholastic-TAB, 1981.

"JUST NORTH MYSTERY ADVENTURE" SERIES; ALL JUVENILE; HIGH-INTEREST/LOW VOCABULARY NOVELS; ALL ILLUSTRATED BY M. E. NEWTON-WHITE

Monster from the Slimes, Highway Book Shop, 1976.
The Chief Commanda Hi-Jack, Highway Book Shop, 1976.
The Thunder Bay Threat, Highway Book Shop, 1977.
The Message to Moosonee, Highway Book Shop, 1977.
Arrest at the Soo, Highway Book Shop, 1977.
The Sudbury Moon Chase, Highway Book Shop, 1977.

ADULT

Gold Camp Pioneer: Roza Brown of Kirkland Lake (history; illustrated by John Slater), Highway Book Shop, 1973.
Jake Englehart (history; illustrated by J. Slater), Highway Book Shop, 1973.
Gold in the Porcupine! (history; illustrated by Alison Barnes), Highway Book Shop, 1975.
Cochrane: The Polar Bear Town (history; illustrated by Muriel E. Newton-White), Highway Book Shop, 1976.
Kirkland Lake, The Town That Stands on Gold (history; illustrated by M. Roberts, Jim Harling and with photographs by Doug Skeggs), Highway Book Shop, 1978.
A Souvenir of Kirkland Lake (nonfiction), Kirkland Lake Chamber of Commerce (Ontario), 1981.
Gateway City: The North Bay Story (history), North Bay Chamber of Commerce (Ontario), 1982.
The Best of Hartley Trussler's North Bay (nonfiction), North Bay Chamber of Commerce, 1982.
Link with a Lonely Land: The Story of the Temiskaming and Northern Ontario Railway (nonfiction), Boston Mills (Ontario), 1985.

(From *Killer in the Bush: The Great Fires of Northeastern Ontario* by Michael Barnes. Photograph from Bob Atkinson collection.)

Fortunes in the Ground: Famous Mines of Northern Ontario (nonfiction), Boston Mills, 1986.
Killer in the Bush: The Great Fires of Northern Ontario (nonfiction), Boston Mills, 1987.
(With others) *Canadians All!,* (young adult/adult nonfiction), Methuen Canada, 1988.
Polar Bear Express (nonfiction), Boston Mills, 1988.
Policing Ontario—The Ontario Provincial Police Today, Boston Mills, in press.

Contributor to the "Language Development Reading" series published by Nelson Canada, 1970-77. Also co-author of several study books and "Readaway Books" in this series.

SIDELIGHTS: "I spent early childhood years in the London, England suburb of East Shene, alternately evacuated to the countryside to escape the bombing. Young people were often left to their own devices then as parents were engaged in the war effort. As a result, we explored and made our own entertainments. These no doubt spurred the imagination. . . .

"I have lived all over Northeastern Ontario in places like Biscotasing, Sudbury, Lively, Wawa, Moose Factory, Cochrane and Kirkland Lake. Each center has added to my experience. While on the isolated settlement of Moose Factory Island set in the Moose River in lower James Bay, I became the James Bay correspondent for the Toronto *Globe and Mail*. From there I began to write for a prominent children's reading series—wrote high interest-low vocabulary texts for slow learners—,

and finally to popular history. Research for these books is done by scholarly means as well as travel over the terrain. I believe that one must present such work for the average reader in a bright and fast-flowing style. The idea must work as the books are found in libraries across Canada.

"I am the most prolific writer 'extant' about Northern Ontario and have also gained a reputation as a police writer. *Police Story* was a Canadian bestseller."

HOBBIES AND OTHER INTERESTS: Exploring old mines, working on his home at Round Lake, south of Kirkland Lake; researching Northern Ontario history and Canadian eccentrics.

FOR MORE INFORMATION SEE:

Northern Ontario Business, December, 1987.
Canadian Geographic, December, 1987.
Writers Union of Canada Member's Guide, June, 1988.

BENHAM, Mary Lile   1914-

PERSONAL: Born October 8, 1914, in Winnipeg, Manitoba, Canada; daughter of William D. and Gussie (Drewry) Love; married Hugh A. Benham (an investment consultant), October 16, 1935; children: Patricia Joan Benham Norrena, Hugh John, William Drewry, Donald Bruce. *Education:* University of Manitoba, B.A., 1935. *Religion:* Anglican. *Home and office:* 249 Waverley St., Winnipeg, Manitoba, Canada R3M 3K4.

MARY LILE BENHAM

CAREER: Writer, 1971—. Worked in public relations division of National War Finance Committee, Winnipeg, Manitoba, 1943-45. Member of board, Canadian Writers' Foundation. *Member:* Writers' Union of Canada; Canadian Authors Association; Canadian Society of Children's Authors, Illustrators, and Performers; Penhandlers; Junior League of Winnipeg. *Awards, honors:* Honorable Mention from the Manitoba Historical Society's Margaret McWilliams Competition for Local History, for *Once More unto the Breach 1883-1983;* Y.W.C.A. Woman of the Year in the Arts, 1984.

WRITINGS:

FOR YOUNG PEOPLE; BIOGRAPHIES

Nellie McClung, Fitzhenry & Whiteside, 1975, new edition, 1984.
Paul Kane, Fitzhenry & Whiteside, 1977.
La Verendrye, Fitzhenry & Whiteside, 1980.

OTHER

Winnipeg (illustrated with photographs by George Mitchell), City of Winnipeg, Manitoba, 1974.
The Manitoba Club: 1874-1974, Manitoba Club, 1974.
Once More unto the Breach 1883-1983, St. George's Anglican Church, 1982.

PLAYS

"Heather and Feather" (three-act children's play), first produced in Winnipeg, Manitoba, at Playhouse Theatre, 1951.
"Little Lost Reindeer" (puppet play), first produced in Winnipeg by Rupert's Puppets, 1974.
"Snow Queen" (puppet play), first produced in Winnipeg by Rupert's Puppets.

"Buster Beaver Builds the Best" (puppet play), produced in Winnipeg by the Junior League of Winnipeg.
"Whose Zoo" (puppet play), produced in Winnipeg by the Junior League of Winnipeg.
"Bats in the Belfry" (puppet play), produced in Winnipeg by the Junior League of Winnipeg.

Author of weekly column, "What Can I Do?," in the *Winnipeg Free Press* during World War II. Contributor of articles, reviews, and poems to magazines, including *Harlequin, Style, Branching Out, Pierian Spring, Manitoba Business, Alumni Journal* (University of Manitoba), *Canadian Hotel and Restaurant, Discovery, Canadian Author and Bookman,* and *Short Story International.* Past-editor of *Peg Leg* (Junior League of Winnipeg magazine).

SIDELIGHTS: "I have always done some writing, but mainly confined my activities to volunteer work until my last child started at the university in 1971. Then I started writing in earnest for markets.

"I am strongly committed to 'The Canadians' series published by Fitzhenry & Whiteside. Primarily designed for school libraries, the books have steady sales in book stores as adults, too, like these easy-reading, profusely illustrated, biographies which weave the contemporary scene into the story of one mover-and-shaker in Canada."

Benham enjoys researching and begins writing when she realizes, "I've read this before! I don't have much of a system, mostly catch-as-catch can."[1]

Writing scripts for puppet plays is her favorite genre. When the characters "took over" the writing, it was both exciting and threatening to her. "I didn't like losing control.

"I would like to write for young adults. But when I read in the newspapers about some of today's teenagers, I wonder if I even understand them. And if I don't understand teenagers, how can I write for them. My grandchildren are either too young or too old to observe."[1]

"With my retired husband, I travel a great deal—so much that I don't have time to write travel articles! We used to spend summers on a tiny island near Keewatin, Ontario, an island shaped like a Chianti bottle, which threatened to sink into the lake under the sheer weight of Benhams, as our offspring and their offspring joined us in the sun. As we got older and creakier, island living became too much for us. As of August, 1984, we have a mainland cottage near Keewatin, Ontario."

A prolific painter until a few years ago, the walls in her home hold her oils featuring bold colors and busy scenes.

FOOTNOTE SOURCES

[1]Betty L. Dyck, "Mary Lile Benham," *Canadian Author and Bookman,* spring, 1987.

FOR MORE INFORMATION SEE:

Winnipeg Free Press, October 13, 1979.

BETANCOURT, Jeanne   1941-

PERSONAL: Born October 2, 1941, in Burlington, Vt.; daughter of Henry (a certified public accountant) and Beatrice (a secretary; maiden name, Mario) Granger; married Lee Minoff (a writer and psychoanalyst), March 5, 1983; children: (first marriage) Nicole. *Education:* College of St. Joseph the Provider,

JEANNE BETANCOURT

(Jacket illustration by Tom Galazinski from *Home Sweet Home* by Jeanne Betancourt.)

B.S., 1964; New York University, M.A., 1974. *Home:* New York City, and Sharon, Conn. *Agent:* Charlotte Sheedy, 145 West 86th St., New York, N.Y. 10024.

CAREER: St. Peters School, Rutland, Vt., teacher, 1961-63; St. Francis deSales Academy, Bennington, Vt., teacher, 1963-64; Edmunds Junior High School, Burlington, Vt., teacher 1964-65; East Islip High School, East Islip, N.Y., teacher, 1965-66; High School for Pregnant Teens, Bronx, N.Y., teacher, 1967-69; Tetard Junior High School, Bronx, teacher 1969-70; John Jay High School, Brooklyn, N.Y., teacher, 1970-71; Prospect Heights High School, Brooklyn, 1971-76; Edward R. Murrow High School, Brooklyn, teacher, 1976-80; New School for Social Research, New York City, faculty member, 1977-80; Tomorrow Entertainment/Medcom Company, New York City, director of development, 1980-81; full-time writer, 1981—. Member of preview committee for first International Film Festival, 1972, of reviewing committee of film division at Brooklyn Public Library, 1974-79, and of board of directors, Media Center for Children, New York City, 1977-87. *Member:* New York Women in Film (president, 1981-82).

AWARDS, HONORS: SMILE! How to Cope with Braces was selected an Outstanding Science Trade Book for Children by the National Science Teachers Association and the Children's Book Council, 1982; Emmy nomination for Outstanding Children's Special, 1986, for "I Want to Go Home," and "Don't Touch," 1987, for "Teen Father," and 1988, for "Supermom's Daughter"; Emmy nomination for Best Children's Script, 1986, for "Don't Touch"; Humanitarian Award from the Los Angeles Council on Assaults against Women, 1987, for "Don't Touch"; Humanitas Award finalist, 1986, for "Don't Touch," and 1987, for "Teen Father"; National Psychology Award for Excellence in the Media from the American Psychological As-

sociation, and Nancy Susan Reynolds Award from the Center for Population Options, both 1987, both for "Teen Father"; Children's Choice Award from the International Reading Association and the Children's Book Council, 1987, for *Sweet Sixteen and Never. . .;* Commendation Award from American Women in Radio and Television, and Mentor Award from the National Association for Youth, both 1988, both for "Supermom's Daughter."

WRITINGS:

NONFICTION

Women in Focus (adult), Pflaum, 1974.
SMILE! How to Cope with Braces (juvenile; illustrated by Mimi Harrison), Knopf, 1982.

JUVENILE

The Rainbow Kid, Avon, 1983.
Turtle Time, Avon, 1985
Puppy Love, Avon, 1986.
Crazy Christmas, Bantam, 1988.

YOUNG ADULT NOVELS

Am I Normal? (adaptation of a film), Avon, 1983, Printed Matter, 1988.
Dear Diary (adaptation of a film), Avon, 1983, Printed Matter, 1988.
The Edge, Scholastic, 1985.
Between Us, Scholastic, 1986.
Sweet Sixteen and Never. . . , Bantam, 1986.
Home Sweet Home, Bantam, 1988.
Not Just Party Girls, Bantam, 1988.

TELEPLAYS; ALL ABC "AFTERSCHOOL SPECIALS"

"I Want to Go Home," 1985.
"Don't Touch," 1985.
"Are You My Mother," 1986.
"Teen Father," 1986.
"Supermom's Daughter," 1987.
"Tattle," 1988.

Author with husband, Lee Minoff of unproduced screenplay "Carolyn and Maggie," based on a novel by Norma Klein for Columbia Pictures. Developer of workshops for librarians and educators on the topic of film programming for adolescents. Contributor of articles and reviews to periodicals, including *Women in Film, Film Library Quarterly, Media Methods,* and *Sightlines.* Contributing editor, *Channels,* 1981-82.

WORK IN PROGRESS: A book on her years as a nun.

SIDELIGHTS: "I grew up in rural Vermont. For many seasons of my childhood I lived across the road from a dairy farm and spent hours upon hours playing in the fields, 'helping' in the barns and hanging out in the big kitchen with our Swedish farmer/neighbors. Those years I never thought of being a writer. I loved my tap dancing classes and wanted to be a Rockette at Radio City Music Hall.

"When I was in high school we moved to Burlington, Vermont. I kept on tapping and went to a Catholic girls high school. On Saturdays I helped teach tap and ballet to children at the studio where I took classes. When I learned that at five feet eight inches I was too tall for the Rockettes tap dancing line of chorus girls I decided I'd be a dancing teacher instead. Late in the eleventh grade, however, I felt I had a calling to the religious life—an idea that I pursued so diligently that after high school I entered a teaching order of nuns—the Sisters of Saint Joseph in Rutland, Vermont. I stayed there for six years. During that time I got my first degree and taught junior high school.

"I left the convent for all sorts of reasons—intellectual, personal and religious. Two years later I was married and living in New York City. For the next fourteen years I taught in inner city public high schools and raised my daughter, Nicole. I got a degree in film studies and designed curriculum in film studies and film making for high school students. My first book, *Women in Focus,* was my masters degree project.

"I wrote my first children's book, *SMILE! How to Cope with Braces,* when my daughter Nicole was having orthodontic treatment. I couldn't find the right book to help her with this new experience, so I researched and wrote one. By the time the book was published Nicole was out of braces, but her picture is on the cover of the book.

"I started writing the Aviva Granger stories (*The Rainbow Kid, Turtle Time, Puppy Love,* and *Crazy Christmas*) when, at nine, Nicole first became a joint custody kid and began to split her life—two weeks at a time—with me and her father.

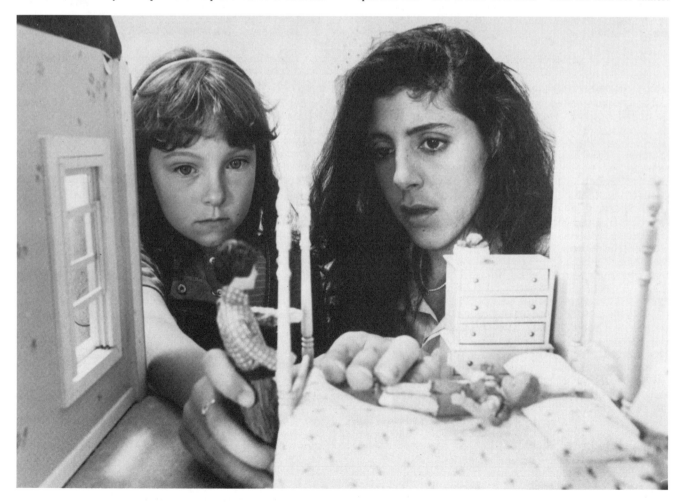

(Niki Scalera and Kelly Wolf star in the "ABC Afterschool Special" "Don't Touch." Copyright © 1985 by ABC, Inc.)

(From the ''ABC Afterschool Special'' ''Teen Father,'' starring Corey Parker. Copyright © 1986 by Capital Cities/ABC, Inc.)

I've given Aviva my maiden name, Granger, and set the stories in Burlington, Vermont.

"Nicole, who is now twenty and a sophomore in college, has been the 'inspiration' for most of my books and some of my 'Afterschool Special' scripts. But when it comes down to writing the story and getting into the head and heart of Aviva, Julie, Cassandra or any of my characters, I have to become the character myself. Nicole can't do that for me.

"The month after *Home Sweet Home* was published Nicole went on a school trip to the Soviet Union. Since one of the characters and voices in *Home Sweet Home* is a Russian foreign exchange student, Nicole decided to take ten copies of *Home Sweet Home* with her to the USSR. She presented the copies to English-speaking students and their teachers. So now Russian kids are reading the story of a close friendship between a Russian girl (Anya) and her new American friend (Tracy) and seeing America through Anya's eyes.

"For all of my books and scripts I do research. For example, for *Home Sweet Home* I read many books about the Soviet Union, visited dairy farms and interviewed farmers. For *Between Us*—a mystery novel that makes a connection between drugs used for medical reasons and drugs sold illegally for recreational use—I spent many mornings in the pharmacy of our local hospital in Sharon, Connecticut learning about drugs and how a hospital pharmacy works.

"I write about tough subjects that emphasize some of the harsher realities of our lives. In the novels: divorce, pre-marital sex, drug abuse, family farm crisis, migrant workers plight. In the

'Afterschool Specials': child molestation, parental kidnapping, cocaine addiction, homelessness, teen parenting. I know that my reader/viewers are either experiencing some of these difficult and challenging situations personally, through their friends and neighbors, or through the media. I want to show, in a story, the aspects of the 'issue' that I feel kids should be aware of. These are important issues that the media sometimes exploits. I want to explore them. I want to help kids grow stronger and wiser through the experience of my stories, to see that they have responsibility and power. Through role models from their own age group I want to show kids what they can and should do for themselves and for others.

"I believe that the antidote to our human problems is based in human values—those little things we can do for one another to alleviate the pain. I've learned, as children must, that bad things happen to good people and good people have no choice but to become better through the process of coping. This is where the writer comes in. Samuel Johnson said it best when he wrote, 'The only end of writing is to enable the reader to enjoy life better or better to endure it.'

"I suffer from the learning disability dyslexia, which for me manifests itself in spelling problems, memory problems for dates and names. I also have trouble following spacial directions and am a very slow reader. To compensate for my disability I have developed a sharply tuned attention to conversation (particularly the rhythms and emotional content of dialogue), heightened visual acuity and memory, and empathy. These are the critical tools I use in my story telling.

"Besides writing and reading, I spend my time gardening, drawing and oil painting. My sporting life is pretty solitary. I've never been good in competitive sports, probably because I have terrible eye/hand coordination; so I swim, cross-country ski, do yoga and ride my bike or motor scoot around the countryside. I still love to dance.

"My daughter, Nicole, is now at Sarah Lawrence College. My husband, Lee Minoff, is a psychoanalyst and writer. He came up with the idea for the Beatles film, 'Yellow Submarine,' and wrote the script. We've written scripts together and he is my first and best editor. I'm very lucky to be married to someone who loves to 'talk story' and who has a writer's mind for character and plot.

"We have a dog—a Wheaton terrier named Willie—who appears on the cover of *Puppy Love*. Lee and I split our time between our apartment and offices in New York and our home in rural Connecticut.

"Some people think that a writer's life is lonely. When I'm writing a story I don't feel lonely because I am actively involved with lots of interesting people—the characters in my books. I love knowing that some day—in the private moment of reading—other people will get to know and care about these people too.''

BRONOWSKI, Jacob 1908-1974

PERSONAL: Surname is pronounced Bron-*off*-ski; born January 18, 1908, in Poland; came to United States in 1964; died August 22, 1974, in East Hampton, N.Y.; son of Abram and Celia (Flatto) Bronowski; married Rita Coblentz, February 17, 1941; children: Lisa Anne, Judith Jill, Nicole Ruth, Clare Beth. *Education:* Jesus College, Cambridge, M.A., 1930, Ph.D., 1933. *Residence:* La Jolla, Calif.

JACOB BRONOWSKI

CAREER: University College, Hull, England, senior lecturer, 1934-42; wartime researcher and head of statistical units dealing with the effects of bombings for British Ministry of Home Security, 1942-45; served with Joint Target Group, Washington, D.C., and as scientific deputy to British Chiefs of Staff mission to Japan, 1945; statistical researcher on economics and industries for British Ministry of Works, 1946-50; National Coal Board of Great Britain, London, England, director of Coal Research Establishment, 1950-59, director-general of Process Development Department, 1959-63; Salk Institute for Biological Studies, San Diego, Calif., research professor, fellow, and director of council for biology in human affairs, 1964-74. Charles Beard Lecturer, Oxford University; Carnegie Visiting Professor, Massachusetts Institute of Technology, 1953; lecturer, American Museum of Natural History, 1965; Eastman Memorial Visiting Professor, University of Rochester, 1965; Condon Lecturer, Oregon State University, 1967; Silliman Lecturer, Yale University, 1967; Bampton Lecturer, Columbia University, 1969; Mellon Lecturer, National Gallery of Art, 1969. Head of projects division, UNESCO, 1948. Commentator on atomic energy and other scientific and cultural subjects for British Broadcasting Corp.; panelist, "Brains Trust" (radio and television program), 1946-59. Lecturer.

MEMBER: World Academy of Art and Science (fellow), Society for Visiting Scientists, Royal Society of Literature (fellow), American Academy of Arts and Sciences (honorary member), Athenaeum Club (London). *Awards, honors:* Thornton Medal; Italia Prize for best dramatic work broadcast throughout Europe during 1950-51, for "The Face of Violence"; Edison Mass Media Award from the Thomas Alva Edison Foundation, 1966, for *Biography of an Atom;* honorary fellow, Jesus College, Cambridge University, 1967.

WRITINGS:

JUVENILE

(With M. E. Selsam) *Biography of an Atom* (illustrated by Weimer Pursell), Harper, 1965.

OTHER

The Poet's Defence, Macmillan, 1939, published as *The Poet's Defense: The Concept of Poetry from Sidney to Yeats,* World, 1966.
Spain 1939: Four Poems, Andrew Marvell Press, 1939.
William Blake, 1757-1827: A Man without a Mask, Secker & Warburg, 1943, Transatlantic, 1945, reissued, Gordon Press, 1976, revised edition, Penguin, 1954, published as *William Blake and the Age of Revolution,* Harper, 1965.
The Common Sense of Science, Heinemann, 1951, Harvard University Press, 1953, reissued, 1978.
The Face of Violence: An Essay with a Play (first produced, 1950), Turnstile Press, 1954, Braziller, 1955, new and enlarged edition, World, 1967.
Science and Human Values, Messner, 1956, revised edition, Penguin, 1964.
(Editor and author of introduction) *William Blake: A Selection of Poems and Letters,* Penguin, 1958.
(Editor with others) *Science: Chemistry, Physics, Astronomy,* Doubleday, 1960.
(With Bruce Mazlish) *The Western Intellectual Tradition: From Leonardo to Hegel,* Harper, 1960.
(Editor with others) *Technology: Man Remakes His World,* MacDonald, 1963, published as *The Doubleday Pictorial Library of Technology,* Doubleday, 1964, revised edition published under original title, Responsive Environments Corp., 1966.
(With others) *Imagination and the University,* University of Toronto Press, 1964.
Insight, Harper, 1964.
The Identity of Man, Natural History Press, 1965, revised edition, 1971.
Science and Human Values [and] *The Abacus and the Rose* (radio program; first produced, 1962), Harper, 1965, revised edition, 1972.
On Being an Intellectual, Smith College, 1968.
Nature and Knowledge: The Philosophy of Contemporary Science, Oregon State System of Higher Education, 1969.
The Ascent of Man (essays based on television series), British Broadcasting Corp., 1973, Little, Brown, 1974.
A Sense of the Future: Essays in Natural Philosophy, M.I.T. Press, 1977.
The Visionary Eye: Essays in the Arts, Literature, and Science, M.I.T. Press, 1978.
Magic, Science, and Civilization, Columbia University Press, 1978.
The Origins of Knowledge and Imagination, Yale University Press, 1978.

Also author of radio dramas, including "The Man without a Mask," 1946, "Journey to Japan," 1948, and "The Closing Years," 1951, an opera (with Peter Racine Fricker), "My Brother Died," 1954, several television documentary series, "Science in the Making," 1953-54, "New Horizon," 1958, "Insight," 1960-61, and "The Ascent of Man," 1973, and numerous papers on mathematics. Contributor of articles to newspapers and journals.

SIDELIGHTS: A mathematician by training, Bronowski, like many of his countrymen, was profoundly shaken by the events of World War II; shaken enough, in fact, that he changed the direction of his life. As he once explained to an interviewer: "Hitler's coming struck a most powerful blow at me and my

Charles Darwin's study at Downe House. ■ (From *The Ascent of Man* by Jacob Bronowski. Photograph courtesy of Sir Hedley Atkins.)

generation. I suddenly realized that being happy, being human, being a scientist, being with friends was not enough. And particularly being an academic, which I was then destined to be, was not going to be enough. Quite suddenly it became clear that whatever one did with one's life after 1932, one had to bear witness for what one believed to be the foundations of human decency. . . .It was no longer enough to be a good person quietly working at your desk. . . .I realized that I was a persuasive person, that coming to England and learning English had given me a gift for the language and for the thought, for the way that English people think about themselves and about eccentrics like me, which was persuasive to other people. And I never looked back. It was then that I began to write about science in general, to address people who were not in university classes, and to go out to do the kind of thing that I became classic for.''

The specific turning point in Bronowski's career came in Nagasaki, Japan, at the end of 1945. As a member of a commission assigned to study the effects of atomic bombing, he noted that ''of course I had seen all the pictures. I had seen all the aerial surveys, and I had seen all the stereo pictures and I thought I knew what it looked like. But coming into that gloomy valley by the sea, with the ships in the harbor, with the broken railways, was an unforgettable experience. I did not know I was in Nagasaki until we were actually at the side of the ships, because everything was such a tangle of wreckage. . . . [I] knew that we had dehumanized the enemy and ourselves in one blow. I saw how much deeper the implica-

tions of great general actions are. And I came back with a totally different sense of how human beings had to react to one another.''

Realizing that scientists could no longer regard themselves as being ''wholly withdrawn from public affairs,'' Bronowski turned more and more towards a study of the relation between art and science. He was firmly convinced that creativity—whether scientific or artistic—springs from the same basic source. ''Science and art,'' he insisted, ''are wonderfully human because they both call on imagination and they both require enormous dedication and integrity. When people say to me 'Oh, I do not much care about science; I never could do arithmetic. I am an arts person,' I know they are just telling me a pack of lies. . . .They are against science just because it happens to be the fashionable culture. No, if you care about art or if you care about science you must have a huge sense of involvement with what is human about those things. Now, about science the answer is quite straightforward. The wonder of science is reading the riddle of man, reading the riddle of human nature, reading the riddle of *life,* if you like. . . .What makes the arts so wonderfully special and so wonderfully human [is] the ability of the human being to identify himself with someone else and to say 'That is universal humanity, that is what we share and what I try to utter and invoke at one and the same moment.' ''

The Ascent of Man was probably Bronowski's most popular achievement. A collection of essays derived from a thirteen-

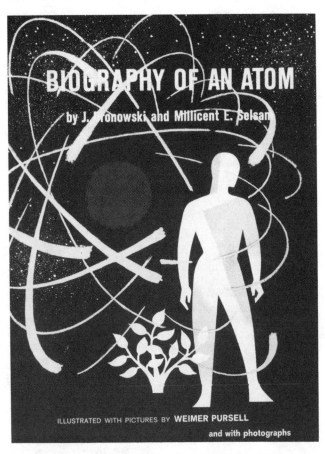

(Jacket illustration by Weimer Pursell from *Biography of an Atom* by Jacob Bronowski and Millicent E. Selsam.)

part BBC-TV series, it was a virtual celebration of the development of man's attempts to understand and control nature from prehistoric times to the present. For children he wrote *Biography of an Atom* with Millicent E. Selsam, which has been in print for more than two decades.

Throughout the years, in spite of what he had observed in man that discouraged him, Bronowski remained optimistic about the future. Having expressed his conviction that acquiring a thorough understanding of the role of violence in modern society is crucial if one seeks to create a "happy society," he speculated on what the future might hold for mankind: "What violence everywhere shows is that there is a real sense of unease in the tension between people as individuals and the society that they believe fulfills them physically but does not yet fulfill their aspirations as individuals. . . .[We must understand] that every man has a right to be himself, and no man. . .has any more right to speak for the state than that man, or you, or you, or I. . . .It is not ecology that is threatened. It is not the environment that is threatened. It is the human structure of society which I believe to be at risk. . . .And happily I am a great optimist. I think we shall win."

FOR MORE INFORMATION SEE:

Christian Science Monitor, June 5, 1958, June 25, 1974.
New Republic, August 18, 1958.
Choice, July, 1974.
New York Times, August 23, 1974.
Washington Post, August 23, 1974.
Newsweek, September 2, 1974, January 27, 1975.
Time, September 2, 1974.
Publishers Weekly, September 2, 1974.

Books and Bookmen, April, 1975.
Jacob Bronowski: Twentieth Century Man (interviews), Salk Institute for Biological Studies, 1976.
Los Angeles Times Book Review, March 25, 1979.

BROWN, Cassie   1919-1986

PERSONAL: Born January 10, 1919, in Rose Blanche, Newfoundland, Canada; died December 30, 1986; daughter of Wilson Gordon (a merchant) and Caroline (Hillier) Horwood; married Donald Frank Brown (a consultant), September 10, 1945; children: Derek, Christine. *Education:* Attended schools in Newfoundland. *Religion:* Protestant. *Home:* St. John's, Newfoundland, Canada.

CAREER: Stenographer for various firms, 1940-46; freelance writer, 1947-59; *Daily News,* St. John's, Newfoundland, journalist, 1959-66; *Newfoundland Woman* (magazine), St. John's, publisher and editor, 1962-65; president of Karwood Ltd., 1966-86. *Member:* Newfoundland Drama Society. *Awards, honors:* Arts and Letters awards from the government of Newfoundland, annually, 1953-57, for short stories and radio plays.

WRITINGS:

NONFICTION

Death on the Ice: The Great Newfoundland Sealing Disaster of 1914, Doubleday, 1972.
A Winter's Tale: The Wreck of the Florizel, Doubleday (Toronto), 1976, (New York), 1977.
Standing into Danger, Doubleday, 1979.

CASSIE BROWN

SCRIPTS

"Down by the Sea" (radio play), CBC Radio, 1966.
"Wreckers" (radio play), CBC Radio, 1967.
"Mamma Was a Mermaid" (radio play), CBC Radio, 1968.
"Act of God" (documentary), CBC Radio, 1973.
"The Wreck of the Florizel" (documentary), CBC Radio, 1974.

Author of plays, adaptations, documentaries, and commentaries for Newfoundland Regional Network of the Canadian Broadcasting Company, including "The Storyteller," 1958-59. Also author of stage plays, including "Down by the Sea," and "Wreckers." Work represented in anthologies, including *The Book of Newfoundland,* edited by J. R. Smallwood, Newfoundland Book Publishers, 1975. Author of weekly column, "The Inside Track," *Daily News,* St. John's, Newfoundland, 1959-66. Contributor to *Atlantic Advocate* and other periodicals.

SIDELIGHTS: "I began writing when I was very young—twelve or thirteen years of age. During my teens I wrote publicity articles for the Newfoundland Hiking Club which were published in a local newspaper. In the 1950s I began writing fiction and plays for radio. At that time I also entered the Arts and Letters competition and was a five-time winner. I have written documentaries and plays for the regional and national networks of the CBC Radio, as well as for schools and broadcasts for the Newfoundland and Maritime Networks.

"In 1966 I left my job with the *Daily News* and began in-depth research into my first book *Death on the Ice,* which was published in 1972. It was serialized in England, Australia, Norway, and Spain; was published in Buenos Aires, Argentina; was in the *Reader's Digest* book section in all of their publications around the world; and is in the schools in many Canadian provinces.

"My second book, *A Winter's Tale,* was in the *Reader's Digest* and is in the Canadian schools."

FOR MORE INFORMATION SEE:

Canada Writes!, Writers' Union of Canada, 1977.
Canadian Children's Literature, number 23/24, 1981.

BRUCK, Lorraine 1921-
(Laurie Bridges)

PERSONAL: Born March 16, 1921, in Omaha, Neb.; daughter of Joseph and Emma (Rubenstein) Stern; married Marvin L. Bruck (a commercial test pilot), December 25, 1942; children: Marvin, Jr., Joseph. *Education:* University of Minnesota, B.S., 1942; University of Bridgeport, M.S., 1964. *Politics:* Independent. *Religion:* "Free thinker." *Home:* HCR5, Box 574-46, Kerrville, Tex. 78028. *Office:* TWN Communications, Inc., 4500 Claire Chennault, Dallas, Tex. 75248.

CAREER: New Haven Regional Center for the Retarded, New Haven, Conn., in public relations, 1965-66; Bruck Industries, Inc., Westport, Conn., in marketing and public relations, 1968-77; Southbury Press, Inc., Southbury, Conn., projects coor-

LORRAINE BRUCK

dinator and writer, 1980-86; Bruck Corporation, Lake Havasu City, Ariz., editor-in-chief, 1982-86; TWN Communications, Inc., Dallas, Tex., president, co-publisher and executive editor of *The Texas Woman's News,* 1984—. *Member:* Women in Communications, Author's Guild, League of Women Voters, Dallas Women's Political Caucus, Dallas Women's Art Caucus (board member), Ninety-Nines (international organization of women pilots), Association of Women Entrepreneurs of Dallas, Radio and Relay League.

WRITINGS:

JUVENILE; "DARK FORCES" SERIES; UNDER PSEUDONYM LAU-RIE BRIDGES

(With Paul Alexander) *Swamp Witch,* Bantam, 1983.
(With P. Alexander), *Magic Show,* Bantam, 1983.
(With P. Alexander), *Devil Wind,* Bantam, 1983.
The Ashton Horror, Bantam, 1984.

Contributor of articles to *Seniority.* Editor-in-chief, *Colorado River Guide,* 1982-86.

WORK IN PROGRESS: Co-publisher and executive editor of a monthly newspaper for, by and about women serving business and professional women in Dallas and Forth Worth, Texas.

SIDELIGHTS: "One major area of interest is the history of women through the ages with an emphasis on American women. I have an active pilot's license with a sea and land rating, and a ham radio operator's license also. I am a collector of coins, stamps and crystals. Traveling across the country in our motor coach is one of my greatest delights. Flying is next. Publishing *The Texas Woman's News* is all-consuming right now—and worth every minute! I'm old enough to retire—but I'm an inveterate entrepreneur so I guess I'll wear out before I rust out. My interest in people, places and projects is insatiable, so my word processor is humming most of the time recording and writing and editing—life is a ball!"

ROBERT BURLEIGH

BURLEIGH, Robert 1936-

PERSONAL: Born January 4, 1936, in Chicago, Ill.; married; children: three. *Education:* Attended DePauw University, l953-57; University of Chicago, l958-62. *Home:* 6134 N. Rockwell, Chicago, Ill. 60659. *Agent:* Barbara Kouts, 788 Ninth Ave., New York, N. Y. 10019. *Office:* Society for Visual Education, 1345 Diversey, Chicago, Ill.

CAREER: Writer, artist. Society for Visual Education, Chicago, Ill., writer, artist, l975—.

WRITINGS:

(With Mary Jane Gray) *Basic Writing Skills,* Society for Visual Education, l976.
The Triumph of Mittens: Poems, Boardwell-Kloner, 1980.
A Man Named Thoreau (juvenile; illustrated by Lloyd Bloom), Atheneum, 1985.

Also author and producer of over one hundred filmstrips and cassettes on all educational subjects.

CARLYON, Richard

PERSONAL: Surname sounds like Care-leon; son of Richard (an army officer) and Honor (Wilkinson) Carlyon; married Tarie Jesse; children: Leo, Tristan, Clarissa. *Education:* University College, London, B.A. (with honors). *Politics:* "People should care for each other." *Religion:* Anglican. *Residence:* London, England.

CAREER: Author. Also film producer, television researcher for current affairs, and editor of quarterly magazine. *Member:* Bloomsbury Skip Raiders (founder and life president), Forbes Society. *Awards, honors:* Peredur Medal for unpublished lyrical enneads.

WRITINGS:

JUVENILE

Battle for Planet Earth (fantasy; illustrated by Chris Orr; photographs by Philip Sayer), G. Whizzard/Andre Deutsch, 1975.
The Dark Lord of Pengersick (fantasy; illustrated by Pauline Ellison), G. Whizzard/Andre Deutsch, 1976, Farrar, Straus, 1980.
(Compiler) *A Guide to the Gods* (reference), Heinemann, 1981, Morrow, 1982, also published as *A Guide to Gods and Goddesses,* Crossroad, 1981.
Firebird (nonfiction), Haynes, 1984.
Mustang (nonfiction), Haynes, 1984.

Also author of articles and monographs.

WORK IN PROGRESS: "Completing poem cycle (seventy-five items) dedicated to 'A Cruel Lady.' Researching seventeenth-century assassination plots for a historical novel."

SIDELIGHTS: "I have been writing since the age of ten, and it is the most important thing in my life, apart from falling in love. As an epileptic, I understand the transition of fantasy

"Come on, lad, come on," called the jester. ■ (From *The Dark Lord of Pengersick* by Richard Carlyon. Illustrated by Pauline Ellison.)

and reality and know that inspiration is a merciless goddess. I am a fencer, an accomplished marksman, and an expert geomancer. I am also a hopeless romantic in the school of Goethe's Werther but am trying hard to grow up. My whole life has been spent in searching for the ideal in art, life, religion, and mental experience. I have uncovered several secrets which will appear embedded in a future series of books, still being planned.

"I find modern life profoundly exciting and yet profoundly disappointing. Two main things bother me: one is the fact that the few inspired people I have met have turned out to be more interested in wordly things, and the other is the kind of clothing men are expected to wear nowadays. I am also perturbed by loud noises, the lack of sunlight in England, materialism, and the great difficulty I experience in obtaining shoes to fit me, for I have very small feet.

"As a child I lived in India, Africa, Germany, and many parts of England. I lived at fourteen different addresses in the first nineteen years of my life. This has contributed greatly to my stability of character and dullness of imagination. But, to look on the bright side, I have been buried to my neck in a snowdrift, seen ghosts, and have been chased by a rabid dog."

CARR, Mary Jane 1899-1988

OBITUARY NOTICE—See sketch in *SATA* Volume 2: Born April 23, 1899, in Portland, Ore.; died January 4, 1988, in Portland, Ore. Journalist and author. Carr wrote the popular children's book *Children of the Covered Wagon,* which was adapted by Walt Disney Film Studios as "Westward Ho! the Wagons" in 1956. The book was also transcribed into Braille, translated into French and Serbo-Croatian, and was the choice of three national book clubs. Prior to writing for children, Carr was associate editor for the *Catholic Sentinel.* She left that publication and began writing for the *Oregonian,* where she created the historical serial *Young Pioneers* that became her first book. Her subsequent writings included: *Young Mac of Fort Vancouver,* a popular boys' book; *Peggy and Paul and Laddy,* a Newbery Medal runner-up; *Stranger at the Apple Ranch;* and *Top of the Morning,* a book of verse for children. Carr's work is included in the Kerlan Collection at the University of Minnesota.

FOR MORE INFORMATION SEE:

Junior Book of Authors (biographical; p.66), edited by Kunitz and Haycraft, H. W. Wilson, 1951.
Huck and Young, *Children's Literature in the Elementary School,* Holt, 1961.
Contemporary Authors, Permanent Series (biographical, p. 111), edited by Clare D. Kinsman, Gale, 1975.

OBITUARIES

Los Angeles Times, January 7, 1988.
Washington Post, January 7, 1988.

DAVIES, Hunter 1936-
(Atticus)

PERSONAL: Born January 7, 1936, in Renfrew, Scotland; son of John Hunter and Marion (Brechin) Davies; married Margaret Forster (a writer), June 11, 1960; children: Caitlin, Jake, Flora. *Education:* University of Durham, B.A., 1957. *Home:* 11 Boscastle Rd., London NW5, England. *Agent:* Richard Scott Simon, 32 College Cross, London N1, England. *Office:* Punch, 27 Tudor St., London EC4, England.

CAREER: Journalist. *Evening Chronicle,* Manchester, England, reporter, 1958-60; *Sunday Times,* London, England, reporter, 1960, columnist under pseudonym Atticus, 1961-67; worked for *Editor* (magazine), 1977-79; *Punch,* London, columnist, 1979—; *Stamps* (magazine), London, columnist, 1987—. Presenter of "Bookshelf" on BBC-Radio 4, 1983-86.

WRITINGS:

FOR YOUNG PEOPLE

Flossie Teacake's Fur Coat (illustrated by Laurence Hutchins), Bodley Head, 1982, Salem House, 1985.
Flossie Teacake—Again! (illustrated by L. Hutchins), Bodley Head, 1983, Salem House, 1985.
Flossie Teacake Strikes Back! (illustrated by L. Hutchins), Bodley Head, 1984, Salem House, 1985.
Come On Ossie!, Bodley Head, 1985.
Ossie Goes Supersonic!, Bodley Head, 1986.
Ossie the Millionaire, Bodley Head, 1987.

ADULT

Here We Go, Round the Mulberry Bush (novel), Heinemann, 1965, Little, Brown, 1966.

It had been one of those long Saturday mornings and Flossie Teacake was very, very bored. ■ (From *Flossie Teacake—Again!* by Hunter Davies. Illustrated by Laurence Hutchins.)

The original five Beatles in 1960: Pete Best, George Harrison, John Lennon, Paul McCartney and Stu Sutcliffe. ■ (From *The Beatles* by Hunter Davies. Photograph by Astrid Kirchherr.)

(Editor) *The New "London Spy": A Discreet Guide to the City's Pleasures* (nonfiction), Blond, 1966, David White, 1967.

The Other Half (nonfiction), Heinemann, 1966, published as *The Other Halves,* Stein & Day, 1968.

The Beatles: The Authorized Biography, McGraw-Hill, 1968, 2nd revised edition, 1985.

(Editor and contributor with others) *I Knew Daisy Smuten* (communal novel), Coward, 1970.

The Rise and Fall of Jake Sullivan (novel; also author of screenplay), Little, Brown, 1970.

A Very Loving Couple (novel), Weidenfeld & Nicolson, 1971.

The Glory Game, Weidenfeld & Nicolson, 1972, St. Martin's, 1973.

Body Charge, Sphere, 1974.

A Walk along the Wall, Weidenfeld & Nicolson, 1974.

George Stephenson (biography), Weidenfeld & Nicolson, 1975.

The Creighton Report, Hamish Hamilton, 1976.

A Walk around the Lakes, Weidenfeld & Nicolson, 1979.

Father's Day, Weidenfeld & Nicolson, 1981.

The Grades: The First Family of British Entertainment, Weidenfeld & Nicolson, 1981.

A Walk along the Tracks, Weidenfeld & Nicolson, 1982.

England!, Futura, 1982.

Great Britain: A Celebration, Hamish Hamilton, 1982.

British Book of Lists, Hamlyn, 1982.

A Walk around London's Parks, Hamish Hamilton, 1983.

The Joy of Stamps, Robson, 1983.

The Good Guide to the Lakes, Forster Davies, 1984.

The Grand Tour, Hamish Hamilton, 1986.

Back in the U.S.S.R., Hamish Hamilton, 1987.

Beatrix Potter's Lakeland, Warne, 1988.

ADAPTATIONS:

"Here We Go, Round the Mulbery Bush" (motion picture), United Artists, 1968.

WORK IN PROGRESS: In Search of Columbus, half biography, half travel, to be published by Hamish Hamilton; *Saturday Night,* a teenage novel for Penguin.

SIDELIGHTS: "I have only recently come into children's books, after publishing almost thirty adult ones. I've now done one every Christmas for the last seven years, starting at precisely three o'clock on Boxing Day and finishing on my birthday, January 7. What fun, what bliss, what escape from the boringness of the draggy post Christmas period. The first three, about Flossie, were based on my own daughter Flora, then aged ten, who used to burst into tears when her big sister, then aged nearly eighteen, used to go out to the pub, or have her boyfriend calling, or doing her Saturday job, or going to the disco. Flora so desperately wanted to be eighteen NOW. So I devised a way in which this could happen. Doing children's books is like working for MI5. No one knows you, you don't get reviewed, it's all secret, but now the fan letters are flooding in as Flossie has caught on with the nation's kids, well, some of them, and a great many in the United States and Japan.

"As for my adult books, or so-called adult books, for so-called adults, look at the list carefully and you'll notice one thing. Go on, have a look. See anything, hmm? Yup. The connection is no connection. There is no denominator, however common. The only running theme is IGNORANCE. I always want to do something new, start a new topic, every time, as I hate going back, hate returning to a similar subject. So every book starts off the same, with my ignorance of the subject.

"Columbus, the subject which obsesses me as I write this, was a closed book, now I have enough written notes for four books. There were two strands. We have a holiday home in Portugal, near where Columbus was supposed to have been shipwrecked (true), and not far from Sagres where he is supposed to have attended Henry the Navigator's School (not true). I'd been looking for a biography in English to read, but could find none more up to date than the famous Samuel Eliot Morrison works, first written over forty years ago. The second strand came in 1986 when we had a holiday in Barbados, an island he did not discover. I realized that 1992 was coming up, the 500th anniversary of America being discovered by Columbus, and the biggest celebrations of any historic event the world will ever see. So, what a neat time and excuse to do a biography. So far I have been to Jamaica, Venezuela, the Bahamas, the United States Virgin Isles, the British Virgin Isles, Puerto Rico, the Dominican Republic, Haiti, plus Italy, Portugal and Spain. I have never travelled so much for a book in my life, nor had such excitement, such stimulation. Now I've got to write it. Wish me luck, and all who sail. . . ."

FOR MORE INFORMATION SEE:

Commentary, April, 1969.
Times Literary Supplement, July 23, 1970.
New York Times, October 29, 1980.
Washington Post, November 13, 1980.

DUCHACEK, Ivo D(uka)   1913-1988
(Ivo Duka; Martin Cermak)

OBITUARY NOTICE: Born February 27, 1913, in Prostejov, Czechoslovakia; immigrated to United States, 1949, naturalized citizen; died of cancer of the pharynx, March 1, 1988, in Kent, Conn. Government official, educator, radio broadcaster, and author. Under the pseudonym Martin Cermak, Duchacek narrated the weekly commentary "Sunday Notebook," which was transmitted over the Voice of America—a radio service of the United States Information Agency—to Czechoslovakia. A refugee from that country following its Communist takeover in 1948, he concealed his true identity from his radio audience for the entire thirty-eight years he was in broadcasting.

Before he fled his homeland in 1948, Duchacek was engaged in the government's diplomatic service and was a member of its Parliament; during the last year of World War II he served as liaison officer to the U.S. Army. After he arrived in the United States, Duchacek lectured and taught at a number of educational facilities, including Yale University and the City College of the City University of New York, where he received two teaching awards. Duchacek was the author or co-author of several fiction and non-fiction books for children and adults, some under the name Ivo Duka. Among them are: *The Secret of Two Feathers, Martin and His Friend from Outer Space, Nations and Men, Rights and Liberties in the World Today, Power-Maps: Comparative Politics of Constitutions,* and *Conflict and Cooperation among Nations,* with K. W. Thompson. *Martin and His Friend from Outer Space* received the Junior Book Award from the Boys' Club of America in

1956. In addition to his books, Duchacek contributed to various political science journals and publications.

FOR MORE INFORMATION SEE:

Writers Directory: 1986-1988, St. James Press, 1986.
Contemporary Authors, New Revision Series, edited by Ann Evory, Volume 1, Gale, 1981.

OBITUARIES

New York Times, March 3, 1988.

DUMAS, Jacqueline (Claudia)   1946-

PERSONAL: Born April 19, 1946, in Castor, Alberta, Canada; daughter of Roger Eugene (a barber) and Cecile (a teacher; maiden name, Cordel) Dumas; married Giuseppe Vannelli, January 7, 1972 (died, February 18, 1973); living with Michael Lash Wayman (a professor of metallurgy); children: Louise Suzanne. *Education:* Attended University of Alberta, 1963-67; Sir George Williams University (now Concordia University), B.A., 1971. *Home:* 11334 78th Ave., Edmonton, Alberta T6G 0M9, Canada.

CAREER: Worked at various jobs, including the University of Alberta Bookstore, Internal Revenue, men's shirts department at Eaton's in Montreal and a two-year stint as a teacher, 1967-77; Aspen Books, Edmonton, Alberta, co-owner, 1978-85; writer, 1985—. Member of board of directors of NeWest Press, Edmonton. *Member:* Writers Guild of Alberta, Alberta Booksellers Association (executive director, 1987-88).

JACQUELINE DUMAS

WRITINGS:

And I'm Never Coming Back (illustrated by Iris Paabo), Annick Press, 1986.

WORK IN PROGRESS: A novel, tentatively entitled *Outskirts*.

SIDELIGHTS: "In January of 1972 I married Joe Vannelli of Montreal and we set off on a long trip. We hitchhiked across Canada, down the western U.S. coast, across Central America, through South America, went on a freighter to the Galapagos Islands and back again. In February, 1973 we were at a beach in the south of Brazil and he drowned. I returned to Canada.

"In 1975 I moved in with Michael Wayman and we have lived together ever since. We have one daughter, Louise, who was born February 26, 1978.

"I love to travel, and apart from Central and South America, I have travelled back and forth from one end of Canada to the other, to the U.S., the Caribbean, Britain, France, Spain, Portugal and Italy. I lived for one year in Paris, France and for one year in Granada, Spain.

"Among my favourite writers are Italo Calvino, Mavis Gallant, Gina Berriault, Julio Cortazar, Gabriel Garcia Marquez, and Jane Yolen, and I have a passion for folk tales of all sorts."

EAGAR, Frances (Elisabeth Stuart)   1940-1978

OBITUARY NOTICE—See sketch in *SATA* Volume 11: Born March 26, 1940, in London, England; died in July, 1978. Educator and author. After her marriage in 1963 to a teacher at Eaton College, Eagar taught at Eaton College Choir School and Faulkner House School, both in England. In the 1970s she began writing novels for children, including *The Little Sparrow, The Donkey Upstairs, The Tin Mine, The Dolphin of the Two Seas,* and *Cuckoo Clock Island*. About her children's books, she once observed that childhood was a "time of particular clarity" for her and that she enjoyed "observing things with the innocent eye of a child."

FOR MORE INFORMATION SEE:

Growing Point, March, 1975.
Contemporary Authors (biographical; p. 169), Volumes 61-64, edited by Cynthia R. Fadool, Gale, 1976.

ELWOOD, Ann   1931-

PERSONAL: Born January 3, 1931, in Ridgewood, N.J.; daughter of E. S. (a carpenter) and Helen (a housewife; maiden name, Buhlman) Elwood. *Education:* Fairleigh Dickinson University, B.A., 1952; University of California at San Diego, M.A., 1985. *Home:* 2442 Montgomery Ave., Cardiff, Calif. 92007.

CAREER: Free-lance writer, 1952-67, 1972—; Glencoe Press, Beverly Hills, Calif., advertising manager, 1967-72. *Awards, honors: Windows in Space* was selected an Outstanding Science Trade Book for Children by the National Science Teachers Association and the Children's Book Council, 1982, and named a Distinguished Work of Nonfiction by the Southern California Council on Literature for Children and Young People, 1983.

WRITINGS:

FOR YOUNG PEOPLE

(With John Raht) *Walking Out* (young adult novel), Grosset, 1979.
(With Carol Orsag and Sidney Solomon) *The Macmillan Illustrated Almanac for Kids* (illustrated by Lindsey Barrett), Macmillan, 1981.
(With Linda C. Wood) *Windows in Space,* Walker, 1982.
(With C. Orsag Madigan) *Brainstorms and Thunderbolts: How Creative Genius Works,* Macmillan, 1983.

Also author with C. O. Madigan of *Kids' World,* 1989.

WORK IN PROGRESS: A biography of Elisabeth De Ranfaing, founder of convents for "fallen women"; research on French nuns, 1630-1792.

ERNST, Lisa Campbell   1957-

PERSONAL: Born March 13, 1957, in Bartlesville, Okla; daughter of Paul Everton (a chemical engineer) and Mardell (a decorating store owner; maiden name, Lemmon) Campbell; married Lee R. Ernst (an art director in advertising), December 27, 1978. *Education:* University of Oklahoma, B.F.A., 1978. *Office:* 207 Westport Rd., Kansas City, Mo. 64111.

CAREER: Ogilvy & Mather (advertising agency), New York, N.Y., assistant art director, 1978; writer, illustrator and designer of books, 1978—. *Awards, honors: Mirror Magic* was included in the American Institute of Graphic Arts Book Show, 1981; *The Bee* and *Up to Ten and Down Again* were both selected one of Child Study Association of America's Children's Books of the Year, 1986.

WRITINGS:

JUVENILE; ALL SELF-ILLUSTRATED, EXCEPT AS NOTED

Sam Johnson and the Blue Ribbon Quilt (Junior Literary Guild selection), Lothrop, 1983.

LISA CAMPBELL ERNST

The Prize Pig Surprise, Lothrop, 1984.
Up to Ten and Down Again, Lothrop, 1986.
The Bee (illustrated by husband, Lee Ernst), Lothrop, 1986.
Hamilton's Art Show, Lothrop, 1986.
Rescue of Aunt Pansy, Viking, 1987.
Nattie Parsons' Good-Luck Lamb (Junior Literary Guild selection), Viking, 1987.
When Bluebell Sang, Bradbury, 1989.

ILLUSTRATOR

Alice Siegel and Margo McLoone, *It's a Girl's Game Too,* Holt, 1980.
Burton Marks and Rita Marks, *Kites for Kids,* Lothrop, 1980.
Louise Murphy, *My Garden: A Journal for Gardening around the Year,* Scribner, 1980.
Seymour Simon, *Mirror Magic* (Junior Literary Guild selection), Lothrop, 1980.
David Cleveland, *The Frog on Robert's Head,* Coward, 1981.
B. Marks and R. Marks, *The Spook Book,* Lothrop, 1981.
Charles L. Blood, *American Indian Games and Crafts,* F. Watts, 1981.
Harriet Ziefert, *Dress Little Bunny,* Viking, 1986.
H. Ziefert, *Play with Little Bunny,* Viking, 1986.
H. Ziefert, *Good Morning, Sun!,* Viking, 1987.
H. Ziefert, *Breakfast Time!,* Viking, 1987.
H. Ziefert, *Let's Get Dressed,* Viking, 1987.
H. Ziefert, *Bye-Bye Daddy!,* Viking, 1987.

HOBBIES AND OTHER INTERESTS: Reading, drawing, gardening.

FLESCH, Yolande (Catarina) 1950- (Yvonne Greene)

PERSONAL: Born August 20, 1950, in Arnhem, Netherlands; immigrated to the United States, 1956; naturalized citizen, 1963; daughter of Renald J. and Petronella (Hogenbirk) Flesch. *Education:* Hunter College of the City University of New York, B.A., 1976. *Home:* 853 7th Ave., Apt. #3B, New York, N.Y. 10019. *Agent:* Edward J. Acton, 928 Broadway, New York, N.Y. 10010. *Office:* Flesch, Inc., 853 7th Ave., Apt. #3B, New York, N.Y. 10019.

CAREER: Wilhelmina Models, New York City, fashion model, 1968-87; writer, 1978—.

WRITINGS:

Free Things for Homeowners, Cornerstone Library, 1981.
Julian Lennon (young adult), Running Press, 1985.

YOUNG ADULT NOVELS; ALL UNDER PSEUDONYM YVONNE GREENE

Little Sister, Bantam, 1981.
Cover Girl, Bantam, 1982.
The Love Hunt, Bantam, 1985.
The Sweet Dreams Model's Handbook, Bantam, 1985.
Discovered! Kelly Blake, Teen Model, Bantam, 1986.
Paris Nights, Bantam, 1987.

WORK IN PROGRESS: Research for a novel about a Jewish girl living in the Netherlands, who survives the Holocaust but finds herself trapped in a world to which she no longer belongs; ''Katrina Smith,'' a six-book series about a teenage designer for young adults, to be published by Angel Entertainment.

YOLANDE FLESCH

SIDELIGHTS: ''I love all things having to do with nature: bird watching, hiking, gardening. I do this whenever I can, but living in the city, I have to be content with two cats, a mouse or two, and window boxes filled with ivy and geraniums. I also love art and music, and try to go to museums and concerts as often as possible. I am active in a women's career group. Other people's occupations fascinate me, especially after a day cooped up in my study behind the word processor!''

FRANK, Daniel B. 1956-

PERSONAL: Born January 4, 1956, in Washington, D.C.; son of Gerald B. and Joan W. (Harris) Frank; married Carol Levine (a social worker), June 23, 1983. *Religion:* Jewish. *Education:* Amherst College, B.A. (magna cum laude), 1979. *Home:* 486 West Deming Pl., Chicago, Ill. 60614.

CAREER: Teacher of American literature, economics, and writing at elementary and secondary schools in Chicago, Ill., 1980-82; Michael Reese Hospital and Medical Center, Chicago, fellow in adolescent clinical research training program, 1983—. Research associate at Family Focus, Inc., 1980-82.

WRITINGS:

Deep Blue Funk and Other Stories: Portraits of Teenage Parents, University of Chicago Press, 1983.

Contributor to *Chicago.*

WORK IN PROGRESS: Perceptions of the Future among Israeli Youth; Self-Image and the Daughters of the Kibbutz; Personal Experience and Social Change; Alienation and Adolescence: A Review of Psychoanalytic Theory.

Julian Lennon. ■ (From *Julian Lennon* by Yolande Flesch. Photograph by Scott Weiner, Retna Ltd.)

SIDELIGHTS: Deep Blue Funk and Other Stories relates true stories of teenage mothers and fathers and explores their fears and fantasies. For his material, Frank spent two years hanging out at Our Place, a community center run by the social service agency, Family Focus, in a black section of Evanstown, Illinois. Frank, who is white and Jewish, tutored black teenagers for their GED (general equivalency diploma) and listened to their stories. In this community where pregnancy is a mark of status for a teenager, these young women—still children themselves—struggle to raise their babies. The young fathers, too, get a chance to express themselves. They relate how they feel excluded from the tight group of mother, child, and grandmother and bewildered over their new responsibilities.

"I am interested in the processes of social change and political conflict as they are experienced privately and personally by individuals. My ideas are influenced by Freud, Marx and Weber in the social sciences and by Faulkner, Proust, and Thomas Mann in literature. Mark Twain and Carl Sandburg are also important to me. I want to bring together the theory of social science and the sensitivity of the poet and novelist."

GOODE, Stephen   1943-

PERSONAL: Born March 5, 1943, in Elkins, W. Va.; son of Ersel Ray (in lumber business) and Dorothy (a licensed practical nurse; maiden name, Vanscoy) Goode. *Education:* Davidson College, B.A., 1965; University of Virginia, M.A., 1968; Rutgers University, Ph.D., 1978; studied in Vienna, Austria and Budapest, Hungary. *Home:* 5820 Black Hawk Dr., Oxon Hill, Md. 20745.

CAREER: Rutgers University, New Brunswick, N.J., lecturer in history, 1971-72; writer, 1972—. *Awards, honors: Affluent Revolutionaries* was selected one of Child Study Association of America's Children's Books of the Year, 1974.

WRITINGS:

YOUNG ADULT

Affluent Revolutionaries: A Portrait of the New Left, F. Watts, 1974.
The Prophet and the Revolutionary: Arab Socialism in the Modern Middle East, F. Watts, 1975.
Guerilla Warfare and Terrorism, F. Watts, 1977.
The National Defense System, F. Watts, 1977.
Assassination! Kennedy, King, Kennedy, F. Watts, 1978.
Eurocommunism, F. Watts, 1980.
The Nuclear Energy Controversy, F. Watts, 1980.
The New Congress, Messner, 1980.
The End of Detente? U.S.-Soviet Relations, F. Watts, 1981.
The Supreme Court, Messner, 1982.
The Controversial Court: Supreme Court Influences on American Life, Messner, 1982.
The CIA, F. Watts, 1982.
Reaganomics: Reagan's Economic Program, F. Watts, 1982.
The Right to Privacy, F. Watts, 1983.
Foreign Policy in the 1980s, F. Watts, 1983.
Violence in America, Messner, 1983.
States Rights Versus the Federal Government, F. Watts, 1983.
The New Federalism: States Rights in American History, F. Watts, 1983.
The Foreign Policy Debate: Human Rights and American Foreign Policy, 1984.

OTHER

(Editor) *CCLM Index: An Annual Index to Literary Magazines,* Volume 1, Penkevill, 1986.

SIDELIGHTS: "I hope that my best characteristics as a writer are clarity and the ability to distill a great deal of information into a readable and interesting book. When I write on politics, I try to present a balanced and complete picture of the issues without advocating one position or another. My training as a historian has given me the historian's bias that nothing can be understood except from a long-range, historic point of view. In my books I stress the origins of present day political conflicts as well as their significance for today.

"Modern politics, especially in the United States and Europe, is my chief interest. An excellent high school teacher encouraged me to write. I've traveled extensively in Europe and the United States and studied for extended periods of time in Vienna and Budapest."

HOBBIES AND OTHER INTERESTS: Jazz, Mozart, most films, cooking.

HAMILTON, Mary (E.)   1927-

PERSONAL: Born April 3, 1927, in Regina, Saskatchewan, Canada; daughter of Austin McPherson (a veterinary surgeon) and Mary Matilda (a high school principal; maiden name, Dawson) McFarlane; married Albert Charles Hamilton (a professor), July 20, 1950; children: Ian, Malcolm, Peter, Ross. *Education:* United College, University of Manitoba, B.A. (with honors), 1946; doctoral study at University of Toronto. *Politics:* Liberal. *Religion:* Christian. *Home:* 50 Edgehill St., Kingston, Ontario, Canada K7L 2T5.

CAREER: Star, Toronto, Ontario, editor, 1946-48; *News of the World,* Cambridge, England, editor, 1950-52; free-lance

MARY HAMILTON

editor, 1952—. Volunteer library worker at St. Mary's of the Lake Hospital, Kingston, Ontario.

WRITINGS:

The Sky Caribou (juvenile; illustrated by Debi Perna), Peter Martin Associates, 1980.
(With Mary Alice Downie) *And Some Brought Flowers: Plants in a New World* (adult; illustrated by Ernest John Revell), University of Toronto Press, 1980.
The Tin-Lined Trunk (juvenile; illustrated by Ron Berg), Kids Can Press, 1980.
(Contributor) Jeffrey M. Heath, editor, *Profiles in Canadian Literature,* Dundurn Press, 1982.
The New World Bestiary (illustrated by Kim LaFave), Douglas & McIntyre, 1985.
Samuel Hearne (juvenile), Grolier (Toronto), 1988.
Wild Treasures (juvenile), Hyperion Press, 1989.

Contributor of poems to magazines, including *Vox* and *Saturday Night.*

WORK IN PROGRESS: A children's book based on the Sutherland "clearances" and the Red River Settlement; *The Poets' Nosegay,* a collection of major poems about flowers, with commentary.

SIDELIGHTS: Hamilton's writing has been "influenced by a prairie childhood, the experience of living in post-war Cambridge, England, and a happy fifteen years in Seattle. I am now enjoying historic Kingston and its French-Canadian connection.

"As a young child, I had botanical training from an uncle, Dr. George Bartlett of Winnipeg. After graduating in English from United College in Winnipeg, I took graduate studies for three years at the University of Toronto. For several years I was a Don at Victoria College. While in England from 1950-52, I worked for *News of the World* in the editorial department, with the job of interpreting the National Health and National Insurance schemes to readers."

HANNA, Nell(ie L.) 1908-
(Nell)

PERSONAL: Born January 26, 1908, in Edmonton, Alberta, Canada; daughter of Nicholas (a farmer) and Hulda (a homemaker; maiden name, Rentz) Martin; married Joseph Hanna, February 6, 1943; children: David, Jane. *Education:* Attended secondary school in Courtenay, British Columbia, Canada. *Religion:* United Church of Canada. *Home:* Sanderson Ave., Peachland, British Columbia, Canada V0H 1X0.

CAREER: Taught for thirty years in rural, private, city and town schools; writer, 1942—.

WRITINGS:

Thistle Creek, Borealis, 1978.
Where the Heart Is, Borealis, 1980.
(Contributor) *South Edmonton Saga,* Friesen, 1983.

Contributor to *Winnipeg Free Press.*

WORK IN PROGRESS: The story of her early childhood.

SIDELIGHTS: "I grew up on a farm and am oriented to rural life. My father's great storytelling gift inspired me to write. At the age of fourteen I won two prizes from the daily paper,

NELL HANNA

the *Edmonton Bulletin,* one for poetry and another for a competition entitled 'The Land of My Forefathers.'

"For years I wrote a good deal of poetry and children's verse and plays for my pupils in various schools. My writings deal largely with life experiences, but I do research historical facts for the sake of authenticity.

"The source of material for *Thistle Creek* is actual happenings in rural schools, and for *Where the Heart Is,* my father's life as an early pioneer of rural Edmonton from 1896-1939 and his life in his 'old' homeland."

HOBBIES AND OTHER INTERESTS: Water-colour painting, gardening.

HARRIS, Steven Michael 1957-

PERSONAL: Born August 31, 1957, in Fall River, Mass.; son of George Edwin (an optician) and Janice (a housewife and real estate agent; maiden name, Paquette) Harris; married Dawn Decker (a massage therapist), April 28, 1985; children: Kameron. *Education:* Attended high school in Pasadena, Calif. *Home:* R.D. #1, Box 180, Salisbury, Vt. 05769.

CAREER: Pasadena Optical Co., Pasadena, Calif., optician, 1976-77; Ringling Brothers and Barnum & Bailey Circus, ringmaster and clown, 1978-79; actor in Broadway production of the musical "Barnum," 1980-82; television actor in New York, N.Y., 1980-85; writer, 1985—. Presents author's programs for children. *Awards, honors: This Is My Trunk* was

STEVEN MICHAEL HARRIS

selected one of Child Study Association of America's Children's Books of the Year, 1985.

WRITINGS:

This Is My Trunk (juvenile; illustrated by Norma Welliver), Atheneum, 1985.

WORK IN PROGRESS: An adult novel; a screenplay; a study leading towards a speaking program and book about Edward De Vere, the seventeenth Earl of Oxford who very possibly wrote the Shakespearean plays.

SIDELIGHTS: "My study of comedy in performance and acting has been valuable in my pursuit of a writing career. It can be applied to *all* kinds of writing. I'm now working on adult fiction. My children's book, *This Is My Trunk,* has been very successful, so I plan to write more juvenile books.

"*This Is My Trunk* is a nonfiction book about circus clowning. I wanted to write something about clowns that was appealing for its truth, with information not usually mentioned about the subject. Most children's books treat clowns as mindless creatures rather than as hard-working artists.

"Of all my performing jobs, being ringmaster for Ringling Brothers and Barnum & Bailey Circus held the most power and magic. The privilege of announcing in a great voice to tens of thousands of people, thirteen times a week, that magic Ringling name, under eight spotlights backed by tympani roll—'Ladies and gentlemen, children of all ages. . .'—often stiffened the hairs on the back of my neck. My job gave me the power to use my voice to sustain the illusion—and sometimes the reality—of the many variations of 'greatest in the world.'"

HOBBIES AND OTHER INTERESTS: "Music, juggling, fishing, stand-up comedy, circus, and any other unusual form of play or adventure or unique skill I have time to explore at least once."

HENBEST, Nigel   1951-

PERSONAL: Born May 6, 1951, in Manchester, Lancashire, England; son of Harold Bernard (a professor) and Rosalind Skone (a psychiatrist; maiden name, James) Henbest. *Education:* University of Leicester, B.S. (with first class honors), 1972; Cambridge University, M.S., 1975. *Home and office:* 55 Colomb St., London SE10 9EZ, England.

CAREER: University of Leicester, Leicestershire, England, research assistant, 1976-77; author, 1978—; *New Scientist,* London, England, astronomy consultant, 1980—; Royal Greenwich Observatory, Sussex, England, consultant, 1982-85. Broadcaster for British radio and British Broadcasting Corporation World Service. *Member:* British Astronomical Association, Royal Astronomical Society. *Award, honors:* Special Award from the New York Academy of Sciences for a series on engineering and technology, 1979, for *Space Frontiers; The Exploding Universe* was chosen one of New York Public Library's Books for the Teen Age, 1981 and 1982; Senior Information Book Award from the *Times Educational Supplement,* 1987, for *Galaxies and Quasars.*

WRITINGS:

The Exploding Universe, Macmillan, 1979.
Spotter's Guide to the Night Sky (juvenile; illustrated by Michael Roffe), Mayflower, 1979.

NIGEL HENBEST

Mysteries of the Universe, Van Nostrand, 1981 (published in England as *The Mysterious Universe,* Ebury Press, 1981).
(With Michael Marten) *The New Astronomy,* Cambridge University Press, 1983.
(Editor) *Observing the Universe,* Blackwell, 1984.
Comets, Stars, Planets, Admiral, 1985.
Halley's Comet, New Science, 1985.
Simply Star Gazing, Telegraph, 1988.

ALL WITH HEATHER COUPER

Space Frontiers (juvenile), edited by Christopher Cooper, Viking, 1978.
All about Space (juvenile), edited by C. Cooper, Marshall Cavendish, 1981, EMC Publishing, 1983.
The Restless Universe, G. Philip, 1982.
Astronomy (juvenile; illustrated by Denis Bishop and others), F. Watts, 1983.
Physics (juvenile), F. Watts, 1983.
The Planets, Pan Books, 1985.
New Worlds: In Search of the Planets, Addison-Wesley, 1986.
The Sun (juvenile), F. Watts, 1986.
The Moon (juvenile; illustrated by Rhoda Burns and others), F. Watts, 1986.
Galaxies and Quasars (juvenile; illustrated by R. Burns and others), F. Watts, 1986.
Telescopes and Observatories (juvenile), F. Watts, 1987.
Spaceprobes and Satellites (juvenile), F. Watts, 1987.
The Stars, Pan Books, 1988.

TELEVISION SCRIPTS

(With G. Jones) "IRAS: The Infrared Eye," British Broadcasting Corporation (BBC-TV), 1985, WGBH-TV, 1986.
(With H. Couper) "The Planets" (based on book of the same title), Channel 4-TV, 1985.
(Consultant) "Halley's Comet," BBC-TV, 1986.

Columnist, *New Scientist,* 1980—, and *Independent,* 1987—; editor, Journal of the British Astronomical Association, London, England, 1985-87. Contributor to encyclopedias, including *Encyclopedia Brittanica, Encyclopedia of Astronomy and Space,* and *Encyclopedia of Space Travel and Astronomy.* Contributor to periodicals, including *Sunday Times, Guardian, Popular Astronomy, Astronomy* (U.S.), *Unexplained, UNESCO Courier, Bild der Wissenschaft* (Germany), *l'Astronomia* (Italy), *Christian Science Monitor,* and *Newton* (Japan).

WORK IN PROGRESS: The Guide to the Galaxy, to be published by Cambridge University Press; several television outlines are at a preliminary stage of discussion.

SIDELIGHTS: "Astronomy is one of the few areas of science that the average person finds fascinating. By writing about the sky, its beauty and its mysteries, an author can not only grip his audience, but also impart—in a most gentle way—an understanding of how science and scientists work.

"When I began my career as an author, I was doing research at Cambridge, under the then Astronomer Royal. As a research scientist, I was learning more and more—about less and less! In my case, that meant the exploding gases from a supernova that went off over four-hundred years ago.

"At the same time, there were very few people with a professional background who could—or who wanted to—explain astronomy to the public. I've always liked writing, and contributed articles to university magazines and magazines produced for amateur astronomy societies. A friend who was a professional editor invited me to contribute to an encyclopedia of science and technology (*How It Works,* Marshall Caven-

dish, 1975). So, I became a professional writer, and (somewhat to my surprise) found a virtually unlimited market for astronomy titles. There is an especially large interest from young people. They have been brought up with ideas of space, and feel more at home with alien worlds and vast distances than many adults.

"Apart from my work as an author, editor and consultant, I broadcast widely on British radio and the BBC World Service. I was fortunate enough, for example, to cover live the encounter of the Giotto spaceprobe with Halley's Comet for an estimated audience of 120 million on the World Service.

"My leisure interests include travelling, both on business and pleasure. The former included a flight to New Zealand on the Concorde (an experience in itself!) to view Halley's Comet, and conferences in places as far away as Colombia.

"Much of these work and leisure activities are done with fellow astronomy writer and broadcaster Heather Couper—the other member of the team known as 'Hencoup Enterprises'!"

HOBBIES AND OTHER INTERESTS: Travel, homemade wine, vegetarian food, music.

FOR MORE INFORMATION SEE:

Times Literary Supplement, February 17, 1984.

HENDERSON, Kathy 1949-

PERSONAL: Born April 22, 1949, in Oxford, England; daughter of William Anthony (an architect) and Inge (a teacher; maiden name, von Schey) Henderson; living with Nick P. Davidson (a writer and filmmaker), 1976; children: Charley, Daniel, Annie. *Education:* Somerville College, Oxford, B.A. (with honors), 1969; attended Chelsea College Centre for Science Education and Technology, London University, 1974-75. *Home:* 69 Woodland Rise, London N10 3UN, England.

KATHY HENDERSON

'PUSH!'

(From *Sam and the Box* by Kathy Henderson. Illustrated by the author.)

CAREER: Weidenfeld & Nicolson, London, England, picture researcher and editor, 1969-71; Penguin Education (division of Penguin Books), Harmondsworth, England, commissioning editor, 1971-74; writer, 1972—; Inner London Education Authority, London, adult literacy teacher, 1974-78; National Community Development Project, London, editor, 1975-77; University of London, London, research fellow at Charing Cross Hospital Medical School, 1979-82; Open University, Milton Keynes, England, consultant, 1982-84; Frances Lincoln Ltd., London, commissioning editor, 1984—. *Awards, honors:* Shortlisted for Smarties Prize, 1986, for *Fifteen Ways to Go to Bed; Sam and the Big Machines* was selected one of *Parents'* (magazine) Best Books for Babies, 1986; *Sam and the Box* was selected one of Book Trust's Ten Best Children's Books of the Year, 1987.

WRITINGS:

JUVENILE

Sam and the Big Machines (self-illustrated), Deutsch, 1985.
Fifteen Ways to Go to Bed (self-illustrated), Macdonald, 1986.
Where Does It Come From? Water (illustrated by Diane Tippell), Macdonald, 1986.
Where Does It Come From? Banana (illustrated by D. Tippell), Macdonald, 1986.
Where Does It Come From? Sweater (illustrated by D. Tippell), Macdonald, 1986.
Where Does It Come From? Lego Brick (illustrated by D. Tippell), Macdonald, 1986.
Sam and the Box (self-illustrated), Deutsch, 1987.
Where Does It Come From? Bread (illustrated by D. Tippell), Macdonald, 1987.
Where Does It Come From? Letter (illustrated by D. Tippell), Macdonald, 1987.
The Babysitter (self-illustrated), Deutsch, 1988.
Don't Interrupt (illustrated by Sue Hellard), Barrons, 1988.

The Baby's Book of Babies (illustrated with photographs by Anthea Sieveking), Frances Lincoln/Windward, 1988.
Fifteen Ways to Get Dressed (self-illustrated), Macdonald, 1989.
Don't Do That! (sequel to *Don't Interrupt;* illustrated by Susan Hellard), Frances Lincoln/Windward, 1989.

ADULT

(With Frankie Armstrong and Sandra Kerr) *My Song Is My Own: One Hundred Women's Songs,* Pluto Press, 1979.

ILLUSTRATOR

Michael Rosen, *Once There Was a King Who Never Chopped Anyone's Head Off* (juvenile), Deutsch, 1974.

Author of children's poetry programs for "Pictures in Your Mind," and "Something to Think About," on BBC-Schools Radio, 1984—.

WORK IN PROGRESS: Children's books: *Sam and the Smoke,* self-illustrated, and *Jim's Winter,* both to be published by Deutsch.

SIDELIGHTS: "I like to write for the ear, to play with rhythm, assonance, alliteration (and other people's expectations), and I've been lucky enough to be asked to write in that way for BBC-Schools Radio, as well as for publication. This may have a little to do with having studied English language and literature. It certainly has a lot to do with a life-long interest in music of all kinds, including oral narrative.

"Classically trained to play the violin, I later 'discovered' by traditional and ethnic music, the oral tradition, not to mention jazz, blues, and so on. Out of this and an involvement in the women's movement in this country came *My Song Is My Own,* a collection of (only) a hundred women's songs from the United

Kingdom. It was my response to the statement that there really was no such thing in this country, and an offering, in slightly unusual form, to the debates of the time. It took two years for the research, and it was finished just in time for my first child, Charley, to be born. In connection with the book, I played the fiddle on the recording of the same name, a set of radio programs, and in a number of concerts with Sandra Kerr, Frankie Armstrong, and Alison McMorland.

"Another strong strand is a fascination with images. I've always drawn and painted, and I work now as an artist and printmaker as well as an illustrator. The way words and pictures work together is a thing I find endlessly interesting. I have explored this in forms ranging from stage design through cartooning, layout and design, editing illustrated books of all kinds (from history of art to contemporary politics), to children's book illustration.

"The combination of all these strands into my picture books for children is fascinating and demanding. Though it preceded them, the process owes a very great deal to my three children and the comic chaos of family life."

HEST, Amy 1950-

PERSONAL: Born April 28, 1950, in New York, N.Y.; daughter of Seymour Cye and Thelma (Goldberg) Levine; married Lionel Hest (a lawyer), May 19, 1977; children: Sam, Kate. *Education:* Hunter College of the City University of New York,

B.A., 1971; C. W. Post College of Long Island University, M.L.S., 1972.

CAREER: New York Public Library, New York City, children's librarian, 1972-75; Viking Press, Inc., New York City, assistant editor, 1977; writer, 1977—. *Member:* Society of Children's Book Writers. *Awards, honors:* Christopher Award, 1987, for *The Purple Coat; Pete and Lily* was selected one of Child Study Association of America's Children's Books of the Year, 1987.

WRITINGS:

JUVENILE

Maybe Next Year. . ., Clarion, 1982.
The Crack-of-Dawn Walkers (illustrated by Amy Schwartz), Macmillan, 1984.
Pete and Lily, Clarion, 1986.
The Purple Coat ("Reading Rainbow" selection; illustrated by A. Schwartz), Four Winds, 1986.
The Mommy Exchange, Four Winds, 1988.
Getting Rid of Krista, Morrow, 1988.

HILDEBRANDT, Greg 1939-
(The Brothers Hildebrandt, The Hildebrandts)

PERSONAL: Born January 23, 1939, in Detroit, Mich.; son of George J. (an executive) and Germaine (Lajack) Hilde-

AMY HEST

GREG HILDEBRANDT

brandt; children: Mary, Laura, Gregory. *Education:* Attended Meinzinger School of Art, 1958. *Agent:* Jean L. Scrocco, 1148 Parsippany Blvd., Parsippany, N. J. 07054.

CAREER: Free-lance illustrator and writer, 1958—. Jam Handy Co., Detroit, Mich., artist in animation department, beginning 1965; creator with twin brother, Tim Hildebrandt, of posters for Coca-Cola's "Camp-us Poster" series, 1977, and Twentieth Century-Fox's movie "Star Wars," 1977. Consultant to Columbia Pictures. *Military service:* U.S. Army, 1957-60.

AWARDS, HONORS: The Giant Panda Book was chosen one of Child Study Association of America's Children's Books of the Year, 1973; (with Tim Hildebrandt) Gold Medal from the Society of Illustrators, 1977, for the cover illustration of *Clive* (Ballantine Books).

WRITINGS:

(With brother, Tim Hildebrandt) *How Do You Build It?* (illustrated with T. Hildebrandt), Platt & Munk, 1974.
(With T. Hildebrandt under joint pseudonym The Brothers Hildebrandt and Jerry Nichols) *Urshurak* (fantasy novel; illustrated with T. Hildebrandt), Bantam, 1979.
Greg Hildebrandt's Favorite Fairy Tales, edited by Lynn Offerman, Simon & Schuster, 1984.
Treasures of Chanukah, Unicorn, 1987.

ILLUSTRATOR

Charles Dickens, *A Christmas Carol,* Simon & Schuster, 1983.
Bram Stoker, *Dracula,* Unicorn, 1985.
Jean L. Scrocco, editor, *Fairy Tales Frieze,* Unicorn, 1985.
Bonnie Worth, *Peter Cottontail's Surprise,* Unicorn, 1985.
Frank L. Baum, *The Wizard of Oz,* Unicorn, 1985.

J. L. Scrocco, editor, *A Christmas Treasury,* Unicorn, 1985.
William McGuire, *From Tolkien to Oz: The Art of Greg Hildebrandt,* Unicorn, 1985.
Poe, Unicorn, 1986.
J. L. Scrocco, editor, *Peter Cottontail's Frieze,* Unicorn, l986.
J. L. Scrocco, editor, *Peter Cottontail's Story and Coloring Book,* Unicorn, l986.
J. L. Scrocco, editor, *Come Play with Peter Cottontail,* Unicorn, l986.
Frank L. Baum, *The Wizard of Oz Frieze,* Unicorn, l986.
Carlo Collodi, *Pinocchio,* Unicorn, l986.
Come Play with Rutherford Raccoon, Unicorn, 1987.
Come Visit with Mr. Caterpillar, Unicorn, l987.
J. M. Barrie, *Peter Pan,* Unicorn, l987.
J. L. Scrocco, editor, *Treasures of Chanukah,* Unicorn, 1987.
J. L. Scrocco, editor, *Learning Adventures with the Wise Old Owl,* Unicorn, 1988.
J. L. Scrocco, *Reading Is Fun with Bobby Bookworm,* Unicorn, 1988.
Gaston Leroux, *Phantom of the Opera,* Unicorn, 1988.
Charles E. Carryl, *Davy and the Goblin,* Unicorn, 1988.

ILLUSTRATOR WITH T. HILDEBRANDT; JUVENILE, EXCEPT AS NOTED

Gary Webster, *The Man Who Found Out Why,* Hawthorn, 1963.
Audrey Hirsch and Harvey Hirsch, *A Home for Tandy* (fiction), Platt & Munk, 1971.
Watty Piper (pseudonym of Mabel C. Bragg), editor, *Mother Goose: A Treasury of Best-Loved Rhymes,* Platt & Munk, 1972.
Aileen Fisher, *Animal Disguises* (fiction), Bowmar, 1973.
Barbara Shook Hazen, *A Nose for Trouble* (fiction), Golden Press, 1973.
Anthony Hiss, *The Giant Panda Book* (nonfiction), Golden Press, 1973.
Gloria Skurzynski, *The Remarkable Journey of Gustavus Bell* (fiction), Abingdon, 1973.
Sarah Keyser, *The Pop-Up Action Circus Book,* Platt & Munk, 1973.
S. Keyser, *The Pop-Up Action Construction Book,* Platt & Munk, 1973.
Simone Zapun, *Games Animals Play* (nonfiction), Platt & Munk, 1974.
Bill Larson, *Let's Go to Animal Town: A Book about Things That Go!,* Golden Press, 1975.
Annie Ingle, *The Big City Book* (fiction), Platt & Munk, 1975.
Winifred Rosen Casey, *The Hippopotamus Book* (nonfiction), Golden Press, 1975.
(Contributing illustrator) J. R. R. Tolkien, *Smith of Wooten Major and Farmer Giles of Ham* (fiction), Ballantine, 1976.
Kathleen N. Daly, *The Wonder of Animals* (nonfiction), Golden Press, 1976.
K. N. Daly, *Dinosaurs* (nonfiction), Golden Press, 1977.
K. N. Daly, *Today's Biggest Animals* (nonfiction), Golden Press, 1977.
(Under joint pseudonym The Brothers Hildebrandt) Terry Brooks, *The Sword of Shannara* (adult fantasy novel), Random House, 1977.
Ruthanna Long, *The Great Monster Contest* (fiction), Golden Press, 1977.
K. N. Daly, *Hide and Defend* (nonfiction), Golden Press, 1977.
K. N. Daly, *Unusual Animals* (nonfiction), Golden Press, 1977.
(Under joint pseudonym The Hildebrandts), *Here Come the Builders!,* Platt & Munk, 1978.
(Under joint pseudonym The Hildebrandts) *Who Runs the City?,* Platt & Munk, 1978.

When the eyes were finished, imagine his astonishment when he perceived that they moved and looked fixedly at him. ■ (From *Pinocchio* by Carlo Collodi. Illustrated by Greg Hildebrandt.)

(From *A Christmas Carol* by Charles Dickens. Illustrated by Greg Hildebrandt.)

(Under joint pseudonym, The Hildebrandts) *Animals!*, Platt & Munk, 1978.
Clement C. Moore, *The Night before Christmas* (poem), Golden Press, 1981.

Illustrator of Merlin calendar adapted from Mary Stewart's book and creator with T. Hildebrandt, of three calendars based on J. R. R. Tolkien's *Lord of the Rings*, 1976-78. Also illustrator of book jackets. Contributor of illustrations to *Omni*.

ADAPTATIONS:

"Animal Disguises" (filmstrip with record or cassette), Bowmar/Noble, 1973.

SIDELIGHTS: Hildebrandt was born in Detroit, Michigan, on January 23, 1939, five minutes before his identical twin brother, Tim. The Hildebrandt family moved from the city to a rural area of Michigan, where they became involved in farming, wood working, and collecting antiques. Growing up on the farm, Greg and his brother shared identical needs, desires and interests. "As far back as I can remember, I was involved with art of one kind or another. I think the first was pencil drawing."

With their parents' encouragement, the twins spent hours drawing their favorite comic book characters, often creating their own stories to accompany their illustrations. Their mother, Germaine Hildebrandt, recalled her earliest recollection of the twins' drawings: "It was a cold afternoon in early winter, and the Christmas season was approaching. My husband sat at the dining room table with crayons and a coloring book, showing the twins how to color. They instantly became involved, taking over the crayons. And wouldn't you know it, they stayed perfectly inside the lines! My husband and I knew it was very premature. From that moment, art became the mainstream of their lives. They were not yet two years old."[1]

By the age of five, Greg Hildebrandt was creating puppets and sculptures from clay, paper, cloth and wood. His drawings were so outstanding that his kindergarten teacher suggested that he attend the Children's Art Institute. By the time he was eight years old, Greg had developed an interest in comic books, sketching them as a favorite pastime. "I was drawing Superman from the cover of a comic book. His arms were outstretched and he was crushing something in his hands. I couldn't draw the hands and the basic anatomy properly. I kept erasing and drawing, erasing and drawing until I finally screamed in frustration and stormed from the house. Eventually I settled down and went back to the same drawing until I improved it. This pattern repeated itself for years. It exasperated my parents but never discouraged them from supporting me."[1]

Throughout his childhood, the young artist demonstrated a vivid imagination, a passion for sketching family and friends, and a love of fantasy. He was particularly impressed with the animated film, "Pinocchio." "Sitting in the darkened theatre next to my mother, I waited anxiously for the film to begin. Minutes into Walt Disney's 'Pinocchio,' I was lost in the magic and mystery of not only a puppet brought to life, but also in the creation of an entire imaginary world. A world where a cunning fox and cat wore clothes and connived and schemed for gleaming gold. A world where an evil coachman lead innocent boys to a land of self-destructive laziness, only to gleefully watch them turn into donkeys. A world where a beautiful fairy guided a puppet in his struggle to become human. A mystical world where good and evil were ever present, and adventure lurked at every turn. Pinocchio's experiences and sacrifices transformed him, just as I believe that our experiences and sacrifices transform us. 'Pinocchio' was the first film I ever saw. It had a lasting impact on me. It's images are powerful and majestic, and it determined the course of my artistic career."[2]

In high school, science fiction was a great Hildebrandt interest, as was set designing and making movies with a hand-wound Brownie movie camera. "The time it took to get the film back was forever! In class I wondered if the mailman had delivered that yellow Kodak box. After school, I ran home to get the film. I watched the animation for hours, enjoying the movement and analyzing its weaknesses, which appeared glaring once projected on the screen."[1]

Labeled "beatniks" during their high school years, Greg and Tim preferred to make homemade movies and "hang out" in coffeehouses.

At the end of his high school years, Greg Hildebrandt knew that he wanted to be an artist, but to fulfill his military obligation, he joined the Army Reserve immediately after graduation. "The six months felt like six years. Circumstances were such that I could not create. My real nature stood at the main gates, waiting in anticipation for me to return."[1]

At the completion of his Army stint, Hildebrandt and his brother entered Meinzinger Art School in Detroit, where they studied color and design, basic drawing, perspective, and anatomy. They withdrew from the school after eight months, however, to work in the animation department of Jam Handy Company. "It is an exciting career. But only if you are willing to pay the price. If that's what you go after, then you can't go after 50 other things. You have to work very hard at it. It has to be an obsession. It has to be the motivating factor of your existence. If it isn't, forget it! Go do something else."[1]

The brothers spent several years in the commercial art field, designing films, creating story boards, doing advertisements, and mastering set design and live-action animation. Their commercial art work included the Purina cat on the cat food box. During this time they also illustrated their first children's book, *The Man Who Found Out Why*.

By the late 1960s, Greg and Tim Hildebrandt had discovered the works of J. R. R. Tolkien. They read his books together and shared his stories with their families and friends. The brothers began making notes and sketching the Tolkien characters, hoping that some day they would be commissioned to illustrate them. The opportunity did not come until 1975 when they discovered a J. R. R. Tolkien calendar. Printed on the back of the calendar was an invitation to artists to submit their drawings for the following year's calendar. The brothers assembled a portfolio and showed it to the art director of the publishing company who commissioned them to illustrate the 1976 calendar. Within the next three months, they completed the project using family and friends as models.

While the success of the 1976 calendar established the Hildebrandt brothers' reputation, the following calendar was even more successful in both an artistic and financial sense. More than two million Tolkien calendars were sold in a three-year period. "The calendars I've painted have primarily been from books, and you have to try and cover the entire book. You have to hit the key characters, environments, moods and lighting conditions. Since people look at the same image for thirty to thirty-one days you have to choose your illustrations carefully. You have to decide what people want to look at every day. Sometimes that gets tricky.

"Calendar images have to be self-contained because there is no text. So, unlike a book illustration, they each have to tell

(Cover illustration by Greg Hildebrandt from *Dracula* by Bram Stoker.)

Peter Cottontail lived beneath a clearing, deep under the ground. ■ (From *Peter Cottontail's Surprise* by Bonnie Worth. Illustrated by Greg Hildebrandt.)

Her voice was so low that at first he could not make out what she said. ■ (From *Peter Pan* by J. M. Barrie. Illustrated by Greg Hildebrandt.)

their own story and they have to be pleasant for people to view. You have to illustrate specific scenes in a general sense.''[1]

Besides the calendars, Greg and his brother created numerous book jackets and art posters, including the 1977 ''Star Wars'' poster for the Twentieth Century-Fox movie. ''It's always a challenge to try and sum up a movie in one image. You have to grab the spirit of the film and condense it. Since movie poster jobs usually have to be done overnight, I really have to gear myself up to produce. So I take a lot of vitamins and just do it.

''If I was painting the 'Star Wars' poster today I might change the composition slightly but in general I still like this painting. In retrospect, I think it's funny that I had to get two of my friends to pose for Luke and Leia because of the deadline, and now years later, I realize just how many people have walked around with these unknown people on their chests.''[1]

Gradually, the Hildebrandt brothers began to work on their own, attempting to find their individual niches in their careers. ''I was extremely nervous during those months and insecure about my art, even about my ability as an artist. The experience of working alone was so unusual that it frequently broke my concentration just enough to make me feel different in front of a sketch pad or painting. It took a while to feel just me in the art.''[1]

In 1983, Greg Hildebrandt illustrated Dicken's *A Christmas Carol* as a solo effort. ''There is a feeling of awe and intimidation when I look at the finished book and see Charles Dickens name and mine on the same spine. I say, 'My God, this is unbelievable. How dare I allow my name to be printed on the same book with this master?' That's the first feeling I have. Then, I wonder, if Mr. Dickens was alive, would he like these pictures? I wonder that always.

''The characters in this classic are so well defined. Scrooge and his miserliness, the Cratchit family, the spirits, the ghosts and all the other characters are ones that I can get involved with in my illustrations. The story itself, the transformation of a human being is great!''[1]

Since Dickens, Hildebrandt has illustrated numerous classics and fairy tales, including *Greg Hildebrandt's Favorite Fairy Tales*, a project that conjured up childhood memories. ''In each of us there is a child and an imaginative person. I'm trying to reach that child.

''Kids are imaginative! They get it worked out of them by growing up. I think that people resent having to grow up and most of us still want to be kids. It's the freedom of imagination that's important and that's what I'm trying to reach with my art.

''In a book like the *Favorite Fairy Tales*, I'm painting individual characters from separate stories. There are more long shots in this type of illustration. It's less centered on the people because I have to sum up the whole story in one image.

''I tried to achieve a single window into each of these tales. I don't know if I have but I certainly hope so. If I succeed in creating a window into another world that allows someone to walk into it, they can walk away from their problems and into an adventure. That's like a vacation! When you're bored you want to escape into romance or action. That's what my art does for me and I hope it does it for other people. It's pure escapism.''[1]

In 1985, Greg Hildebrandt began sketches for a book, *Peter Cottontail's Surprise*, the first book about this character, who

had been conceived in the 1950s with the popular song, ''Here Comes Peter Cottontail.'' ''At first I approached Peter Cottontail on a very negative level. I had done so many animal books before the *Lord of the Rings*, which was the kind of art I really wanted to do. At that time, I was taking all the work I could get to make a living and stay in the business.

''Don't take me wrong. I love animal classics. I loved them in Disney and *Aesop's Fables*, but it was tough for me to try and get a handle on this rabbit and figure out an approach I wanted to take. I didn't know if I wanted it to be cartoony and then I decided I would approach it the same way I did the classics.

''That's when Peter became a challenge and an original. I realized I hadn't done this before. This was a whole new approach for me with animals.''[1]

Although many of Hildebrandt's works are set in imaginary worlds, the artist uses reality as the foundation for his illustrations. ''I'm a realist and a representationalist. Obviously realism does not apply to a painting of a Balrog from the *Lord of the Rings*. But I paint it realistically even though it doesn't really exist. To paint a picture of a creature like a vampire or a monster like the Balrog, you have to go to nature. They each have elements of human shapes so you need to derive them from reality. Nature is always there, even with the most fantasmagorical situation. If I want to paint an imaginary world, I still have to use the laws of this world. An example of those laws is the way light affects a given subject regarding highlights and shadows; and how the color of the light affects the colors of the objects. I have to study what each light source does to any given color and then apply that to each fantastic situation.

''If you paint a scene of an imaginary world, even though it's on another planet in another solar system, you still have to paint that scene with your knowledge of light that's based on the spectrum of the natural world—our natural world.

''I'm like *Alice through the Looking Glass*. I move through the experience—through the invented world; and then get out of it all kinds of unexpected things. I say I leave this world, yet I totally depend on this world to invent the world I am going to escape into. I can go and invent a world, whatever it may be, and get totally lost in it. I can travel anywhere, go anyplace on my drawing board. I can climb mountains or go into outer space. I can do that with my art and probably get almost the same thrill as those who really do it. I think this idea connects to the idea that it is a lot better to fight wars on paper than it is in reality. And that's one way I think fantasy art is good. You can swing swords and go on all kinds of adventures and you don't have to hurt anybody.

''I get involved with the characters and environments. There is a wonderful thing about this kind of art. I become a part of all the people and the trees and the sky. I feel it and smell it.''[1]

Hildebrandt works diligently on his art projects, averaging ten to twelve hours a day, six days a week, all year long. ''For me, art is my life. It is the center of my being. I need it like my body needs my heart to pump my blood or my lungs to breathe. It is absolutely necessary to sustain my life. The act of living by itself is not enough for me. My life exists for creating art.

''I think the whole idea is to keep developing, to keep evolving up a spiral. You start, and you go higher and higher, and you learn more and more, and you keep getting better and better.

She hugged the soft, stuffed body of the Scarecrow in her arms. ■ (From *The Wizard of Oz* by L. Frank Baum. Illustrated by Greg Hildebrandt.)

You never want to stop on your way up the spiral and say, 'This is it.'"[1]

In reviewing his life and art career, Hildebrandt commented: "There are obviously things I would change, but overall I think I'm headed in the right direction. I'm never really totally satisfied with my work. I think that's what drives me on. I feel the next piece will be it—the one that's going to be perfect. And yet if I really face it, I know that it won't be! That goes on and on. You never know. You can't project on a scale of 1 to 10 and think you're going to end up with a 10. I know I'm after perfection. If I get rational about it, I would say, 'NO,' I'll never find it. I would say that it's a quest. It's exploration; but I never explore the territory completely."[1]

To aspiring young artists, Hildebrandt offered this advice: "I believe like Salvador Dali said, 'Go learn how to paint like the masters and then do what you want to do.' And that's very true. Take any person you are inspired by, and imitate...them. Do it like crazy, and then your own style will gradually emerge. There was an obsession with style while I was growing up. Even now people say, 'I feel that I have to come up with a personal style.' Well, a style evolves like a personality does. You're inspired by other people and you imitate them and you grow from them."[1]

The artists who greatly influenced Hildebrandt include: N.C. Wyeth, Howard Pyle, the Renaissance masters, and early Disney. "I consider even the early Disney art realism. The form that it took was a cartoon but it moved and conveyed a story. It made you cry! It made you laugh! It terrified you! It inspired you! That's what the early illustrators did for me and I'm trying to do it with my art."[1]

FOOTNOTE SOURCES

[1]William McGuire, *From Tolkien to Oz: The Art of Greg Hildebrandt,* Unicorn, 1985.
[2]Greg Hildebrandt, "Illustrator's Note," *Pinocchio,* Unicorn, 1986.

FOR MORE INFORMATION SEE:

Ian Summers, *The Art of the Brothers Hildebrandt,* Ballantine, 1979.
R. Dahlin, "Brothers Hildebrandt Create First Novel; Bantam to Publish It in September," *Publishers Weekly,* May 14, 1979.

HILDEBRANDT, Tim(othy) 1939- (The Brothers Hildebrandt, The Hildebrandts)

PERSONAL: Born January 23, 1939, in Detroit, Mich.; son of George J. (an executive) and Germaine (Lajack) Hildebrandt; married Rita Murray, July 10, 1965; children: Charles. *Education:* Attended Meinzinger School of Art, 1958. *Home:* New Jersey.

CAREER: Free-lance illustrator, 1958—. Worked for four years as an artist in animation department and as film designer for Jam Handy Co., Detroit, Mich., 1959-63; worked for six years as head of film department and filmmaker for Society for the Propagation of the Faith, New York, N.Y. With twin brother, Greg Hildebrandt, illustrated poster for the film "Star Wars," 1977. Sole illustrator for the poster for the film "The Secret of NIMH," 1984. Work has been exhibited in major shows in New York, Philadelphia, and San Francisco; (retrospective) Tokyo, 1979. *Military service:* U.S. Army, 1957-60.

TIM HILDEBRANDT

AWARDS, HONORS: The Giant Panda Book was chosen one of Child Study Association of America's Children's Books of the Year, 1973; (with Greg Hildebrandt) Gold Medal from the Society of Illustrators, 1977, for the cover illustration of *Clive* (Ballantine Books); Children's Choice from the International Reading Association and the Children's Book Council, 1984, for *Hector McSnector and the Mail-Order Christmas Witch;* Award of Merit at the Society of Illustrators Annual Show, 1987, for cover illustration of *The Children of Arabel* (New American Library); Golden Eagle Award for the film "Project Hope."

WRITINGS:

(With brother, Greg Hildebrandt) *How Do They Build It?* (illustrated with G. Hildebrandt), Platt & Munk, 1974.
(With G. Hildebrandt under joint pseudonym The Brothers Hildebrandt, and Jerry Nichols) *Urshurak* (fantasy novel; illustrated with G. Hildebrandt), Bantam, 1979.
(With wife, Rita Hildebrandt) *The Rita and Tim Hildebrandt Fantasy Cookbook* (self-illustrated), Bobbs-Merrill, 1983.
(With R. Hildebrandt) *Merlin and the Dragons of Atlantis* (self-illustrated), Bobbs-Merrill, 1984.
The Unicorn Journal II: An Illustrated Book with Space for Notes, Running Press, 1985.

ILLUSTRATOR

Othello Bach, *Lilly, Willy, and the Mail-Order Witch* (juvenile fiction), Caedmon, 1983.
O. Bach, *Hector McSnector and the Mail-Order Christmas Witch,* Caedmon, 1984.
Michael G. Coney, *Fang, the Gnome,* New American Library, 1988.
Bruce Coville, *The Unicorn Treasury,* Doubleday, 1988.

(From *Fang, the Gnome* by Michael G. Coney. Illustrated by Tim Hildebrandt.)

ILLUSTRATOR; ALL WITH G. HILDEBRANDT; JUVENILE, EXCEPT AS NOTED

Gary Webster, *The Man Who Found Out Why,* Hawthorn, 1963.

Audrey Hirsch and Harvey Hirsch, *A Home for Tandy* (fiction), Platt & Munk, 1971.

Watty Piper (pseudonym of Mabel C. Bragg), editor, *Mother Goose: A Treasury of Best-Loved Rhymes,* Platt & Munk, 1972.

Aileen Fisher, *Animal Disguises* (fiction), Bowmar, 1973.

Anthony Hiss, *The Giant Panda Book* (nonfiction), Golden Press, 1973.

Barbara Shook Hazen, *A Nose for Trouble* (fiction), Golden Press, 1973.

Gloria Skurzynski, *The Remarkable Journey of Gustavus Bell* (fiction), Abingdon, 1973.

Sarah Keyser, *The Pop-Up Action Circus Book,* Platt & Munk, 1973.

S. Keyser, *The Pop-Up Action Construction Book,* Platt & Munk, 1973.

Simone Zapun, *Games Animals Play* (nonfiction), Platt & Munk, 1974.

Bill Larson, *Let's Go to Animal Town: A Book about Things That Go!,* Golden Press, 1975.

Annie Ingle, *The Big City Book* (fiction), Platt & Munk, 1975.

Winifred Rosen Casey, *The Hippopotamus Book* (nonfiction), Golden Press, 1975.

(Contributing illustrator) J. R. R. Tolkien, *Smith of Wooten Major and Farmer Giles of Ham* (fiction), Ballantine, 1976.

Kathleen N. Daly, *The Wonder of Animals* (nonfiction), Golden Press, 1976.

K. N. Daly, *Dinosaurs* (nonfiction), Golden Press, 1977.

K. N. Daly, *Today's Biggest Animals* (nonfiction), Golden Press, 1977.

K. N. Daly, *Hide and Defend* (nonfiction), Golden Press, 1977.

K. N. Daly, *Unusual Animals* (nonfiction), Golden Press, 1977.

(Under joint pseudonym The Brothers Hildebrandt) Terry Brooks, *The Sword of Shannara* (adult fantasy novel), Random House, 1977.

Ruthanna Long, *The Great Monster Contest* (fiction), Golden Press, 1977.

(Under joint pseudonym The Hildebrandts) *Here Come The Builders!,* Platt & Munk, 1978.

(Under joint pseudonym The Hildebrandts) *Animals!,* Platt & Munk, 1978.

(Under joint pseudonym The Hildebrandts) *Who Runs the City?,* Platt & Munk, 1978.

Clement C. Moore, *The Night before Christmas* (poem), Golden Press, 1981.

Illustrator, working solo and in partnership with G. Hildebrandt, of covers for numerous books. Also illustrator with G. Hildebrandt of three calendars based on J. R. R. Tolkien's *Lord of the Rings,* 1976-78.

ADAPTATIONS:

''Animal Disguises'' (filmstrip with cassette or record), Bowmar/Noble, 1973.

WORK IN PROGRESS: A how-to-art book, with own illustrations, for Watson-Guptill; illustrations for book covers, numerous children's books, and the Book of Revelations from the *Bible;* collector plates for the Hamilton Group; game cover and game board for Milton Bradley; a calendar.

SIDELIGHTS: Timothy ''Tim'' Hildebrandt was born five minutes after his brother, Greg, on January 23, 1939, in Detroit, Michigan. From the time of his birth Tim was intimately associated with his brother, sharing identical needs and interests, and displaying a precocious artistic ability. ''I began to draw at about the age of four.''[1]

As far back as he can remember, Tim Hildebrandt was fascinated by comic books, science-fiction books and movies, and would draw many of his favorite cartoon strips with his brother. Later, the brothers created hand puppets, dolls, and marionettes, imitating the Bairds, Edgar Bergen and Lou Bunin. It was the hand puppets, ''Kukla'' and ''Ollie,'' however, that created trouble for Tim and his brother. In order to create ''Ollie,'' the brothers used fur ''borrowed'' from their mother's new fur coat. Although their mother was upset to find her fur damaged, she and her husband continued to encourage the boys to pursue their artistic inclinations.

Tim and Greg especially enjoyed the Disney films and the science-fiction movies of the 1950s. ''The outstanding influences on me as a child were the animated films of Walt Disney, such as 'Snow White and the Seven Dwarfs,' 'Pinocchio,' 'Fantasia,' and 'Bambi.' I also remember seeing around our house the classics illustrated by N. C. Wyeth, and these stuck in my head. Later on, other influences were Hal Foster's

Sunday comic strip, 'Prince Valient,' and the science-fiction films of George Pal, including 'The War of the Worlds' and 'The Time Machine.' Minor influences go on and on—Hieronymus Bosch, Bruegel, and the Impressionists among them—but the greatest still remains Disney. The Disney films continue to give me inspiration, and I feel they are, as Peter Ustinov once said, 'among the wonders of the world'."[1] Reading choices corresponded with his interests in science fiction with works by H. G. Wells, Jules Verne, and Edgar Rice Burroughs.

In high school, Tim and his brother continued to share identical interests in animation, drawing and model building. Considered antisocial by many of their peers, the brothers preferred to make home movies rather than to date or go to school functions. On graduation day from Avondale High School in 1957, they spent the day at the movies watching a science-fiction thriller.

Tim and brother Greg joined the Army Reserve program after high school graduation. During their six-month army stint, the twins discovered that they shared extrasensory powers and "dream sharing." Frequently their dreams were identical and if one suffered a restless night, the other would know something was wrong.

Following their brief army stint, the brothers enrolled in the Meinzinger School of Art in Detroit, Michigan for a few months. The experience was enough to convince them that they should pursue careers in art, particularly in animation.

They were hired by the Jam Handy Company, "which produced industrial films, television commercials, and theatrical productions. I worked in the animation department, starting from the bottom with basic painting tasks. I worked my way up to background painter, storyboard artist, production designer, and animator. It was a small department, and one could be involved on all these levels. Handy's boasted having employed the great Max Fleisher, creator of all those great Popeye cartoons of the 1930s.

"I stayed for four years at Handy's, and I designed several films that won various awards, including the Golden Eagle Award. I then came to New York to make documentary films for a religious organization headed by Bishop Fulton J. Sheen, a leading television personality of the 1950s. I stayed there several years, traveling around the world shooting, directing, editing, and writing various productions. While making these films, I had let my drawing go. It dawned on me one day that I was wasting my talent, so I got a portfolio together and presented it to several publishers of children's books in New York. I began to get so many assignments that I quit making documentary films and went full time into illustrating."[1]

In 1965, Tim met future wife Rita Murray, and eventually settled in northern New Jersey near brother Greg. "During the 1970s my twin brother. . .and I created hundreds of illustrations for books, magazines, and advertising."[1]

Along with their inherent psychic abilities, Tim and his brother shared identical, interchangeable artistic techniques. They were

(From *Lilly, Willy and the Mail-Order Witch* by Othello Bach. Illustrated by Tim Hildebrandt.)

(From the 1977 Tolkien calendar, illustrated by The Brothers Hildebrandt.)

able to paint in shifts, one brother taking over when the other tired. They were also able to work on a picture simultaneously.

Until they were commissioned to illustrate the J. R. R. Tolkien calendars in 1976, the Hildebrandt twins were relatively unknown. The popularity of the calendars changed their status. In 1977, they illustrated the "Star Wars" poster, also a commercial success, using their ability to paint interchangeably to complete the poster in just two days by alternating on a twenty-four hour basis.

After painting forty-five major paintings for the Tolkien calendars within three years, Tim and Greg Hildebrandt decided to let someone else illustrate them, and turned their attention instead toward the creation of their own fantasy story about a kingdom called Urshurak. "After the three Tolkien calendars, we thought about a fantasy calendar of our own, one telling a story."[2] Then they decided to do a book of their own.

Brother Greg, however, came up with the idea of doing a book and a movie as a single project. They engaged a friend, writer Jerry Nichols, to tell the story of Urshurak, a land of elves, Amazons, wizards and witches. Tim said: "We'd already broken down all the cultures—the Amazon culture, the dwarf culture—economics, architecture, even burial rituals. We drew a city. We drew maps.

"Urshurak is the culmination of 40 years of fixation on fantasy."[2]

In addition to Urshurak, Tim and his brother illustrated over fifty books, many book jackets, and art posters. By the early 1980s, however, Tim and Greg gradually began to search for their separate identities. Subsequently, Tim Hildebrandt illustrated a fantasy cookbook and a fantasy storybook that his wife, Rita wrote. More recently, Tim has written and illustrated The Unicorn Journal II.

About his work, Tim commented: "My favorite medium is acrylic. However, I do use watercolor and pen-and-ink. On very rare occasions I have used oils."[1]

HOBBIES AND OTHER INTERESTS: "I collect the old Scribner books illustrated by N. C. Wyeth, along with books illustrated by Maxfield Parrish and by Howard Pyle—the grandfather of American illustration."[1] Classical music, collecting antiques.

FOOTNOTE SOURCES

[1]Contemporary Authors, Volume 122, Gale, 1987.
[2]R. Dahlin, "Brothers Hildebrandt Create First Novel; Bantam to Publish It in September," Publishers Weekly, May 14, 1979.

FOR MORE INFORMATION SEE:

Ian Summers, The Art of the Brothers Hildebrandt, Ballantine, 1979.

HOPF, Alice (Martha) L(ightner)   1904-1988
(Alice Hopf, A. M. Lightner, Alice Lightner)

OBITUARY NOTICE—See sketch in *SATA*, Volume 5: Born October 11, 1904, in Detroit, Mich.; died February 3, 1988, in Upper Black Eddy, Bucks County, Pa. Naturalist and author. Books were a major family interest during Hopf's childhood, since her father, a lawyer, founded the Detroit Public Library. When she grew up, Hopf worked as a secretary, writing science-fiction and nature books for children in her spare time under various pseudonyms.

Besides writing and secretarial work, Hopf had an avocational interest as a lepidopterist and ecologist/conservationist. Among her hobbies was tagging and rearing Monarch butterflies. Her children's book *Monarch Butterflies* resulted. Hopf's success and popularity among students and teachers alike derived from her skill in providing stimulating and informative reading that was easily comprehended by young people. Among her non-fiction writings are: *Wild Traveler: The Story of the Coyote,* the award-winning *Misunderstood Animals,* and *Wild Cousins of the Cat.*

She was also the author of a series of books on the lives of various animals and birds, which was published from 1971 to 1981 and won several science book awards from the National Association of Science Teachers. The series contained *Biography of an Octopus, . . .of a Reindeer, . . .of a Snowy Owl,* and *. . .of a Komodo Dragon,* among other titles. Her fiction includes such titles as *The Rock of Three Planets, The Thursday Toads,* and *The Space Gypsies.* Additionally, Hopf was the author of a number of uncollected short stories, which she contributed to various periodicals.

FOR MORE INFORMATION SEE:

Contemporary Authors, New Revision Series, edited by Ann Evory and Linda Metzger, Volume 9, Gale, 1983.
Twentieth-Century Science-Fiction Writers, 2nd edition, St. James Press, 1986.

OBITUARIES

New York Times, March 11, 1988.

JOHNS, W(illiam) E(arl)   1893-1968
(William Earle, Jon Early, Captain W. E. Johns)

PERSONAL: Born February 5, 1893, in Bengeo, Hertfordshire, England; died of a coronary thrombosis, June 21, 1968; son of Richard Eastman (a tailor) and Elizabeth (Earl) Johns; married Maude Hunt in 1914 (died, 1961); children: William Earl Carmichael. *Education:* Educated at local grammar schools. *Residence:* Hampton Court, Middlesex, England.

CAREER: Journalist and author of books for children. Was apprenticed to a local surveyor at age 16, but entered the Army in 1913, serving in the Middle East, 1915-17, transferred to the Royal Flying Corps (now Royal Air Force), 1917-29, serving on flying duties at home and abroad; shot down over Germany, September, 1918, and was a prisoner of war for the remainder of the war; retired to the Reserves, 1930, retaining rank of captain; took up journalism as an air correspondent to several British and overseas newspapers and magazines; aviation illustrator, beginning, 1927; writer, beginning 1930s.

W. E. Johns with his parents and younger brother, Russell, about 1908. ■ (Photograph courtesy of Margaret Collins.)

Lectured to air cadets, 1939, and worked for the Ministry of Information, 1939-45.

WRITINGS:

JUVENILE; ALL UNDER NAME CAPTAIN W. E. JOHNS, EXCEPT AS INDICATED

Champion of the Main (illustrated by H. Gooderman), Oxford University Press, 1938.
Sinister Service (illustrated by Stuart Tresilian), Oxford University Press, 1942.
Comrades in Arms (illustrated by Leslie Stead), Hodder & Stoughton, 1947.
The Rustlers of Rattlesnake Valley, T. Nelson, 1948.
Adventure Bound (illustrated by Douglas Relf), T. Nelson, 1955.
Adventure Unlimited (illustrated by D. Relf), T. Nelson, 1957.
Adventures of the Junior Detection Club, M. Parrish, 1960.
Where the Golden Eagle Soars (illustrated by Colin Gibson), Hodder & Stoughton, 1960.

"BIGGLES" SERIES; JUVENILE FICTION; ALL UNDER NAME CAPTAIN W. E. JOHNS, EXCEPT AS INDICATED

(Under name W. E. Johns) *The Camels Are Coming* (self-illustrated), J. Hamilton, 1932.
The Cruise of the Condor (illustrated by H. Leigh), J. Hamilton, 1933, reissued as *Biggles in the Cruise of the Condor,* Thames, 1961.
Biggles of the Camel Squadron (illustrated by H. Leigh), J. Hamilton, 1934, reissued, Thames, 1961, also published as *Biggles Goes to War,* Boys' Friend Library, 1983 (not

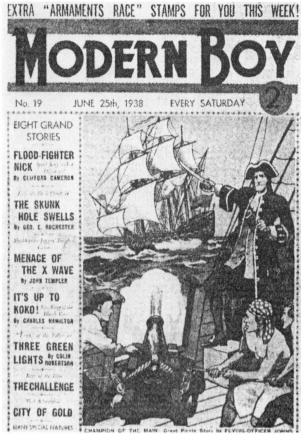

EXTRA "ARMAMENTS RACE" STAMPS FOR YOU THIS WEEK!

MODERN BOY

No. 19   JUNE 25th, 1938   EVERY SATURDAY   2ᵈ

EIGHT GRAND STORIES

FLOOD-FIGHTER NICK
By CLIFFORD CAMERON

THE SKUNK HOLE SWELLS
By GEO. E. ROCHESTER

MENACE OF THE X WAVE
By JOHN TEMPLER

IT'S UP TO KOKO!
By CHARLES HAMILTON

THREE GREEN LIGHTS By COLIN ROBERTSON

THE CHALLENGE

CITY OF GOLD

(The cover of this weekly magazine featured an illustration for the Johns' story, "Champion of the Main.")

same book as *Biggles Goes to War,* Oxford University Press, 1938).

Biggles Flies Again (illustrated by H. Leigh), J. Hamilton, 1934, reissued, Thames, 1961.

The Black Peril: A "Biggles" Story, J. Hamilton, 1935, reissued as *Biggles and the Black Peril,* Thames, 1961, also published as *Biggles Flies East,* Boys Friend Library, 1938 (not same book as *Biggles Flies East,* Oxford University Press, 1935).

Biggles Flies East (illustrated by H. Leigh and Alfred Sindall), Oxford University Press, 1935, reissued, May Fair Books, 1963.

Biggles Hits the Trail (illustrated by H. Leigh and A. Sindall), Oxford University Press, 1935.

Biggles in France, Boys' Friend Library, 1935.

Biggles Learns to Fly (paperback edition; illustrated by L. Stead), Boys' Friend Library, 1935, (hardcover edition) Brockhampton, 1951, reissued, May Fair Books, 1963.

Biggles in Africa (illustrated by H. Leigh and A. Sindall), Oxford University Press, 1936, reissued, May Fair Books, 1965.

Biggles & Co. (illustrated by H. Leigh and A. Sindall), Oxford University Press, 1936.

Biggles Flies West (illustrated by H. Leigh and A. Sindall), Oxford University Press, 1937.

Biggles—Air Commodore (illustrated by H. Leigh and A. Sindall), Oxford University Press, 1937, reissued, Collins, 1966.

Biggles Flies South (illustrated by H. Leigh and Jack Nicolle), Oxford University Press, 1938.

Biggles Goes to War (illustrated by H. Leigh and Martin Tyas), Oxford University Press, 1938.

The Biggles Omnibus (contains *Biggles Flies East, Biggles Hits the Trail,* and *Biggles & Co.*), Oxford University Press, 1938.

The Rescue Flight: A Biggles Story, (illustrated by H. Leigh and A. Sindall), Oxford University Press, 1939, reissued as *Biggles, the Rescue Flight,* May Fair Books, 1965.

Biggles Flies North (illustrated by H. Leigh and Will Narraway), Oxford University Press, 1939.

Biggles in Spain (illustrated by H. Leigh and J. Abbey), Oxford University Press, 1939, reissued, May Fair Books, 1963.

Biggles—Secret Agent (illustrated by H. Leigh and A. Sindall), Oxford University Press, 1940.

The Biggles Flying Omnibus (contains *Biggles Flies North, Biggles Flies South,* and *Biggles Flies West*), Oxford University Press, 1940.

Biggles in the South Seas (illustrated by Norman Howard), Oxford University Press, 1940.

Biggles in the Baltic (illustrated by H. Leigh and A. Sindall), Oxford University Press, 1940, reissued, May Fair Books, 1963.

The Third Biggles Omnibus (contains *Biggles in Spain, Biggles Goes to War,* and *Biggles in the Baltic*), Oxford University Press, 1941.

Biggles Defies the Swastika (illustrated by H. Leigh and A. Sindall), Oxford University Press, 1941, reissued, May Fair Books, 1965.

Biggles Sees It Through (illustrated by H. Leigh and A. Sindall), Oxford University Press, 1941.

Spitfire Parade: Stories of Biggles in War-Time (illustrated by Ratcliffe Wilson), Oxford University Press, 1941, reissued, Transworld, 1956.

Biggles Sweeps the Desert (illustrated by L. Stead), Hodder & Stoughton, 1942.

Biggles in the Jungle (illustrated by Terence Cuneo), Oxford University Press, 1942.

Biggles "Fails to Return" (illustrated by L. Stead), Hodder & Stoughton, 1943.

Biggles Charter Pilot (illustrated by Mendoza), Oxford University Press, 1943, reissued, May Fair Books, 1965.

Biggles in Borneo (illustrated by S. Tresilian), Oxford University Press, 1943.

"BIGGLES" SERIES; JUVENILE FICTION; ALL UNDER NAME CAPTAIN W. E. JOHNS; ALL ILLUSTRATED BY L. STEAD, EXCEPT AS INDICATED

Biggles in the Orient, Hodder & Stoughton, 1945, reissued, May Fair Books, 1963.

Biggles Delivers the Goods, Hodder & Stoughton, 1946.

Sergeant Bigglesworth CID, Hodder & Stoughton, 1947, reissued, May Fair Books, 1963.

Biggles Second Case, Hodder & Stoughton, 1948.

Biggles Hunts Big Game, Hodder & Stoughton, 1948, reissued, Brockhampton Press, 1965.

Biggles Breaks the Silence, Hodder & Stoughton, 1949, published as *Biggles in the Antarctic,* Armada Books, 1970.

Biggles Takes a Holiday, Hodder & Stoughton, 1949.

Biggles Gets His Men, Hodder & Stoughton, 1950, reissued, May Fair Books, 1965.

Biggles Goes to School, Hodder & Stoughton, 1951.

Another Job for Biggles, Hodder & Stoughton, 1951.

Biggles Works It Out, Hodder & Stoughton, 1951.

Biggles—Air Detective, Latimer House, 1952, reissued, Dean, 1967.

Biggles Follows On, Hodder & Stoughton, 1952.

Biggles Takes the Case, Hodder & Stoughton, 1952.

The First Biggles Omnibus, (contains *Biggles Sweeps the Desert, Biggles in the Orient, Biggles Delivers the Goods,* and *Biggles Fails to Return*), Hodder & Stoughton, 1953.

Biggles in the Blue, Brockhampton, 1953.
Biggles and the Black-Raider, Hodder & Stoughton, 1953.
Biggles in the Gobi, Hodder & Stoughton, 1953.
Biggles, Foreign Legionnaire, Hodder & Stoughton, 1953.
Biggles of the Special Air Police, Thames, 1953, reissued, Dean, 1962.
Biggles Pioneer Air Fighter, Thames, 1954, reissued, 1961.
Biggles and the Pirate Treasure and Other Biggles Adventures, Brockhampton, 1954.
Biggles Cuts It Fine, Hodder & Stoughton, 1954.
Biggles Follows On, Transworld, 1955.
Biggles' Chinese Puzzle and Other Biggles Adventures, Brockhampton, 1955.
Biggles in Australia, Hodder & Stoughton, 1955.
The Biggles Air Detective Omnibus, (contains *Sergeant Bigglesworth CID*, *Biggles' Second Case*, *Another Job for Biggles*, and *Biggles Works It Out*), Hodder & Stoughton, 1956.
No Rest for Biggles, Hodder & Stoughton, 1956, reissued, May Fair Books, 1963.
Biggles of 266, Thames, 1956, reissued, Dean, 1962.
Biggles Takes Charge, Brockhampton, 1956.
Biggles Makes Ends Meet, Hodder & Stoughton, 1957.
Biggles of the Interpol, Brockhampton, 1957, reissued, 1965.
Biggles on the Home Front, Hodder & Stoughton, 1957.
Biggles Presses On, Brockhampton, 1958.
Biggles Buries a Hatchet, Brockhampton, 1958.
Biggles on Mystery Island, Hodder & Stoughton, 1958.
Biggles in Mexico, Brockhampton, 1959.
Biggles Combined Operation, Hodder & Stoughton, 1959.

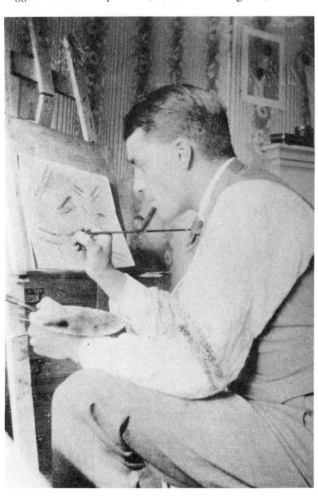

W. E. Johns, 1919.

Biggles at World's End, Brockhampton, 1959.
Biggles and the Leopards of Zinn, Brockhampton, 1960.
Biggles Goes Home, Hodder & Stoughton, 1960.
Biggles and the Missing Millionaire, Brockhampton, 1961.
Biggles Forms a Syndicate, Hodder & Stoughton, 1961.
Biggles and the Poor Rich Boy, Brockhampton, 1961.
Biggles Goes Alone, Hodder & Stoughton, 1962.
Orchids for Biggles, Brockhampton, 1962.
Biggles Sets a Trap, Hodder & Stoughton, 1962.
Biggles and the Plane That Disappeared: A Story of the Air Police, Hodder & Stoughton, 1963.
Biggles Takes It Rough, Brockhampton, 1963.
Biggles' Special Case, Brockhampton, 1963.
Biggles Flies to Work, Dean, 1963.
Biggles Takes a Hand, Hodder & Stoughton, 1963.
Biggles and the Black Mask, Hodder & Stoughton, 1964.
Biggles Investigates and Other Stories of the Air Police, Brockhampton, 1964.
Biggles and the Lost Sovereigns, Brockhampton, 1964, published as *Biggles and the Lost Treasure*, Knight, 1978.
Biggles and the Plot That Failed, Brockhampton, 1965.
Biggles and the Blue Moon, Brockhampton, 1965.
Biggles Looks Back: A Story of Biggles and the Air Police, Hodder & Stoughton, 1965.
Biggles Scores a Bull, Hodder & Stoughton, 1965.
The Biggles Adventure Omnibus, (contains *Biggles Gets His Men*, *No Rest for Biggles*, *Another Job for Biggles*, and *Biggles Takes a Holiday*), Hodder & Stoughton, 1965.
Biggles in the Terai, Brockhampton, 1966.
Biggles and the Gun Runners, Brockhampton, 1966.
Biggles and the Penitent Thief, Brockhampton, 1967.
Biggles Sorts It Out, Brockhampton, 1967.
Biggles and the Dark Intruder (paperback), Knight, 1967, (hardcover) Brockhampton, 1970.
Biggles in the Underworld, Brockhampton, 1968.
The Boy Biggles, Dean, 1968.
Biggles and the Deep Blue Sea, Brockhampton, 1968.
Biggles and the Little Green God, Brockhampton, 1969.
Biggles and the Noble Lord, Brockhampton, 1969.
Biggles Sees Too Much, Brockhampton, 1970.
Biggles of the Royal Flying Corps (selections), edited by Piers Williams, Purnell, 1978.

"GIMLET" SERIES; JUVENILE; ALL ILLUSTRATED BY L. STEAD, EXCEPT AS INDICATED

King of the Commandos, University of London Press, 1943, reissued (illustrated by Walter Foster), May Fair Books, 1963.
Gimlet Goes Again, University of London Press, 1944, reissued, May Fair Books, 1963.
Gimlet Comes Home, University of London Press, 1946.
Gimlet Mops Up, Brockhampton, 1947, reissued, May Fair Books, 1963.
Gimlet's Oriental Quest, Brockhampton, 1948, reissued, May Fair Books, 1963.
Gimlet Lends a Hand, Brockhampton, 1949, reissued, May Fair Books, 1964.
Gimlet Bores In, Brockhampton, 1950.
Gimlet Off the Map, Brockhampton, 1951.
Gimlet Gets the Answer, Brockhampton, 1952.
Gimlet Takes a Job, Brockhampton, 1954, reissued (illustrated by Walter Foster), May Fair Books, 1963.

"WORRALS" SERIES; ALL ILLUSTRATED BY L. STEAD

Worrals of the WAAF, Lutterworth, 1941.
Worrals Flies Again, Hodder & Stoughton, 1942.
Worrals Carries On, Lutterworth, 1942.
Worrals on the Warpath, Hodder & Stoughton, 1943.
Worrals Goes East, Hodder & Stoughton, 1944.

(This 1933 issue, edited by Captain Johns, contained the Biggles story "Beauty and the Beast.")

Worrals of the Islands: A Story of the War in the Pacific, Hodder & Stoughton, 1945.
Worrals in the Wilds, Hodder & Stoughton, 1947.
Worrals Down Under, Lutterworth, 1948.
Worrals Goes Afoot, Lutterworth, 1949.
Worrals in the Wastelands, Lutterworth, 1949.
Worrals Investigates, Lutterworth, 1950.

SCIENCE FICTION; JUVENILE; ALL UNDER NAME CAPTAIN W. E. JOHNS; ALL ILLUSTRATED BY L. STEAD

Kings of Space: A Story of Interplanetary Exploration, Hodder & Stoughton, 1954.
Return to Mars, Hodder & Stoughton, 1955.
Now to the Stars, Hodder & Stoughton, 1956.
To Outer Space, Hodder & Stoughton, 1957.
The Edge of Beyond, Hodder & Stoughton, 1958.
The Death Rays of Ardilla, Hodder & Stoughton, 1959.
To Worlds Unknown: A Story of Interplanetary Exploration, Hodder & Stoughton, 1960.
The Quest for the Perfect Planet, Hodder & Stoughton, 1961.
Worlds of Wonder: More Adventures in Space, Hodder & Stoughton, 1962.
The Man Who Vanished into Space, Hodder & Stoughton, 1963.

NONFICTION; ALL UNDER NAME CAPTAIN W.E. JOHNS, EXCEPT AS INDICATED

(Under name W. E. Johns, with Harry M. Schofield) *The Pictorial Flying Course* (adult; self-illustrated), J. Hamilton, 1932.
Fighting Planes and Aces (juvenile; illustrated by Howard Leigh), J. Hamilton, 1932.

Johns in the 1930's.

Some Milestones in Aviation (adult), J. Hamilton, 1935.
The Air VC's (adult), J. Hamilton, 1935.
The Passing Show: A Garden Diary by an Amateur Gardener (adult; illustrated by H. Leigh), My Garden, 1937.
(Under name W. E. Johns) *The Modern Boy's Book of Pirates* (juvenile), Amalgamated, 1939.
The Biggles Book of Heroes (juvenile), M. Parrish, 1959.
The Biggles Book of Treasure Hunting (juvenile; illustrated by William Randell), M. Parrish, 1962.

ANTHOLOGIES; EDITOR

Wings: A Book of Flying Adventures (adult), J. Hamilton, 1931.
The Modern Boy's Book of Aircraft (juvenile), Amalgamated, 1931.
(Under name Captain W. E. Johns) *Thrilling Flights* (adult; illustrated by H. Leigh), J. Hamilton, 1936.

ADULT; ALL UNDER NAME CAPTAIN W.E. JOHNS, EXCEPT AS INDICATED

(Under pseudonym William Earle) *Mossyface* (novel), Mellifont, 1932.
The Spy Flyers (novel; illustrated by H. Leigh), J. Hamilton, 1933.
The Raid (short stories), J. Hamilton, 1935.
(Under pseudonym Jon Early) *Blue Blood Runs Red,* Newnes, 1936.
Desert Night: A Romance (novel), J. Hamilton, 1938.
The Unknown Quantity (novel), J. Hamilton, 1940.
Doctor Vane Answers the Call (short stories), Latimer House, 1950.
Short Stories (short stories), Latimer House, 1950.
Sky Fever and Other Stories, Latimer House, 1953.

No Motive for Murder (novel), Hodder & Stoughton, 1958, Washburn, 1959.

The Man Who Lost His Way (novel), Macdonald, 1960.

(With R. A. Kelly) *No Surrender,* Harrap, 1969.

"STEELEY" SERIES; ADULT; ALL UNDER NAME CAPTAIN W.E. JOHNS

Sky High (novel), Newnes, 1936, revised edition, Latimer House, 1951.

Steeley Flies Again (novel), Newnes, 1936, revised edition, Latimer House, 1951.

Murder by Air (novel), Newnes, 1937, revised edition, Latimer House, 1951.

The Murder at Castle Deeping (novel), J. Hamilton, 1938, revised edition, Latimer House, 1951.

Wings of Romance: A "Steeley" Adventure (novel), Newnes, 1939, revised edition, Latimer House, 1951.

Det forsuunne dagboksblad (title means "The Missing Page"; appeared in *Thriller,* October 16, 1937), Forlagshuset (Norway), 1939.

RADIO PLAYS, BOTH WITH G. R. RANIER

"The Machine That Disappeared," BBC Home Service, 1942.
"The Charming Mrs. Nayther," BBC Home Service, 1942.

Also author of many adult short stories published in Great Britain and the United States, some of which were dramatized and broadcast; illustrator of Covington Clarke's *Desert Wings,*

1931. Contributor of technical aircraft drawings and illustrations to periodicals including *Illustrated London News, Modern Boy,* and *Graphic.* Contributor of short stories and articles to periodicals and newspapers, including *Modern Boy, Popular Flying, Pearson's, Thriller, Gem, Extension, Woman's Journal, Boys' Book of Adventure, Wonder Book of Comics, Daily Mail, Colliers, Maclean's, Eagle, Junior Mirror, Liverpool Daily Post, Boys' Own Paper,* and *Girls' Own Paper.* Founder and editor of *Popular Flying,* 1932-39, and *Flying,* 1938-39. Author of columns in periodicals, including "What Plane Was That?," 1930-32, and "Let's Look Around," 1938-39, both in *Modern Boy,* and "The Passing Show," in *My Garden,* (London), 1936-44.

ADAPTATIONS:

"Biggles" series (radio), Amalgamated Wireless Ltd. (Australia), 1949-1955.

"The Cruise of the Condor" (comic strip adaptation in book form), Juvenile Productions, May, 1955.

"Biggles" (television series), Granada Television, 1960.

"Biggles Learns to Fly" (cassette), Ivan Berg Associates (London), 1977.

RADIO DRAMATIZATIONS; ALL PRODUCED ON "CHILDREN'S HOUR," BBC HOME SERVICE

"Biggles Flies West," 1948.
"Biggles Flies North," 1948.
"Biggles in the Jungle," 1949.
"Biggles Hunts Big Game," 1950.

(From *Biggles Breaks the Silence* by Captain W. E. Johns. Illustrated by L. Stead.)

(Jacket from Johns' third book.)

Johns with Doris.

A 1970's Biggles comic.

"Biggles in the Blue," 1953.
"Biggles and the Pirate Treasure," 1955.
"Biggles' Chinese Puzzle," 1957.
"Biggles of the Interpol," 1957.
"Biggles Presses On," 1959.

Comic strip adaptation of "Biggles" appeared in *Express Weekly,* 1950s-60s; "The Adventures of 'Biggles'" (comic books), Action Comic Pty. (Sydney, Australia) and Strato Publications (London, England), 1950s.

SIDELIGHTS: Born **February 5, 1893** on Mole Wood Road, Bengeo, in the outskirts of Hertford, England. Johns' father, like his father before him, was a tailor. His mother, Elizabeth Earl Johns, was the daughter of a master butcher. "Yesterday, my mother came to see me. . .she. . .smells faintly of lavender. Perhaps that is why I, too, am a little *triste* today and why I grow lavender in my garden. And why I caress it with my hand in passing. . . ."[1]

Even in childhood, gardens were an important part of his life. "When I was a small boy my uncle Harry gave my mother some crocus bulbs, which, after discussion, were planted under the tulip tree at the end of the lawn. I can see my father planting them now, awkwardly, for he was no gardener. Did he but know it, he was planting a living spirit in that garden for, before the year was out, my uncle was no longer with us. He was killed in the Boer War. But in the Spring we were cheered by 'Uncle Harry's bulbs' which, as you may suppose, had acquired a new significance. Now observe the joy of such a gift and the wisdom of the giver, for that same pleasure was repeated every Spring for nearly thirty years. Every March we would say, one to another, 'Have you seen Uncle Harry's bulbs?' I never saw him again, the years rolled on, and his

face became a hazy memory (so soon does youth forget) but he lived with us always in that simple gift.

"At first the bulbs occupied perhaps a foot of ground; the last time I saw them they were a gleaming carpet, covering many yards."[1]

January 26, 1905. Johns was admitted to Hertford Grammar School. His headmaster was a retired military officer who rode his horse during cadet corps exercises. "It may be some consolation to readers of my books, who have failed their examinations, to know that I have never passed an examination in my life; yet I have managed to get all the things I coveted, although some of them appeared as remote as the moon."[1]

"Breathing heavily over my shoulder [my math teacher] would go through an equation with infinite pains. At the end he would say: 'Now do you understand?' All I could do was hang my head and whisper, 'No.' Making funny noises in his throat he would walk away like a man going to the scaffold. Wretched fellow. I must have put years on his life."[1]

Not clever in other areas either, he recalled that he had "never been able to make, or even mend, an article of wood, metal or anything else. . . .I have never been able to knock a nail in straight. On the rare occasions when I have been forced to try, it was usually my thumb that came under the hammer. As a small boy I once tried to fix the mast of a toy boat. It was too long. Fetching the carving knife I hit it a smart crack—and away went half the tip of the finger of my left hand. There is a simple answer to this handicap. Get someone else to do it."[1]

He aspired to become a soldier. "It is impossible for a boy of today to realise the enthusiasm the boys of 1900 had for any-

(Biggles was the cover story for this December, 1934 magazine.)

Johns at Park House shortly before his death.
■ (Photograph courtesy of Marjorie Ellis.)

thing military. Soldiers were gods. Mind you, in those days a soldier in full dress uniform was something to look at. When troops went overseas they did not creep away furtively, for security reasons, in the middle of the night. They marched through cheering crowds in broad daylight, bands playing, colours flying, flowers in their caps. We boys, decorated with as much red, white and blue ribbon as we could afford to buy, marched with them to the railway station and yelled our heads off as the train steamed out, whistle screaming and fog signals thundering under the wheels.''[1]

1907-1912. Left Hertford Grammar School. ''My father had. . .ideas about my career. I arrived home one day to be introduced to a county municipal surveyor to whom I was to be articled for the next four years. So I went to work. My pocket money was sixpence a week. This taught me the value of money.''[1] Johns didn't stop studying, however, taking music and art lessons three times a week. He also played piano at local moviehouses.

During one of his concerts, three pretty girls, daughters of the local vicar Rev. John Hunt, were in the audience. Johns began to attend Hunt's church in Little Dunham, near Swaffham and was often invited for supper, or musical evenings, tennis parties or fundraisers for the church. He became close to Maude Penelope Hunt, who was eleven years older than he was. The couple married two years later.

October 4, 1913. Joined the Territorial Army with the Norfolk Yeomanry, a calvary regiment. When Great Britain went to war with Germany, his life changed dramatically. ''To many, August 4th, 1914, was to be a parting of the ways: almost as abrupt as the closing of a door; the end of one life and the

beginning of a new. We did not know it then. We only perceive it now by looking down the vista of the years, route-marked by the mocking milestones of what-might-have-been.

''I little dreamed, on that fateful morning when I put away my compasses and T-square. . .that I should never take them out again. When I said goodbye to the men and boys whom I had known since childhood, many of them friends of school boy days, not for one moment did it occur to me that I was bidding most of them farewell for ever—or I might have said, like Brutus:

''‘Fare thee well, and if for ever
Still for ever fare thee well.'

''A yeoman, I led my mare from the stables, and, slashing with my sword at imaginary foes, galloped down the drive to what, in my youthful folly, I supposed was going to be death or glory. I had yet to learn that in war there is plenty of death but little glory; that in war only death is real; that the glory is simply gilt and tinsel to wrap around the other so that it looks less like what it really is.''[1]

In September of 1915, Johns was ordered overseas. Maude was pregnant. ''I remember clearly the first man whom I saw die. . . .His name was George Bellingham. We were amateur soldiers in the amateur cavalry (sometimes called yeomanry) and we had gone to the rifle range at Colchester to do our firing practice. For a time I sat on a pile of horse-blankets behind the firing point, talking to George, who was standing up. He was telling me, I remember, about a mare he had at home. He was not to know, of course, that he was never going

(Cover illustration from *Biggles Learns to Fly* by Captain W. E. Johns.)

home. At that moment there was nothing to indicate that in precisely one minute of time he would be a dead man.

"I got up—I don't really know why, unless it was to stretch my legs. Anyway, if there was a reason, I've forgotten it. George sat down. As he did so there was a sharp bang somewhere near at hand, and almost simultaneously a sort of dull *phut*. Looking up to see what it was I became aware of a curious silence. The troops were all staring at me—or rather, at my feet. I looked down. I did more than that. I stared fascinated by what I saw. George was on his back, twitching.

"The silence was broken by a man who started repeating, with parrot-like monotony, 'I didn't know it was loaded. . .I didn't know it was loaded. . . .' They marched him away.''[1]

Johns was sent to Gallipoli and by mid-October was in the trenches. ''. . .If there is one thing calculated to give an ordinary human being the screaming willies, it is crawling about in the pitch-dark, catching your chin on barbed wire, and sliding into water-logged shell-craters. When, added to these pleasantries, you remember (and you never forget it) that there is a chance that at any moment you may trip over a land-mine, walk into a line of bullets discharged by a windy machine-gunner, or bump into a thug with a dagger in one hand and a life-preserver in the other, you'll see what I mean about a patrol not being all fun and games.

"By the time you've dodged out of the way of a lunatic who is amusing himself by broadcasting grenades, and lain in a few

puddles while another maniac blazes away with star shells, you don't know whether you're coming or going. Even if you do remember, you're likely to have forgotten the password, in which case you'll probably be greeted at the firestep by a poke in the eye from a bayonet. If you've got the password on the tip of your tongue, you might strike a pal who forgets to ask for it before he pulls the trigger.

"These guys who moan because the only news they get is 'our night patrols were active' ought to do one. Just one. This is the way it goes.

"Six of you, or maybe a dozen, crawl out of the trench into a wilderness that goes by the cheerful name of No-Man's Land. Now don't get the idea that all you have to do is stroll to the nearest shell-hole and sit there for an hour before going back with the glad news that everything is O.K. Oh no, it isn't as easy as that. You always have to do something. Maybe your job is to catch a prisoner and bring him home alive. It needs no great imagination to perceive that this is likely to be an exhilarating pastime besides which the stalking of a mad tiger with your bare hands would be a tame pursuit. Germans don't stand about waiting to come clean. Most of them object to your invitations and they back up their protests in a most unfriendly manner.

"All the time you are out, vague sounds assail your ears. These sounds may be quite different, but they have one thing

The Captain's son was attacked by fierce sea birds and enormous crabs. ■ (From *The Biggles Book of Treasure Hunting* by Captain W. E. Johns. Illustrated by William Randell.)

in common—they are all sinister. A foot being dragged out of the slush somewhere near at hand gives you a tingling sensation at the nape of the neck. A grunted oath a few paces away makes you hold your breath while a line of vague shadows goes past. The hollow groans of some poor devil who has collided with a piece of hot metal travelling in the opposite direction makes your blood run cold.

"Just as you reach the stage when you feel you can't bear it any longer, or it is time you went home, anyway, somebody decides to start a war. Probably it is quite unofficial. It just happens—starting with ordinary bullets and ending in a barrage from the 'heavies' of both sides. And you're in the middle of it."[1] By Christmas Day, Johns had arrived in Egypt, to defend the Suez Canal.

The war years took their toll. "Take ten million men at random from between those man-made boundaries which we call frontiers, and ask them if they want to leave their homes to fight, perhaps die. Not one will answer 'Yes.' Yet when the time comes they will go, straining to be at the throats of other poor fools as helpless as themselves. Why will they go? They will go because the handful of men who control their destinies will, by the subtle means at their disposal, by lies and lies, and still more lies, make it impossible for them to stay at home without appearing contemptible cravens. Being one of the fools, I shall probably go myself, and presently find myself destroying the home of a man who has done no more harm to me than I to him. Oh no; I have no delusions left about war. When you have seen such sights as I have, you won't either.

"I once discussed this very point with a dying German on the Oriovika Road. A lad of perhaps eighteen, he had been thrown off a GS Wagon for dead, but when I came upon him he was still alive. He asked me for a drink. I gave him one. We talked. He knew he was going to die, and wept at the thought of it. Not for himself, I think, but for his mother to whom he sent, by me, a rosary that hung around his neck. She never received it because a nurse stole it from me in Salonika—as a souvenir. A souvenir! Turn that over in your mind, and ask yourself, a souvenir of what? When you rub off the gilt and tinsel you will find that it was a souvenir of the agony of two poor souls who probably did no one any harm. Well, that's war."[1]

1917. Johns contracted malaria and while in the hospital in Salonika he decided to apply for a transfer to the Royal Flying Corps. On September 26, he received a temporary commission as a second lieutenant in the R.F.C. He was sent home, to Oxford, for training.

"Tickled to death with myself I soared, in ever increasing circles, until I lost my way and finally returned home—more by luck than judgement—after having been in the air for ninety minutes. Which must be pretty well a record for a first solo. I was told not to be more than ten minutes."[1] Soon after, he received his wings and was made a flight instructor.

July, 1918. Johns was sent to France. His orders were lost somehow, so he hitched a ride with another British pilot going to France. He gambled away what money he had, and for days continued to hitch rides around France, trying to find out where he was supposed to report for duty. Finally he joined No. 55 Squadron whose job was bombing and reconaissance. "The first dog fight I was ever in, it seemed to me that one minute we—that is, my formation—were sailing along all merry and bright, and the next minute the air was full of machines, darting all over the place. I didn't see where they came from or where they went. I didn't see where my formation went either.

"By the time I had grasped the fact that the fight had started and I was looking to see who the dickens was perforating my

(From *The Camels Are Coming* by W. E. Johns.)

plane, the show was all over. Two machines lay smoking on the ground and everybody else had disappeared.

"While I was considering what the dickens I should do I suddenly discovered that I was flying back in formation again! The fellows had come back to pick me up and formed up around me. I didn't even see where they came from!"[1]

Besides the threat of enemy attacks, airplanes at this time were unpredictable, sometimes falling apart in mid-air, and often crashing. Johns twice shot off his own propeller, and once had to land with a bomb hanging out of the fusilage because it had failed to release.

On September 16, 1918, he was shot down over Germany. "Sick with fright and fury, I looked around for help, but from horizon to horizon stretched the unbroken blue of a summer sky. Bullets were striking the machine all the time like whip-lashes, so I put her in a steep bank and held her there while I considered the position. For perhaps five minutes we tore round and round, the enemy getting in a burst now and then and me 'browning' the whole bunch of them, but I could not go on indefinitely. My ammunition was running low and I was still over forty miles from home. . . .Things looked bad. To try to make forty miles against ten or a dozen enemy machines (several others were joining in the fun) was going to be difficult. In fact, I strongly suspected that my time had come.

"I had seen the vapour and what followed it before. That was my worst moment. I switched off and literally flung the machine into a vertical sideslip, but she still smoked as the petrol ran over the hot engine. Suddenly the joystick went loose in my hand as the controls broke somewhere; we spun, half came out and spun again.

"Every detail of that field is stamped on my memory with vivid clarity. I knew I was going to crash, but curiously enough I do not think I was afraid: (I have been much more scared on other occasions). I hadn't time to be scared. My brain was whirling at full revs.—should I jump as we hit the ground—should I unfasten my belt—and so on, and all the time I was automatically trying to get the machine on an even keel. Twice her nose nearly came up of her own accord as she tried to right herself, and it was in that position that we struck."[1]

He was taken to Strasbourg jail and interrogated for several days. He attempted to escape with another prisoner, but was caught and thrown in solitary for ten days. "Day after day I sat on my bed, consisting of three planks, in a tiny stone cell. It was cold and damp. But the worst thing was having absolutely nothing to do. I didn't know the time. I hardly knew if it was day or night. Hour after hour I just sat and stared at the opposite wall. The solitude was broken twice in twenty-four hours. At twelve noon a warder brought me a plate of soup and some water. He did the same at 6 p.m. From 6 p.m. until twelve the next day seemed a life time. Only those who have been through it can form the slightest conception of how slowly time can go."[1]

He was then transferred to a P.O.W. camp, at Landshut on an island in a river. ". . .One shares quarters with the other fellows, and that is not bad. The talk is all of one thing—

They were congregating with excited gestures.
■ (From _Biggles Delivers the Goods_ by Captain W. E. Johns. Illustrated by Leslie Stead.)

escape. I must have spent more than half the hours I was a prisoner talking about ways and means of escape. It isn't easy. The knowledge that guards are standing around with loaded rifles is distinctly discouraging."[1]

Johns did escape, alone, but after five days was caught by a German farmer while trying to steal an apple. He returned to Landshut for ten more days in solitary. Then he was transferred to a stronghold for prisoners who had attempted escape. "Prison camps differed a good deal. Once you had tried to escape, it usually meant that you were sent to a punishment camp where conditions were bad. One just had to put up with it. Guards were changed frequently, so that you never got to know one well enough to risk offering a bribe for assistance in an escape. The eternal barbed wire and fixed bayonets had a depressing effect on one, particularly if one's vitality was lowered through bad and indifferent food. Some fellows just became ill and died under the strain of it. Luckily I was never ill, but I lost a lot of weight. I went in weighing eleven stone and came home weighing seven! One developed rather a nasty smell through undernourishment. This was helped by one's clothes, which, of course, got very dirty."[1]

November 11, 1918. Armistice was declared, and nineteen days later, he was released. Two days before Christmas he embarked for England. "After crossing the Channel in a terrific gale, I arrived home on Christmas Day, causing a small sensation, for although I did not know it, I had simply been reported 'missing' and given up for dead. When I walked in at the back door, dressed in odd bits of old French uniform, the parlourmaid who first saw me let out a yell, dropped the saucepan of potatoes she was just lifting off the range, and flopped down in a faint. I must have looked an odd sort of ghost, if that's what she took me for. Anyway, having been nearly starved to death, for months, I certainly tucked away some pudding that day. . . ."[1]

1919. Remaining in the Royal Air Forces, he was sent to Cranwell as a flight instructor. Four months later he was demobilized and returned to Little Dunham with Maude and Jack. By November, 1920, he was reinstated in the R.A.F. as a full lieutenant and recruiting officer.

Unemployment was rampant and many former officers were enlisting in the ranks just to have work. Among them was T. E. Lawrence, the famed Lawrence of Arabia, whom Johns recruited. "One day, a thin, pale-faced chap walked in. There was something so off-hand about his manner, almost amounting to insolence, that I took an instinctive dislike to him. I had got to know the type. He was 'different' from the other recruits and he was letting me know."[1]

Lawrence gave the name of John Hume Ross. "By this time everyone on the station knew who Ross was. Certainly Lawrence knew that I knew, because I had a long talk with him while he was waiting for the train to take him to Uxbridge. When he went he left me with the memory of a cold, clammy handshake.

"I then rang up Flight Lieutenant Nelson, my opposite number at Uxbridge, to warn him of who was on the way, for by this time Lawrence was making it clear that he had no time for junior officers. Lawrence himself soon saw to it that everyone knew who he was.

"Lawrence went on, and wherever he went word of who he was preceded him: officers are officers and, I hope, gentlemen, and no one was going to let down a comrade by failing to put him wise as to the real identity of the aircraftsman 2nd class who spent weekends with Cabinet Ministers."[1]

Meanwhile his marriage to Maude lay in shambles. She was ill with arthritis since the birth of their son, and Jack, too, was sickly. They tried, briefly, to live together in London, but Maude and Jack returned to her father's vicarage. Johns had asked to divorce, but the idea was repudiated by Maude and her father. She therefore remained his legal wife until her death in 1961. He continued to support them and saw Jack occasionally.

Johns became enamoured with the "girl next door." He and Doris Leigh began living together when he was given a new posting to Newcastle. Doris opened a guest house to supplement their income. Here Johns began to paint, especially illustrations of airplanes, and began to write articles under the pen name William Earl, later William Earle. His first spread of pictures, four full-color prints, appeared in the *Illustrated London News*.

After retiring from the R.A.F., he and Doris settled into a small cottage in Kingfield, Sussex, and he began a new career as aviation illustrator. Soon they moved to a larger cottage next door, and Doris' family moved into the little one. Johns took up gardening at the four-hundred-year-old thatched cottage, a hobby that remained with him all his life. He loved the outdoors, especially his own garden and mountain climbing. "What is it about these harsh, bare rocks, so grim and stark, that calls us back, and back again. Is it the solitude, the joy of breaking away from the clutches of the monster we ourselves have made, the ogre called Civilization? Is it the relief of being able to gaze once more at an infinite distance, instead of a brick wall? Is it the silence, after the everlasting turmoil of the cities, or the purity of the air, after their poisonous vapours? Is it the freedom that we share with the eagles, soaring in the smokeless blue? I will tell you. It is all these things which together make that indefinable condition called peace. Not the mere peace of warring nations, but real peace, which is peace of mind, body and soul."[1]

1929. Began selling illustrations and short articles to *Modern Boy* and *Ranger*. By 1931 he was editing, illustrating and contributing articles to *The Modern Boys' Book of Aircraft,* and edited an anthology called *Wings: A Book of Flying Adventures.*

He was asked by his publisher, John Hamilton, to edit a magazine for adults to be called *Popular Flying.* "Before going to press with the first number of *Popular Flying,* we tried hard to find out just how much it would mean to people in the aeronautical world, and how ready the public were for a non-technical journal devoted entirely to aviation. We went to some pains to enquire what was most needed, likely to be of service to the industry and of interest to the ordinary reader. The question of how much space to devote to current events, pure fiction, civil and Service flying, and so on, present difficulties which may work themselves out as we proceed.

"Broadly speaking, *Popular Flying* will cover the whole field of aviation without necessarily segregating each section into separate departments. So far as current events are concerned we may find it impossible to publish in detail the mass of indiscriminate information which reaches us daily. If so, we shall select such items as appear to be of lasting significance and set them down with any general relevant information or appropriate historical background; this should be sufficient to give the regular reader a clear idea of how aviation is progressing. Those who wish to learn more about flying generally will find it presented in a new form which we believe will be more digestible than the old."[1]

Later issues featured short stories by "William Earle" about James Bigglesworth, a young R.A.F. pilot who would become

his most famous character. The first of these stories was called "The White Fokker" and appeared in April, 1932. These first stories about Biggles were republished in *The Camels are Coming* late in 1932.

"Captain James Bigglesworth is a fictitious character, yet he could have been found in any RFC mess during those great days of 1917 and 1918 when air combat had become the order of the day and air dueling was a fine art. . . .He developed under the stress of war into the sort of man most men would like to be: fearless but modest, efficient and resolute in what he undertook. . . .The exploits with which he has been credited have nearly all been built on a foundation of truth, although needless to say they were not all the efforts of a single individual. Students of air-war history may have no difficulty in recognising the actual incidents and the names of the officers associated with them. . . ."[1]

Johns also described Biggles as, ". . .a shadowy figure created by my admiration for the courage and resource displayed by some of the men with whom it was my good fortune to spend several years of my life. Having had some experience of air warfare, and knowing my own limitations, I was better able to appreciate what these fellows did.

"In a way, he is myself."[1]

The Biggles books were immensely popular. Johns had used various by-lines, many of them the pen names William Earle, W. E. Johns, Flying Officer W. E. Johns and Captain W. E. Johns. After 1939 he settled on Captain W. E. Johns, a rank from his early Royal Flying Corps service.

By 1939 he had produced forty books. In addition to the Biggles books, he wrote an adult thriller series called "The Raffles" whose hero was Steeley Delaroy. He also wrote several romances, one under the pseudonym Jon Early, and several books about pirates.

His editorials against the British government, particularly the Air Ministers, led to his release from the editorship of both *Popular Flying* and *Flying.* "For years past, inspired by heaven only knows what false information, most of the feature writers in the daily press had been belittling the bomber as a potent factor of warfare, and/or making groundless claims that our few antiquated interceptors could stop enemy bombers. And it was that as much as anything that drove me into incoherence on these pages. Oh, I had some raps over the knuckles for those Editorials, make no mistake about that. But I had a power behind me. It was Truth. And judging from my correspondence, most readers recognised it.

"Well, that's the story. It's all over, I think, except for the final bang. We have nearly finished eating humble pie. If Hitler or his henchmen ever had the idea of breaking the British Empire, they've lost their chance. But the very fact that they might once have done it is not pleasant to contemplate."[1]

He still had his other columns and was asked to write another for *Pearson's Magazine* called "What Men Are Talking About." Later this year, on September 3, 1939, Britain declared war on Germany. Johns was forty-six and considered returning to uniform, but was persuaded to write and lecture for the Air Defense Cadet Corps, a junior branch of the R.A.F. which trained school boys. He also started a regular column in *The Boys Own Paper* on the Air Training Corps and in the *Girls Own Paper* on the Women's Auxiliary Air Force.

1941. *Worrals of the WAAF* appeared. Johns said of his heroine, Joan Worralson, "She undertook some remarkable missions but none (although for security reasons this couldn't be divulged at the time) more desperate than were actually being made by girls in the same Service."[1] He eventually wrote eleven books about her.

The strain of war time bombing led Johns and Doris to move to Scotland, where they rented a large house called Pitchroy Lodge. "Enemy action at last forced me to abandon my home. What has happened and what is happening to the garden, I do not know. Nor do I care particularly. No one, I imagine, can garden with enthusiasm in a sort of minor Hades, with an occasional shower of bricks and mortar. It seemed to me that if I was to go away I might as well remove myself as far as possible from the clamour which I have endured for nearly five years. So, to the serene heart of the Highlands of Scotland I took myself, [to] a remote glen where no man goes from one year to another."[1]

He kept a regular routine of early rising, working in his study, reading mail and newspapers, with a cocktail before dinner and more work after dinner if he and Doris weren't entertaining. He wrote longhand with a fountain pen and hired a typist to type his manuscripts. In late summer he would hunt, and in the fall he would go to London to see his publisher and agent. Then on to Paris, and the Sologne region of France, or perhaps the Riviera, returning to Scotland in late winter.

For nine years they kept up their routine of travel with spring and summer in Scotland. Then, as Johns turned sixty, they decided to move to London, where they bought a large Queen Anne mansion called Park House in Hampton Court. In its large garden, Johns returned to his beloved flowers. His upstairs study overlooked the Royal Paddock, where the royal family rode.

The backbone of Johns' stories is "the urge which is still the dominant driving force in the young human male. Adventure. It may last all his life. If his environment forbids active expression he will satisfy the craving secondhand by reading. Subconsciously, perhaps, a boy sees himself doing what his hero is doing, and hopes to do it himself one day. Security, which is the offspring of fear, is not for him.

"Remember, you are catering for brains that are fresh, eager, receptive; brains not yet warped by the ugly side of life or political propaganda; brains not yet disillusioned; clean, healthy youth that still believes in the basic principles of decent behaviour—courage, loyalty, fair play, knight-errantry. All boys, of every race, colour and creed, believe in these things—or so I judge, as my books sell as well in the Orient as in Iceland. And you must believe in them too, or shatter the confidence of your reader should your insincerity be exposed."[1]

Johns' heroes never drank, swore, or had sex. Biggles had an early love with Marie Jonis, a spy, but was broken hearted and never loved again. Johns' fans often protested when romance was introduced. Yet Johns was aware that with time, his readers were changing: "For better or worse, the boy of today is not the boy of yesterday. Born into an age of wonders that he accepts as a matter of course, he keeps pace with the times more easily than his elders. He sees what's going on around him, and more often than not knows more about technical and scientific developments than his parents. He is a well-informed and unforgiving critic. Let the author make one boob and his fan mail may shock him. I once took a chance and made an aircraft fly 200 miles farther than its official endurance range allowed. In poured letters from outraged readers demanding to be told how this miracle had been achieved. You may gloss over mechanical details with adults but not with youngsters.

By the mid-sixties, Biggles was in disrepute with many librarians and teachers and was often banned on the basis that he was prejudiced, fascist, sexist and violent. Such accusations continued well after Johns' death. ". . .I give boys what they want, not what their elders and betters think they ought to read. I teach at the same time, under a camouflage. Juveniles are keen to learn, but the educational aspect must not be too obvious or they become suspicious of its intention. I teach a boy to be a man, for without that essential qualification he will never be anything. I teach sportsmanship according to the British idea. One doesn't need blood and thunder to do that. In more than forty novels about my hero Biggles he has only once struck a man, and that was a matter of life and death. I teach that decent behaviour wins in the end as a natural order of things. I teach the spirit of team-work, loyalty to the Crown, the Empire, and to rightful authority."[2]

1965-1968. In his last years, Johns continued to write, to garden and to travel, although he had come to dislike flying and always took a ship to the Continent. He continued to make public appearances and gave occasional interviews. In fact, his routines continued as usual until he died on June 21, 1968, of coronary thrombosis at the age of seventy-five.

Books in Johns' "Biggles" series have been translated into many foreign languages, including French and German.

FOOTNOTE SOURCES

[1]Peter Berresford Elis and Piers Williams, *By Jove, Biggles! The Life of Captain W. E. Johns,* W. H. Allen (London), 1981.
[2]Geoffrey Trease, *Tales Out of School,* Heinemann, 1964.

FOR MORE INFORMATION SEE:

Brian Doyle, editor, *The Who's Who of Children's Literature,* Schocken Books, 1968.
W. O. G. Lofts and D. J. Adley, *The Men behind Boys' Fiction,* Howard Baker, 1970.
Children's Literature in Education, number 15, 1974.
Margery Fisher, *Who's Who in Children's Books,* Holt, 1975.
D. L. Kirkpatrick, editor, *Twentieth-Century Children's Writers,* St. Martin's, 1978, new edition, 1983.
John Pearson, *Biggles: The Authorised Biography,* Sidgwick & Jackson, 1979.
Biggles Annual, World International Publishing, 1980.
F. H. Winstanley, "Capt. W. E. Johns' Biggles Stories," *Book and Magazine Collector,* July, 1984 (p.5).
H. Carpenter and M. Pritchard, *The Oxford Companion to Children's Literature,* Oxford University Press, 1984.

OBITUARIES

Time, June 28, 1968 (p. 56).

KIDDELL-MONROE, Joan 1908-

PERSONAL: Born August 9, 1908, in Clacton-on-Sea, Essex, England; daughter of William and Lallah Ethel Frances (Lloyd) Kiddell-Monroe; married Webster Murray (a portrait painter and illustrator), 1939 (died, 1951); children: James Euan. *Education:* Attended Willesden School of Art, and Chelsea School of Art. *Home:* Ca'n Murray, Camino del Murtara, Soller, Mallorca, Baleareas, Spain.

CAREER: Free-lance artist and illustrator. Worked in an advertising studio early in her career. *Member:* Royal Zoological Society (fellow). *Awards, honors:* Carnegie Medal Commendation from the British Library Association, 1955, for En-

(From ''My Long Journey to Eisenhower: A Story of World War II'' by Ernest W. Michel in *The Secret Weapon and Other Stories of Faith and Valor*, selected, translated and edited by Azriel Eisenberg and Leah Ain Globe. Illustrated by Joan Kiddell-Monroe.)

glish *Fables and Fairy Stories;* Boys' Club Award from the Boys' Club of America, and Lewis Carroll Shelf Award, both 1961, both for *Grishka and the Bear; The Curse of Cain* was chosen one of Child Study Association of America's Children's Books of the Year, 1968.

WRITINGS:

ALL SELF-ILLUSTRATED

In His Little Black Waistcoat, Longmans, Green, 1939.
Little Skunk, Nicholson & Watson, 1942.
Ingulabi, Nicholson & Watson, 1943.
Wau-Wau the Ape, Methuen, 1947.
In His Little Black Waistcoat to China, Longmans, Green, 1947.
The Irresponsible Goat, Methuen, 1948.
In His Little Black Waistcoat to India, Longmans, Green, 1948.
In His Little Black Waistcoat to Tibet, Longmans, Green, 1949.

ILLUSTRATOR

Thomas Wyatt Bagshawe, *Pompey Was a Penguin,* Oxford University Press, 1940.
David Severn, *Rick Afire,* John Lane, 1942.
Patricia Lynch, *Longears: The Story of a Little Grey Donkey,* Dent, 1943.
D. Severn, *Wagon for Five,* John Lane, 1944.
Pearl S. Buck, *The Water-Buffalo Children,* Methuen, 1945.
Mary Norton, *The Magic Bed-Knob,* Dent, 1945.
P. S. Buck, *The Dragon Fish,* Methuen, 1946.
Dorothy Martin, *Munya the Lion,* Oxford University Press, 1946.
D. Severn, *Forest Holiday,* John Lane, 1946.
D. Severn, *Ponies and Poachers,* John Lane, 1947.
Patricia M. Donahue, *Whiskery Jinks and the Donkey Cart,* Methuen, 1948, British Book Center, 1953.
D. Severn, *The Cruise of the ''Maiden Castle,''* Bodley Head, 1948.

Frank F. Darling, *Sandy, the Red Deer,* Oxford University Press, 1949.
Hugh Gardner, *Tales from the Marble Mountain,* Oxford University Press, 1949, Meredith, 1969.
D. Severn, *Hermit in the Hills,* John Lane, 1949.
D. Severn, *Treasure for Three,* Bodley Head, 1949.
Maribel Edwin, *This Way to Greenacres,* Longmans, Green, 1950.
E. Dixon, editor, *Fairy Tales from the Arabian Nights,* Dent, 1951, Dutton, 1952.
(With others) P. S. Buck, *One Bright Day, and Other Stories for Children,* Methuen, 1952.
R. Forbes-Watson, *Ambari!,* Oxford University Press, 1952.
Rene Guillot, *Sama,* translation by Gwen Marsh, Oxford University Press, 1952.
Barbara L. Picard, reteller, *The Odyssey of Homer* (ALA Notable Book), Walck, 1952.
P. Lynch, *The Boy at the Swinging Lantern,* Dent, 1952.
D. Severn, *Burglars and Bandicoots,* Bodley Head, 1952.
M. Edwin, *Curlew Jon,* T. Nelson, 1953.
R. Guillot, *Sirga, Queen of the African Bush,* translation by G. Marsh, Oxford University Press, 1953, Criterion, 1959.
P. Lynch, *Delia Daly of Galloping Green,* Dent, 1953.
B. L. Picard, *Tales of the Norse Gods and Heroes,* Oxford University Press, 1953.
R. Guillot, *Oworo,* translation by G. Marsh, Oxford University Press, 1954.
Eileen O'Faolain, *Irish Sagas and Folk-Tales,* Walck, 1954.
P. Lynch, *Orla of Burren,* Dent, 1954.
Mary Elwyn Patchett, *Tam, the Untamed,* Lutterworth, 1954.
Barbara Ker Wilson, *Scottish Folk-Tales and Legends,* Oxford University Press, 1954.
Lorna Wood, *The People in the Garden,* Dent, 1954.
James Reeves, reteller, *English Fables and Fairy Stories,* Oxford University Press, 1954, Walck, 1966.
M. Edwin, *Zigzag Path,* T. Nelson, 1955.
Margherita Fanchiotti, *Stories from the Bible,* Oxford University Press, 1955.
Emmeline Garnett, *Hills of Sheep,* Hodder & Stoughton, 1955.
R. Guillot, *Kpo the Leopard,* translation by G. Marsh, Oxford University Press, 1955.
B. L. Picard, *French Legends, Tales and Fairy Stories,* Walck, 1955.
Gwyn Jones, *Welsh Legends and Folk-Tales,* Oxford University Press, 1955, Walck, 1965.
M. E. Patchett, *Treasure of the Reef,* Lutterworth, 1955.
M. E. Patchett, *Undersea Treasure Hunters,* Lutterworth, 1955.
G. Jones, *Scandinavian Legends and Folk-Tales,* Oxford University Press, 1956.
M. E. Patchett, *Return to the Reef,* Lutterworth, 1956.
Muriel Sherrington, *Poetical Pig,* Brockhampton Press, 1956.
L. Wood, *Rescue by Broomstick,* Dent, 1956.
Charles Downing, *Russian Tales and Legends,* Walck, 1957.
Nada Curcija-Prodanovic, *Yugoslav Folk-Tales,* Oxford University Press, 1957.
R. Guillot, *Animal Kingdom,* translation by G. Marsh, Oxford University Press, 1957.
Fritz Muller-Guggenbuehl, *Swiss-Alpine Folk-Tales,* translation by Katharine Potts, Walck, 1958.
B. L. Picard, *German Hero-Sagas and Folk-Tales,* Walck, 1958.
Helen McAlpine and William McAlpine, *Japanese Tales and Legends,* Walck, 1959.
Hester Burton, *The Great Gale,* Oxford University Press, 1960.
R. Guillot, *Grishka and the Bear* (ALA Notable Book), translated by G. Marsh, Abelard, 1960.
Eulenspiegel, *The Owl and the Mirror,* edited and translated by Godfrey Freeman, Basil Blackwell, 1960, Duell, Sloan & Pearce, 1961.

On came the great sea-monster, coasting along like a huge black galley. . . . ■ (From *The Heroes* by Charles Kingsley. Illustrated by Joan Kiddell-Monroe.)

B. L. Picard, reteller, *The Iliad of Homer,* Oxford University Press, 1960.

Henry Wadsworth Longfellow, *The Song of Hiawatha,* Dutton, 1960.

The Aeneid of Virgil, Walck, 1961.

Aesop, *Fables,* translation by John Warrington, Dent, 1961, Dutton, 1966.

Cyril Birch, *Chinese Myths and Fantasies,* Walck, 1961.

John E. Gray, *India's Tales and Legends,* Walck, 1961.

Robert Graves, *Myths of Ancient Greece,* Cassell, 1961.

Eugenie Fenton, *Sher, Lord of the Jungle,* Benn, 1962.

Kathleen Arnott, *African Myths and Legends,* Oxford University Press, 1962, Walck, 1963.

Homer, *The Adventures of Odysseus,* retold by Andrew Lang, Dutton, 1962.

Frederick Grice, *The Moving Finger,* Oxford University Press, 1962.

Charles Kingsley, *The Heroes,* Dutton, 1963.

Ogden Nash, *Girls Are Silly,* Dent, 1964.

Roger L. Green, editor, *Book of Myths,* Dutton, 1965.

(With Carl Craig) Philip Manderson Sherlock, *West Indian Folk-Tales,* Walck, 1966.

Azriel Eisenberg and Leach Ain Globe, selectors, translators, and editors, *The Secret Weapon and Other Stories of Faith and Valor,* Soncino Press, 1966.

Ivan Southall, *The Curse of Cain,* St. Martin's, 1968.

I. Southall, *The Sword of Esau,* Angus & Robertson, 1968.

Strate Tsirka, *Aisopeioi mythoi,* Chryses Ekdoseis (Athens), 1968.

L. Wood, *Hags by Starlight,* Dent, 1970.

Also illustrator of numerous additional books, including Kitty Barne's, *The Secret of the Sandhills,* 1955, and Hazel M. Peel's, *Fury, Son of the Wilds,* 1959.

WORK IN PROGRESS: Illustrating books; a novel set in Mallorca; reminiscences.

SIDELIGHTS: Began working in an advertising studio at eighteen; left after a number of years (''the soul-destroying work almost finished me as an artist'') to free-lance as an artist and illustrator. ''I am my own architect, remaking two houses. My son and I have two Ibizian hounds—tall, incredibly narrow dogs—descendents of the old Egyptian hunting dogs, an enormous red Setter, and the offspring of one of the hounds and the Setter. . . .I cannot spell—a drawback for an author—like the Spanish typewriter. I speak a very bad Spanish, with no grammar, but in some extraordinary way seem to get by unless it is a serious matter.''

''I continue illustrating—but writing for children, no more. My several styles have not changed, but I have added to them, and now that I have more time from illustrating, I paint portraits, landscapes and what not in oils.''[1]

FOOTNOTE SOURCES

[1]Lee Kingman and others, compilers, *Illustrators of Children's Books, 1957-1966,* Horn Book, 1968.

FOR MORE INFORMATION SEE:

B. M. Miller and others, compilers, *Illustrators of Children's Books, 1946-1956,* Horn Book, 1958.

Brian Doyle, *The Who's Who of Children's Literature,* Schocken Books, 1968.

Martha E. Ward and Dorothy A. Marquardt, *Illustrators of Books for Young People,* Scarecrow, 1975.

COLLECTIONS

Kerlan Collection at the University of Minnesota.

KING, Stephen (Edwin) 1947-
(Richard Bachman)

PERSONAL: Born September 21, 1947, in Portland, Me.; son of Donald (a merchant seaman) and Nellie Ruth (Pillsbury) King; married Tabitha Jane Spruce (a poet), January 2, 1971; children: Naomi, Joseph Hill, Owen. *Education:* University of Maine at Orono, B.Sc., 1970. *Politics:* Democrat. *Home:* Bangor and Center Lowell, Maine. *Office:* P.O. Box 1186, Bangor, Me. 04401. *Agent:* Kirby McCauley, Blassingame, McCauley & Wood, 432 Park Ave., S., Suite 1205, New York, N.Y. 10016.

CAREER: Writer. Has worked as a janitor, laundry worker, and in a knitting mill; Hampden Academy (high school), Hampden, Me., English teacher, 1971-73; University of Maine at Orono, writer-in-residence, 1978-79. *Member:* Authors Guild, Authors League of America.

AWARDS, HONORS: Carrie was included on *School Library Journal*'s Book List, 1974; Hugo Award nomination from the World Science Fiction Convention, 1978, for *The Shining; Salem's Lot* was selected one of American Library Association's Best Books for Young Adults, 1978, and *Firestarter,* 1981; Balrog Award, second place for best novel for *The Stand,* and second place for best collection, for *Night Shift,* both 1979; *Firestarter* was selected one of New York Public Library's Books for the Teen Age, 1981 and 1982, and *Cujo,* 1982; Best Fiction Writer of the Year from *Us* magazine, 1982; Golden Pen Award from the Young Adult Advisory Committee of the

STEPHEN KING

Spokane Public Library, 1986, for "the author who has given the committee members the most reading pleasure."

WRITINGS:

NOVELS

Carrie, Doubleday, 1974, movie edition, New American Library, 1976.
Salem's Lot, Doubleday, 1975, television edition, New American Library, 1979.
The Shining, Doubleday, 1977, movie edition, New American Library, 1980.
The Stand, Doubleday, 1978.
The Dead Zone, Viking, 1979, movie edition published as *The Dead Zone: Movie Tie-In,* New American Library, 1980.
Firestarter, Viking, 1980.
Cujo, Viking, 1981.
Different Seasons, Viking, 1982.
Creepshow, New American Library, 1982, (movie), starring Hal Holbrook and Fritz Weaver), Warner Bros., 1982.
Pet Sematary, Doubleday, 1983, large print edition, G. K. Hall, 1984.
Christine, Viking, 1983.
(With Peter Straub) *The Talisman,* Viking, 1984.
The Eyes of the Dragon, Philtrum Press, 1984, another edition illustrated by David Palladini, Viking, 1987, large print edition, G. K. Hall, 1988.
Cycle of the Werewolf (illustrated by Bernie Wrightson), New American Library, 1985, new edition published as *Silver Bullet,* 1985.
The Bachman Books: Four Early Novels, New American Library, 1985.
Bare Bones, Underwood Miller, 1986.
It, Viking, 1986.
Maximum Overdrive, New American Library, 1986.
Misery, Viking, 1987.
The Tommyknockers, Putnam, 1987.
Nightmares in the Sky, Viking, 1988.
Night Visions, Dark Harvest, 1988.

SHORT STORIES

Night Shift: Excursions into Horror, Doubleday, 1978.
Skeleton Crew, Putnam, 1985.

NONFICTION

Stephen King's Danse Macabre, Everest House, 1981.

UNDER PSEUDONYM RICHARD BACHMAN

Rage, New American Library, 1977.
The Long Walk, New American Library, 1979.
Roadwork: A Novel of the First Energy Crisis, New American Library, 1981.
The Running Man, New American Library, 1982.
Thinner, New American Library, 1984, large print edition, G. K. Hall, 1986.

Also author of screenplays, "The Shining," "Creepshow," and "Silver Bullet." Author of numerous short stories. Contributor to periodicals, including *Startling Mystery Stories, Cavalier, Fantasy and Science Fiction, Gallery, Ellery Queen's Mystery Magazine, Oui, Rolling Stone, American Bookseller, Adelina,* and *Playboy.*

ADAPTATIONS:

MOVIES

"Carrie," starring Sissy Spacek, William Katt, and John Travolta, United Artists, 1976, (theater play), script by Law-

("Christine" is no ordinary red 1958 Plymouth Fury. From the 1983, Columbia Pictures film "Christine.")

rence Cohen, first produced May 12, 1988 at Virginia Theater (closed after five performances).

"Salem's Lot" (television mini-series), starring David Soul, Lane Kerwin, James Mason and Bonnie Bedelia, CBS, 1979.

"The Shining," starring Jack Nicholson and Shelley Duvall, Warner Bros., 1980.

"Cujo," starring Dee Wallace, Daniel Hugh-Kelly, Danny Pintauro, Ed Lauter and Christopher Stone, Warner Bros., 1983.

"Christine," starring Keith Gordon, John Stockwell and Robert Prosky, Columbia, 1983.

"The Dead Zone" (also Beta or VHS videocassette), starring Christopher Walken, Brooke Adams, Tom Skerritt, and Martin Sheen, Paramount, 1983.

"Stephen King's Children of the Corn" (based on the short story from *Night Shift*), starring John Franklin and Peter Horton, New World Pictures, 1984.

(Also director) "Firestarter," starring David Keith, George C. Scott, Martin Sheen and Drew Barrymore, Universal, 1984.

"Stephen King's Silver Bullet," starring Gary Busey and Corey Haim, Dino De Laurentiis Entertainment Group, 1985.

"Cat's Eye" (based on three short stories: "Quitters, Inc.," "The General," and "The Ledge"), starring Drew Barrymore, Alan King, James Woods, Kenneth McMillan, Robert Hays, and Candy Clark, Metro-Goldwyn-Mayer, 1985.

(Also director) "Maximum Overdrive" (based on the short story "Trucks"), starring Emilio Estevez and Pat Hingle, Dino De Laurentiis Entertainment Group, 1986.

"Stand by Me" (based on novella "The Body"), starring Wil Wheaton, River Phoenix, Corey Feldman, Jerry O'Connell, Kiefer Sutherland, and Richard Dreyfuss, Columbia, 1986.

"The Running Man," starring Arnold Schwarzenegger, Tri-Star, 1987.

"Creepshow II," starring Dorothy Lamour and George Kennedy, New World Pictures, 1987.

CASSETTES

"Rita Hayworth and Shawshank Redemption: Different Seasons I," Recorded Books, 1984.

"The Body: Different Seasons II," Recorded Books, 1984.

"Apt Pupil: Different Seasons III," Recorded Books, 1984.

"The Breathing Method: Different Season IV," Recorded Books, 1984.

"The Ballad of the Flexible Bullet: Skeleton Crew," Recorded Books, 1985.

"Gramma: From Skeleton Crew," Recorded Books, 1985.

"The Mist: From Skeleton Crew," Recorded Books, 1985.

"Night Shift," Warner Audio, 1985.

"Mrs. Todd's Shortcut" (from anthology *Skeleton Crew*), Warner Audio.

"Nona: Skeleton Crew," Recorded Books, 1985.

"Skeleton Crew" (Book One and Book Two), Recorded Books, 1985.

"Skeleton Crew: The Monkey," Warner Audio.

"Stories from Night Shift," Warner Audio, 1985.

"Stories from Skeleton Crew," Warner Audio, 1985.

("Here's Johnny!" Jack Nicholson terrified audiences in Warner Brothers' 1980 film "The Shining.")

(A unique double cover was used for the Signet edition of *Misery*—this interior cover spoofed the popular horror writer. From *Misery* by Stephen King.)

''Thinner,'' Listen for Pleasure, 1985.
''The Dark Tower: The Gunslinger,'' New American Library, 1988.

SIDELIGHTS: King was born **September 21, 1947,** in Portland, Maine, the second son of Donald and Nellie Ruth Pillsbury King. Two years later, his father, a merchant seaman, went to the grocery store for a pack of cigarettes and never returned. King's mother was left to raise her two sons in near-poverty conditions taking jobs as laundry presser and doughnut baker to make ends meet. The one thing that was not in short supply, however, was love.

''Home was always rented. Our outhouse was painted blue and that's where we contemplated the sins of life. Our well was always going dry. I'd have to lug water from a spring in another field, and even now I'm nervous about our wells.''¹ There were no bathing facilities, so a hot bath meant a half a mile trek to Aunt Ethelyn's house, an especially difficult task during the icy Maine winter.

King fell prey to conflicting emotions as a child. He had friends, yet often felt estranged from others his age. He was overweight and uncoordinated which contributed to his feelings of unhappiness. ''My nightmares. . .were always inadequacy dreams.

Dreams of standing up to salute the flag and having my pants fall down. Trying to get to a class and not being prepared. When I played baseball I was always the kid who got picked last. 'Ha, ha, you got King' the others would say.

''Without a father I needed my own power trips. My alter ego as a child was Cannonball Cannon, a daredevil. Sometimes I went out West if I was unhappy, but most of the time I stayed home and did good deeds.''¹

An active imagination coupled with the same day-to-day anxieties and insecurities suffered by many children were part of King's baggage. He went through a period when he harbored fears of suddenly going crazy—walking down the street one minute and totally losing control the next.

Then there were adolescent periods of suppressed violence. Aided by television violence, he became terrified and preoccupied with death—death in general and his own in particular. Convinced he would never see twenty, he fantasized dark deserted streets; strange figures leaping at him from behind bushes. His fascination and intrigue with the subject culminated in a scrapbook of Fifties mass murderer Charlie Starkweather who with his girlfriend cut a bloody trail through the Midwest slaughtering nine or ten people. King pasted these newsclippings into a book in hope of unraveling the inner horror behind Starkweather's face.

As a kid, King went to every horror and science-fiction movie he could cram into a Saturday. ''If you love horror movies. . .you turn into the kind of person who would watch 'Attack of the Crab Monsters' four times. You know how. . .it is, but there's something that appeals to you.''²

He recalled one striking incident in October, 1957, while watching a science-fiction/horror movie ''Earth Vs. the Flying Saucers,'' starring Hugh Marlowe. During a critical point, the screen went blank, the lights went on, and the theater manager took center stage to announce that the Russians had just launched ''Sputnik,'' the first space satellite to orbit the Earth. King immediately connected the film he was watching with an enemy satellite circling the earth, carrying A-bombs, or H-bombs, or. . . .The fictional horror intersected sharply with the potential horror of annihilation. King sat frozen with fear for the remainder of the performance.

He discovered that his fascination with the macabre might have been inherited from his father who had at one time submitted his own science-fiction/horror tales to major men's magazines. None of the stories were published, however.

''When I was a sophomore in high school, I did a sophomoric thing which got me in a pot of fairly hot water, as sophomoric didoes often do. I wrote and published a small satiric newspaper called 'The Village Vomit.' In this little paper I lampooned a number of teachers at Lisbon (Maine) High School, where I was under instruction. These were not very gentle lampoons; they ranged from the scatological to the downright cruel.

''Eventually, a copy of this little newspaper found its way into the hands of a faculty member, and since I had been unwise enough to put my name on it (a fault, some critics would argue, of which I have still not been entirely cured), I was brought into the office. The sophisticated satirist had by that time reverted to what he really was: a fourteen-year-old kid who was shaking in his boots and wondering if he was going to get a suspension. . .what we called a 'three-day vacation' in those dim days of 1964.

"I wasn't suspended. I was forced to make a number of apologies—they were warranted, but they still tasted like dog-dirt in my mouth—and spent a week in detention hall. And the guidance counselor arranged what he no doubt thought of as a more constructive channel for my talents. This was a job—contingent upon the editor's approval—writing sports for the Lisbon *Enterprise,* a twelve-page weekly of the sort with which any small-town resident will be familiar. This editor was the man who taught me everything I know about writing in ten minutes. His name was John Gould. . . . "[3]

Gould simply proceeded to edit King's piece, paring it down, leaving only the salient points of the story. " 'I only took out the bad parts, you know,' he said. 'Most of it's pretty good.' 'I know,' I said, meaning both things: yes most of it was good, and yes, he had only taken out the bad parts. 'I won't do it again.'

" 'If that's true,' he said, 'you'll never have to work again. You can do *this* for a living.' Then he threw back his head and laughed.

"And he was right: I *am* doing this for a living, and as long as I can keep on, I don't expect ever to have to work again."[3]

1966. Attended University of Maine at Orono. "[My mother] was a very hardheaded person when it came to success. She knew what it was like to be on her own without an education and she was determined that [brother] David and I would go to college. 'You're not going to punch a time clock all your life,' she told us. She always told us that dreams and ambitions can cause bitterness if they're not realized and she encouraged me to submit my writings.

"We both got scholarships to the University of Maine. When we were there she'd send us $5 nearly every week for spending money. After she died, I found she had frequently gone without meals to send that money we'd so casually accepted. It was very unsettling."[1]

In college King studied under an English teacher named Burton Hatlen who became a mentor. Often Hatlen would be heard to mumble in the classroom: " 'Is there such a thing as white soul? Is there suburban soul?'

"Something in all of that reached out to me because I liked McDonald's and Dairy Queen and things like that. You'd see people bopping in there and it seemed to me they *did* have white soul. . . .I once wrote a story ('The Mist') and thought more of Burt while writing it than anything else. These people are stuck in a supermarket. Awful bugs are crawling up the walls and the people are cowering back by the Heinz spaghetti sauce. . . .I kept hearing Burt say 'That's it! That's myth!' "[4]

1970. Graduated from the University of Maine. With his degree in hand he landed a job pumping gas in a filling station, then pressing sheets in an industrial laundry for $60 a week. Alas, there was a glut on the teaching market.

1971. Married Tabitha Jane Spruce. "We got married on a Saturday because the laundry was closed on Saturday afternoons. . . .Everyone wished me well, but I still was docked for not being in that Saturday morning."[5]

Daughter, Naomi, was born; two years later, his son Joseph. "By having children you're able to reexperience everything you experienced as a child, only from a more mature perspective. It's like completing the wheel. At that point you can give your childhood up."[5]

King finally got a job teaching English at the local high school, Hampden Academy, but his real love was writing. After a

(From the movie "Cujo," starring Dee Wallace, Warner Brothers, 1983.)

(From the movie "Stand by Me," starring Wil Wheaton, River Phoenix, Jerry O'Connell and Corey Feldman. Directed by Rob Reiner, it was produced by Columbia Pictures in 1986.)

long day of teaching, he would squeeze himself into the furnace room and do battle with vampires and monsters.

By 1972, he had written countless short stories and completed his fourth novel, *The Running Man*, but success continued to elude him. "I was really depressed. I began to think that only cousins of editors get books published."[6]

Family finances were depressed as well. His wife was juggling mountains of unpaid bills, the children were in hand-me-downs, the 1965 Buick Special was self destructing, and the phone wires were snipped.

"I started writing [*Carrie*] but after four pages thought it stank and threw it in the rubbish. I came home later and found Tabby had taken them out and had left a note. 'Please keep going—it's good.' Since she's really stingy with her praise, I did."[1]

March, 1973. *Carrie* was submitted to Doubleday and accepted. "Remembering where you were and what you were doing when you found out your first novel had been accepted for publication is as easy as remembering where you were on Pearl Harbor Day or on November 22, 1963—although the circumstances are much more pleasant. I was prepping an American Lit class in the teacher's room one rainy afternoon in March of 1973 when my wife called, so excited and out of breath she could barely talk. She had a telegram which read: 'CARRIE OFFICIALLY A DOUBLEDAY BOOK. $2500 ADVANCE AGAINST ROYALTIES. CONGRATS, KID— THE FUTURE LIES AHEAD. BILL.'"[3]

"[*Carrie*] was based on a couple of real people. . .one I went to school with was a very peculiar girl who came from a very peculiar family. Her mother wasn't a religious nut like the mother in *Carrie*; she was a game nut, a sweepstakes nut who subscribed to magazines for people who entered contests. And she won things—weird things. She won a year's supply of BeBop pencils, but the big thing she won was Jack Benny's old Maxwell. They had it out in the front yard for years, with weeds growing up around it. They didn't know what to do with it.

"This girl had one change of clothes for the entire school year, and all the other kids made fun of her. I have a very clear memory of the day she came to school with a new outfit she'd bought herself. She was a plain-looking country girl, but she'd changed the black skirt and white blouse—which was all anybody had ever seen her in—for a bright-colored checked blouse with puffed sleeves and a skirt that was fashionable at the time. And everybody made worse fun of her because nobody wanted to see her change the mold. Later she married a man who was a weather forecaster on top of Mt. Washington—a very strange man, a man as peculiar as she was. She had three kids and then hung herself one summer."[7]

"*Carrie*. . .lives out a nightmare that all teen-agers go through. Not being accepted by peers. And all high school kids are full of suppressed violence. Remember how you used to go home and throw your books across a room if you'd flunked a quiz? *Carrie* lets people relive that violent urge of adolescence."[8]

"If it had any thesis to offer, this deliberate updating of 'High School Confidential,' it was that high school is a place of almost bottomless conservatism and bigotry."[9]

1975. *Salem's Lot* published. "I was teaching *Dracula*...at Hampden Academy. . . .I was also teaching Thornton Wilder's *Our Town* in freshman English. . . .I could really identify with the nature of a very small town. I grew up in Durham, Maine, a really small town. . . .We had an eight-party line. You could

(The prom scene from United Artists' 1976 release "Carrie," starring Sissy Spacek and William Katt.)

always count on the heavy breathing of the fat old lady up the street when you talked to your girl friend on the phone. There was a lot to love in that little town. But there was a lot of nastiness too. . . .

"We were eating supper in our crummy little trailer and I was spouting off about *Dracula*. Tabby said suddenly, 'What would happen if *Dracula* came back today? Not to London, but to Herman?' where we were living. I sort of shrugged it off. But good ideas stick to you like burrs—they won't let go.'"[1]

"Actually, *Invasion of the Body Snatchers* had a much greater effect. The thing that had stayed in my mind was the situation at the end, where Kevin McCarthy and Dana Wynter are the last two humans in town, all the other townspeople have been replaced by pods and they're closing in. I just thought that was so romantic, two against this whole town, and that's pretty well reflected in *Salem's Lot*.'"[10]

Most of King's ideas are extensions of other ideas. "I've had about three original ideas in my life. The rest of them were bounces. I sense the limitation of where my talents are.'"[11]

Carrie was derived from a grade-B flick "The Brain from Planet Arous''; *The Shining* was influenced by Shirley Jackson's *The Haunting of Hill House; The Stand* owes its debt to George R. Stewart's *Earth Abides* and M. P. Shiel's *The Purple Cloud; Firestarter* had a number of science-fictional antecedents. *Salem's Lot* bears intentional similarity to Stoker's *Dracula*.

1976. Motion picture "Carrie" released, directed by Brian DePalma. "I liked DePalma's film of *Carrie* quite a bit. The attitude of the film was different from my book; I tended to view the events straight-on, humorlessly, in a straight point-

to-point progression. . .while I think DePalma saw a chance to make a movie that was a satirical view of high school life in general and high school peer-groups in particular. A perfectly viable point of view. Sissy Spacek was excellent, but right behind her—in a smaller part than it should have been—was John Travolta. He played the part of Billy Nolan the way I wish I'd written it, half-funny and half-crazy.'"[12]

The movie became one of the top-grossing films of 1976. "That happy sound of people clutching their pacemakers, I love it. Every shriek is a wonderful moment. My pleasure comes in getting them in there and getting that happening. Close all the doors so they can't get out and just scare the hell out of 'em.'"[13] "The movie made the book and the book made me.'"[10]

"When I was writing *The Shining* there was a scene I was terrified of having to face writing. Writing is a pretty intense act of visualization. I won't say it's magic, but it's pretty close to magic. There was this woman in the tub, dead and bloated for years, and she gets up and starts to come for the boy who can't get the door open. I didn't want to have to face that unspeakable thing in the tub any more than the boy did. Two or three nights running, before I got to that section, I dreamed there was a nuclear explosion on the lake where we lived. The mushroom cloud turned into a huge red bird that was coming for me.'"[1]

"As I worked, I found myself thinking, 'In about eight days I'll be rewriting the bathtub scene.' Then it was, 'In five days I'll be rewriting the bathtub scene.' And then it was, 'Today—the bathtub scene!' And I really got tense and nervous about doing it, because when you write, you live your story, and no reader ever has a reaction as tight about your book as your own. . . .The way he hears the thump when something comes

(From the movie "Maximum Overdrive," starring Emilio Estevez. Directed by King, it was produced by Dino De Laurentiis in 1986.)

to greet him, the way that knob starts to go back and forth. . . .Boy, things like that really get to me."[7]

The list of King's fears is long. "I don't like elevators, or closed-in places. I don't like the dark, or sewers, or funerals, or the idea of being buried alive. Cancer, heart attacks, the possibility of being squished under a car lift, running into a stone wall on my motorcycle, having my brains pureed, swallowing a fishbone and choking on it."[14]

And he has his share of superstitions. "Throwing salt over your shoulders. Don't walk under ladders. Don't light three on a match. Whatever is the worst thing that could happen in a situation is what crosses my mind."[14]

"At night, when I go to bed, I still am at pains to be sure that my legs are under the blankets after the lights go out. I'm not a child anymore but. . .I don't like to sleep with one leg sticking out. Because if a cool hand ever reached out from under the bed and grasped my ankle, I might scream. Yes, I might scream to wake the dead. . . .The thing under my bed waiting to grab my ankle isn't real. I know that, and I also know that if I'm careful to keep my foot under the covers, it will never be able to grab my ankle."[1]

King has always been an exceedingly prolific writer. As a result, his novel *Rage* was published under the pseudonym of Richard Bachman because King's publishers were loathe to print so much work yearly under a single author's name. "I do wonder betimes from whence this idea came that a really *decorous* novelist only publishes a book every two or three years. If you do it more often than that, you begin to get a reputation, like the girl of easy virtue who has to leave town every two years or so to visit her Aunt Cora in Idaho. I've begun to have a sense that what these critics would *really* like

to say is something like, 'You have scattered literary bastards all over the landscape, King—didn't your mother ever teach you to keep your pen in your pocket once in a while?'"[15]

1978. Son Owen born; novel *The Stand* published, a long and difficult book for King to write. "It got to the point where I began describing it to friends as my own little Vietnam, because I kept telling myself that in another hundred pages or so I would begin to see light at the end of the tunnel."[16]

"*The Stand* starts with a plague that wipes out most of the world's population, and it develops into a titanic struggle that Christianity figures in. But it's not about God, like some of the reviews claimed. Stuart Redman isn't Christ, and the Dark Man isn't the Devil. It's the same with *Salem's Lot*—Christianity is there, but it isn't the most important thing. The important thing is that we are dealing with two elemental forces—White and Black—and I really do believe in White force. . . .There are a lot of horror writers who deal with this struggle, but they tend to concentrate on the Black. But the other force is there, too; it's just a lot tougher to deal with.'"[7]

"In my own books, the power of God doesn't play a passive part at all. (Call it the power of White, if you prefer; sometimes I do, although the White concept is more pagan than Christian). . . .Good wins out over evil in *Salem's Lot* and *The Shining* and at least earns a draw in *Carrie*. Anyhow, this whole question is very central to my new book, *The Stand*.

"I'm religious in terms of the White, but I don't go to church. God and the devil—the White and Black forces—proceed from the *inside*—that's where the power comes from. Churches make morals, which, I suppose, is useful. . . .So is Tupperware, in its way."[12]

(Stephen King and family in front of their Victorian mansion. Photograph copyright James Roderick Photography.)

(From the 1985 MGM film ''Cat's Eye,'' starring Drew Barrymore.)

1979. Novel *The Dead Zone* published; "Salem's Lot" released as a television miniseries. King feels horror hasn't fared well on television because it is difficult to write a horror story in a world already full of horrors: thousand megaton warheads and nuclear power plants.

Television, according to King, is too fainthearted and unimaginative and often overlooks one simple fact when dealing with horror: "you gotta scare the audience. Sooner or later you gotta put on the gruesome mask and go booga-booga!"[17]

"There are only two scenes in recent memory that match the moment [in the film 'Alien'] when the alien comes bursting out of that hapless fellow's stomach at the dinner table: one occurs when the dead black man takes a chomp out of his wife's shoulder in 'Dawn of the Dead,' the other comes in William Friedkin's 'The Exorcist' when Linda Blair's head does a complete 360. . . .'Alien' is all very well, but there is still left in me a lot of the kid who went to see Steve McQueen in 'The Blob' (not once but four times. . .). Every now and then I long for a renewal of the Attack of the Killer B's. . . ."[18]

"The Shining" was released, directed by Stanley Kubrick. "The first time he called, it was 7:30 in the morning. I was standing in the bathroom in my underwear, shaving, and my wife comes in and her eyes are bugging out. I thought one of the kids must be choking in the kitchen or something. She says, 'Stanley Kubrick is on the phone!' I mean, I was just floored. I didn't even take the shaving cream off my face."[19]

"When it happened, I hadn't had a No. 1 on the hard-cover list or anything. And I'd see my friends, and they'd say, 'What's happening?' And I'd say, 'Well, I guess Stanley Kubrick's going to make a film out of my new book.' And they'd say, 'Oh, yeah. Right.'"[20]

King recalls his first Hollywood pre-production meeting. "We sat around the table talking seriously about people to play roles in the movie. 'What do you think of Robert DeNiro for the father?' someone says. Somebody else says, 'I think Jack Nicholson would be terrific.' And I say, 'Don't you think Nicholson is too old for the part?' And so it goes. We're tossing around these names from the fan magazines—except it's for real. Then the check comes and it's $140 without drinks, and somebody picks it up without batting an eye.

"Then I come back to Maine and pick up the toys and check if the kids brush in the back of their mouths, and I'm smoking too many cigarettes and chewing aspirins alone in this office and the glamour people aren't here.

"There is a curious loneliness. You have to produce day after day and you have to deal with doubts—that what you're producing is trivial and, besides not even good. So, in a way, when I go there, to New York City, I feel like I've earned it. I'm getting my due."[21]

Unfortunately, the film was a disappointment to King. "Stanley Kubrick's stated purpose was to make a horror picture and I don't think he understood the genre."[13]

"The worst problem was that it was uninformed. They wanted to make a horror film, but they had no understanding of what's been done before in the field. The snapper, the gimmick at the end, it's been done twelve, fourteen times on TV. It wasn't a failure of talent. It was a failure of experience."[22]

"Could it have been done better? Over the years I've come to believe that it probably could not. The film is cold and disappointingly loveless—but chilling."[23]

1980. Novel *Firestarter* published. King became the only author ever to have three different books simultaneously on the *New York Times'* bestseller list: *Firestarter, The Dead Zone,* and *The Shining.*

"[*Firestarter* is] more about paranoia than about horror. Paranoia is a good way to get an effect across to a reader. I went to college in the '60s, man: I'm a product of my times. The government was up to a lot. . .in the '60s. This is actually the closest I'll ever get to writing about that period, when all that energy and promise led us to nothing, to the '70s. The '80s. I see the '80's going right down the chute."[24]

"We're killing ourselves; we're fiddling while Rome burns. I mean, while we've got enough explosives to turn planet Earth into the second asteroid belt, the largest weekly magazine in the country is talking about where celebrities shop, and why people in Hollywood don't want to serve finger foods any more."[19]

"We are living in a nervous time, but nervous times provide the perfect climate for horror. Horror movies and books are very reassuring because they end. You walk out of the theater or put down the book and the monster is dead and everything is all right."[25]

As the name suggests, *Firestarter* is about a young girl with pyrotechnic abilities. King often uses children as his main characters. "They epitomize the powers of good. They're cleareyed. They're very useful in fantasy because they have a broad spectrum of perceptions."[5]

"Kids don't fight shock the way adults do; they go with it, maybe because kids are in a semipermanent state of shock until they're 13 or so."[26]

King bought a second house outside of Bangor, Maine—a huge Victorian mansion with twin turrets, wrought iron fences, indoor swimming pool and whirlpool. He has a housekeeper and a secretary. "Everything is going so well for us that I keep expecting the doctor to tell me I have cancer or one of our kids has leukemia."[27]

With all these amenities, his lifestyle remains simple and unpretentious: "I am my work to a large extent. Work takes most of the energy. It's what gives me pleasure. It *is* the toy. I don't feel the need to fill up my life with tape decks and amplifiers. It's nice, but I can take it or leave it."[5]

The Kings rise at 6 a.m., get the kids off to school, then he and Tabitha settle down to work for several hours. He writes every day but Christmas and his birthday. "I work on what's important to me in the morning, for three hours. Usually, in the afternoon, I have what I call my 'toy truck,' a story that might develop or might not, but meanwhile it's fun to work on."[7]

"I'm not a fast writer, but I stick to it. I write 1500 words a day, and the stuff just piles up. It's a constant secretion. I have the feeling that if I stop, I won't be able to do it again."[6]

1981. Published the novel *Cujo* and a non-fiction work entitled *Danse Macabre,* "an informal overview" of the horror genre from 1950 through 1980. "The work of horror. . .is a dance—a moving rhythmic search. . .[for] the place where you, the viewer or reader live at your most primitive level." He asserts that horror is "beneath its fangs and fright wig as conservative as an Illinois Republican in a three-piece suit," a "rehearsal for death" but also "a reaffirmation of life and good will and simple imagination—just one more pipeline to the infinite."[16]

(From the movie ''Firestarter,'' starring Drew Barrymore and George C. Scott. Produced by Dino De Laurentiis, 1984.)

''Almost all horror stories mirror specific areas of free-forming anxieties. And that sounds like a mouthful, a lot of intellectual bullshit, but what I mean is, when you read a horror novel or see a horror film, you make a connection with the things you're afraid of in your own life.

''People are always asking why you write those things, which I think is a question that can't be answered. The mind is like a table, and it's on a tilt; you put a marble on it and it rolls in a different direction from mine. . . .I doubt that anyone goes up to Louis L'Amour and asks him why he writes western stories. He does, and they accept it. But they always ask horror writers things like that.''[7]

King speculated on his future. ''I don't feel the urge to change. I don't always intend to do horror, but somehow things almost always head that way. If they don't, I'm not going to fight it. You go where you feel you have to go. Writing is like that. You can't always tell yourself you're going to write one particular thing and that's that. You get the story and the story takes hold, and away you go.''[7]

''I don't want there to be a time when I think that Steve King should be exclusively a horror writer. The temptation is great, though. You say to yourself, if I don't produce horror stories, I won't have any more Number Ones—and it's very satisfying to have Number Ones.''[28]

1982. Among many other awards, King was named Best Fiction Writer of the Year in a national poll conducted by *Us* magazine.

Different Seasons was published, a collection of four stories which included ''The Body''—an intensely autobiographical story about King's childhood and his best friends. ''I never had any friends later on like the ones I had when I was twelve. Jesus, does anyone?'' The film ''Stand by Me,'' directed by Rob Reiner was based on ''The Body.'' ''I had to be alone after I saw it because it shook me. It's a wonderful picture, and I think it will be nominated for awards. It's as simple as that.''[29]

The film ''Creepshow,'' a series of stories that spoofed the horror genre, was released. ''The comic-book form allowed us to pare the motivations and characterizations down to a bare minimum and let us just go for scares.

'''Creepshow'. . .[had] to be funny to really work. But comic in the way that the Shakespearean tragedies were comic—with a couple of gravediggers yucking it up. You get the audience laughing every once in a while, and it keeps them plugged in; they can't turn away completely, so the fright channels stay open. That's what Hitchcock was great at.''[30]

His son Joe appeared as Billy in ''Creepshow,'' as did King himself in the roll of a shirttail farmer who unearths a meteor.

1984. Novel *Thinner* published under the pseudonym of Richard Bachman. ''I used to weigh 236 pounds, and I smoked heavily. I went to see the doctor. He said: 'Listen, man, your triglycerides are really high. In case you haven't noticed it, you've entered heart attack country.' That line is in the book.''[31]

(King experienced his own horror—directing "Maximum Overdrive.")

Novel *The Talisman,* co-written with Peter Straub, was published. "Peter Straub is one of the best. I know I'm chewing off a big bite here, but I think *Ghost Story* is one of the best gothic horror novels of the past century."[7] Stephen Spielberg picked up the film option immediately. Twenty-four hours after its release, the novel made back the author's advances and sales began like no other book in the history of publishing.

It was also King's first attempt at working with a word processor: "It makes me feel like that man in the James Bond movie, where he's caught in the exercise machine. I get into it and can't get out. It just scrolls up and up and up and I feel like those words are all under glass."[32] Nonetheless, once he switched to the computer, King's output literally doubled.

The Eyes of the Dragon published in limited edition. "I wrote it deliberately with my daughter in mind because she doesn't like horror stories and gross things. She never read anything that I had written and, in a way, that hurt. So, I thought, 'All right, if she won't come to me, I'll go to her.' I sat down to write this story, which I started when she was about eleven. . . .I tried to write this fantasy and deliberately tried not to talk down to her. The best novels are *just* novels. Really. No children novels, no adult novels."[29]

"People like Doris Lessing, John Updike, Joyce Carol Oates. . .do books about extraordinary people in ordinary situations, while I'm more fetched by the exact opposite. . .ordinary people in a pressure-cooker, in a crunch situation. Preferably one where events have skewed from the unusual to the unnatural to the out-and-out unbelievable."[12]

"Would I rather have critical or popular success? Well, I used to walk around saying people don't want tunas with good taste, people want tunas that taste good. I think my stuff is good."[14]

Of his first eleven novels, every one of them has topped the book charts and has either been optioned or made into a film.

1985. *Skeleton Crew,* a collection of short stories written over seventeen years, was published. One story, "Cain Rose Up," is a retelling of Charles Whitman's Texas Tower murders. Writing is a therapeutic process for King during which he is allowed to exorcise all of the demons, all of the violence, the rage, the frustrations, all that is dark within him onto a sheet of paper.

After eight years and five novels under the pseudonym of Richard Bachman, people finally connected the writing style to its real author. "It should have been in *Time*'s 'Milestones,' 'Died, Richard Bachman, of cancer of the pseudonym.'"[11]

1986. Directed his first movie, "Maximum Overdrive." "People tell me they don't go to my movies anymore because they don't find me on the screen. . .I was intensely curious to find out if I could translate whatever was in my heart and brain—the stuff that's between the lines in the books—onto film. . . .I went in with the idea that I was going to make a moron movie. . . .They're the best kind of movies as far as I'm concerned. 'Back to the Future' is a moron movie, 'Rambo' is a moron movie. I loved them both.

"I wish someone had told me how little I knew and how grueling (directing) was going to be. I didn't know how little I knew about mechanics and the politics of filmmaking. People tiptoe around the director with this 'Don't wake the baby' attitude. Nobody wants to tell you this, that or the other thing if it's bad news."[33]

"It's a primitive way to create: eighty people drinking Gatorade waiting for the clouds to clear to get one shot."[34]

"You've got to remember that they didn't hire me because I did a wonderful job on 'The Magnificent Seven.' Dino De Laurentiis is not a stupid man. He felt if I directed this picture, that in itself would mean a big first weekend. It's like what Samuel Johnson said about women preachers and dancing dogs. You don't expect to see it done well, you pay to see it done at all."[29]

Maximum Overdrive was at first censored with an X-rating. "The basic problem is that sex and violence on screen are being rated by people who can't distinguish between fact and imagination. These are people who have no imagination."[34]

"You can't traumatize a kid for life by taking him to see one or two horror movies. Kids might get a few nights of bad dreams, but horror movies won't make them go home and kill their grandmothers. To traumatize a kid for life, it takes about fourteen years of television. I would rather take any kid in America out to see 'Night of the Living Dead' or 'Halloween II' than have him watch 'The Dukes of Hazzard' on TV. 'The Dukes of Hazzard' says it's good fun to go out and drive at 90 miles an hour. No horror movie does that."[25]

King's attitude toward censorship naturally flows over into books: "I resent people who take the attitude that says, 'I know more about this than you do, sonnybuns. I'll tell you what you can read and what you can't read.' That's fascism.

"Every book that I've ever had published, with the exception of two, has been banned from one public high school library or another. *Cujo* has been banned so often now that it is on the American Civil Liberties Union's [ACLU] list of the top ten banned books. And I'm very proud of that, because I'm never going to win a Nobel Prize or a National Book Award. But being on that list of banned books, I'm in the company of greats: Flannery O'Connor, Harper Lee, J. D. Salinger, and John Updike.

"When it comes to censorship involving high school libraries, I love it, man. Somebody writes me a letter and says, 'Do you want to come and defend this book?' I say 'Absolutely not— let them jerk it. Just make sure to tell the kids that whatever is taken off the shelves is probably what they need to know the most.' That will get their asses running to a public library or a bookstore. When a book gets banned, kids will read it.

"My book *The Shining* may be pulled from library shelves because people believe it's bad for children to read a story about how a father ends up hunting down his own son. But *Hansel and Gretel* is all right for children, a story in which a stepmother orders her husband to disembowel his two children and bring her their hearts. The father decides to leave the kids in the woods to starve to death instead of killing them outright—which we're supposed to interpret as kindness. The children arrive at a witch's house, and it's stated she's going to. . .eat them! That's cannibalism! *The Shining* is not all right for kids, but *Hansel and Gretel* is—it's staple reading."

1986. *It* published. "I thought of the fairy tale called *The Three Billy-Goats Gruff* and wondered what I would do if a troll called out from beneath me, 'Who is trip-trapping upon my bridge.' All of a sudden I wanted to write a novel about a real troll under a real bridge. . . .Then, one night about six months later—after a while these things seem to pick up their own blind urgency—I thought of how such a story might be cast; how it might be possible to create a ricochet effect, interweaving the stories of children and the adults they became. The idea was so good it was horrible. It was also irresistible."[35]

1987. *Misery* and *Tommyknockers* were published. "[*Misery* is]. . .gruesome and the one people are going to sit and read

(John Franklin plays the demonic leader of a pack of murderous youngsters in Stephen King's "Children of the Corn." Released by New World Pictures, 1984.)

without stopping. It's interesting because it's a far better book than *Cujo,* yet it's set in an even smaller compass of space. Very claustrophobic book."[29]

Tommyknockers was number one on the *New York Times* Bestseller List, and *Misery* was ranked number fourteen. "Which leads me to an almost mandatory piece of advice for the beginning novelist: Don't write your novel with best-seller lists or movie companies or rich paperback houses in mind. Don't, in fact, even write it with publication in mind. Write it for yourself. It's the only way you can come out of one of the world's most grueling projects still able to face rejection with your equanimity intact.

"Start by believing in yourself."[3]

FOOTNOTE SOURCES

[1]Mel Allen, "The Man Who Writes Nightmares," *Yankee,* March, 1979.
[2]Stanley Wiater, "Stephen King and George Romero: Collaboration in Terror," *Fangoria,* number 6, n.d.
[3]*Writer,* June, 1975.
[4]Erik Hedegaard, "Mentors: Students Who Made It and the Teachers Who Made the Difference," *Rolling Stone,* April 15, 1982.
[5]Michael J. Bandler, "The King of the Macabre at Home," *Parents,* January, 1982.
[6]Carol Lawson, "Behind the Best Sellers," *New York Times Book Review,* September 23, 1979.
[7]Charles L. Grant, "Stephen King: I Like to Go for the Jugular," *Twilight Zone,* Volume 1, number 1, 1981.
[8]Lois Lowry, "King of the Occult," *Down East,* 1978.
[9]"King, Stephen (Edwin)," *Current Biography,* October, 1981.
[10]David Chute, "King of the Night: An Interview with Stephen King," *Take One,* January, 1979.
[11]Stefan Kanfer, "King of Horror," *Time,* October 6, 1986.
[12]Peter S. Perakos, "Stephen King on *Carrie, The Shining,* Etc.," *Cinefantastique,* winter, 1979.
[13]"Stephen King: 'Firestarter,'" *Universal News,* April 9, 1984.
[14]Susin Shapiro, "One Picture Is Worth a Million Words," *Daily News* (N. Y.), July 13, 1986.
[15]Stephen King, "The Irish King," *Daily News* (N. Y.), March 16, 1984.
[16]S. King, *Danse Macabre,* Everest House, 1981.
[17]S. King, "You Gotta Put on the Gruesome Mask and Go Booga-Booga!" *TV Guide,* December 5, 1981.
[18]S. King, "A Year in the Dark: The Horror of '79," *Rolling Stone,* December 27, 1979-Jan. 10, 1980.
[19]Darrell Ewing and Dennis Myers, "King of the Road," *American Film,* June, 1986.
[20]William Wilson, "Riding the Crest of the Horror Craze," *New York Times Magazine,* May 11, 1980.
[21]M. Allen, "Witches and Aspirin," *Writers Digest,* June, 1977.
[22]Martin Burden, "King-Sized Complaints: Horror Author Horrified by That H'wood Touch," *New York Post,* April 16, 1985.
[23]S. King, "Horrors!" *TV Guide,* October 30, 1982.

[24]Bill Kelley, "Author of 'The Shining' Stephen King Reveres the Relevance of Horror," *Aquarian Weekly*, November 19-26, 1980.

[25]Mark Sullivan, "King of Terror in a World of Big Macs," *Women's Wear Daily*, August 23, 1982.

[26]Constance Adler, "Prince of Darkness: In His Reign of Best-Selling Terror, Author Stephen King Remains Absolute Master of the Scary Story," *Philadelphia*, August, 1985.

[27]"Couples," *People*, May 18, 1981.

[28]Edwin McDowell, "Behind the Best Sellers: Stephen King," *New York Times Biographical Service*, September, 1981.

[29]Edward Gross, "Stephen King Takes a Vacation," *Fangoria*, October, 1986.

[30]Ron Hansen, "Creepshow: The Dawn of a Living Horror Comedy," *Esquire Film Quarterly*, January, 1982.

[31]Stephen P. Brown, "Secretly Hidden behind the Pen Name of Richard Bachman Was Stephen King," *Daily News* (N. Y.), May 19, 1985.

[32]William Goldstein, "A Coupl'a Authors Sittin' around Talkin'," *Publisher's Weekly*, May 11, 1984.

[33]Jessie Horsting, "Stephen King Gets behind the Wheel," *Fangoria*, August, 1986.

[34]Stephen Schaefer, "King in Overdrive," *Boston Herald*, July 27, 1986.

[35]*Book of the Month Club News*, October, 1986.

FOR MORE INFORMATION SEE:

Psychology Today, September, 1975.

John F. Baker, "Stephen King," *Publishers Weekly*, January 17, 1977.

New York Times, March 1, 1977, August 17, 1979.

Frank Sleeper, "Stephen King Makes Millions by Scaring Hell Out of Three Million Readers," *People*, March 7, 1977.

Stephen King, "The Fright Report," *Oui*, January, 1978.

"Horror Teller," *Horizon*, February, 1978.

Washington Post Book World, October 1, 1978.

Washington Post, November 23, 1978, August 30, 1979.

Maclean's, December 18, 1978.

Nyclatops, Volume 1, number 7, 1978.

New Yorker, January 15, 1979.

America, February 17, 1979.

Chicago Tribune, September 18, 1979.

Daily News (N. Y.), September 23, 1979.

Detroit News, September 26, 1979.

S. King, "A Pilgrim's Progress," *American Bookseller*, January, 1980.

Fantasy Newsletter, February, 1980.

S. King, "How I Became a Brand Name," *Adelina*, February, 1980.

Newsweek, May 26, 1980.

Paul R. Gagne, "Stephen King," *Cinefantastique*, summer, 1980.

Time, June 2, 1980, August 30, 1982.

S. King, "Imagery and the Third Eye," *Writer*, October, 1980.

Boston, October, 1980.

"A Mild Down-Easter Discovers Terror Is the Ticket," *People*, December 29, 1980.

Dan Christensen, "Stephen King: Living in 'Constant, Deadly Terror,'" *Fangoria*, number 3, n.d.

S. King, "Why We Crave Horror Movies," *Playboy*, January, 1981.

Stephen Rubin, "The Shining of Stephen King," *Daily News*, (N. Y.), March 25, 1981.

P. R. Gagne, "Stephen King," *Cinefantastique*, spring, 1981.

"Stephen King's Guilty Pleasures," *Film Comment*, May/June, 1981.

"Now You Take Bambi or Snow White—That's Scary," *TV Guide*, June 13, 1981.

"Notes on Horror," *Quest*, June, 1981.

S. King, "A Master of Horror Stories Has Some Provocative Thoughts about Tots, Terror and TV," *TV Guide*, June 13, 1981.

"Why We Crave Horror Movies," *Oui*, August, 1981.

"King and Straub to Write Novel; Co-publishers Named," *Publishers Weekly*, October 2, 1981.

S. King, "Between Rocks and a Soft Place," *Playboy*, January, 1982.

Penthouse, April, 1982.

P. Gray, "Master of Postliterate Prose," *Time*, August 30, 1982.

Douglas E. Winter, *The Reader's Guide to Stephen King*, Borgo, 1982.

Tim Underwood and Chuck Miller, editors, *Fear Itself: The Horror Fiction of Stephen King*, Underwood Miller, 1982.

Life, January, 1983.

A. Thompson, "The Thrills, Chills and Skills of Stephen King," *McCall's*, February, 1983.

Playboy, June, 1983.

American Libraries, July/August, 1983.

Rob Baker, "The King Zone," *Daily News* (N. Y.), October 23, 1983.

Richard Zoglin, "Giving Hollywood the Chills," *Time*, January 9, 1984.

David Sherman, "The Stephen King Interview," *Fangoria*, April, 1984.

Leo Siligsohn, "The King of Horror," *Newsday*, May 6, 1984.

People, May 28, 1984, January 28, 1985, August 18, 1986.

"Why I Am for Gary Hart," *New Republic*, June 4, 1984.

Andrea Chambers, "Author Stephen King's Spooky Amex Commerical Caps a Decade of 'Do You Know Me's?,'" *People*, August 27, 1984.

Richard Rothenstein, "Two Terror Titans Team Up," *Daily News* (N. Y.), October 14, 1984.

C. Leerhsen, "The Titans of Terror," *Newsweek*, December 24, 1984.

Daniel Cohen, *Masters of Horror*, Clarion, 1984.

D. E. Winter, *Stephen King: The Art of Darkness*, New American Library, 1984, revised edition, 1986.

R. Sutton, "Screaming in Unison," *School Library Journal*, January, 1985.

"Trade News," *Publishers Weekly*, March 22, 1985.

Tim Hewitt, "Cat's Eye," *Cinefantastique*, May, 1985.

Kim Foltz and Penelope Wang, "An Unstoppable Thriller King," *Newsweek*, June 10, 1985.

"Fire—Ice Cream," *Mademoiselle*, November, 1985.

American Spectator, December, 1985.

Michael R. Collings and David Engebretson, *The Shorter Works of Stephen King*, Starmont House, 1985.

M. R. Collings, *Stephen King as Richard Bachman*, Starmont House, 1985.

S. Schaefer, "The Director Is King," *Film Comment*, May/June, 1986.

T. Underwood and C. Miller, *Kingdom of Fear: The World of Stephen King*, New American Library, 1986.

M. R. Collings, *Stephen King Concordance*, Starmont House, 1986.

"Everything You Need to Know about Writing Successfully—in Ten Minutes," *Writer*, July, 1986.

Stephen Holder, "Rob Reiner Films Unusual Teen Drama," *New York Times*, August 8, 1986.

"The Roots of Terror," *Maclean's*, August 11, 1986.

Stefan Kanfer, "King of Horror," *Time*, October 6, 1986.

M. R. Collings, *Stephen King Phenomenon*, Starmont House, 1986.

S. King, "What's Scaring Stephen King," *Omni*, February, 1987.

P. Gagne, *Stephen King Goes to the Movies*, Underwood Miller, 1987.

S. King, "Writing the #1 Bestseller: How It Happened," *Writer*, April, 1987.
S. King, "'Ever Et Raw Meat?' and Other Weird Questions," *New York Times Book Review* December 6, 1987.

KLEIN, Robin 1936-

PERSONAL: Born February 28, 1936, in Kempsey, Australia; daughter of Leslie Macquarie (a farmer) and Mary (a homemaker; maiden name, Cleaver) McMaugh; married Karl Klein, August 18, 1956 (divorced, April, 1978); children: Michael, Peter, Ingrid, Rosalind. *Education:* Attended schools in New South Wales, Australia. *Home:* Belgrave, Victoria 3160, Australia. *Agent:* Curtis Brown, P.O. Box 19, Paddington, Sydney NSW 2021, Australia.

CAREER: Writer, 1981—. Worked as a "tea lady" at a warehouse, and as a bookshop assistant, library assistant, nurse, copper enamelist, and program aide at a school for disadvantaged children. *Awards, honors:* Special Mention from the Critici in Erba Awards at the Bologna Children's Book Fair, 1979, for *The Giraffe in Pepperell Street;* Australian Junior Book of the Year Award from the Children's Book Council of Australia, 1983, for *Thing;* Book of the Year Award Highly Commended Citation from the Children's Book Council of Australia, 1984, for *Penny Pollard's Diary;* Senior Fellowship Grant from the Arts Council of Australia Literature Board, 1985.

WRITINGS:

JUVENILE

The Giraffe in Pepperell Street (illustrated by Gill Tomblin), Hodder & Stoughton, 1978.
Honoured Guest, Macmillan, 1979.
Thing (illustrated by Alison Lester), Oxford University Press, 1982.
People Might Hear You, Penguin, 1983, Viking, 1987.
Junk Castle (illustrated by Rolf Heimann), Oxford University Press, 1983.

ROBIN KLEIN

(Cover illustration by Drew Aitken from *Hating Alison Ashley* by Robin Klein.)

Penny Pollard's Diary (illustrated by Ann James), Oxford University Press, 1983.
Oodoolay, Era Publications, 1984.
Hating Alison Ashley, Penguin, 1984, Viking, 1987.
Brock and the Dragon, Hodder & Stoughton, 1984.
Thalia the Failure, Ashton Scholastic, 1984.
Thingnapped! (sequel to *Thing;* illustrated by A. Lester), Oxford University Press, 1984.
Penny Pollard's Letters (illustrated by A. James), Oxford University Press, 1984.
Ratbags and Rascals (illustrated by A. Lester), Dent, 1984.
Halfway across the Galaxy and Turn Left, Penguin, 1985.
The Enemies, Angus & Robertson, 1985.
Penny Pollard in Print, Oxford University Press, 1986.
The Princess Who Hated It, Omnibus Books, 1986.
Snakes and Ladders: Poems about the Ups and Downs of Life, Dent, 1985, Merrimack, 1986.
(With Max Dunn) *The Lonely Hearts Club*, Oxford University Press, 1986.
Boss of the Pool, Omnibus Books, 1986.
Games, Viking, 1986.
Birk the Berserker (illustrated by A. Lester), Omnibus Books, 1987.
Robin Klein's Crookbook, Methuen, 1987.
Christmas, Methuen, 1987.
I Shot an Arrow (illustrated by Geoff Hocking), Viking Kestrel, 1987.
Don't Tell Lucy, Methuen, 1987.
Laurie Loved Me Best (young adult), Viking Kestrel, 1988.

Contributor of stories, poems, and plays to *New South Wales School Magazine* and publications of the Victorian Department of Education.

WORK IN PROGRESS: Amy's Bed, a picturebook to be published by Omnibus Books; *Penny Pollard's Passport*, to be published by Oxford University Press; a teenage/late primary age novel about drugs.

SIDELIGHTS: "I write for children because I adore their company, honesty, and sense of fun. I'm addicted to writing and can feel quite physically ill if more than three days go by and I haven't been able to get to a typewriter. (It makes me a dreadful hostess!) The letters I've received from children more than make up for the long hours of isolated work, and I've never wanted to move into any other field of writing.

"I wrote my first book, *The Giraffe in Pepperell Street*, while sitting in a railway station watching a kid trying to entice an enormous stray dog home with her. Since then I've become an eager 'child watcher' and get many ideas from incidents I see on public transport and at shopping centers. I also use material gathered from bringing up my own four children and working in various jobs where children were involved. However, I don't sit down and write consciously for children as a particular audience, or use modified vocabulary for their benefit.

"Most of my books seem to have a strong female character, capable of dealing with any problem that arises, perhaps because I was a very cowardly child and admired people like that. I also have a soft spot for the 'underdog,' and many of my characters are awkward misfits who still manage to achieve goals. Without really meaning to, I find that I'm most at ease writing in a humorous vein. I suppose that what I admire most in people is their ability to laugh when facing quite sad circumstances in their lives; it seems to me a very moving gallantry that often goes unpraised."

HOBBIES AND OTHER INTERESTS: Gardening, embroidery, reading, shopping, handcrafts.

FOR MORE INFORMATION SEE:

P. Lloyd, *How Writers Work*, Methuen, 1987.
Belle Alderman, editor, *The Inside Story*, Children's Book Council of Australia, 1987.
The Storymakers, Oxford University Press, 1987.

LASKI, Marghanita   1915-1988
(Sarah Russell)

PERSONAL: Born October 24, 1915, in London, England; died February 6, 1988, in Dublin, Ireland; daughter of Neville J. (a King's counsel) and Phina (maiden name, Gaster) Laski; married John Eldred Howard (a publisher), 1937; children: Rebecca, Jonathan. *Education:* Sommerville College, Oxford, B.A., 1936. *Agent:* David Higham Associates Ltd., 5-8 Lower John St., Golden Square, London W1R 4HA, England.

CAREER: Journalist, broadcaster, critic, and author. Member of Annan Committee of Inquiry in Future of Broadcasting, 1974-77. *Member:* P.E.N., Women's Press Club of London, Arts Council of Great Britain (vice-chairman, 1982-86). *Awards, honors:* Honorary fellow, Manchester Polytechnic, 1971; *Jane Austen and Her World* was named one of New York Public Library's Books for the Teen Age, 1980, 1981, and 1982.

WRITINGS:

NOVELS

Love on the Supertax (illustrated by W. Stein), Cresset, 1944.
(Under pseudonym Sarah Russell) *To Bed with Grand Music*, Pilot Press, 1946.
Tory Heaven; or, Thunder on the Right, Cresset, 1948, published as *Toasted English*, Houghton, 1949.
Little Boy Lost, Houghton, 1949.
The Village, Houghton, 1952.
The Victorian Chaise-Longue, Cresset, 1953, Houghton, 1954.
Ferry, the Jerusalem Cat (juvenile), Deutsch, 1983.

OTHER

Mrs. Ewing, Mrs. Molesworth, and Mrs. Hodgson Burnett (criticism), Arthur Barker, 1950, Oxford University Press (New York), 1961, reissued, Norwood, 1977.
Apologies (illustrated by Anton), Harvill, 1955.
The Offshore Island (three-act television play), Cresset, 1959.
(Contributor) Antoinette Pirie, editor, *Survivors: Fiction Based on Scientific Fact*, Campaign for Nuclear Disarmament (London), 1960.
Ecstasy: A Study of Some Secular and Religious Experiences, Cresset, 1961, Indiana University Press, 1962.
(Contributor) R. M. Wilson, editor, *English Association: Essays and Studies*, Humanities Press, 1966.
Jane Austen and Her World: Her Life and Work, Viking, 1969, revised edition, Scribner, 1975.
God and Man, edited by Anthony Bloom, Darton, Longman & Todd, 1971.
George Eliot and Her World, Thames & Hudson, 1973, Scribner, 1978.
Everyday Ecstasy, Thames & Hudson, 1980.
From Palm to Pine: Kipling at Home and Abroad, Facts on File, 1987.

EDITOR

The Patchwork Book (juvenile anthology), Pilot Press, 1946.
Stories of Adventure (juvenile), Pilot Press, 1946.
(With Georgina Battiscombe) *A Chaplet for Charlotte Yonge*, Cresset, 1965.
Kipling's English History, BBC Publications, 1974, Parkwest, 1988.

Also author of *Domestic Life in Edwardian England*, 1964, and *The Secular Responsibility: Conway Memorial Lecture*, 1967, and editor of *Victorian Tales*, 1948. Contributor of articles and reviews to newspapers and periodicals, including the *Times* (London), and *Vogue*, and to *Oxford English Dictionary* supplements.

ADAPTATIONS:

"Little Boy Lost" (movie), starring Bing Crosby, Paramount, 1953.

SIDELIGHTS: "I was born in London. . . .When I was two. . .we went to live in Manchester. . . .I went to an excellent school there. . .and got a very good education. When I was thirteen. . .we moved to London where I went to St. Paul's. . . ; I passed the appropriate exams and got no real education at all. I left at sixteen, spent a year learning to be a dress-designer, decided I wasn't good enough, and managed to get into Somerville College, Oxford, at a day's notice and without any entrance exam—a feat unsurpassed in the annals of the college. I had a wonderful time at Oxford, went to thousands of parties and studied Anglo-Saxon philology. Indeed, I meant to be a philologist, but my tutor said I would be a better journalist, so a journalist I obediently became.

(From the movie "Little Boy Lost," starring Bing Crosby and Christian Fourcade. Produced by Paramount, 1953.)

"I met my husband (who is. . .my publisher) at Oxford, married him in Paris when I was twenty-one, and spent the pre-war years traveling around Europe with him as far and as often as we could afford. During the war I did nursing, ran a dairy farm, worked in Intelligence, and had two children. It was while I was in the hospital after the second was born that I wrote my first novel, *Love on Super-Tax.* . . .''[1]

Two of Laski's early novels were set in the realm of fantasy. *Love on the Supertax,* for example, is a comic account of an England transformed by war. In *Toasted English,* Laski created a mock utopia in which the caste system is revived in England. She has written other books, including books for children, and one play, *The Offshore Island.*

Laski's first serious novel, *Little Boy Lost,* set against the bleak background of post-World War II France, tells about a father's search for his missing son. Laski also writes books of biographical criticism. Her first, *Mrs. Ewing, Mrs. Molesworth, and Mrs. Hodgson Burnett,* is a study of three Victorian writers of children's books. The volume traces the lives and careers of the authors as well as the tradition of children's literature. Although Laski was known primarily as a writer of fiction, the publication of *Jane Austen and Her World* led critics to regard her as a capable biographer as well as a skillful novelist.

Widely known as a radio broadcaster, Laski was one of the original panelists on the television program "What's My Line?"

FOOTNOTE SOURCES

[1]Stanley J. Kunitz, editor, *Twentieth Century Authors,* 1st supplement, H. W. Wilson, 1955.

FOR MORE INFORMATION SEE:

San Francisco Chronicle, April 26, 1949, June 16, 1954.
Chicago Sun, April 27, 1949.
New Yorker, April 30, 1949, December 24, 1949, August 1, 1977.
New York Herald Tribune Book Review, May 1, 1949, December 18, 1949, January 20, 1952, June 15, 1952, June 13, 1954.
New York Times Book Review, May 1, 1949, June 1, 1952.
Christian Science Monitor, May 5, 1949, December 21, 1949, November 28, 1969.
Atlantic Monthly, May, 1949, July, 1952.
Saturday Review, June 4, 1949, December 31, 1949, March 29, 1952, July 19, 1952, August 14, 1954, August 4, 1962, November 8, 1969.
Times Literary Supplement, September 23, 1949, February 1, 1952, November 6, 1953, November 24, 1961, August 28, 1969, June 29, 1973, June 6, 1980.
Spectator, September 30, 1949, February 1, 1952, November 17, 1961.
New York Times, December 11, 1949, June 13, 1954, April 26, 1978.
Wilson Library Bulletin, January, 1951.
Catholic World, September, 1952.

MARGHANITA LASKI

RONA LAURIE

Current Biography 1951, H. W. Wilson, 1952.
Manchester Guardian, October 23, 1953.
New Statesman and Nation, December 5, 1953, November 17, 1961.
Anthony Bloom, *God and Man*, Darton, Longman & Todd, 1971.

OBITUARIES

Detroit Free Press, February 8, 1988.
Times (London), February 8, 1988.
Chicago Tribune, February 9, 1988.
New York Times, February 9, 1988.
Washington Post, February 10, 1988.

LAURIE, Rona   1916-

PERSONAL: Born September 16, 1916, in Derby, England; daughter of Alan Rupert (a physician) and Alexandrina (Ross) Laurie; married Edward Lewis Neilson (a commander in the Royal Navy), August 28, 1961. *Education:* University of Birmingham, B.A. (with honors), 1939; also attended Royal Academy of Dramatic Art, 1939. *Home:* 21 New Quebec St., London W1H 7DE, England. *Office:* Department of Speech and Drama, Guildhall School of Music and Drama, Barbican, London EC2Y 8DT, England.

CAREER: Professional actress in London, England, 1939-58; Guildhall School of Music and Drama, London, examiner and lecturer in drama, 1958—, head of department of drama in education, 1970—; Royal College of Music Opera School, drama coach, 1985—. Drama tutor for Studio 68 and Academy of Live and Recorded Arts; teacher of courses on London

Theatre to American university students. *Member:* Guild of Drama Adjudicators (chairperson, 1969-72), Society of Teachers of Speech and Drama (chairperson, 1977-79), British Federation of Music Festivals (adjudicator, 1958—), Poetry Society (Gold Medal adjudicator). *Awards, honors:* Fellowship from Guildhall School of Music and Drama, 1967.

WRITINGS:

(Editor with Edita Maisie Cobby) *Speaking Together*, Books I and II, Pitman, 1964.
(Editor with Daniel Roberts) *The Eighth Anthology*, Guildhall School of Music and Drama, 1964.
(Editor) *A Hundred Speeches from the Theatre*, Evans Brothers, 1966, revised edition published as *One Hundred Speeches from the Theater*, Crowell-Collier Press, 1973.
(With E. M. Cobby) *Adventures in Group-Speaking*, Pitman, 1967.
(Editor) *Scenes and Ideas*, Pitman, 1967.
(Editor with John Holgate) *The Eleventh Anthology*, Guildhall School of Music and Drama, 1969.
(Editor with J. Holgate) *The Thirteenth Anthology*, Guildhall School of Music and Drama, 1973.
Festivals and Adjudication: The Organisation of Music and Drama Festivals, Pitman, 1975.
Children's Plays from Beatrix Potter, Warne, 1980.
(Co-editor) *The Seventeenth Anthology*, Guildhall School of Music and Drama, 1981.
Auditioning, J. Garnet Miller, 1985.
Mrs. Tiggy-Winkle and Friends, Puffin, 1986.
The Actor's Art and Craft, J. Garnet Miller, 1989.

Contributor to *Speech and Drama* and *Onstage*.

SIDELIGHTS: "I am an identical twin. We are the eldest children of a family of four girls. My father was a pioneer in radiology, and, as a hobby he and my mother were both passionately interested in the theatre and acted with the Derby Shakespeare Society. I was brought up on Shakespeare and, from the age of four, knew that I wanted to go into the theatre. My first appearance on the stage was in the Shakespeare Society's production of *A Midsummer Night's Dream*—as Moth. Later I played Titania for the Society. While I was at the University of Birmingham reading for an honours English degree, I was lucky enough to have Helen Gardner, later the editor of the *New Oxford Book of English Verse,* as my tutor. Throughout my time at the University I was acting in plays and also directing them.

"My interest in writing had always lain dormant until I won the essay prize at the Royal Academy of Dramatic Art. When I went into the theatre I had plenty of time in the dressing room to plan books. And so, when I became a professor at the Guildhall School of Music and Drama, I already had the idea of a collection of audition speeches which would be useful to actors. This was published under the title *A Hundred Speeches from the Theatre. Scenes and Ideas* followed as a result of my appointment as Head of Drama in Education at the Guildhall School. By now I was adjudicating at drama festivals throughout the United Kingdom and as far afield as Hong Kong. I found the Chinese children avid for acting material and anything I could suggest was eagerly taken up. I had always loved the Beatrix Potter stories and managed to persuade the publisher Warne to let me dramatize six of them. *Children's Plays from Beatrix Potter* was the result. This was a labour of love. Whenever I visit a house where there are children I am asked to play Miss Beatrix Potter while they act out the plays.

"My book *Auditioning* is designed for anyone interested in the theatre but particularly for youngsters who are contemplating a stage career.

"I live in an old house (1760) on an old street in Marylebone, London. I love my work and especially the contacts I have with children at music and speech festivals. I have dedicated *Auditioning* 'To my students in gratitude for all that they have taught me.'"

HOBBIES AND OTHER INTERESTS: Bird watching, anything to do with the theatre.

LAWRENCE, R(onald) D(ouglas) 1921-

PERSONAL: Born September 12, 1921, in Vigo, Spain; son of Thomas Edward (a journalist) and Esther (a housewife; maiden name, Rodriguez) Lawrence; married Joan Frances Gray, September 18, 1962 (died, June 7, 1969); married Sharon Janet Frise (a teacher), December 16, 1973. *Education:* Educated at private schools in Barcelona, Spain, and by a private tutor. *Home and office address:* P.O. Box 47, Gooderham, Ontario K0M 1R0, Canada. *Agent:* Wallace & Sheil Agency, Inc., 177 East 70th St., New York, N.Y. 10021.

CAREER: Writer, 1934—; *Daily Mirror,* London England, journalist, 1948-54; logger and cattle farmer on homestead in northern Ontario, 1954-57; *Free Press,* Winnipeg, Manitoba, night editor, 1957-61; *Telegram,* Toronto, Ontario, worked as reporter, entertainment and financial editor, and publisher of affiliate suburban weekly newspaper, 1960-70. *Military service:* British Army, Military Intelligence, Tank Corps, 1939-44. *Member:* American Society of Mammalogists, Canadian Authors Association, Mark Twain Society (honorary mem-

R. D. LAWRENCE

ber), Canadian Nature Federation, Society for Conservation Biology. *Awards, honors:* Frank H. Kortright Award from the Toronto Sportsman's Show, 1967, and 1968, for excellence in writing in the field of conservation; *The North Runner* was named one of New York Public Library's Books for the Teen Age, 1980, 1981, and 1982, and *Secret Go the Wolves,* 1982; Award for Best Nonfiction from the Canadian Authors Association, 1984, for *The Ghost Walker; Cry Wild* was exhibited at the Bologna International Children's Book Fair, 1985.

WRITINGS:

Wildlife in Canada, M. Joseph, 1966.
The Place in the Forest, M. Joseph, 1967.
Where the Water Lilies Grow, M. Joseph, 1968.
The Poison Makers, T. Nelson, 1968.
Maple Syrup, T. Nelson, 1970.
Cry Wild, T. Nelson, 1970, condensed edition, Reader's Digest Press, 1986.
Wildlife in North America: Mammals, T. Nelson, 1974.
Wildlife in North America: Birds, T. Nelson, 1974.
Paddy: A Naturalist's Story of an Orphan Beaver Rescued, Adopted and Observed, Knopf, 1976, condensed edition, Reader's Digest Press, 1978.
The North Runner, Holt, 1979, condensed edition, Reader's Digest Press, 1979.
Secret Go the Wolves, Holt, 1980, condensed edition, Reader's Digest Press, 1982.
The Study of Life: A Naturalist's View, Myrin Institute, 1980.
The Zoo That Never Was, Holt, 1981.
Voyage of the Stella, Holt, 1982.
The Ghost Walker, Holt, 1983.
Canada's National Parks, Collins (Canada), 1983.
Teeth below the Waters, McClelland & Stewart, 1985.

The yellow eyes bored into mine. ■ (Jacket illustration by Norman Adams from *The North Runner* by R. D. Lawrence.)

The Shark: Nature's Masterpiece, McClelland & Stewart, 1985.
In Praise of Wolves, Holt, 1986.
The Trans-Canada Highway, Collins (Canada), 1986.
The Natural History of Canada, Key Porter, 1988.
The White Puma, Holt, 1989.
For the Love of Mike, Stoddart, 1989.

SIDELIGHTS: "The single most potent motivating force is my consuming interest in living things, from mouse to man, and it was on this subject that I wrote a diary of wildlife which I later expanded into my first book, *Wildlife in Canada.*

"I began writing about nature as a child; I explored nature as a child, but perhaps the greatest influence in my life and writings comes from Thoreau. At fourteen I read *Walden* and was deeply impressed by one of Thoreau's sentences: 'In wildness is the preservation of the world.'

"Over the years I have received, and continue to receive, thousands of letters from readers of my work; this is the greatest stimulation that I obtain from my writings. The knowledge that so many people share my passion for life lived in mutual respect and toleration keeps me elevated during those times (which are now occurring with greater frequency) when the insanity of man's politics begins to debase and depress me.

"My writing is always guided by personal experience with animals in the field as well as by continuous biological re-

search, albeit I try to adopt an interesting style while hoping to teach laymen about the importance of the natural world.

"Perhaps the most encouragement that I have received lately stems from the fact that publishers the world over are now seeking out my work. This tells me that more and more people are becoming aware of their natural heritage and would wish to see it preserved, which, of course, is my greatest wish also.

"As an example of research in the field, I returned from an intensive study of wolves, and I raised a male and female of this species. Kept in a two-acre enclosure, my wife, Sharon and I relate with them closely on a daily basis, finding as I have done many times in the past, that the wolf is probably the most intelligent of all mammals, the most social (perhaps even more social than our own species), and an animal that can teach mankind how to manage our affairs in harmony with our world and at peace with each other. Our wolves are now four years old.

"I live on a 100-acre property composed of wilderness that is located some 130 miles north of the city of Toronto. Here, living in a two story log house, my wife and I monitor the affairs of the wild, which stretches for a number of miles north of our domicile. Here too I do my writing, alternating between bouts at the computer, long walks through the wilderness and communion with our two wolves. Occasionally, I must leave our refuge and return to the world of cities and bustle for short periods of time, but I am always most glad to return to this oasis of sanity in a world that moves much too quickly for its own good."

Lawrence's books have been translated into thirteen languages and have been published in sixteen countries.

HOBBIES AND OTHER INTERESTS: "My work is my hobby—other interests include endocrinology, behavior studies, photography, canoeing, and wilderness travel and exploration."

FOR MORE INFORMATION SEE:

Irma McDonough, editor, *Profiles,* Canadian Library Association, 1971, revised edition, 1975.
Washington Post Book World, April 17, 1979.

LAWSON, Joan 1906-

PERSONAL: Born January 30, 1906, in London, England; daughter of Robb (a critic and public relations officer) and Edith Marion (a singer; maiden name, Usherwood) Lawson. *Education:* Attended Choreographic School in Moscow, Leningrad Choreographic School, and Seraphina Astafieva School of Dance. *Home and office:* 11 Hallswelle Rd., London NW11 ODH, England.

CAREER: Critic for *Dancing Times,* 1940-60; Royal Ballet School, London, England, teacher of classical and national dance and history of ballet, 1963-83. Lecturer to military forces for Advisory Council for Education, 1940-47. *Member:* International Folk Music Society, Critics' Circle, Imperial Society of Teachers of Dancing (national vice-chairman, 1952—), Society for Theatre Research. *Awards, honors:* Imperial Award for special services to national dance, 1964.

WRITINGS:

(Translator, with Stephen Garry) Valerian Mikhailovich Bogdanov-Berezovsky, *Ulanova and the Development of the Soviet Ballet,* MacGibbon & Kee, 1952.

European Folk Dance: Its National and Musical Characteristics, Pitman, 1953, reissued, Imperial Society of Teachers of Dancing, 1976, Arno, 1980.

Mime: The Theory and Practice of Expressive Gesture, with a Description of Its Historical Development, Pitman, 1957, Dance Horizons, 1973.

(With Peter Revitt) *Dressing for the Ballet,* A. & C. Black, 1958.

Classical Ballet: Its Style and Technique, A. & C. Black, 1960.

A History of Ballet and Its Makers, Pitman, 1964, Dance Horizons, 1972.

(Editor and translator) Tamara Stepanovna Tkachenko, *Soviet Dances,* Imperial Society of Teachers of Dancing, 1964.

(Editor and translator) T. S. Tkachenko, *More Soviet Dances,* Imperial Society of Teachers of Dancing, 1967.

(Editor) T. S. Tkachenko, *A Third Set of Soviet Dances,* Imperial Society of Teachers of Dancing, 1968.

The Teaching of Classical Ballet: Common Faults in Young Dancers and Their Training, Theatre Arts, 1973.

Teaching Young Dancers: Muscular Coordination in Classical Ballet, Theatre Arts, 1975.

The Story of Ballet, Taplinger, 1976.

Beginning Ballet: A Concentrated Primer for Ballet Students of All Ages, A. & C. Black, 1977.

Ballet Stories, Mayflower, 1978, Smith, 1979.

The Principles of Classical Dance, A. & C. Black, 1979.

The Kay Ambrose Ballet Companion, A. & C. Black, 1979.

Flint Cottage, Dobson, 1981.

Ballet Class, A. & C. Black, 1984.

Also author of *Pas de deuce,* 1978. Contributor to *Oxford Union Encyclopedia, Enciclopedia Della Spectaccolo* and *Encyclopaedia Britannica.* Contributor to dance journals.

WORK IN PROGRESS: A textbook on choreography.

SIDELIGHTS: "I started dancing at the age of six, after recovering from a serious illness. I have traveled widely in professional dance companies throughout England and Europe. I have worked with an orthopedic surgeon on the rehabilitation of dancers after serious injuries."

LEAF, Margaret P. 1909(?)-1988

OBITUARY NOTICE: Born about 1909, in East Orange, N.J.; died of cancer, February 24, 1988, in Rockville, Md. Administrator, social activist, and author. Leaf was an executive in the home-building business, but spent much of her time on children's causes. While living in Connecticut during the 1940s, for example, she participated in efforts to bring disadvantaged children into mainstream school programs and also volunteered in programs to aid Hungarian refugees. She is perhaps best remembered, however, as the widow of Munro Leaf, the author of the classic children's book, *The Story of Ferdinand the Bull,* which has been translated into more than sixty languages, and has sold more than two and a half million copies. It was also made into a Walt Disney cartoon. During the 1960s she and her husband became part of the U.S. State Department's cultural exchange program, traveling abroad and discussing children's books. They visited several countries, including India, Japan, and the Soviet Union. In later years, Leaf wrote a children's book entitled *Eyes of the Dragon,* which was published in 1987. To commemorate the fiftieth anniversary of *The Story of Ferdinand the Bull,* Leaf lectured frequently to children's audiences about the book.

FOR MORE INFORMATION SEE:

OBITUARIES

Washington Post, February 27, 1988.

LeVERT, (William) John 1946-

PERSONAL: Born June 14, 1946, in Brighton, Mass.; son of William (a salesman) and Rita (a housewife; maiden name, Moan) LeVert; married Cynthia Ballenger (a teacher), May 7, 1975; children: Michael, Catherine. *Education:* Columbia University, B.A., 1968. *Politics:* "Left." *Home:* Natick, Mass. *Agent:* RLR Associates Ltd., 7 West 51st St., New York, N.Y. 10019.

CAREER: Carpenter and builder, 1970—; author, 1986—. *Member:* National Writers Union. *Awards, honors:* Fellow, Massachusetts Artists Foundation, 1983, and 1987; *The Flight of the Cassowary* was selected one of American Library Association's Best Books for Young Adults, 1986, and Best Young Adult Book of the Year by the Young Adult Caucus of the Michigan Library Association, 1987.

WRITINGS:

The Flight of the Cassowary (young adult novel), Atlantic Monthly Press, 1986.

WORK IN PROGRESS: A second novel.

I soared, my back hot under the sun, and the wind making my eyes all teary. . . . ■ (Jacket illustration by Paul Mock from *The Flight of the Cassowary* by John LeVert.)

SIDELIGHTS: "I am a carpenter by trade, and building and writing have always seemed complimentary activities to me. Both begin with a love for the material itself, whether wood or words, and a love for working with the material that goes beyond whatever specific thing you are trying to make. Both demand intense concentration and attention to detail, and in each it is the work you put into the details that keeps the whole thing from falling apart.

"Both carpentry and writing are combinations of hard work and play, and both have a similar goal: to make something strong and true that will last."

HOBBIES AND OTHER INTERESTS: Natural history, most sports.

LOBEL, Anita (Kempler)   1934-

PERSONAL: Born June 3, 1934, in Cracow, Poland; came to United States in 1952; naturalized citizen, 1956; daughter of Leon and Sofia (Grunbereg) Kempler; married Arnold Stark Lobel (a writer and illustrator of books for children), April, 1955 (died, December 4, 1987); children: Adrianne, Adam. *Education:* Pratt Institute, B.F.A., 1955; attended Brooklyn Museum Art School, 1975-76. *Home and office:* New York, N.Y.

CAREER: Free-lance textile designer, 1957-64; writer and illustrator of books for children, 1964—. *Awards, honors: Sven's Bridge* was selected one of *New York Times* Best Illustrated

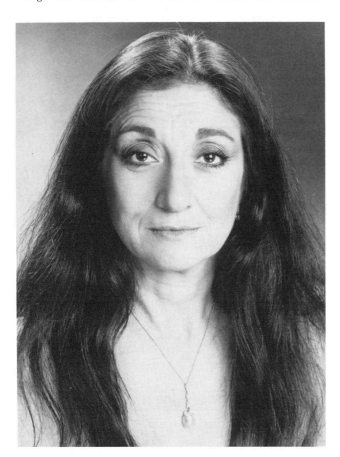

ANITA LOBEL

Picture Books of the Year, 1965, and *On Market Street,* 1981; *Potatoes, Potatoes* was selected one of American Institute of Graphic Arts Children's Books, 1967-68, and *The Seamstress of Salzburg,* 1970; *Indian Summer* was selected one of Child Study Association's Children's Books of the Year, 1968, *Under a Mushroom,* 1971, *Clever Kate,* 1973, *King Rooster, Queen Hen,* 1975, *Peter Penny's Dance,* 1976, and *On Market Street* and *The Rose in My Garden,* 1985; *Book World's* Children's Spring Book Festival Picture Book Award, 1972, for *Little John; A Birthday for the Princess* and *Little John* were both included in the American Institute of Graphic Arts Children's Book Show, 1973-74, *Peter Penny's Dance,* 1976, *A Treeful of Pigs,* 1980, and *On Market Street,* 1982; *A Birthday for the Princess* was included in the Children's Book Showcase of the Children's Book Council, 1974, and *Peter Penny's Dance,* 1977.

Peter Penny's Dance was selected one of *New York Times* Outstanding Books, 1976, *How the Rooster Saved the Day,* 1977, and *On Market Street,* 1981; *Peter Penny's Dance* was selected one of *School Library Journal's* Best Books of the Year, 1976, *A Treeful of Pigs,* 1979, *Singing Bee!,* 1982, and *The Rose in My Garden,* 1984; *How the Rooster Saved the Day* was chosen one of *School Library Journal's* Best Books for Spring, 1977; Children's Choice from the International Reading Association and the Children's Book Council, 1979, for *The Pancake,* and 1980, for *Fanny's Sister; Boston Globe-Horn Book* Award Honor for Illustration, 1981, for *On Market Street,* and 1984, for *The Rose in My Garden;* Caldecott Honor Book, and American Book Award finalist, both 1982, both for *On Market Street.*

WRITINGS:

SELF-ILLUSTRATED

Sven's Bridge, Harper, 1965.
The Troll Music, Harper, 1966.
Potatoes, Potatoes, Harper, 1967.
The Seamstress of Salzburg, Harper, 1970.
Under a Mushroom, Harper, 1971.
A Birthday for the Princess, Harper, 1973.
(Reteller) *King Rooster, Queen Hen,* Greenwillow, 1975, large print edition, 1975.
(Reteller) *The Pancake,* Greenwillow, 1978, large print edition, 1978.
(Adapter) *The Straw Maid,* Greenwillow, 1983, large print edition, 1983.

ILLUSTRATOR

Paul Kapp, *Cock-a-Doodle Doo! Cock-a-Doodle Dandy!,* Harper, 1966.
Meindert De Jong, *Puppy Summer,* Harper, 1966.
The Wishing Penny, and Other Stories (anthology), Parents Magazine Press, 1967.
F. N. Monjo, *Indian Summer,* Harper, 1968.
Alice Dalgliesh, *The Little Wooden Farmer,* Macmillan, 1968.
Benjamin Elkin, *The Wisest Man in the World,* Parents Magazine Press, 1968.
Barbara Borack, *Someone Small,* Harper, 1969.
Doris Orgel, *The Uproar,* McGraw, 1970.
Mirra Ginsburg, editor, *Three Rolls and One Doughnut: Fables from Russia,* Dial, 1970.
B. Elkin, *How the Tsar Drinks Tea,* Parents Magazine Press, 1971.
Theodore Storm, *Little John,* retold by D. Orgel, Farrar, 1972.
John Langstaff, editor, *Soldier, Soldier, Won't You Marry Me?,* Doubleday, 1972.

(From *Potatoes, Potatoes* by Anita Lobel. Illustrated by the author.)

Cynthia Jameson, *One for the Price of Two,* Parents Magazine Press, 1972.

Elizabeth Shub, adapter, *Clever Kate,* Macmillan, 1973.

Carolyn Meyer, *Christmas Crafts: Things to Make the Days before Christmas,* Harper, 1974.

Janet Quin-Harkin, *Peter Penny's Dance,* Dial, 1976.

Arnold Lobel, *How the Rooster Saved the Day,* Greenwillow, 1977.

Arnold Lobel, *A Treeful of Pigs* (Junior Literary Guild selection), Greenwillow, 1979.

Penelope Lively, *Fanny's Sister* (*Horn Book* honor list), Elsevier-Dutton, 1980.

Arnold Lobel, *On Market Street* (*Horn Book* honor list), Greenwillow, 1981.

Jane Hart, compiler, *Singing Bee! A Collection of Favorite Children's Songs* (ALA Notable Book), Lothrop, 1982, published in England as *Sing a Song of Sixpence! The Best Song Book Ever,* Gollancz, 1983.

Arnold Lobel, *The Rose in My Garden* (Junior Literary Guild selection), Greenwillow, 1984.

Clement C. Moore, *The Night before Christmas,* Knopf, 1984.

Harriet Ziefert, *A New Coat for Anna,* Knopf, 1986.

B. P. Nichol, *Once: A Lullaby,* Greenwillow, 1986.

Steven Kroll, *Looking for Daniela: A Romantic Adventure,* Holiday House, 1988.

ADAPTATIONS:

"The Little Wooden Farmer" (filmstrip with cassette), Threshold Filmstrips, 1974.

"King Rooster, Queen Hen" (cassette), Random House.

"Peter Penny's Dance," (filmstrip with cassette), Weston Woods, 1978.

"A Treeful of Pigs," (filmstrip with cassette), Random House.

"On Market Street" (filmstrip with cassette; read-along cassette; VHS or Beta videocassette), Random House.

"The Rose in My Garden" (cassette), Random House.

"A New Coat for Anna" (filmstrip with cassette), Random House, 1987.

SIDELIGHTS: Anita Lobel was born in Poland on June 3, 1934. "I was born into a relatively comfortable merchant family. Hitler put a stop to those comforts. My parents separated for practical reasons, believing we would all have better chances for survival, which proved to be true. My brother and I were left in the care of a Polish woman with whom we stayed and drifted around Poland for the next four and one half years."[1]

"I had a wonderful nanny, and when. . .I was 5 years old. . .the nanny took me and my young brother into the Polish countryside—which was primitive, nasty, raw and Catholic. That was on one side and the Nazis on the other. Aside from the fact that there was an outside force that hated us and chased us, I always felt my brother and I were protected by this person who chose to protect us. I loved her and she loved us, and I think that this was very important. I really feel Nanny's affection colors my work, because I don't feel I have to portray the awful bleakness of the time."[2]

"Toward the end of the war, my brother and I were captured and sent to a concentration camp in Germany, from which we were rescued in 1945. We were eventually reunited with our

I will be king and you will be my queen. ■ (From *King Rooster, Queen Hen* by Anita Lobel. Illustrated by the author.)

parents in Stockholm. I did not go to school until I was 13, but was taught how to read and write. I came from Sweden to New York against my will because my parents wanted to reclaim some long, lost relatives they had in this country."[1]

The family moved to New York in 1952 and Lobel graduated from high school and entered Pratt Institute, where she met her future husband, artist Arnold Lobel. She met him on stage when she was cast in a play he was directing. Acting was a major influence on her work. "I wanted to be in the theatre at one time. When I am illustrating a manuscript, I do it as if it might be a stage play."[1]

"Picture books are like screenplays. How do you translate very terse text into some kind of visual context? Really and truly, if you don't know anything about the theater, it is very difficult to illustrate children's books."[2]

Lobel graduated from Pratt Institute in 1955, the same year she was married. "For several years after graduation I worked as a textile designer. Then Susan Hirschman, who had 'discovered' Arnold, asked me to do a book. I thought I couldn't but Susan and Arnold encouraged me and I came through with *Sven's Bridge*."[3]

Lobel's first book grew from an idea and a character sketch of a kindly man. "At first I thought only of illustrating stories by other authors but found, with a little effort, I, too, could supply a story to go with the pictures. When I begin a book, I have a specific style in mind, for instance, a historical period. *The Troll Music* was mainly inspired by the bottom parts of medieval tapestries with all the vegetation and little animals running around. I got the idea for *Potatoes, Potatoes* partly from childhood memories of Poland."[1]

Potatoes, Potatoes told the story of two brothers who became enemies in war and of their wise mother who would not give them or their starving comrades so much as one potato peel until all of them promised to lay down their swords and their guns. "I like *Potatoes, Potatoes* because of its theme. But I do not take it as seriously as some of the reviewers have."[1]

For many years Lobel and her husband worked constantly from nine in the morning until late afternoon and then, after spending time with their two children, Adrianne and Adam, returned to their work until 2 a.m. About her work, Lobel once commented: "I feel very strongly that an artist working in the field of children's book illustration should by no means compromise on the graphic design quality of his work. Our senses are bombarded by so much ugliness from our earliest days that it is to be hoped that picture books do open a child's eyes and start at least a germ for a future esthetic sense. I have always loved to draw flowers and I love needlework and tapestries as well as embroidery. During my years as an art student, I spent most of my time drawing and painting monumental figures. When I had to make a living I became a textile designer. Picture books have opened to me an opportunity to bring back some of my old fat friends and put them in landscapes filled with floral design! I usually plan a book as a play. The pictures become 'scenes' with 'principals' and 'chorus' grouped and regrouped according to what is then happening in the story."[4]

Lobel and her husband, unlike many husband and wife teams, did not collaborate on their books. "I think maybe we take ideas from each other, but it is not a conscious thing. Whenever germs of ideas start with each of us, they are entirely different.

"In our illustrations we both like to show someone's dignity being mocked. I think it is something that appeals whether you are writing a story of your own or illustrating the manuscript of someone else. That is why I like peasant tales—there is always somebody who is made a damn fool of by somebody else.

"I must have been influenced by old fairy tales, tales that have a logical beginning, a middle and then retribution in the end for someone and happiness for someone else."[5]

Arnold Lobel eventually wrote several manuscripts especially for Anita. One of them, *A Treeful of Pigs*, was "...written specifically for me to illustrate, the way an author might write a star part for an actress. There were few noises of objection coming in my direction during the execution of the pictures. The nice thing about having the illustrator and the author together in the same studio is that we can decide to change or rethink little details while the work is in progress. For many years we tried to keep our work separate but, when we discovered this extra bonus, we nodded and bowed graciously to each other, and giggled with a sense of a new discovery. That discovery I felt is especially a gift to me."[3]

(From *Sven's Bridge* by Anita Lobel. Illustrated by the author.)

Throughout her long and distinguished career, Lobel has produced several award winning children's books and illustrated numerous books by other authors. "Writing and illustrating books for children is a form of drama for me. . . .Some books take the form of zany farces (*King Rooster, Queen Hen* and *The Pancake*). Others, like *Peter Penny's Dance*, are a bit like *Around the World in Eighty Days*, a sort of movie or musical. *The Seamstress of Salzburg* and *A Birthday for the Princess* are more like operettas. *On Market Street* was constucted like a series of solos in a ballet, held together by a prologue and epilogue, with an implied divertimento for a score."[6]

FOOTNOTE SOURCES

[1]Lee Bennett Hopkins, *Books Are by People*, Citation Press, 1969.

[2]John F. Berry, "The Lobels: A Marriage of Two Drawing Boards," *Washington Post Book World*, June 13, 1982.

[3]*Junior Literary Guild*, March, 1979.

[4]Lee Kingman and others, compilers, *Illustrators of Children's Books: 1957-1966*, Horn Book, 1968.

[5]*Publishers Weekly*, May 17, 1971.

[6]D. L. Kirkpatrick, editor, *Twentieth-Century Children's Writers*, 2nd edition, St. Martin's, 1983.

FOR MORE INFORMATION SEE:

Times Literary Supplement, June 26, 1969.

Horn Book, February, 1971, August, 1981.

Selma G. Lanes, *Down the Rabbit Hole*, Atheneum, 1971.

Doris de Montreville and Donna Hill, editors, *Third Book of Junior Authors*, H. W. Wilson, 1972.

Martha E. Ward and Dorothy A. Marquardt, *Illustrators of Books for Young People*, 2nd edition, Scarecrow, 1975.

L. Kingman and others, compilers, *Illustrators of Children's Books: 1967-1976*, Horn Book, 1978.

COLLECTIONS

Kerlan Collection, University of Minnesota.

(From *On Market Street* by Arnold Lobel. Illustrated by Anita Lobel.)

LOBEL, Arnold (Stark)   1933-1987

PERSONAL: Born May 22, 1933, in Los Angeles, Calif.; died December 4, 1987, in New York, N.Y.; son of Joseph (a salesman) and Lucille (a secretary; maiden name, Stark) Lobel; married Anita Kempler (a writer and illustrator of children's books), April, 1955; children: Adrianne, Adam. *Education:* Pratt Institute, B.F.A., 1955.

CAREER: Writer and illustrator of books for children, 1959-87. Early in career worked as an illustrator for an advertising agency. *Exhibitions:* "Art and the Alphabet," Museum of Fine Arts, Houston, Tex., 1978.

AWARDS, HONORS: A Holiday for Mister Muster was selected one of *New York Times* Best Illustrated Books of the Year, 1963, *The Man Who Took the Indoors Out* and *Miss Suzy's Birthday,* 1974, *As Right As Right Can Be,* 1976, *Merry, Merry FIBruary,* 1977, *The Headless Horseman Rides Tonight,* 1980, and *On Market Street,* 1981; *Someday* was chosen one of the National Education Association's and American Library Association's Outstanding Children's Books of 1964-65; *Let's Get Turtles* was chosen one of Library of Congress' Children's Books of 1965, *Benny's Animals and How He Put Them in Order* and *Oscar Otter,* 1966, *Let's Be Early Settlers with Daniel Boone,* 1967, and *Ants Are Fun,* 1968.

Red Fox and His Canoe was chosen one of Child Study Association of America's Children's Books of the Year, 1964, *Benny's Animals and How He Put Them in Order,* 1966, *Sam the Minuteman, Junk Day on Juniper Street,* and *Small Pig,* 1969, *Frog and Toad Are Friends,* 1970, *The Master of Miracle,* and *Hansel and Gretel,* 1971, *Miss Suzy's Easter Surprise, Frog and Toad Together, Seahorse,* and *Mouse Tales,* 1972, *The Clay Pot Boy,* 1973, *The Man Who Took the Indoors Out, Dinosaur Time, Circus,* and *Miss Suzy's Birthday,* 1974, *Owl at Home,* and *As I Was Crossing Boston Common,* 1975, *Frog and Toad All Year,* and *As Right As Right Can Be,* 1976, *On Market Street,* 1981, *The Rose in My Garden,* 1984, and *Whiskers and Rhymes,* 1985; Boys' Club Award

ARNOLD LOBEL

Toad made Frog a cup of hot tea. ■ (From *Frog and Toad Are Friends* by Arnold Lobel. Illustrated by the author.)

Certificate, 1966-67, for *Benny's Animals and How He Put Them in Order.*

Frog and Toad Are Friends and *The New Vestments* were each selected one of American Institute of Graphic Arts Children's Books, both 1970; Caldecott Honor Book from the American Library Association, 1971, for *Frog and Toad Are Friends,* 1972, for *Hildilid's Night,* and 1982, for *On Market Street;* National Book Award finalist from the Association of American Publishers, 1971, for *Frog and Toad Are Friends; The Master of Miracle* was chosen one of *New York Times* Outstanding Books of the Year, 1971, *Frog and Toad Together,* 1972, *Owl at Home,* 1975, *Frog and Toad All Year,* 1976, *How the Rooster Saved the Day,* 1977, *Fables* and *The Headless Horseman Rides Tonight,* 1980, and *On Market Street,* 1981.

Christopher Award, 1972, for *On the Day Peter Stuyvesant Sailed into Town,* and 1977, for *Frog and Toad All Year; Hildilid's Night* and *On the Day Peter Stuyvesant Sailed into Town* were chosen for the Children's Book Showcase of the Children's Book Council, 1972, *Frog and Toad Together* and *Seahorse,* 1973, *The Clay Pot Boy,* 1974, *The Man Who Took the Indoors Out,* 1975, *As I Was Crossing Boston Common,* 1976, and *As Right As Right Can Be* and *Nightmares,* 1977; *Book World*'s Children's Spring Book Festival Award for picturebooks, and *Library Journal*'s book list, both 1972, and Newbery Honor Book from the American Library Association, and Brooklyn Art Books for Children citation, both 1973, all for *Frog and Toad Together;* Irma Simonton Black Award from Bank Street College of Education, 1973, for *Mouse Tales,* and honor book, 1982, for *Uncle Elephant; Mouse Tales* was included in the American Institute of Graphic Arts Book Show, 1973-74, *As Right As Right Can Be* and *Nightmares,* 1976, *A Treeful of Pigs,* 1980, *On Market Street,* 1982, and *The Book of Pigericks,* 1984.

Garden State Children's Book Award from the New Jersey Library Association, 1977, for *Dinosaur Time,* 1978, for *Owl at Home,* and 1981, for *Grasshopper on the Road; How the Rooster Saved the Day* was chosen one of *School Library Journal*'s Best Books for Spring, 1977; Recognition of Merit Award from the George G. Stone Center for Children's Books, 1978, for *Frog and Toad* series; Children's Choice from the International Reading Association and the Children's Book Council, 1979, for *The Mean Old Mean Hyena, Grasshopper on the Road,* and *Gregory Griggs and Other Nursery Rhyme People,* 1981, for *The Tale of Meshka the Kvetch,* and 1982, for *On Market Street; A Treeful of Pigs,* and *Tales of Oliver Pig* were selected one of *School Library Journal*'s Best Books of the Year, 1979, *Uncle Elephant,* 1981, *The Random House Book of Poetry for Children,* 1983, and *The Rose in My Garden,* 1984.

American Book Award (paperback), finalist, 1980, for *Frog and Toad Are Friends;* Caldecott Medal from the American Library Association, 1981, for *Fables; Boston Globe-Horn Book* Award Honor Book for Illustration, 1981, for *On Market Street,* and 1984, for *The Rose in My Garden;* Parents' Choice Award for Illustration from the Parents' Choice Foundation, 1982, for *Ming Lo Moves the Mountain;* American Book Award nomination, 1982, for *On Market Street;* Lucky Four-Leaf Clover Award from Scholastic, 1982; University of Southern Mississippi Medallion, 1985, for ''Distinguished Service to Children's Literature''; Laura Ingalls Wilder Medal nomination, 1986, for ''Distinguished, Enduring Contributions to Children's Literature.''

WRITINGS:

ALL SELF-ILLUSTRATED, EXCEPT AS NOTED

A Zoo for Mister Muster, Harper, 1962.
A Holiday for Mister Muster, Harper, 1963.
Prince Bertram the Bad, Harper, 1963.
Lucille, Harper, 1964, large print edition, 1964.
Giant John, Harper, 1964.
The Bears of the Air, Harper, 1965.
Martha the Movie Mouse, Harper, 1966.
The Great Blueness and Other Predicaments, Harper, 1968.
Small Pig, Harper, 1969, large print edition, 1969.
Frog and Toad Are Friends (ALA Notable Book; *Horn Book* honor list), Harper, 1970, large print edition, 1970.
The Ice-Cream Cone Coot and Other Rare Birds, Parents Magazine Press, 1971.
On the Day Peter Stuyvesant Sailed into Town (ALA Notable Book), Harper, 1971.
Frog and Toad Together (ALA Notable Book), Harper, 1972, large print edition, 1972.
Mouse Tales (*Horn Book* honor list), Harper, 1972, large print edition, 1972.
The Man Who Took the Indoors Out, Harper, 1974.
Owl at Home (*Horn Book* honor list), Harper, 1975, large print edition, 1975.
Frog and Toad All Year (ALA Notable Book; *Horn Book* honor list), Harper, 1976, large print edition, 1976.
How the Rooster Saved the Day (illustrated by Anita Lobel), Greenwillow, 1977, large print edition, 1977.
Mouse Soup, Harper, 1977, large print edition, 1977.

Grasshopper on the Road (*Horn Book* honor list), Harper, 1978, large print edition, 1978.
(Selector) *Gregory Griggs and Other Nursery Rhyme People,* Greenwillow, 1978, large print edition, 1978.
Days with Frog and Toad (*Horn Book* honor list), Harper, 1979.
A Treeful of Pigs (Junior Literary Guild selection; illustrated by Anita Lobel), Greenwillow, 1979, large print edition, 1979.
Fables (*Horn Book* honor list), Harper, 1980.
The Frog and Toad Coloring Book, Harper, 1981.
Uncle Elephant, Harper, 1981, large print edition, 1982.
Frog and Toad Tales (collection), World's Work, 1981.
On Market Street (*Horn Book* honor list; illustrated by Anita Lobel), Greenwillow, 1981, large print edition, 1981.
Ming Lo Moves the Mountain (ALA Notable Book), Greenwillow, 1982.
The Book of Pigericks: Pig Limericks (ALA Notable Book), Harper, 1983.
The Rose in My Garden (Junior Literary Guild selection; illustrated by Anita Lobel), Greenwillow, 1984, large print edition, 1984.
Whiskers and Rhymes (poems), Greenwillow, 1985.
(Compiler) *The Random House Book of Mother Goose: A Treasury of 306 Timeless Nursery Rhymes,* Random House, 1986.
The Frog and Toad Pop-Up Book, Harper, 1986.
(Contributor) *Once Upon a Time: Celebrating the Magic of Children's Books in Honor of the Twentieth Anniversary of Reading Is Fundamental,* Putnam, 1986.
The Turnaround Wind, Harper, 1988.
Humpty Dumpty Book and Doll Set, Random House, 1988.

ILLUSTRATOR

Sol Scharfstein, *Bibletime: With 14 Full-Page Bible Pasteups and 84 Full-Color Perforated Bible Stamps,* Ktav, 1958.
(With Ezekiel Schloss) Edythe Scharfstein, *Book of Chanukah: Poems, Riddles, Stories, Songs and Things to Do,* Ktav, 1958.
S. Scharfstein, *Hebrew Dictionary: Activity Funbook,* Ktav, 1958.
S. Scharfstein, *Holiday Dictionary: With 90 Religious Objects to Color and 84 Full-Page Color Perforated Religious Objects Stamps,* Ktav, 1958.
Morris Epstein, *All about Jewish Holidays and Customs,* Ktav, 1959, revised edition, 1970.
Frederick B. Phleger, *Red Tag Comes Back,* Harper, 1961.
Susan Oneacre Rhinehart, *Something Old, Something New,* Harper, 1961.
Peggy Parish, *Let's Be Indians,* Harper, 1962.
Millicent E. Selsam, *Terry and the Caterpillars,* Harper, 1962.
Betty Baker, *Little Runner of the Longhouse,* Harper, 1962.
M. E. Selsam, *Greg's Microscope,* Harper, 1963.
Charlotte Zolotow, *The Quarreling Book,* Harper, 1963.
Mildred Myrick, *The Secret Three,* Harper, 1963.
Nathaniel Benchley, *Red Fox and His Canoe,* Harper, 1964.
Miriam Young, *Miss Suzy,* Parents Magazine Press, 1964.
Phil Ressner, *Dudley Pippin,* Harper, 1965.
M. E. Selsam, *Let's Get Turtles,* Harper, 1965.
C. Zolotow, *Someday,* Harper, 1965.
Felice Holman, *The Witch on the Corner,* Norton, 1966.
Lilian Moore, *The Magic Spectacles and Other Easy-to-Read Stories,* Parents Magazine Press, 1966.
N. Benchley, *Oscar Otter,* Harper, 1966.
M. E. Selsam, *Benny's Animals and How He Put Them in Order,* Harper, 1966.
Andrea DiNoto, *The Star Thief,* Macmillan, 1967.
P. Parish, *Let's Be Early Settlers with Daniel Boone,* Harper, 1967.

(From *The Devil and Mother Crump* by Valerie Scho Carey. Illustrated by Arnold Lobel.)

(From the filmstrip "On Market Street." Produced by Random House/Miller Brody Productions, 1982.)

N. Benchley, *The Strange Disappearance of Arthur Cluck*, Harper, 1967.
M. Myrick, *Ants Are Fun*, Harper, 1968.
(With E. Schloss) E. Scharfstein, *My First Book of Prayers*, Ktav, 1968.
Edward Lear, *The Four Little Children Who Went around the World*, Macmillan, 1968.
Sara C. Martin, *The Comic Adventures of Old Mother Hubbard and Her Dog*, Bradbury, 1968.
L. Moore, *Junk Day on Juniper Street: And Other Easy-to-Read Stories*, Parents Magazine Press, 1968.
Judith Viorst, *I'll Fix Anthony*, Harper, 1969.
N. Benchley, *Sam the Minuteman*, Harper, 1969.
E. Lear, *The New Vestments*, Bradbury, 1970.
Jack Prelutsky, *The Terrible Tiger*, Macmillan, 1970.
Laura Cathon, *Tot Botut and His Little Flute*, Macmillan, 1970.
Cheli Duran Ryan, *Hildilid's Night*, Macmillan, 1971.
Sulamith Ish-Kishor, *The Master of Miracle: A New Novel of the Golem*, 1971.
Jakob Grimm and Wilhelm Grimm, *Hansel and Gretel*, Delacorte, 1971.
M. Young, *Miss Suzy's Easter Surprise*, Parents Magazine Press, 1972.
Robert A. Morris, *Seahorse*, Harper, 1972.
M. Young, *Miss Suzy's Christmas*, Parents Magazine Press, 1973.
Paula Fox, *Good Ethan* (Junior Literary Guild selection), Bradbury, 1973.
Cynthia Jameson, *The Clay Pot Boy*, Coward, 1973.
M. Young, *Miss Suzy's Birthday*, Parents Magazine Press, 1974.
J. Prelutsky, *Circus*, Macmillan, 1974.
P. Parrish, *Dinosaur Time*, Harper, 1974.

Norma Farber, *As I Was Crossing Boston Common* (*Horn Book* honor list), Dutton, 1975.
J. Prelutsky, *Nightmares: Poems to Trouble Your Sleep*, Greenwillow, 1976.
Anne Rose, *As Right As Right Can Be*, Dial, 1976.
Doris Orgel, *Merry, Merry FIBruary*, Parents Magazine Press, 1977.
J. Prelutsky, *The Mean Old Mean Hyena*, Greenwillow, 1978.
Jean Van Leeuwen, *Tales of Oliver Pig* (Junior Literary Guild selection), Dial, 1979.
Carol Chapman, *The Tale of Meshka the Kvetch*, Dutton, 1980.
J. Prelutsky, *The Headless Horseman Rides Tonight: More Poems to Trouble Your Sleep*, Greenwillow, 1980.
J. Van Leeuwen, *More Tales of Oliver Pig* (ALA Notable Book; Junior Literary Guild selection), Dial, 1981.
J. Prelutsky, editor, *The Random House Book of Poetry for Children* (ALA Notable Book), Random House, 1983.
Maxine Kumin, *The Microscope*, Harper, 1984.
Laura Geringer, *A Three Hat Day* (ALA Notable Book; "Reading Rainbow" selection), Harper, 1985.
Harriet Ziefert, *Bear All Year*, Harper, 1986.
H. Ziefert, *Bear Gets Dressed*, Harper, 1986.
H. Ziefert, *Bear Goes Shopping*, Harper, 1986.
H. Ziefert, *Bear's Busy Morning*, Harper, 1986.
H. Ziefert, *Where's the Dog?*, Harper, 1987.
H. Ziefert, *Where's the Guinea Pig?*, Harper, 1987.
H. Ziefert, *Where's the Turtle?*, Harper, 1987.
H. Ziefert, *Where's the Cat?*, Harper, 1987.
Valerie S. Carey, *The Devil and Mother Crump*, Harper, 1987.
J. Prelutsky, *Tyrannosaurus Was a Beast*, Greenwillow, 1988.

Contributor to record "Cricket and Other Friends" and to *Cricket's Choice*, Open Court, 1974.

ADAPTATIONS:

CASSETTE WITH BOOK

"As I Was Crossing Boston Common," Listening Library, 1978.
"Days with Frog and Toad," Harper, 1985.
"Frog and Toad All Year," Harper, 1985.
"Frog and Toad Are Friends," Harper, 1985.
"Frog and Toad Together," Harper, 1985.
"Mouse Tales," Harper, 1985.
"Uncle Elephant," Children's Book and Music Center, 1985.
"Ming Lo Moves the Mountain," Scholastic, 1986.
"Mouse Soup," Harper, 1986.
"Owl at Home," Harper, 1987.
"On Market Street," Random House.
"Fables," Random House.
"The Book of Pigericks," Random House.
"The Rose in My Garden," Random House.
"Tales of Oliver Pig," Listening Library.
"More Tales of Oliver Pig," Listening Library.
"Frog and Toad" (contains *Frog and Toad Are Friends, Frog and Toad Together, Frog and Toad All Year,* and *Days with Frog and Toad*), Listening Library.

FILMSTRIPS WITH RECORD OR CASSETTE

"Prince Bertram the Bad," Harper, 1974.
"Strange Disappearance of Arthur Cluck," Harper, 1974.
"A List" (based on *Frog and Toad Together*), Miller-Brody, 1976.
"Cookies" (based on *Frog and Toad Together*), Miller-Brody, 1976.
"The Garden" (based on *Frog and Toad Together*), Miller-Brody, 1976.
"Dragons and Giants" (based on *Frog and Toad Together*), Miller-Brody, 1976.

(From *More Tales of Oliver Pig* by Jean Van Leeuwen. Illustrated by Arnold Lobel.)

I had a little husband,
No bigger than my thumb;
I put him in a pint-pot
And there I bid him drum.
I bought a little horse
That galloped up and down;
I bridled him and saddled him
And sent him out of town.
I gave him a pair of garters
To garter up his hose,
And a little silk handkerchief
To wipe his snotty nose.

(From *The Random House Book of Mother Goose,* selected by Arnold Lobel. Illustrated by Arnold Lobel.)

"The Dream" (based on *Frog and Toad Together*), Miller-Brody, 1976.
"A Lost Button" (based on *Frog and Toad Are Friends*), Miller-Brody, 1976.
"A Swim" (based on *Frog and Toad Are Friends*), Miller-Brody, 1976.
"Spring" (based on *Frog and Toad Are Friends*), Miller-Brody, 1976.
"The Story" (based on *Frog and Toad Are Friends*), Miller-Brody, 1976.
"The Letter" (based on *Frog and Toad Are Friends*), Miller-Brody, 1976.
"Frog and Toad Together," Miller-Brody, 1976.
"Frog and Toad Are Friends," Random House.
"As I Was Crossing Boston Common," Listening Library, 1978.
"Mouse Soup," Random House.
"Someday," Educational Enrichment Materials, 197?.
"Fables" (ALA Notable Filmstrip), Miller-Brody, 1981.
"Tales of Oliver Pig," Listening Library.
"On Market Street," Random House, 1982.
"A Treeful of Pigs," Random House.
"Fables II," Random House.
"Whiskers and Rhymes," Random House, 1986.

RECORD/CASSETTE

"Frog and Toad Are Friends," Newbery Award Records, 1976.
"Frog and Toad Together," Newbery Award Records, 1976.

VIDEOCASSETTE

"Fables," Random House.
"Arnold Lobel Video Showcase" (VHS; BETA; contains selections from "Frog and Toad Are Friends," selections from "Frog and Toad Together," "Fables," "Mouse Soup," and "Meet the Newbery Author: Arnold Lobel"), Random House.
"On Market Street" (VHS; BETA), Random House.

Dinosaur Time, Frog and Toad All Year, Giant John, and *Mouse Tales* have been adapted into Braille, and *Frog and Toad Are Friends, Frog and Toad Together,* and *Small Pig* have been adapted into talking books.

SIDELIGHTS: Arnold Lobel was born on May 22, 1933 in Los Angeles, California. "My parents had gone from Schenectady, New York, to Los Angeles to find their fortunes. Of course there were not fortunes to be found in 1933, so they returned to Schenectady and to eventual divorce. There I continued to live through a rather unhappy and neurotic childhood until I finally escaped to college in my late teens."[1]

Lobel found temporary solace in reading, however. "From my house in Schenectady. . .the long walk to the library was downhill all the way. I would return the books that I had borrowed and would quickly stock up on five new selections. Five—as I remember, that was the limit of the number of books that one could take out at a time.

"Then I would begin the journey back. What I would feel, as I climbed uphill toward home with these five books, was not the anticipation of the stories and pictures that I was to pore over and enjoy, but an overwhelming feeling of absolute possession. These books were mine, all mine, and the inevitability of having to return them to the library in two weeks never entered my thoughts. I was the true owner of these pleasantly hard, rectangular objects I carried under my arm and that was that. . . .

"There was a large tree in my front yard and I would flop down in the shady grass. I savored my new acquisitions—

And soon you will have a garden. ■ (From *Frog and Toad Together* by Arnold Lobel. Illustrated by the author.)

savored them mostly, as I recall, because every hand-picked one of them belonged to me."[2]

Having made an early decision to pursue an art career, Lobel entered Pratt Institute, where he discovered that book illustration was his speciality. He also met Anita Kempler, a fellow artist and Pratt student. They were married, following graduation in 1955.

Although Lobel began his art career in advertising, he was illustrating books by the late 1950s. "I began in the field as an artist. I did not intend to be a writer. I went to art school and I started out as an illustrator. But in the beginning there is the portfolio, and when artists today ask me, 'How do you make a start in the field?' I think I say to them that there is only one way, and that is exactly what I did: You make a portfolio, you make appointments with editors, and you pound the pavements. It is debasing, it is humiliating, it is time-wasting, but it is the only way to get your foot in the door.

"I started with the smaller publishers first, thinking I would have a better chance with them and I got absolutely nowhere. I remember in one particular case; well, they look through your portfolio. They're flipping through the pages of your soul, your life, your blood. They're saying nothing except, 'Don't call us we'll call you.' I remember one lady was doing this, looking through my portfolio, and she wrote something on a little card and then her phone rang and she swiveled around in her chair to answer. Naturally, I looked to see what she had written on the card and she had written, 'OK for flats.' And I thought, HUMPH!, anybody who calls a picture book a flat, I wouldn't want to work for anyway. As it turned out I didn't have the opportunity because she didn't give me any jobs, she didn't give me a chance to refuse.

"Finally, I stumbled into Harper and Row. I worked my way up to the best publisher in the business and to my great surprise I was given a manuscript to illustrate. Most of my portfolio was very art schooly, but I had one very realistic illustration of a cricket in my portfolio and when Susan Hirschman, the editor at Harper and Row, saw that cricket she said, 'Oh you can do this kind of drawing, too. Can you draw salmon?' And I said, 'Oh yes, I do it all the time!' I thought that salmon was that pink stuff that comes in a can. But I was given a trial period, and I went home and I drew salmon as though my life depended on it, which of course it did. I got the job. It was a manuscript that I don't think you could give to a more established illustrator. It was 24 pages of a salmon swimming upstream to spawn, possibly the sexiest book ever written for children. But I did it, and even today. . .I think that is a pretty good fish. Anita. . .looked at the finished drawings and she thought, yes the fish were good but the water looked like hair. I think she was right.

"Reading my first contract, I discovered that if I wrote my own stories I would not have to share the royalty with another author, which was a very good incentive to begin to become a writer. My first book, *A Zoo for Mister Muster* was modestly done in two colors. I didn't want them to say we couldn't possibly print this book in full color because you're unknown.

"I was in my mid-twenties, and I had two children who were very small. My wife and I lived in a small apartment with these two children. I know it sounds very bizarre today, but people, young people, did things like that back in the 1950s. But there we were in our small apartment with two children. We were both working; Anita was a textile designer and I was just beginning this career as a children's book illustrator and writer. I'm afraid we succumbed to putting the children in front of the television set and watching those little eyes glaze over because we knew that during that period of time we could both work. It was a very hard time for us, to work and take care of small children at the same time. I think, looking at my style, I was looking over those heads at the television screen. For, indeed, the style of all these early books reflects a kind of television cartooniness. But I knew at the time that it wasn't quite comfortable on a picture book page. Nevertheless it was all I knew how to do so I did it. It's perfectly obvious that I was being influenced by my children, or at least what they were watching on television, even at this early stage.

"A book from that same period was *Prince Bertram the Bad,* again overly cartoony. I had not yet learned that good illustration for a picture book must not be a cartoon, it must be a humorous drawing. And there is a difference. But at this point in my career I was doing cartoons and rather stiff cartoons, too. I did have a good feeling even then for the distribution of design on a page.

"Another book I did in that period was called *Giant John,* because I thought it would be fun to work with big elements and little elements. But again it was very cartoony, rather stiff and quite influenced by what I was seeing on television. Again, a nice distribution of forms on the page, but I do wish it was not quite so cartoony. Still, that was the way I was working at that time, and I was glad to be doing that work, I can tell you, glad to be given the opportunity.

"Something wonderful was happening to me at the time, although I didn't know it. And it's the kind of thing that doesn't happen anymore to young illustrators, unfortunately. Harper and Row was giving me a real apprenticeship. When a manuscript would come into the house and they didn't know who to give it to, and they didn't know who would want to do it, they would call me. My editor, would say, 'Arnold, I have a manuscript.' And I would say, 'Send it right over, I'll illustrate it.' Without even reading it, without even knowing what it was. So, in a sense it was an apprenticeship for me, a baptism of fire, because I was being forced to illustrate books that I really wasn't quite capable of illustrating.

"From that same period, I illustrated a science book about a little girl who finds a cocoon and watches it develop into a cecropia moth. I had to learn to draw a cecropia moth. I had to learn to draw a little girl in various positions watching that moth. They weren't necessarily manuscripts I cared much for, had much feeling for. But I needed the money and I had to do it, and I did it. It was that kind of situation.

"Every artist has to be allowed to fail. One of my failures was a book called *Greg's Microscope.* It was supposed to be an early reader, but the poor organization of material, the scattered pictures, the scattered type, to me, would discourage any young reader from being able to plow through those words at all. The color was bad. The color separations were bad. The faces looked jaundiced and the little boy's head looked absolutely encephalic. But again, I was working all the time. I was struggling. I was failing, but I was moving forward, and that's what the important part of my career was at that time.

"Every art school student thinks he is going to grow up to be Picasso. He is going to paint wonderful paintings to hang in museums, and I was no exception. And in those years, in addition to the books, I was also painting. Somehow, in your mid-twenties, you can raise two children, do children's books and paint at the same time. Don't ask me how. But somehow I had the energy to do it and I was doing a whole series of paintings based on old photographs. I had found an album of old photographs of my family. I was hypnotized by them, fascinated by them. I did a series of oil paintings, all of which I have destroyed except for two. These paintings still have a kind of haunting quality that I like. However, I was painting in addition to doing my children's books. Perhaps in my mind I had not quite decided that I really was ever going to be able to make an impression as a picture book person. Perhaps I was painting to give myself another outlet.

"If happiness is hard work then we must have been extremely happy. Anita was a textile designer and I was doing my illustrations. We would take turns: she would take the children for the morning, I would take the children for the afternoon, and we would both babysit. It was mutual babysitting. We were, without even knowing it, a truly liberated family. In those days, you never saw a father pushing a baby in a stroller. It was absolutely unheard of to see that. It seems odd to think that now, but in those days it was an unseen phenomenon, but I did it all the time and I was looked at with great askance by the other mothers of the sandbox.

"During all the time, until the mid-sixties, I was extremely bothered by the stiffness, the cartoony stiffness in my work. It was ever present and was always bothering me and I knew it was wrong. Knowing is not necessarily being able to do much about it. But in the book *Red Fox and His Canoe,* written by Nathaniel Benchley, I specifically tried a different technique to get out of that stiffness. I used a fountain pen as a dip and I think I succeeded. It did become less of a cartoon and more of a humorous drawing. There was a flow to the

(From ''The Elephant and His Son'' in *Fables* by Arnold Lobel. Illustrated by the author.)

(From *On the Day Peter Stuyvesant Sailed into Town* by Arnold Lobel. Illustrated by the author.)

line that heretofore had not been seen in my drawing. So I think that was another little step forward.

"The first time I was able to use my beloved Brooklyn as a backdrop for my book was in a collection of short stories written by another author and it was the first time that I had ever had trouble with an author. Because this was a collection of obviously autobiographical stories about his own life, when he saw my pictures he looked at my Brooklynscapes and said, 'But this is not the neighborhood in which I grew up!' I was absolutely speechless. What could I say except, 'Well, if you wanted to draw the neighborhood you grew up in you should have drawn it yourself. How could I get into your head and know that?' He had to agree that was true so I ended up with my Brooklyn drawings. And it was in pencil; I was always able to draw well in pencil. The name of the book is *Dudley Pippen*.

"There is probably only one book I ever did that, if it is still

on the shelves, should be banned. Right after the book was published it was discovered that these little turtles that they sell in pet stores gave a disease to children. The title of the books should really be called, "Let's Get Salmonella!" I did like the cover, however; it has a lot of verve. Some of the pictures inside aren't quite as good.

"In 1965, my wife was a textile designer and most of the work she had done were florals. Occasionally she would do textile designs with figures on them. She was most unhappy because I was doing picture books with my name all over them and her textile designs didn't have her name on them at all; it was totally anonymous. So she was fussing and fuming about that. Susan Hirschman saw one of her textile designs one day and said, 'Why don't you do a picture book, why don't you try it?'

"Anita is never one to do anything in a halfway manner. She began to work in a great passion and frenzy. I remember I had just learned to drive that summer and we were taking a motor trip through New England. I woke up at 4:00 a.m. in this grubby little motel room and I was alarmed to find her not in the bed. I saw a crack of light under the bathroom door, I opened the door, and saw her sitting there, in the only seat in that bathroom with a tracing pad on her lap frantically working on the sketches for a book. Not a moment should be lost. And her passion paid off because the book turned out to be beautiful. It was selected as one of the ten best books by the *New York Times,* which isn't bad on a first try. . . .This was her first color separation. It was blue and black and yellow and I think she did a masterful job with creating a cold wintery atmosphere. It's really quite a triumph of a book, I think. She went on to become, from that time on, a children's book person just like myself. . . .

"I love mice. I had two mice when I was a child and it was in no time at all that I had forty mice. I was raised by my grandparents and it was truly a traumatic experience for all of us. My grandfather tried to drown them but he didn't have the heart to do it. I don't know, I think they found somebody to take those mice. But when my son wanted a pet and we felt that our apartment was too small for a dog and a cat, I allowed him to buy one male mouse and we had Seymour.

"Mice are extremely difficult to take care of. They tend to overeat in captivity, particularly if they are celibate, as this mouse had to have been. And even though I built a house for him, with wonderful little ramps for him to climb up and down for exercise, obesity set in. But he was a wonderful pet and I do think mice are marvelously jewel-like creatures. The mouse lead [sic] directly to a book that I did called *Martha the Movie Mouse.*

"I was beginning to realize that one could not write children's books arbitrarily. They had to come out of the things that I, as an author, was passionately interested in. I loved the movies and I liked mice so I decided to combine both interests and write a children's book about both. So, I wrote a book about a mouse who lives in a movie theater. In one illustration, there is a lady in the box office doing her finger nails with an emery board. I've always been fond of that picture.

"In another spread from the same book, Martha, in the tradition of all show business stories, becomes a star. The movie projector breaks down and she jumps on the stage and dances and sings. I had been very much taken by Judy Garland at the time and Judy used to sit at the edge of the stage at the end of each performance and establish rapport with the audience. I had Martha doing the same thing.

"But, even then not all my books were a joy and delight. I was still doing books to make a living. I was still doing books to keep the pot boiling.

"A book called *Ants Are Fun* was an itchy project. There were red ants and black ants in this book and they were fighting with each other. Which ants would be the black ants and which ants would be the red ants and how would I do which ant on which color separation? I did the pictures in Vermont where we were summering in a rented house. I finally said, 'I can't bear it anymore!' And I went down to the lake and I sat down and watched the boats. As I was sitting there by the lake I was being bitten by something on my legs. I looked down and saw that I was bitten by ants that were half black and half red and I thought I was losing my mind. I later found out that there were such things, and I was very happy to know it. The point is, I was still in the position to have to do books that I didn't absolutely love.

"It is terrible to do a book that you don't really love. Because a picture book such as an 'I Can Read' book is 64 pages. It means three separate pieces of art work for each page, 192 separate pieces of artwork per book. To drag yourself up to a drawing table for six to nine months when you're really not having a good time is true drudgery.

"Every artist does his 'Mother Hubbard,' and I did mine. I achieved something that I had never been able to achieve before. I achieved a drawing that was not just a cartoon but that was also a graphic design. The scales on the fish, the scales on the roof, the rhythm of the piling, the rhythm of the folds on the dress, all worked together to make not only a humorous drawing but also a strong graphic design.

"If Beatrix Potter is my artistic mother than Edward Lear is my artistic father. I feel a great kinship to that man, he haunts me all the time. He stands over my drawing table morning, noon, and night, whenever I work. I love his work. I love everything about him. I love his period, all the things he did. When I was asked to illustrate a book called *The Four Little Children Who Went around the World,* a manuscript that he did not illustrate terribly well, I jumped at the chance. It was my great desire to illustrate the book in crosshatch black and white pen. It has a wonderful Victorian feeling. It is the hardest of all techniques for an artist to do because what you're doing is taking many, many hard ink lines, putting them together to make something soft. It requires a great, great deal of technical virtuosity which, unfortunately, in 1967 when this book was done, I didn't have. I tried, I struggled for weeks, for months. And finally I had to call my publisher and say I'm going to have to do the book in pencil because I can't master this black and white ink technique. So I did it in pencil and it turned out quite well anyway. The book was not as well printed as it could have been, but I think that the organization of the material is progress.

"In 1968, I believe it was, I attempted my first picture book in the grand manner, that is to say, full color. I don't know why it took me so long to do it, but it did take me that long.

And Papa began. ■ (From *Mouse Tales* by Arnold Lobel. Illustrated by the author.)

This is the cat with the tattered ear,
That chases the fieldmouse shaking in fear. . . .
■ (From *The Rose in My Garden* by Arnold Lobel. Illustrated by Anita Lobel.)

(From *The Book of Pigericks: Pig Limericks* by Arnold Lobel. Illustrated by the author.)

Full color, large, large pictures, lots of detail. The pictures were influenced by Brueghel, a bit. It was about a wizard who discovered the gray world, discovers each color separately, blue, yellow, red, and learns to put them together. I thought it would be a nice instructional book for children to learn about color, and teachers tell me that indeed it is. I think that I took the phrase 'full color' perhaps a little too seriously; the last page is full color to beat the band.

"The pig in *Lucille* was given his very own book. It was called *Small Pig* and I think there is progress in the pig when you compare it with that little wooden thing I drew so many years before. This pig has animation and life and he sits down and stands up and he sleeps and he runs and it's just a general improvement over the old pig.

"I was still doing books that I didn't enjoy much doing, such as *Sam the Minuteman,* about the Revolutionary war. I don't like drawing guns, I don't like drawing men shooting each other, and I don't like drawing bodies on the ground. But I did all of it in one picture, not having a very good time. I think the dreariness kind of shows in the picture. It is called making a living, which I had to do.

"But something wonderful happened to me in 1970. I guess you call it a watershed year. If you're lucky, if you are an artist and you're lucky, it happens to you: all of a sudden all of the things that didn't work in your work up until that time suddenly come together. After 1970, with almost no exceptions, well maybe one or two small exceptions, I was pretty pleased with everything that I did. The style, the drawing, was no longer overly cartoony.

"We didn't believe in sending our children to summer camp. We thought that was legalized desertion. So we took them with us every summer. We rented a house in Vermont. We did it for three or four years and the children would frolic by themselves and we would work there in the house, and when we had time we would frolic. It was an absolutely marvelous arrangement. I love Vermont.

"This mountain brings us nothing but unhappiness," said the wife of Ming Lo. "Husband, you must move the mountain. . . ." ■ (From *Ming Lo Moves the Mountain* by Arnold Lobel. Illustrated by the author.)

"During those summers my children caught many frogs and toads. The frogs we couldn't keep in captivity because they wouldn't eat in captivity. But the toads made absolutely marvelous house pets. You put them in an aquarium. You give them milk baths; they drink through their skin. They'll eat anything you give them if you wiggle it. We took them home to New York and put them in an aquarium. We hibernated them for the winter and then we took them back to Vermont the next summer and put them back in the same place where we found them. They must have been very confused toads.

"But I loved those little creatures and I think they led to the creation of my two most famous characters, Frog and Toad. As I said before, I thought that one of the secrets of writing good books for children is that you can't really write books for children; you must write books for yourself and about yourself. And somehow in the writing of the manuscript for *Frog and Toad* I was, for the first time, able to write about myself.

Frog and Toad are really two aspects of myself. If they have validity and truth it is because they are the validity and truth in myself.

"Shortly after that, in the early '70s, I received in the mail the best text of a picture book written by someone else that I have ever received. It's called *Hildilid's Night,* and it was an absolutely beautiful manuscript about an old lady who hates the night so much that she tries to boil it in a cauldron, she tries to tie it to the tree with vines, she tries to sing it a lullaby. It was a very simple poetic manuscript. And it gave me as an illustrator a great range, a great freedom to do anything I wanted with it. I also felt that the illustration of this manuscript had to be black and white pen and ink technique. I couldn't get away with pencil this time because it needed the rich black feeling of night that only pen and ink would give me. So I really struggled and this time I succeeded with pen and ink. I also succeeded in doing something I had never done before in any of my illustrations. I achieved a very strong psychological feeling in these pictures. At the end of the story, she is totally defeated by the night. She's tried everything but she cannot get rid of the night, it's still there. In the picture you have the sense of the immensity of this black world stretching behind her and this little figure turning around in defeat and going home to sleep. The irony of it is, she goes to sleep and the sun comes up, she's asleep in the daytime. But for the first time I got a strong feeling of psychological validity to a picture.

"Nobody has done a good *Hansel and Gretel* in this day and age, in my opinion. *Hansel and Gretel* is a horrifying story and, if you excuse the pun, nobody has ever made it grim enough. My own version, like other versions of the present day, turns out to be very sanitized, I think. It is truly a horrific story; maybe I should try again and really bring out the horror and grimness of it.

"I had a good time in the early '70s doing books that I was really enjoying for the first time. I no longer had to do books that I didn't want to do just to keep the pot boiling. I could do books that I like[d] to do and I was probably a much nicer person to be with because of that.

"I love doing science books. . . . I love the Sherlock Holmes kind of research that comes with doing a science book. You think you know what something looks like until you go to draw it and then you realize you have no idea what it looks like. For an "I Can Read" book, which you know are small, my problem was getting giant dinosaurs into the format of the little "I Can Read" book. But I invented a new technique for the book, a combination of pencil and pen and ink which was fun to do. The research for the creature was easy. In New York, all I had to do was go down to the IRT subway and look at the other riders. You see creatures like that all the time every day walking around there.

"When you do a science book you become a kind of mini expert on what you're doing, what you're drawing. I learned that sea horses use their noses as vacuum cleaners to eat with. I learned which fin makes a sea horse go forward and which fin makes him go backward. I learned that sea horses are the only species in which the male gives birth to the children. Absolutely fascinating information comes when you're working on a science book and I love doing them and I hope to do more. . . .

"It is funny where you do get your ideas. I was. . .raised—in Schenectady, New York, which has a very strong Dutch heritage. I had a fourth-grade teacher who was Dutch and there were a lot of children in my class with Dutch names. We were very, very aware of our Dutch heritage in Schenectady. My teacher was just bananas about Dutch heritage. It was just forced down our throats all year and I was fascinated by the period, fascinated by the costumes and the whole Dutch ancestry thing. And I thought it would be fun to write a comic book about Peter Stuyvesant, for truly he is a comic character in his own way. So I did; I wrote a book called *On the Day Peter Stuyvesant Sailed into Town*. It was a very hard book to do and required a great deal of research about what the colony of New Amsterdam looked like when Peter Stuyvesant arrived there. I was pretty careful about putting all the houses in the right place.

"The book was not a success, I think, partly because I did not do it in full color as I should have. I had some idea I would use blue and yellow to make the whole book look like a Dutch tile. People told me it was too regional. But I thought that all school children learned about the thirteen original colonies. The book did not sell particularly well. I loved doing it however.

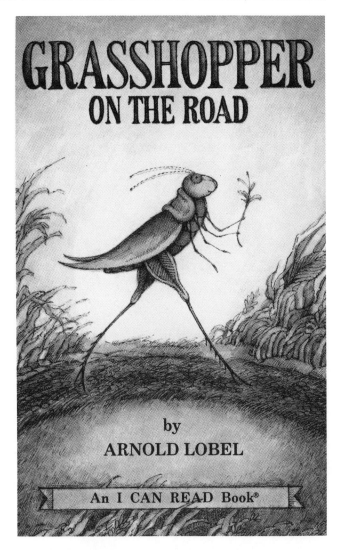

(From *Grasshopper on the Road* by Arnold Lobel. Illustrated by the author.)

"When you're working in children's books it's so important to have a concept of the past, of books that have been done in the past, of Beatrix Potter, of Edward Lear, of Walter Crane, of all the great people of the turn of the century and before. I'm not an old-book collector myself. I have a few old things that I've been given as gifts but there have been some wonderful modern anthologies of old books that have been put out and I have those. I love the way that the covers of old children's books look. For the book *Mouse Tales*, I tried to recapture that look and I think I did a pretty good job. The lettering is very nice, I think, for a non-letterer like myself. It has a nice feeling. I went into self portraiture again. Children are fascinated by the fact that Mouse looks like me. I'm constantly getting letters asking, 'Is that a self-portrait?' and it was. The number of children was not.

"I said I was happy with almost everything I did after 1970. One of the books that I wasn't so happy with was a book called *Circus*. These are wonderful verses by Jack Prelutsky, but I don't like the circus very much. It's kind of frightening, I think, and I never know what to look at. It's too busy and too scary; I used to take my children to the circus and I would come out a nervous wreck. And I'm afraid I was all too accurate in getting that feeling into the book. It was too busy and too much was going on and I was not particularly happy

Pigs were growing in the trees like apples. ■ (From *A Treeful of Pigs* by Arnold Lobel. Illustrated by Anita Lobel.)

with it. I don't think I served Jack too well as an illustrator in this particular case, except for the page with the aerialists. I do like that; it has a nice sweep to the page, the way the aerialists jump into the air.

"You set problems for yourself when you do a book. One of the problems I set for myself when I started to write *Owl at Home* was to create a character; write five chapters, five different stories in it, and make a character who talks to no one but himself and inanimate objects. In other words, do a monologue. Try to do it. See if you can do it. Sit down with pencil in your hand and try to do it. It usually works for me. My imagination seems to take fire when I give it limitations of that nature. *Owl at Home* was, indeed, a total monologue. He speaks to no one else in the book except, of course, himself; he talks to himself a lot.

"I had become quite successful in writing 'I Can Read' books. I think I'm the grand old man, the dean of the 'I Can Read' book at this point. I write in repetition, which is of course very handy and successful in a text for an 'I Can Read' book. I thought if the words in an 'I Can Read' book reappear, why not try to write a story in which you use the same picture repeated again and again and again with variations. So that was the problem that I set for myself. I finally was able to do it in a story from a book called *Mouse Soup*. Stones don't go anywhere, so it was very easy just to draw one picture, but of course things happen inside the picture. Like a bird comes and sits down and a mouse comes and the weather changes, but

essentially it is the same picture. I like these stones because they remind me of Abbott and Costello.

"The wonderful thing about illustrating other people's manuscripts is that you are freed from your own imagination. If I only illustrated books that I wrote myself I'd be trapped inside my own head. When I illustrate somebody else's books I can stretch myself. It's like playing a part in another author's play. I have to become someone else. Jack Prelutsky wrote two books, one is called *Nightmares* and one is called *The Headless Horseman Rides Tonight*, truly terrifying poems, not for the little children, but for what I would call the Dracula set, the nine- to ten-year-old group. For once I could leave my role as lovable Arnold Lobel and become evil and monstrous and do these drawings.

"For *Nightmares* it was great fun drawing the mummy with all those bandages. But there was no way I could have written a poem because my imagination could not have written a poem to go with the picture.

"As I said, Edward Lear is my father, my artistic father. By the time I had written so many 'I Can Read' books with simple words, I decided that I wanted to write a book with longer words, consciously longer words. So I created a story about a man who takes his furniture out for a walk, called *The Man Who Took the Indoors Out*. I could write lines like, 'a preposterous sort of procession began.' I could never get away with a line like that in an 'I Can Read' book. So that was fun to do. It was a very hard book to do in terms of time and technique and detail and color. It took me almost a year to do the pictures.

"My favorite part of children's books is doing the sketch dummies. I do very finished dummies. I'm told that I do the most finished dummies of any artist in the field. I don't know whether that is true or not, I don't see anyone elses' dummies. I do it for two reasons. One, because I think it is important for the finished art, and the other reason is that I love doing it so much. I love meeting something coming out of absolutely nothing the way a dummy does.

"I say I love to do research. For *Grasshopper on the Road,* I did do my grasshopper research. I went to the library and I looked at grasshopper photographs, and I sketched and drew from real grasshoppers. And then when I went to draw for the printer for the finished artwork, I thought 'that doesn't look like a grasshopper at all, that looks like a green rabbit.' What

could I do? This grasshopper was such a wonderfully elegant, cosmopolitan, charming man, and suddenly I thought, Fred Astaire! That saved the day. I was able somehow to create the character just thinking about him. His proportion, and how he moved, that's how I got my grasshopper in this particular case.

"Something new happened in our life when I was working on a story in the late '70s for myself to illustrate. It was a European folktale and I suddenly realized that the style of the story was much more appropriate for my wife to illustrate. So I generously gave her the story to illustrate. For the first time in my life I was on the other side of the picture. I was the writer having his words illustrated by somebody else. I must say that when she began the pictures I looked at the drawings and said, 'What on earth are you doing to my stories?' I learned to keep my mouth shut. . . ."[3]

During the late seventies and into the eighties the Lobels occupied side-by-side drawing boards, creating award-winning

"Ah," he said. "The creaks in my feet are gone." ◼ (From *Uncle Elephant* by Arnold Lobel. Illustrated by the author.)

children's books from their Victorian townhouse in Brooklyn, New York. Their children, both in their twenties, were also talented and established in their artistic careers; Adam as a video consultant, photographer and rock guitarist, and Adrianne as a New York set designer.

Of the numerous books that Lobel did, many were given awards. His success in the children's book field was based on a personal belief that "satisfaction will come to those who please themselves."[3]

Applying that conviction to his work often meant humorous rewrites, as in the case of one of his favorite books, *Uncle Elephant*. "It does take courage, to say 'This is lousy!' I was very angry about the whole thing. With a thick black marker, I crossed out all of the things in the manuscript that I didn't like. I took the chapters of the book and shuffled them and I threw the whole mess into a drawer. I thought to myself, 'Is it too late to go to auto mechanic's school?' I felt terribly discouraged that day. But the next day I pulled myself together, I opened that drawer and I reread the manuscript. Somehow the changes that I had made and the reshuffling of the chapters altered the manuscript just enough so I knew that there was some life—that they would live, that the ailing patient would survive....Perhaps that's the real secret of the problem. Perhaps it's just a matter of gritting one's teeth and hanging on, just having the courage to hang on. I love making books for children and I most certainly am willing to do that."[3]

This perseverance and meticulous attention to detail, eventually produced *Fables,* which received a Caldecott Medal in 1981. "The creation of most picture books for children is not dramatic. It is a matter of daily, patient, single-minded effort. It is a matter of writing some words on a page in a silent room. It is the soft sound of a pencil or a pen sweeping across a bit of drawing paper. To see a book appearing in front of one's eyes where before there was nothing is a pleasure and a joy. But this elation comes quietly. This was not true, however, in the case of *Fables*....The conception and birth of *Fables* was a fable in itself. A saga with the ups and downs, the climaxes and anticlimaxes, of a real plot.

"Children have fallen heir to the fables of Aesop because of the anthropomorphic use of animals therein. I soon realized that these fables were not originally created for children at all. There were no children, as we know them, in Aesop's time. There were only younger and smaller Greeks. I found dogs tearing sheep into pieces. I found snakes strangling ravens. I found deer being chewed to bits by lions. I came upon harsh cruelties and bitter ironies of every sort. The adaptations I was reading were heavily laden with the cautionary moralism of the nineteenth century. Surely it was very interesting, but it was a far cry from *Frog and Toad*....

"Day by day, to my great surprise, they told me their stories, and I wrote them. For once the pages of my notebook were not empty. Anita went off to dance class every day. She would return in the early evening and ask in hushed tones, 'Did you write another one?' My exuberant answer would almost always be, 'Yes I did!' and then I would read her my latest effort. I thank her for her approval and support. . . .

"In a great passion, I rushed to do the pictures, for as wary as I am of writing, I do love to draw. I chose to do my first drawings as color paintings instead of the black-and-white pencil sketches that I usually make. The camel wearing a tutu, the pig floating through a dreamlike cosmos, the baboon clutching his ventilated umbrella—these images clicked into being. In no time at all I had a preliminary dummy, stories and pictures all pasted neatly into place. It was ready to be

"Ah!" said the weasel. "I am going to make mouse soup." ■ (From *Mouse Soup* by Arnold Lobel. Illustrated by the author.)

presented to Harper. I thought the book was damned good, but how hard it is to be objective about one's own work! Perhaps I was very wrong. There are always the doubts."[4]

During the thirty years that Lobel wrote and illustrated childrens books he developed into a "natural illustrator," but remained apprehensive about completing the text, writing laboriously. "As I go through the process of making a book for children, I find that I am a rather confident illustrator and much at ease in that role.

"But when it comes to the writing of the stories for my books, my approach is far more cautious and apprehensive. I supply myself with a not very intimidating notebook and an unassuming set of sharpened yellow pencils. I find a quiet and comfortable corner of the house and I begin. It can be a long and a frustrating time for me. For every good day when things are ripping along nicely, there are two or three days when nothing whatsoever happens—except that I draw the ends off of a great many of those yellow pencils. I've learned to persist and to be patient, however, and eventually I arrive at a text that I believe is finished enough to begin drawing the pictures for. I still keep changing, or rather eliminating—for I try to take out every word that does not really have to be there. When it comes to the words of a picture book, less is almost always very definitely more.

"When the first sketches are finished, I type the text and paste it down near the drawings. I go back to that quiet and comfortable corner of the house and slowly turn the pages, reading aloud to myself—getting the feeling of how the words and the pictures are working together—as well they must. When all goes well; when the combination 'clicks,' it is a great satisfaction to me.''

Lobel died, at the age of fifty-four, at Doctors Hospital in New York on December 4, 1987. ''It is a kind of pleasant omnipotence that I feel at the drawing board. There is a little world at the end of my pencil. I am the stage director, the costume designer, and the man who pulls the curtain. If I'm in the mood, I can admit to being despotic, too, for when a character is not behaving as I would wish him to he can be quickly dismissed with a wave of my eraser. This is certainly part of the joy of making books for children.''

FOOTNOTE SOURCES

[1]Lee Bennett Hopkins, ''Anita and Arnold Lobel,'' *Books Are by People*, Citation Press, 1969.
[2]Arnold Lobel, ''This Book Belongs to Me!,'' in *Once Upon a Time*, Putnam, 1986.
[3]A. Lobel, ''A Quick Backward Glance,'' *New Books for Young Readers*, University of Minnesota, 1982.
[4]A. Lobel, ''Caldecott Medal Acceptance Speech,'' *Horn Book*, August, 1981.

FOR MORE INFORMATION SEE:

Lee Kingman and others, compilers, *Illustrators of Children's Books: 1957-1966*, Horn Book, 1968.
National Observer, November 4, 1968.
Horn Book, August, 1969, October, 1970, April, 1971, December, 1971, June, 1972, December, 1972.
Publishers Weekly, May 17, 1971, February 26, 1973, February 25, 1974, August 22, 1986, January 29, 1988 (p. 395).
Martha E. Ward and Dorothy A. Marquardt, *Authors of Books for Young People*, 2nd edition, Scarecrow, 1971.
Selma G. Lanes, *Down the Rabbit Hole*, Atheneum, 1971.
Graphis 155, Volume 27, 1971/72.
Doris de Montreville and Donna Hill, editors, *Third Book of Junior Authors*, H. W. Wilson, 1972.
Top of the News, April, 1972.
Donnarae MacCann and Olga Richard, *The Child's First Books*, H. W. Wilson, 1973.
Jacqueline S. Weiss, ''Arnold Lobel'' (videocassette), Profiles in Literature, Temple University, 1973.
Contemporary American Illustrators of Children's Books, Rutgers University Art Gallery, 1974.
Bea J. Pepan, ''Author Meets His Fans—All Children,'' *Milwaukee Journal*, April 25, 1974.
R. Natov and G. DeLuca, ''Interview with Arnold Lobel,'' *Lion and the Unicorn*, number 1, 1977.
''Meet the Newbery Author: Arnold Lobel'' (filmstrip with record or cassette), Miller-Brody, 1978.
L. Kingman and others, compilers, *Illustrators of Children's Books: 1967-1976*, Horn Book, 1978.
D. L. Kirkpatrick, editor, *Twentieth-Century Children's Writers*, St. Martin's, 1978, 2nd edition, 1983.
''Arnold Lobel, the Natural Illustrator, the Entertainer,'' *Early Years* (now *Teaching preK-8*), November, 1980.
Betsy Hearne and Marilyn Kaye, editors, *Celebrating Children's Books: Essays on Children's Literature in Honor of Zena Sutherland*, Lothrop, 1981.
John F. Berry, ''The Lobels: A Marriage of Two Drawing Boards,'' *Washington Post Book World*, June 13, 1982.
Jim Roginski, compiler, *Newbery and Caldecott Medalists and Honor Book Winners: Bibliographies and Resource Material through 1977*, Libraries Unlimited, 1982.
Lucy Rollin, ''The Astonished Witness Disclosed: An Interview with Arnold Lobel,'' *Children's Literature in Education*, winter, 1984.

OBITUARIES

New York Times, December 7, 1987.
Day (New London, Conn.), December 9, 1987.
Publishers Weekly, December 25, 1987.
School Library Journal, January, 1988.

COLLECTIONS

De Grummond Collection, University of Southern Mississippi.
Kerlan Collection, University of Minnesota.
Free Library of Philadelphia.
Iowa City Public Library.

MacEWEN, Gwendolyn (Margaret) 1941-1987

OBITUARY NOTICE—See sketch in *SATA* Volume 50: Born September 1, 1941, in Toronto, Ontario, Canada; died November 30, 1987, in Toronto, Ontario, Canada. Educator, poet, and author. MacEwen left school at the age of eighteen to devote her time exclusively to writing poetry and prose. Her first volume of poetry was published by the time she was twenty. She was writer-in-residence at the University of Western Ontario and at the University of Toronto during the 1980s, and received several Canadian awards, including the Governor General's Award for Poetry.

Collections of her poems include *Selah, The Shadow-Maker, The Armies of the Moon, The Fire-Eaters, Afterworlds*, and *Dragon Sandwiches*, a volume of poetry for children. Her other books for young people are *The Chocolate Moose*, illustrated by Barry Zaid, *The Honey Drum: Seven Tales from Arab Lands*, which she translated, and *Noman's Land: Stories*. MacEwen also wrote *King of Egypt, King of Dreams: A Novel*, several documentaries, verse dramas, and radio plays. She once stated that she wrote ''. . .in order to make sense of the chaotic nature of experience, of reality—and also to create a bridge between the inner world of the *psyche* and the 'outer' world of things. For me, language has enormous, almost magical power, and I tend to regard poetry in much the same way as the ancients regarded the chants or hymns used in holy festivals: as a means of involving the mysterious forces which move the world and shape our destinies.'' Besides her original writings, MacEwen was also a translator of Greek poetry and a contributor to numerous anthologies and literary magazines. Her poetry was translated into many languages, including Spanish, Swedish, French, Italian and Portuguese.

FOR MORE INFORMATION SEE:

D. G. Jones, *Butterfly on Rock: A Study of Themes and Images in Canadian Literature*, University of Toronto Press, 1970.
Canadian Literature, summer, 1970, summer, 1977.
Saturday Night, January, 1972.
Frank Davey, ''Gwendolyn MacEwen: The Secret of Alchemy,'' *Open Letter*, spring, 1973.
Frank Davey, *From There to Here*, Press Porcepic, 1974 (pp.31-32).
Gary Geddes, ''Now You See It. . .,'' *Books in Canada*, July, 1976.
Ellen Warwick, ''To Seek a Single Symmetry,'' *Canadian Literature*, winter, 1976 (pp.21-34).
David Staines, editor, *The Canadian Imagination*, Harvard University Press, 1977 (pp. 97-122).
Contemporary Literary Criticism, Volume XIII, Gale, 1980.
Patricia Keeney Smith, ''WQ Interview with Gwendolyn MacEwen,'' *Cross Canada Writers Quarterly*, Volume 5, number 1, 1983.

Jan Bartley, *Invocations: The Poetry and Prose of Gwendolyn MacEwen*, University of British Columbia Press, l983.
M. Atwood, "MacEwen's Muse," *Second Words*, Anasi, l984.
Dictionary of Literary Biography, Volume LIII: *Canadian Writers since l960*, Gale, l986.
Globe and Mail (Toronto), February 22, l986.
Deborah A. Straub, editor, *Contemporary Authors, New Revision Series*, Volume 22, Gale, l988 (pp. 290-291).

MAYERSON, Evelyn Wilde   1935-

PERSONAL: Born January 12, 1935, in New York, N.Y.; daughter of Arthur C. and Charlotte (Goodman) Wilde; married Don A. Mayerson (an attorney), June 17, 1953; children: Gary, Robert. *Education:* University of Miami, Coral Gables, Fla., B.A., 1963; Goddard College, M.A., 1973; Laurence University of California, Ed.D., 1975. *Home:* One Grove Isle, No. 702, Coconut Grove, Fla. 33133. *Agent:* Maryanne C. Colas, Cantrell-Colas, Inc., 229 East 79th St., New York, N.Y. 10021. *Office:* Department of English, University of Miami, Coral Gables, Fla. 33124.

CAREER: Temple University, Philadelphia, Pa., assistant professor of psychiatry, 1971-77; University of South Florida, Tampa, assistant professor of psychiatry, 1977-78; University of Miami, Coral Gables, Fla., assistant professor of English, until 1984, associate professor of English, director of composition, 1984—. Member of board of directors of North Miami Beach Public Library, 1962-63; consultant to U.S. Department of Commerce and U.S. Civil Service Commission; member of board of directors, Florida Council of Libraries, 1982—; grant review panelist for literature, state of Florida, 1984. *Awards, honors: If Birds Are Free* was selected one of New York Public Library's Books for the Teenage, 1981.

WRITINGS:

Putting the Ill at Ease, Harper, 1976.
Shoptalk, Saunders, 1979.
Sanjo, Lippincott, 1979.

EVELYN WILDE MAYERSON

If Birds Are Free, Lippincott, 1980.
Coydog, Scribner, 1981.
No Enemy but Time, Doubleday, 1983, Talking Books for the Blind, 1984.
Princess in Amber, Doubleday, 1985.

Author of "Introduction to Psychiatry" (videocassette series), Lippincott, 1975.

SIDELIGHTS: "I represent a battalion of writers who write on a daily basis, regardless of other career or family obligations. Most of us have learned to shave time, so that two hours in the early morning (before daybreak) and an hour waiting for a plane to take off are not wasted, but are spent scribbling corrections on a dog-eared draft of our latest manuscript.

"Ideally, it would be nice to have nothing to do but write. I can't imagine the luxury. Because the majority of my day is spent on a university campus, I write under pressure. Sometimes other people tell me that they too will write when they have the time. I think they imagine time as some inviting, yawning, cavern. I usually tell them that if they wait that long, by the time they get there, they will likely forget what it was they wanted to say in the first place.

"Writing for me is both joy and misery, joy when everything works, when the right words convey an exact meaning, when everything flows smoothly and when wonderful metaphors are dredged up mysteriously through the action of some primeval pump; misery when I know it's hiding somewhere in my cortex, refusing to be dislodged." Mayerson has recently completed a play, "A Long and Lovely Suicide."

McHUGH, (Berit) Elisabet   1941-

PERSONAL: Born January 26, 1941, in Stoede, Sweden; came to the United States in 1971, naturalized citizen, 1982; daughter of Nils G. O. (a journalist) and Rut E. (a homemaker; maiden name, Gradin) Oejerhag; married Richard G. McHugh (a commander in the U.S. Navy), February 14, 1972 (divorced March, 1982); children: (adopted) Fred R., Lee Ann, Erin V., Jan M., Ryan C., Karen E. *Education:* Royal Naval College, Stockholm, Sweden, graduated, 1961. *Home:* 2131 Robinson Park Rd., Moscow, Idaho 83843. *Agent:* Barbara S. Kouts, 788 Ninth Ave., New York, N.Y. 10019.

CAREER: Writer, 1979—. Has worked as a radio officer in Sweden.

WRITINGS:

JUVENILE

Raising a Mother Isn't Easy, Greenwillow, 1983.
Karen's Sister, Greenwillow, 1983.
Karen and Vicki, Greenwillow, 1984.
Beethoven's Cat, Atheneum, 1988.

WORK IN PROGRESS: A sequel to *Beethoven's Cat*, to be published by Atheneum; a juvenile book; an adult murder mystery.

SIDELIGHTS: "I spent twelve years traveling around the world as a radio officer. I worked in East Africa and Australia. I lived in West Berlin. I never had any thought of becoming a writer and I had no desire to write.

"In 1979 my husband and I separated. At that time we lived on a mountain in Idaho with seven children [including a foster child], three of whom were pre-schoolers. Having no money, no income, no skills, I started to write and began to sell articles to magazines and newspapers. I had to learn everything the hard way. In 1982 I was offered a contract for my first book.

"I now live in the country. Most of the children are gone. I write full-time and usually start my day by walking five miles. In the wintertime I go cross country skiing. I am a compulsive reader."

McKENDRICK, Melveena (Christine) 1941-

PERSONAL: Born March 23, 1941, in Glamorgan, Wales; daughter of James Powell (a teacher) and Catherine Letitia (a housewife; maiden name, Richards) Jones; married Neil McKendrick (a historian), March 18, 1968; children: Olivia, Cornelia. *Education:* King's College, London B.A. (first class honors), 1963; Girton College, Cambridge, Ph.D., 1967. *Home:* Howe House, Huntingdon Rd., Cambridge CB3 OLY, England. *Office:* Girton College, Cambridge University, Cambridge CB3 OJG, England.

CAREER: Cambridge University, Girton College, Cambridge, England, research fellow, 1967-70, tutor, 1970-83, senior tutor, 1974-82, lecturer in Spanish, 1970—. *Member:* British Association of Hispanus, International Association of Hispanus. *Awards, honors: Ferdinand and Isabella* was named one of New York Public Library's Books for the Teen Age, 1980, and 1982.

WRITINGS:

Ferdinand and Isabella, American Heritage, 1968.
A Concise History of Spain, McGraw, 1972.
Woman and Society in the Spanish Drama of the Golden Age, Cambridge University Press, 1974.
Cervantes, Little, Brown, 1982.
The Spanish Theatre in the Sixteenth and Seventeenth Centuries, Cambridge University Press, 1989.

Contributor to *Calderon: Critical Studies,* edited by J. E. Varey, 1973, to *Women in Hispanic Literature,* edited by Beth Miller, and to language and Spanish studies journals. Editor of and contributor to *Golden Age Studies in Honor of A. A. Parker,* 1984.

WORK IN PROGRESS: A composite edition of Calderon's *El magico prodigioso* with A. A. Parker; a study of the seventeenth-century Spanish theatre.

MEIER, Minta 1906-

PERSONAL: Surname is pronounced "Meyer." Born May 26, 1906, in Dayton, Wash; married Ronald W. Meier (a lawyer), June 21, 1935 (deceased); children: Peter, Madeline Meier Moskonas. *Education:* Whitman College, B.A.; University of Washington, M.A. *Religion:* Episcopalian. *Home:* 2011 20th N.E., Oak Harbor, Wash. 98277.

CAREER: Writer, 1930—. Taught drama and directing to amateur theater groups. Member of board of public television station KCTS-9.

WRITINGS:

PLAYS

The Little Shepherd, Coach House, 1955.
The Children, Coach House, 1955.

Cat on the Oregon Trail, Coach House, 1959.

Author of short stories and articles in periodicals, including *Ladies' Home Journal, Colliers, Parent,* and *Today's Health.*

WORK IN PROGRESS: A novel.

SIDELIGHTS: "I worked in a church group and we needed plays, so I wrote them."

FOR MORE INFORMATION SEE:

Lee Brainard, "'Til Death Did Us Part. . .," *Whidbey News-Times* (Wash.), December 11, 1985 (p. 14).

MOWAT, Farley (McGill) 1921-

PERSONAL: Born May 12, 1921, in Belleville, Ontario, Canada; son of Angus McGill (a librarian) and Helen Elizabeth (Thomson) Mowat; married Francis Thornhill, 1947 (marriage ended, 1959); married Claire A. (a writer; maiden name, Wheeler), March, 1964; children: (first marriage) Robert Alexander, David Peter. *Education:* University of Toronto, B.A., 1949. *Residence:* Port Hope, Ontario, Canada, and Cape Breton, Nova Scotia. *Address:* c/o McClelland & Stewart Ltd., 481 University Ave., Toronto, Ontario M5G 2E9, Canada.

CAREER: Author. *Military service:* Canadian Army, Infantry and Intelligence Corps, 1939-46; became captain. *Awards, honors:* President's Medal for Best Canadian Short Story of 1952 from the University of Western Ontario for "Eskimo Spring"; Anisfield-Wolfe Award for contribution to interracial relations, 1954, for *People of the Deer;* Governor General's

FARLEY MOWAT

Medal for juvenile literature, 1957, Book of the Year for Children Award from the Canadian Association of Children's Librarians, and International Board on Books for Young People Honour List (Canada), both 1958, all for *Lost in the Barrens;* Canadian Women's Clubs Award, 1958, for *The Dog Who Wouldn't Be;* Boys' Club Junior Book Award from the Boys' Club of America, 1963, for *Owls in the Family;* National Association of Independent Schools Award, 1963, for juvenile books; Hans Christian Andersen Honour List, 1965, for juvenile books; Canadian Centennial Medal, 1967; Leacock Medal from the Stephen Leacock Foundation, 1970, and L'Etoile de la Mer Honours List, 1972, both for *The Boat Who Wouldn't Float;* D.Lit., Laurentian University, 1970, University of Victoria, 1982, and Lakeland University, 1986; Vicky Metcalf Award from the Canadian Authors' Association, 1971, for his body of work; Doctor of Law from Lethbridge University, and University of Toronto, both 1973, and University of Prince Edward Island, 1979; Curran Award, 1977, for "contributions to understanding wolves"; Queen Elizabeth II Jubilee Medal, 1978; Knight of Mark Twain, 1980; New York Public Library's Books for the Teen Age, 1980, for *The Great Betrayal,* and 1981, for *And No Birds Sang;* Officer, Order of Canada, 1981.

WRITINGS:

NONFICTION

People of the Deer, Atlantic-Little Brown, 1952, revised edition, McClelland & Stewart, 1975.

The Regiment, McClelland & Stewart, 1954, revised edition, 1973.

The Dog Who Wouldn't Be (juvenile; illustrated by Paul Galdone), Atlantic-Little Brown, 1957.

(Editor) Samuel Hearne, *Coppermine Journey: An Account of a Great Adventure,* Atlantic-Little, Brown, 1958.

The Grey Seas Under, Atlantic-Little, Brown, 1958.

The Desperate People, Atlantic-Little, Brown, 1959, revised edition, McClelland & Stewart, 1976.

(Editor) *Ordeal by Ice,* McClelland & Stewart, 1960, revised edition, 1973, Atlantic-Little, Brown, 1961.

The Serpent's Coil, McClelland & Stewart, 1961, Atlantic-Little, Brown, 1962.

Owls in the Family (juvenile; ALA Notable Book; illustrated by Robert Frankenberg), Atlantic-Little, Brown, 1961, revised edition, McClelland & Stewart, 1973.

Never Cry Wolf, Atlantic-Little, Brown, 1963, revised edition, McClelland & Stewart, 1973.

Westviking: The Ancient Norse in Greenland and North America (illustrated by wife, Claire Wheeler), Atlantic-Little, Brown, 1965.

(Editor) *The Polar Passion: The Quest for the North Pole,* McClelland & Stewart, 1967, revised edition, 1973, Atlantic-Little, Brown, 1968.

Canada North, Atlantic-Little, Brown, 1967, revised edition published as *The Great Betrayal: Arctic Canada Now,* 1976 (published in Canada as *Canada North Now: The Great Betrayal* [illustrated by Shin Sugini], McClelland & Stewart, 1976).

This Rock within the Sea: A Heritage Lost (illustrated with photographs by John de Visser), Atlantic-Little, Brown, 1969, new edition, McClelland & Stewart, 1976.

The Boat Who Wouldn't Float, McClelland & Stewart, 1969, Atlantic-Little, Brown, 1970.

The Siberians, Atlantic-Little, Brown, 1970 (published in Canada as *Sibir: My Discovery of Siberia,* McClelland & Stewart, 1970, revised edition, 1973).

A Whale for the Killing, Atlantic-Little, Brown, 1972.

Wake of the Great Sealers (illustrated by David Blackwood), Atlantic-Little, Brown, 1973.

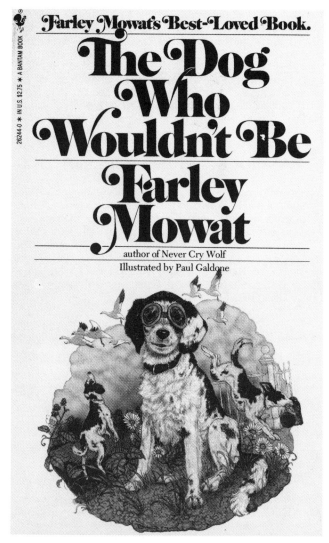

During his first few weeks with us Mutt astonished us all by his maturity of outlook. ■ (From *The Dog Who Wouldn't Be* by Farley Mowat. Illustrated by Paul Galdone.)

(Editor) *Tundra: Selections from the Great Accounts of Arctic Land Voyages,* McClelland & Stewart, 1973.

Top of the World Trilogy (includes *Ordeal by Ice, The Polar Passion,* and *Tundra*), McClelland & Stewart, 1976.

Death of a People, 2 volumes, McClelland & Stewart, 1976.

And No Birds Sang (autobiography), Atlantic-Little, Brown, 1979, large print edition, Gatefold, 1982.

The World of Farley Mowat: A Selection from His Works, edited by Peter Davison, Atlantic-Little, Brown, 1980.

Sea of Slaughter, McClelland & Stewart, 1984, Atlantic-Little, Brown, 1985.

My Discovery of America, McClelland & Stewart, 1985, Atlantic-Little, Brown, 1986.

Woman in the Mists: The Story of Dian Fossey and the Mountain Gorillas of Africa, Warner, 1987.

FICTION

Lost in the Barrens (young adult novel; illustrated by Charles Geer), Atlantic-Little, Brown, 1956, published as *Two against the North* (illustrated by Alan Daniel), Scholastic-TAB, 1977.

The Black Joke (juvenile novel; illustrated by D. Johnson), McClelland & Stewart, 1962, revised edition, 1973,

American edition (illustrated by Victor Mays), Atlantic-Little, Brown, 1963.

The Curse of the Viking Grave (juvenile novel; illustrated by C. Geer), Atlantic-Little, Brown, 1966.

The Snow Walker (adult short-story collection), Atlantic-Little, Brown, 1975.

Also author of television screenplays "Sea Fare" and "Diary of a Boy on Vacation," both 1964. Contributor to *Cricket's Choice,* Open Court, 1974, and to magazines, including *Saturday Evening Post, Argosy, Maclean's,* and *Cricket.* Mowat's books have been translated into thirty languages and anthologized in more then 150 works.

ADAPTATIONS:

"A Whale for the Killing" (movie), ABC-TV, February 1, 1981, (cassette), Books on Tape.

"Never Cry Wolf" (movie), Disney, 1983, (cassette), Books on Tape, 1986, (cassette; voice by Mowat) Bantam, 1988.

"Grey Seas Under" (cassette), Books on Tape, 1986.

"Lost in the Barrens" (cassette), Books on Tape.

"People of the Deer" (cassette), Books on Tape.

"The Snow Walker" (cassette), Books on Tape, 1986.

WORK IN PROGRESS: Farley's Bestiary, a collection of light verse; collaboration with a number of ecology writers on a massive book on conservation; *Born Naked,* "the first volume of my autobiography"; two feature films.

SIDELIGHTS: "I was conceived in a green canoe on the Bay of Quinte and born in a taxi between Trenton and Belleville."[1]

An auspicious beginning for a man who would spend much of his life moving around. "I grew up pretty much an outcast.

For a variety of reasons, one of which was that I was rootless. My father was a librarian and went from job to more prestigious job in Belleville, Windsor, Toronto and Saskatoon, where he was chief librarian. It seemed we were always picking up and leaving. Another thing that made me an outcast was that I was very small for my age and always looked much younger. In addition, I had no interest in sports whatsoever, partly owing to my small stature. I was a passionate birdwatcher and, to cap it all off, a writer. My teachers thought this was great, but the other kids were pretty suspicious of a boy who spent most of his time on poetry.

"I spent monstrous amounts of time in the libraries my father directed. To his everlasting credit, he never directed my reading. He gave me carte blanche. In some of his libraries they kept the 'bad books' under the counter. These I would spirit home by the armful and devour in solitary splendor. My father, of course, knew full well and gave me nothing but encouragement for my writing as well as for my reading.

"It was he who suggested that I send one of my pieces to the *Saskatchewan Star Phoenix,* which had a weekly supplement for kids called *Prairie Pals.* They liked what I sent and gave me a regular column. If memory serves, I was about ten years old. I was more than ready for the challenge, for I'd been publishing my own little magazine, *Nature Lore,* which we mimeographed on the library machine.

"*Nature Lore* was put out by the members of the Beaver Club that I had formed. Nobody else could write, so I did all the articles and used the other kids' names. Each copy sold for five cents, and somehow or other we usually managed to sell out our 'print runs,' as I would later learn to say.

"I guess I shouldn't overdramatize my solitary childhood. I always had one or two friends my own age—outcasts like

There was a ledge right across the river halfway down where a huge curling backwave reared up. . . . ■ (From *The Curse of the Viking Grave* by Farley Mowat. Illustrated by Charles Geer.)

myself, probably—and good adult companions. One of the most important people in my life was my uncle, Frank Farley. He was a naturalist of the old school some hundred years ago. Which means that he was an avid collector of bird eggs, bird specimens, and a tireless maker of lists: lists of eggs, lists of specimens, lists of most everything he saw and handled. He indoctrinated me, and, for the first years of my life, I, too, was a naturalist of the old school. I went out with my shotgun and shot all the little birds and then stuffed them with cotton wool, called 'study skins.' Every museum in the world has enormous, cavernous rooms filled with metal cabinets which in turn are filled with drawer after drawer of birds and animals laid out flat on their backs. The Royal Ontario Museum probably has half a million, and that is by no means unusual. Literally hundreds of millions of specimens of birds and animals have been killed simply to provide study skins for museums. It's a horrible thought and a worse reality. As a lad I felt quite the scientist tromping through the woods murdering things and contemplating corpses in the hallowed halls of museums.

"It was my Uncle Farley who first took me to the far north where I saw the great herds of caribou migrating across the tundra. It would prove momentous in my life. I returned to the Arctic after the war to recapture the thrill I felt upon first seeing those splendid herds.''[2] The spectacle figured prominently in *People of the Deer* and *Never Cry Wolf*. His research into the caribou's relations with the wolves and Eskimos proved revolutionary, upsetting decades of mistaken scientific assumptions.

"My father's enormous, extremely flamboyant presence was the biggest star in the sky under which I grew up. In fact, he was crazy, which I didn't mind a bit. Some kids would have said, 'Christ, why can't he be like everyone else.' Not me. I rather admired him for it. Without him, I never would have become the writer I am. Unfortunately, he and I never really understood each other once I reached maturity. I think he always felt that I had let him down. He had wanted to be a novelist, and wrote two or three bad novels. They weren't terrible books, but they weren't very good. His dream was beyond his reach, and like so many men, he wanted his son to accomplish what he could not. I think he harbored a resentment that I did not pick up the torch and do what he wanted.

"I look back on my childhood as quite idyllic. The incidents recounted in *The Dog Who Wouldn't Be* and *Owls in the Family* really happened. As a kid I was aware of tensions between my parents but didn't understand what they signified. In fact I did not understand until my father, at the age of seventy-two, left my mother for a thirty-five-year-old redhead and never came back. It would be years before I had any real sense of my mother. As a boy I had always taken the side of my father, who called my mother 'PDH' for Poor Dear Helen. He was mocking her, of course, for being so long-suffering. Quite late in her life, I moved to the town in which she lived. We became good friends, and I still feel guilty for not having taken her part. It took a lot of personal experience to bring me beyond macho male attitudes and assumptions.''[2]

"On the second day of September, 1939, I was painting the porch of our clapboard house in the rural Ontario town of Richmond Hill when my father pulled into the driveway at the helm of his red convertible. He looked as if he might have had a drink or two—high-colored and exhilarated.

"'Farley, my lad, there's bloody big news! *The war is on!* Nothing official yet, but the Regiment's been ordered to mobilize, and I'm to go back in with the rank of major, bum arm and all. There'll be a place for you too. You'll have to sweat

NOW A MAJOR MOTION PICTURE FROM WALT DISNEY PRODUCTIONS

FARLEY MOWAT

NEVER CRY WOLF

THE SPELLBINDING BESTSELLER. THE INCREDIBLE TRUE STORY OF LIFE AMONG ARCTIC WOLVES.

(Cover illustration by Walt Disney Productions from *Never Cry Wolf* by Farley Mowat.)

a bit for it, of course, but if you keep your nose clean and work like hell there'll be the King's Commission.'

"He spoke as if he was offering me a knighthood or, at the very least, membership in some exceedingly exclusive order.

"Slim, wiry and sharply handsome, my father still carried himself like the young soldier who had gone off in 1915 to fight in the Great War, fired by the ideals of Empire—a Soldier of the King—one of those gay young men whose sense of right, of chivalry, was to bait them into the uttermost reaches of hell. Although he had come back from Hades with his right arm made useless by German bullets, he nevertheless remained an impassioned supporter of the peacetime volunteer militia, and in particular of his own outfit, the Hastings and Prince Edward Regiment, an infantry unit composed of countrymen and townsmen from southeastern Ontario, which was familiarly if inelegantly known as the Hasty Pees.

"My father's news excited me tremendously, for I had long been inflamed by his fulminations against the Russophobe French, British and U.S. politicians and industrialists who had connived at the growth and spread of fascism, concealing their real admiration for it beneath the public explanation that it was the only trustworthy 'bulwark against communism.'. . .I believed that every healthy young man in the freedom-espousing countries was duty-bound to take up arms against the fascist plague and, in particular, the singularly bestial German brand.''[3]

"Well, of course, it's the old lie. My father believed it, and so, at first, did I. But the war changed my thinking radically.

I had had no real sense of fear, cruelty, madness, and horror before seeing combat in Italy. I thought I had, but I was wrong. I saved myself during the last part of my infantry experience by writing what would eventually become *The Dog Who Wouldn't Be.* Amid the bombs, grenades, strafing, death and dying, I tried to steep myself in the funny, idyllic world of my childhood. I also drew sustenance from the great poets of World War I, particularly Rupert Brooke and Wilfred Owen. I did not realize then that I would write a book about my experience during the war, and in fact the only reason I did so was out of fear that with Vietnam, the whole thing was about to happen all over again. I felt I had to raise my voice in protest against the possibility of more global carnage.''[2]

And No Birds Sang, which was published in 1979, was hailed as a masterpiece of its genre, on par with such classics as *The Red Badge of Courage* and *All Quiet on the Western Front.* Certainly it contains some of Mowat's most impassioned, vivid and precise prose: ''The blast flung me through the empty doorway with such violence that I sprawled full-length on top of a prone human figure who emitted a horrid gurgling belch. It was an unconscious protest, for he and two of his three companions—gray-clad paratroopers—were dead, their bodies mired in the muck and goat manure on the floor. The fourth man—dimly seen in that dim place—was sitting upright in a corner of the little unroofed room and his eyes met mine as I struggled to my hands and knees.

''In that instant I was so convinced that I had had it—that he would shoot me where I knelt—that I did not even try to reach for the carbine slung across my back. I remained transfixed for what seemed an interminable time, then in an unconscious reflex effort to cheat death, I flung myself sideways and rolled to my feet. I was lurching through the doorway when his thin voice reached me.

'' 'Vasser. . .haff. . .you. . .vasser?'

''I checked my rush and swung up against the outer wall, knowing then that I was safe, that he posed no threat. And I felt an inexplicable sense of recognition, almost as if I had heard his voice before. Cautiously I peered back through the doorway.

''His left hand was clasping the shattered stump where his right arm had been severed just below the elbow. Dark gore was still gouting between his fingers and spreading in a black pool about his outthrust legs. Most dreadful was a great gash in his side from which protruded a glistening dark mass which must have been his liver. Above this wreakage, his eyes were large and luminous in a young man's face, pallid to the point of translucency.

'' 'Vasser. . .please giff. . .vasser.'

''Reluctantly I shook my head. 'Sorry, chum, I've got none. *Nein* vasser. Only rum, and that's no good for you.'

''The eyes, so vividly alive in the dying body, pleaded with me. Oh, hell, I thought, he's going anyway. What harm!

''I held the water bottle to his lips and he swallowed in deep, spasmodic gulps until I took it back and drank from it myself. And so. . .the two of us got drunk together. And in a little while he died.''[3]

''I was demobilized in 1946 and, after buying a jeep, headed for Saskatchewan on a field trip to collect birds. I roamed the province, spending most of my time with the Indians. It was here that I lost all further interest in massacring little birds and

abandoned my plan to become a professional biologist. I began to consider a writing career, but attempts to write about the war proved abortive, although I did write a lot of poetry.

''I then took part in a two-man expedition to the Nueltin Lake area of central Keewatin nominally as a field biologist. But after the first few weeks, I decided to abandon 'shotgun biology' for good. I joined a young halfbreed on a canoe trip from Nueltin to Brochet, Manitoba and back with a canoe load of freight. On that journey I met the Eskimos and Indians and became enraged at their condition. I also saw the caribou migration I had seen a dozen years earlier. I prepared a 'Caribou Study Plan' and attempted to gain the support of the Arctic Institute but it was the federal government which took up the plan and agreed to employ me as a student biologist to implement it. I became enmeshed in the problems of the Eskimo, however, although I did spend considerable time studying wolves and caribou, and the government fired me. I then began to work seriously at writing and drew up the outline of material for *People of the Deer.* I sent the outline to *Atlantic Monthly,* and received enthusiastic support for the book which was subsequently published.''[4]

''After the war, I deliberately sought out solitude. I wanted to get away from my own species. I didn't like myself for being one of them. And going to the Arctic was marvelously salutary because I met the Eskimos—who were not of the damnable tribe called 'civilized man,' but rather suffering 'civilization's' effects—as well as the caribou and the wolves. To be more precise, it was not solitude I craved, although I thought so then, but isolation from my own kind.''[2]

Mowat spent two years living in an area called the Barrens, approximately half a million square miles west of Hudson Bay, with a tribe called the Ihalmiut (''People of the Deer''). The Ihalmiut, whose numbers had dwindled to about forty (only two of whom were women of childbearing age), were a flourishing tribe until the first white settlers arrived in 1900. At the turn of the century, they were still living as they had been since the Stone Age, off caribou that migrated through their lands four times a year. White traders persuaded them to hunt fox, which they could sell on the international market, in exchange for flour, sugar, lard, and baking powder. When the world market for fox fur collapsed, the traders left, leaving the Ihalmiut without food or supplies. The tribe, which had been subsisting for a generation on an unnatural diet had ceased training its young to hunt caribou. The result was mass starvation.

People of the Deer turned out to be an extremely controversial book. Mowat was viciously attacked by many in the Canadian scientific and political establishment for what they construed as errors and the author's excessive impressionability and preference for readability over accuracy. A cabinet minister went so far as to call Mowat a liar during a parliamentary debate. This did not surprise Mowat. It was his intention to skewer those whose policies and practices had made life difficult and, at times, impossible for the Ihalmiut Eskimos. So passionate, acrimonious and public was the controversy that almost overnight Mowat became a famous crusader. Criticism notwithstanding, the publication of *People of the Deer,* along with its sequel, *The Desperate People,* eventually resulted in fundamental changes by the Canadian government in the way it handled its dealings with the Eskimos in the Arctic territories.

The book also garnered a good deal of praise and admiration, not only for the author but for the ''People of the Deer.'' Albert Hubbell wrote in the *New Yorker:* ''To study the Ihalmiut, Mowat not only lived with them but undertook to learn the Eskimo language—something few white explorers or trav-

Mowat and his retriever, Edward, face a frigid Lake Ontario. ■ (Photograph copyright © by Thomas Victor.)

ellers have ever bothered to do. Two men of the tribe instructed him. Mowat did not know it at the time, but they devised a 'basic' Eskimo for his lessons, teaching him only one noun, and none of its variants, for a given object, and only one verb form for an action. The Ihalmiut spoke to him solely in this pidgin tongue and used it exclusively when talking among themselves in his presence. . . .He later became aware that the language is extraordinarily flexible and complex, that it can express many shades of meaning and many abstract thoughts, and that, grammatically, it is one of the toughest languages in the world, with verbs that can have up to five hundred endings and nouns that have nine cases. Mowat cites this experience as typical of the Eskimos' code of politeness and helpfulness; he believes that the Ihalmiut, who have respect for the white man but no very high opinion of his powers, felt that he would never be able to learn their language properly in the year or so he would be among them. . . .

"It is not often that a writer finds himself the sole chronicler of a whole human society, even of a microcosmic one like the Ihalmiut, and Mowat has done marvellously well at the job, despite a stylistic looseness and a tendency to formlessness. Also, his justifiable anger at the Canadian government's neglect of the Ihalmiut, who are its wards, intrudes in places where it doesn't belong, but then, as I said, Mowat is something of a fanatic on this subject. His book, just the same, is a fine one.''[5]

Writing in the *New York Times Book Review,* Walter O'Hearn called Mowat ''Canada's angriest young man'' and added that ''if we are at last fumbling toward a grasp of the Eskimo problem, the goading of Farley Mowat is one of the reasons. He has convictions and he can express them in prose that sears the conscience.''[6]

"Looking back on *People of the Deer,* I think perhaps I was a little too romantic. I don't say this because I would revise by one iota my indictment of the treatment the Ihalmiut suffered at the hands of what we generally refer to as 'civilization.' There are three reasons: one, I was very young; two, I really didn't know what the hell I was doing; three, I was desperate to see in my own species evidence of the values that had been destroyed for me during the Second World War. I don't think I shirked in the sense that I *totally* whitewashed primitive man. And I use 'primitive' in the best sense of the word. Primitive societies, as well as so-called civilized ones, can burst their bounds and become dangerous to themselves. There does exist aberration among primitive people. There is an incident I recount in *People of the Deer* which has to do with madness. Every so often, a member of the tribe would succumb to homicidal madness. That person had to be murdered, for the sake of the tribe, and he was. I am to this day of the opinion that primitive peoples generally deal with aberration in a much healthier, cleaner and contained way than do modern societies. Western societies tend to call these aberrations 'evil' and devise all sorts of complicated mindsets, mythologies and plans of action to deal with it. Primitive peoples tend not to judge. Their view would be that the aberrant person had become a bad animal in its environment, and consequently had to be eliminated. In primitive societies one cannot live at cross-purposes to the natural environment and survive.''[2]

The Desperate People, which appeared seven years after *People of the Deer,* got equally strong, if not stronger, reviews. For *Saturday Review,* the British critic Ivan Sanderson wrote that Mowat ''leans over backwards to be fair to [the Catholic and Protestant churches, the Royal Canadian Mounted Police and the Hudson's Bay Company, all of whom share responsibility for the demise of the People of the Deer]. . . .There are many damning quotes in this book. The pay-off is probably that of

(From the movie "Never Cry Wolf," starring Charles Martin Smith as a young biologist air-dropped into the Arctic wilderness to study wolves. Released by Walt Disney Productions, 1983.)

a government official, a Dr. Porsild, who stated, after the publication of Mr. Mowat's former book, 'I am sure that Farley Mowat is pleased with [an] award and perhaps a little amused too—for he has a keen sense of humor—that his plea for the understanding help without which these people will vanish from the earth has been heard. What worries me is that the Ihalmiut people never did exist except in Mowat's imagination.' So speaks authority, science, religion, and non-Eskimo 'humanity.' Not only the Ihalmiuts' existence but their plight has been fully documented for almost two decades in the files of the Canadian Government's departments concerned with their affairs. . . .Accounts of millions deliberately killed in prison camps are bad enough, but the story of a gentle people just as deliberately starved into virtual extinction in the name of 'kindness,' and religious 'soul-saving' is so utterly disgusting that it comes very close to destroying any respect one may have remaining for our own race.''[7]

Mowat's *Never Cry Wolf,* which became a best-seller and was made into a film both popularly and critically acclaimed, was in its way as controversial as his *People of the Deer*. When the book appeared in the Soviet Union, the title was translated as *Wolves, Please Don't Cry!*, a linguistic error that pleases Mowat because it nonetheless penetrated his thesis that wolves are among the most misunderstood and maligned animals on earth. Mowat's initial assignment, from the Wildlife Service of the Canadian government, was to investigate reports that hordes of wolves were slaughtering the Arctic caribou, thereby wreaking havoc on the ecosystem of the Barrens. He was dropped by airplane onto the frozen tundra where he spent approximately two years studying a particular family of wolves at unprecedented close range.

Mowat concluded that the wolves were not slaughtering the

caribou for the simple reason that wolves, as he was the first to discover, do not subsist on caribou meat, but rather on mice.

"I suppose it was only because my own wolf indoctrination had been so complete, and of such a staggeringly inaccurate nature, that it took me so long to account for the healthy state of the wolves in the apparent absence of any game worthy of their reputation and physical abilities. The idea of wolves not only eating, but actually thriving and raising their families on a diet of mice was so at odds with the character of the mythical wolf that it was really too ludicrous to consider. And yet, it was the answer to the problem of how my wolves were keeping the larder full.''[8]

"Now, I knew people in the scientific establishment who would think me insane—the mouse-wolf relationship was revolutionary. So I had to prove my thesis that mice were sufficiently nutritious to keep the wolf going. I needed a controlled experiment and a subject. As I was virtually the only one around, I selected myself as the subject for my experiment. Which meant that I would attempt to subsist wholly on a diet of mice.''[2]

"There being no time like the present, I resolved to begin the experiment at once. Having cleaned the basinful of small corpses which remained from my morning session of mouse skinning, I placed them in a pot and hung it over my primus stove. The pot gave off a most delicate and delicious odor as the water boiled, and I was in excellent appetite by the time the stew was done.

"Eating these small mammals presented something of a problem at first because of the numerous minute bones; however, I found that the bones could be chewed and swallowed without

(Cover illustration from *The Serpent's Coil* by Farley Mowat.)

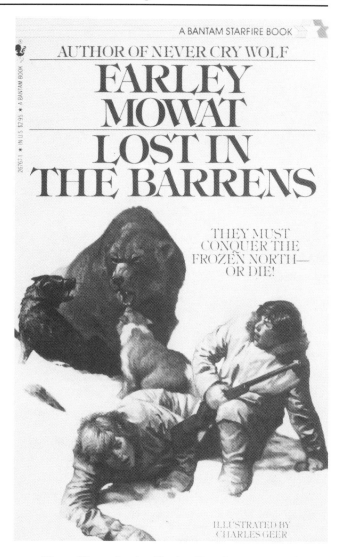

(Cover illustration by Charles Geer from *Lost in the Barrens* by Farley Mowat.)

much difficulty. The taste of the mice—a purely subjective factor and not in the least relevant to the experiment—was pleasing if rather bland. As the experiment progressed, this blandness led to a degree of boredom and a consequent loss of appetite and I was forced to seek variety in my methods of preparation.

"Of the several recipes which I developed, the finest by far was Creamed Mouse. . . ."[8] *Never Cry Wolf* is duly graced with Mowat's recipe for *Souris a la Creme.*

"Much of what I discovered about wolves flies in the face of our received notions about this species. I learned that wolves mate for life, live in devoted family groups which absorb widowed relations as members of the nuclear family unit, are extremely affectionate and playful, and are far less violent than man. I never saw a wolf commit a wanton act of destruction, cruelty, or maliciousness.

"But our attitudes die hard. Even after close to two years of living at very close range to my family of wolves I had a reaction one day that absolutely horrified me. The one thing left for me to do was to enter the family's den. I finally did, when I thought the wolves were not at home. To my astonishment, at least one adult and pup were there. I was terrified, certain for the instant that they would kill me for having tres-

passed. I hate to say this, but if I had had my rifle with me, I think I might have killed them."[2]

"Mine had been the fury of resentment born of fear: resentment against the beasts who had engendered naked terror in me and who, by so doing, had intolerably affronted my human ego.

"I was appalled at the realization of how easily I had forgotten, and how readily I had denied, all that. . .the wolves had taught me about them. . .and about myself. I thought of Angeline and her pup cowering at the bottom of the den where they had taken refuge. . .and I was ashamed.

"Somewhere to the eastward a wolf howled; lightly, questioningly. I knew the voice, for I had heard it many times before. It was George, sounding the wasteland for an echo from the missing members of his family. But for me it was a voice which spoke of a lost world which once was ours before we chose the alien role; a world which I had glimpsed and almost entered. . .only to be excluded, at the end, by my own self."[8]

"We must develop a new ethos whereby we apply the same morality to other forms of life that we apply to our own species. That old notion of 'scientific objectivity' and the practice of observing from afar is not only useless as far as I'm concerned but egregious. Not by those means will we ever penetrate the inner sanctum of animal life. You have to be subjective, you have to use your senses, your emotions, your viscera. Your intellect alone will never win you access. In this sense I am proud to say that I am not a scientist. I am not a 'picker-up' of facts. I live life and that is a distinction most scientists don't understand. Nobody really knows very much about what goes on in the heads of other animals, but those of us who have had tiny glimpses into the intimate lives of other, particularly mammalian, species all say essentially the same thing: these animals are more closely related to us than previously was imagined. The primates, for instance, have in embryo all of the faculties and capacities that humans possess. We know they feel pain. A lot of people still refuse to concede that other animals feel pain, even though it has been demonstrated clinically that some species feel pain to a greater degree than humans. There is no question in my mind that animals feel everything we feel. The only difference may be the matter of degree. We must act upon this recognition. Otherwise, we will lose any possibility remaining to us for harmony on this planet."[2]

One of Mowat's saddest books, *A Whale for the Killing,* grew out of a community's apparent disbelief that whales suffer pain after the slaughter of a pregnant Fin Whale that had wandered mistakenly into the village's inlet. The village was Burgeo, an outport in the Canadian Maritimes where Mowat and his wife had lived for several years in what they thought was

harmony with the locals. It was perhaps the enormity of the animal that hardened people to her, made them think she was invincible. A fisherman who approached Mowat for help, described the spectacle this way:

"'Twas something like I never seen before. There was that crowd from down The Reach, one of them fellers on every point, and carrying on like they had all gone right foolish. There was yelling and jumping, and hauling away on bottles, and shooting at the whale, and yelling some more. There was bullets flying every which way. 'Twas a wonder some of them never killed the others. . . .

"The creature was drove clean crazy! She got herself into the shoal water on the eastward side of the Pond, the farthest she could get from them fellers, and there wasn't no more than just enough water to keep her afloat. And beat the water! My dear man, her tail and flippers was flying in the air! 'Twas a desperate sight, I tell you. And all the while you could hear the thump of them bullets just a-pounding into her.'"[9]

Saving the whale became a consuming passion for Mowat. He and a small circle of friends tried valiantly for days to guide her back to the open sea, but she was too wounded and disoriented. Mowat also waged a media offensive to make the violent ones desist. But many in the town saw the whale as a beginning of what might be a lucrative tourist trade for Burgeo. (And many did come to see the whale in her strange captivity.) Mowat was made the butt of malicious jokes and

(From the television movie, "A Whale for the Killing," starring Kathryn Walker with Peter Strauss and Richard Widmark. Presented on ABC's "Sunday Night Movie," February 1, 1981.)

a public smear campaign. "Moby Joe is dead and gone/Farley Mowat, he won't stay long, . . ." crowds chanted as Mowat made his way through the village.

The whale eventually died a gruesome, excruciating death. She presented a health hazard owing to the infections resulting from her numerous open wounds. Many in the town feared that her proximity to the Burgeo fish canning plant would force it to close, causing unemployment. Her gigantic corpse would be a peril to ship traffic. In the ensuing pandemonium which broke out among local officials, Mowat, his wife and their close companions mourned.

"For the first time since the trapped whale vanished, I became fully aware of a rending sense of loss. It was dark, and there was none to know that I was weeping. . .weeping not just for the whale that died, but because the fragile link between her race and mine was severed.

"I wept, because I knew that this fleeting opportunity to bridge, no matter how tenuously, the ever-widening chasm that is isolating mankind from the totality of life, had perished in a welter of human stupidity and ignorance—some part of which was mine.

"I wept, not for the loneliness which would now be Claire's and mine as aliens among people we had grown to love, but for the inexpressibly greater loneliness which Man, having made himself the ultimate stranger on his own planet, has doomed himself to carry into the silence of his final hour."[9]

Mowat, in his continuing search for an explanation, cannot bring himself to make a blanket indictment of the whale's killers. "The point is, the people who killed the whale had been infected with the virus of western civilization. They had left the outport to work on ships plying the Great Lakes; many had lived for a while in the cities of Toronto and Hamilton. They brought the virus with them. Those who fished Burgeo's waters in an unbroken chain over generations did not participate in the massacre."[2]

He contends that, of all his books, *Sea of Slaughter* was by far the most difficult to write. A number of reviewers, including those within the international scientific establishment, cited it as Mowat's most ambitious, and most important work to date. It is, in sum, a history from 1500-1980 of man's over-exploitation of the North Atlantic, which has resulted in legion numbers of extinct, dying and seriously reduced species. Using captains' logs, the records of shipping and trading companies, personal diaries and correspondence as well as other primary material, Mowat documents four centuries of mass killing-for-profit from the standpoint of the victims. One of the most striking of his findings is the vast amount of waste entailed in commercial fishing.

"[There is] a misconception that has been of great service to those responsible for the recent 'management' of the seal herds: namely that the number of seals *destroyed* has always been, and remains, essentially the same as the number of sculps *landed*. Even in the net fishery this assumption is untrue, since a very large percentage of netted seals are pregnant females, the death of each of which represents two lives lost.

"As applied to the gun fishery, it is also false. Prior to the breeding season, when they are still fat but not fully buoyant, at least half the adult harp seals killed in open water will sink before they can be recovered. In addition, most of those hit are only wounded and will dive and not be seen again. Of those adults killed outright in the water *after* the breeding season, when the fat reserves of both sexes have largely been

exhausted, as many as four out of five will sink and so be lost."[10]

Mowat also documents the horror that routinely has been part of commercial expeditions after birds, fish and fowl. The following account is from the writings of one Aaron Thomas, who worked Funk Island (so named because of the incredible stench resulting from the killing of the island's wildlife) toward the end of the eighteenth century, "While you abide on this Island you are in the constant practice of horrid cruelties, for you not only Skin [the Penguins] *Alive,* but you burn them *Alive* also. . .You take a Kettle with you and kindle the fire under it, and this fire is absolutely made from the unfortunate Penguins themselves."[10]

"Writing this book was the most terrible five years of my life I wish I could forget. It was a descent into Dante's innermost circle of hell. Three times I told myself, 'You can't go on with this.' I had started out to do a rather slim book on recent extinctions. A little pamphleteering, let us say. But as so often happens with me, the book took charge. Which means my subconscious took charge and led me to do a book I had not intended.

"The research for *Sea of Slaughter* yielded tens of thousands of pages. Fortunately, I had hired two undergraduates from the University of Montreal to amass documents. I had a good idea of what I was looking for and where it might be, so they weren't totally untethered. Quite apart from the psychic wear and tear, the physical job of going through and selecting source material was arduous.

"My purpose, of course, was not simply to depress everyone, including myself, but it was a warning that we must change our attitudes toward the species with which we inhabit this earth. We must, in every sense, *share* the planet with them, or we will become its ultimate destroyers. I could not effectively make my warning without impressing upon people that the earth was once *very different and much richer* than it presently is. We humans have a marvelous capacity for forgetting that which we don't wish to remember. People can easily lose sight of the fact that when they were kids, there were a hell of a lot more birds around, for example. We have a terrible tendency to assume that what we see is what always was. Not so. We have a responsibility to look back in anger and to use that anger to try to salvage the present and ensure the future."[2]

Sea of Slaughter became controversial beyond Mowat's wildest imaginings. On the morning of April 23, 1985 he was scheduled to leave for an extended publicity tour in the U.S., but was turned back by United States Immigrations and Naturalization Service [INS] officials at the Toronto airport, who disallowed him from entering the country because his name was listed in the *Lookout Book*. The *Lookout Book* dates from the 1922 McCarran-Walter Act which bars the admission of individuals who are suspected of being Communists, anarchists or spies. Both the law and the book are vehemently contested by a number of Congressional members as well as by the American Civil Liberties Union, which has called attention to what it considers notable errors in the listings, which include such cultural luminaries as Gabriel Garcia Marquez, Carlos Fuentes and Ernesto Cardenal Martinez, a Roman Catholic priest, poet and Nicaragua's Minister of Culture. According to the INS, Mowat's name landed in the *Lookout Book* because in 1968 he showed his objection to the United States flying SAC aircraft loaded with hydrogen bombs over the Canadian Prairies by firing his .22 calibre rifle at the planes from his backyard. In *My Discovery of America*, in which Mowat details his odyssey with the INS, Mowat disputes this contention. "Do you think I'm mad? Why, suppose I'd brought one down!

Mowat and his Labrador, Tom, frolic on the lawn. ■ (Photograph by John de Visser.)

The consequent explosion would have eliminated half of Newfoundland."[11]

Further digging by journalists revealed a strong possibility that anti-environmentalists and the gun lobby were behind the State Department's inclusion of Mowat in the *Lookout Book*. Mowat is utterly convinced that this is the case. When U.S. officials finally agreed to compromise by 'paroling' him and thereby allowing him to enter the country to do his tour—by then hopelessly off-schedule—Mowat responded, "I'm the injured party here. So my bottom line is a free trip to Los Angeles in Air Force One, *after* it has delivered President Reagan's letter of apology."[11]

Mowat has not traveled to the U.S. and has no plans to make the attempt. "I had a sweet revenge, after all. Not only did I get mountains of supportive mail from every corner of the United States but *Sea of Slaughter* got more publicity than otherwise it would have. Thanks, INS! And for my following book, *Woman in the Mists*, I got to stay home and do my publicity 'tour' by satellite—eighteen cities at one time."[2]

Woman in the Mists, Mowat's latest book, is a biography of Dian Fossey, the renowned "gorilla lady" of Rwanda. American-born Fossey spent decades living in the African jungle doing ground-breaking research on gorillas. In December, 1985, she was found brutally murdered in her cabin. By all accounts, Fossey was passionate, temperamental, charismatic, driven,

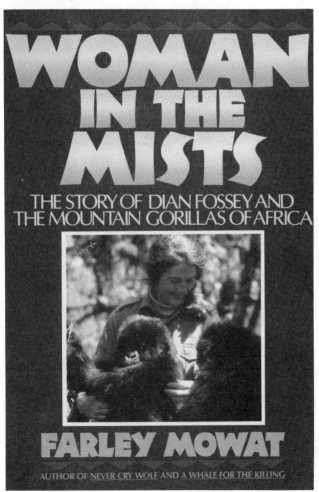

(Jacket photograph by Robert Campbell from *Woman in the Mists: The Story of Dian Fossey and the Mountain Gorillas of Africa* by Farley Mowat.)

difficult to work with and zealously devoted to the well-being of African gorillas. She tirelessly fought government tourist agencies, zoos, certain environmental organizations and fellow scientists she perceived as withholding support for her project or competing with her.

"This was a book I did not want to do, for the simple reason that I had never before written a book at someone else's suggestion. Against my principles. But once I started reading her diaries and correspondence, I was hooked. Here was a great woman. I incorporated a lot of material from her own writings because she was a strong and powerful writer. For me to have read and paraphrased her work would have been an indecency."[2]

"[Writing *Woman in the Mists*] was a disturbing experience. It's almost as though I were possessed. I wasn't the master. I fought for mastery but I didn't win. It really was a transcendental experience and I'm uncomfortable with it."[12]

He found Fossey's tragically misunderstood life and violent death profoundly disturbing. "Practically all accusations against her are false. She drank heavily when things were unbearable, but she wasn't an alcoholic. She wasn't a nymphomaniac but she liked to make love. Bestiality wasn't her thing, not even in fantasy life. And she wasn't a racist. What impressed me was her honesty. She was always willing to face herself. Her touchstone was integrity. She did betray her integrity on occasion and she went through hell. She wasn't essentially an extraordinary person. . . .but she was indomitable. . . ., I learned a lot about people. I learned that the evil within us is endemic. It probably should not be called evil. I learned that every single. . .[one] of us is victimized, and that we victimize ourselves. We do it against our best wishes or intentions."[12]

Mowat, who has written books for young as well as adult readers, says he prefers writing for kids and adolescents. "Once people become adults, you can't get through to them anymore. A shame, really, because we can learn and change all through our lives if we let ourselves.

"I'm a storyteller in the same tradition as the old saga men who told their tales to a live audience. The saga man was a moralist, in a sense, passing on sugar-coated ethical concepts. But it's the *tale* that grabs people's attention, the tale they can't get out of their minds, long after the telling of it has passed.

"Now, of course, the ancient saga men were *tellers* of tales, I am a writer. I do use a lot of oral material in my work, bits I've overheard, parts of legends, stories and conversations. I do this in all of my work, but perhaps nowhere more so than in *The Snow Walker*."[2]

The Snow Walker, fictional stories based on his time in the Arctic, was generally well-received in the press. The *New York Times Book Review* was particularly laudatory. "[It] is a book of tales about the Eskimo, stories ranging from the ancient to the overwhelmingly modern. It is passionate, harsh, with a mythic density that puts a great strain on the reader. In fact, the reader will assuredly come up feeling more than vaguely unclean.

"History is forgetful but ultimately unforgiving, and in *The Snow Walker* Mowat draws us into the beauty and anguish of an extirpated culture, perhaps more than a culture, a microcosmic civilization. The beauty of the tales purge, exhaust, draw us out of our skin, but the pain involved is so deep that we feel the free-floating remorse that characterizes modern man on those rare occasions he has the wit and humility to turn around and look at his spoor."[13]

Asked if he was optimistic or pessimistic regarding the future of homo sapiens, Mowat answered, "If I have one little bit of blind hope this is it: I don't believe that even we will have the capacity for totally eliminating life on this planet. We may come pretty bloody close, but I don't think we can do it. I suspect that the impulse of life is so enormously powerful that one bad species, one bad apple, so to speak, can't rot the whole barrel."²

FOOTNOTE SOURCES

¹Terry McDougall, "The Wanderer at Home," *Canadian Heritage*, October, 1980.

²Based on an interview by Marguerite Feitlowitz for *Something about the Author*.

³Farley Mowat, *And No Birds Sang*, McClelland & Stewart, 1979.

⁴*Something about the Author*, Volume 3, Gale, 1972.

⁵Albert Hubbell, "Two from up North," *New Yorker*, April 26, 1952.

⁶Walter O'Hearn, "People of the Deer," *New York Times Book Review*, November 1, 1959.

⁷Ivan Sanderson, "Book in the News," *Saturday Review*, November 28, 1959.

⁸F. Mowat, *Never Cry Wolf*, Bantam, 1964.

⁹F. Mowat, *A Whale for the Killing*, Bantam, 1972.

¹⁰F. Mowat, *Sea of Slaughter*, Atlantic Monthly Press, 1984.

¹¹F. Mowat, *My Discovery of America*, Atlantic Monthly Press, 1985.

¹²Beverly Slopen, "Farley Mowat," *Publishers Weekly*, October 2, 1987.

¹³Jim Harrison, "The Snow Walker," *New York Times Book Review*, February 22, 1976.

FOR MORE INFORMATION SEE:

Saturday Evening Post, July 29, 1950, April 13, 1957.
New Yorker, April 26, 1952, May 11, 1968, March 17, 1980.
Illustrated London News, September 20, 1952.
Spectator, November 21, 1952.
Wilson Library Bulletin, February, 1961.
Scientific American, March, 1964.
Maclean's, March, 1968, October 8, 1979.
Nation, June 10, 1968.
Joseph E. Carver, "Farley Mowat, an Author for All Ages," *British Columbia Library Bulletin*, April, 1969.
Christian Science Monitor, May 15, 1969, May 10, 1970, April 15, 1971, March 6, 1974.
Times Literary Supplement, March 19, 1971, February 16, 1973.
Dorothy A. Marquardt and Martha E. Ward, *Authors of Books for Young People*, 2nd edition, Scarecrow, 1971.
Economist, January 15, 1972.
Book World, December 31, 1972.
Doris de Montreville, editor, *Third Book of Junior Authors*, H. W. Wilson, 1972.
Audubon, January, 1973.
Observer, March 4, 1973.
F. Mowat, "A Message from the Patron," *Canadian Library Journal*, September-October, 1973.
F. Mowat, "Owls in the Family," *Cricket*, March, 1974.
Canadian Geographical Journal, June, 1974.
Canadian Forum, July, 1974, March, 1976.
Saturday Night, November, 1975.
John Wakeman, *World Authors: 1950-1970*, H. W. Wilson, 1975.
Alec Lucas, "Farley Mowat: Writer for Young People," *Canadian Children's Literature*, number 5-6, 1976 (p. 40).
A. Lucas, *Farley Mowat* (critical study), McClelland & Stewart, 1976.
Sierra, September, 1978.

D. L. Kirkpatrick, editor, *Twentieth-Century Children's Writers*, St. Martin's, 1978, 2nd edition, 1983.
Time, February 18, 1980 (p. 87), May 6, 1985, October 26, 1987.
"Disney Taps Ballard for 'Wolf' Feature; Gives Points in Pic," *Variety*, March 5, 1980.
Cheryl McCall, "To Canadian Author Farley Mowat, the Place Where No Birds Sang Was a Chilling Wasteland," *People Weekly*, March 31, 1980 (p. 65).
"In Search of Farley Mowat" (biographical film), National Film Board of Canada, 1981.
"Meet the Author: Farley Mowat" (cassette; filmstrip with cassette), Mead Sound Filmstrips, 1986.
Kit Pearson, "A Second Look: Owls in the Family," *Horn Book*, July-August, 1987 (p. 440).

COLLECTIONS

Mowat's manuscripts are housed at McMaster University, Hamilton, Ontario, Canada.

NAKATANI, Chiyoko   1930-1981

PERSONAL: Born January 16, 1930, in Tokyo, Japan; died December 26, 1981; daughter of Teisuke (an industrial engineer) and Toshiko (Sato) Nagano; married Sadahiko Nakatani (a university professor and painter), March 5, 1953. *Education:* Tokyo National University of Fine Arts and Music, B.A., 1952; also studied in France and Switzerland. *Home:* Tokyo, Japan.

CAREER: Writer and illustrator of books for children. Has also given painting lessons to children. *Member:* Japanese Board on Books for Young People. *Awards, honors:* New York Herald Tribune's Children's Spring Book Festival Honor Book, 1968, for *The Brave Little Goat of Monsieur Sequin; The Brave Little Goat of Monsieur Seguin* was chosen one of Child Study Association of America's Children's Books of the Year, 1968, *The Lion and the Bird's Nest*, 1973; Prize from Kodansha Publishing Co., 1970, for *Machi no nezumi to inaka no nezumi*.

WRITINGS:

SELF-ILLUSTRATED

The Day Chiro Was Lost, Bodley Head, 1968, World Publishing, 1969.
Taro to iruka, Fukuinkan, 1969, translation published as *Fumio and the Dolphins: A Picture Story from Japan*, World Publishing, 1970.
Machi no nezumi to inaka no nezumi (adapted from Ruri Nagano's translation of an English adaptation of Aesop's fable, "A Town Mouse and a Country Mouse"), Fukuinkan, 1971.
Boku no uchi no dobutsuen, Fukuinkan, 1971, translation published as *The Zoo in My Garden*, Crowell, 1973.
My Teddy Bear, Crowell, 1976.
My Day on the Farm, Crowell, 1976.
My Treasures, Bodley Head, 1979.
My Animal Friends, Bodley Head, 1979.
Feeding Babies, Bodley Head, 1981.
Animal Opposites, Heian International, 1981.

ILLUSTRATOR

Eriko Kishida, *Hippopotamus*, Prentice-Hall, 1963.
E. Kishida, *Wake Up, Hippopotamus*, Bodley Head, 1967.
E. Kishida, *The Hippo Boat*, Bodley Head, 1967, World Publishing, 1968.
Trude Alberti, *The Animals' Lullaby*, World Publishing, 1967.

CHIYOKO NAKATANI

Alphonse Daudet, *The Brave Little Goat of Monsieur Seguin,* World Publishing, 1968.

Soya Kiyoshi, *Raru no tanjobi* (title means ''The Kitten Ru- ru's Birthday''), [Japan], 1971.

E. Kishida, *The Lion and the Bird's Nest,* Crowell, 1973.

Also illustrator of Mutsuko Watari's, *The Little Old Lady in the Strawberry Patch,* Bodley Head.

SIDELIGHTS: ''Since my childhood I have liked drawing pic- tures imagining scenes of my favorite fairy tales. After grad- uating from the university I held after-school painting classes for children in my home. It was in those days that I began to illustrate children's books with enthusiasm. I wanted to make good picture books for children in order to add a good element to their environment.

''I am interested in traveling. I especially like to go to places, such as mountains and stock farms, which are not contami- nated by modern civilization. I have a country house at the seaside, one hundred fifty kilometers from Tokyo. The house is situated in a beautiful place between the Pacific Ocean and the mountains. I draw pictures and do lithographs there. Dur- ing the spring and summer holidays, my beloved nephews often come from Tokyo to stay for several days. I enjoy taking a walk, fishing, and swimming with them. While observing children's emotions, new ideas for books spring up inside me.

''When I illustrate children's books, I like to draw realistic pictures to express the scenes of the stories. I consider the rhythms of lines and the harmony of colors to be most important.''

FOR MORE INFORMATION SEE:

Bettina Hurlimann, *Picture-Book World,* World Publishing, 1969.

Martha E. Ward and Dorothy A. Marquardt, *Illustrators of Books for Young People,* Scarecrow, 1975.

B. Hurlimann, *Seven Houses,* Bodley Head, 1976.

Lee Kingman and others, compilers, *Illustrators of Children's Books: 1967-1976*, Horn Book, 1978.

NORTHCOTT, (William) Cecil   1902-1987
(Mary Miller, Arthur Temple)

OBITUARY NOTICE: Born April 5, 1902, in Buckfast, Devonshire, England; died November 10, 1987. Clergyman, editor, journalist, and author. An ordained Congregationalist minister, Northcott is best remembered as the editorial secretary of the United Society for Christian Literature, a post he assumed in 1952. He was also involved with many other religious organizations, including the London Missionary Society, the World Council of Churches, and the United Council for Missionary Education, and served as an editor for Lutterworth Press from 1952 to 1972. Affiliated with religious periodicals such as *Congregational Monthly* and *Christian Century*, Northcott served as the church's correspondent for the London *Daily Telegraph*.

A prolific writer as well as an able editor, Northcott wrote numerous religious books. Using the pseudonym Mary Miller, he wrote several for children, including *Bible Encyclopedia for Children, Jesus, the Good Shepherd, Jesus, the Saviour, Great Stories of the Bible, The Greatest Name of All*, and *Children's Prayers and Praises*. Occasionally using the pseudonym Arthur Temple, he wrote numerous adult books on religious subjects as well, including *Who Claims the World? An Attempt to Present the Case for the Christian Missionary Enterprise, No Strangers Here: Meditations on the Gospel and the Church in the World*, and *Religious Liberty*. Northcott was also greatly interested in the exploration of Africa, and penned the biographies *Robert Moffat: Pioneer in Africa* and *David Livingstone: His Triumph, Decline, and Fall*, among others.

FOR MORE INFORMATION SEE:

Clare D. Kinsman and Mary Ann Tennenhouse, editors, *Contemporary Authors*, Volumes 9-12, Gale, 1974.

OBITUARIES

Times (London), November 12, 1987.
Washington Post, February 27, 1988.

ORMEROD, Jan(ette Louise)   1946-

PERSONAL: Born September 23, 1946, in Bunbury, Western Australia; daughter of Jack and Thelma (Harvey) Hendry; married Paul Ormerod (an information scientist), January 21, 1971; children: Sophie, Laura. *Education:* Western Australian Institute of Technology, Associateship in Graphic Design, 1966, Associateship in Art Teaching, 1973; Claremont Teachers College, Perth, Western Australia, Teacher's Certificate, 1967. *Home:* Cambridge, England. *Agent:* Laura Cecil, 17 Alwyne Villas, London N1 2HG, England.

CAREER: Western Australian Education Department, Bunbury, Applecross, art teacher, 1968-72; Mt. Lawley College of Advanced Education, Perth, Western Australia, lecturer in art education, 1973-75; Western Australian Institute of Technology, Perth, part-time lecturer in drawing and basic design, 1976-79; author and illustrator of children's books, 1981—. *Member:* Society of Authors. *Awards, honors:* Mother Goose Award, Australian Picture Book of the Year Award from the Australian Children's Book Council, and Kate Greenaway Award Commendation from the British Library Association,

JAN ORMEROD

all 1982, all for *Sunshine; Dad's Back, Messy Baby, Reading, Sleeping*, and *Young Joe* were each selected one of Child Study Association of America's Children's Books of the Year, 1985.

WRITINGS:

JUVENILE; SELF-ILLUSTRATED

Sunshine (ALA Notable Book), Lothrop, 1981.
Moonlight (ALA Notable Book), Lothrop, 1982.
Be Brave, Billy, Dent, 1983.
101 Things to Do with a Baby, Lothrop, 1984.
Young Joe, Lothrop, 1985.
(Reteller) *The Story of Chicken Licken* (ALA Notable Book), Walker, 1985, Lothrop, 1986.
Just Like Me, Lothrop, 1986.
Our Ollie, Lothrop, 1986.
Silly Goose, Lothrop, 1986.
Bend and Stretch (ALA Notable Book), Lothrop, 1987.
Making Friends (ALA Notable Book), Lothrop, 1987.
Mom's Home (ALA Notable Book), Lothrop, 1987.
This Little Nose (ALA Notable Book), Lothrop, 1987.

"JAN ORMEROD BABY BOOK" SERIES; SELF-ILLUSTRATED

Dad's Back (ALA Notable Book), Lothrop, 1985.
Messy Baby (ALA Notable Book), Lothrop, 1985.
Sleeping (ALA Notable Book), Lothrop, 1985.
Reading (ALA Notable Book), Lothrop, 1985.

ILLUSTRATOR

Jan Mark, *Hairs in the Palm of the Hand*, Kestrel, 1981.
Margaret Mahy, *The Chewing Gum Rescue and Other Stories*, Dent, 1982.

Pat Thompson, compiler, *Rhymes around the Day,* Lothrop, 1983.

Karin Lorentzen, *Lanky Longlegs,* translated by Joan Tate, Atheneum, 1983.

Sarah Hayes, *Happy Christmas, Gemma,* Lothrop, 1986.

J. M. Barrie, *Peter Pan,* Lothrop, 1988.

S. Hayes, *Eat up Gemma,* Lothrop, 1988.

S. Hayes, *Stamp Your Feet,* Lothrop, 1988.

WORK IN PROGRESS: The Saucepan Game; Two for the Zoo.

SIDELIGHTS: "In retrospect, nothing in my life was irrelevant. Everything I've experienced was part of a long, long buildup to the work I'm doing now. I trained as a graphic designer and taught art education. My husband, Paul, worked primarily as a college librarian, but he became a children's librarian for a brief time—just at the right time—when our daughter Sophie was born.

"When Paul brought children's books home for Sophie, he hooked me too! Sophie was absolutely fascinated by stories about the complexities of her life, and she showed great enjoyment in looking at pictures of other children. Her response motivated me. I became interested in recording stories. This new interest coincided with what I was learning about human relationships and having a marriage turn into a family.

"Paul and I decided that I should get a portfolio together to show what I could do—and we'd go to London and see if it could happen. Things were good in Australia at the time, so we felt confident. We resigned our jobs, rented our house, packed up our child, and off we went.

"In London I got on the phone and made appointments, and knocked on doors, and just turned up. Unconventional, but it worked."

Ormerod's family enjoys sharing books. "It must come from the way [my husband] uses books. Books are so much a part of his life, and he always wants to share them with other people.

"Sophie often reads to me now. She has picked up the feeling that to communicate with books and about books is a very warm and meaningful way to share ideas. This starts at the very beginning, in infancy. A book is rarely looked at by a child alone. The parent and the child share the story. Some of the best times I have with my girls come while sharing books. That's the way my books are conceived in my mind—as a joint experience. I have great sympathy for, and I identify with, young parents. I'm talking to them as well as to their children.

"Sophie. . .was the model for the little girl in both *Sunshine* and *Moonlight.* Her sister Laura. . .was the baby in the 'Baby Books,' and the model for the girl in *Silly Goose.* In fact, Laura now claims that she is the girl in *Sunshine* and *Moonlight.*"

Children's responses to Ormerod's books have made her more aware of her work. "I didn't think of *Sunshine* going out into

(From *Sunshine* by Jan Ormerod. Illustrated by the author.)

the world. It just seemed such a fantastic thing to have a book in print. Then I began to get so many reactions! I received a tape of a child talking it through, telling her mother what the story was.

"Once you've had such a response, your internal dialogue about what you are doing and what you hope to get out of it comes a lot clearer. I want children to have to search my drawings. On the surface they seem simple, but there is more in the drawings than the surface shows.

"When Laura was born, Sophie was seven. I was just delighted to see their relationship; they looked so beautiful together—I wanted to draw them. *101 Things to Do with a Baby* comes very directly from our family experience. In one series of pictures, the father is holding the baby, and the text doesn't say anything about the older child's jealousy and wish to be held. The expression of great satisfaction on her face and resigned amusement on his face when he pays attention to her too has to be looked for and interpreted. The joy and the jealousy are all part of life's rich mix.

"I like to see children who communicate with the whole of themselves. That's what I try to bring to the page. . .the expressive quality a movement can add."

Parents and children need to talk about the emotions they see in a book. "That was not one of my aims when I started, but it is now—very much. It's of profound importance for a child and an adult to have that sort of dialogue. If this habit is established when a child is a toddler, it will continue when the family is facing more complex issues later on."

A nurturing father is included in her books. "It's what I see around me. Since Laura was born, Paul has been the houseperson. He takes care of all the traditional female duties so I can keep working."

"The 'Baby Books' started with a set of ideas about a crawling baby and a cat exploring the house together. I was intrigued by the parallels between the cat and the baby. They seemed to be at the same stage. Both were intensely curious—they would look into a box in the same way. The cat has since dropped behind. Father appeared of his own free will in a drawing and suddenly it seemed a much richer concept.

"I find reality so fabulous. All I want to do is observe and record.

"I have recently moved to Cambridge, England where I live within a mile of the city centre."

FOR MORE INFORMATION SEE:

Times Literary Supplement, July 24, 1981, July 23, 1982.
New York Times, November 29, 1982.

OSBORNE, Mary Pope 1949-

PERSONAL: Born May 20, 1949, in Fort Sill, Okla.; daughter of William P. (a U.S. Army colonel) and Barnette (Dickens) Pope; married Will Osborne (an actor), May 16, 1976. *Education:* University of North Carolina at Chapel Hill, B.A., 1971. *Home and office:* 325 Bleecker St., #18, New York, N.Y. 10014. *Agent:* Sheldon Fogelman, 10 East 40th St., New York, N.Y. 10016.

CAREER: Writer. *Member:* PEN International, Authors Guild. *Awards, honors:* Woodward Park School Annual Book Award

MARY POPE OSBORNE

(Brooklyn, N.Y.), and Children's Choice from the International Reading Association and the Children's Book Council, both 1983, and chosen Most Popular Children's Novel of the Northern Territory of Australia, 1986, all for *Run, Run, as Fast as You Can; Last One Home* was selected one of Child Study Association of America's Children's Books of the Year, 1986.

WRITINGS:

FOR YOUNG PEOPLE

Run, Run, as Fast as You Can, Dial, 1982.
Love Always, Blue, Dial, 1983.
Best Wishes, Joe Brady, Dial, 1984.
Mo to the Rescue (illustrated by Dyanne Disalvo-Ryan), Dial, 1985.
Last One Home, Dial, 1986.
(Reteller) *Beauty and the Beast* (illustrated by Winslow Pinney Pels), Scholastic, 1987.
Christopher Columbus: Admiral of the Sea, Dell, 1987.
Pandora's Box (illustrated by Lisa Amoroso), Scholastic, 1987.
(With husband, Will Osborne) *Jason and the Argonauts,* Scholastic, 1988.
(With W. Osborne) *Deadly Power of Medusa,* Scholastic, 1988.

WORK IN PROGRESS: A collection of Greek myths retold for young people.

SIDELIGHTS: "My childhood was spent on different Army posts with my parents, two brothers, and sister. We lived mostly in the southern United States with a three year stay in Salzburg, Austria. When I was fifteen my father retired and my family settled permanently in North Carolina. After graduation from the University of North Carolina at Chapel Hill in 1971, I resumed my travels. I lived in Europe and spent a year traveling overland through Asia to Nepal. Back in the States in 1973, I settled in Monterey, California, and worked as a medical assistant. In 1974, I moved to Washington, D.C., and began work as a travel agent, specializing in Eastern European and Russian tours. I moved to New York in 1975 and worked with the Russian Travel Bureau until I married actor Will

One night Beauty dreamed of her father. ■ (From *Beauty and the Beast*, retold by Mary Pope Osborne. Illustrated by Winslow Pinney Pels.)

Osborne in the spring of 1976. The day after our wedding we took off on a theater tour.

"While on the road with Will, I began writing. In 1979, I wrote a young adult novel, *Run, Run, as Fast as You Can*, about a girl whose family retires from the military and settles in the South. Dial Press bought the manuscript, and my editor, Amy Ehrlich, helped me develop it. Amy has also been a big influence on other young adult books, including *Love Always, Blue, Best Wishes, Joe Brady* and *Last One Home*. I have recently begun to supplement my fiction writing with retellings of mythology and fairy tales and biographies of people I am interested in. I feel that the years I spent traveling in Asia, the different jobs I've held, the theater career of my husband, our life in New York among a small community of writers, actors, musicians, and artists, my southern military background, my family, my editor, my work with runaway teenagers, and my interests in philosophy and mythology have all informed and shaped my work."

FOR MORE INFORMATION SEE:

Baltimore Sun, May 16, 1982.
London Times, August 25, 1983.
Times Literary Supplement, September 30, 1983.

PECK, Richard 1934-

PERSONAL: Born April 5, 1934, in Decatur, Ill.; son of Wayne M. (a merchant) and Virginia (a dietician; maiden name, Gray) Peck. *Education:* Attended University of Exeter, 1954-55; DePauw University, B.A., 1956; Southern Illinois University, M.A., 1959; further graduate study at Washington University, 1960-61. *Home:* 155 East 72nd St., New York, N.Y. 10021. *Agent:* Sheldon Fogelman, 10 East 40th St., New York, N.Y. 10016.

CAREER: Southern Illinois University at Carbondale, instructor in English, 1958-60; Glenbrook North High School, Northbrook, Ill., teacher of English, 1961-63; Scott, Foresman Co., Chicago, Ill., textbook editor, 1963-65; Hunter College of the City University of New York and Hunter College High School, New York, N.Y., instructor in English and education, 1965-71; writer, 1971—. Assistant director of the Council for Basic Education, Washington, D.C., 1969-70. *Military service:* U.S. Army, 1956-58; served in Stuttgart, Germany. *Member:* Authors Guild, Authors League of America.

AWARDS, HONORS: Sounds and Silences was selected one of Child Study Association of America's Children's Book of the Year, 1970, *Mindscapes*, 1971, and *Blossom Culp and the Sleep of Death*, 1986; Writing Award from the National Council for the Advancement of Education, 1971; Edgar Allan Poe Award runner-up from the Mystery Writers of America, 1974, for *Dreamland Lake; Representing Super Doll* was selected one of American Library Association's Best Books of the Year, 1974, *Are You in the House Alone?*, 1976, and *Ghosts I Have Been*, 1977.

Friends of American Writers Award, 1976, for *The Ghost Belonged to Me;* Edgar Allan Poe Award for Best Juvenile Mystery Novel, 1976, for *Are You in the House Alone?; Are You in the House Alone?* was selected one of *School Library Journal*'s Best Books of the Year, 1976, *Ghosts I Have Been*, 1977, and *Remembering the Good Times,* 1985; *Ghosts I Have Been* was selected one of *New York Times* Outstanding Book of the Year, 1977; Illinois Writer of the Year from the Illinois

RICHARD PECK

Association of Teachers of English, 1977; Author's Award from the New Jersey Institute of Technology, 1978, for *Are You in the House Alone?*; *Dreamland Lake* and *Father Figure* were each chosen one of *School Library Journal*'s Best of the Best 1966-1978.

Pictures That Storm inside My Head, Ghosts I Have Been, and *Are You in the House Alone?* were each chosen one of New York Public Library's Books for the Teen Age, 1980, 1981, and 1982, and *Close Enough to Touch,* 1982; *Close Enough to Touch* was selected one of American Library Association's Best Books for Young Adults, 1981, *Remembering the Good Times,* 1985, and *Princess Ashley,* 1987; *Close Enough to Touch* was selected one of *School Library Journal*'s Best Books for Young Adults, 1981, *This Family of Women,* 1983, *Remembering the Good Times,* 1985, and *Blossom Culp and the Sleep of Death,* 1987; *Are You in the House Alone?* and *Ghosts I Have Been* were each selected one of the Young Adult Services Division of the American Library Association's Best of the Best Books 1970-1983.

WRITINGS:

YOUNG ADULT NOVELS

Don't Look and It Won't Hurt, Holt, 1972.
Dreamland Lake, Holt, 1973.
Through a Brief Darkness, Viking, 1973.
Representing Super Doll, Viking, 1974.
The Ghost Belonged to Me (ALA Notable Book), Viking, 1975.
Are You in the House Alone? (teacher's guide available), Viking, 1976.
Ghosts I Have Been (sequel to *The Ghost Belonged to Me*), Viking, 1977.
Father Figure, Viking, 1978.
Secrets of the Shopping Mall, Delacorte, 1979.
Close Enough to Touch, Delacorte, 1981.
The Dreadful Future of Blossom Culp (sequel to *Ghosts I Have Been*), Delacorte, 1983.
Remembering the Good Times (ALA Notable Book), Delacorte, 1985.
Blossom Culp and the Sleep of Death, Delacorte, 1986.
Princess Ashley, Delacorte, 1987.
Those Summer Girls I Never Met, Delacorte, 1988.

JUVENILE

Monster Night at Grandma's House (illustrated by Don Freeman), Viking, 1977.

ADULT NOVELS

Amanda/Miranda, Viking, 1980.
New York Time, Delacorte, 1981.
This Family of Women, Delacorte, 1983.

EDITOR

(With Ned E. Hoopes) *Edge of Awareness: Twenty-five Contemporary Essays,* Dell, 1966.
Sounds and Silences: Poetry for Now, Delacorte, 1970.
Mindscapes: Poems for the Real World, Delacorte, 1971.
Leap into Reality: Essays for Now, Dell, 1972.
Urban Studies: A Research Paper Casebook, Random House, 1973.
Transitions: A Literary Paper Casebook, Random House, 1974.
Pictures That Storm inside My Head (poetry anthology), Avon, 1976.

OTHER

(With Norman Strasma) *Old Town, A Complete Guide: Strolling, Shopping, Supping, Sipping,* 2nd edition, [Chicago], 1965.

(Cover illustration from *Ghosts I Have Been* by Richard Peck.)

(With Mortimer Smith and George Weber) *A Consumer's Guide to Educational Innovations,* Council for Basic Education, 1972.
(With Stephen N. Judy) *The Creative Word 2,* (Peck was not associated with other volumes), Random House, 1974.
(Contributor) Kenneth L. Donelson and Alleen Pace Nilsen, *Literature for Today's Young Adults,* Scott, Foresman, 1980.
(Contributor) Donald R. Gallo, editor, *Sixteen: Short Stories by Outstanding Young Adult Writers,* Delacorte, 1984.
(Contributor) D. R. Gallo, editor, *Visions: Nineteen Short Stories by Outstanding Writers for Young Adults,* Delacorte, 1987.

Author of column on the architecture of historic neighborhoods for the *New York Times.* Contributor of poetry to several anthologies, *Saturday Review,* and *Chicago Tribune Magazine.* Contributor of articles to periodicals, including *American Libraries, PTA,* and *Parents'.*

ADAPTATIONS:

"The Ghost Belonged to Me" (cassette), Live Oak Media, 1976.
"Are You in the House Alone?" (television movie), CBS, 1977.

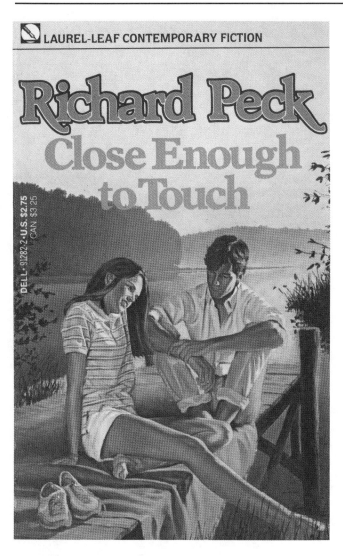

LAUREL-LEAF CONTEMPORARY FICTION

(Cover illustration from *Close Enough to Touch* by Richard Peck.)

"Child of Glass" (television movie; based on *The Ghost Belonged to Me*), Walt Disney Productions, 1979.

"Father Figure" (television movie), Time-Life Production, 1980.

"Don't Look and It Won't Hurt" (listening cassette; filmstrip with cassette), Random House.

"Remembering the Good Times" (cassette; with teacher's guide), Listening Library, 1987.

SIDELIGHTS: "When you write novels you hope young people will read, you do well never to invoke that fatal phrase: 'When I was your age. . . .' However, give me a moment."[1]

April 5, 1934. Born in Decatur, Illinois "in *middle* Middle America."[2]

"The neighborhood is any kid's first nation, and we lived on the border. It was the white frame house on the corner where Dennis Avenue ends at Fairview Park. I spent eighteen years growing up there.

"In a neighborhood where other people's fathers went off to offices every morning in white collars and Plymouth sedans, my dad was apt to roar away astride a Harley-Davidson. Like the teenagers, he'd also gone scrounging in the junkyard and found an historic 1928 Packard coupe to drive to work. It was

the size of a Sherman tank, but louder. It cornered like an aircraft carrier and had a rumble seat, and it loomed large among the Plymouth sedans.

"Like any midwestern boy, my first romance was with the automobile. I sat on my dad's lap and pretended to steer the Packard while his hand rested on the lower rim of the wheel, the diamond in his Masonic ring glittering and giving him away. I learned words by naming the oncoming cars: DeSoto, Terraplane, Lincoln Zephyr, LaSalle, Oldsmobile, Hydramatic—the streamlined poetry of progress."[3]

Peck's vocabulary was also enriched by the stories he heard at his father's Phillips 66 gas station, "where elderly men—old truckers and farmers and railroaders—hung out, telling tales. Large, twelve-year-old boys rolled their newspapers at the station too, and so when I was way too young to be hearing it, I began to learn the uses of vocabulary.

"The old-timers had honed their stories with years of retelling and flavored them with tobacco juice. The newspaper boys worked hard on their macho vocabulary and hoped to be believed. I was bombarded from both sides by the language of other generations, and from these rough tale-tellers I began to learn *style*.

"From my father I learned nostalgia as an art form. I fell on Mark Twain's stories of middle-American boyhood because they merged with my dad's memories. He supped and drank for the rest of his life on his recollections of a boyhood full of hunting and fishing in the Sangamon River bottoms and staying out all night. He'd swapped seventh grade for the adventure of work. Wearing overalls over his serge suit, he hopped freights up to the Dakotas to work on a team running a steam threshing machine for the wheat harvest."[3]

Surrounded by "elders of all ages," Peck listened to stories of Victorian days told to him by his maternal grandmother, aunts and uncles, "farm folk. . .and old settlers, but only as dignified as they needed to be. In memory the card table is always set up in the front yard, and the ice-cream freezer is already packed with rock salt and waiting in the cellar to be cranked. Rural electrification had not found them, and so they trimmed wicks and filled lamps and lit their world with mellow coal-oil flame and laughter.

"Little wonder that old folks stalk through my novels about being young. Madame Malevich, the wise, disillusioned drama teacher in the smug suburb of *Are You in the House Alone?* Uncle Miles, the rapscallion great-uncle of *The Ghost Belonged to Me* who derived from my own great-uncle, Miles Peck. Miss Gertrude Dabney, the eccentric recluse with a ghost in her pantry of *Ghosts I Have Been.* Polly Prior in her wheelchair, the third oldest woman in the township of *Remembering the Good Times*.

"When you write to young readers, you need the wisdom of those people at the other end of life. I came to writing with an entire crew of seasoned elders on my side.

"I marched into kindergarten on the day Germany marched into Poland. I too was fortified. My mother had read to me, making me hungry for books and school and the world. Because of this, I wanted to be a writer before I could read. Luckily, I was born too early to have to learn my first language from 'Sesame Street,' from a large crepe-paper bird speaking out of a small box. I heard my first book-stories in my mother's voice. A satisfactory substitute for this has yet to be found."[3]

While World War II expanded Peck's grammar school world, the post war era brought him into ". . .Decatur High

There was only a little light from outside to show Toby the way. ■ (From *Monster Night at Grandma's House* by Richard Peck. Illustrated by Don Freeman.)

School. . .the least provincial setting I was ever to inhabit with the possible exception of the army. It was racially integrated long before that was fashionable, and the children of every walk of life were thrust together, two thousand of us. Somehow, it seemed bigger than the town it served.

"Even the most privileged and prominent people in town sent their children to the public schools because private schools were considered undemocratic. The almost invisible children of the very poor were there too, kids like Carol Patterson, the heroine of my first novel, *Don't Look and It Won't Hurt*. There was even a splinter group who climbed down out of yellow buses straight from the farm, a blending of worlds that crops up in *Representing Super Doll*.

"We seem to have been the last youthful generation who were kept really busy. It was the final moment before television blanketed the earth, and I for one was afraid to go to school without my homework done. On Saturdays I bagged groceries

at the A & P for the wage of $7.45 which went farther then. A good deal of it went for wrist corsages since our social life revolved entirely around dancing, the more formal the better. By junior year I'd achieved a shawl-collared white dinner jacket worn over a maroon cummerbund. Spiffy.

"I wasn't falling for high school though. I was scanning the horizon for college and farther fields than that. By the summer I was sixteen I went to visit a distant relative who'd married a dignitary assigned to the United Nations and lived in the mythic city of New York. I raked yards and shoveled snow for a chair-car ticket on the Pennsylvania Railroad and was on my way.

"It came as quite a relief to me that the outside world was really there and somewhat better than the movies. I began to explore the streets of New York and plumb the depths of the subway system all the way to Coney Island. It occured to me that this was the place I'd been homesick for all along, this

In the year of 1914 my class went from being eighth graders at Horace Mann School to being freshmen at Bluff City High School. . . . ■ (From *The Dreadful Future of Blossom Culp* by Richard Peck.)

place and London. That first trek into the Great World ended on June 25, 1950, the day the Korean War began. The postwar era we'd waited for all through grade school had turned out to run less than five years, and the 1950s had truly begun.''[3]

''When I was [a] teenager, the world was run by adults. When you were out of sight of your parents, you were still within range of people who knew your parents well. My English teacher, who could have used some Christian charity, sat in the pew ahead of us at church—even Sundays weren't safe. My math teacher moonlighted in the suit department at Sears. You couldn't even go *shopping,* for Pete's sake. They had us outflanked.

''In the 1950s, adolescents were an underclass with plenty of dues yet to be paid. The chief authority figure in a boy's life was the looming figure of the head of the local draft board, yet another adult in the world full of them. Back then adolescence didn't meld seamlessly with the lifestyle of the Yuppie. A boy knew when his adolescence was over. A notice to that effect came in the mail.

''Like any normally paranoid teenager, I assumed I was behind an entire frame of eight balls all my own. I believed that if I

didn't get straight 'As, I wasn't going to win the necessary scholarship for college, assuming, always, the draft board would grant a college deferment.

''I grubbed for grades, yearned for the scholarship, dreaded Korea, and feared the formless future. Moreover, I hadn't been born into the class of society that provided lemon-yellow Studebaker convertibles for their offspring. I managed to keep this genealogical outrage down to minor irritation somewhere around acne and two or three other afflictions that will remain nameless. Still, as a youth I was a worried man.''[1]

Peck won the scholarship he had been pursuing through high school, and entered DePauw University in Indiana rather than the army. ''If a boy didn't maintain a college grade point average in the upper half of his class, the university informed his local draft board, and he soon found himself in Korea. When I was a freshman, one of the seniors in the fraternity house allowed his grades to slip and was drafted out of school in mid-semester. This had an electrifying effect on the rest of us, and we all became a lot more scholarly than we'd meant to be. Silent study hours were invoked and homework seminars were set up in the dining room. It was far from an animal-house environment.

''In fact the entirety of college life then is hard to describe now. At DePauw no student was allowed to have a car, and drinking led directly to expulsion. Strangely, the college had a widespread reputation for its brisk social life. It was the

(Cover illustration from *Secrets of the Shopping Mall* by Richard Peck.)

high-water mark of the fraternity/sorority system. Girls dazzling to behold descended long curving staircases to claim their wrist corsages, and we danced away to formal evenings, cheek to cheek and sober as judges.

"I entered college with the full complement of late-adolescent complexes. For one thing I had this secret itch to be a writer, though I wouldn't have admitted any such long shot. Instead, I planned to be a teacher, which seemed to be my nearest approach to the written word."[3]

Peck's interests in literature and history led to a year in the southwest of England where he took, "most of my literature courses at Exeter University. . . .I'd obtained a dispensation from my draft board to leave the country for a year. Then, any undrafted twenty-year-old was regarded as a potential fugitive.

"But it was all worth the effort. Every late adolescent should be cut out of the pack to find out who he is."[3]

1955-1956. "I returned to DePauw University in Indiana, heavily tweeded and with midwestern accent blurred, for senior year and all the grim courses needed for a teaching credential. . . .Graduation day came, and not long after I was marched off, on cue, to the army."[3]

1956-1958. Served his mandatory two-year military stint in an army field post outside Ansbach, Germany. "It was in this unlikely, muddy locale, that I found out the advantage of writing. I learned that if you can type, punctuate, spell, and improvise in mid-sentence, you can work in a clean dry office near a warm stove. Otherwise, you're at the mercy of the elements and the sergeants. I became an army clerk, and then I invented a whole new career for myself. I became a ghost-writer of sermons for chaplains (all denominations). That way, I passed a pious, pleasant, and perfectly dry army hitch and sensed the power of the written word.

"The army is a more instructive experience than college, but I wouldn't sell my university days short."[4]

When he returned stateside, Peck spent a year at Southern Illinois University working on a masters degree. "And I was learning to be alone, which is of course the only way a writer can work, whenever he begins to do it in earnest."[4]

He became a teaching assistant in the English Department while earning a masters degree. "Teaching was what I did because I thought I couldn't be a writer. I wanted to be a writer from the very beginning, but I allowed myself to be discouraged by people who said, 'Oh, you can't make a living in that field.' I realize now that those people were not very well informed. Also, I came from Middle America, a long way from the publishing world. I didn't understand the publishing process; nor did my teachers. So I became a teacher because teachers were the people in my hometown whom I admired and who were interested in the things I was interested in. Then I fell in love with teaching. And I would have made it as a teacher, all the way through to retirement, had it not been for that historic happenstance when the schooling in this country fell apart. In my early years of teaching, it was more or less in place, and I loved it a lot. When I was doing it, I thought of teaching as an end in itself. Teaching is a lifetime, not a nine-to-five job; I didn't have time to think of anything but that. I got terribly interested in the kids, and that did lead on to writing for them."[5]

Peck became familiar with adolescent problems while teaching English at Glenbrook North High School in Northbrook, Illi-

nois, an affluent Chicago suburb. "In our country an extraordinary number of fiction writers come from three fields: journalism, advertising, and teaching. What these three fields as seedbeds seem to offer the prospective writer are evocative language, communication with strangers, and deadlines.

"I chose teaching. In the classroom I identified my potential readers: they were the students who could be won to reading. I learned that the best, most independent, most promising students are the thoughtful, quiet ones—often in the back row—who'll reach for a book in search of themselves, the ones who often get overlooked in our crisis-oriented schools."[4]

1965. Moved to New York City where he taught English at Hunter College High School. "I came to the end of my teaching years at a school for academically gifted girls on Park Avenue in New York City, far from the suburbs. The world of the young, and their teachers, was changing fast. For the first time I was teaching junior-high level students and looking high and low for books that reflected their realities, books that were 'relevant,' the battle cry of the age. It was a time when students were excused from school to march on Washington in masses to protest the war in Vietnam, a war they couldn't find on the map."[4]

Frustrated by his failure to persuade students to learn, Peck began to re-examine and re-evaluate teaching. "Many young people today are just like young people have always been—anxious to be as adult as possible. But many are not. Many

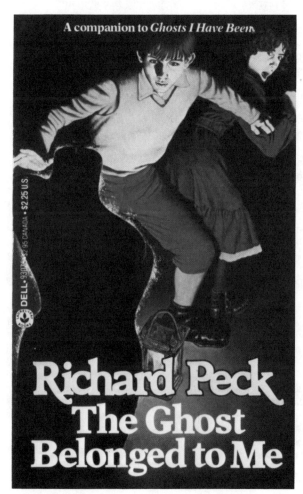

We had a ghost and she haunted our barnloft. ■ (From *The Ghost Belonged to Me* by Richard Peck.)

are patients in the remedial reading clinic. Some of them appear to be terminal cases. The permissive home and the watered-down school curriculum have betrayed them. The basic skills were not imposed, and attention spans were not stretched. There are college freshmen abroad in the land who aren't ready for a seventh-grade textbook.''[6]

''I was burning out as a teacher. I think at that point it would have been scarier for me to go on teaching. I was just getting to that age where a few of the older guys in the faculty room were beginning to compute their time until retirement in days, and some of them had twenty-four years to go! I wasn't going to do that.

''I quit teaching at Hunter. . .at a time when the Vietnam War protest was at its peak, when the school was being racially integrated from without and racially segregated from within on the following day by the students. I was being held legally responsible for the whereabouts of students I had never met because, at the height—or the depth—of the protest movement, it was considered fascist to call roll, lest there be some seventh grader who was, in fact, in Washington marching against the government. I realized I was not in control of the classroom, and I thought nothing would get better in teaching. As it happened, nothing ever did. In short, I quit teaching when I could no longer teach as I had been taught.''[5]

''As a teacher, I'd already learned that you can only teach those who are willing to be taught. . . .I didn't want to [quit], but it seemed to me that teaching had begun to turn into something that looked weirdly like psychiatric social work—a field in which I was not trained or interested. I turned in my pension and hospitalization plan and my attendance book—which was, come to think of it, the first work of fiction I ever wrote. I moved my typewriter out into the garden of the brick barn in Brooklyn where I live. And I began writing a novel to some of the young people I'd left behind in the classroom.''[7]

Four months later, _Don't Look and It Won't Hurt,_ a young adult novel about teenage pregnancy, was finished. ''It was junior-high students, the puberty people, who taught me how to be a writer. They taught me what I hadn't learned elsewhere: that people don't read fiction to be educated. They read fiction to be reassured, to be given hope. As a novelist I wasn't going to give them happy endings every time. They have television for that. But I knew never to leave the reader without hope for the future and a new beginning. My students reminded me that puberty, the time of life when you're too old for a Care Bear and too young for a driver's license, is a rough passage. From books such readers want fictional friends as companions and role models.

''_Don't Look and It Won't Hurt_...was based on the experiences of my close friends, Jean and Richard Hughes, who took into their home in suburban Chicago girls from a local home for unwed mothers. In the end, I wrote the story not from the viewpoint of the unwed teenaged mother-to-be, but from the viewpoint of her younger sister. I cared more about the young person who wasn't already in the kind of trouble that adults can no longer overlook. I identified Carol with the quiet students who'd always sat at the back of the classroom, wondering what life had to offer for them, and what they had to contribute.

''I hand-carried this first manuscript to George Nicholson who was Juveniles Editor-in-Chief of Holt, Rinehart and Winston. On the following day, after I had a restless night, he called me up and said, 'You can start your second novel.' And so I did.''[3]

1976. _Are You in the House Alone?,_ a controversial novel about a teenage girl who is raped, met with critical approval and won the Edgar Allan Poe Award. ''I wrote that novel because the chief victim of rape is not a woman, but a teenage girl—a teenage girl who doesn't have her own lawyer, who doesn't have mobility, who doesn't have a lot of the things that she will need to be strong in her situation. But I have never received a letter from a teenage girl who says she was a rape victim. Yet I have a lot of letters from librarians who said _they_ were rape victims. So it seems that it is adults who can respond in that direct way, and that kids will not thank you for invading their privacy.

''On the other hand, you get letters that are ambiguously written, the sort of letter that says, 'I had this friend who. . . .' and you realize that the friend is the self. They are interested in other people's problems, and they can identify very closely with them. That's important, because the young are running each other today. The peer group is in command of their lives, not adults. Anything that can be done to make that peer group a little more compassionate is worth doing. And nothing is being done about it in schools. Gang leaders are being celebrated. The status quo of the youth culture, which is very cruel and intolerant, is indemnified by schools; administrations say they can do nothing about students social activities, and ad-

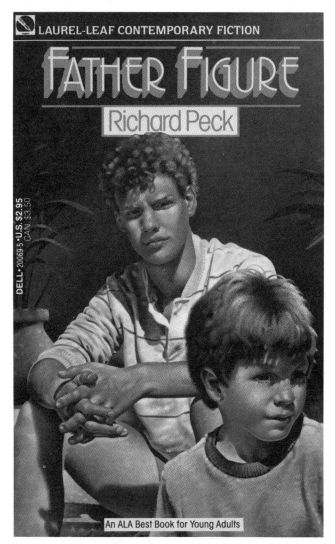

Even at a distance I like to believe I can hear him thinking. . . .■ (From _Father Figure_ by Richard Peck.)

ministrators are glad they pursue most of them off the school property. . . ."[5]

"*Are You in the House Alone?* is not a book to reassure, nor even to please. If it's to be honest, the story's victim continues to be victimized by public opinion in many small ways. And the story cannot have a happy ending: in fact it can't really have an ending at all."[8]

The book was adapted into a prime-time television movie. "It was a relief when they didn't do what I was terribly worried they would—change the ending to show everything working out all right; the criminal rehabilitated: justice triumphing and so on."[2]

While he has written ghost stories, romances and thrillers, Peck is best known for his books about teenagers caught up in personal problems, such as *Father Figure,* which he considers ". . .my best book. It may be the best book I can do. It's the story of a defensive seventeen-year-old boy who has to make an unthinkable sacrifice before he can begin to grow up. The book is devoid of sexual content because the boy's passions are directed elsewhere. He's clinging ardently to role-playing the part of father to his small eight-year-old brother. When their mother dies, these brothers are reunited with their own, unknown father. The novel chronicles a rocky father-son relationship. It wonders if the members of a suddenly all-male family can move beyond macho posturing to a shared commitment. In the end the teenaged son is able to surrender his little brother to their real father. In this, his first mature act, he rids himself of anger."[9]

To keep his topics relevant, Peck has travelled widely, meeting young people first hand. In the course of the usual speaking engagements common to authors, Peck encountered his first censor—a mother of a thirteen-year-old girl who had effectively banned his favorite novel from her daughter's school library. "My cliched view of successful censors is that they neither read the book in question nor let you see them. I was about to be wrong twice. My guard wasn't up either. You'd have to give my collected young adult works a close reading if you were scanning for rough language or sexual content. Even then, you'd come up disappointingly short in the sensation department. I've never thought you could build a faithful constituency of young readers with shock value. I've always believed they read to be reassured and recognized.

"As it happened, there'd been earlier rumblings of censorship about a novel of mine called *Are You in the House Alone?* I'd even heard of librarians who wouldn't give it shelf space for fear it might occasion trouble. It's my best seller. Evidently the censor I was about to meet had never heard of that book. The book she'd efficiently purged is *Father Figure.*

"While the administrators and the librarian stood back, she came forth: a handsome woman, well-dressed. She was a prominent doctor's wife, in fact, with an air of cool command. Quite a bit younger than I am too. All expectation of seeing her as an illiterate crank withered within me. I can't quote our conversation verbatim. I'm in no sense wired to record encounters this unexpected; all my best response came days too late, in the middle of the night. I couldn't feign ignorance either. She knew I knew who she was. From the first moment I marveled at how completely she appeared to be in control of her universe—and a corner of mine.

"After finding a copy of *Father Figure* in her daughter's possession, she'd read it herself. I know because she booktalked my own book to me from start to finish with admirable economy. She'd disliked it from beginning to end.

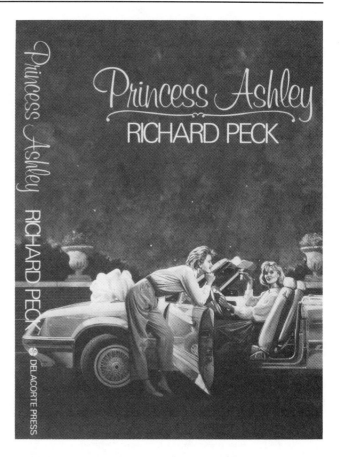

(Cover illustration by Frank Morris from *Princess Ashley* by Richard Peck.)

"*Father Figure* begins with the death of a mother. Worse, this character takes her own life because she's suffering a terminal illness. The removal of a maternal character so early was clearly repugnant to this reader, however, she spoke mainly of the immorality of suicide. She harped on nothing and moved swiftly to the central issues of the book. All were equally unsuitable: another book about divorced parents; the angry disrespect of a son for his father; the inability of a parent to shape his child.

"Her tone was so reasoned that there seemed promise of dialogue. I pointed out that nearly half of my potential readers are the children of divorced parents, that their special problems are meant to be recognized in this book.

" 'That isn't my daughter's situation,' she said, 'nor her friends. They have been drawn mainly from our church.'

"Another mother, implying she was able to choose, even screen, her thirteen-year-old child's friend, would have made me gravely skeptical. I was less sure about this one. For a sentence or so I clung to the argument that attention must be paid to the needs of readers from broken homes. She wasn't interested. She was even less interested in the particular problems of emotional communication between fathers and sons. She had no sons, and referred to her husband only obliquely with the pronoun *we:* 'We set a good standard for our daughter, and we don't want to be undermined.'

"It was several days before I took serious offense to the suggestion that any book of mine undermines parental authority. Until this moment, I hadn't thought that parents had enough authority to be undermined. Had I wished other parents were more like this one? I was sinking fast. And it was useless to suggest a larger view. She didn't have to be reminded that her daughter attends a public school with classmates from all backgrounds, and that the girl couldn't live as circumscribed a life as her own mother.

''Because her interest was limited to her daughter, I cited which of my books she might find more suitable for her. Her face began to close; she'd given my work all the attention it deserves. She turned to go. There was nothing whatever wrong with her timing.

'''I can respect any parent who cares enough to oversee her child's reading,' I said, 'but I think that no parent has the right to withhold a book from other readers.'

''She almost smiled at this impertinence. She hadn't come here to be criticized. But at the door she spoke again, with the first note of uncertainty in her voice. 'I am able to direct my daughter now,' she said, 'but I don't know about the future.'

''There, I thought, I could reassure her. 'If you can dominate her at puberty,' I said, 'I expect you can hold her for life.'

''She seemed to take that more kindly than it was meant and walked away down the empty hallway of the school.

''And so, I have met and faced my first censor. In the way of adversaries she wasn't at all what I'd expected. She hadn't clothed her arguments in religion or politics; she was clearly no joiner. She was interested in power of her own. I sensed that power early on, from across a crowded room. She didn't need to follow any prescribed procedure to have a book eliminated from a library. She removed it with the force of her personality, augmented by her position in the community. My only faint hope lies in the librarian quietly reshelving the book once the daughter moves on to high school.

''Power is always a problem for writers. We never think we have any. Only the youngest among us believe our words will change the world in measurable ways. We're awed by authority we don't have: the powers of publishers to accept and reject, the crisp pronouncements of reviewers, the blinding might of television.

''I lost some days in wondering at the efficient power of a woman out to purify her daughter's environment. I wagged my chin at how hard it is to write a book and how easy to eradicate it. But I got over that, though that parent lingered in my mind. I kept puzzling over why she'd broken cover. Surely she hadn't thought I was an instrument of the devil she had to see to believe. Surely she hadn't come to protect the assembled students; she betrayed no interest in other people's children. I couldn't even believe she was flaunting her authority over a system she'd already brought down. Finally I thought she must be frightened and was reaching out. She appeared to be too literate to fear a book, but there are less-tangible fears—of a world that threatens her authority and will, in the long run, claim her daughter.

''I also wondered if she wasn't lonely in the aftermath of her easy triumph. A system meant to be strong enough to protect and educate her daughter had fallen at her feet. The administrators had bowed before her without reading the book at issue. Their colleague, the librarian, had found the rug jerked out from under her so suavely it didn't merit mention in the local newspaper. I wondered if this woman, like a thirteen-year-old girl herself, hadn't been testing a system in the hope it would hold firm, that she'd come to us all for some obscure assurance.

''Given the vulnerabilities of parents today, I wondered if I could even blame her. I decided I could. She is after all the enemy. Though her powers are ultimately limited, they proved ample enough to dispatch my book. She wants a perfect world, on her terms, for her daughter. In a more nearly perfect world, she'd have been held accountable. She would have needed to muster more reasons than she had to eliminate any book from a community of readers. She would have needed to gather considerable support for her viewpoint from like-minded readers. She would have had to endure a defense of the book, of books by people alerted to the danger of her. She'd have had to go public. If it had been necessary, she may have gone through the process. I wish it had been necessary.

''But this isn't even close to a perfect world. With stunning regularity, school administrators knuckle under to the standards of communities that in fact don't have any. Librarians live for the interludes between the censorship wars when they can put the right books into the right hands. Writers wonder when the creeping illiteracy fostered by soft schools and empty homes will eliminate our last readers. Even one mighty mother looked a little forlorn after her victory.

''And so, in a picture-perfect town and an orderly schoolhouse, I've met my first censor, but she hasn't met her first writer, though she went out of her way to do so. She was deaf to the notion that I cared as much in my way for a group of young readers as she cared in her way about only one. She was proof against any suggestion I may have made that books are meant to ready young readers for the world. Prisoners of civilization both, we didn't raise our voices, and neither of us budged from who we'd been. Each thought the other immoral. Each wouldn't mind running the other out of the community, though only one of us succeeded in that.

''There's another offstage character in this squalid, genteel little drama. It's the daughter, that young stranger finding her way through a school day not yet completely monitored by her mother. If she finished reading my book, she either reacted to it or not. If she hadn't been allowed to finish it, my book may lay a greater claim upon her than it deserves to have.''[9]

Whether condemned or revered by critics and readers, Peck maintains that he writes for teenagers, who are ''. . .the most important people in my life, and in the lives of booksellers who hope to have a next generation of book buyers. We've got to find them where they live if we're to survive a decade when a high-school graduate who can read his own diploma is increasingly being called 'gifted.'

''Looking for the pubescent and adolescent who lives in a separate state is what I do for a living.

''Being a writer is no laughing matter. Being a writer is sitting in an empty room trying to make a blank page speak. Being a writer is yearning for the telephone to ring to prove you haven't turned into another hermetically sealed J. D. Salinger—because you don't have his backlist. Then the telephone does ring, and it's the IRS, and they want to know how we can make livings without being employed. We wonder ourselves. Writing may well be the last unexplained phenomenon.

''In a world full of people going off to salaried jobs with paid vacations and negotiated coffee breaks, we writers are on duty, awake or asleep. And our job is to make bricks without straw, something out of nothing. Therefore we value our colleagues, because our enemies are so much better organized.''[10]

Peck defines his readers as ''. . .a generation whose grade-school years were informed and enlivened by Betsy Byars,

(From the television movie ''Are You in the House Alone?'' starring Kathleen Beller and Scott Colomby. Broadcast on CBS-TV, 1977.)

who teaches the basic lesson to the next generation of book buyers: that a novel must entertain first before it can do anything else. But I don't get these readers until they hit puberty. They haven't even budded, and already the Blume is off. I don't get them till puberty, and it's the darkest moment of life. For while puberty is the death of childhood, it isn't the birth of reason.

"Puberty is the same gulag we all once did time in, robbed of the certainties of grade school and still years away from a driver's license. Puberty is waking up every morning wondering which sex you are, if any. Puberty is the practice of strict sexual segregation with all the girls on one side of an invisible line and all the boys on the other: big women, little men. Like a Shaker meeting but without the hope of eternal life. Puberty is no fun, and changing the name of the junior high to the middle school has fooled nobody. In America puberty is deciding at the age of twelve or so to divorce your own parents, charging irreconcilable differences. The children of the underclass hit the streets then and are thereafter out of reach of home and school and books. The children of the middle class recede to their rooms and lock themselves into elaborate sound systems, paid for by parents, that eliminate the possibility of a parental voice. They are free of us at twelve.

"I write for these people whose own parents haven't seen them for days. In our impotence we've reasoned that children must be given freedoms in order to learn how to handle them. But it doesn't work that way. The prematurely emancipated young transfer all their need for a dominating, problem-solving authority from weak adults at home and school to the peer group. The only government they recognize is the vengeful law-giving of each other.

"That's what I write: counterculture literature of individuality to a conformist readership. I write books for the knapsacks of young soldiers of both sexes going forth every school day hoping to survive the 'Chocolate War.' I write for the inmates of schools where you cannot win a letter sweater for literacy. You can win a letter sweater only for mindless conformity, for listening to language from the coach that would get the librarian into big trouble. I write for a generation of young people who don't have to drop by the library, even on the way to the Gifted Program. They don't have to drop by anywhere except, perhaps, the shopping mall."[10]

The shopping mall is the setting and focus of another popular Peck novel, *Secrets of the Shopping Mall.* "I wrote the novel asking the kids why they felt they had to report to the shopping mall every day, even though home and school were now optional. Was it possibly because even in the cradle they had been conditioned by television commercials to buy happiness with unearned money? Or is it that they're in the suburbs and there is no other center in these rootless, blank communities? Or—and here's the real reason—is the shopping mall a place where you can eliminate even the *possibility* of adult authority? So I took reality one step beyond and said, if you want to spend all your waking hours in a shopping mall, how about spending all your sleeping hours there too? How about living there? And I wrote it as a satire, with these kids as pioneers on the last American frontier—Lord & Taylor at the mall."[5]

"The book is a satire, and when you write satire for seventh-graders, you have some explaining to do. It's a novel that asks a question. . . .How about just moving into the mall, safe at last from the cruel rules of home and school?

"The secret in my shopping mall is that it's being run all night, every night, by a peer group of runaway suburban teens, ruled with a rod of iron by a permissively reared little female Hitler

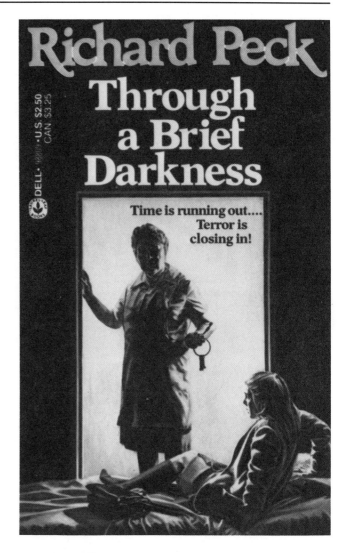

(Cover illustration from *Through a Brief Darkness* by Richard Peck.)

named Barbie, whose preppy consort is just naturally named Ken. They run a typically totalitarian youth culture nocturnally in the furniture department. I experienced Andy Warhol's fifteen minutes of fame when *Time* magazine called this novel a 'Lord & Taylor of the Flies.'

"On the other side of satire I have to mention a newer book of mine, *Remembering the Good Times.* I wrote it because a boy in real life went to seventh grade in a school and told twelve of his—better not call them friends, better call them classmates—that he would kill himself. He went home that night and did. Later, people asked these twelve why they hadn't said anything. But the thought of informing adults hadn't occurred to them. They don't deal much with adults. People asked them if they knew there were social agencies in the community to help people who are in despair, suicidal. But the seventh-graders had never heard of them. The only government they recognize is their own. I've written *Remembering the Good Times* to dramatize the classic warning signs of suicide for the young themselves in the hope they'll reach out to one another—though they're beyond our reach."[10]

Peck believes that communication—or lack of it—is a number one problem among today's young adults as is the age old problem of the need to conform. ". . .In every one of my novels, somebody has to grow up. That isn't true of my readers. Growing up is optional for them. They can go along with

The guys stayed on one side of an invisible line, and girls stayed on the other. It's some rule of junior high nature. . . . ■ (From *Remembering the Good Times* by Richard Peck.)

the gang. They can drift through high school and still get into college, because colleges today need them. They can drift into the Yuppiedom of adulthood still taking money from home. *Or* they can stand up on their own feet. In my novels, somebody always has to do that. . . .In each of my novels, one of the characters takes a step toward adulthood, and it almost always means taking a step away from the peer group.

"It's not an attractive message, of course, because most young people have no intention of being rejected by the peer group, and in many cases that would be physically dangerous. But I think they ought to know that the possibility exists. They ought to know that, if you are going to do anything in this world, you will be doing it on your own, just as I have to write a novel alone. I think they need to know that you can grow up with a clean body. You do not have to be polluted by alcohol and drugs, although many would feel that those things are necessary concomitants to their social structure and grownups don't know anything about it. They also feel drugs, alcohol, and cigarettes can't hurt them, because they cannot die. I can even commit suicide, a young person says to himself, and I'll be back in school Monday morning. We had these feelings of unreality too, but they are exaggerated now in the mind of the permissively reared child who has been given everything.

"I have a particular interest in the male relationships in families, and the emotional content of men and boys, which gets a bad snubbing by books. So that's what *Father Figure* and *Close Enough to Touch* are about. And that is why *Remembering the Good Times* is told in the voice of a boy who had a strong relationship with his father. I'm going to go on and do a body of work in defining men's and boys' emotions, because women and girls are acting as if they don't know they are there. You will not see it in Harlequin romances. And that's uphill work. Even a certain publisher said recently that it is almost impossible to promote a book told from a boy's viewpoint to high schools today. That means we're going backwards. That means, too, we do not have the committed help of the largely female library establishment. I'm sorry about that, because I believe there's a lot of damage being done to boys *and* girls because boys do not have outlets for their emotions. Boys don't know they can cry; they don't know that, in fact, their emotional needs are the same as girls'. Also, half of them are not living in the same homes as their fathers; they do not have the role modeling of a man because there is no father figure in the home. And some of them who *do* live in the same homes as their fathers do not have that role modeling because there is no real dialogue. That, I think, is our number-one problem. The irony is, I don't know anybody else who regards that as a problem. They think the problem is suicide and rape and alcoholism. I think it's the male's inability to communicate."[5]

In speaking about the future of young adult fiction, Peck predicts themes that have ". . .nothing to do with the sexual revolution, the drug culture, and racial politics. The young now and in the future are not going to be able to solve these problems. It's a sickness from the '60s that we ever expected them to. They're going to continue to draw back from such problems in search of smaller, safer worlds. Possibly the writers' challenge will be to write adventurous books on 'safe' subjects.

"Books that explore friendship, which is a more potent preoccupation than sex to the young, and easier to contemplate. Books that continue to examine the family structure rather than celebrating collectivist alternatives. Books set in suburbs that still purvey a liberating hint of larger, more stimulating worlds.

"A second generation of such books might do well to include dimension now missing. We might continue plumbing the coming-of-age theme and then follow our young characters into adult life. That way we could depict not only actions, but their ultimate consequences. And I'm not talking about cautionary tales that warn young unwed mothers and fathers that they've blighted their entire lives. Such a message might not even be true.

"But it would be pleasantly expansive to indicate to the young that all of life need not be as cruelly conformist and conservative as adolescence—unless you want it to be. That the most truly successful men and women were not high-school hotshots, beauty queens, super jocks, or manipulative gang leaders.

"But maybe that's expecting too much. I imagine that the most acceptable new titles of the 1990s will be books about the sorrows of friendship and the painful necessity of growing up in a world new to no one but yourself. Books that include a little cautious nudge of optimism to offset what is blaring from a TV without an off knob. Books that invite the young to think for themselves instead of for each other."[11]

Peck's own literary future includes more YA books as well as novels for adults. "I will never give up writing for teenagers unless they give me up—or unless the field does crumble under the weight of illiteracy."[5]

FOOTNOTE SOURCES

[1]Richard Peck, "Growing Up Suburban: 'We Don't Use Slang, We're Gifted,'" *School Library Journal,* October, 1985.

[2]Jean F. Mercier, "PW Interviews: Richard Peck," *Publishers Weekly,* March 14, 1980.

[3]*Something about the Author Autobiography Series,* Volume 2, Gale, 1986.

[4]*Something about the Author,* Volume 18, Gale, 1980.

[5]*Contemporary Authors New Revisions Series,* Volume 19, Gale, 1987.

[6]R. Peck, "In the Country of Teenage Fiction," *American Libraries,* April, 1973.

[7]*Contemporary Authors,* Volumes 85-88, Gale, 1980.

[8]D. L. Kirkpatrick, editor, *Twentieth-Century Children's Writers,* St. Martin's, 1978.

[9]R. Peck, "The Genteel Unshelving of a Book," *School Library Journal,* May, 1986.

[10]R. Peck, "Young Adult Books," *Horn Book,* September/October, 1986.

[11]*Contemporary Literary Criticism,* Volume 21, Gale, 1982.

FOR MORE INFORMATION SEE:

Washington Post Children's Book World, November 5, 1972.

Letty Cottin Pogrebin, "Dreams for Children, Nightmares for Teen-agers," *New York Times Book Review,* November 12, 1972.

"For Ages 4, 5. . .15: *Dreamland Lake,*" *New York Times Book Review,* January 13, 1974 (p. 10).

Joan Goldman Levine, "The Spirits Are Willing: *The Ghost Belonged to Me,*" *New York Times Book Review,* July 27, 1975 (p. 8).

Horn Book, October, 1975, February, 1977, April, 1983, September, 1985, October, 1986.

English Journal, February, 1976.

Alix Nelson, "Ah, Not to Be Sixteen Again," *New York Times Book Review,* November 14, 1976 (p. 29).

Bulletin of the Center for Children's Books, March, 1977.

Times Literary Supplement, March 25, 1977, August 21, 1981.

Jack Forman, "Children's Books: *Secrets of the Shopping Mall,*" *New York Times Book Review,* December 2, 1979 (p.40).

"Richard Peck" *Children's Literature in Education,* Volume 11, number 3, 1980.

Kenneth L. Donelson and Alleen Pace Nilson, editors, *Literature for Today's Young Adults,* Scott, Foresman, 1980.

Los Angeles Times, April 3, 1981.

Voice of Youth Advocates, October, 1981.

Washington Post Book World, May 1, 1983.

D. L. Kirkpatrick, editor, *Twentieth-Century Children's Writers,* 2nd edition, St. Martin's, 1983.

"Children's Book and Author Breakfast," *Publishers Weekly,* June 20, 1986 (biographical).

COLLECTIONS

De Grummond Collection at the University of Southern Mississippi.

Kerlan Collection at the University of Minnesota.

POLLACK, Merrill S. 1924-1988

OBITUARY NOTICE: Born July 24, 1924, in Middle Village, Long Island, N. Y.; died of a stroke, February 14, 1988, in Parkersberg, W. Va. Journalist, editor, and author. Pollack worked as a reporter on the staffs of the *Bronx Home News* and *New York Post* in the late 1940s before serving as an associate editor for the publishing company Simon & Schuster;

he later worked for W. W. Norton & Company and Viking Press.

Pollack went into farming in 1974; at that time he also established Seneca Books, Inc. His writings include the children's works *Shem and Doon,* and *Phaethon,* and for adults, *How to Cope with. . .* and *O Is for Overkill.* He also contributed articles and short stories to *Boys' Life* magazine, as well as other periodicals.

FOR MORE INFORMATION SEE:

"Life among the Editors," *Saturday Evening Post,* January 16, 1954.

Barbara Harte and Carolyn Riley, editors, *Contemporary Authors,* Volumes 5-8, Gale, 1969 (p. 902).

OBITUARIES

Publishers Weekly, March 11, 1988.

RAWDING, F(rederick) W(illiam) 1930-

PERSONAL: Born May 19, 1930, in London, England; son of Wilfrid Wulstan (in the British army) and Lilian (Garrett) Rawding. *Education:* St. Mary's College, student, 1950-52; London University Institute of Education, certificate of education, 1952; King's College, Cambridge, B.A. (honors), 1973, M.A., 1977. *Politics:* Centre Conservative. *Religion:* Roman Catholic. *Home:* "Roshanara," High Road, Newton, Near Wisbech, Cambridgeshire PE13 5HR, England. *Agent:* c/o Cambridge University Press, Edinburgh Building, Shaftesbury Rd., Cambridge CB2 2RU, England.

CAREER: Educator. Territorial Army, Royal Artillery, 1949-52, became lieutenant; Regular Army, captain, 1952-57, major, 1964-68, retired to reserve, 1968; British Army Educational Corps, Korea, Malaya, Singapore, Persian Gulf, Saudi Arabia, Oman, Yemen Arab Republic, school inspector, administrator of education, and director and chief instructor in a variety of military training establishments, 1974-85. *Awards,*

F. W. RAWDING

honors: Received military campaign medals for service in Korea, Malaya, and South Arabia; James Prize from King's College, l97l, and l972, for poetry; "Smuts Fund" Award from Cambridge University, l973, and l976, for research.

WRITINGS:

Mr. Parkin's Travels (English reader), Ministry of Education (Saudi Arabia), l966.
The Buddha, Cambridge University Press, l975, Lerner, l979.
The Rebellion in India, l857, Cambridge University Press, l977.
Gandhi, Cambridge University Press, l980, published in the United States as *Gandhi and the Struggle for India's Independence,* Lerner, l982.

Also author of numerous articles for the Saudi Arabian English Language Press.

WORK IN PROGRESS: A comparative grammar of Nepali and Newari; memoirs of service in Arabia; a book about his travels in India, Pakistan, Nepal, and Sri Lanka; short stories with backgrounds in Korea, Japan, Hong Kong, Thailand, Arabia, Bahrain, Oman, the Yemen Arab Republic, and Muslim North Africa.

SIDELIGHTS: "Having served and travelled as a Regular Army officer and later as a civilian all over Asia and the Middle East, I became intensely interested in the languages, people, and cultures of those regions. I acquired fluency in Nepali, Malay, Hindi, Urdu and Arabic. My studies, both in the army and later at Cambridge, reinforced these interests and I continue to write and travel. I also continue to add to my collection of papers and research material in the South Asian Archive of the University of Cambridge.

"I have had the very interesting and privileged opportunity of serving in the British Army before the end of the empire in South East Asia and East Africa. The most formative period of my service was with the Brigade of Gurkhas in Hong Kong, Singapore and Malaya between l954 and l966. I also have trekked for hundreds of miles in the Himalayas before that region became widely accessible to tourists.

"I retain an active interest in and support the social and educational work of the Jesuit fathers and brothers of the Chicago Province in Nepal."

HOBBIES AND OTHER INTERESTS: Travel, photography, languages, anthropology.

RAYNER, William 1929-

PERSONAL: Born January 1, 1929, in Barnsley, Yorkshire, England; son of Thomas (a civil servant) and Lily (Fisher) Rayner; married Pamela Ross (a secretary), November 1, 1954; children: Simon Thomas, Christopher Philip, William Ian. *Education:* Wadham College, Oxford University, B.A. (with honors), 1952. *Politics:* Social Democrat. *Religion:* "Uncertain." *Home:* Spurriers Close, West Porlock, near Minehead, Somerset, England. *Agent:* William Collins Sons Ltd., 14 St. James's Place, London SW1A 1PS, England.

CAREER: Writer. Has worked as a teacher of English in England and Africa.

WILLIAM RAYNER

WRITINGS:

The Reapers, Faber, 1961.
The Tribe and Its Successors: An Account of African Traditional Life and European Settlement of Southern Rhodesia (nonfiction), Praeger, 1962.
The Barebones, Faber, 1963.
The Last Days, Morrow, 1968.
The Knifeman: The Last Journal of Judas Iscariot, Morrow, 1969.
The World Turned Upside Down, Morrow, 1970, published as *Redcoat,* Sphere (London), 1971.
Stag Boy (young adult novel), Collins, 1972, Harcourt, 1973.
The Bloody Affray at Riverside Drive, Collins, 1972, published in America as *Seth and Belle and Mr. Quarles and Me: The Bloody Affray at Lakeside Drive,* Simon & Schuster, 1973.
Big Mister (young adult novel), Collins, 1974.
The Trail to Bear Paw Mountain, Collins, 1974, Ballantine, 1976.
A Weekend with Captain Jack, Collins, 1975, Ballantine, 1977.
The Day of Chaminuka, Collins, 1976, Atheneum, 1977.
Eating the Big Fish, Collins, 1977, published as *The Interface Assignment,* Atheneum, 1977.
Chief Joseph and His People (juvenile biography), Collins, 1978.

WORK IN PROGRESS: "I am at present involved in widescale research concerning the period of the Industrial Revolution in its social and political as well as its economic aspects, including developments in America as well as in England. I hope a series of novels will result eventually."

HOBBIES AND OTHER INTERESTS: Vegetable gardening, history, comparative religion, and politics.

FOR MORE INFORMATION SEE:

D. L. Kirkpatrick, editor, *Twentieth-Century Children's Writers,* St. Martin's, 1978.

REIGOT, Betty Polisar 1924-

PERSONAL: Surname is pronounced *Rye*-got; born March 9, 1924, in Brooklyn, N.Y.; daughter of Joseph Marco (a physician) and Pauline (a homemaker; maiden name, Blumberg) Polisar; married Marvin Schwartz, August 1, 1944 (divorced, 1962); married Jack Reigot, October 25, 1970 (deceased); children: (first marriage) Jonathan P., Paula A., D. Jean. *Education:* Smith College, B.A., 1944; attended Hofstra University, 1963-65, and Columbia University, 1982-83. *Home and office:* 508 Dogwood Dr., Chapel Hill, N.C. 27516.

CAREER: Harcourt Brace Jovanovich, Inc., New York City, editorial secretary in trade department, 1944-46; *New York Times,* New York City, editorial assistant to associate editor, 1965-66, assistant to executive vice-president, 1966-70; Ergonomics, Inc., Great Neck, N.Y., associate editor, 1970; Institute for Research and Evaluation, Hempstead, N.Y., deputy director, 1970-72; writer and lecturer, 1975—. Member of Committee on Aging, American Jewish Committee, 1972-75; volunteer worker, American Museum of Natural History. *Member:* Authors Guild, Authors League of America, Society of Children's Book Writers, League of Women Voters (president of Long Island chapter, 1958-59), New York Academy of Sciences, Bank Street Writers Workshop, Mercantile Library Writers Group, Writers Room, Common Cause, Ansonia Democratic Club, Smith College Club of New York. *Awards, honors:* Lucky Four-Leaf Clover Award, 1983.

WRITINGS:

JUVENILE

Wake Up—It's Night: A Science Book about Nocturnal Animals, Scholastic, 1978.
Wolves, Scholastic, 1980.
A Book about Planets (illustrated by Ted Hanke), Scholastic, 1981.
Questions and Answers about Bees (illustrated by Robert Andrew Parker), Scholastic, 1983.
Space Traveler: To Space and Back on the Shuttle, Scholastic, 1983.
A Book about Planets and Stars, Scholastic, 1988.

Contributor to *Family Weekly.*

SIDELIGHTS: "I subscribe to the connection that exists between science and the arts, best known through C. P. Snow's *The Two Cultures.* I must have sensed the stirrings and rumblings that preceded the tidal wave of technology and decided it was important to understand the physical world we inhabit. That was the beginning. Now I'm hooked.

"Having had little science in my formal education, it was an absorbing challenge to do extensive research on a particular scientific subject and explain it as clearly and interestingly as I could. It's been enlightening and rewarding; and I hope as much so for my readers—most of whom are young."

HOBBIES AND OTHER INTERESTS: Music, gardening, tennis.

RODD, Kathleen Tennant 1912-1988 (Kylie Tennant)

OBITUARY NOTICE—See sketch in *SATA* Volume 6: Born March 12, 1912, in Manly (one source says Sydney), New South Wales, Australia; died February 28, 1988, in Sydney, Australia. Editor and author. A full-time writer except for a ten-year stint as an editor and advisor for the Macmillan publishing firm, Rodd was one of Australia's best known authors of realistic fiction and books for children.

All of her work was published under the name Kylie Tennant, including her first novel, *Tiburon,* which won the S. H. Prior Memorial Prize for Best Australian Novel in 1935. *The Battlers,* Rodd's most famous work, won the Australian Literary Society's Gold Medal in 1941. Her children's novel *All the Proud Tribesmen* was named Children's Book of the Year in 1960 by the Children's Book Council of New South Wales. The book was written about the Australian Aborigines, whose welfare was a concern of Rodd's.

Besides writing fiction and non-fiction books for adults and children, Rodd also wrote plays for children in the 1950s, "My husband was a headmaster and could not find suitable plays for his pupils," she said, "so I would write plays according to the number of characters that he wanted and after the children had acted them and tried them out, they were published."

FOR MORE INFORMATION SEE:

Ann Evory, editor, *Contemporary Authors: New Revision Series,* Volume 5, Gale, 1982.
Contemporary Novelists, St. Martin's, 1986.
Kylie Tennant, *The Missing Heir: The Autobiography of Kylie Tennant,* Macmillan, 1986.

OBITUARIES

Times (London), March 10, 1988.

ROGERS, Jean 1919-

PERSONAL: Born October 1, 1919, in Wendell, Idaho; daughter of John Harvey and Maud (Powers) Clark; married George W. Rogers (a research economist), November 27, 1942; children: Shelley Rogers Eldridge, Geoffrey, Sidney Rogers Sisikin, Gavin (deceased), Sabrina, Garth. *Education:* University of California, Berkeley, B.A., 1943. *Home:* 1790 Evergreen Ave., Juneau, Alaska 99801.

CAREER: Author of children's books, 1982—. Member of board of directors, 1975-83, past chairman of board, Capital Community Broadcasting, Inc.; member, Alaska Public Offices Commission, 1982-87, and Alaska Public Broadcasting Commission, 1988-1992. *Member:* American Library Association, Alaska Library Association. *Awards, honors:* Honored Author Citation from the Alaska State Reading Association, 1980; Literacy Award from the International Reading Association, and Literacy Award from the Juneau Reading Council, both 1985, both for service to libraries and the promotion of reading; *The Secret Moose* was selected one of Child Study Association of America's Children's Books of the Year, 1985.

WRITINGS:

FOR YOUNG PEOPLE

Goodbye, My Island (illustrated by Rie Munoz), Greenwillow, 1983.

JEAN ROGERS

The Secret Moose (illustrated by Jim Fowler), Greenwillow, 1985, large print edition, 1985.
King Island Christmas (illustrated by R. Munoz), Greenwillow, 1985.
Runaway Mittens, Greenwillow, 1988.
Dinosaurs Are 568, Greenwillow, 1988.

SIDELIGHTS: "My writing is definitely an outgrowth of my lifelong pleasure in reading. I am honored to be described as a children's book author. A great deal of very fine writing is done in that field, and it has long been a keen interest of mine.

"I was interested in writing in elementary school and did considerable writing for school newspapers both in high school and college. I knew I didn't want a career in journalism—books were always the goal.

"When our last two children were in high school I realized that there was creative energy I could spare for writing. That was when I began writing again in earnest.

"I help in the library at a local school as well as read my stories to children. I try to do this once a week when I am at home in Juneau. Children at school ask me why I like writing. I always reply that it is because I love reading so much. They also ask if I plan to write books about adults. I tell them I probably will never go beyond the eighth grade."

HOBBIES AND OTHER INTERESTS: "Choir singing, opera, going to plays, cooking, eating, people watching, READING, pushing books."

ROOT, Phyllis 1949-

PERSONAL: Born February 14, 1949, in Fort Wayne, Ind.; daughter of John Howard and Esther (Traut) Root; married James Elliott Hansa (a mason); children: Amelia Christin, Ellen Rose. *Education:* Valparaiso University, B.A., 1971. *Home:* Minneapolis, Minn.

CAREER: Writer. Has worked as architectural drafter, costume seamstress, bicycle repair person, and administrative assistant. *Member:* Society of Children's Book Writers. *Awards, honors: Moon Tiger* was selected one of Child Study Association of America's Children's Books of the Year, and was exhibited at the Bologna International Children's Book Fair, both 1985.

WRITINGS:

JUVENILE

Hidden Places (illustrated by Daniel San Souci), Carnival Press, 1983.
(With Carol A. Marron) *Gretchen's Grandma* (illustrated by Deborah K. Ray), Carnival Press, 1983.
(With C. A. Marron) *Just One of the Family* (illustrated by George Karn), Carnival Press, 1984.
(With C. A. Marron) *No Place for a Pig* (illustrated by Nathan Y. Jarvis), Carnival Press, 1984.
My Cousin Charlie (illustrated by Pia Marella), Carnival Press, 1984.
Moon Tiger (Junior Literary Guild selection; illustrated by Ed Young), Holt, 1985.
Soup for Supper (Junior Literary Guild selection; illustrated by Sue Truesdell), Harper, 1986.

Contributor to periodicals, including *Cricket* and *Children's Magic Window*.

ADAPTATIONS:

"Just One of the Family" (cassette), Raintree, 1985.

WORK IN PROGRESS: Kiri, a fantasy novel for children, and *Contrary Bear*, a picture book, both for Harper.

SIDELIGHTS: "As far back as I can remember, I made up stories, poems, and songs. In first grade I wrote a poem about love and a dove, and in second grade I won a class essay contest for my four-sentence story about the Sahara desert. In fifth grade I had a remarkable and wonderful teacher, Mrs. Keller, a gentle Quaker lady who encouraged me to write. It was in her class that I decided I would be an 'authoress' when I grew up.

"The idea for *Soup for Supper* came to me during a thunderstorm in the middle of the night. I had gotten up to comfort my daughter Amelia, and remembered how, when I was a child, my sister and I had sat on the bed with our parents, watching the lightning and rain. 'Don't let the thunder scare you,' they reassured us. 'It's just the noise potatoes make spilling out of the giant's cart.'

"Listening to the thunder with my own daughter, I suddenly saw the giant with his cart of vegetables and a wee small woman chasing after him. The next morning I wrote down the first draft of *Soup for Supper.*

"When I was thirty, I took my first class in writing for children with Marion Bauer, a gifted writer and teacher, who gave me the tools I needed to begin to write.

A tear trickled down her face and splashed on the parsley. ■ (From *Soup for Supper* by Phyllis Root. Illustrated by Sue Truesdell.)

''Perhaps because I devoured fairy tales and fantasies, both as a child and as an adult, I strongly believe that children need good fantasies.

''I believe that stories help children (and adults) to make some sense out of our world. I believe in imagination and fantasy, and the power they have to help a child grow and be healed. I believe in feelings, that they should be recognized and named and accepted, and that feelings are often the place where our lives touch.

''I know that some stories come to me unbidden, out of wherever stories come from. They are like my children—I don't necessarily understand them, but I feel blessed to have been given them.''

ROSENBERG, Maxine B(erta) 1939-

PERSONAL: Born August 6, 1939, in New York, N.Y.; daughter of Stanley (in sales) and Martha (a buyer; maiden name, Kleinman) Schick; married Paul A. Rosenberg (a dentist), June 5, 1960; children: Mark, David, Seth, Karin. *Education:* Hunter College of the City University of New York, A.B., 1961, M.S., 1969; Columbia University, graduate study, 1963. *Religion:* Jewish. *Home:* 31 Stephenson Ter., Briarcliff, N.Y. 10510. *Agent:* Carol Mann, 55 Fifth Ave., New York, N.Y. 10003; and Dorothy Markinko, McIntosh & Otis, 310 Madison Ave., New York, N.Y. 10017.

CAREER: Public School #26, Bronx, N.Y., teacher, 1961-64; homebound and special education teacher in Peekskill, N.Y., 1977; free-lance writer, 1977—. *Awards, honors: Being a Twin, Having a Twin* was selected one of Child Study Association of America's Children's Books of the Year, 1985, and *Making a New Home in America,* 1986; Carter Woodson Award Honorable Mention from the National Council for Social Studies, 1986, for *Living in Two Worlds.*

WRITINGS:

JUVENILE

My Friend, Leslie: The Story of a Handicapped Child (ALA Notable Book; illustrated with photographs by George Ancona), Lothrop, 1983.
Being Adopted (ALA Notable Book; illustrated with photographs by G. Ancona), Lothrop, 1984.
Being a Twin, Having a Twin (illustrated with photographs by G. Ancona), Lothrop, 1985.
Making a New Home in America (illustrated with photographs by G. Ancona), Lothrop, 1986.
Living in Two Worlds (illustrated with photographs by G. Ancona), Lothrop, 1986.
Artists of Handcrafted Furniture at Work (illustrated with photographs by G. Ancona), Lothrop, 1988.
Finding a Way: Living with Exceptional Brothers and Sisters, Lothrop, 1988.

Contributor to magazines and newspapers, including *New York Times.*

WORK IN PROGRESS: Not My Family, a book about the feelings of children of alcoholics, to be published by Bradbury; another adoption book.

SIDELIGHTS: ''My education centered on teaching the visually handicapped and emotionally disturbed. I have also taught non-disabled fourth and fifth graders.

''I am most interested in the inner feelings of people, not only the way they act to the rest of the world, but what they experience inside themselves. The adoption of my Korean-born daughter raised my consciousness to this issue. I learned that an outward smile may be masking an insecurity or inner pain.

''A handicapped child, an adopted one, a twin, a child emigrating from another country or a child born of two races, all have joys and pains they want to share. By putting their feelings in books, I offer children in special situations the comfort of knowing there are others like them with the same or similar agonies and ecstasies.

''One of my greatest joys is visiting schools and talking to children about my books—how they came to be written and the 'behind-the-scenes' cover-ups and near crises. The responses of the kids run the gamut from unfolding sensitive experiences in their own lives to hysterical anecdotes that would make a parent want to hide. I love speaking to adult groups too, but when I can get a child to feel comfortable enough to express his feelings before others, I've achieved what I've hoped for in my writing.

''Before I begin writing any of my books, I do extensive research on the subject. Usually this research is focused on the areas of psychology and sociology to gain further understanding about the young people I intend to interview. Before I actually interview the children and their parents (and I interview many more than I need for my book), I meet with a psychologist to go over the questions I propose to ask. Since many of my books deal with sensitive issues, I want to be careful not to offend people or be intrusive in their private

MAXINE B. ROSENBERG

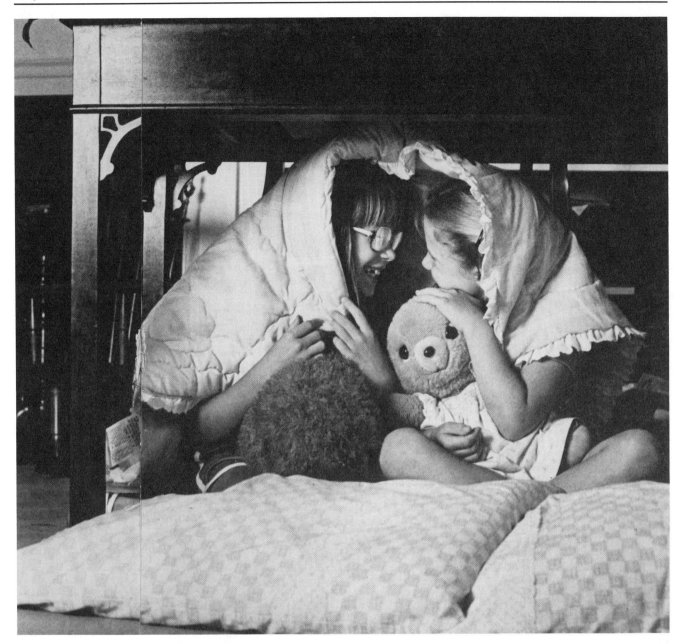

Being a twin means having someone special in your life forever. ■ (From *Being a Twin/Having a Twin* by Maxine B. Rosenberg. Illustrated by George Ancona.)

lives. I am in a delicate position when I interview families; I am a writer, not a therapist. And I do not pretend to be the latter.

"Through the research, interviewing, and writing, I am the one who has grown most in the understanding of children. Often what I hypothesized does not hold true. Children in all types of situations are resilient. If given love, care, warmth, and a secure home, with time they are able to overcome handicaps and discrimination—and often with a sense of humor.

"Sometimes before I investigate a subject, I hold a notion that children in a particular stressful situation will be scarred and not be able to develop positive feelings about themselves. Over and over again, I am proven wrong—happily! I love hearing the laughter and joy of kids who with patience, time, and hard work have found happiness where they never dreamed it existed."

HOBBIES AND OTHER INTERESTS: Jazz, gourmet cooking, sewing, jogging, travel (Europe, Israel, Mexico, the Caribbean).

FOR MORE INFORMATION SEE:

New York Times, March 16, 1984.

ROYDS, Caroline   1953-

PERSONAL: Born June 26, 1953, in Calcutta, India; daughter of Alexander (a journalist) and Pamela (an editor; maiden name, Maycock) Royds; children: Thomas Hans Eilenberg. *Education:* University of York, B.A. (with honors), 1975; University of Bristol, Post-Graduate Certificate in Education, 1976. *Politics:* Labour. *Home:* 74 Hemingford Rd., London N1, England. *Office:* Kingfisher Books, 20-22 Great Titchfield St., London W1P 7AD, England.

CAREER: Sheldon School, Chippenham, Wiltshire, England, English teacher, 1975; Kingfisher Books, London, England, assistant editor, 1976-79; senior editor of children's fiction and history books, 1979-88; Bodley Head, London, England, senior editor in the children's book department, 1988—.

WRITINGS:

EDITOR

The Christmas Book: Stories, Poems, and Carols for the Twelve Days of Christmas (illustrated by Annabel Spenceley), Putnam, 1985.
The Animal Tale Treasury (illustrated by A. Spenceley), Putnam, 1986 (published in England as *The Hare and the Tortoise and Other Stories*, Kingfisher, 1986).
Poems for Young Children, Doubleday, 1986 (published in England as *Read Me a Poem*, Kingfisher, 1986).
A Treasury of Dragons, Giants and Monsters, Kingfisher, 1988.

SALLIS, Susan (Diana) 1929-
(Susan Meadmore)

PERSONAL: Born November 7, 1929, in Gloucester, England; daughter of Clement (a railwayman) and Marjorie (a teacher; maiden name, Hill) Meadmore; married Brian Sallis, March 3, 1951 (died, December 31, 1983); children: Jane, John, Michael. *Education:* Girls High School, teaching certificate, 1970. *Religion:* Church of England. *Home:* 21 Kingston Ave., Clevedon, Avon BS21 6DS, England. *Agent:* Mary Irvine, 11 Upland Park, Oxford OX2 7RU, England.

CAREER: Author, 1959—; primary schoolteacher, 1969-74. *Member:* Romantic Novelists' Association. *Awards, honors: Only Love* was selected one of American Library Association's Best Books for Young Adults, 1979, and one of New York Public Library's Books for the Teen Age, 1981, and 1982; *A Time for Everything* was selected one of New York Public Library's Books for the Teen Age, 1980, and 1981.

WRITINGS:

YOUNG ADULT NOVELS

An Open Mind, Harper, 1978.
A Time for Everything, Harper, 1979, published under pseudonym Susan Meadmore as *Thunder in the Hills*, Hale, 1981.
Only Love, Harper, 1979, published as *Sweet Frannie*, Heinemann, 1981.
Secret Places of the Stairs, Harper, 1984.

ADULT NOVELS

Return to Linstowel, Hale, 1975.
Troubled Waters, Hale, 1975.
Richmond Heritage, Corgi, 1977.
Four Weeks in Venice, Corgi, 1978.
(Under pseudonym Susan Meadmore) *Behind the Mask*, Hale, 1980.
(Under pseudonym Susan Meadmore) *Mary, Mary*, Hale, 1982.
A Scattering of Daisies, Corgi, 1984.
April Rising, St. Martin's, 1984.
The Daffodils of Newent, Corgi, 1985.
Bluebell Windows, Corgi, 1987.
Rosemary for Remembrance, Corgi, 1987.
Summer Visitors, Corgi, 1988.

WORK IN PROGRESS: A Kind of Honour, a novel.

SIDELIGHTS: "I was an only child, very protected within a secure extended family yet with plenty of opportunities to be alone in our countryside environment. I remember the shock of being 'invaded' when an enormous army camp was built in my very own fields and occupied at various times during the war by British, Polish, Canadian, and American troops as well as Italian and German P.O.W.s. I tried to recapture this period in *A Time for Everything*.

"*Only Love* sprang from my knowledge of a local hospital full of 'life' patients. I saw how a few of them refused to become institutionalized and how their spirits rose above their damaged bodies; my heroine, Frannie, celebrates this indomitable courage.

"*Secret Places of the Stairs* is also based on a true incident and is a similarly serious subject to which I have tried to bring humour.

"A quartet of books about my mother's family and home town of Gloucester is now finished. The first book had a title taken from an old rhyme: *A Scattering of Daisies*, and after that it seemed appropriate to keep a flower in each title: *The Daffodils of Newent*, *Bluebell Windows*, and *Rosemary for Remembrance*.

"My latest book is based in a Cornish fishing village, where 'my family' go regularly for their summer holidays. We saw them for that holiday period over a period of forty years; the book is called *Summer Visitors*.

"I am now working on a book about friendship, its loyalties and disloyalties, how it endures. It will be called *A Kind of Honour*. After that I would very much like to do another book for young people."

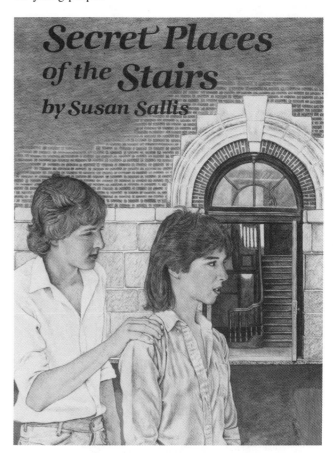

He led me out toward the bulk of the railway station. . . . ■ (Jacket illustration by Bob Marstall from *Secret Places of the Stairs* by Susan Sallis.)

HOBBIES AND OTHER INTERESTS: "I still teach occasionally. I swim most days. Work in my small garden. Read avidly. Do housework unenthusiastically. Iron clothes terribly. Enjoy things."

FOR MORE INFORMATION SEE:

COLLECTIONS

De Grummond Collection at the University of Southern Mississippi.
Kerlan Collection at the University of Minnesota.

SCOTT, Jane (Harrington) 1931-

PERSONAL: Born February 14, 1931, in New York, N.Y.; daughter of Heisler (a chemical engineer) and Ethel (a homemaker; maiden name, Ecker) Harrington; married Anthony Scott (a physical chemist), August 22, 1953; children: Elizabeth Marenakos, Robert, Anne. *Education:* Wheaton College, B.A., 1952; Institute of Children's Literature, Redding Ridge, Conn., M.A., 1979. *Religion:* Episcopalian. *Home and office:* Box 313, Mendenhall, Pa. 19357.

CAREER: John Wiley & Sons, New York, N.Y., sales correspondent, 1952-54; author and illustrator. Past-president, board of trustees, The Children's Home, Wilmington, Del.; board member, Delaware Nature Education Society, 1977-83. *Member:* Author's Guild, Society of Children's Book Writers, Philadelphia Children's Reading Round Table, Garden Club of America (member of editorial board, 1984-87).

JANE SCOTT

WRITINGS:

(With F. M. Mooberry) *Grow Native Shrubs in Your Garden* (self-illustrated), Brandywine Conservancy, 1980.
Cross Fox, Atheneum, 1980.
To Keep an Island, Atheneum, 1983.
Botany in the Field: An Introduction to Plant Communities for the Amateur Naturalist (self-illustrated), Prentice-Hall, 1984.

Contributor of articles to *American Horticulturist. Cross Fox* has been published in Japan.

ILLUSTRATOR

Claude Phillips, *Wildflowers of Delaware and the Eastern Shore,* Delaware Natural Education Society, 1978.
Elizabeth N. duPont, *Landscaping with Native Plants in the Middle Atlantic Region,* Brandywine Conservancy, 1980.

WORK IN PROGRESS: The Chinese Box, a children's book; a book on the natural history of the Delmarva Peninsula to be published by Tidewater.

SIDELIGHTS: "I've always loved books. I remember sitting on my mother's lap and following along while she read a story. In fact, that's how I learned to read. I soon graduated to fairy tales, the 'Oz' books (I owned thirty-one out of a possible thirty-three at one time), animal tales, horse stories, and mysteries. We lived in the Connecticut countryside surrounded by dogs and horses. There were also numbers of half-wild cats in the barn. They were there to keep rats and mice out of the stable, but of course they had kittens regularly in the hayloft. At times it was a bit like Wanda Gag's *Millions of Cats.*

"There was a stream behind our house and a patch of rocky Connecticut woods where I spent a lot of time making up stories, pretending to be each character in turn. That was during World War II, so most of my stories had to do with dramatic escapes through the French countryside. When I was in the eighth grade, my best friend and I made a pact to write a book together; the first one to quit before it was finished must submit to having her hair cut off by the other! The book, as I remember, included several handsome RAF flyers and a nasty little German kid who had been sent to live with his English cousins. Of course, he saw the light in the end. (We read a lot of Nevil Shute and Elswyth Thane in those days.)

"When I was fifteen my parents sent me to boarding school. I didn't like it much. I remember rushing through all my homework before dinner, so that I could spend the evening study hall in the library, where I started with Pearl Buck and A. J. Cronin and worked straight through the fiction shelves to T. H. White and Thomas Wolfe.

"In college I majored in English literature and wrote obscure poetry in the style of T. S. Eliot. On graduation I got a job with a technical book publisher in New York writing sales blurbs and answering mail from foreign bookstores. The books I wrote about had titles like *Imperfections in Nearly Perfect Crystals* and *Nuclear Moments.* Luckily the authors supplied me with the proper information because I had no idea what they were about!

"Considering all this, it is perhaps strange that I didn't get around to actually writing a book until I was in my forties and had brought up three children. Actually, it was reading their books that prodded me to try, for it seemed to me that I could easily do as well. I gave myself a year, but it actually took two; and two more after that to sell it! Writing a book was not as easy as I thought.

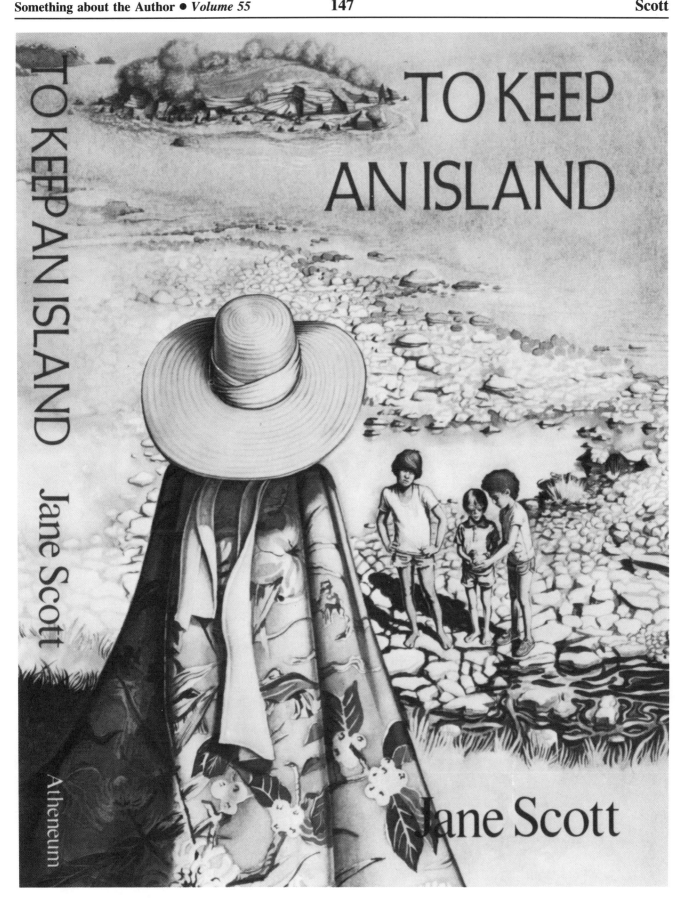

The children swung around to see Mrs. Wetherill standing above them on the rise from the beach. ■ (Jacket illustration by Tom Stoerrle from *To Keep an Island* by Jane Scott.)

"The first publisher I sent my manuscript to kept it six months and wrote me encouraging letters, but in the end decided against it. The second publisher lost it! When I inquired after not hearing for weeks, they said they had never received any manuscript. I, in a panic, put a tracer through the mail and settled down to type another original from my carbon. I had no sooner finished when a battered package arrived from the publisher. They had had it all the time, no doubt buried at the bottom of the 'slush pile.' Meanwhile the brand new typed copy went off to a third publisher who, in due time, accepted it! *Cross Fox* was published in 1980 by Margaret McElderry Books, and was followed in 1983 by *To Keep an Island*. Both are for the nine to twelve age group. Currently I am finishing a third, tentatively called *The Chinese Box*.

"My other love is gardening. (I read *The Secret Garden* early on!) I also love to draw. This naturally led to illustrating books about plants. My first two were published by non-profit organizations, the Delaware Natural Education Society (1978) and the Brandywine Conservancy (1980). Luckily they attracted the attention of Prentice-Hall, and I was soon writing and illustrating a book for amateur plant enthusiasts called *Botany in the Field*. It was published in 1984 and is suitable for high school age as well as grown-ups.

"The books I loved best as a child transported me into someone else's life and world. I loved reading fantasy but, so far, I haven't written any. The children in my stories are absorbed in trying to understand the world around them. I try to give the story a strong sense of place and to people it with interesting characters, grown-ups as well as children, with plenty of faults as well as strengths. I start with a plot idea, but it often changes as the children lead me deeper into the story.

"Today, my husband and I still live in the country, in Pennsylvania now instead of Connecticut. The children come and go as they begin lives of their own, but we still have two Welsh Corgis, a Golden Retriever, and one (fixed) cat."

FOR MORE INFORMATION SEE:

News Journal (Wilmington, Del.), July 11, 1982.

SELMAN, LaRue W. 1927-

PERSONAL: Born August 27, 1927, in Scipio, Utah; daughter of Myron William (a teacher) and Flossie (a housewife; maiden name, Reynolds) Wasden; married Orrin M. Selman (an educator), August 27, 1946, (died, July, 1986); children: Thelma (Mrs. Maugham Guymon), Carolyn Erickson, Kathy (Mrs. Rex Firth), Sandra (Mrs. Jim Anderson), LaMar, Alan, Anita (Mrs. Tom Lott), Lorraine (Mrs. Karl Cameron), Gwen, Richard. *Education:* Brigham Young University, B.S., 1966. *Politics:* Independent. *Religion:* Church of Jesus Christ of Latter-Day Saints. *Home:* Salt Lake City, Utah. *Office:* CAI, Inc., Salt Lake City, Utah.

CAREER: Fruit farmer in Orem and Genola, Utah, 1964-83; Carbon County School District, Price, Utah, substitute teacher, 1970-76; College of Eastern Utah, Price, instructor, 1970's; CAI, Inc., (computer educational software company), Salt Lake City, Utah, courseware development, 1985-86, member of board of directors, 1986—.

WRITINGS:

JUVENILE

Sammy Skunk Plays the Clown, ARO Publishing, 1981.
Boots, Two, ARO Publishing, 1981.

LaRUE W. SELMAN

The Hero, Two, ARO Publishing, 1981.
JD and the Bee, ARO Publishing, 1981.
Rain Frog, ARO Publishing, 1981.

WORK IN PROGRESS: "Writing with English Grammar," a series of computer tutorials; a series of children's books on values.

SIDELIGHTS: "As the daughter of a dedicated and gifted educator and the wife of another, I became infused with the desire to help young people learn to 'live well' in our world.

"My husband and I decided that we wanted a large family (before we married), so, as the children arrived I began teaching them—then taught all ages in church organizations (at various times), and later, I taught all ages (pre-school to graduate school) in various schools.

"I have since learned to see people of all ages as students at various levels of learning and development and I've learned to love and appreciate them all.

"My husband was co-founder of a company (CAI, Inc.) that devised a way to manage 'competency-based' education in conjunction with the Utah State Adult Education Association, and it seems to have the potential for solving most of the current problems of education. I am involved with it as a member of the board of directors and in courseware development.

"Telling stories to our ten children and forty grandchildren inspired me to write and illustrate my own stories. I am studying oil and watercolor painting, illustration, and wood sculpting.

"As an outgrowth of writing books for children I have developed an interest in creating unique, one-of-a-kind cloth toys, of which I make about fifty a year. I call them my 'Weirdly Other-Worldly Creatures.' Each has an original 'other-worldly' name and a special personality all it's own.

"Raising and marketing fruits, traveling widely in the U.S., particularly traveling and camping in the western mountains and deserts, spending a month in India studying their education system, caring for my father and my husband in their final illnesses, maintaining good relationships with my children, in-laws and families, grandchildren, brothers and sisters and their families, all of whom we see often, has tended to broaden my outlook and deepen my capacity for caring.

"People are very important to me, and helping them the best way I can receives my highest priority."

HOBBIES AND OTHER INTERESTS: "I enjoy gardening, walking, cooking, travelling and learning new information about our universe and the people in it. I am currently learning Tai Chi."

SMITH, Betsy Covington 1937-

PERSONAL: Born July 29, 1937, in Omaha, Neb.; daughter of William S. (a stockbroker) and Elizabeth (a homemaker; maiden name, Morse) Covington; married Charles Carter Smith, Jr. (a publisher), July 4, 1959; children: Elizabeth Adair, Charles Carter III, Adam Covington. *Education:* Vassar College, B.A., 1959. *Politics:* Democrat. *Religion:* Episcopalian. *Home and office:* P.O. Box 101, West Woods Rd., Sharon, Conn. 06069.

CAREER: Author, 1975—. Member of board of directors, Housatonic Center for Mental Health, Lakeville, Conn.; past member of women's boards of Chicago Symphony Orchestra, St. Luke's Hospital, and Chicago Urban League. *Awards, honors: Breakthrough: Women in Religion* was selected one of New York Public Library's Books for the Teen Age, 1980, 1981, and 1982, and *Breakthrough: Women in Television,* 1982.

BETSY COVINGTON SMITH

WRITINGS:

JUVENILE

A Day in the Life of a Firefighter (illustrated with photographs by Catherine Noren), Troll Associates, 1981.
A Day in the Life of an Actress (illustrated with photographs by F. Reid Buckley Jr. and Marianne Berstein), Troll Associates, 1984.

YOUNG ADULT

Breakthrough: Women in Religion, Walker, 1978.
Breakthrough: Women in Television, Walker, 1981.
(With Jeanne Gardener) *Breakthrough: Women in Law,* Walker, 1984.
Jimmy Carter, President, Walker, 1986.

Chairman of *Miss Porter's School Alumnae Bulletin,* 1977—.

ADAPTATIONS:

"A Day in the Life of a Firefighter" (cassette), Troll Associates, 1981.
"A Day in the Life of an Actress" (cassette), Troll Associates, 1985.

SIDELIGHTS: "Several years ago, after I'd published a couple of books for young adults, a childhood friend complimented me on my writing. 'You always were the best writer in our class, ever since sixth grade,' she said.

"Her comment really irritated me. If I write decently now, I told her, that's solely because I've worked harder at writing than anything I've ever worked at in my life. Few writers are naturally gifted, and I'm not one of them. In fact, the last thing I thought I'd ever be when I graduated from college was a writer. Writing seemed too lonely, too hard, too much like school. It was not until I was in my early thirties and had moved to New York City with my husband and three young children that I turned to writing. At first it was therapy, nothing more. I wrote lots of rambling short stories with me as the thinly-disguised central character. Gradually, I stopped writing about me and got hooked on the craft of writing. The satisfaction of having written one good paragraph, to have said what I wanted to say, remains an exhilarating experience.

"Primarily, I write biographies about contemporary women. I always interview people I write about. Although I've interviewed several famous women (such as Sandra Day O'Connor), I far prefer interviewing and writing about ordinary women who have made everyday decisions and choices about their lives that seem quite heroic and extraordinary. After I've interviewed someone whose story has moved me (which doesn't always happen, of course), I go away feeling both elated and terribly, terribly frightened. 'Can I do it?' I ask myself. To convey that person's life story onto a piece of paper, to make that person as alive and unique to the reader as he/she was to me seems an awesome responsibility. Life would be much easier, I sometimes think, if I were writing about Greek vases!

"But people and the human condition are what fascinate me. These people have led me into worlds I never would have known—worlds occupied by women priests, symphony orchestra musicians, veterinarians caring for exotic animals, television producers, and so on. It is amazing that I once thought writing a lonely occupation. It has been just the opposite."

STEARNS, Monroe (Mather) 1913-1987

OBITUARY NOTICE—See sketch in *SATA* Volume 5: Born September 28, 1913, in New York, N.Y.; died of an apparent respiratory ailment, December 17, 1987. Educator, editor, translator, and author. Stearns taught for fifteen years at institutions including Rutgers University before embarking on a career in publishing, first as an editor for Prentice-Hall and later as managing editor of Bobbs-Merrill. In addition, he was the author of historical books and works for children, among them *Casimir's Journey, Gabriel and His Magic Wand, The Story of New England,* and *Wolfgang Amadeus Mozart.* He also translated *Angelique and the King, The Soldier and the Rose,* and *Wherever They May Be*.

FOR MORE INFORMATION SEE:

Ann Evory, editor, *Contemporary Authors: New Revision Series,* Volume 2, Gale, 1981.
The Writers Directory: 1982-1984, Gale, 1981.

OBITUARIES

New York Times, December 31, 1987.

STEFANIK, Alfred T. 1939-

PERSONAL: Born July 5, 1939, in Copaigue, N.Y.; son of Alfred F. (a building superintendent) and Julia H. (a homemaker; maiden name, Gnaudowski) Stefanik; married Claire Helen Affourtit (a psychologist), October 3, 1969; children: Stefan, Anastasia; stepchildren: Daniel, Sean, Thomas, Ted, Donald. *Education:* Cathedral College, B.A., 1961; Catholic University, S.T.B., 1965; St. Michael's College, M.A.T.E.S.L., 1970. *Religion:* Episcopalian. *Home:* 30 Hayes Ave., South Burlington, Vt. 05403. *Office:* Episcopal Diocesan Center, Rock Point, Burlington, Vt. 05401.

CAREER: Roman Catholic priest. St. Frances de Chantal, Wantagh, N.Y., parish priest, 1965-69; St. John's, Riverhead, N.Y., parish priest, 1969; St. Michaels College, Winooski, Vt., fellow, 1969-70; State of Vermont, social worker, 1971-81, adoption social worker, 1981-82; private counsellor, Cambridge, Vt., 1978-85; University of Vermont, Burlington, Episcopal/Lutheran chaplain, 1983—. *Member:* American As-

ALFRED T. STEFANIK

sociation of Counselling and Development, Association for Religious Values in Counselling.

WRITINGS:

Copycat Sam: Developing Ties with a Special Child (illustrated by Laura Huff), Human Sciences Press, 1982.

WORK IN PROGRESS: A biography about his maternal grandmother, her superstitions and her earthy, peasant-like approach to life's mysteries.

SIDELIGHTS: "My grandmother provided the safest place in the world from which I had absolute freedom to explore the woods and swamp near her home. She also instructed me about gardening and animal husbandry in a non-sentimental way that allowed me to respect and use creation.

"She was as mysterious as she was caring. Though she never explained her religious practices, praying to saints and the Mother of God (represented by icons), attending mass, etc., I came to understand her practices by participating in them as I chose to do so.

"Mysticism has always been present. Fostered by my mother who set many fairy tales firmly in my imaginative life and carried on by my youthful desire to read every mythology I could locate, this desire to look for things unseen was given a rational encouragement by the Catholic liturgies which weaved in and out of our yearly cycle. I later developed the ability to separate the overburdensome religious institutionality from spirituality due to my grandmother's cunning. My desire to dream and to play with my dreams continues well past the stage when I was expected to 'grow up' largely because of my father's spiritual sensitivity and idealism which expressed itself in many kind acts for other people."

HOBBIES AND OTHER INTERESTS: Walking, weight lifting, bass fishing, cross country skiing, alpine skiing.

TCHUDI, Stephen N. 1942-
(Stephen Judy, Stephen N. Judy)

PERSONAL: Original surname, Judy; name legally changed October 22, 1982; born January 31, 1942, in Waterbury, Conn.; son of John Nelson (a chemist) and Anna Louise (a consultant; maiden name, May) Judy; married Susan Jane Schmidt (a writer and college teacher), June 3, 1979; children: Stephen, Emily, Michael, Christopher. *Education:* Hamilton College, B.A., 1963; Northwestern University, M.A., 1964, Ph.D., 1967. *Home:* 2011 Pawnee Trail, Okemos, Mich. 48864. *Office:* Department of English, Morrill Hall, Michigan State University, East Lansing, Mich. 48824.

CAREER: Northwestern University, Evanston, Ill., assistant professor of English and education, 1967-69; Michigan State University, East Lansing, Mich., assistant professor, 1969-71, associate professor, 1971-76, professor of English, 1976—, director of the Center for Literacy and Learning, 1987—. Visiting professor, University of British Columbia, 1975, Northeastern University, 1981, 1983, University of Sydney, 1986. *Member:* National Council of Teachers of English (past president), Educational Press Association, Conference on College Composition and Communication, Conference on English Education, Michigan Council of Teachers of English, National Storytelling Association, Society for the Preservation of Barbershop Quartet Singing in America.

STEPHEN TCHUDI

AWARDS, HONORS: Eight awards from the Educational Press Association for excellence in educational journalism, for *English Journal;* Charles Carpenter Fries Award from the Michigan Council of Teachers of English, 1978, for distinguished service to the profession of English teaching; *The Burg-O-Rama Man* was chosen as a Notable Children's Trade Book in the Field of Social Studies by the National Council for Social Studies and the Children's Book Council, 1985; *Soda Poppery* was selected one of Child Study Association of America's Children's Books of the Year, 1987.

WRITINGS:

(Under name Stephen Judy; with wife, Susan J. Judy) *Gifts of Writing Creative Projects with Words and Art,* Scribner, 1980.

(Under name Stephen Judy; with S. J. Judy) *Putting on a Play: A Guide to Writing and Producing Neighborhood Drama,* Scribner, 1982.

(With S. J. Tchudi) *Teaching Writing in the Content Areas: Elementary School,* National Education Association, 1983.

(With Margie C. Huerta) *Teaching Writing in the Content Areas: Middle School/Junior High,* National Education Association, 1983.

(With Joanne Yates) *Teaching Writing in the Content Areas: Senior High School,* National Education Association Professional Library, 1983.

(With S. J. Tchudi) *The Young Writer's Handbook: A Practical Guide for the Beginner Who Is Serious about Writing,* Scribner, 1984.

The Burg-O-Rama Man (young adult), Delacorte, 1984.

(Editor) *Language, Schooling, and Society,* Boynton Cook, 1985.

Soda Poppery: The History of Soft Drinks in America (juvenile), Scribner, 1986.

(Editor) *English Teachers at Work: Ideas and Strategies from Five Countries,* Boynton Cook, 1986.

The Green Machine and the Frog Crusade (young adult novel), Delacorte, 1987.

The Young Learner's Handbook: A Guide to Solving Problems, Mastering Skills, Thinking Creatively, Scribner, 1987.

UNDER NAME STEPHEN N. JUDY

(With others) *The Creative Word,* six volumes, Random House, 1973-74.

Explorations in the Teaching of Secondary English: A Source Book for Experimental Teaching, Dodd, 1974, 2nd edition published as *Explorations in the Teaching of English,* Harper, 1981, 3rd edition, 1988.

(With James Edwin Miller) *Writing in Reality,* Harper, 1978.

(With S. J. Judy) *The English Teacher's Handbook: Ideas and Resources for Teaching English,* Winthrop Publishers, 1979.

(Editor) *Teaching English: Reflections on the State of the Art,* Hayden Book, 1979.

The ABCs of Literacy: A Guide for Parents and Educators, Oxford University Press, 1980.

(With S. J. Judy) *An Introduction to the Teaching of Writing,* Wiley, 1981.

(Editor) *Publishing in English Education,* Boynton Cook, 1982.

Editor of *English Journal,* 1973-80.

WORK IN PROGRESS: Explaining the Unknown, nonfiction young adult; *The Valedictorian,* a young adult novel; a monograph on English curriculum studies for the Association for Curriculum Development and Supervision.

SIDELIGHTS: "I began my writing career by doing various textbooks for teachers, but in the 1980s I have moved in the direction of fiction and nonfiction for young adults. I especially enjoy writing for kids, who are both more candid in their dislikes and more demonstrative of their appreciation than adults are.

"I am interested in the publication of young people's writing in all forms—from one-of-a-kind handbound books to authentic printed books. I teach and sponsor young writers' workshops with this in mind, and take pride in helping unpublished writers get their work in print, particularly young writers who are normally excluded from participation in formal school publications.

"My writing for young adults tends to be a permutation of current or past experiences. *Soda Poppery* was triggered by childhood memories of homemade root beer. *The Green Machine* traces its origins to my days as a frog collector. *The Valedictorian* does *not* reflect immediate experience—I wasn't the top student by a long shot—but explores some of my high school and college experiences with academic competition. *The Young Learner's Handbook* comes from my work in a teacher education program at Michigan State University. People

"Man cannot live by milkshakes alone," he said . . . "Or woman, either." I insisted. ■ (Jacket illustration by Joe Csatari from *Burg-O-Rama Man* by Stephen Tchudi.)

accuse me of taking up hobbies so I can write books on them. If so, readers can expect books on barbershop quartets, madrigal singing, bicycling, and harmonica playing."

FOR MORE INFORMATION SEE:

Washington Post Book World, January 6, 1980.

THOMPSON, Julian F(rancis) 1927-

PERSONAL: Born November 16, 1927, in New York, N.Y.; son of Julian Francis (a playwright; in business) and Amalita (Stagg) Thompson; married Polly Nichy (an artist), August 11, 1978. *Education:* Princeton University, A.B., 1949; Columbia University, M.A., 1955. *Home address:* P.O. Box 138, West Rupert, Vt. 05776. *Agent:* Curtis Brown Ltd., 575 Madison Ave., New York, N.Y. 10022.

CAREER: Lawrenceville School, Lawrenceville, N.J., history teacher, athletic coach, and director of Lower School, 1949-61, 1965-67; Changes, Inc. (alternative high school), East Orange, N.J., director and teacher, 1971-77; writer, 1978—. *Member:* Authors Guild, Authors League of America. *Awards, honors: A Band of Angels* was selected one of American Library Association's Best Books for Young Adults, 1986; *Booklist*'s Editor's Choice, 1987, for *Simon Pure.*

WRITINGS:

YOUNG ADULT NOVELS

The Grounding of Group 6, Avon, 1983.
Facing It, Avon, 1983.
A Question of Survival, Avon, 1984.
Discontinued, Scholastic, 1986.
A Band of Angels, Scholastic, 1986.
Simon Pure, Scholastic, 1987.
The Taking of Mariasburg, Scholastic, 1988.

WORK IN PROGRESS: "A novel about half finished; another novel for Scholastic, tentative title, *Goofbang Value Daze*—'goofbang' being one of Kerouac's great words in *On the Road.* It's about the rather vexing problem of whether 'values' can (or should) be taught in public school or not."

SIDELIGHTS: "I started to write young adult novels in 1978. Not long before, I'd resigned after seven years as janitor/teacher/director at a wonderful, exhausting alternative high school that some kids and I had banded together to found, and my wife had gone back to being a full-time student. I'd done my own assignments in a writing workshop at the school all seven years, and I thought I might have taught myself something about writing, and even found a voice that seemed to be my own.

"It was an old friend, Perry Knowlton, president of Curtis Brown Ltd., the literary agency, who first told me that the book I was writing in 1980 would probably be perceived as a 'young adult' novel. I'd never heard the expression before, so I asked him what one was, and he said it was a book that was (mostly) about kids but wasn't *Lord of the Flies* or *Catcher in the Rye.* He also put me in the hands of his executive vice-president Marilyn Marlow, which meant I had the finest agent imaginable.

"To be honest, I didn't care what anybody called my books, as long as somebody published them and other people got to read them, and I still don't. My only strategy is to write down whatever story comes to my mind, as well as I can, and let other people put the labels on. It seems to me that some of

JULIAN F. THOMPSON

my books work at least as well for people beyond their teens—many of whom have told me so—but of course that's a matter of opinion.

"There are a number of reasons for my choosing to write novels that have teen-aged protagonists. First of all, I *did* spend over thirty years with people that age, in settings ranging from a state reformatory (on one extreme) to a selective private school (on another). And I really did enjoy the kids I met in all those different places. Naturally, I had a lot of roles and titles through the years, like 'teacher,' 'coach,' 'counselor,' and 'director,' but the one I liked most—corny as this sounds—was 'friend.' I enjoyed hanging out with people that age, not *all* the time (for sure) but some of it. And so it really pleases me to write books that some of them enjoy. I like to think that kids are (somehow) reassured and feel approved by what they read in my books. I take kids seriously. I want them to know that a lot of the 'answers' that grown-ups give to many questions should not be swallowed whole. I want them to hold onto their hopefulness and wonder and to their own real selves.

"A lot of people have told me that my stuff is 'controversial,' but that's not part of my purpose; it doesn't seem that way to me. I realize, though, that anything a person writes about such things as peer and parent relationships, nuclear and conventional war, or the educational system can be labeled controversial by someone who disagrees with what is written—and I suppose that accounts, in part, for those opinions. It's possible, too, that some readers take what I write completely literally. That would be a bad mistake; by and large, my novels

have (as, thank heaven, reviewers have noticed) a certain amount of surrealistic (and even black) humor in them. I'm pretty sure most kids—and all but the most conservative adults—understand and relax with what I'm up to, sometimes even before they learn what it's called."

THOMSON, David (Robert Alexander) 1914-1988

OBITUARY NOTICE—See sketch in *SATA* Volume 46: Born February 17, 1914, in Quetta, India; died in February, 1988. English broadcaster, educator, and author. In 1932 Thomson began his career as a tutor in Ireland, a post he held until 1943, when he became a writer and producer with the British Broadcasting Corporation (BBC).

Thomson, who wrote both fiction and nonfiction for children and adults, was the author of the "Danny Fox" series for children. He is best remembered, however, for his evocative use of a novelistic technique in his autobiographies, *Woodbrook* and *Nairn in Darkness and Light*. The latter book won the first McVities Award for Scottish Book of the Year in 1987. He also wrote *The People of the Sea: A Journey in Search of the Seal Legend* and *Ronan and Other Stories;* the novels *Daniel* and *Break in the Sun;* and the nonfiction work *In Camden Town*. With Moyra McGusty he edited *The Irish Journals of Elizabeth Smith, 1840-1850: A Selection*. Thomson said that he could only write well, ". . .when I put something

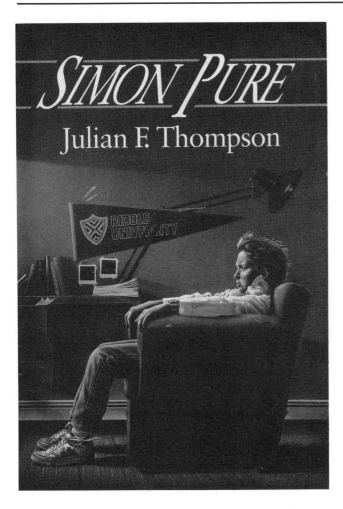

(Jacket painting by Jeff Walker from *Simon Pure* by Julian F. Thompson.)

of my own into the subject I am dealing with. It must come from the heart. And it isn't easy. In fact it's very hard work. But in the end you enjoy it.''

FOR MORE INFORMATION SEE:

Hal May, editor, *Contemporary Authors*, Volume l07, Gale, l983.
International Authors and Writers Who's Who, l0th edition, International Biographical Centre, l986.
The Writers Directory: l986-l988, St. James Press, l986.

OBITUARIES

Times (London), March l, l988.

TOLLIVER, Ruby C(hangos)   1922-

PERSONAL: Born May 29, 1922, in Forth Worth, Tex.; daughter of George Nicolas (a restaurant owner) and Lena (Brock) Changos; married B(owers) H(arbert) Tolliver, Jr. (a construction engineer and consultant), November 4, 1944; children: Elizabeth Tolliver Wright, Dotty Tolliver Brown, Steve. *Education:* Attended Port Arthur Business College. *Religion:* Baptist. *Residence:* Conroe, Tex. *Agent:* Lettie Lee, Ann Elmo Agency, 60 East 42nd St., New York, N.Y. 10165. *Office:* 1806 Pin Oak, Conroe, Tex. 77302.

CAREER: War Manpower Commission, Jasper, Tex., and Port Arthur, Tex., interviewer, 1942-44; U.S. Navy, Corpus Christi, Tex., civil service clerk, 1944-45; South Carolina State Ration Board, Columbia, S.C., clerk, 1945; Texas Employment Commission, Conroe, Tex., clerk, 1959-60; Montgomery County Tax Office, Conroe, deputy tax assessor, 1960-71; Mims Memorial Baptist Church, Conroe, secretary, 1972-73; writer. Volunteer instructor in English as a second language. *Member:* Hughie Call Scribblers Club. *Awards, honors:* Texas Institute of Letters Young Adult Book Award, 1987, and Opie Award from Radio Station WRR-FM (Dallas), 1988, both for *Muddy Banks*.

WRITINGS:

YOUNG ADULT NOVELS

Summer of Decision, Broadman, 1979.
Decision at Sea, Broadman, 1980.
More Than One Decision, Broadman, 1981.
Decision at Brushy Creek, Broadman, 1982.
A Question of Doors, Broadman, 1984.
Muddy Banks, Texas Christian University Press, 1987.

Contributor of short stories to magazines, including *War Cry!*, *Alive!*, *Living Message*, *Mature Living*, and *Home Life*.

WORK IN PROGRESS: Sara's Story.

SIDELIGHTS: ''I never planned to be a writer. I was forty-three years old before I wrote my first short story. I joined a writers' club in 1965 because my friends belonged to one. I am a Christian and very involved with children and young people in our church, so I chose to write for denominational magazines. After I retired from full-time work, I began to write idealistic novels about real situations. At the time, too many writers for young people were writing the realistic fiction that seemed to leave young people without hope—drug users, incest, divorce, drop-outs, and their problems. I felt young people needed 'escape' novels that would help them deal with the pressures being forced on them.

''My first four books are job-oriented, or fishing-and-boats-oriented. I gleaned my material being with my husband during his work as construction engineer for an oil company in Texas and Louisiana. The first five of my books are Christian-oriented without being preachy. I think it important to write about the problems of young people and how they solved them. I feel good kids can have exciting adventures, too. I have tried to offer interesting information about oil production, boats, tankers, shrimping, conservation, and bass fishing—as well as to entertain.

''I wrote *Muddy Banks* when I discovered I was reared within ten miles of the battle that for several months stopped the invasion of Texas by Union troops during the Civil War. I knew then that if the battle was presented from the viewpoint of a young person, the history would be more real.

''I like doing the necessary research. I get many ideas from reading newspapers, too. I have taken several creative writing courses since I started writing, but the only formal education in creative writing was a journalism course in high school. Being an avid reader helped me become a writer more than anything else.''

FOR MORE INFORMATION SEE:

Royal Service, October, 1978, December, 1979.

RUBY C. TOLLIVER

TORGERSEN, Don Arthur   1934-

PERSONAL: Born September 27, 1934, in Chicago, Ill.; son of Arthur Arvid (a sales representative in the steel industry) and Bernice (a legal secretary; maiden name, Malstrom) Torgersen; married Sabina Elizabeth Platt, 1964 (divorced, 1966); married Kathleen Jean Pucillo (a homemaker), January 27, 1967; children: Scott Arthur, Dana Falcon, Guy Eric, Jane Anne. *Education:* Attended University of Hawaii, 1953-54, and University of Chicago, 1961-62; University of Illinois, B.A., 1961. *Home and office:* 1062 Old Mill Dr., Palatine, Ill. 60067.

CAREER: Writer, 1961—; Science and Mechanics Publishing Company, Chicago, Ill., editor and contributor, 1961-62; Chicago International Manuscripts, Chicago, editor and publisher of radio and television scripts, literary magazines, and scientific journals, 1962-67; Science Research Associates, Chicago, mathematics editor, 1963-65; WXFM-Radio, Chicago, producer and moderator of "Nine Faces of the Muse," (weekly program), 1964-67; Allied News Co., Chicago, managing editor, 1965-70; Chicago City College (Wright) Chicago, instructor, 1970-72; Society for Visual Education, Chicago, manager of producers, 1971-75; Don Arthur Torgersen Productions (publishing, advertising, and audiovisual production firm), Palatine, Ill., founder and owner, 1976—. Producer of International Poetry Festival, Chicago, 1967. Member of Aspen Chamber of Commerce; president of Palatine Boys Baseball, 1982-83; director of Palatine Baseball Association (Palatine Park District), 1984-1988; manager and general manager of Palatine American Legion Post 690 baseball team. *Military service:* U.S. Navy, 1952-55.

MEMBER: Authors Guild, American Association of College Baseball Coaches, Chicago Audiovisual Producers, Chicago Unlimited, University of Illinois Alumni Association, Masons, American Legion. *Awards, honors:* University of Illinois Honorarium, 1966, and Award from the Friends of the Chicago Library, 1967, both for *Port Chicago Poets;* Northminster Fellowship, 1977; Award from Norwegian-American Literary Society, 1978, for *The Troll's Three Christmas Wishes;* Award

from the Children's Reading Round Table, 1980, for *The Scariest Night in Troll Forest,* and 1983, for *The Last Days of Gorlock the Dragon;* Award from the Illinois Young Authors Conference, 1983, for *The Last Days of Gorlock the Dragon,* and for contributions to children's literature.

WRITINGS:

JUVENILE

Gandhi, Childrens Press, 1968, revised edition, 1984.
Encyclopaedia Britannica Biology Program, Encyclopaedia Britannica Educational Corp., 1977.
Troll Tales of Tumble Town, Random House, 1978.
The Girl Who Tricked the Troll, Childrens Press, 1978.
The Troll's Three Christmas Wishes, Vinland, 1978.
The Troll Who Lived in the Lake, Childrens Press, 1979.
The Scariest Night in Troll Forest, Childrens Press, 1979.

"ANIMAL LIFE STORIES" SERIES

Ziggy the Elephant, Encyclopaedia Britannica Educational Corp., 1977.
The Polar Bears and the Seals, Encyclopaedia Britannica Educational Corp., 1977.
The Mountain Gorilla, Encyclopaedia Britannica Educational Corp., 1977.
The Golden Eagles, Encyclopaedia Britannica Educational Corp., 1977.
The Great Tigers of India, Encyclopaedia Britannica Educational Corp., 1977.
The Wolves of Isle Royale, Encyclopaedia Britannica Educational Corp., 1977.
Big Gator of the Everglades, Encyclopaedia Britannica Educational Corp., 1977.
The Porpoises and the Sailor, Encyclopaedia Britannica Educational Corp., 1977.
Prairie Dog Town, Encyclopaedia Britannica Educational Corp., 1977.
The Wild Ostrich of the Kalahari, Encyclopaedia Britannica Educational Corp., 1977.
The Cheetahs of the Serengeti Plain, Encyclopaedia Britannica Educational Corp., 1977.
The Blue Shark, Encyclopaedia Britannica Educational Corp., 1977.

JUVENILE; ALL ILLUSTRATED BY TOM DUNNINGTON

The Troll Who Went to School, Childrens Press, 1980.
The Angry Giants of Troll Mountain, Childrens Press, 1980.
The Wicked Witch of the Troll Cave, Childrens Press, 1981.
The Gnomes of Pepper Tree Forest, Random House, 1981.
Huff and Puff and the Troll Hole, Childrens Press, 1982.
The Secret of Cathedral Lake, Childrens Press, 1982.
Torrek and the Elfin Girl, Childrens Press, 1982.
The Last Days of Gorlock the Dragon, Childrens Press, 1982.

"ANIMAL SAFARI NATURE LIBRARY" SERIES; JUVENILE; ILLUS-TRATED WITH OWN PHOTOGRAPHS AND PHOTOGRAPHS BY LEE TRAIL

Elephant Herds and Rhino Horns, Childrens Press, 1982.
Lion Prides and Tiger Tracks, Childrens Press, 1982.
Giraffe Hooves and Antelope Horns, Childrens Press, 1982.
Killer Whales and Dolphin Play, Childrens Press, 1982.
Bear Claws and Furry Tails, Childrens Press, 1983.
Wolf Fangs and Fox Dens, Childrens Press, 1983.
Turtles, Snakes, and Alligator Jaws, Childrens Press, 1983.
Great Apes and Monkey Tails, Childrens Press, 1983.

OTHER

The Poet and Truth, Chicago International Manuscripts, 1963.
(Editor and contributor) *Port Chicago Poets,* Chicago International Manuscripts, 1966.

DON ARTHUR TORGERSEN

Morte De Gaulle: The Experiment Anthology, Chicago City College, 1971.

EDUCATIONAL DOCUMENTARY FILM SCRIPTS; ALSO PRODUCER

"New Dimensions in Decimals and Percent," Society for Visual Education, 1974.

"The History of Impeachment," Society for Visual Education, 1974.

"Impeachment Procedure: How it Works," Society for Visual Education, 1974.

"Planning the Human Community," Society for Visual Education, 1974.

"Exploring Careers," Society for Visual Education, 1975.

"The Scuba Diver," Society for Visual Education, 1975.

"The Farm Equipment Mechanic," Society for Visual Education, 1975.

(With Robert Burleigh) "Stories from the Old West," Society for Visual Education, 1975.

(With Donald and Barbara Smetzer) "Israel: The Making of a Modern Nation," Society for Visual Education, 1975.

"The Middle East: Facing a New World Role," Society for Visual Education, 1976.

(With R. Burleigh) "The American Example," Society for Visual Education, 1976.

"DOCUMENTARY ON CANADA" SERIES

"The Fishermen of Nova Scotia," Society for Visual Education, 1973.

"Quebec City and the French Canadians," Society for Visual Education, 1973.

"Pinawa—Suburb for Atomic Energy," Society for Visual Education, 1973.

"Yellowknife—Capitol of the Northwest Territories," Society for Visual Education, 1973.

"Canada's Arctic Settlements," Society for Visual Education, 1973.

"Port of Vancouver: Canada's Pacific Gateway," Society for Visual Education, 1973.

"CUBA AND ITS REFUGEES" SERIES

"Cuba: The Island Country," Society for Visual Education, 1973.

"Miami's Cuban Community," Society for Visual Education, 1973.

"THE NEW JAPAN" SERIES; WITH MARTHA COOPER GUTHRIE AND STEWART GUTHRIE

"Tokyo—World's Largest City," Society for Visual Education, 1974.

"A Traditional Japanese Family," Society for Visual Education, 1974.

"Japan's Life from the Sea," Society for Visual Education, 1974.

"Silk Farming at Takatoya," Society for Visual Education, 1974.

"Nagasaki and Her Ship Builders," Society for Visual Education, 1974.

"Okinawa—Keystone of the Pacific," Society for Visual Education, 1974.

"THE BRITISH ISLES" SERIES; WITH RICHARD HERBERT

"London and the Mother of Parliaments," Society for Visual Education, 1974.

"Bath and the English Countryside," Society for Visual Education, 1974.

"Scotland—A Separate Way of Life," Society for Visual Education, 1974.

"The Orkneys—Isolated Islanders," Society for Visual Education, 1974.

"Wales—Land of the Red Dragon," Society for Visual Education, 1974.

"Ireland—A People Divided," Society for Visual Education, 1974.

"THE AMERICAN EXPERIENCE IN DEMOCRACY" SERIES

"Give Us Independence," Society for Visual Education, 1975.

"Working Together—The U.S. Constitution," Society for Visual Education, 1975.

"The Living Constitution," Society for Visual Education, 1975.

"The Chief Executive," Society for Visual Education, 1975.

"Profile of Congress," Society for Visual Education, 1975.

"The Supreme Court," Society for Visual Education, 1975.

"WILDLIFE STORIES" SERIES; ALL WITH WORTHLEY N. L. BURBANK

"Curly and Simba: Twin African Lions," Society for Visual Education, 1975.

"Beishung: The Giant Panda," Society for Visual Education, 1975.

"Buffy: The Sea Otter," Society for Visual Education, 1975.

"Coco and Chacha: The Coatis," Society for Visual Education, 1975.

"Windy: The Snow Goose," Society for Visual Education, 1975.

"Koolah: The White Koala," Society for Visual Education, 1975.

Contributor to the 1983 edition of *Raintree Illustrated Science Encyclopedia;* managing and contributing editor of *Catalyst,* 1962-64.

WORK IN PROGRESS: Wolf Song and Bristlecone, "eco-poems and nature photographs"; *Tipi and Totem Pole Tales,* native American folk tales; *Thieves of the Cherry Trees,* memoirs of author's Chicago boyhood; *Arinbjorn,* a Viking novel; additional books for the "Animal Safari Nature Library" series for Childrens Press; more troll and gnome books; with Helen Fletre translated from the Swedish Nels Ryden's *Fredrik's Secret;* an animated feature film based on the troll and gnome tales; *The Dragons of Asklepios,* a novel about the ancient Greek physicians who set the standards for the profession of medicine and the American surgeon who betrayed them.

SIDELIGHTS: "I am fortunate to have had many opportunities to write, publish, produce, and find creative expression in all media. I have been able to make significant contributions to the educational and trade publishing markets, as well as to the fields of journalism, broadcasting, advertising, and documentary filmmaking. I have developed interdisciplinary materials for social studies programs, natural and applied sciences, sports, art, music, mathematics, and literature.

"Children's literature has been a very productive area for me. As a child, I was deeply impressed by the classical fairy tales which were read aloud to me and which quickly seized my imagination: the heroic myths and legends and the great epic poems. Many of those initial literary impressions helped to nourish my intellectual development and eventually influenced some of my own works. I see myself in the tradition of the storyteller, skald, and bard, spinning new tales and poems from threads of folklore and fragments of ancient myth. Many of my stories are similar in genre to the German 'Maerchen'—tales that move through fabulous, somewhat unreal worlds filled with marvelous, terrifying, and delightful events. I enjoy giving life and character to trolls, gnomes, witches, giants, dragons, trees, rocks, insects, and animals, and creating complex plots with conflicts and unexpected turnings. The protagonists often struggle against great odds but persevere to discover a joyous ending, self worth, and a secure future. Aren't these the gifts we would like to give to our children?

"We live in an amazing electronic age. Commercial television, computers, video games, and other audiovisual devices proliferate in great numbers and dramatize visual effects at the expense of sound dialogue. The action is exciting, but the storyline is not believable. We begin to yearn for the logic, the believability, and the psychological satisfaction gained from reading or hearing a well-crafted tale. Video systems *interface* with computers and many forms of electronic equipment; human beings *interact* with many levels of intelligence and many layers of emotion. As writers, we need to assimilate the new electronic tools and formats into our craft, but not be overwhelmed or enfeebled by them. We must not lose sight of the *interpersonal role* of the storyteller: his oral and poetic traditions, his wisdom and humor, his affection for the story *and* his audience, and his unique influence on the psychological development of the child.

"It is important for the storyteller to enter the children's circle and keep the oral traditions alive: to give shape and sound to

A young elephant likes to have its tongue tickled. ∎
(From *Elephant Herds and Rhino Horns* by Don Arthur Torgersen. Photograph by Lee Trail and Don Torgersen.)

(From the "Wildlife Stories" filmstrip "Beishung: The Giant Panda." Produced by Society for Visual Education, Inc., 1975.)

words, rhythm to phrases, voice and feeling to characters, familiarity to strangeness, significance and meaning to the tale; to excite, challenge, and delight; to encourage spontaneous interruption, animated discussion, and interplay of personalities; to cause children to probe deeply into their intelligence and their imagination; to bring them as close as possible to the center of the tale and its creative sources; and to leave them with happy, lasting memories."

HOBBIES AND OTHER INTERESTS: Nature and animal photography, skiing, sailing, mountain climbing, playing the piano, composing folk songs, enjoying opera and classical music, competitive sports.

FOR MORE INFORMATION SEE:

Chicago Tribune, January 29, 1966 (p. 16), March 7, 1966, January 26, 1982 (p. 16).
Chicago Sun Times, June 28, 1966 (p. 46), July 11, 1966 (p. 32)

Chicago Tribune Magazine, November 12, 1967 (p. 77), January 25, 1987 (p. 8).
Vinland, February 13, 1969 (p. 4), December 21, 1978 (p. 1), April 16, 1981 (p. 6).
Social Studies, February, 1970 (p. 94).
School Library Journal, September, 1978 (p. 126).
University of Illinois Alumni News, March, 1979 (p. 9).
Palatine Countryside, July 22, 1981 (p. 1).
Arlington Heights Daily Journal, September 21, 1982 (p. 2).
Booklist, January 15, 1983 (p. 680).

TOWNSEND, Sue   1946-

PERSONAL: Born April 2, 1946, in Leicester, England. *Politics:* Socialist. *Religion:* Atheist. *Agent:* Giles Gordon, 43 Doughty St., London, England.

CAREER: Author. Worked a variety of jobs, including a garage attendant, a saleswoman and factory worker. Has also worked for the BBC. Trained as a community worker and has worked in the community on various projects. *Member:* Leicester Phoenix Playwright's Association. *Awards, honors:* Thames Television Bursary, 1980, for play "Womberang"; *The Adrian Mole Diaries* was chosen one of American Library Association's Best Books for Young Adults, 1986.

WRITINGS:

The Secret Diary of Adrian Mole Aged 13 3/4 (young adult; illustrated by Caroline Holden; monologue first produced on BBC-Radio 4, 1981), Methuen, 1982, Avon, 1984.

The Growing Pains of Adrian Mole (young adult), Methuen, 1984, Grove, 1986.

The Adrian Mole Diaries: A Novel (contains *The Secret Diary of Adrian Mole Aged 13 3/4* and *The Growing Pains of Adrian Mole*), Methuen, 1985, Grove, 1986.

The Secret Diary of Adrian Mole Aged 13 3/4 Song Book, Methuen, 1985.

Rebuilding Coventry, Methuen, 1988.

PLAYS

"The Ghost of Daniel Lambert," first produced at Phoenix Arts Centre and Leicester Haymarket Theatre, Leicester, England, 1981.

"Dayroom," first produced at Croydon Warehouse Theatre, Croyden, England, 1981.

"Captain Christmas and the Evil Adults," first produced at Phoenix Arts Centre, Leicester, 1982.

SUE TOWNSEND

(Cover illustration by Caroline Holden from *The Secret Diary of Adrian Mole Aged 13 3/4* by Sue Townsend.)

"Are You Sitting Comfortably," first produced at Croydon Warehouse Theatre, Croyden, 1983.

Bazaar and Rummage; Groping for Words; Womberang: Three Plays ("Womberang" first produced at Soho Poly, 1980; "Bazaar and Rummage" first produced at Royal Court Theatre Upstairs, 1982, also produced on BBC-TV, 1983; "Groping for Words" first produced at Croydon Warehouse Theatre, 1983), Methuen, 1983.

The Great Celestial Cow (first produced at Royal Court Theatre, 1984), Methuen, 1984.

The Secret Diary of Adrian Mole Aged 13 3/4: The Play (music and lyrics by Ken Howard and Alan Blaikley; first produced at Phoenix Theatre, Leicester, England, September 6, 1984), Methuen, 1985.

Contributor to BBC-TV series "Revolting Women," 1981; author with Carole Hayman of a comedy series "The Refuge," BBC-Radio 4, 1987. Also contributor to periodicals, including *Times, New Statesman,* and *Airport.* Regular contributor of column to *Woman's Realm,* 1983-85.

ADAPTATIONS:

"The Secret Diary of Adrian Mole Aged 13 3/4" (seven-part radio series), BBC-Radio 4, 1982, (cassette), Talking Tape,

(From the television series, "The Secret Diary of Adrian Mole Aged 13 3/4." Presented on Thames Television, September 16, 1985.)

1983, (six-part television series), Thames Television, 1985, (computer game), Mosaic, 1985.
"The Growing Pains of Adrian Mole" (five-part series), BBC-Radio 4, 1984, (cassette), EMI Records/Listen for Pleasure, 1985, (television series; starring Lulu), Thames Television, 1987, (computer game), Mosaic, 1987.

WORK IN PROGRESS: Second series of "The Refuge" for BBC-Radio 4; a stage play.

SIDELIGHTS: "I think I always knew I'd be a writer one day. Certainly I'd been a secret scribbler for nineteen years before the birth of Adrian Mole when I finally 'came out of the closet.' I suppose hiding my writing was partly due to society's conditioning that women aren't supposed to want to do anything other than stay in the kitchen, although hopefully that's changing now. But whenever I hear a woman say, 'Oh, I'd love to write if only I had the time,' I feel saddened. All that inbuilt guilt about neglected housework stopping them. Mine gets sandwiched in between the writing and, if it had been the other way round, let's face it, maybe I'd still be struggling to become known. . . .

"Like most writers, I've been an avid reader since I was a child (though I couldn't read until I was eight years old) and

I'm often asked which authors have most influenced me. Without doubt, Richmal Crompton with her 'Just William' books have to head the list. I adored them. Now I realise why—because they gave a child's eye view of the society of the period, something I hope *Adrian Mole's Diary* also does. Then there's P. G. Wodehouse and the Russian 'greats' because they produced real 'meaty' books. *Crime and Punishment* is a wonderful read and Dostoevsky is probably my favourite. In fact, I've just made a sort of pilgrimage to Russia mainly to see his grave in Leningrad. And, would you believe it, it was exactly opposite my hotel bedroom window! How's that for a bizarre coincidence?

"I love diaries, too, so I suppose that's why I started Adrian Mole's. Grossmith's *The Diary of a Nobody* is a classic. If you were to ask me to choose one book to take on to a desert island, it would have to be *The Diaries of Evelyn Waugh*. They're absolutely marvellous. I do believe it's through reading voraciously that you develop your own style though, of course, you write what you are. I know all my writing will have to be touched by humour because that's me. I've always been able to see the funny side of things—that's how I make sense of the world which is what every writer does, really.

"Another habit that I think is essential is to be insatiably curious. As a child, I'd spend hours and hours just watching everything and everyone around me. Subconsciously absorbing life. I suppose, because after all that is one's raw material and we have to learn to look behind the facade which is all that most see.

"One thing I would like to stress, though, is that having a formal higher education is not a prerequisite for becoming a writer. I left school at fifteen and had a succession of menial jobs, both before I got married and produced three children, and after. But working in such places as a dress shop and a hot-dog stall, allowed me to observe people and added to my experience of life on which I've been able to draw in my writing. And when it comes to English grammar, well, Adrian and I are educating ourselves with the help of Usborne's *Book of Children's Grammar* because his isn't too great, either. And you've only got to think of, say, Arnold Bennett and Alan Sillitoe to know that lack of 'education' doesn't stop you being a good writer.

"When I began, it was in the kitchen of a small terraced house on a desk that, often as not, would have hot dishes straight from the oven dumped on it. Inevitably, that desk fell apart and I now have a large 'cheapo' secondhand one in a much bigger room, surrounded by the clutter all writers seem to acquire.

"I don't think environment is all that important, though. I could write [i]n Waterloo station, if I had to—but maybe that's just me. Incidentally, I write in longhand with a fine felt-tip pen on pads of lined A4 paper. At first, I used to send my manuscripts to an agency to be typed and then Colin (the man in my life) taught himself and actually typed up *The Secret Diary* for me despite having a broken arm at the time. Since then, my sister, Kate, has taken over as my secretary.

"Colin has played a big part in my writing success because it was he who persuaded me to join the Leicester Phoenix Playwright's Association several years ago. Then Ian Giles, the director at the Phoenix, unbeknown to me, submitted 'Womberang' for a Thames TV bursary in 1980. When I was shortlisted and called for an interview, I could hardly believe it. John Mortimer was one of the panel of judges and the fact that he'd memorised some of my lines gave my confidence a tremendous boost. By the time I arrived back home, there was a telegram waiting to say I'd been awarded 2,500 pounds which was to pay my wages for a year as writer-in-residence at the Phoenix. Then the really hard work began.

"During those twelve months, I wrote play after play and, because I was so inexperienced, I broke all the rules and got away with it. I mean, thirteen characters in a half-hour play! But what a lot I learned and isn't that the only way to learn your craft—by doing?

"It was in 1980 that I had a huge stroke of luck when Janet Fillingham, a literary agent, who was trying to build up a 'stable' of playwrights, took me on. I'd already written some of the *Adrian Mole Diary* and she suggested I turn it into a thirty-minute radio play. At first, it was rejected. . .but. . .eventually accepted. . . .Janet Fillingham then sent it to Methuen where Geoffrey Strachen, the managing director, loved it and commissioned a paperback edition. . . .

"I'm sometimes asked if the success of Adrian Mole has made a difference to my life and, of course, it would be stupid to deny that it has. Basically, it's given me freedom from the everyday money worries I've known all my life until now. But I hope it hasn't changed me. I keep asking people I've known a long time 'I haven't changed, have I?' And it's very reassuring when they smile and shake their heads. Anyway, just look at me now—no makeup, jeans and sweatshirt, tins of paint everywhere, books piled up in corners and every door inside the house off its hinges. Hardly the conventional image

of a successful writer, would you say? In any case, you're only as good as your last book or play.

"Another question I'm asked is how I was able to get into an adolescent boy's mind. Well, I don't think there's any difference between the sexes as regards their emotions. It's just that boys, unfortunately, learn to repress them, so there's a lot of me in him. I think he was actually conceived when my daughter was a baby. I caught my son looking at me with that cold objective eye of the adolescent and knew he was seeing me as a person rather than Mum for perhaps the first time. (Have you ever noticed how teenagers often have seemingly blank faces as if there's nothing going on behind them? There is, of course—their minds are actually busily churning away behind those facades). It was then I started writing Adrian's diary. I intended it as a serious social commentary, told in a humorous vein, because that's the only way I can write. He started out as Nigel originally, but Adrian somehow seemed totally non-threatening and absolutely right. I think your characters' names are vitally important.

"One of the nicest things about the *Diary*'s popularity is the number of letters I get from schoolboys, middle-aged men and even from men in prison, saying how much they've enjoyed reading it and that they've been able to identify with Adrian. The illustrations are super. . . .They're by Caroline Holden who, by coincidence, also used to live in Leicester.

"It's also brought me a lot of unsolicited manuscripts and, while I sympathise with beginners wanting help, obviously it's

(From the third episode of Thames Television's serialization, "The Secret Diary of Adrian Mole Aged 13 3/4.")

impossible for me to criticise them all. The best advice I can give to any would-be writer is, if you want to write plays, join a playwright's association. I consider that invaluable, particularly if you have professional actors willing to read the parts as I did at the Phoenix.

"Finally, if you want to be a writer, you really only need two pieces of equipment—a pen and some paper. Then, if you're quite sure you want to write and are prepared for all the hard work involved, do just that—write. And I wish you all every success."[1]

FOOTNOTE SOURCES

[1]Nancy Smith, "The Writing Life of Adrian Mole's Mum," *Writers' Monthly,* December, 1985.

HOBBIES AND OTHER INTERESTS: Walking, reading, eating, drinking, canoeing, and travelling alone.

FOR MORE INFORMATION SEE:

New Statesman, November 26, 1982.
Publishers Weekly, February 24, 1984, August 23, 1985, March 21, 1986.
Book World, May 13, 1984.
School Library Journal, September, 1984, February, 1987.
Times (London), November 28, 1984.
Times Literary Supplement, November 30, 1984.
Drama, winter, 1984.
Booklist, May 1, 1986.
Voice of Youth Advocates, December, 1986.

VINTON, Iris 1906(?)-1988

OBITUARY NOTICE—See sketch in *SATA* Volume 24: Born about 1906 in West Point, Miss.; died of breast cancer, February 6, 1988, in Manhattan, N. Y. Editor and author. Vinton, who grew up in the Gulf of Mexico area, taught in a two-room Texas schoolhouse early in her career. Her teaching experiences combined with her Texas background later provided her with rich material for her adventure stories. Vinton's first writings were short plays such as *Just Babies,* published in 1939. *Laffy of the Navy Salvage Divers,* published in 1944, was her first fiction book.

Vinton was best known for her novels for young people, including *Flying Ebony,* which was adapted as a motion picture, "The Mooncussers." Among her other works are a sequel to *Flying Ebony* titled *The Black Horse Company,* and adventure stories based on real incidents, *Longbow Island* and *Look out for Pirates!* In addition, she wrote a number of biographies for children, including *The Story of Robert E. Lee* and *The Story of President Kennedy.* Vinton contributed to several "Nancy Drew" mysteries and compiled a book of games from around the world entitled *The Folkways Omnibus of Children's Games.* She also served as editor of *You and Your Child* magazine during the late 1930s, as associate editor for Breskin Publishing Company in the early 1940s, and was director of publications for the Boys' Club of America for twenty years.

FOR MORE INFORMATION SEE:

New York Times, July 6, 1947, June 23, 1957.
Saturday Review of Literature, May 13, 1950.
Christian Science Monitor, August 29, 1970.
Contemporary Authors, Volumes 77-80, Gale, 1979.

OBITUARIES

New York Times, February 9, 1988.

WICKER, Ireene 1905(?)-1987

OBITUARY NOTICE: Name originally Irene Seaton; born November 24, 1905 (some sources indicate 1900 or 1901), in Quincy, Ill.; died November 17 (one source says November 16), 1987, in West Palm Beach, Fla. Broadcasting personality, scriptwriter, and author of juvenile literature. Early in her radio career, Wicker changed the spelling of her first name to "Ireene" when she was told that adding one more letter would bring her success.

Wicker gained notoriety as a storyteller on radio and television between 1930 and 1975. Popularly known as the "Lady with a Thousand Voices," she starred in "The Singing Story Lady" show which became one of radio's most successful programs and eventually prospered on television. Wicker provided all the voices for the show's characters, and occasionally wrote the stories she performed—several of which became books or sound recordings for children.

Early in her career, Wicker was featured in the radio soap operas "Today's Children" and "Harold Teen"—a favorite with teenagers—and during the 1930s and 1940s she produced a weekly series called "The Ireene Wicker Musical Plays" in which she dramatized operas and folk legends with guest performers, such as Don Ameche, John Houseman, and Agnes Moorehead. The recipient of at least thirty awards, including the prestigious George Foster Peabody Award for lifetime achievement and an Emmy Award from the Academy of Television Arts and Sciences, Wicker also devoted much effort to eliminating violence from broadcasting. In the early 1950s she and Gypsy Rose Lee were wrongly accused of being Communist sympathizers; charges which were soon dismissed.

Wicker published a number of works for children, including *The Singing Lady's Favorite Stories, Young Master Artists: Boyhoods of Famous Artists, Children's Stories of Famous Composers and Artists, The Legend of the Christmas Rose,* and *How The Ocelots Got Their Spots.* She wrote many songs for children, adapted operas for juvenile audiences, and made a number of recordings for young people. Among her sound recordings and tape cassettes are: "Kipling's Just So Stories,""Grimm's Fairy Tales," "The Owl and the Pussycat and Other Stories," and "Andersen's Fairy Tales," all for the Record Guild of America.

FOR MORE INFORMATION SEE:

Contemporary Authors, Volumes 69-72, Gale, 1978.
L. Dumont, "First Ladies of Radio," *Hobbies,* August, 1978.
Who's Who in America, 42nd edition, Marquis, 1982.

OBITUARIES

Los Angeles Times, November 18, 1987.
New York Times, November 19, 1987.
Chicago Tribune, November 20, 1987.

WIGHT, James Alfred 1916-
(James Herriot)

PERSONAL: Born October 3, 1916, in Sunderland, County Tyne and Werr, England; son of James Henry (a musician) and Hannah (a professional singer; maiden name, Bell) Wight; married Joan Catherine Danbury, November 5, 1941; children: James, Rosemary. *Education:* Glasgow Veterinary College, M.R.C.V.S., 1938. *Religion:* Protestant.

CAREER: General practitioner in veterinary medicine, Yorkshire, England, 1938—; writer, 1966—. *Military service:* Royal

Wight with his Border terrier, Bodie. ■ (From *The Best of James Herriot* by James Herriot.)

Air Force, 1943-45. _Member:_ British Veterinary Association (honorary member), Royal College of Veterinary Surgeons (fellow). _Awards, honors: All Things Bright and Beautiful_ was chosen one of American Library Association's Best Young Adult Books, 1974, and _All Creatures Great and Small_, 1975; Officer of the British Empire, 1979; D. Litt., Watt University (Scotland), 1979; honorary D. Vsc., Liverpool University, 1984.

WRITINGS:

If Only They Could Talk, M. Joseph, 1970, large print edition, G. K. Hall, 1977.
It Shouldn't Happen to a Vet, M. Joseph, 1972.
All Creatures Great and Small (contains _If Only They Could Talk_ and _It Shouldn't Happen to a Vet_), St. Martin's, 1972, large print edition, G. K. Hall, 1973.
Let Sleeping Vets Lie, M. Joseph, 1973.
Vet in Harness, M. Joseph, 1974.
All Things Bright and Beautiful (contains _Let Sleeping Vets Lie_ and _Vet in Harness_), St. Martin's, 1974, large print edition, G. K. Hall, 1975.
Vets Might Fly, M. Joseph, 1976.
Vet in a Spin, M. Joseph, 1977.
All Things Wise and Wonderful (contains _Vets Might Fly_ and _Vet in a Spin_), St. Martin's, 1977, large print edition, G. K. Hall, 1977.
James Herriot's Yorkshire, St. Martin's, 1979.
(With others) _Animals Tame and Wild,_ Sterling, 1979, published as _Animal Stories: Tame and Wild,_ Sterling, 1985.
The Lord God Made Them All, St. Martin's, 1981, large print edition, G. K. Hall, 1982.
The Best of James Herriot, St. Martin's, 1983.
Moses the Kitten (juvenile; illustrated by Peter Barrett), St. Martin's, 1984.
Only One Woof, (juvenile; illustrated by P. Barrett), St. Martin's, 1985.
James Herriot's Dog Stories, St. Martin's, 1986, large print edition, G. K. Hall, 1987.
The Christmas Day Kitten (illustrated by Ruth Brown), St. Martin's, 1986.
Bonny's Big Day (illustrated by R. Brown), St. Martin's, 1987.
Blossom Comes Home (illustrated by R. Brown), St. Martin's, 1988.

Also author of _James Herriot's Yorkshire Calendar._

ADAPTATIONS:

"All Creatures Great and Small" (movie with screenplay by Hugh Whitemore), starring Simon Ward, Lisa Harrow and Anthony Hopkins, EMI Productions, 1975, presented as a television special on Hallmark Hall of Fame, NBC-TV, February 4, 1975, (television series), starring Robert Hardy, Peter Davison, Christopher Timothy and Carol Drinkwater, British Broadcasting Corp., 1978, PBS-TV, 1979, (listening cassette), Listen for Pleasure, 1980.
"All Things Bright and Beautiful" (motion picture; also released as "It Shouldn't Happen to a Vet"), starring John Alderton, Colin Blakely and Lisa Harrow, BBC-TV, 1979, (listening cassette), Listen for Pleasure, 1980.
"All Things Wise and Wonderful" (cassette), Cassette Book.
"The Lord God Made Them All" (listening cassette), Listen for Pleasure, 1982.
"Stories from the Herriot Collection" (cassette), Listen for Pleasure.

SIDELIGHTS: Readers of all ages have enjoyed the best-selling books of James Wight, written under the pseudonym James Herriot. Wight's memoirs chronicle over forty years of his life as a country vet in the uplands of Yorkshire, England—commencing with his first harrowing year as a newly-qualified

veterinary surgeon during the late 1930s, and continuing through the early days of his marriage, the turbulent years of World War II when he served in the R.A.F., and the post-war years.

1916. James Alfred Wight, or "Alf," as he's known locally, was born in Sunderland, a small town in Yorkshire on October 3. Three weeks later, the family moved to Glasgow. As the son of a mother who sang professionally and a father who played piano and organ, music played a large part in the household, and Wight grew up with an especial love for Elgar, Beethoven, and Mozart. He lived in Hillhead near Glasgow, Scotland, and attended Hillhead High School.

"I was an only child, but I had the good luck to be born into a household which was full of books so I was never lonely. I became an avid reader, discovering at an early age that reading is the most satisfying recreation of all. Like most children I began with comics but very soon I began to look through my father's shelves of books with authors like H. G. Wells, Conan Doyle and Rider Haggard, and that was the end of the comics. This love of reading has remained with me to this day and, in fact, I often think that as I grow older I enjoy it more than ever.

"When I was at school I didn't think I liked it—not, anyway, as modern children seem to like school—because discipline was very strict and, as I had the unfortunate habit of laughing in class I was a regular recipient of several strokes of the 'twase,' the leather belt which was used for punishment in Scottish schools in those days. In retrospect, I realise that I really had a good time and a first class education to boot.

"In fact, I had what I can only describe as an idyllic childhood, because, although I grew up in the big city of Glasgow, my home was only a few miles from the beauties of Loch Lomond and the Scottish hills.

"I spent much of my childhood and adolescence walking with my dog, camping and climbing among the highlands of Scotland so that at an early age three things were implanted in my character; a love of animals, reading and the countryside. It is small wonder that I am a happy man!"[1]

1929. "When I was thirteen I read in my _Meccano_ magazine an article describing a vet's life and that did it. Nothing could shake my determination to train as an animal vet and I got into Glasgow Veterinary School even though they were somewhat underwhelmed, if that's the word, by my poor science record."[2]

1938. "When I graduated, it was the height of the Depression. I was 22. My friends were reduced to taking jobs in the shipyards, but I had a lucky break. I spotted an advertisement and got the job of assistant to a vet in a small North Yorkshire town. . . .I'd hoped to deal with dogs and cats. Being confronted with cows and pigs was a bit of a shock. . . ."[2]

"I knew nothing about agriculture or about farm animals and though, during the years in college, I learned about these things, I could see only one future for myself; I was going to be a small animal surgeon. This lasted right up to the time I qualified—a kind of vision of treating people's pets in my own animal hospital where everything would be not just modern but revolutionary. The fully equipped operating theatre, laboratory and X-ray room; they had all stayed crystal clear in my mind until I had graduated M.R.C.V.S.

"How on earth, then, did I come to be sitting on a high Yorkshire moor in shirt sleeves and Wellingtons, smelling vaguely of cows?

(From *Bonny's Big Day* by James Herriot. Illustrated by Ruth Brown.)

Wight examines a baby lamb for an infectious disease. ■ (Photograph by Barry Lewis/Network.)

"The change in my outlook had come quite quickly—in fact almost immediately after my arrival. . . .The job had been a godsend. . . , but only, I had thought, a stepping-stone to my real ambition. But everything had switched round, almost in a flash.

"Maybe it was something to do with the incredible sweetness of the air which still took me by surprise when I stepped out into the old wild garden at Skeldale House every morning. Or perhaps the daily piquancy of life in the graceful old house with my gifted but mercurial boss, Siegfried, and his reluctant student brother, Tristan. Or it could be that it was just the realisation that treating cows and pigs and sheep and horses had a fascination I had never even suspected; and this brought with it a new concept of myself as a tiny wheel in the great machine of British agriculture. There was a kind of solid satisfaction in that.

"Probably it was because I hadn't dreamed there was a place like the Dales. I hadn't thought it possible that I could spend all my days in a high, clean-blown land where the scent of grass or trees was never far away; and where even in the driving rain of winter I could snuff the air and find the freshness of growing things hidden somewhere in the cold clasp of the wind.

"Anyway, it had all changed for me and my work consisted now of driving from farm to farm across the roof of England with a growing conviction that I was a privileged person."[3]

Thirsk in the Vale of York—Darrowby in his books—is fertile land fed by an impressive river system, bordered by the bleak North Moors to the east and the Yorkshire Dales to the west. The land supports mixed farming, with the fields marked out by drystone walls which caterpillar over the fields and fells. Wight grew to love the wild landscape and its rugged farming population. The two were to become the central ingredients for the books he was to write thirty years later. "I fell heavily for the Pennine countryside. This was it. This (apart from Scotland) was where I wanted to live. I was completely smitten. . . ."[2]

Beginning as an obviously inexperienced vet, straight out of college, Wight had to earn the farmers' trust. It was not simply a question of trying to cure the animals; for many farmers a fatal disease amongst their herd meant bankruptcy and ruin. At the end of his first year in the practice he wrote: "There were people who thought I was a pretty fair vet, some who regarded me as an amiable idiot, a few who were convinced I was a genius and one or two who would set their dogs on me if I put a foot inside their gates."[4]

"The difficult thing about being a country vet is that first you have to catch your patient. I can remember rounding up a litter of sixteen piglets. . . .They hurtled around like little pink racehorses. I spent a long time diving frantically after them, only to see the other group escaping while I rounded up their brothers and sisters. And when you're taking a calf from its mother, you may spend hours with your arm in the cow's vagina, she squeezing it so tightly that the circulation virtually stops."[5]

There are other hazards. "Take the prolapsed uterus in a pig. I've tried everything with that type of condition: directing a hose on the everted organ, pushing, straining, sweating over the great mass of flesh, trying to push it back through that absurdly small vagina. And most of the time not succeeding, with the result that the pig eventually becomes pork pies. You have no idea how tough it is, lying on cold concrete, fighting to get that uterus back into the animal until your breath gives out, your feet braced against the wall and shoving, gasping, shoving, gasping, until you're completely exhausted.

"It's not for nothing that I have steel tips in my Wellington boots. Cows like almost nothing better than standing on your feet. I say 'almost' nothing because they also like kicking. Most of the time they catch you on the knee or shin bone, which is bad enough. But there have been occasions when both hind feet have lashed out and hit me simultaneously, sailing me out through the barn door. That's when the farmer often says laconically, 'Aye, she's allus had a habit of that.' If the kick is low enough, he's liable to add a certain amount of additional ripe comment, embracing the possible effect on my future sex life. I'm particularly wary of black cows; they're the worst."[5]

Although tractors had already been introduced, draught horses were still in use when he began to practice, and he treated them in their last days as working horses before they were put out to grass forever. The young vet worked at all hours, seven days a week, often being summoned from his warm bed in the early hours of the morning to attend to a sick calf or sheep— "I developed my half-awake technique."[6] Even so, he never lost his delight at helping to deliver a live calf or lamb. "This was always the best part, the wonder that was always fresh, the miracle you couldn't explain."[6]

Although, Wight cared for his animals with great compassion and dedication, much of the treatment in those early years was little more than guesswork. "Hoping for the best was something that vets did a lot of in the thirties."[6] He was forced to work in tandem not only with local farming lore but with quack doctors who maintained that their wares were more effective than the professionals.

For example, while treating a sick ewe one day with no known cure available, Wight discovered that administering a painkiller could by itself aid recovery. "That ewe's life had been saved not by medicinal therapy but simply by stopping her pain and allowing nature to do its own job of healing. It was a lesson I have never forgotten; that animals confronted with severe continuous pain and the terror and shock that goes with it will often retreat even into death, and if you can remove that pain amazing things can happen. It's difficult to explain rationally but I know that it is so."[6]

"In those days a veterinarian was practically a practitioner in black magic. A vet was almost like a witch. Farmers would stick an onion up the backside of a sick animal hoping to cure it, and the vet would be labelled a miracle-worker because he'd pull out the onion and the animal would get better. Common sense and trial and error were the most important tools in a vet's black bag. I can remember [my partner] telling me one day, 'Alf, there is more to be learned up a cow's arse than in many an encyclopaedia.'

"If you couldn't think of anything else for curing the animal, you'd send him on a bloody good gallop, often with spectacular results. Enemas were the most common cure for everything. I remember another old vet telling me, 'Keep the bowels open and trust to God.' I would take a long rubber stomach tube, pump two gallons of warm water rich in formalin and

sodium chloride into the cow, and it made me feel like Napoleon sending in the battalions of the Old Guard at Waterloo. If that wouldn't work, nothing would."[5]

Practicing in the days before penicillin or steroids, he witnessed the enormous changes which transformed the life of farmers and vets alike as the century progressed. "The dispensary was an important place in the days before penicillin and the sulphonamides. Rows of gleaming Winchester bottles lined the white walls from floor to ceiling. I savoured the familiar names: Sweet Spirits of Nitre, Tincture of Camphor, Chlorodyne, Formalin, Salamoniac, Hexamine, Sugar of Lead, Linimentum Album, Perchloride of Mercury, Red Blister."[3]

Despite their romantic names, the mixtures were often pitifully inadequate. Wight gives testament to the thrill of first using the new medicines. These seem commonplace nowadays, but as he observes, "I had witnessed the beginning of the revolution. . .the tremendous therapeutic breakthrough which was to sweep the old remedies into oblivion. . . .We have good results now but no miracles, and I feel I was lucky to be one of the generation which was in at the beginning when wonderful things did happen."[6]

A few more advanced treatments were already available, and some, like the calcium injection produced instant results. "It was one of the most satisfying experiences of my working life, not clever but a magical transfiguration; from despair to hope, from death to life within minutes."[6]

1941. Married Joan Catherine Danbury (Helen in his books), and was made a partner of the Yorkshire practice on the same day. Catherine was the daughter of a local farmer, and she obligingly spent her honeymoon helping her husband tuberculin test multiple herds of cows. Their accident prone courtship is humourously described in *All Creatures Great and Small*.

For eight years, the couple lived on the top floor of the veterinary practice (Skeldale House in the books), with a view of the town and the surrounding hills. It was an ivy clad Georgian house which fronted the street and boasted lawns and a rockery at the back.

"In those days the wisteria covered the entire rear of the house, thrusting fragrant blooms into the open windows. . . .The French window at the foot of the house opens on to the surgery waiting room, but in those days of my books that lovely room with the glass-fronted cabinet over the fireplace was where Siegfried, Tristan and I spent so many happy bachelor hours. . . .After the war,. . .this was our family sitting room, open on summer days to the sunlit garden.

"They were a hard but happy eight years. Siegfried had married and moved a few miles out into the country, but this was still the practice headquarters to which the farmers sent their calls on that ever-jangling phone, and we saw the dogs and cats in the long offshoot on the left. But most of all it was home for Helen and me, where we had our early struggles and where we raised our children from babyhood."[7]

Their quarters furnished from house sales, they were contented despite their spartan accomodation. "The long games of bezique by the fireside in our bed-sitter, tense battles on the push-ha'penny board; we even used to throw rings at hooks on a board on the wall. Kids' games after a long hard slog round the practice, but even now as I look down the years I know I have never found a better way of living."[8]

1943. On his twenty-seventh birthday, Wight's call up papers for the R.A.F. arrived. Reluctantly, he tore himself away from

(From the fourth television series of ''All Creatures Great and Small'' in which Christopher Timothy portrayed Wight. Co-produced by the British Broadcasting Corp. and Arts & Entertainment Cable Network, broadcast here in 1988.)

his new wife and the job he loved, and left for active service. Afraid that he would forget his new found skills, he took with him a bulky volume of Black's *Veterinary Dictionary* to read in any spare time he might have.

Reporting for duty at the famous Lords Cricket Ground at St. John's Wood in London, he was subjected to rigorous training and, appropriately for a vet, shared his meals with other recruits at London Zoo. He was then posted to Scarborough in Yorkshire for further training.

"It is the Grand Hotel that has the most memories because of those six months in the war when we slept in the uncarpeted rooms with the windows nailed open, marched around the echoing corridors under the shouts of the S.P.'s and clattered up and down the stone service stairs.

"After the war I got a tremendous kick out of taking Helen to dine in the elegant room that was once an open terrace where I learned to use an Aldis lamp. It was glass fronted when we went there in peace time, and as we ate we looked down at the lights of the town winking in the gathering dusk. It was very pleasant, too, to sit in the richly carpeted lounge and drink tea and listen to a string orchestra playing selections from *Rose Marie,* and know with happy certainty that nobody could order me to do anything.

"Scarborough is of course divided into two. There is the North and the South Bay, both fine and spacious with splendid beaches. The bays are divided by a headland where the ruins of the twelfth century castle stand.

"I spent a lot of time among those ruins during the war, because that is where they marched us to practice shooting with every imaginable kind of firearm. In fact, there are few streets in Scarborough which have not heard the thump of my R.A.F. boots or the slither of my sneakers. Scarborough is where the R.A.F. converted me from a slightly tubby, pampered, newly-married man into a kind of human greyhound."[7]

He was delighted with his Scarborough post since it allowed him the opportunity to play truant and escape to see Joan who was expecting their first child.

February 13, 1944. Son, James, was born in the Sunnyside Nursing Home with the help of a mid-wife, Nurse Bell. "I was, of course, playing hookey from Scarborough. . .and I hadn't expected to find I was a father when the bus rolled into Thirsk."[7] Wight underwent a "sympathetic" pregnancy, convinced he "carried" his son.[8] Although used to delivering animals, he had never before seen a newborn baby, and asked to see another to check that all was well with his son. It was.

Sent to flying school at Windsor in the south of England, Wight was several years older than most of the other recruits, and was delighted to be the third in his group to make a solo flight. He was then posted to Manchester but his flying days were shortlived, since he was forced to have an operation after which he was declared unfit to fly.

In 1945 he returned home to take up his place in the Yorkshire practice once more. He has been there ever since, watching

(From *Moses the Kitten* by James Herriot. Illustrated by Peter Barrett.)

children he knew as babies take over their fathers' positions in running the farm.

Helping a fellow vet operate on a dog one day, he realized that his heart was now in the outdoor life rather than that of a small animal surgery. "I had no regrets, the life which had been forced on me by circumstances had turned out to be a thing of magical fulfillment. It came to me with a flooding certainty that I would rather spend my days driving over the unfenced roads of the high country than stooping over that operating table."[6]

Between visits to farmers, Wight would relax in the countryside with his dog. "Stretched on the turf, gazing with half closed eyes into the bright sky, luxuriating in the sensation of being detached from the world and its problems.

"This form of self-indulgence had become part of my life, and still is; a reluctance to come down from the high country; a penchant for stepping out of the stream of life and loitering on the brink for a few minutes as an uninvolved spectator."[6]

1949. Daughter, Rosemary, was born in the same room as Jimmy. "This was peace time a little more than four years later, and I was directly involved in the dramatic preliminaries which I had missed the first time. We had been to Harrogate on our half-day, and Helen had begun to experience funny little pains in the cinema. These increased on the way home in the car, and we had a restless few hours of scares and alarms till 6 a.m. when Helen announced that there was no time to be lost—young Rosie was definitely on her way.

"Shaking with panic, I whisked her round to the little nursing home on the green, and the first person I saw when I burst into the place was Cliff, Nurse Bell's husband, at his breakfast.

"I should think at that moment the most anxious man in the town was confronting the calmest. Cliff was a perpetually smiling, unflappable, supremely amiable man. He was a lorry driver for a local contractor and over the years he had seen a long succession of distraught husbands standing in that kitchen.

"He grinned up at me from his laden plate as Helen was ushered upstairs. 'Now then, Jim, it's a grand mornin'.'

"It was the ninth of May, and the rising sun brought promise of a fine day, but I wasn't in the mood to notice.

"'Yes, Cliff, yes. . .' I muttered, most of my attention focused on the creaking of the floorboards in the bedroom above.

"He speared one of a selection of sausages that lay among mounds of bacon, eggs and tomatoes, and he sliced into it. By his side stood an empty porridge bowl, and a pile of cut bread and marmalade awaited his further attention. He was a very large man but I felt he would not suffer from malnutrition before lunch time.

"As he chewed he smiled at me again. 'Don't worry, lad,' he said. 'It'll be right.'

"And it was right—at eleven o'clock that morning. After hours of classical floor pacing and repeated attempts to read the newspaper upside down, I rushed to the surgery phone."[7] It was a sister for Jimmy.

1966. Wight first began to write, settling down with a notebook in front of the television after a hard day's work. "The life of a country vet was dirty, uncomfortable, sometimes dangerous. It was terribly hard work and I loved it. I felt vaguely

that I ought to write about it and every day for twenty-five years I told my wife of something funny that had happened and said I was keeping it for the book.

"She usually said 'Yes, dear' to humour me but one day, when I was fifty, she said: 'Who are you kidding? Vets of fifty don't write first books.' Well, that did it. I stormed out and bought some paper and taught myself to type.

"Then I started to put it all down and the story didn't work. All I managed to pick out on the machine was a very amateur school essay. So I spent a year or two learning my craft, as real writers say. I read *How to Be a Writer* and *Teach Yourself to Write* and I bombarded newspapers, magazines and the BBC with unreadable short stories. They came back, every one, without a word of comment. Not even 'You show promise.' There's a special noise that a rejected manuscript makes when it comes through the letter-box and hits the doormat. It's more recognisable than that of a ewe in labour or a cow with a prolapsed uterus. I would call it a sick thud and it was a noise I learned to hate.

"Then I read Salinger and Hemingway and Dickens and Conan Doyle, all with a learner's eye. In the end, I got away from my awful Macaulay's essays style, with its beautifully balanced sentences and florid adjectives. And I learned the art of flashbacks from Budd Schulberg's book about Scott Fitzgerald, *The Disenchanted*."[2]

"When I wrote all my books, I was a full-time working vet—seven days a week, through the night, twenty-five hours a day.

Skeldale House. ■ (From *James Herriot's Yorkshire* by James Herriot. Photograph by Derry Brabbs.)

The movie version of a town meeting in Darrowby. ■ (From the television movie "All Creatures Great and Small," presented on NBC.)

I wrote in little tiny bursts of half an hour in front of the television. Then I'd be out and gone. I don't like sitting."[9]

"By the end of eighteen months, I knew I had a book. My first choice as a potential publisher was the London company, Michael Joseph, who had done a whole series of books called *Doctor in the House* which were very successful in Britain. I thought a book about a vet would fit right into their publishing philosophy. But a friend told me not to send it to the Joseph company and suggested another firm instead. The manuscript stayed at the other publisher's for eighteen months and to this day I don't know whether they spent any time reading it. Finally the book came back. . . .I threw in a drawer and it would have been there to this day if Joan hadn't ordered me to take it out and do something with it. I sent it to a literary agent. Within a week the agent had sent me a letter saying he liked the book enormously and that I'd have no trouble in getting it published. When I finally met the agent in London I asked him which publisher he'd sent the book to. He told me Michael Joseph. I'd wasted eighteen months."[10]

1970. The book, *If Only They Could Talk,* was published in England under the pseudonym James Herriot. "It's against the ethics of the veterinary profession to advertise and when I first started writing my books, I was afraid some of my peers might think it unprofessional of me to write under my own name. So, I was sitting in front of the TV tapping out one of my stories and there was this fellow James Herriot playing such a good game of soccer for Birmingham that I just took his name."[5]

His first book sold a meager 1,200 copies.

1972. "It was America that gave me the real breakthrough. After I had written my second book [*It Shouldn't Happen to* *a Vet*], Tom McCormack of St. Martin's Press published the two books in one volume [*All Creatures Great and Small*]. It was an instant best seller. In fact it was almost too much of a success. I know I should be grateful when I get as many as twenty or thirty fans waiting after surgery for me to sign their books. I am, of course, but I prefer my privacy.

"They track me down even though I've never mentioned the exact location of the vet's practice. I've even trained the local people to point in the wrong direction when admirers find the town and ask where I am."[2]

Like the rest of the series Wight has since written, the majority of incidents he describes are autobiographical, although most place and character names are fictitious, including the name "Siegfried," based on his partner, Donald Sinclair.

"When I look down on the map. . .of Yorkshire, I can see and recall all the places so clearly; where I have calved cows, foaled mares, found heady success and abject failure, laughed or had my heart nearly broken.

"I have put a lot of it in my books, but of course the names of places and people are all changed. . . .I thought it would stop at one book and nobody would ever discover the identity of the obscure veterinary surgeon who had scribbled his experiences in snatched moments of spare time.

"This has caused a lot of nice people all over the world much puzzlement as they searched their travel books in vain. Where, for instance, is Darrowby? I really don't know myself. It is a composite town; a bit of Thirsk, something of Richmond, Leyburn and Middleham and a fair chunk of my own imagination."[7]

The narratives are told with a self-deprecating humour which captures the affection which Wight bears towards the Yorkshire landscape, its farmers and his patients. Despite their strong local flavor, Wight's tetralogy has been translated into every European language as well as Japanese, and the idiosyncratic characters of the Yorkshire Dales have become popular world wide with over fifty million books sold.

"I know some writers dream of best sellerdom and the best table in the restaurants and all that, but not me. I just had this compulsion to write down what it was like to be a vet in those funny old days in the 1930s before I forgot. If I could find a publisher and my stories amused a few people well, that was the summit of my ambition.

"The description of the veterinary practice at Darrowby and of Siegfried Farnon's great charm and uncertain temper is completely accurate. He really did say: 'Ah, James, the very man I'm looking for!' Siegfried's brother, Tristan, is also true to life and in his retirement he's making a bob or two lecturing all over the place on 'My Life with James Herriot.'

"As for me, I was the colourless, heavily intimidated character I describe. Damon Runyon had a guy who simply lived on Broadway and observed the life around him and that's me."[2]

"Professional critics tend to be nice, but a bit condescending. They acknowledge that it sells, but manage to imply that it's all rather lightweight stuff, not too taxing on the intellect. I agree with them, actually. It's only the Americans who get very intense about my writing. They read into it all kinds of weighty, humanitarian, sociological meanings—it astonishes me, something I can't see. Not many round here can see it either. A local farmer once told me that 'the books are about nowt.' I've just stopped asking myself too many questions about writing. I'm much too busy being a vet."[4]

1974. The movie "All Creatures Great and Small" was filmed. Simon Ward played Herriot; Anthony Hopkins, Siegfried; Lisa Harrow, Helen. "Thousands of times in my veterinary work, and on countless days for pleasure, I have driven over. . .the

I looked irresolutely at the huge, lethal animal. ■ (From *The Best of James Herriot: Favourite Memories of a Country Vet* by James Herriot. Illustrated by Victor Ambrus.)

highway to Scarborough and the coast. . . .One particularly memorable expedition to this enchanting countryside was when Helen and I went to see them making my first film, 'All Creatures Great and Small.' This was a tremendous novelty for me because I had never had a book filmed nor had either of us ever met an actor, and there were some very famous ones waiting there over the hill. . . .''[7]

They located the film crew in Farndale, ''that long, beautiful valley, famous for its blaze of daffodils in the spring and so like a Pennine dale with its walls creeping up to the untamed moorland.

''I could see at a glance that they were filming the episode of the Clydesdale horse with pus in its hoof. I had described it in my first book, *All Creatures Great and Small,* and as I looked down the hillside at the actors, I was snatched back to that first day when I went to Darrowby and met Siegfried.

''There below me were Anthony Hopkins and Simon Ward driving up to the farm in a marvelous old car of the thirties. Their clothes, when they alighted, were of that great period, too, and I watched entranced as the farmer led out the horse and Simon Ward lifted the foot and seated over it as I had done so many years ago.

''People have always asked me if I felt a thrill at seeing my past life enacted then, but strangely, the thing which gave me the deepest satisfaction was to hear the words I had written spoken by those fine actors. Both of them have magnificent voices, and every word came up to me and pierced me in a way I find hard to describe.

''The next thing, of course, was to meet these people, and I must say I felt very diffident about that. I waited in some apprehension as the scene was shot and reshot a dozen times—something which I was to learn was inseparable from film-making—then the director took Helen and me down the slope, and the moment had arrived.

''I have always been puzzled by the fact that Simon Ward, who was playing me, told me later that he was absolutely petrified at the prospect of meeting me. For a man who had just made a great name for himself playing Winston Churchill, it seemed odd. An obscure country vet was surely insignificant by contrast.''[7]

1978. BBC Television screened its serial ''All Creatures Great and Small'' based on Wight's first four books. Christopher Timothy played James Herriot. ''Timothy got right inside the part. . .he was terrific. It's an odd feeling watching someone playing your life. Christopher Timothy became the James Herriot I wrote about.''

1979. An Officer of the British Empire (O.B.E.) was conferred by Prince Charles. In the same year, *James Herriot's Yorkshire* was published, and the movie, ''All Things Bright and Beautiful'' was released in America. Wight began to extract sections from his books to use as the basis for children's stories, and brought out *Moses the Kitten,* illustrated by Peter Barrett in 1984.

1983. Mrs. Marjorie Warner of Sowerby in North Yorkshire, the woman on whom Wight based the character Mrs. Pumphrey died, leaving 90,000 pounds for needy old people. In his books she is the owner of the pampered Pekinese, Tricki Woo, who feasted on chopped chicken, pate on toast, trifle, cake and other delicacies. When the dog ''had become hugely fat, like a bloated sausage with a leg at each corner,'' Wight rescued him by removing Tricki Woo for a few weeks and

(From *All Things Bright and Beautiful* by James Herriot.)

treating him as if he were on a health farm. There Tricki Woo was put on a strict diet and took his exercise along with the household hounds until he was fit enough to return to his owner. Mrs. Pumphry later acquired a pet pig which she hoped to keep indoors.

Despite the enormous success of his books, Wight is still a working vet, driving out to his patients in the surrounding fields, accompanied by his border terrier, Bodie. ''I can't put in five days a week at the practice any more. In any case the small farmer I wrote about is a thing of the past. The modern farmer wears a white coat and knows more about the science of his job. So he's more willing to take advice which is all to the good, I suppose.

''But one thing hasn't changed. If a farmer calls me out to a sick cow, he couldn't care less if I were George Bernard Shaw. If we discuss anything other than work, it's the fortunes of Sunderland Football Club. I'm a fanatical Sunderland supporter in the middle of Leeds and Middlesbrough county.

''I don't drive an expensive car or anything like that. It's the same old S-registration Peugot. We take pretty good holidays. As a student I used to go camping round Dumgoyne or in the Trossachs [in Scotland]. Now we go and find the sun.

''I've got enough ideas written down as chapter headings, to fill another five or six books, but I'll never write them. *The Lord God Made Them All* is my last. . . .

"I look at the last ten years and realise how much experience has been lost while I tapped away at a typewriter. Not enough time has been devoted to my grandchildren. I'm missing their youth and the fun of doing things with them.

"There's so much gardening neglected and so many walks never taken over the fells, when the air was warm and the pale sun fingering the heather. But there's one day to which I still look forward. It's the one when I open my surgery curtains in the morning and there's no one outside pointing a camera at me."[2]

Although he proclaims that he has given up writing, Wight is known to have bought a word processor, and it is rumoured that another book is likely. "[I] might get what they call a rush of blood. Besides, I'm not so good at pushing the horses and cows about as I used to be."[11] His son, James, now works at the practice where his father began his career, and his daughter, Rosemary, is a doctor also living and working locally.

Although most of his book earnings have gone to the British government—"I wrote six books at 83% percent tax, and at the end of it my accountant said, 'You've written six books, and five of them you wrote for the tax man.'"[11]—Wight would still prefer to stay in his beloved fells then to follow the "rich and famous" to a more lucrative exile. He plans to live there until he dies, "like so many good vets, in a cow byre, doing a tough job. If you get married and have kids, that's the main thing, isn't it? And I've lived in this beautiful district, having the great pleasure of being associated with animals. Oh, aye, it's been a marvelous life."[9]

FOOTNOTE SOURCES

[1]Excerpt from a letter to Cathy Courtney for *Something about the Author*, from James Wight, February, 1988.
[2]"James Herriot Talking to William Foster," *Scotsman*, October 16, 1981.
[3]James Herriot, *All Creatures Great and Small*, St. Martin's Press, 1972.
[4]David Taylor, "It Could Only Happen to a Vet," *Radio Times*, January, 1978.
[5]Arturo F. Gonzalez, *Saturday Review*, May/June, 1986.
[6]James Herriot, *All Things Bright and Beautiful*, Pan, 1978.
[7]James Herriot, *James Herriot's Yorkshire*, St. Martin's Press, 1979.
[8]James Herriot, *All Things Wise and Wonderful*, Pan, 1979.
[9]"*Life* Visits Herriot Country," *Life*, March, 1988.
[10]"Interview with James Herriot," *Macleans* (Canada), May 29, 1978.
[11]Monty Brower, "Long a Success as 'James Herriot,' Yorkshire Vet Jim Wight Says *All Things* Must Come to an End," *People Weekly*, March 18, 1985.

FOR MORE INFORMATION SEE:

Observer, February 13, 1972, May 27, 1973, August 22, 1976.
New Statesman, March 10, 1972, August 20, 1976.
New York Times, December 14, 1972, September 24, 1974.
Time, February 19, 1973, June 29, 1981.
Books and Bookmen, October, 1973.
English Journal, December, 1973.
American Veterinary Medical Association Journal, February 1, 1974, October 15, 1975, August 1, 1979.
Atlantic Monthly, August, 1974, October, 1974.
Timothy Green, "Best-Selling Vet Practices as Usual," *Smithsonian*, November, 1974.
Book World, December 8, 1974, September 14, 1975, December 5, 1976, September 11, 1977.
National Observer, December 28, 1974.
House and Garden, December, 1975.

London Times, July 23, 1976.
Sunday Times Magazine (London), November 25, 1976.
Arturo F. Gonzales, Jr., "America's Favorite Animal Doctor," *50 Plus*, September, 1978.
Suzanne Del Balso, "The Wise, Wonderful World of the Real James Herriot," *Good Housekeeping*, March, 1979.
Time, June 29, 1981.
The Writers Directory: 1984-86, St. James Press, 1983.
Publishers Weekly, January 1, 1986, September 26, 1986.

WILSON, Budge 1927-
(Marjorie Wilson)

PERSONAL: Name originally Marjorie MacGregor Archibald; born May 2, 1927, in Halifax, Nova Scotia, Canada; daughter of Maynard Brown (a judge) and Helen MacGregor (a secretary; maiden name, Dustan) Archibald; married Alan Wilson (a professor), July 31, 1953; children: Glynis Wilson Boultbee, Andrea. *Education:* Attended University of King's College, 1945-46; Dalhousie University, B.A., 1949, Teaching Certificate, 1953; graduate study, University of Toronto, 1949-51. *Home:* North West Cove, R.R. #1 Hubbards, Nova Scotia, Canada B0J 1T0 (summer).

CAREER: Halifax Ladies' College (now Armbrae Academy), Halifax, Nova Scotia, teacher of English and art, 1951-52; University of Toronto, Institute of Child Study, Toronto, Ontario, began as filing clerk, became staff artist and editor, 1953-57; Toronto Public Library, Toronto, librarian for Boys' and Girls' House, 1954; Acadia University Nursery School, Wolfville, Nova Scotia, teacher, 1956-57; Peterborough County Board of Education and Young Women's Christian Associa-

BUDGE WILSON

tion, Peterborough Ontario, fitness instructor, 1968-87; writer, 1978—. Has worked as free-lance editor, journalist, commercial artist, and photographer. *Member:* Writers' Union of Canada; Canadian Society of Children's Authors, Illustrators, and Performers; Writers' Federation of Nova Scotia.

AWARDS, HONORS: Canadian Broadcasting Corporation Literary Competition, first prize in short adult fiction, 1981, for "The Leaving"; *Chatelaine* Short Story Contest, second prize, 1983, for "The Metaphor"; Canada Council Grant, 1985; *Atlantic* Writing Competition, first prize in short adult fiction, 1986, for "My Cousin Clarette"; *The Best/Worst Christmas Present Ever* was chosen one of *Emergency Librarian*'s Twelve Best Canadian Paperback Children's Books, 1986; *Mr. John Bertrand Nijinsky and Charlie* was named "Chickadee Choice" by *Chickadee* magazine, 1986; Ontario Arts Council Grant, 1988.

WRITINGS:

The Best/Worst Christmas Present Ever (juvenile novel; "Blue Harbour" series), Scholastic-TAB, 1984.
A House Far from Home (juvenile novel; "Blue Harbour" series), Scholastic-TAB, 1986.
Mr. John Bertrand Nijinsky and Charlie (picture book; illustrated by Terry Roscoe Boucher), Nimbus, 1986.
Mystery Lights at Blue Harbour (juvenile novel; "Blue Harbor" series), Scholastic-TAB, 1987.
Breakdown (young adult novel), Scholastic-TAB, 1988.
Fourteen Never Changes (young adult novel), Scholastic-TAB, 1989.
Mulligan Chee-Chaw, Scholastic-TAB, 1989.

Work represented in anthologies, including *Canadian Children's Annual*, Potlatch, 1983, *Inside Stories 2*, Harcourt, 1987, *Winter Welcomes*, Nelson Canada, 1987, and *Royal Family Fables*, Tree Frog Press. Child care columnist for the Toronto *Globe and Mail* in the mid-1960s under name Marjorie Wilson. Contributor of child care articles to periodicals under name Marjorie Wilson in the 1960s. Contributor of short stories to *Magook, Chatelaine, Atlantis, Crackers, Dinosaur Review, University of Windsor Review, Antigonish Review, Sunday Star*, and *Herizons*.

ADAPTATIONS:

"The Leaving," CBC Radio, 1981.

WORK IN PROGRESS: A collection of short adult fiction; another book in the "Blue Harbor" series titled *Gretchen's Diary;* a book of nonsense poems for children.

SIDELIGHTS: "I grew up in Nova Scotia, Canada, and have spent much of my life in that province. Most of the action in my juvenile fiction and in my adult work is located there, it also is the setting for many of my stories.

"I was more interested in drawing than in writing until ten years ago, although I made up hundreds of stories for my children when they were little. And even today, two strong influences on my writing are my grade ten English teacher and an English professor from long ago at Dalhousie University.

"When I did start to write, I found that I loved it more than any other thing I had tried to do. Writing centers me and makes me peaceful. If I haven't written anything for a while, I start to feel like a jig-saw puzzle before it has been made up. When I am writing and just after I've finished a book, I feel as though all those pieces are in place. I feel like I know who I am, and I'm at home with that knowledge.

"I've travelled a great deal in Canada, reading my stories and talking about creative writing with school children in cities in very remote northern regions and to native communities. As a result of doing this, I know that many children want to be writers when they grow up; and many of them have already started to write excellent stories and poems. It is very exciting to see this happening—to see young people loving to read and to tell stories, and wanting to live a life that is based on the writing of books. A person who loves to write is never lonely; within his or her own head, a writer always has a safe and very interesting place to go."

WINTERFELD, Henry 1901-
(Manfred Michael)

PERSONAL: Born April 9, 1901, in Hamburg, Germany; came to the United States in 1940, naturalized citizen, 1946; son of Max (a composer) and Rosa (Wagner) Winterfeld; married Elsbeth Michael (a toy designer), April 9, 1923; children: Thomas. *Education:* Attended Stern's Academy of Music. *Home:* Roque Bluffs, Machias, Maine 04654. *Agent:* Joan Daves, 21 West 26th St., New York, N.Y. 10010.

CAREER: Playwright and screenwriter, 1923-45; author of books for children, 1937—. *Awards, honors: Mystery of the Roman Ransom* was selected one of Child Study Association of America's Children's Books of the Year, 1971.

WRITINGS:

JUVENILE; TRANSLATED INTO ENGLISH

(Under pseudonym Manfred Michael) *Timpetill: Die Stadt ohne Eltern*, Corrodi, 1937, translation by Kyrill Schabert pub-

HENRY WINTERFELD

lished (under name Henry Winterfeld) as *Trouble at Timpetill*, Harcourt, 1965.

Caius ist ein Dummkopf: Eine lustige und spannende Detektivgeschichte fuer Kinder, Blanvalet, 1953, translation by Richard Winston and Clara Winston published as *Detectives in Togas* (illustrated by Charlotte Kleinert), Harcourt, 1956.

Kommt ein Maedchen geflogen: Eine fast unglaubliche Geschichte fuer Kinder, Blanvalet, 1956, translation by K. Schabert published as *Star Girl* (illustrated by Fritz Wegner; Parents' Magazine Book Club selection), Harcourt, 1957, Avon, 1976.

Telegramm aus Lilliput: Eine phantastische Geschichte nur fuer Kinder, Blanvalet, 1958, translation by K. Schabert published as *Castaways in Lilliput* (Weekly Reader Children's Book Club selection), Harcourt, 1960.

Caius geht ein Licht auf, Blanvalet, 1969, translation by Edith McCormick published as *Mystery of the Roman Ransom* (illustrated by Fritz Biermann), Harcourt, 1971.

OTHER

Pimmi Pferdeschwanz: Eine koenigliche Unterhaltung fuer junge Maedchen (title means "Pimmy Ponytail"), Blanvalet, 1967.

Der Letzte der Sekundaner: Eine haarstraeubende Erzaehlung (title means "The Last of the Sekundaner"), Blanvalet, 1971.

Caius in der Klemme (title means "Caius in Trouble"), Blanvalet, 1976.

PLAYS

"Schloss im Nebel" (title means "Manor in the Fog"), first produced in Ostrava, Czechoslovakia, 1937.

SCREENPLAYS

"Privatsekretaerin" (title means "Private Secretary"), Universium Film Aktiengesellschaft (UFA), 1929.

"Maedchen zum Heiraten" (title means "Girls to Marry"), UFA, 1931.

"Einer Frau muss man alles verzeihen" (title means "You Have to Forgive a Woman"), UFA, 1932.

"Das Frauenparadies" (title means "A Paradise for Women"), [Vienna], 1936.

SIDELIGHTS: "I started studying the piano at Stern's Academy of Music in Berlin, together with Claudio Arrau and Frederick Loewe. I couldn't compete with them and switched to the profession of writing.

"In 1933 I left Germany and went to Austria. There I wrote *Timpetill*. I wanted somehow to entertain my son Thomas, who was sick with scarlet fever. Surprisingly other people liked the story too. Since then I have written only children's books. It's painful but I do it because I love children so much. Most of my best friends are children.

"We live in Maine, on the ocean, and even have a little private beach all to ourselves. Each summer we give a young people's garden party for the children of our friends, the lobster men, clam diggers, and other neighbors. It's great fun!"

Winterfeld's books have been published in Switzerland, England, the Netherlands, France, Norway, Sweden, Japan, Germany, Spain, Italy, Australia, and Yugoslavia.

FOR MORE INFORMATION SEE:

Doris de Montreville and Donna Hill, editors, *Third Book of Junior Authors*, H.W. Wilson, 1972.

WITTANEN, Etolin 1907-

PERSONAL: Accent on first syllable, *Witt*-anen; born August 11, 1907, in Wrangell, Ala.; daughter of Fred A. (a policeman) and Marie (a midwife; maiden name, Stender) Campen; married Clarence Wittanen (retired from U.S. Forest Service), March 23, 1936; children: Frederick, Claire. *Education:* Attended University of Oregon, 1926-29, San Francisco State College, summer, 1950, and University of Alaska at Juneau, evening classes, 1956-72; Western Washington University, B.A., 1966. *Religion:* Protestant. *Home:* 352 South Forest St., Bellingham, Wash. 98225 (winter); P.O. Box 372, Juneau, Alaska 99802 (summer).

CAREER: Kodiak Public Schools, Kodiak, Alaska, teacher, 1929-30; Chilkoot Territorial School, Haines, Alaska, teacher, 1930-31; Minfield Territorial School, Juneau, Alaska, teacher, 1933-36, 1942-44; Douglas Public Schools, Douglas, Alaska, teacher, 1946-56; Juneau-Douglas Public Schools, Juneau, teacher, 1956-72. *Member:* National Retired Teachers, Alaska State Retired Teachers, Pioneers of Alaska, women's church groups.

WRITINGS:

Auke Lake Tales (illustrated by Nikolai Alenov and Lydia Alenov), Synaxis Press, 1978.

Contributor of poems to *New World Anthology of Poetry*, Helicon, 1929. Contributor of articles to *Tlingit Herald, Southeastern Alaska Log, Writer's Companion, Herald* (Bellingham, Wash.), church newsletters and school annuals.

WORK IN PROGRESS: Gathering material on family background for family members, not for publication.

SIDELIGHTS: "I started writing verse when I was about eleven years old. All through school I contributed verse, short stories and articles to school publications and local newspapers.

"A term paper written by me for a required course for teachers, 'Teaching Tlingit (Indian) Children,' is filed in the Alaska

ETOLIN WITTANEN

State Library at Juneau. It caught the eye of the Russian Orthodox priest who worked among the Tlingit in that area. He was also the editor of the *Tlingit Herald,* a journal published by his order.

"He gained permission to print my paper, 'The Child in Early Tlingit Culture,' in his journal. At that time he asked me to submit a story each month for the children's section of the journal. 'Just write the stories,' he said when I complained I had little knowledge of the Orthodox faith, 'and I will "orthodox" them.' Later he brought out the stories as written in the book *Auke Lake Tales.* There is also an Orthodox edition. He tells me this version is found in many Orthodox communities throughout the world.

"My father went to the vast territory of Alaska during the famed gold rush of 1898, a mere boy of nineteen years. He didn't find any gold, so later returned to San Francisco and married a girl with golden hair. He couldn't get Alaska out of his blood, so in 1906, with his wife and infant son, he returned. I was born the next year, a sister two years later, and by that time Alaska was home.

"I listed him as a policeman, which was what he finally settled into after establishing the first shingle mill in Alaska, building bridges over roaring rivers, and even building a boat and trying life as a fisherman. Later he built his own five bedroom log house, felling and razing the trees by himself, depending only upon an old white horse borrowed from a neighbor to haul the logs out of the forest and assist in raising them onto the structure.

"From my father I gained a love and respect for the land and its wild inhabitants, and an appreciation for the natural phenomena of the seasons. I recall being roused from my warm bed, to stand shivering on the porch while awed by the wanton display of the Aurora Borealis, or to trace out constellations in a cold, vivid sky.

"From my mother I inherited a love of children. Be they white, like me and my brother and sister, or little brown bundles, she stood ready and happy to assist in their arrival into this world.

"Teaching school gave me a natural outlet. Alaska has never had reservations and our schools were integrated at an early date. I had a special affection for the Tlingit children whose quiet presence graced my classrooms. Later, I was privileged to have two part-Tlingit grandchildren. They and their red headed cousin (our daughter's son) are the characters in *Auke Lake Tales.* The house on the edge of the lake was built by my husband. It was there we raised our family, and where our son and his family now live. (We have a small retirement place nearby.) The incidents in the book are taken from actual occurrences or events that could have reasonably taken place.

"We now spend our winters in a warmer climate, but we will always love Alaska, the land of our birth, and we return every summer."

HOBBIES AND OTHER INTERESTS: Camping, travel, needlework, study groups.

FOR MORE INFORMATION SEE:

Tlingit Herald, Volume 4, number 4, 1977.

YADIN, Yigael   1917-1984

PERSONAL: Original surname, Sukenik; name legally changed; born March 21, 1917, in Jerusalem, Israel; died of a heart attack, June 28, 1984, in Hadera, Israel; son of Eleazar (an archaeologist) and Chassia (Feinsod) Sukenik; married Carmella Ruppin, December 22, 1941; children: Orly, Littal (daughters). *Education:* Hebrew University, Jerusalem, M.A., 1946, Ph.D., 1955. *Religion:* Jewish. *Residence:* Jerusalem, Israel. *Office:* Hebrew University, Jerusalem, Israel.

CAREER: Archaeologist, educator, military leader, translator, editor and author. Served in Haganah (underground Jewish defense corps that later became Israel Defense Forces), 1932-47, instructor in small arms, 1937, instructor in officer training school, 1940-41, adjutant to chief of staff, 1941-45, chief of planning department, 1945-47; Israel Defense Forces, chief of operations, 1947-48, chief of general staff, 1949-52, became lieutenant general; Hebrew University, Jerusalem, Israel, lecturer, 1955-59, associate professor, 1959-63, professor of archaeology, 1963-84; Government of Israel, Jerusalem, deputy prime minister and member of Knesset, 1977-81. Director of archaeological expeditions to Megiddo and Hazor, 1955-58, to caves near Dead Sea, 1960-61, and to Masada, 1963-65. Chairman of Democratic Movement for Change Party, 1977-81.

MEMBER: Israel Academy of Science and Humanities, British Academy (corresponding fellow), French Academy (corresponding fellow). *Awards, honors:* Israel Prize in Jewish Studies, 1956, for *Megilat milkheimet bneior, bivnei hoshekh;* honorary degrees from Brandeis University, 1959, and Hebrew Union College, 1963; William Frank Memorial Award for Children's Literature, and Charles and Bertie G. Swartz Juvenile Award, both from the Jewish Book Council, and chosen one of Child Study Association of America's Children's Books of the Year, all 1969, all for *The Story of Masada.*

WRITINGS:

New Light on the Dead Sea Scrolls (lecture), American Israel Society, 1954.
(Editor and author of introduction) *Megilat milkheimet bneior, bivnei hoshekh,* Bialik Institute (Jerusalem), 1955, translation by Batya Rabin and Chaim Rabin published as *The Scroll of the War of the Sons of Light against the Sons of Darkness,* Oxford University Press, 1962.
(Translator and transcriber with Nahman Avigad) *A Genesis Apocryphon: A Scroll from the Wilderness of Judea,* Magnes Press, 1956.
The Message of the Scrolls, Simon & Schuster, 1957.
Hazor, Volume I, Magnes Press, 1958, Volume II: (with Yohanan Aharoni, Ruth Amiran, and Trude Dothan) *An Account of the Second Season of Excavations, 1956,* Magnes Press, 1960, Volumes III-IV: (with others) *An Account of the Third and Fourth Seasons of Excavations, 1957-58,* Oxford University Press, 1965.
(Editor with Abe Harman) *Israel,* introduction by David Ben-Gurion, Doubleday, 1958.
(Editor with C. Rabin) *Aspects of the Dead Sea Scrolls,* Oxford University Press, 1958, 2nd edition, Magnes Press, 1965.
Military and Archaeological Aspects of the Conquest of Canaan in the Book of Joshua, Department for Education and Culture in the Diaspora of the Jewish Agency, 1960, 3rd edition, Hahevra Leheker Hamikra, 1965.
(With Yoshinori Maeda and John Kenneth Galbraith) *The Past Speaks to the Present, Television for Teaching,* [and] *The Language of Economics* (the first by Yadin, the second by Maeda, the third by Galbraith), Granada TV Network (Manchester), 1962.
Torat ha-milhamah be-artsot ha-mikra, International Publishing, 1963, translation by Moshe Pearlman published as

Yigael Yadin, leader of the expedition, supervising work atop Masada. ■ (From *The Story of Masada* by Yadin. Retold by Gerald Gottleib.)

The Art of Warfare in Biblical Lands in the Light of Archaeological Study, two volumes, McGraw, 1963.
The Finds from the Bar Kokhba Period in the Cave of Letters, Israel Exploration Society, 1963.
(Author of introductions and commentary) *The Ben Sira Scroll from Masada,* Israel Exploration Society (Jerusalem), 1965.
The Excavation of Masada, 1963-64, Preliminary Report, Israel Exploration Society, 1965.
(Translator) William Foxwell Albright, *Ha-Ark-he'ologyah shel erets yisrae* (translation of *The Archaeology of Palestine*), Am-Oved, 1965.
Metsadah, Ma'ariv & Shikmona, 1966, translation by M. Pearlman published as *Masada: Herod's Fortress and the Zealots' Last Stand,* Random House, 1966.
The Story of Masada, adapted for young readers by Gerald Gottlieb, Random House, 1969.
Tefillin from Qumran, Israel Exploration Society, 1969.
Bar-Kokhba: The Rediscovery of the Legendary Hero of the Second Jewish Revolt against Rome, Random House, 1971.
Hazor: With a Chapter on Israelite Meggido (Schweich lectures), Oxford University Press for British Academy, 1972.
Hazor: The Rediscovery of a Great Citadel of the Bible, Random House, 1975.
(Editor) *Jerusalem Revealed: Archaeology in the Holy City, 1968-1974,* translation by R. Grafman, Israel Exploration Society, 1976.
Megillah ha Gimiqdush (title means ''The Temple Scroll''), three volumes, Israel Exploration Society, 1978.
Hazor: The Head of All Those Kingdoms, Joshua 11:10, with a Chapter on Israelite Meggido, State Mutual Book, 1979.

The Temple Scroll: The Hidden Law of the Dead Sea Sect, Random House, 1985.

SIDELIGHTS: Yadin is ''virtually a household name'' in Israel, wrote Morton Kondracke in the *New Republic.* Military chief of staff in Israel's 1948 war of independence and appointed deputy prime minister of Israel, Yadin was seldom out of the public eye. But he is best known as an archaeologist ''in a country where,'' according to Naomi Shepherd in the *New Statesman,* ''archaeology is a modern religion.''

Following in the footsteps of his father, Eleazar Sukenik, the archaeologist who is credited with identifying the Dead Sea Scrolls, Yadin built an international reputation in the same field. He managed to acquire for Israel four of the Dead Sea Scrolls, and several of his books are transliterations and/or explications of them. The expedition he led at Hazor has, Yadin claimed, confirmed the Biblical narrative of the Book of Joshua, and his exploration at Masada—the fortress where, in 73 A.D., a group of Jewish defenders, besieged for three years by Roman attackers, preferred suicide to surrender—produced a text identical to that of a Dead Sea Scroll found at Qumran. His discovery of the letters of Simon Bar Kokhba, the Jewish insurgent chief who led the last revolt against the Romans in 132-135 A.D., provided the first confirmation of Bar Kokhba's existence.

Besides his expeditions and books, Yadin also taught archaeology at Hebrew University until his death in 1984. ''I find it the greatest challenge to tell the intelligent layman of my scientific discoveries—not to 'talk down' or 'up,' not to impress him with my knowledge, but rather with my finding—and make him understand. . . .That is the reward!''

FOR MORE INFORMATION SEE:

Times Literary Supplement, February 27, 1964.
New York Times, September 28, 1966.
Shane Miller, *Desert Fighter: The Story of General Yigael Yadin and the Dead Sea Scrolls,* Hawthorn, 1967.
Gray Poole and Lynn Poole, *Men Who Dig Up History,* Dodd, 1968.
Best Sellers, May 1, 1969.

Morris Rosenblum, *Heroes of Israel,* Fleet Press, 1972.
New Statesman, June 11, 1976.
Newsweek, June 14, 1976.
Time, January 24, 1977.
New Republic, February 26, 1977.

OBITUARIES

New York Times, June 29, 1984.
Los Angeles Times, June 29, 1984.
Times (London), June 30, 1984.
Newsweek, July 9, 1984.
Time, July 9, 1984.

Cumulative Indexes

Illustrations Index

(In the following index, the number of the volume in which an illustrator's work appears is given *before* the colon, and the page on which it appears is given *after* the colon. For example, a drawing by Adams, Adrienne appears in Volume 2 on page 6, another drawing by her appears in Volume 3 on page 80, another drawing in Volume 8 on page 1, and another drawing in Volume 15 on page 107.)

YABC

Index citations including this abbreviation refer to listings appearing in *Yesterday's Authors of Books for Children,* also published by the Gale Research Company, which covers authors who died prior to 1960.

Aas, Ulf, *5:* 174
Abbé, S. van. *See* van Abbé, S.
Abel, Raymond, *6:* 122; *7:* 195; *12:* 3; *21:* 86; *25:* 119
Abrahams, Hilary, *26:* 205; *29:* 24-25; *53:* 61
Abrams, Kathie, *36:* 170
Abrams, Lester, *49:* 26
Accorsi, William, *11:* 198
Acs, Laszlo, *14:* 156; *42:* 22
Adams, Adrienne, *2:* 6; *3:* 80; *8:* 1; *15:* 107; *16:* 180; *20:* 65; *22:* 134-135; *33:* 75; *36:* 103, 112; *39:* 74
Adams, John Wolcott, *17:* 162
Adams, Norman, *55:* 82
Adamson, George, *30:* 23, 24
Addams, Charles, *55:* 5
Adkins, Alta, *22:* 250
Adkins, Jan, *8:* 3
Adler, Peggy, *22:* 6; *29:* 31
Adler, Ruth, *29:* 29
Adragna, Robert, *47:* 145
Agard, Nadema, *18:* 1
Agre, Patricia, *47:* 195
Ahl, Anna Maria, *32:* 24
Aichinger, Helga, *4:* 5, 45
Aitken, Amy, *31:* 34
Akaba, Suekichi, *46:* 23; *53:* 127
Akasaka, Miyoshi, *YABC 2:* 261
Akino, Fuku, *6:* 144
Alain, *40:* 41
Alajalov, *2:* 226
Albrecht, Jan, *37:* 176
Albright, Donn, *1:* 91
Alcorn, John, *3:* 159; *7:* 165; *31:* 22; *44:* 127; *46:* 23, 170
Alda, Arlene, *44:* 24
Alden, Albert, *11:* 103
Aldridge, Andy, *27:* 131
Alex, Ben, *45:* 25, 26
Alexander, Lloyd, *49:* 34
Alexander, Martha, *3:* 206; *11:* 103; *13:* 109; *25:* 100; *36:* 131
Alexeieff, Alexander, *14:* 6; *26:* 199
Aliki. *See* Brandenberg, Aliki
Allamand, Pascale, *12:* 9
Allan, Judith, *38:* 166
Alland, Alexander, *16:* 255
Alland, Alexandra, *16:* 255
Allen, Gertrude, *9:* 6
Allen, Graham, *31:* 145

Allen, Pamela, *50:* 25, 26-27, 28
Allen, Rowena, *47:* 75
Allison, Linda, *43:* 27
Almquist, Don, *11:* 8; *12:* 128; *17:* 46; *22:* 110
Aloise, Frank, *5:* 38; *10:* 133; *30:* 92
Althea. *See* Braithwaite, Althea
Altschuler, Franz, *11:* 185; *23:* 141; *40:* 48; *45:* 29
Ambrus, Victor G., *1:* 6-7, 194; *3:* 69; *5:* 15; *6:* 44; *7:* 36; *8:* 210; *12:* 227; *14:* 213; *15:* 213; *22:* 209; *24:* 36; *28:* 179; *30:* 178; *32:* 44, 46; *38:* 143; *41:* 25, 26, 27, 28, 29, 30, 31, 32; *42:* 87; *44:* 190; *55:* 172
Ames, Lee J., *3:* 12; *9:* 130; *10:* 69; *17:* 214; *22:* 124
Amon, Aline, *9:* 9
Amoss, Berthe, *5:* 5
Amundsen, Dick, *7:* 77
Amundsen, Richard E., *5:* 10; *24:* 122
Ancona, George, *12:* 11; *55:* 144
Anderson, Alasdair, *18:* 122
Anderson, Brad, *33:* 28
Anderson, C. W., *11:* 10
Anderson, Carl, *7:* 4
Anderson, Doug, *40:* 111
Anderson, Erica, *23:* 65
Anderson, Laurie, *12:* 153, 155
Anderson, Wayne, *23:* 119; *41:* 239
Andrew, John, *22:* 4
Andrews, Benny, *14:* 251; *31:* 24
Angel, Marie, *47:* 22
Angelo, Valenti, *14:* 8; *18:* 100; *20:* 232; *32:* 70
Anglund, Joan Walsh, *2:* 7, 250-251; *37:* 198, 199, 200
Anno, Mitsumasa, *5:* 7; *38:* 25, 26-27, 28, 29, 30, 31, 32
Antal, Andrew, *1:* 124; *30:* 145
Apple, Margot, *33:* 25; *35:* 206; *46:* 81; *53:* 8
Appleyard, Dev, *2:* 192
Aragonés, Sergio, *48:* 23, 24, 25, 26, 27
Araneus, *40:* 29
Archer, Janet, *16:* 69
Ardizzone, Edward, *1:* 11, 12; *2:* 105; *3:* 258; *4:* 78; *7:* 79; *10:* 100; *15:* 232; *20:* 69, 178; *23:* 223; *24:* 125; *28:* 25, 26, 27, 28, 29,

30, 31, 33, 34, 35, 36, 37; *31:* 192, 193; *34:* 215, 217; *YABC 2:* 25
Arenella, Roy, *14:* 9
Armer, Austin, *13:* 3
Armer, Laura Adams, *13:* 3
Armer, Sidney, *13:* 3
Armitage, David, *47:* 23
Armitage, Eileen, *4:* 16
Armstrong, George, *10:* 6; *21:* 72
Arno, Enrico, *1:* 217; *2:* 22, 210; *4:* 9; *5:* 43; *6:* 52; *29:* 217, 219; *33:* 152; *35:* 99; *43:* 31, 32, 33; *45:* 212, 213, 214
Arnosky, Jim, *22:* 20
Arrowood, Clinton, *12:* 193; *19:* 11
Arting, Fred J., *41:* 63
Artzybasheff, Boris, *13:* 143; *14:* 15; *40:* 152, 155
Aruego, Ariane, *6:* 4
See also Dewey, Ariane
Aruego, Jose, *4:* 140; *6:* 4; *7:* 64; *33:* 195; *35:* 208
Asch, Frank, *5:* 9
Ashby, Gail, *11:* 135
Ashby, Gwynneth, *44:* 26
Ashley, C. W., *19:* 197
Ashmead, Hal, *8:* 70
Assel, Steven, *44:* 153
Astrop, John, *32:* 56
Atene, Ann, *12:* 18
Atherton, Lisa, *38:* 198
Atkinson, J. Priestman, *17:* 275
Atkinson, Wayne, *40:* 46
Attebery, Charles, *38:* 170
Atwood, Ann, *7:* 9
Augarde, Steve, *25:* 22
Austerman, Miriam, *23:* 107
Austin, Margot, *11:* 16
Austin, Robert, *3:* 44
Auth, Tony, *51:* 5
Averill, Esther, *1:* 17; *28:* 39, 40, 41
Axeman, Lois, *2:* 32; *11:* 84; *13:* 165; *22:* 8; *23:* 49
Ayer, Jacqueline, *13:* 7
Ayer, Margaret, *15:* 12; *50:* 120

B.T.B. *See* Blackwell, Basil T.
Babbitt, Bradford, *33:* 158
Babbitt, Natalie, *6:* 6; *8:* 220

Bachem, Paul, *48:* 180
Back, George, *31:* 161
Bacon, Bruce, *4:* 74
Bacon, Paul, *7:* 155; *8:* 121; *31:* 55;
   50: 42
Bacon, Peggy, *2:* 11, 228; *46:* 44
Baker, Alan, *22:* 22
Baker, Charlotte, *2:* 12
Baker, Jeannie, *23:* 4
Baker, Jim, *22:* 24
Baldridge, Cyrus LeRoy, *19:* 69;
   44: 50
Balet, Jan, *11:* 22
Balian, Lorna, *9:* 16
Ballantyne, R. M., *24:* 34
Ballis, George, *14:* 199
Baltzer, Hans, *40:* 30
Bang, Molly Garrett, *24:* 37, 38
Banik, Yvette Santiago, *21:* 136
Banner, Angela. *See* Maddison, Angela
   Mary
Bannerman, Helen, *19:* 13, 14
Bannon, Laura, *6:* 10; *23:* 8
Baptist, Michael, *37:* 208
Bare, Arnold Edwin, *16:* 31
Bare, Colleen Stanley, *32:* 33
Bargery, Geoffrey, *14:* 258
Barker, Carol, *31:* 27
Barker, Cicely Mary, *49:* 50, 51
Barkley, James, *4:* 13; *6:* 11; *13:* 112
Barks, Carl, *37:* 27, 28, 29, 30-31, 32,
   33, 34
Barling, Tom, *9:* 23
Barlow, Perry, *35:* 28
Barlowe, Dot, *30:* 223
Barlowe, Wayne, *37:* 72
Barner, Bob, *29:* 37
Barnes, Hiram P., *20:* 28
Barnett, Moneta, *16:* 89; *19:* 142;
   31: 102; *33:* 30, 31, 32; *41:* 153
Barney, Maginel Wright, *39:* 32, 33,
   34; *YABC 2:* 306
Barnum, Jay Hyde, *11:* 224; *20:* 5;
   37: 189, 190
Barrauds, *33:* 114
Barrer-Russell, Gertrude, *9:* 65; *27:* 31
Barrett, Angela, *40:* 136, 137
Barrett, John E., *43:* 119
Barrett, Peter, *55:* 169
Barrett, Ron, *14:* 24; *26:* 35
Barron, John N., *3:* 261; *5:* 101;
   14: 220
Barrows, Walter, *14:* 268
Barry, Ethelred B., *37:* 79;
   YABC 1: 229
Barry, James, *14:* 25
Barry, Katharina, *2:* 159; *4:* 22
Barry, Robert E., *6:* 12
Barry, Scott, *32:* 35
Bartenbach, Jean, *40:* 31
Barth, Ernest Kurt, *2:* 172; *3:* 160;
   8: 26; *10:* 31
Barton, Byron, *8:* 207; *9:* 18; *23:* 66
Barton, Harriett, *30:* 71
Bartram, Robert, *10:* 42
Bartsch, Jochen, *8:* 105; *39:* 38
Bascove, Barbara, *45:* 73
Baskin, Leonard, *30:* 42, 43, 46, 47;
   49: 125, 126, 128, 129, 133

Bass, Saul, *49:* 192
Bassett, Jeni, *40:* 99
Batchelor, Joy, *29:* 41, 47, 48
Bate, Norman, *5:* 16
Bates, Leo, *24:* 35
Batet, Carmen, *39:* 134
Batherman, Muriel, *31:* 79; *45:* 185
Battaglia, Aurelius, *50:* 44
Batten, John D., *25:* 161, 162
Battles, Asa, *32:* 94, 95
Bauernschmidt, Marjorie, *15:* 15
Baum, Allyn, *20:* 10
Baum, Willi, *4:* 24-25; *7:* 173
Baumann, Jill, *34:* 170
Baumhauer, Hans, *11:* 218; *15:* 163,
   165, 167
Bayley, Dorothy, *37:* 195
Bayley, Nicola, *40:* 104; *41:* 34, 35
Baynes, Pauline, *2:* 244; *3:* 149;
   13: 133, 135, 137-141; *19:* 18,
   19, 20; *32:* 208, 213, 214;
   36: 105, 108
Beame, Rona, *12:* 40
Beard, Dan, *22:* 31, 32
Beard, J. H., *YABC 1:* 158
Bearden, Romare, *9:* 7; *22:* 35
Beardsley, Aubrey, *17:* 14; *23:* 181
Bearman, Jane, *29:* 38
Beaton, Cecil, *24:* 208
Beaucé, J. A., *18:* 103
Beck, Charles, *11:* 169; *51:* 173
Beck, Ruth, *13:* 11
Becker, Harriet, *12:* 211
Beckett, Sheilah, *25:* 5; *33:* 37, 38
Beckhoff, Harry, *1:* 78; *5:* 163
Beckman, Kaj, *45:* 38, 39, 40, 41
Beckman, Per, *45:* 42, 43
Bedford, F. D., *20:* 118, 122; *33:* 170;
   41: 220, 221, 230, 233
Bee, Joyce, *19:* 62
Beeby, Betty, *25:* 36
Beech, Carol, *9:* 149
Beek, *25:* 51, 55, 59
Beerbohm, Max, *24:* 208
Behr, Joyce, *15:* 15; *21:* 132; *23:* 161
Behrens, Hans, *5:* 97
Beisner, Monika, *46:* 128, 131
Belden, Charles J., *12:* 182
Belina, Renate, *39:* 132
Bell, Corydon, *3:* 20
Bell, Graham, *54:* 48
Beltran, Alberto, *43:* 37
Bemelmans, Ludwig, *15:* 19, 21
Benda, Wladyslaw T., *15:* 256;
   30: 76, 77; *44:* 182
Bendick, Jeanne, *2:* 24
Bennett, F. I., *YABC 1:* 134
Bennett, Jill, *26:* 61; *41:* 38, 39;
   45: 54
Bennett, Rainey, *15:* 26; *23:* 53
Bennett, Richard, *15:* 45; *21:* 11, 12,
   13; *25:* 175
Bennett, Susan, *5:* 55
Bentley, Carolyn, *46:* 153
Bentley, Roy, *30:* 162
Benton, Thomas Hart, *2:* 99
Berelson, Howard, *5:* 20; *16:* 58;
   31: 50
Berenstain, Jan, *12:* 47

Berenstain, Stan, *12:* 47
Berg, Joan, *1:* 115; *3:* 156; *6:* 26, 58
Berg, Ron, *36:* 48, 49; *48:* 37, 38
Berger, William M., *14:* 143;
   YABC 1: 204
Bering, Claus, *13:* 14
Berkowitz, Jeanette, *3:* 249
Bernadette. *See* Watts, Bernadette
Bernath, Stefen, *32:* 76
Bernstein, Michel J., *51:* 71
Bernstein, Ted, *38:* 183; *50:* 131
Bernstein, Zena, *23:* 46
Berrill, Jacquelyn, *12:* 50
Berry, Erick. *See* Best, Allena.
Berry, William A., *6:* 219
Berry, William D., *14:* 29; *19:* 48
Berson, Harold, *2:* 17-18; *4:* 28-29,
   220; *9:* 10; *12:* 19; *17:* 45;
   18: 193; *22:* 85; *34:* 172; *44:* 120;
   46: 42
Bertschmann, Harry, *16:* 1
Beskow, Elsa, *20:* 13, 14, 15
Best, Allena, *2:* 26; *34:* 76
Bethers, Ray, *6:* 22
Bettina. *See* Ehrlich, Bettina
Betts, Ethel Franklin, *17:* 161,
   164-165; *YABC 2:* 47
Bewick, Thomas, *16:* 40-41, 43-45,
   47; *54:* 150; *YABC 1:* 107
Bezencon, Jacqueline, *48:* 40
Biamonte, Daniel, *40:* 90
Bianco, Pamela, *15:* 31; *28:* 44, 45, 46
Bible, Charles, *13:* 15
Bice, Clare, *22:* 40
Biggers, John, *2:* 123
Bileck, Marvin, *3:* 102; *40:* 36-37
Bimen, Levent, *5:* 179
Binks, Robert, *25:* 150
Binzen, Bill, *24:* 47
Birch, Reginald, *15:* 150; *19:* 33, 34,
   35, 36; *37:* 196, 197; *44:* 182;
   46: 176; *YABC 1:* 84;
   YABC 2: 34, 39
Bird, Esther Brock, *1:* 36; *25:* 66
Birmingham, Lloyd, *12:* 51
Biro, Val, *1:* 26; *41:* 42
Bischoff, Ilse, *44:* 51
Bjorklund, Lorence, *3:* 188, 252;
   7: 100; *9:* 113; *10:* 66; *19:* 178;
   33: 122, 123; *35:* 36, 37, 38, 39,
   41, 42, 43; *36:* 185; *38:* 93;
   47: 106; *YABC 1:* 242
Blackwell, Basil T., *YABC 1:* 68, 69
Blades, Ann, *16:* 52; *37:* 213; *50:* 41
Blair, Jay, *45:* 46; *46:* 155
Blaisdell, Elinore, *1:* 121; *3:* 134;
   35: 63
Blake, Quentin, *3:* 170; *10:* 48; *13:* 38;
   21: 180; *26:* 60; *28:* 228; *30:* 29,
   31; *40:* 108; *45:* 219; *46:* 165,
   168; *48:* 196; *52:* 10, 11, 12, 13,
   14, 15, 16, 17
Blake, Robert, *54:* 23
Blake, Robert J., *37:* 90; *53:* 67
Blake, William, *30:* 54, 56, 57, 58,
   59, 60
Blass, Jacqueline, *8:* 215

Blegvad, Erik, *2:* 59; *3:* 98; *5:* 117;
    7: 131; *11:* 149; *14:* 34, 35;
    18: 237; *32:* 219; *YABC 1:* 201
Bliss, Corinne Demas, *37:* 38
Bloch, Lucienne, *10:* 12
Bloom, Lloyd, *35:* 180; *36:* 149;
    47: 99
Blossom, Dave, *34:* 29
Blumenschein, E. L., *YABC 1:* 113,
    115
Blumer, Patt, *29:* 214
Blundell, Kim, *29:* 36
Boardman, Gwenn, *12:* 60
Bobri, *30:* 138; *47:* 27
Bock, Vera, *1:* 187; *21:* 41
Bock, William Sauts, *8:* 7; *14:* 37;
    16: 120; *21:* 141; *36:* 177
Bodecker, N. M., *8:* 13; *14:* 2;
    17: 55-57
Boehm, Linda, *40:* 31
Bohdal, Susi, *22:* 44
Bolian, Polly, *3:* 270; *4:* 30; *13:* 77;
    29: 197
Bolognese, Don, *2:* 147, 231; *4:* 176;
    7: 146; *17:* 43; *23:* 192; *24:* 50;
    34: 108; *36:* 133
Bond, Arnold, *18:* 116
Bond, Barbara Higgins, *21:* 102
Bond, Bruce, *52:* 97
Bond, Felicia, *38:* 197; *49:* 55, 56
Bonn, Pat, *43:* 40
Bonners, Susan, *41:* 40
Bonsall, Crosby, *23:* 6
Booth, Franklin, *YABC 2:* 76
Booth, Graham, *32:* 193; *37:* 41, 42
Bordier, Georgette, *16:* 54
Boren, Tinka, *27:* 128
Borja, Robert, *22:* 48
Born, Adolf, *49:* 63
Bornstein, Ruth, *14:* 44
Borten, Helen, *3:* 54; *5:* 24
Bossom, Naomi, *35:* 48
Boston, Peter, *19:* 42
Bosustow, Stephen, *34:* 202
Bottner, Barbara, *14:* 46
Boucher, Joelle, *41:* 138
Boulat, Pierre, *44:* 40
Boulet, Susan Seddon, *50:* 47
Bourke-White, Margaret, *15:* 286-287
Boutet de Monvel, M., *30:* 61, 62, 63,
    65
Bowen, Richard, *42:* 134
Bowen, Ruth, *31:* 188
Bower, Ron, *29:* 33
Bowser, Carolyn Ewing, *22:* 253
Boyd, Patti, *45:* 31
Boyle, Eleanor Vere, *28:* 50, 51
Bozzo, Frank, *4:* 154
Brabbs, Derry, *55:* 170
Bradford, Ron, *7:* 157
Bradley, Richard D., *26:* 182
Bradley, William, *5:* 164
Brady, Irene, *4:* 31; *42:* 37
Bragg, Michael, *32:* 78; *46:* 31
Braithwaite, Althea, *23:* 12-13
Bram, Elizabeth, *30:* 67
Bramley, Peter, *4:* 3
Brandenberg, Aliki, *2:* 36-37; *24:* 222;
    35: 49, 50, 51, 52, 53, 54, 56, 57

Brandenburg, Jim, *47:* 58
Brandi, Lillian, *31:* 158
Brandon, Brumsic, Jr., *9:* 25
Bransom, Paul, *17:* 121; *43:* 44
Brenner, Fred, *22:* 85; *36:* 34; *42:* 34
Brett, Bernard, *22:* 54
Brett, Harold M., *26:* 98, 99, 100
Brett, Jan, *30:* 135; *42:* 39
Brewer, Sally King, *33:* 44
Brewster, Patience, *40:* 68; *45:* 22,
    183; *51:* 20
Brick, John, *10:* 15
Bridge, David R., *45:* 28
Bridgman, L. J., *37:* 77
Bridwell, Norman, *4:* 37
Briggs, Raymond, *10:* 168; *23:* 20, 21
Brigham, Grace A., *37:* 148
Bright, Robert, *24:* 55
Brinckloe, Julie, *13:* 18; *24:* 79, 115;
    29: 35
Brion, *47:* 116
Brisley, Joyce L., *22:* 57
Brock, Charles E., *15:* 97; *19:* 247,
    249; *23:* 224, 225; *36:* 88; *42:* 41,
    42, 43, 44, 45; *YABC 1:* 194,
    196, 203
Brock, Emma, *7:* 21
Brock, Henry Matthew, *15:* 81;
    16: 141; *19:* 71; *34:* 115; *40:* 164;
    42: 47, 48, 49; *49:* 66
Brodkin, Gwen, *34:* 135
Brodovitch, Alexi, *52:* 22
Bromhall, Winifred, *5:* 11; *26:* 38
Brooke, L. Leslie, *16:* 181-183, 186;
    17: 15-17; *18:* 194
Brooker, Christopher, *15:* 251
Broomfield, Maurice, *40:* 141
Brotman, Adolph E., *5:* 21
Brown, Buck, *45:* 48
Brown, David, *7:* 47; *48:* 52
Brown, Denise, *11:* 213
Brown, Ford Madox, *48:* 74
Brown, Judith Gwyn, *1:* 45; *7:* 5;
    8: 167; *9:* 182, 190; *20:* 16, 17,
    18; *23:* 142; *29:* 117; *33:* 97;
    36: 23, 26; *43:* 184; *48:* 201, 223;
    49: 69
Brown, Marc Tolon, *10:* 17, 197;
    14: 263; *51:* 18; *53:* 11, 12, 13,
    15, 16-17
Brown, Marcia, *7:* 30; *25:* 203;
    47: 31, 32, 33, 34, 35, 36-37, 38,
    39, 40, 42, 43, 44; *YABC 1:* 27
Brown, Margery W., *5:* 32-33; *10:* 3
Brown, Palmer, *36:* 40
Brown, Paul, *25:* 26; *26:* 107
Brown, Ruth, *55:* 165
Browne, Anthony, *45:* 50, 51, 52
Browne, Dik, *8:* 212
Browne, Gordon, *16:* 97
Browne, Hablot K., *15:* 65, 80;
    21: 14, 15, 16, 17, 18, 19, 20;
    24: 25
Browning, Coleen, *4:* 132
Browning, Mary Eleanor, *24:* 84
Bruce, Robert, *23:* 23
Brude, Dick, *48:* 215
Brule, Al, *3:* 135
Bruna, Dick, *43:* 48, 49, 50

Brundage, Frances, *19:* 244
Brunhoff, Jean de, *24:* 57, 58
Brunhoff, Laurent de, *24:* 60
Brunson, Bob, *43:* 135
Bryan, Ashley, *31:* 44
Brychta, Alex, *21:* 21
Bryson, Bernarda, *3:* 88, 146; *39:* 26;
    44: 185
Buba, Joy, *12:* 83; *30:* 226; *44:* 56
Buchanan, Lilian, *13:* 16
Bucholtz-Ross, Linda, *44:* 137
Buchs, Thomas, *40:* 38
Buck, Margaret Waring, *3:* 30
Buehr, Walter, *3:* 31
Buff, Conrad, *19:* 52, 53, 54
Buff, Mary, *19:* 52, 53
Bull, Charles Livingston, *18:* 207
Bullen, Anne, *3:* 166, 167
Burbank, Addison, *37:* 43
Burchard, Peter, *3:* 197; *5:* 35; *6:* 158,
    218
Burger, Carl, *3:* 33; *45:* 160, 162
Burgeson, Marjorie, *19:* 31
Burgess, Gelett, *32:* 39, 42
Burkert, Nancy Ekholm, *18:* 186;
    22: 140; *24:* 62, 63, 64, 65;
    26: 53; *29:* 60, 61; *46:* 171;
    YABC 1: 46
Burn, Doris, *6:* 172
Burnett, Virgil, *44:* 42
Burningham, John, *9:* 68; *16:* 60-61
Burns, Howard M., *12:* 173
Burns, Jim, *47:* 70
Burns, M. F., *26:* 69
Burns, Raymond, *9:* 29
Burns, Robert, *24:* 106
Burr, Dane, *12:* 2
Burra, Edward, *YABC 2:* 68
Burri, René, *41:* 143; *54:* 166
Burridge, Marge Opitz, *14:* 42
Burris, Burmah, *4:* 81
Burroughs, John Coleman, *41:* 64
Burroughs, Studley O., *41:* 65
Burton, Marilee Robin, *46:* 33
Burton, Virginia Lee, *2:* 43; *44:* 49,
    51; *YABC 1:* 24
Busoni, Rafaello, *1:* 186; *3:* 224;
    6: 126; *14:* 5; *16:* 62-63
Butchkes, Sidney, *50:* 58
Butterfield, Ned, *1:* 153; *27:* 128
Buzonas, Gail, *29:* 88
Buzzell, Russ W., *12:* 177
Byard, Carole M., *39:* 44
Byars, Betsy, *46:* 35
Byfield, Barbara Ninde, *8:* 18
Byfield, Graham, *32:* 29
Byrd, Robert, *13:* 218; *33:* 46

Caddy, Alice, *6:* 41
Cady, Harrison, *17:* 21, 23; *19:* 57, 58
Caldecott, Randolph, *16:* 98, 103;
    17: 32-33, 36, 38-39; *26:* 90;
    YABC 2: 172
Calder, Alexander, *18:* 168
Calderon, W. Frank, *25:* 160
Caldwell, Doreen, *23:* 77
Caldwell, John, *46:* 225

Callahan, Kevin, 22: 42
Callahan, Philip S., 25: 77
Cameron, Julia Margaret, 19: 203
Campbell, Ann, 11: 43
Campbell, Robert, 55: 120
Campbell, Rod, 51: 27
Campbell, Walter M., YABC 2: 158
Camps, Luis, 28: 120-121
Canright, David, 36: 162
Caras, Peter, 36: 64
Caraway, James, 3: 200-201
Carbe, Nino, 29: 183
Carigiet, Alois, 24: 67
Carle, Eric, 4: 42; 11: 121; 12: 29
Carlson, Nancy L., 41: 116
Carr, Archie, 37: 225
Carrick, Donald, 5: 194; 39: 97;
    49: 70; 53: 156
Carrick, Malcolm, 28: 59, 60
Carrick, Valery, 21: 47
Carroll, Lewis. See Dodgson, Charles
    L.
Carroll, Ruth, 7: 41; 10: 68
Carter, Barbara, 47: 167, 169
Carter, Harry, 22: 179
Carter, Helene, 15: 38; 22: 202, 203;
    YABC 2: 220-221
Cartlidge, Michelle, 49: 65
Carty, Leo, 4: 196; 7: 163
Cary, 4: 133; 9: 32; 20: 2; 21: 143
Cary, Page, 12: 41
Case, Sandra E., 16: 2
Cassel, Lili. See Wronker, Lili Cassel
Cassel-Wronker, Lili.
    See also Wronker, Lili Cassel
Cassels, Jean, 8: 50
Castellon, Federico, 48: 45, 46, 47, 48
Castle, Jane, 4: 80
Cather, Carolyn, 3: 83; 15: 203;
    34: 216
Cauley, Lorinda Bryan, 44: 135;
    46: 49
Cayard, Bruce, 38: 67
Cazet, Denys, 52: 27
Cellini, Joseph, 2: 73; 3: 35; 16: 116;
    47: 103
Chabrian, Debbi, 45: 55
Chabrian, Deborah, 51: 182; 53: 124
Chagnon, Mary, 37: 158
Chalmers, Mary, 3: 145; 13: 148;
    33: 125
Chamberlain, Christopher, 45: 57
Chamberlain, Margaret, 46: 51
Chambers, C. E., 17: 230
Chambers, Dave, 12: 151
Chambers, Mary, 4: 188
Chambliss, Maxie, 42: 186
Chandler, David P., 28: 62
Chapman, C. H., 13: 83, 85, 87
Chapman, Frederick T., 6: 27; 44: 28
Chapman, Gaynor, 32: 52, 53
Chappell, Warren, 3: 172; 21: 56;
    27: 125
Charles, Donald, 30: 154, 155
Charlip, Remy, 4: 48; 34: 138
Charlot, Jean, 1: 137, 138; 8: 23;
    14: 31; 48: 151
Charlton, Michael, 34: 50; 37: 39
Charmatz, Bill, 7: 45

Chartier, Normand, 9: 36; 52: 49
Chase, Lynwood M., 14: 4
Chastain, Madye Lee, 4: 50
Chauncy, Francis, 24: 158
Chen, Tony, 6: 45; 19: 131; 29: 126;
    34: 160
Cheney, T. A., 11: 47
Cheng, Judith, 36: 45; 51: 16
Chermayeff, Ivan, 47: 53
Cherry, Lynne, 34: 52
Chess, Victoria, 12: 6; 33: 42, 48, 49;
    40: 194; 41: 145
Chessare, Michele, 41: 50
Chesterton, G. K., 27: 43, 44, 45, 47
Chestnutt, David, 47: 217
Chevalier, Christa, 35: 66
Chew, Ruth, 7: 46
Chifflart, 47: 113, 127
Chin, Alex, 28: 54
Cho, Shinta, 8: 126
Chodos, Margaret, 52: 102, 103, 107
Chollick, Jay, 25: 175
Chorao, Kay, 7: 200-201; 8: 25;
    11: 234; 33: 187; 35: 239
Christelow, Eileen, 38: 44
Christensen, Gardell Dano, 1: 57
Christiansen, Per, 40: 24
Christy, Howard Chandler,
    17: 163-165, 168-169; 19: 186,
    187; 21: 22, 23, 24, 25
Chronister, Robert, 23: 138
Church, Frederick, YABC 1: 155
Chute, Marchette, 1: 59
Chwast, Jacqueline, 1: 63; 2: 275;
    6: 46-47; 11: 125; 12: 202;
    14: 235
Chwast, Seymour, 3: 128-129; 18: 43;
    27: 152
Cirlin, Edgard, 2: 168
Clairin, Georges, 53: 109
Clark, Victoria, 35: 159
Clarke, Harry, 23: 172, 173
Claverie, Jean, 38: 46
Clayton, Robert, 9: 181
Cleaver, Elizabeth, 8: 204; 23: 36
Cleland, T. M., 26: 92
Clement, Charles, 20: 38
Clevin, Jörgen, 7: 50
Clifford, Judy, 34: 163; 45: 198
Coalson, Glo, 9: 72, 85; 25: 155;
    26: 42; 35: 212; 53: 31
Cober, Alan E., 17: 158; 32: 77;
    49: 127
Cochran, Bobbye, 11: 52
CoConis, Ted, 4: 41; 46: 41; 51: 104
Coerr, Eleanor, 1: 64
Coes, Peter, 35: 172
Cogancherry, Helen, 52: 143
Coggins, Jack, 2: 69
Cohen, Alix, 7: 53
Cohen, Vincent O., 19: 243
Cohen, Vivien, 11: 112
Coker, Paul, 51: 172
Colbert, Anthony, 15: 41; 20: 193
Colby, C. B., 3: 47
Cole, Herbert, 28: 104
Cole, Olivia H. H., 1: 134; 3: 223;
    9: 111; 38: 104
Collier, David, 13: 127

Collier, John, 27: 179
Collier, Steven, 50: 52
Colonna, Bernard, 21: 50; 28: 103;
    34: 140; 43: 180
Condon, Grattan, 54: 85
Cone, Ferne Geller, 39: 49
Cone, J. Morton, 39: 49
Conklin, Paul, 43: 62
Connolly, Jerome P., 4: 128; 28: 52
Connolly, Peter, 47: 60
Conover, Chris, 31: 52; 40: 184;
    41: 51; 44: 79
Converse, James, 38: 70
Cook, G. R., 29: 165
Cookburn, W. V., 29: 204
Cooke, Donald E., 2: 77
Cooke, Tom, 52: 118
Coomaraswamy, A. K., 50: 100
Coombs, Charles, 43: 65
Coombs, Patricia, 2: 82; 3: 52;
    22: 119; 51: 32, 33, 34, 35, 36-
    37, 38, 39, 40, 42, 43
Cooney, Barbara, 6: 16-17, 50; 12: 42;
    13: 92; 15: 145; 16: 74, 111;
    18: 189; 23: 38, 89, 93; 32: 138;
    38: 105; YABC 2: 10
Cooper, Heather, 50: 39
Cooper, Mario, 24: 107
Cooper, Marjorie, 7: 112
Copelman, Evelyn, 8: 61; 18: 25
Copley, Heather, 30: 86; 45: 57
Corbett, Grahame, 30: 114; 43: 67
Corbino, John, 19: 248
Corcos, Lucille, 2: 223; 10: 27; 34: 66
Corey, Robert, 9: 34
Corlass, Heather, 10: 7
Cornell, James, 27: 60
Cornell, Jeff, 11: 58
Corrigan, Barbara, 8: 37
Corwin, Judith Hoffman, 10: 28
Cory, Fanny Y., 20: 113; 48: 29
Cosgrove, Margaret, 3: 100; 47: 63
Costabel, Eva Deutsch, 45: 66, 67
Costello, David F., 23: 55
Courtney, R., 35: 110
Couture, Christin, 41: 209
Covarrubias, Miguel, 35: 118, 119,
    123, 124, 125
Coville, Katherine, 32: 57; 36: 167
Cox, 43: 93
Cox, Charles, 8: 20
Cox, Palmer, 24: 76, 77
Craft, Kinuko, 22: 182; 36: 220;
    53: 122, 123, 148, 149
Craig, Helen, 49: 76
Crane, Alan H., 1: 217
Crane, H. M., 13: 111
Crane, Jack, 43: 183
Crane, Walter, 18: 46-49, 53-54,
    56-57, 59-61; 22: 128; 24: 210,
    217
Crawford, Will, 43: 77
Credle, Ellis 1: 69
Crews, Donald, 32: 59, 60
Crofut, Susan, 23: 61
Crowell, Pers, 3: 125
Cruikshank, George, 15: 76, 83;
    22: 74, 75, 76, 77, 78, 79, 80,
    81, 82, 84, 137; 24: 22, 23

Crump, Fred H., *11:* 62
Cruz, Ray, *6:* 55
Csatari, Joe, *44:* 82; *55:* 152
Cuffari, Richard, *4:* 75; *5:* 98; *6:* 56;
   7: 13, 84, 153; *8:* 148, 155; *9:* 89;
   11: 19; *12:* 55, 96, 114; *15:* 51,
   202; *18:* 5; *20:* 139; *21:* 197;
   22: 14, 192; *23:* 15, 106; *25:* 97;
   27: 133; *28:* 196; *29:* 54; *30:* 85;
   31: 35; *36:* 101; *38:* 171; *42:* 97;
   44: 92, 192; *45:* 212, 213; *46:* 36,
   198; *50:* 164; *54:* 80, 136, 137,
   145
Cugat, Xavier, *19:* 120
Cumings, Art, *35:* 160
Cummings, Chris, *29:* 167
Cummings, Pat, *42:* 61
Cummings, Richard, *24:* 119
Cunette, Lou, *20:* 93; *22:* 125
Cunningham, Aline, *25:* 180
Cunningham, David, *11:* 13
Cunningham, Imogene, *16:* 122, 127
Curry, John Steuart, *2:* 5; *19:* 84;
   34: 36
Curtis, Bruce, *23:* 96; *30:* 88; *36:* 22

Dabcovich, Lydia, *25:* 105; *40:* 114
Dain, Martin J., *35:* 75
Daley, Joann, *50:* 22
Dalton, Anne, *40:* 62
Daly, Niki, *37:* 53
Dalziel, Brothers, *33:* 113
D'Amato, Alex, *9:* 48; *20:* 25
D'Amato, Janet, *9:* 48; *20:* 25; *26:* 118
Daniel, Alan, *23:* 59; *29:* 110
Daniel, Lewis C., *20:* 216
Daniels, Steve, *22:* 16
Dann, Bonnie, *31:* 83
Danska, Herbert, *24:* 219
Danyell, Alice, *20:* 27
Darley, F.O.C., *16:* 145; *19:* 79, 86,
   88, 185; *21:* 28, 36; *35:* 76, 77,
   78, 79, 80-81; *YABC 2:* 175
Darling, Lois, *3:* 59; *23:* 30, 31
Darling, Louis, *1:* 40-41; *2:* 63; *3:* 59;
   23: 30, 31; *43:* 54, 57, 59
Darrow, Whitney, Jr., *13:* 25; *38:* 220,
   221
Darwin, Beatrice, *43:* 54
Darwin, Len, *24:* 82
Dastolfo, Frank, *33:* 179
Dauber, Liz, *1:* 22; *3:* 266; *30:* 49
Daugherty, James, *3:* 66; *8:* 178;
   13: 27-28, 161; *18:* 101; *19:* 72;
   29: 108; *32:* 156; *42:* 84;
   YABC 1: 256; *YABC 2:* 174
d'Aulaire, Edgar, *5:* 51
d'Aulaire, Ingri, *5:* 51
David, Jonathan, *19:* 37
Davidson, Kevin, *28:* 154
Davidson, Raymond, *32:* 61
Davis, Allen, *20:* 11; *22:* 45; *27:* 222;
   29: 157; *41:* 99; *47:* 99; *50:* 84;
   52: 105
Davis, Bette J., *15:* 53; *23:* 95
Davis, Dimitris, *45:* 95
Davis, Jim, *32:* 63, 64

Davis, Marguerite, *31:* 38; *34:* 69, 70;
   YABC 1: 126, 230
Davisson, Virginia H., *44:* 178
Dawson, Diane, *24:* 127; *42:* 126;
   52: 130
Dean, Bob, *19:* 211
de Angeli, Marguerite, *1:* 77; *27:* 62,
   65, 66, 67, 69, 70, 72;
   YABC 1: 166
Deas, Michael, *27:* 219, 221; *30:* 156
de Bosschère, Jean, *19:* 252; *21:* 4
De Bruyn, M(onica) G., *13:* 30-31
De Cuir, John F., *1:* 28-29
Degen, Bruce, *40:* 227, 229
De Grazia, *14:* 59; *39:* 56, 57
de Groat, Diane, *9:* 39; *18:* 7; *23:* 123;
   28: 200-201; *31:* 58, 59; *34:* 151;
   41: 152; *43:* 88; *46:* 40, 200;
   49: 163; *50:* 89; *52:* 30, 34;
   54: 43
de Groot, Lee, *6:* 21
Delacre, Lulu, *36:* 66
Delaney, A., *21:* 78
Delaney, Ned, *28:* 68
de Larrea, Victoria, *6:* 119, 204;
   29: 103
Delessert, Etienne, *7:* 140; *46:* 61, 62,
   63, 65, 67, 68; *YABC 2:* 209
Delulio, John, *15:* 54
Demarest, Chris L., *45:* 68-69, 70
De Mejo, Oscar, *40:* 67
Denetsosie, Hoke, *13:* 126
Dennis, Morgan, *18:* 68-69
Dennis, Wesley, *2:* 87; *3:* 111;
   11: 132; *18:* 71-74; *22:* 9;
   24: 196, 200; *46:* 178
Denslow, W. W., *16:* 84-87;
   18: 19-20, 24; *29:* 211
de Paola, Tomie, *8:* 95; *9:* 93; *11:* 69;
   25: 103; *28:* 157; *29:* 80; *39:* 52-
   53; *40:* 226; *46:* 187
Detmold, Edward J., *22:* 104, 105,
   106, 107; *35:* 120; *YABC 2:* 203
Detrich, Susan, *20:* 133
DeVelasco, Joseph E., *21:* 51
de Veyrac, Robert, *YABC 2:* 19
DeVille, Edward A., *4:* 235
de Visser, John, *55:* 119
Devito, Bert, *12:* 164
Devlin, Harry, *11:* 74
Dewey, Ariane, *7:* 64; *33:* 195;
   35: 208
   See also Aruego, Ariane
Dewey, Kenneth, *39:* 62; *51:* 23
de Zanger, Arie, *30:* 40
Diamond, Donna, *21:* 200; *23:* 63;
   26: 142; *35:* 83, 84, 85, 86-87,
   88, 89; *38:* 78; *40:* 147; *44:* 152;
   50: 144; *53:* 126
Dick, John Henry, *8:* 181
Dickens, Frank, *34:* 131
Dickey, Robert L., *15:* 279
DiFate, Vincent, *37:* 70
DiFiori, Lawrence, *10:* 51; *12:* 190;
   27: 97; *40:* 219
Di Grazia, Thomas, *32:* 66; *35:* 241
Dillard, Annie, *10:* 32
Dillon, Corinne B., *1:* 139

Dillon, Diane, *4:* 104, 167; *6:* 23;
   13: 29; *15:* 99; *26:* 148; *27:* 136,
   201; *51:* 29, 48, 51, 52, 53, 54,
   55, 56-57, 58, 59, 60, 61, 62;
   54: 155
Dillon, Leo, *4:* 104, 167; *6:* 23;
   13: 29; *15:* 99; *26:* 148; *27:* 136,
   201; *51:* 29, 48, 51, 52, 53, 54,
   55, 56-57, 58, 59, 60, 61, 62;
   54: 155
DiMaggio, Joe, *36:* 22
Dinan, Carol, *25:* 169
Dines, Glen, *7:* 66-67
Dinesen, Thomas, *44:* 37
Dinnerstein, Harvey, *42:* 63, 64, 65,
   66, 67, 68; *50:* 146
Dinsdale, Mary, *10:* 65; *11:* 171
Disney, Walt, *28:* 71, 72, 73, 76, 77,
   78, 79, 80, 81, 87, 88, 89, 90,
   91, 94
Dixon, Maynard, *20:* 165
Doares, Robert G., *20:* 39
Dobias, Frank, *22:* 162
Dobrin, Arnold, *4:* 68
Docktor, Irv, *43:* 70
Dodd, Ed, *4:* 69
Dodd, Lynley, *35:* 92
Dodgson, Charles L., *20:* 148;
   33: 146; *YABC 2:* 98
Dodson, Bert, *9:* 138; *14:* 195; *42:* 55;
   54: 8
Dohanos, Stevan, *16:* 10
Dolch, Marguerite P., *50:* 64
Dolesch, Susanne, *34:* 49
Dolson, Hildegarde, *5:* 57
Domanska, Janina, *6:* 66-67;
   YABC 1: 166
Dominguez, Elías, *53:* 94
Domjan, Joseph, *25:* 93
Donahue, Vic, *2:* 93; *3:* 190; *9:* 44
Donald, Elizabeth, *4:* 18
Donna, Natalie, *9:* 52
Doré, Gustave, *18:* 169, 172, 175;
   19: 93, 94, 95, 96, 97, 98, 99,
   100, 101, 102, 103, 104, 105;
   23: 188; *25:* 197, 199
Doremus, Robert, *6:* 62; *13:* 90;
   30: 95, 96, 97; *38:* 97
Dorfman, Ronald, *11:* 128
Doty, Roy, *28:* 98; *31:* 32; *32:* 224;
   46: 157
Dougherty, Charles, *16:* 204; *18:* 74
Douglas, Aaron, *31:* 103
Douglas, Goray, *13:* 151
Dowd, Vic, *3:* 244; *10:* 97
Dowden, Anne Ophelia, *7:* 70-71;
   13: 120
Dowdy, Mrs. Regera, *29:* 100.
   See also Gorey, Edward
Doyle, Richard, *21:* 31, 32, 33;
   23: 231; *24:* 177; *31:* 87
Draper, Angie, *43:* 84
Drath, Bill, *26:* 34
Drawson, Blair, *17:* 53
Drescher, Joan, *30:* 100, 101; *35:* 245;
   52: 168
Drew, Patricia, *15:* 100
Drummond, V. H., *6:* 70

du Bois, William Pène, *4:* 70; *10:* 122; *26:* 61; *27:* 145, 211; *35:* 243; *41:* 216
Duchesne, Janet, *6:* 162
Dudash, Michael, *32:* 122
Duer, Douglas, *34:* 177
Duffy, Joseph, *38:* 203
Duffy, Pat, *28:* 153
Duke, Chris, *8:* 195
Dulac, Edmund, *19:* 108, 109, 110, 111, 112, 113, 114, 115, 117; *23:* 187; *25:* 152; *YABC 1:* 37; *YABC 2:* 147
Dulac, Jean, *13:* 64
Dumas, Philippe, *52:* 36, 37, 38, 39, 40-41, 42, 43, 45
Dunn, Harvey, *34:* 78, 79, 80, 81
Dunn, Phoebe, *5:* 175
Dunn, Iris, *5:* 175
Dunnington, Tom, *3:* 36; *18:* 281; *25:* 61; *31:* 159; *35:* 168; *48:* 195
Dutz, *6:* 59
Duvoisin, Roger, *2:* 95; *6:* 76-77; *7:* 197; *28:* 125; *30:* 101, 102, 103, 104, 105, 107; *47:* 205
Dypold, Pat, *15:* 37

E.V.B. *See* Boyle, Eleanor Vere (Gordon)
Eachus, Jennifer, *29:* 74
Eagle, Michael, *11:* 86; *20:* 9; *23:* 18; *27:* 122; *28:* 57; *34:* 201; *44:* 189
Earle, Olive L., *7:* 75
Earle, Vana, *27:* 99
Eastman, P. D., *33:* 57
Easton, Reginald, *29:* 181
Eaton, Tom, *4:* 62; *6:* 64; *22:* 99; *24:* 124
Ebel, Alex, *11:* 89
Ebert, Len, *9:* 191; *44:* 47
Echevarria, Abe, *37:* 69
Eckersley, Maureen, *48:* 62
Ede, Janina, *33:* 59
Edens, Cooper, *49:* 81, 82, 83, 84, 85
Edgar, Sarah E., *41:* 97
Edrien, *11:* 53
Edwards, Freya, *45:* 102
Edwards, George Wharton, *31:* 155
Edwards, Gunvor, *2:* 71; *25:* 47; *32:* 71; *54:* 106
Edwards, Jeanne, *29:* 257
Edwards, Linda Strauss, *21:* 134; *39:* 123; *49:* 88-89
Eggenhofer, Nicholas, *2:* 81
Egielski, Richard, *11:* 90; *16:* 208; *33:* 236; *38:* 35; *49:* 91, 92, 93, 95, 212, 213, 214, 216
Ehlert, Lois, *35:* 97
Ehrlich, Bettina, *1:* 83
Eichenberg, Fritz, *1:* 79; *9:* 54; *19:* 248; *23:* 170; *24:* 200; *26:* 208; *50:* 67, 68, 69, 70, 71, 72, 73, 74, 75, 77, 79, 80, 81; *YABC 1:* 104-105; *YABC 2:* 213
Einsel, Naiad, *10:* 35; *29:* 136
Einsel, Walter, *10:* 37
Einzig, Susan, *3:* 77; *43:* 78

Eitzen, Allan, *9:* 56; *12:* 212; *14:* 226; *21:* 194; *38:* 162
Eldridge, H., *54:* 109
Eldridge, Harold, *43:* 83
Elgaard, Greta, *19:* 241
Elgin, Kathleen, *9:* 188; *39:* 69
Ellacott, S. E., *19:* 118
Elliott, Sarah M., *14:* 58
Ellison, Pauline, *55:* 21
Emberley, Ed, *8:* 53
Emberley, Michael, *34:* 83
Emery, Leslie, *49:* 187
Emmett, Bruce, *49:* 147
Engle, Mort, *38:* 64
Englebert, Victor, *8:* 54
Enos, Randall, *20:* 183
Enright, Maginel Wright, *19:* 240, 243; *39:* 31, 35, 36
Enrique, Romeo, *34:* 135
Epstein, Stephen, *50:* 142, 148
Erhard, Walter, *1:* 152
Erickson, Phoebe, *11:* 83
Erikson, Mel, *31:* 69
Ernst, Lisa Campbell, *47:* 147
Escourido, Joseph, *4:* 81
Esté, Kirk, *33:* 111
Estoril, Jean, *32:* 27
Estrada, Ric, *5:* 52, 146; *13:* 174
Etchemendy, Teje, *38:* 68
Ets, Marie Hall, *2:* 102
Eulalie, *YABC 2:* 315
Evans, Katherine, *5:* 64
Ewing, Juliana Horatia, *16:* 92

Falconer, Pearl, *34:* 23
Falls, C. B., *1:* 19; *38:* 71, 72, 73, 74
Falter, John, *40:* 169, 170
Farmer, Andrew, *49:* 102
Farmer, Peter, *24:* 108; *38:* 75
Farquharson, Alexander, *46:* 75
Farrell, David, *40:* 135
Fatigati, Evelyn, *24:* 112
Faul-Jansen, Regina, *22:* 117
Faulkner, Jack, *6:* 169
Fava, Rita, *2:* 29
Fax, Elton C., *1:* 101; *4:* 2; *12:* 77; *25:* 107
Fay, *43:* 93
Federspiel, Marian, *33:* 51
Feelings, Tom, *5:* 22; *8:* 56; *12:* 153; *16:* 105; *30:* 196; *49:* 37
Fehr, Terrence, *21:* 87
Feiffer, Jules, *3:* 91; *8:* 58
Feigeles, Neil, *41:* 242
Feller, Gene, *33:* 130
Fellows, Muriel H., *10:* 42
Felts, Shirley, *33:* 71; *48:* 59
Fennelli, Maureen, *38:* 181
Fenton, Carroll Lane, *5:* 66; *21:* 39
Fenton, Mildred Adams, *5:* 66; *21:* 39
Ferguson, Walter W., *34:* 86
Fetz, Ingrid, *11:* 67; *12:* 52; *16:* 205; *17:* 59; *29:* 105; *30:* 108, 109; *32:* 149; *43:* 142
Fiammenghi, Gioia, *9:* 66; *11:* 44; *12:* 206; *13:* 57, 59; *52:* 126, 129
Field, Rachel, *15:* 113

Fine, Peter K., *43:* 210
Finger, Helen, *42:* 81
Fink, Sam, *18:* 119
Finlay, Winifred, *23:* 72
Fiorentino, Al, *3:* 240
Firmin, Charlotte, *29:* 75; *48:* 70
Fischel, Lillian, *40:* 204
Fischer, Hans, *25:* 202
Fisher, Leonard Everett, *3:* 6; *4:* 72, 86; *6:* 197; *9:* 59; *16:* 151, 153; *23:* 44; *27:* 134; *29:* 26; *34:* 87, 89, 90, 91, 93, 94, 95, 96; *40:* 206; *50:* 150; *YABC 2:* 169
Fisher, Lois, *20:* 62; *21:* 7
Fisk, Nicholas, *25:* 112
Fitschen, Marilyn, *2:* 20-21; *20:* 48
Fitzgerald, F. A., *15:* 116; *25:* 86-87
Fitzhugh, Louise, *1:* 94; *9:* 163; *45:* 75, 78
Fitzhugh, Susie, *11:* 117
Fitzsimmons, Arthur, *14:* 128
Fix, Philippe, *26:* 102
Flack, Marjorie, *21:* 67; *YABC 2:* 122
Flagg, James Montgomery, *17:* 227
Flax, Zeona, *2:* 245
Fleishman, Seymour, *14:* 232; *24:* 87
Fleming, Guy, *18:* 41
Floethe, Richard, *3:* 131; *4:* 90
Floherty, John J., Jr., *5:* 68
Flora, James, *1:* 96; *30:* 111, 112
Florian, Douglas, *19:* 122
Flory, Jane, *22:* 111
Floyd, Gareth, *1:* 74; *17:* 245; *48:* 63
Fluchère, Henri A., *40:* 79
Flynn, Barbara, *7:* 31; *9:* 70
Fogarty, Thomas, *15:* 89
Folger, Joseph, *9:* 100
Folkard, Charles, *22:* 132; *29:* 128, 257-258
Foott, Jeff, *42:* 202
Forberg, Ati, *12:* 71, 205; *14:* 1; *22:* 113; *26:* 22; *48:* 64, 65
Ford, George, *24:* 120; *31:* 70, 177
Ford, H. J., *16:* 185-186
Ford, Pamela Baldwin, *27:* 104
Foreman, Michael, *2:* 110-111
Forrester, Victoria, *40:* 83
Fortnum, Peggy, *6:* 29; *20:* 179; *24:* 211; *26:* 76, 77, 78; *39:* 78; *YABC 1:* 148
Foster, Brad W., *34:* 99
Foster, Genevieve, *2:* 112
Foster, Gerald, *7:* 78
Foster, Laura Louise, *6:* 79
Foster, Marian Curtis, *23:* 74; *40:* 42
Foucher, Adèle, *47:* 118
Fowler, Mel, *36:* 127
Fox, Charles Phillip, *12:* 84
Fox, Jim, *6:* 187
Fracé, Charles, *15:* 118
Frame, Paul, *2:* 45, 145; *9:* 153; *10:* 124; *21:* 71; *23:* 62; *24:* 123; *27:* 106; *31:* 48; *32:* 159; *34:* 195; *38:* 136; *42:* 55; *44:* 139
Francois, André, *25:* 117
Francoise. *See* Seignobosc, Francoise
Frank, Lola Edick, *2:* 199
Frank, Mary, *4:* 54; *34:* 100
Franké, Phil, *45:* 91

Frankel, Julie, *40:* 84, 85, 202
Frankenberg, Robert, *22:* 116; *30:* 50; *38:* 92, 94, 95
Franklin, John, *24:* 22
Frascino, Edward, *9:* 133; *29:* 229; *33:* 190; *48:* 80, 81, 82, 83, 84-85, 86
Frasconi, Antonio, *6:* 80; *27:* 208; *53:* 41, 43, 45, 47, 48
Fraser, Betty, *2:* 212; *6:* 185; *8:* 103; *31:* 72, 73; *43:* 136
Fraser, Eric, *38:* 78; *41:* 149, 151
Fraser, F. A., *22:* 234
Frazetta, Frank, *41:* 72
Freas, John, *25:* 207
Freeman, Don, *2:* 15; *13:* 249; *17:* 62-63, 65, 67-68; *18:* 243; *20:* 195; *23:* 213, 217; *32:* 155; *55:* 129
Fregosi, Claudia, *24:* 117
French, Fiona, *6:* 82-83
Friedman, Judith, *43:* 197
Friedman, Marvin, *19:* 59; *42:* 86
Frinta, Dagmar, *36:* 42
Frith, Michael K., *15:* 138; *18:* 120
Fritz, Ronald, *46:* 73
Fromm, Lilo, *29:* 85; *40:* 197
Frost, A. B., *17:* 6-7; *19:* 123, 124, 125, 126, 127, 128, 129, 130; *YABC 1:* 156-157, 160; *YABC 2:* 107
Fry, Guy, *2:* 224
Fry, Rosalie, *3:* 72; *YABC 2:* 180-181
Fry, Rosalind, *21:* 153, 168
Fryer, Elmer, *34:* 115
Fuchs, Erich, *6:* 84
Fuchshuber, Annegert, *43:* 96
Fufuka, Mahiri, *32:* 146
Fujikawa, Gyo, *39:* 75, 76
Fulford, Deborah, *23:* 159
Fuller, Margaret, *25:* 189
Funai, Mamoru, *38:* 105
Funk, Tom, *7:* 17, 99
Furchgott, Terry, *29:* 86
Furukawa, Mel, *25:* 42

Gaberell, J., *19:* 236
Gackenbach, Dick, *19:* 168; *41:* 81; *48:* 89, 90, 91, 92, 93, 94; *54:* 105
Gaetano, Nicholas, *23:* 209
Gag, Flavia, *17:* 49, 52
Gág, Wanda, *YABC 1:* 135, 137-138, 141, 143
Gagnon, Cécile, *11:* 77
Gál, László, *14:* 127; *52:* 54, 55, 56
Galazinski, Tom, *55:* 13
Galdone, Paul, *1:* 156, 181, 206; *2:* 40, 241; *3:* 42, 144; *4:* 141; *10:* 109, 158; *11:* 21; *12:* 118, 210; *14:* 12; *16:* 36-37; *17:* 70-74; *18:* 111, 230; *19:* 183; *21:* 154; *22:* 150, 245; *33:* 126; *39:* 136, 137; *42:* 57; *51:* 169; *55:* 110
Gallagher, Sears, *20:* 112
Galloway, Ewing, *51:* 154
Galster, Robert, *1:* 66

Galsworthy, Gay John, *35:* 232
Gammell, Stephen, *7:* 48; *13:* 149; *29:* 82; *33:* 209; *41:* 88; *50:* 185, 186-187; *53:* 51, 52-53, 54, 55, 56, 57, 58; *54:* 24, 25
Gannett, Ruth Chrisman, *3:* 74; *18:* 254; *33:* 77, 78
Gantschev, Ivan, *45:* 32
Garbutt, Bernard, *23:* 68
Garcia, *37:* 71
Gardner, Earle, *45:* 167
Gardner, Joan, *40:* 87
Gardner, Joel, *40:* 87, 92
Gardner, John, *40:* 87
Gardner, Lucy, *40:* 87
Gardner, Richard. *See* Cummings, Richard, *24:* 119
Garland, Michael, *36:* 29; *38:* 83; *44:* 168; *48:* 78, 221, 222; *49:* 161
Garnett, Eve, *3:* 75
Garnett, Gary, *39:* 184
Garraty, Gail, *4:* 142; *52:* 106
Garrett, Agnes, *46:* 110; *47:* 157
Garrett, Edmund H., *20:* 29
Garrison, Barbara, *19:* 133
Gates, Frieda, *26:* 80
Gaughan, Jack, *26:* 79; *43:* 185
Gaver, Becky, *20:* 61
Gay, Zhenya, *19:* 135, 136
Geary, Clifford N., *1:* 122; *9:* 104; *51:* 74
Gee, Frank, *33:* 26
Geer, Charles, *1:* 91; *3:* 179; *4:* 201; *6:* 168; *7:* 96; *9:* 58; *10:* 72; *12:* 127; *39:* 156, 157, 158, 159, 160; *42:* 88, 89, 90, 91; *55:* 111, 116
Gehm, Charlie, *36:* 65
Geisel, Theodor Seuss, *1:* 104-105, 106; *28:* 108, 109, 110, 111, 112, 113
Geldart, William, *15:* 121; *21:* 202
Genia, *4:* 84
Gentry, Cyrille R., *12:* 66
George, Jean, *2:* 113
Gérard, Jean Ignace, *45:* 80
Gérard, Rolf, *27:* 147, 150
Gergely, Tibor, *54:* 15, 16
Geritz, Franz, *17:* 135
Gerlach, Geff, *42:* 58
Gerrard, Roy, *47:* 78
Gershinowitz, George, *36:* 27
Gerstein, Mordicai, *31:* 117; *47:* 80, 81, 82, 83, 84, 85, 86; *51:* 173
Gervase, *12:* 27
Getz, Arthur, *32:* 148
Gibbons, Gail, *23:* 78
Gibbs, Tony, *40:* 95
Gibran, Kahlil, *32:* 116
Giesen, Rosemary, *34:* 192-193
Giguère, George, *20:* 111
Gilbert, John, *19:* 184; *54:* 115; *YABC 2:* 287
Gilbert, W. S., *36:* 83, 85, 96
Giles, Will, *41:* 218
Gill, Margery, *4:* 57; *7:* 7; *22:* 122; *25:* 166; *26:* 146, 147
Gillen, Denver, *28:* 216

Gillette, Henry J., *23:* 237
Gilliam, Stan, *39:* 64, 81
Gilman, Esther, *15:* 124
Giovanopoulos, Paul, *7:* 104
Githens, Elizabeth M., *5:* 47
Gladstone, Gary, *12:* 89; *13:* 190
Gladstone, Lise, *15:* 273
Glanzman, Louis S., *2:* 177; *3:* 182; *36:* 97, 98; *38:* 120, 122; *52:* 141, 144
Glaser, Milton, *3:* 5; *5:* 156; *11:* 107; *30:* 26; *36:* 112; *54:* 141
Glass, Andrew, *36:* 38; *44:* 133; *48:* 205
Glass, Marvin, *9:* 174
Glasser, Judy, *41:* 156
Glattauer, Ned, *5:* 84; *13:* 224; *14:* 26
Glauber, Uta, *17:* 76
Gleeson, J. M., *YABC 2:* 207
Glegg, Creina, *36:* 100
Gliewe, Unada, *3:* 78-79; *21:* 73; *30:* 220
Glovach, Linda, *7:* 105
Gobbato, Imero, *3:* 180-181; *6:* 213; *7:* 58; *9:* 150; *18:* 39; *21:* 167; *39:* 82, 83; *41:* 137, 251
Goble, Paul, *25:* 121; *26:* 86; *33:* 65
Goble, Warwick, *46:* 78, 79
Godal, Eric, *36:* 93
Godfrey, Michael, *17:* 279
Goembel, Ponder, *42:* 124
Goffstein, M. B., *8:* 71
Golbin, Andrée, *15:* 125
Goldfeder, Cheryl, *11:* 191
Goldsborough, June, *5:* 154-155; *8:* 92, *14:* 226; *19:* 139; *54:* 165
Goldstein, Leslie, *5:* 8; *6:* 60; *10:* 106
Goldstein, Nathan, *1:* 175; *2:* 79; *11:* 41, 232; *16:* 55
Goodall, John S., *4:* 92-93; *10:* 132; *YABC 1:* 198
Goode, Diane, *15:* 126; *50:* 183; *52:* 114-115
Goodelman, Aaron, *40:* 203
Goodenow, Earle, *40:* 97
Goodman, Joan Elizabeth, *50:* 86
Goodwin, Harold, *13:* 74
Goodwin, Philip R., *18:* 206
Goor, Nancy, *39:* 85, 86
Goor, Ron, *39:* 85, 86
Gordon, Gwen, *12:* 151
Gordon, Margaret, *4:* 147; *5:* 48-49; *9:* 79
Gorecka-Egan, Erica, *18:* 35
Gorey, Edward, *1:* 60-61; *13:* 169; *18:* 192; *20:* 201; *29:* 90, 91, 92-93, 94, 95, 96, 97, 98, 99, 100; *30:* 129; *32:* 90; *34:* 200. *See also* Dowdy, Mrs. Regera
Gorsline, Douglas, *1:* 98; *6:* 13; *11:* 113; *13:* 104; *15:* 14; *28:* 117, 118; *YABC 1:* 15
Gosner, Kenneth, *5:* 135
Gotlieb, Jules, *6:* 127
Gough, Philip, *23:* 47; *45:* 90
Gould, Chester, *49:* 112, 113, 114, 116, 117, 118
Govern, Elaine R., *26:* 94
Grabianski, *20:* 144

Grabiański, Janusz, *39:* 92, 93, 94, 95
Graboff, Abner, *35:* 103, 104
Graham, A. B., *11:* 61
Graham, L., *7:* 108
Graham, Margaret Bloy, *11:* 120;
    18: 305, 307
Grahame-Johnstone, Anne, *13:* 61
Grahame-Johnstone, Janet, *13:* 61
Grainger, Sam, *42:* 95
Gramatky, Hardie, *1:* 107; *30:* 116,
    119, 120, 122, 123
Grandville, J. J., *45:* 81, 82, 83, 84,
    85, 86, 87, 88; *47:* 125
Granger, Paul, *39:* 153
Grant, Gordon, *17:* 230, 234; *25:* 123,
    124, 125, 126; *52:* 69;
    YABC 1: 164
Grant, (Alice) Leigh, *10:* 52; *15:* 131;
    20: 20; *26:* 119; *48:* 202
Graves, Elizabeth, *45:* 101
Gray, Harold, *33:* 87, 88
Gray, Reginald, *6:* 69
Green, Eileen, *6:* 97
Green, Michael, *32:* 216
Greenaway, Kate, *17:* 275; *24:* 180;
    26: 107; *41:* 222, 232;
    YABC 1: 88-89; *YABC 2:* 131,
    133, 136, 138-139, 141
Greenwald, Sheila, *1:* 34; *3:* 99; *8:* 72
Gregorian, Joyce Ballou, *30:* 125
Gregory, Frank M., *29:* 107
Greiffenhagen, Maurice, *16:* 137;
    27: 57; *YABC 2:* 288
Greiner, Robert, *6:* 86
Gretter, J. Clemens, *31:* 134
Gretz, Susanna, *7:* 114
Gretzer, John, *1:* 54; *3:* 26; *4:* 162;
    7: 125; *16:* 247; *18:* 117; *28:* 66;
    30: 85, 211; *33:* 235
Grey Owl, *24:* 41
Gri, *25:* 90
Grieder, Walter *9:* 84
Grifalconi, Ann, *2:* 126; *3:* 248;
    11: 18; *13:* 182; *46:* 38; *50:* 145
Griffin, Gillett Good, *26:* 96
Griffin, James, *30:* 166
Griffiths, Dave, *29:* 76
Gringhuis, Dirk, *6:* 98; *9:* 196
Gripe, Harald, *2:* 127
Grisha, *3:* 71
Gropper, William, *27:* 93; *37:* 193
Grose, Helen Mason, *YABC 1:* 260;
    YABC 2: 150
Grossman, Nancy, *24:* 130; *29:* 101
Grossman, Robert, *11:* 124; *46:* 39
Groth, John, *15:* 79; *21:* 53, 54
Gruelle, Johnny, *35:* 107
Gschwind, William, *11:* 72
Guggenheim, Hans, *2:* 10; *3:* 37;
    8: 136
Guilbeau, Honoré, *22:* 69
Gundersheimer, Karen, *35:* 240
Gusman, Annie, *38:* 62
Gustafson, Scott, *34:* 111; *43:* 40
Guthrie, Robin, *20:* 122
Gwynne, Fred, *41:* 94, 95
Gyberg, Bo-Erik, *38:* 131

Haas, Irene, *17:* 77
Hack, Konrad, *51:* 127
Hader, Berta H., *16:* 126
Hader, Elmer S., *16:* 126
Hafner, Marylin, *22:* 196, 216; *24:* 44;
    30: 51; *35:* 95; *51:* 25, 160, 164
Hague, Michael, *32:* 128; *48:* 98, 99,
    100-101, 103, 105, 106-107, 108,
    109, 110; *49:* 121; *51:* 105
Halas, John, *29:* 41, 47, 48
Haldane, Roger, *13:* 76; *14:* 202
Hale, Irina, *26:* 97
Hale, Kathleen, *17:* 79
Haley, Gail E., *43:* 102, 103, 104, 105
Hall, Chuck, *30:* 189
Hall, Douglas, *15:* 184; *43:* 106, 107
Hall, H. Tom, *1:* 227; *30:* 210
Hall, Sydney P., *31:* 89
Hall, Vicki, *20:* 24
Hallinan, P. K., *39:* 98
Halpern, Joan, *10:* 25
Halverson, Janet, *49:* 38, 42, 44
Hamberger, John, *6:* 8; *8:* 32; *14:* 79;
    34: 136
Hamil, Tom, *14:* 80; *43:* 163
Hamilton, Bill and Associates, *26:* 215
Hamilton, Helen S., *2:* 238
Hamilton, J., *19:* 83, 85, 87
Hammond, Chris, *21:* 37
Hammond, Elizabeth, *5:* 36, 203
Hampshire, Michael, *5:* 187;
    7: 110-111; *48:* 150; *51:* 129
Hampson, Denman, *10:* 155; *15:* 130
Hampton, Blake, *41:* 244
Handforth, Thomas, *42:* 100, 101,
    102, 103, 104, 105, 107
Handville, Robert, *1:* 89; *38:* 76;
    45: 108, 109
Hane, Roger, *17:* 239; *44:* 54
Haney, Elizabeth Mathieu, *34:* 84
Hanley, Catherine, *8:* 161
Hann, Jacquie, *19:* 144
Hannon, Mark, *38:* 37
Hanson, Joan, *8:* 76; *11:* 139
Hanson, Peter E., *52:* 47; *54:* 99, 100
Hardy, David A., *9:* 96
Hardy, Paul, *YABC 2:* 245
Harlan, Jerry, *3:* 96
Harnischfeger, *18:* 121
Harper, Arthur, *YABC 2:* 121
Harrington, Richard, *5:* 81
Harris, Susan Yard, *42:* 121
Harrison, Florence, *20:* 150, 152
Harrison, Harry, *4:* 103
Harrison, Jack, *28:* 149
Hart, William, *13:* 72
Hartelius, Margaret, *10:* 24
Hartshorn, Ruth, *5:* 115; *11:* 129
Harvey, Bob, *48:* 219
Harvey, Gerry, *7:* 180
Hassall, Joan, *43:* 108, 109
Hassell, Hilton, *YABC 1:* 187
Hasselriis, Else, *18:* 87; *YABC 1:* 96
Hauman, Doris, *2:* 184; *29:* 58, 59;
    32: 85, 86, 87
Hauman, George, *2:* 184; *29:* 58, 59;
    32: 85, 86, 87
Hausherr, Rosmarie, *15:* 29

Hawkinson, John, *4:* 109; *7:* 83;
    21: 64
Hawkinson, Lucy, *21:* 64
Haxton, Elaine, *28:* 131
Haydock, Robert, *4:* 95
Hayes, Geoffrey, *26:* 111; *44:* 133
Haywood, Carolyn, *1:* 112; *29:* 104
Healy, Daty, *12:* 143
Hearon, Dorothy, *34:* 69
Hechtkopf, H., *11:* 110
Hedderwick, Mairi, *30:* 127; *32:* 47;
    36: 104
Hefter, Richard, *28:* 170; *31:* 81, 82;
    33: 183
Heigh, James, *22:* 98
Heighway, Richard, *25:* 160
Heinly, John, *45:* 113
Hellebrand, Nancy, *26:* 57
Heller, Linda, *46:* 86
Hellmuth, Jim, *38:* 164
Helms, Georgeann, *33:* 62
Helweg, Hans, *41:* 118; *50:* 93
Henderson, Kathy, *55:* 32
Henderson, Keith, *35:* 122
Henkes, Kevin, *43:* 111
Henneberger, Robert, *1:* 42; *2:* 237;
    25: 83
Henriksen, Harold, *35:* 26; *48:* 68
Henry, Everett, *29:* 191
Henry, Thomas, *5:* 102
Hensel, *27:* 119
Henstra, Friso, *8:* 80; *36:* 70; *40:* 222;
    41: 250
Hepple, Norman, *28:* 198
Herbert, Wally, *23:* 101
Herbster, Mary Lee, *9:* 33
Hergé. See Rémi, Georges
Hermanson, Dennis, *10:* 55
Hermes, Gertrude, *54:* 161
Herrington, Roger, *3:* 161
Heslop, Mike, *38:* 60; *40:* 130
Hess, Richard, *42:* 31
Hester, Ronnie, *37:* 85
Heustis, Louise L., *20:* 28
Heyduck-Huth, Hilde, *8:* 82
Heyer, Hermann, *20:* 114, 115
Heyman, Ken, *8:* 33; *34:* 113
Heywood, Karen, *48:* 114
Hickling, P. B., *40:* 165
Higginbottom, J. Winslow, *8:* 170;
    29: 105, 106
Higham, David, *50:* 104
Hildebrandt, Greg, *8:* 191; *55:* 35, 36,
    38, 39, 40, 42, 46
Hildebrandt, Tim, *8:* 191; *55:* 44, 45,
    46
Hilder, Rowland, *19:* 207
Hill, Gregory, *35:* 190
Hill, Pat, *49:* 120
Hillier, Matthew, *45:* 205
Hillman, Priscilla, *48:* 115
Himler, Ronald, *6:* 114; *7:* 162; *8:* 17,
    84, 125; *14:* 76; *19:* 145; *26:* 160;
    31: 43; *38:* 116; *41:* 44, 79;
    43: 52; *45:* 120; *46:* 43; *54:* 44,
    83
Himmelman, John, *47:* 109
Hinds, Bill, *37:* 127, 130
Hines, Anna Grossnickle, *51:* 90

Hiroshige, *25:* 71
Hirsh, Marilyn, *7:* 126
Hitz, Demi, *11:* 135; *15:* 245
Hnizdovsky, Jacques, *32:* 96
Ho, Kwoncjan, *15:* 132
Hoban, Lillian, *1:* 114; *22:* 157;
   26: 72; *29:* 53; *40:* 105, 107, 195;
   41: 80
Hoban, Tana, *22:* 159
Hoberman, Norman, *5:* 82
Hockerman, Dennis, *39:* 22
Hodgell, P. C., *42:* 114
Hodges, C. Walter, *2:* 139; *11:* 15;
   12: 25; *23:* 34; *25:* 96; *38:* 165;
   44: 197; *45:* 95; *YABC 2:* 62-63
Hodges, David, *9:* 98
Hodgetts, Victoria, *43:* 132
Hofbauer, Imre, *2:* 162
Hoff, Syd, *9:* 107; *10:* 128; *33:* 94
Hoffman, Rosekrans, *15:* 133; *50:* 219
Hoffman, Sanford, *38:* 208
Hoffmann, Felix, *9:* 109
Hofsinde, Robert, *21:* 70
Hogan, Inez, *2:* 141
Hogarth, Burne, *41:* 58
Hogarth, Paul, *41:* 102, 103, 104;
   YABC 1: 16
Hogarth, William, *42:* 33
Hogenbyl, Jan, *1:* 35
Hogner, Nils, *4:* 122; *25:* 144
Hogrogian, Nonny, *3:* 221; *4:* 106-107;
   5: 166; *7:* 129; *15:* 2; *16:* 176;
   20: 154; *22:* 146; *25:* 217;
   27: 206; *YABC 2:* 84, 94
Hokusai, *25:* 71
Holberg, Richard, *2:* 51
Holdcroft, Tina, *38:* 109
Holden, Caroline, *55:* 159
Holder, Heidi, *36:* 99
Holiday, Henry, *YABC 2:* 107
Holl, F., *36:* 91
Holland, Brad, *45:* 59, 159
Holland, Janice, *18:* 118
Holland, Marion, *6:* 116
Holldobler, Turid, *26:* 120
Holling, Holling C., *15:* 136-137
Hollinger, Deanne, *12:* 116
Holmes, B., *3:* 82
Holmes, Bea, *7:* 74; *24:* 156; *31:* 93
Holmes, Dave, *54:* 22
Holmgren, George Ellen, *45:* 112
Holt, Norma, *44:* 106
Holtan, Gene, *32:* 192
Holz, Loretta, *17:* 81
Homar, Lorenzo, *6:* 2
Homer, Winslow, *YABC 2:* 87
Honigman, Marian, *3:* 2
Honoré, Paul, *42:* 77, 79, 81, 82
Hood, Susan, *12:* 43
Hook, Frances, *26:* 188; *27:* 127
Hook, Jeff, *14:* 137
Hook, Richard, *26:* 188
Hoover, Carol A., *21:* 77
Hoover, Russell, *12:* 95; *17:* 2;
   34: 156
Hoppin, Augustus, *34:* 66
Horder, Margaret, *2:* 108
Horen, Michael, *45:* 121
Horvat, Laurel, *12:* 201

Horvath, Ferdinand Kusati, *24:* 176
Hotchkiss, De Wolfe, *20:* 49
Hough, Charlotte, *9:* 112; *13:* 98;
   17: 83; *24:* 195
Houlihan, Ray, *11:* 214
Housman, Laurence, *25:* 146, 147
Houston, James, *13:* 107
How, W. E., *20:* 47
Howard, Alan, *16:* 80; *34:* 58; *45:* 114
Howard, J. N., *15:* 234
Howard, John, *33:* 179
Howard, Rob, *40:* 161
Howe, Stephen, *1:* 232
Howell, Pat, *15:* 139
Howell, Troy, *23:* 24; *31:* 61; *36:* 158;
   37: 184; *41:* 76, 235; *48:* 112
Howes, Charles, *22:* 17
Hubley, Faith, *48:* 120-121, 125, 130,
   131, 132, 134
Hubley, John, *48:* 125, 130, 131, 132,
   134
Hudnut, Robin, *14:* 62
Huffaker, Sandy, *10:* 56
Huffman, Joan, *13:* 33
Huffman, Tom, *13:* 180; *17:* 212;
   21: 116; *24:* 132; *33:* 154; *38:* 59;
   42: 147
Hughes, Arthur, *20:* 148, 149, 150;
   33: 114, 148, 149
Hughes, David, *36:* 197
Hughes, Shirley, *1:* 20, 21; *7:* 3;
   12: 217; *16:* 163; *29:* 154
Hugo, Victor, *47:* 112
Hülsmann, Eva, *16:* 166
Hummel, Berta, *43:* 137, 138, 139
Hummel, Lisl, *29:* 109;
   YABC 2: 333-334
Humphrey, Henry, *16:* 167
Humphreys, Graham, *25:* 168
Hunt, James, *2:* 143
Hurd, Clement, *2:* 148, 149
Hurd, Peter; *24:* 30, 31, *YABC 2:* 56
Hurd, Thacher, *46:* 88-89
Hugo, Victor, *47:* 112
Hürlimann, Ruth, *32:* 99
Hustler, Tom, *6:* 105
Hutchins, Laurence, *55:* 22
Hutchins, Pat, *15:* 142
Hutchinson, William M., *6:* 3, 138;
   46: 70
Hutchison, Paula, *23:* 10
Hutton, Clarke, *YABC 2:* 335
Hutton, Kathryn, *35:* 155
Hutton, Warwick, *20:* 91
Huyette, Marcia, *29:* 188
Hyatt, John, *54:* 7
Hyman, Trina Schart, *1:* 204; *2:* 194;
   5: 153; *6:* 106; *7:* 138, 145; *8:* 22;
   10: 196; *13:* 96; *14:* 114; *15:* 204;
   16: 234; *20:* 82; *22:* 133; *24:* 151;
   25: 79, 82; *26:* 82; *29:* 83; *31:* 37,
   39; *34:* 104; *38:* 84, 100, 128;
   41: 49; *43:* 146; *46:* 91, 92, 93,
   95, 96, 97, 98, 99, 100, 101, 102,
   103, 104-105, 108, 109, 111, 197;
   48: 60, 61; *52:* 32

Ichikawa, Satomi, *29:* 152; *41:* 52;
   47: 133, 134, 135, 136

Ide, Jacqueline, *YABC 1:* 39
Ilsley, Velma, *3:* 1; *7:* 55; *12:* 109;
   37: 62; *38:* 184
Inga, *1:* 142
Ingraham, Erick, *21:* 177
Innocenti, Roberto, *21:* 123
Inoue, Yosuke, *24:* 118
Ipcar, Dahlov, *1:* 124-125; *49:* 137,
   138, 139, 140-141, 142, 143, 144,
   145
Irvin, Fred, *13:* 166; *15:* 143-144;
   27: 175
Irving, Jay, *45:* 72
Irving, Laurence, *27:* 50
Isaac, Joanne, *21:* 76
Isadora, Rachel, *43:* 159, 160; *54:* 31
Ishmael, Woodi, *24:* 111; *31:* 99
Ives, Ruth, *15:* 257

Jackson, Michael, *43:* 42
Jacobs, Barbara, *9:* 136
Jacobs, Lou, Jr., *9:* 136; *15:* 128
Jacques, Robin, *1:* 70; *2:* 1; *8:* 46;
   9: 20; *15:* 187; *19:* 253; *32:* 102,
   103, 104; *43:* 184; *YABC 1:* 42
Jagr, Miloslav, *13:* 197
Jakubowski, Charles, *14:* 192
Jambor, Louis, *YABC 1:* 11
James, Derek, *35:* 187; *44:* 91
James, Gilbert, *YABC 1:* 43
James, Harold, *2:* 151; *3:* 62; *8:* 79;
   29: 113; *51:* 195
James, Robin, *50:* 106; *53:* 32, 34, 35
James, Will, *19:* 150, 152, 153, 155,
   163
Janosch. *See* Eckert, Horst
Jansons, Inese, *48:* 117
Jansson, Tove, *3:* 90; *41:* 106, 108,
   109, 110, 111, 113, 114
Jaques, Faith, *7:* 11, 132-33; *21:* 83,
   84
Jaques, Frances Lee, *29:* 224
Jauss, Anne Marie, *1:* 139; *3:* 34;
   10: 57, 119; *11:* 205; *23:* 194
Jeffers, Susan, *17:* 86-87; *25:* 164-165;
   26: 112; *50:* 132, 134-135
Jefferson, Louise E., *4:* 160
Jenkyns, Chris, *51:* 97
Jeruchim, Simon, *6:* 173; *15:* 250
Jeschke, Susan, *20:* 89; *39:* 161;
   41: 84; *42:* 120
Jessel, Camilla, *29:* 115
Joerns, Consuelo, *38:* 36; *44:* 94
John, Diana, *12:* 209
John, Helen, *1:* 215; *28:* 204
Johns, Jeanne, *24:* 114
Johnson, Bruce, *9:* 47
Johnson, Crockett. *See* Leisk, David
Johnson, D. William, *23:* 104
Johnson, Harper, *1:* 27; *2:* 33; *18:* 302;
   19: 61; *31:* 181; *44:* 46, 50, 95
Johnson, Ingrid, *37:* 118
Johnson, James David, *12:* 195
Johnson, James Ralph, *1:* 23, 127
Johnson, Jane, *48:* 136
Johnson, John E., *34:* 133
Johnson, Larry, *47:* 56

Johnson, Margaret S., *35:* 131
Johnson, Milton, *1:* 67; *2:* 71; *26:* 45; *31:* 107
Johnson, Pamela, *16:* 174; *52:* 145
Johnson, William R., *38:* 91
Johnston, David McCall, *50:* 131, 133
Johnstone, Anne, *8:* 120; *36:* 89
Johnstone, Janet Grahame, *8:* 120; *36:* 89
Jonas, Ann, *50:* 107, 108, 109
Jones, Carol, *5:* 131
Jones, Chuck, *53:* 70, 71
Jones, Elizabeth Orton, *18:* 124, 126, 128-129
Jones, Harold, *14:* 88; *52:* 50
Jones, Jeff, *41:* 64
Jones, Laurian, *25:* 24, 27
Jones, Robert, *25:* 67
Jones, Wilfred, *35:* 115; *YABC 1:* 163
Joseph, James, *53:* 88
Joyner, Jerry, *34:* 138
Jucker, Sita, *5:* 93
Judkis, Jim, *37:* 38
Juhasz, Victor, *31:* 67
Jullian, Philippe, *24:* 206; *25:* 203
Jupo, Frank, *7:* 148-149
Justice, Martin, *34:* 72

Kahl, M. P., *37:* 83
Kahl, Virginia, *48:* 138
Kakimoo, Kozo, *11:* 148
Kalett, Jim, *48:* 159, 160, 161
Kalin, Victor, *39:* 186
Kalmenoff, Matthew, *22:* 191
Kalow, Gisela, *32:* 105
Kamen, Gloria, *1:* 41; *9:* 119; *10:* 178; *35:* 157
Kandell, Alice, *35:* 133
Kane, Henry B., *14:* 90; *18:* 219-220
Kane, Robert, *18:* 131
Kappes, Alfred, *28:* 104
Karalus, Bob, *41:* 157
Karlin, Eugene, *10:* 63; *20:* 131
Kasuya, Masahiro, *41:* 206-207; *51:* 100
Katona, Robert, *21:* 85; *24:* 126
Kauffer, E. McKnight, *33:* 103; *35:* 127
Kaufman, Angelika, *15:* 156
Kaufman, Joe, *33:* 119
Kaufman, John, *13:* 158
Kaufmann, John, *1:* 174; *4:* 159; *8:* 43, 1; *10:* 102; *18:* 133-134; *22:* 251
Kaye, Graham, *1:* 9
Kazalovski, Nata, *40:* 205
Keane, Bil, *4:* 135
Keats, Ezra Jack, *3:* 18, 105, 257; *14:* 101, 102; *33:* 129
Keegan, Marcia, *9:* 122; *32:* 93
Keely, John, *26:* 104; *48:* 214
Keen, Eliot, *25:* 213
Keeping, Charles, *9:* 124, 185; *15:* 28, 134; *18:* 115; *44:* 194, 196; *47:* 25; *52:* 3; *54:* 156
Keith, Eros, *4:* 98; *5:* 138; *31:* 29; *43:* 220; *52:* 91, 92, 93, 94

Kelen, Emery, *13:* 115
Keller, Arthur I., *26:* 106
Keller, Dick, *36:* 123, 125
Keller, Holly, *45:* 79
Keller, Ronald, *45:* 208
Kelley, True, *41:* 114, 115; *42:* 137
Kellogg, Steven, *8:* 96; *11:* 207; *14:* 130; *20:* 58; *29:* 140-141; *30:* 35; *41:* 141; *YABC 1:* 65, 73
Kelly, Walt, *18:* 136-141, 144-146, 148-149
Kemble, E. W., *34:* 75; *44:* 178; *YABC 2:* 54, 59
Kemp-Welsh, Lucy, *24:* 197
Kennedy, Paul Edward, *6:* 190; *8:* 132; *33:* 120
Kennedy, Richard, *3:* 93; *12:* 179; *44:* 193; *YABC 1:* 57
Kent, Jack, *24:* 136; *37:* 37; *40:* 81
Kent, Rockwell, *5:* 166; *6:* 129; *20:* 225, 226, 227, 229
Kepes, Juliet, *13:* 119
Kerr, Judity, *24:* 137
Kessler, Leonard, *1:* 108; *7:* 139; *14:* 107, 227; *22:* 101; *44:* 96
Kesteven, Peter, *35:* 189
Ketcham, Hank, *28:* 140, 141, 142
Kettelkamp, Larry, *2:* 164
Key, Alexander, *8:* 99
Kiakshuk, *8:* 59
Kiddell-Monroe, Joan, *19:* 201; *55:* 59, 60
Kidder, Harvey, *9:* 105
Kidwell, Carl, *43:* 145
Kieffer, Christa, *41:* 89
Kiff, Ken, *40:* 45
Kilbride, Robert, *37:* 100
Kimball, Yeffe, *23:* 116; *37:* 88
Kincade, Orin, *34:* 116
Kindred, Wendy, *7:* 151
King, Colin, *53:* 3
King, Robin, *10:* 164-165
King, Tony, *39:* 121
Kingman, Dong, *16:* 287; *44:* 100, 102, 104
Kingsley, Charles, *YABC 2:* 182
Kingston, Maxine Hong, *53:* 92
Kipling, John Lockwood, *YABC 2:* 198
Kipling, Rudyard, *YABC 2:* 196
Kipniss, Robert, *29:* 59
Kirchherr, Astrid, *55:* 23
Kirchhoff, Art, *28:* 136
Kirk, Ruth, *5:* 96
Kirk, Tim, *32:* 209, 211
Kirmse, Marguerite, *15:* 283; *18:* 153
Kirschner, Ruth, *22:* 154
Klapholz, Mel, *13:* 35
Klein, Robert, *55:* 77
Kleinman, Zalman, *28:* 143
Kliban, B., *35:* 137, 138
Knight, Ann, *34:* 143
Knight, Christopher, *13:* 125
Knight, Hilary, *1:* 233; *3:* 21; *15:* 92, 158-159; *16:* 258-260; *18:* 235; *19:* 169; *35:* 242; *46:* 167; *52:* 116; *YABC 1:* 168-169, 172
Knotts, Howard, *20:* 4; *25:* 170; *36:* 163
Kobayashi, Ann, *39:* 58

Kocsis, J. C. *See* Paul, James
Koehn, Ilse, *34:* 198
Koering, Ursula, *3:* 28; *4:* 14; *44:* 53
Koerner, Henry. *See* Koerner, W.H.D.
Koerner, W.H.D., *14:* 216; *21:* 88, 89, 90, 91; *23:* 211
Koffler, Camilla, *36:* 113
Kogan, Deborah, *8:* 164; *29:* 238; *50:* 112, 113
Koide, Yasuko, *50:* 114
Komoda, Kiyo, *9:* 128; *13:* 214
Konashevicha, V., *YABC 1:* 26
Konigsburg, E. L., *4:* 138; *48:* 141, 142, 144, 145
Kooiker, Leonie, *48:* 148
Korach, Mimi, *1:* 128-129; *2:* 52; *4:* 39; *5:* 159; *9:* 129; *10:* 21; *24:* 69
Koren, Edward, *5:* 100
Kossin, Sandy, *10:* 71; *23:* 105
Kostin, Andrej, *26:* 204
Kovacević, Zivojin, *13:* 247
Krahn, Fernando, *2:* 257; *34:* 206; *49:* 152
Kramer, Anthony, *33:* 81
Kramer, Frank, *6:* 121
Krantz, Kathy, *35:* 83
Kraus, Robert, *13:* 217
Kredel, Fritz, *6:* 35; *17:* 93-96; *22:* 147; *24:* 175; *29:* 130; *35:* 77; *YABC 2:* 166, 300
Krementz, Jill, *17:* 98; *49:* 41
Kresin, Robert, *23:* 19
Krieger, Salem, *54:* 164
Krupp, Robin Rector, *53:* 96, 98
Krush, Beth, *1:* 51, 85; *2:* 233; *4:* 115; *9:* 61; *10:* 191; *11:* 196; *18:* 164-165; *32:* 72; *37:* 203; *43:* 57
Krush, Joe, *2:* 233; *4:* 115; *9:* 61; *10:* 191; *11:* 196; *18:* 164-165; *32:* 72, 91; *37:* 203; *43:* 57
Kubinyi, Laszlo, *4:* 116; *6:* 113; *16:* 118; *17:* 100; *28:* 227; *30:* 172; *49:* 24, 28; *54:* 23
Kuhn, Bob, *17:* 91; *35:* 235
Kunhardt, Dorothy, *53:* 101
Künstler, Mort, *10:* 73; *32:* 143
Kurchevsky, V., *34:* 61
Kurelek, William, *8:* 107
Kuriloff, Ron, *13:* 19
Kuskin, Karla, *2:* 170
Kutzer, Ernst, *19:* 249

LaBlanc, André, *24:* 146
Laboccetta, Mario, *27:* 120
Laceky, Adam, *32:* 121
La Croix, *YABC 2:* 4
La Farge, Margaret, *47:* 141
Laimgruber, Monika, *11:* 153
Laite, Gordon, *1:* 130-131; *8:* 209; *31:* 113; *40:* 63; *46:* 117
Lamarche, Jim, *46:* 204
Lamb, Jim, *10:* 117
Lambert, J. K., *38:* 129; *39:* 24
Lambert, Saul, *23:* 112; *33:* 107; *54:* 136

Lambo, Don, *6:* 156; *35:* 115; *36:* 146
Landa, Peter, *11:* 95; *13:* 177; *53:* 119
Landau, Jacob, *38:* 111
Landshoff, Ursula, *13:* 124
Lane, John, *15:* 176-177; *30:* 146
Lane, John R., *8:* 145
Lang, G. D., *48:* 56
Lang, Jerry, *18:* 295
Lange, Dorothea, *50:* 141
Langner, Nola, *8:* 110; *42:* 36
Lantz, Paul, *1:* 82, 102; *27:* 88;
    34: 102; *45:* 123
Larrecq, John, *44:* 108
Larsen, Suzanne, *1:* 13
Larsson, Carl, *35:* 144, 145, 146, 147,
    148-149, 150, 152, 153, 154
Larsson, Karl, *19:* 177
La Rue, Michael D., *13:* 215
Lasker, Joe, *7:* 186-187; *14:* 55;
    38: 115; *39:* 47
Latham, Barbara, *16:* 188-189; *43:* 71
Lathrop, Dorothy, *14:* 117, 118-119;
    15: 109; *16:* 78-79, 81; *32:* 201,
    203; *33:* 112; *YABC 2:* 301
Lattimore, Eleanor Frances, *7:* 156
Lauden, Claire, *16:* 173
Lauden, George, Jr., *16:* 173
Laune, Paul, *2:* 235; *34:* 31
Lauré, Jason, *49:* 53; *50:* 122
Lavis, Stephen, *43:* 143
Lawrence, John, *25:* 131; *30:* 141;
    44: 198, 200
Lawrence, Stephen, *20:* 195
Lawson, Carol, *6:* 38; *42:* 93, 131
Lawson, George, *17:* 280
Lawson, Robert, *5:* 26; *6:* 94; *13:* 39;
    16: 11; *20:* 100, 102, 103; *54:* 3;
    YABC 2: 222,
    224-225, 227-235, 237-241
Lazare, Jerry, *44:* 109
Lazarevich, Mila, *17:* 118
Lazarus, Keo Felker, *21:* 94
Lazzaro, Victor, *11:* 126
Lea, Tom, *43:* 72, 74
Leacroft, Richard, *6:* 140
Leaf, Munro, *20:* 99
Leander, Patricia, *23:* 27
Lear, Edward, *18:* 183-185
Lebenson, Richard, *6:* 209; *7:* 76;
    23: 145; *44:* 191
Le Cain, Errol, *6:* 141; *9:* 3; *22:* 142;
    25: 198; *28:* 173
Lee, Doris, *13:* 246; *32:* 183; *44:* 111
Lee, Manning de V., *2:* 200; *17:* 12;
    27: 87; *37:* 102, 103, 104;
    YABC 2: 304
Lee, Robert J., *3:* 97
Leech, John, *15:* 59
Leeman, Michael, *44:* 157
Lees, Harry, *6:* 112
Legènisel, *47:* 111
Legrand, Edy, *18:* 89, 93
Lehrman, Rosalie, *2:* 180
Leichman, Seymour, *5:* 107
Leighton, Clare, *25:* 130; *33:* 168;
    37: 105, 106, 108, 109
Leisk, David, *1:* 140-141; *11:* 54;
    30: 137, 142, 143, 144
Leloir, Maurice, *18:* 77, 80, 83, 99

Lemke, Horst, *14:* 98; *38:* 117, 118,
    119
Lemke, R. W., *42:* 162
Lemon, David Gwynne, *9:* 1
Lenski, Lois, *1:* 144; *26:* 135, 137,
    139, 141
Lent, Blair, *1:* 116-117; *2:* 174;
    3: 206-207; *7:* 168-169; *34:* 62
Leone, Leonard, *49:* 190
Lerner, Sharon, *11:* 157; *22:* 56
Leslie, Cecil, *19:* 244
Lester, Alison, *50:* 124
Le Tord, Bijou, *49:* 156
Levai, Blaise, *39:* 130
Levin, Ted, *12:* 148
Levine, David, *43:* 147, 149, 150,
    151, 152
Levit, Herschel, *24:* 223
Levy, Jessica Ann, *19:* 225; *39:* 191
Lewin, Betsy, *32:* 114; *48:* 177
Lewin, Ted, *4:* 77; *8:* 168; *20:* 110;
    21: 99, 100; *27:* 110; *28:* 96, 97;
    31: 49; *45:* 55; *48:* 223
Lewis, Allen, *15:* 112
Lewis, Richard W., *52:* 25
Leydon, Rita Flodén, *21:* 101
Lieblich, Irene, *22:* 173; *27:* 209, 214
Liese, Charles, *4:* 222
Lightfoot, Norman R., *45:* 47
Lignell, Lois, *37:* 114
Lilly, Charles, *8:* 73; *20:* 127; *48:* 53
Lilly, Ken, *37:* 224
Lim, John, *43:* 153
Limona, Mercedes, *51:* 183
Lincoln, Patricia Henderson, *27:* 27
Lindberg, Howard, *10:* 123; *16:* 190
Linden, Seymour, *18:* 200-201;
    43: 140
Linder, Richard, *27:* 119
Lindman, Maj, *43:* 154
Lindsay, Vachel, *40:* 118
Line, Les, *27:* 143
Linell. *See* Smith, Linell
Lionni, Leo, *8:* 115
Lipinsky, Lino, *2:* 156; *22:* 175
Lippman, Peter, *8:* 31; *31:* 119, 120,
    160
Lisker, Sonia O., *16:* 274; *31:* 31;
    44: 113, 114
Lisowski, Gabriel, *47:* 144; *49:* 157
Lissim, Simon, *17:* 138
Little, Harold, *16:* 72
Little, Mary E., *28:* 146
Lively, Lorna, *19:* 216
Llerena, Carlos Antonio, *19:* 181
Lloyd, Errol, *11:* 39; *22:* 178
Lo, Koon-chiu, *7:* 134
Lobel, Anita, *6:* 87; *9:* 141; *18:* 248;
    55: 85, 86, 87, 88, 100, 104
Lobel, Arnold, *1:* 188-189; *5:* 12;
    6: 147; *7:* 167, 209; *18:* 190-191;
    25: 39, 43; *27:* 40; *29:* 174;
    52: 127; *55:* 89, 91, 93, 94, 95, 97,
    98, 99, 101, 102, 103, 105, 106
Loefgren, Ulf, *3:* 108
Loescher, Ann, *20:* 108
Loescher, Gil, *20:* 108
Lofting, Hugh, *15:* 182-183
Loh, George, *38:* 88

Lonette, Reisie, *11:* 211; *12:* 168;
    13: 56; *36:* 122; *43:* 155
Long, Sally, *42:* 184
Longtemps, Ken, *17:* 123; *29:* 221
Looser, Heinz, *YABC 2:* 208
Lopshire, Robert, *6:* 149; *21:* 117;
    34: 166
Lord, John Vernon, *21:* 104; *23:* 25;
    51: 22
Lorenz, Al, *40:* 146
Loretta, Sister Mary, *33:* 73
Lorraine, Walter H., *3:* 110; *4:* 123;
    16: 192
Loss, Joan, *11:* 163
Louderback, Walt, *YABC 1:* 164
Lousada, Sandra, *40:* 138
Low, Joseph, *14:* 124, 125; *18:* 68;
    19: 194; *31:* 166
Lowenheim, Alfred, *13:* 65-66
Lowitz, Anson, *17:* 124; *18:* 215
Lowrey, Jo, *8:* 133
Lubell, Winifred, *1:* 207; *3:* 15; *6:* 151
Lubin, Leonard B., *19:* 224; *36:* 79,
    80; *45:* 128, 129, 131, 132, 133,
    134, 135, 136, 137, 139, 140,
    141; *YABC 2:* 96
Ludwig, Helen, *33:* 144, 145
Lufkin, Raymond, *38:* 138; *44:* 48
Luhrs, Henry, *7:* 123; *11:* 120
Lupo, Dom, *4:* 204
Lustig, Loretta, *30:* 186; *46:* 134, 135,
    136, 137
Luzak, Dennis, *52:* 121
Lydecker, Laura, *21:* 113; *42:* 53
Lynch, Charles, *16:* 33
Lynch, Marietta, *29:* 137; *30:* 171
Lyon, Elinor, *6:* 154
Lyon, Fred, *14:* 16
Lyons, Oren, *8:* 193
Lyster, Michael, *26:* 41

Maas, Dorothy, *6:* 175
Maas, Julie, *47:* 61
Macaulay, David, *46:* 139, 140-141,
    142, 143, 144-145, 147, 149, 150
Macdonald, Alister, *21:* 55
MacDonald, Norman, *13:* 99
Macdonald, Roberta, *19:* 237; *52:* 164
MacDonald, Suse, *54:* 41
Mace, Varian, *49:* 159
Macguire, Robert Reid, *18:* 67
Machetanz, Fredrick, *34:* 147, 148
MacInnes, Ian, *35:* 59
MacIntyre, Elisabeth, *17:* 127-128
Mack, Stan, *17:* 129
Mackay, Donald, *17:* 60
MacKaye, Arvia, *32:* 119
MacKenzie, Garry, *33:* 159
Mackinlay, Miguel, *27:* 22
MacKinstry, Elizabeth, *15:* 110;
    42: 139, 140, 141, 142, 143, 144,
    145
Maclise, Daniel, *YABC 2:* 257
Madden, Don, *3:* 112-113; *4:* 33, 108,
    155; *7:* 193; *YABC 2:* 211
Maddison, Angela Mary, *10:* 83

Maestro, Giulio, *8:* 124; *12:* 17; *13:* 108; *25:* 182; *54:* 147

Magnuson, Diana, *28:* 102; *34:* 190; *41:* 175

Maguire, Sheila, *41:* 100

Mahony, Will, *37:* 120

Mahood, Kenneth, *24:* 141

Maik, Henri, *9:* 102

Maisto, Carol, *29:* 87

Maitland, Antony, *1:* 100, 176; *8:* 41; *17:* 246; *24:* 46; *25:* 177, 178; *32:* 74

Makie, Pam, *37:* 117

Malsberg, Edward, *51:* 175

Malvern, Corinne, *2:* 13; *34:* 148, 149

Mandelbaum, Ira, *31:* 115

Manet, Edouard, *23:* 170

Mangurian, David, *14:* 133

Manham, Allan, *42:* 109

Manniche, Lise, *31:* 121

Manning, Samuel F., *5:* 75

Maraja, *15:* 86; *YABC 1:* 28; *YABC 2:* 115

Marcellino, Fred, *20:* 125; *34:* 222; *53:* 125

Marchesi, Stephen, *34:* 140; *46:* 72; *50:* 147

Marchiori, Carlos, *14:* 60

Margules, Gabriele, *21:* 120

Mariana. *See* Foster, Marian Curtis

Mariano, Michael, *52:* 108

Marino, Dorothy, *6:* 37; *14:* 135

Markham, R. L., *17:* 240

Marks, Cara, *54:* 9

Marokvia, Artur, *31:* 122

Marriott, Pat, *30:* 30; *34:* 39; *35:* 164, 165, 166; *44:* 170; *48:* 186, 187, 188, 189, 191, 192, 193

Mars, W. T., *1:* 161; *3:* 115; *4:* 208, 225; *5:* 92, 105, 186; *8:* 214; *9:* 12; *13:* 121; *27:* 151; *31:* 180; *38:* 102; *48:* 66

Marsh, Christine, *3:* 164

Marsh, Reginald, *17:* 5; *19:* 89; *22:* 90, 96

Marshall, Anthony D., *18:* 216

Marshall, James, *6:* 160; *40:* 221; *42:* 24, 25, 29; *51:* 111, 112, 113, 114, 115, 116, 117, 118, 119, 120, 121

Marstall, Bob, *55:* 145

Martchenko, Michael, *50:* 129, 153, 155, 156, 157

Martin, David Stone, *23:* 232

Martin, Fletcher, *18:* 213; *23:* 151

Martin, René, *7:* 144; *42:* 148, 149, 150

Martin, Richard E., *51:* 157

Martin, Ron, *32:* 81

Martin, Stefan, *8:* 68; *32:* 124, 126

Martinez, John, *6:* 113

Martucci, Griesbach, *52:* 106

Marx, Robert F., *24:* 143

Masefield, Judith, *19:* 208, 209

Mason, George F., *14:* 139

Massie, Diane Redfield, *16:* 194

Massie, Kim, *31:* 43

Mathewuse, James, *51:* 143

Mathieu, Joseph, *14:* 33; *39:* 206; *43:* 167

Matsubara, Naoko, *12:* 121

Matsuda, Shizu, *13:* 167

Matte, L'Enc, *22:* 183

Mattelson, Marvin, *36:* 50, 51

Matthews, F. Leslie, *4:* 216

Matulay, Laszlo, *5:* 18; *43:* 168

Matus, Greta, *12:* 142

Mauldin, Bill, *27:* 23

Mawicke, Tran, *9:* 137; *15:* 191; *47:* 100

Max, Peter, *45:* 146, 147, 148-149, 150

Maxie, Betty, *40:* 135

Maxwell, John Alan, *1:* 148

Mayan, Earl, *7:* 193

Mayer, Marianna, *32:* 132

Mayer, Mercer, *11:* 192; *16:* 195-196; *20:* 55, 57; *32:* 129, 130, 132, 133, 134; *41:* 144, 248, 252

Mayhew, Richard, *3:* 106

Mayo, Gretchen, *38:* 81

Mays, Victor, *5:* 127; *8:* 45, 153; *14:* 245; *23:* 50; *34:* 155; *40:* 79; *45:* 158; *54:* 91

Mazal, Chanan, *49:* 104

Mazza, Adriana Saviozzi, *19:* 215

Mazzetti, Alan, *45:* 210

McBride, Angus, *28:* 49

McBride, Will, *30:* 110

McCaffery, Janet, *38:* 145

McCann, Gerald, *3:* 50; *4:* 94; *7:* 54; *41:* 121

McCay, Winsor, *41:* 124, 126, 128-129, 130-131

McClary, Nelson, *1:* 111

McClintock, Theodore, *14:* 141

McCloskey, Robert, *1:* 184-185; *2:* 186-187; *17:* 209; *39:* 139, 140, 141, 142, 143, 146, 147, 148

McClung, Robert, *2:* 189

McClure, Gillian, *31:* 132

McConnel, Jerry, *31:* 75, 187

McCormick, A. D., *35:* 119

McCormick, Dell J., *19:* 216

McCrady, Lady, *16:* 198; *39:* 127

McCrea, James, *3:* 122; *33:* 216

McCrea, Ruth, *3:* 122; *27:* 102; *33:* 216

McCully, Emily Arnold, *2:* 89; *4:* 120-121, 146, 197; *5:* 2, 129; *7:* 191; *11:* 122; *15:* 210; *33:* 23; *35:* 244; *37:* 122; *39:* 88; *40:* 103; *50:* 30, 31, 32, 33, 34, 35, 36-37; *52:* 89, 90

McCurdy, Michael, *13:* 153; *24:* 85

McDermott, Beverly Brodsky, *11:* 180

McDermott, Gerald, *16:* 201

McDonald, Jill, *13:* 155; *26:* 128

McDonald, Ralph J., *5:* 123, 195

McDonough, Don, *10:* 163

McEntee, Dorothy, *37:* 124

McFall, Christie, *12:* 144

McGee, Barbara, *6:* 165

McGregor, Malcolm, *23:* 27

McHugh, Tom, *23:* 64

McIntosh, Jon, *42:* 56

McKay, Donald, *2:* 118; *32:* 157; *45:* 151, 152

McKeating, Eileen, *44:* 58

McKee, David, *10:* 48; *21:* 9

McKie, Roy, *7:* 44

McKillip, Kathy, *30:* 153

McKinney, Ena, *26:* 39

McLachlan, Edward, *5:* 89

McLean, Sammis, *32:* 197

McLoughlin, John C., *47:* 149

McMahon, Robert, *36:* 155

McMillan, Bruce, *22:* 184

McMullan, James, *40:* 33

McNaught, Harry, *12:* 80; *32:* 136

McNaughton, Colin, *39:* 149; *40:* 108

McNicholas, Maureen, *38:* 148

McPhail, David, *14:* 105; *23:* 135; *37:* 217, 218, 220, 221; *47:* 151, 152, 153, 154, 155, 156, 158-159, 160, 162-163, 164

McPhee, Richard B., *41:* 133

McQueen, Lucinda, *28:* 149; *41:* 249; *46:* 206; *53:* 103

McVay, Tracy, *11:* 68

McVicker, Charles, *39:* 150

Mead, Ben Carlton, *43:* 75

Mecray, John, *33:* 62

Meddaugh, Susan, *20:* 42; *29:* 143; *41:* 241

Melo, John, *16:* 285

Menasco, Milton, *43:* 85

Mendelssohn, Felix, *19:* 170

Meng, Heinz, *13:* 158

Mero, Lee, *34:* 68

Merrill, Frank T., *16:* 147; *19:* 71; *YABC 1:* 226, 229, 273

Meryman, Hope, *27:* 41

Meryweather, Jack, *10:* 179

Meth, Harold, *24:* 203

Meyer, Herbert, *19:* 189

Meyer, Renate, *6:* 170

Meyers, Bob, *11:* 136

Meynell, Louis, *37:* 76

Micale, Albert, *2:* 65; *22:* 185

Middleton-Sandford, Betty, *2:* 125

Mieke, Anne, *45:* 74

Mighell, Patricia, *43:* 134

Mikolaycak, Charles, *9:* 144; *12:* 101; *13:* 212; *21:* 121; *22:* 168; *30:* 187; *34:* 103, 150; *37:* 183; *43:* 179; *44:* 90; *46:* 115, 118-119; *49:* 25

Miles, Jennifer, *17:* 278

Milhous, Katherine, *15:* 193; *17:* 51

Millais, John E., *22:* 230, 231

Millar, H. R., *YABC 1:* 194-195, 203

Millard, C. E., *28:* 186

Miller, Don, *15:* 195; *16:* 71; *20:* 106; *31:* 178

Miller, Edna, *29:* 148

Miller, Frank J., *25:* 94

Miller, Grambs, *18:* 38; *23:* 16

Miller, Jane, *15:* 196

Miller, Marcia, *13:* 233

Miller, Marilyn, *1:* 87; *31:* 69; *33:* 157

Miller, Mitchell, *28:* 183; *34:* 207

Miller, Shane, *5:* 140

Mills, Yaroslava Surmach, *35:* 169, 170; *46:* 114

Millsap, Darrel, *51:* 102
Minor, Wendell, *39:* 188; *52:* 87
Mitsuhashi, Yoko, *45:* 153
Miyake, Yoshi, *38:* 141
Mizumura, Kazue, *10:* 143; *18:* 223; *36:* 159
Mochi, Ugo, *8:* 122; *38:* 150
Mock, Paul, *55:* 83
Modell, Frank, *39:* 152
Mohr, Nicholasa, *8:* 139
Moldon, Peter L., *49:* 168
Momaday, N. Scott, *48:* 159
Montresor, Beni, *2:* 91; *3:* 138; *38:* 152, 153, 154, 155, 156-157, 158, 159, 160
Moon, Carl, *25:* 183, 184, 185
Moon, Eliza, *14:* 40
Moon, Ivan, *22:* 39; *38:* 140
Moore, Agnes Kay Randall, *43:* 187
Moore, Mary, *29:* 160
Mora, Raul Mina, *20:* 41
Mordvinoff, Nicolas, *15:* 179
Morgan, Tom, *42:* 157
Morrill, Les, *42:* 127
Morrill, Leslie, *18:* 218; *29:* 177; *33:* 84; *38:* 147; *44:* 93; *48:* 164, 165, 167, 168, 169, 170, 171; *49:* 162
Morris, *47:* 91
Morris, Frank, *55:* 133
Morrison, Bill, *42:* 116
Morrow, Gray, *2:* 64; *5:* 200; *10:* 103, 114; *14:* 175
Morton, Lee Jack, *32:* 140
Morton, Marian, *3:* 185
Moses, Grandma, *18:* 228
Moskof, Martin Stephen, *27:* 152
Moss, Donald, *11:* 184
Moss, Geoffrey, *32:* 198
Most, Bernard, *48:* 173
Mowry, Carmen, *50:* 62
Moyers, William, *21:* 65
Moyler, Alan, *36:* 142
Mozley, Charles, *9:* 87; *20:* 176, 192, 193; *22:* 228; *25:* 205; *33:* 150; *43:* 170, 171, 172, 173, 174; *YABC 2:* 89
Mueller, Hans Alexander, *26:* 64; *27:* 52, 53
Mugnaini, Joseph, *11:* 35; *27:* 52, 53; *35:* 62
Müller, Jörg, *35:* 215
Muller, Steven, *32:* 167
Mullins, Edward S., *10:* 101
Mullins, Patricia, *51:* 68
Munari, Bruno, *15:* 200
Munowitz, Ken, *14:* 148
Muñoz, William, *42:* 160
Munsinger, Lynn, *33:* 161; *46:* 126
Munson, Russell, *13:* 9
Murphy, Bill, *5:* 138
Murphy, Jill, *37:* 142
Murr, Karl, *20:* 62
Murray, Ossie, *43:* 176
Mussino, Attilio, *29:* 131
Mutchler, Dwight, *1:* 25
Myers, Bernice, *9:* 147; *36:* 75
Myers, Lou, *11:* 2

Nachreiner, Tom, *29:* 182
Nakai, Michael, *30:* 217; *54:* 29
Nakatani, Chiyoko, *12:* 124
Nash, Linell, *46:* 175
Naso, John, *33:* 183
Nason, Thomas W., *14:* 68
Nasser, Muriel, *48:* 74
Nast, Thomas, *21:* 29; *28:* 23; *51:* 132, 133, 134, 135, 136, 137, 138, 139, 141
Natti, Susanna, *20:* 146; *32:* 141, 142; *35:* 178; *37:* 143
Navarra, Celeste Scala, *8:* 142
Naylor, Penelope, *10:* 104
Nebel, M., *45:* 154
Neebe, William, *7:* 93
Needler, Jerry, *12:* 93
Neel, Alice, *31:* 23
Neely, Keith R., *46:* 124
Negri, Rocco, *3:* 213; *5:* 67; *6:* 91, 108; *12:* 159
Neill, John R., *18:* 8, 10-11, 21, 30
Ness, Evaline, *1:* 164-165; *2:* 39; *3:* 8; *10:* 147; *12:* 53; *26:* 150, 151, 152, 153; *49:* 30, 31, 32
Neville, Vera, *2:* 182
Newberry, Clare Turlay, *1:* 170
Newfeld, Frank, *14:* 121; *26:* 154
Newman, Ann, *43:* 90
Newsom, Carol, *40:* 159; *44:* 60; *47:* 189
Newsom, Tom, *49:* 149
Ng, Michael, *29:* 171
Nicholson, William, *15:* 33-34; *16:* 48
Nicklaus, Carol, *45:* 194
Nickless, Will, *16:* 139
Nicolas, *17:* 130, 132-133; *YABC 2:* 215
Niebrugge, Jane, *6:* 118
Nielsen, Jon, *6:* 100; *24:* 202
Nielsen, Kay, *15:* 7; *16:* 211-213, 215, 217; *22:* 143; *YABC 1:* 32-33
Niland, Deborah, *25:* 191; *27:* 156
Niland, Kilmeny, *25:* 191
Ninon, *1:* 5; *38:* 101, 103, 108
Nissen, Rie, *44:* 35
Nixon, K., *14:* 152
Noble, Trinka Hakes, *39:* 162
Noguchi, Yoshie, *30:* 99
Nolan, Dennis, *42:* 163
Noonan, Julia, *4:* 163; *7:* 207; *25:* 151
Nordenskjold, Birgitta, *2:* 208
Norman, Mary, *36:* 138, 147
Norman, Michael, *12:* 117; *27:* 168
Numeroff, Laura Joffe, *28:* 161; *30:* 177
Nussbaumer, Paul, *16:* 219; *39:* 117
Nyce, Helene, *19:* 219
Nygren, Tord, *30:* 148

Oakley, Graham, *8:* 112; *30:* 164, 165
Oakley, Thornton, *YABC 2:* 189
Obligado, Lilian, *2:* 28, 66-67; *6:* 30; *14:* 179; *15:* 103; *25:* 84
Obrant, Susan, *11:* 186
O'Brien, Anne Sibley, *53:* 116, 117
O'Brien, John, *41:* 253

Odell, Carole, *35:* 47
O'Donohue, Thomas, *40:* 89
Oechsli, Kelly, *5:* 144-145; *7:* 115; *8:* 83, 183; *13:* 117; *20:* 94
Offen, Hilda, *42:* 207
Ogden, Bill, *42:* 59; *47:* 55
Ogg, Oscar, *33:* 34
Ohlsson, Ib, *4:* 152; *7:* 57; *10:* 20; *11:* 90; *19:* 217; *41:* 246
Ohtomo, Yasuo, *37:* 146; *39:* 212, 213
O'Kelley, Mattie Lou, *36:* 150
Oliver, Jenni, *23:* 121; *35:* 112
Olschewski, Alfred, *7:* 172
Olsen, Ib Spang, *6:* 178-179
Olugebefola, Ademola, *15:* 205
O'Neil, Dan IV, *7:* 176
O'Neill, Jean, *22:* 146
O'Neill, Michael J., *54:* 172
O'Neill, Rose, *48:* 30, 31
O'Neill, Steve, *21:* 118
Ono, Chiyo, *7:* 97
Orbaan, Albert, *2:* 31; *5:* 65, 171; *9:* 8; *14:* 241; *20:* 109
Orbach, Ruth, *21:* 112
Orfe, Joan, *20:* 81
Ormerod, Jan, *55:* 124
Ormsby, Virginia H., *11:* 187
Orozco, José Clemente, *9:* 177
Orr, Forrest W., *23:* 9
Orr, N., *19:* 70
Osborne, Billie Jean, *35:* 209
Osmond, Edward, *10:* 111
O'Sullivan, Tom, *3:* 176; *4:* 55
Otto, Svend, *22:* 130, 141
Oudry, J. B., *18:* 167
Oughton, Taylor, *5:* 23
Övereng, Johannes, *44:* 36
Overlie, George, *11:* 156
Owens, Carl, *2:* 35; *23:* 521
Owens, Gail, *10:* 170; *12:* 157; *19:* 16; *22:* 70; *25:* 81; *28:* 203, 205; *32:* 221, 222; *36:* 132; *46:* 40; *47:* 57; *54:* 66, 67, 68, 69, 70, 71, 72, 73
Oxenbury, Helen, *3:* 150-151; *24:* 81

Padgett, Jim, *12:* 165
Page, Homer, *14:* 145
Paget, Sidney, *24:* 90, 91, 93, 95, 97
Pak, *12:* 76
Palazzo, Tony, *3:* 152-153
Palladini, David, *4:* 113; *40:* 176, 177, 178-179, 181, 224-225; *50:* 138
Pallarito, Don, *43:* 36
Palmer, Heidi, *15:* 207; *29:* 102
Palmer, Jan, *42:* 153
Palmer, Juliette, *6:* 89; *15:* 208
Palmer, Lemuel, *17:* 25, 29
Palmquist, Eric, *38:* 133
Panesis, Nicholas, *3:* 127
Panton, Doug, *52:* 99
Papas, William, *11:* 223; *50:* 160
Papin, Joseph, *26:* 113
Papish, Robin Lloyd, *10:* 80
Paradis, Susan, *40:* 216
Paraquin, Charles H., *18:* 166
Paris, Peter, *31:* 127

Park, Seho, *39:* 110
Park, W. B., *22:* 189
Parker, Lewis, *2:* 179
Parker, Nancy Winslow, *10:* 113;
    22: 164; *28:* 47, 144; *52:* 7
Parker, Robert, *4:* 161; *5:* 74; *9:* 136;
    29: 39
Parker, Robert Andrew, *11:* 81;
    29: 186; *39:* 165; *40:* 25; *41:* 78;
    42: 123; *43:* 144; *48:* 182; *54:* 140
Parks, Gordon, Jr., *33:* 228
Parnall, Peter, *5:* 137; *16:* 221; *24:* 70;
    40: 78; *51:* 130
Parnall, Virginia, *40:* 78
Parrish, Anne, *27:* 159, 160
Parrish, Dillwyn, *27:* 159
Parrish, Maxfield, *14:* 160, 161, 164,
    165; *16:* 109; *18:* 12-13;
    YABC 1: 149, 152, 267;
    YABC 2: 146, 149
Parry, David, *26:* 156
Parry, Marian, *13:* 176; *19:* 179
Partch, Virgil, *45:* 163, 165
Pascal, David, *14:* 174
Pasquier, J. A., *16:* 91
Paterson, Diane, *13:* 116; *39:* 163
Paterson, Helen, *16:* 93
Paton, Jane, *15:* 271; *35:* 176
Patterson, Geoffrey, *54:* 75
Patterson, Robert, *25:* 118
Paul, James, *4:* 130; *23:* 161
Paull, Grace, *24:* 157
Payne, Joan Balfour, *1:* 118
Payson, Dale, *7:* 34; *9:* 151; *20:* 140;
    37: 22
Payzant, Charles, *21:* 147
Peake, Mervyn, *22:* 136, 149; *23:* 162,
    163, 164; *YABC 2:* 307
Pearson, Larry, *38:* 225
Peat, Fern B., *16:* 115
Peck, Anne Merriman, *18:* 241;
    24: 155
Pederson, Sharleen, *12:* 92
Pedersen, Vilhelm, *YABC 1:* 40
Peek, Merle, *39:* 168
Peet, Bill, *2:* 203; *41:* 159, 160, 161,
    162, 163
Pels, Winslow Pinney, *55:* 126
Peltier, Leslie C., *13:* 178
Pendle, Alexy, *7:* 159; *13:* 34;
    29: 161; *33:* 215
Pennington, Eunice, *27:* 162
Peppé, Mark, *28:* 142
Peppe, Rodney, *4:* 164-165
Perl, Susan, *2:* 98; *4:* 231; *5:* 44-45,
    118; *6:* 199; *8:* 137; *12:* 88;
    22: 193; *34:* 54-55; *52:* 128;
    YABC 1: 176
Perry, Patricia, *29:* 137; *30:* 171
Perry, Roger, *27:* 163
Perske, Martha, *46:* 83; *51:* 108, 147
Pesek, Ludek, *15:* 237
Petersham, Maud, *17:* 108, 147-153
Petersham, Miska, *17:* 108, 147-153
Peterson, R. F., *7:* 101
Peterson, Russell, *7:* 130
Petie, Haris, *2:* 3; *10:* 41, 118;
    11: 227; *12:* 70
Petrides, Heidrun, *19:* 223

Peyo, *40:* 56, 57
Peyton, K. M., *15:* 212
Pfeifer, Herman, *15:* 262
Phillips, Douglas, *1:* 19
Phillips, F. D., *6:* 202
Phillips, Thomas, *30:* 55
Philpot, Glyn, *54:* 46
"Phiz." *See* Browne, Hablot K.
Piatti, Celestino, *16:* 223
Picarella, Joseph, *13:* 147
Pickard, Charles, *12:* 38; *18:* 203;
    36: 152
Picken, George A., *23:* 150
Pickens, David, *22:* 156
Pienkowski, Jan, *6:* 183; *30:* 32
Pimlott, John, *10:* 205
Pincus, Harriet, *4:* 186; *8:* 179;
    22: 148; *27:* 164, 165
Pinkney, Jerry, *8:* 218; *10:* 40;
    15: 276; *20:* 66; *24:* 121; *33:* 109;
    36: 222; *38:* 200; *41:* 165, 166,
    167, 168, 169, 170, 171, 173,
    174; *44:* 198; *48:* 51; *53:* 20
Pinkwater, Daniel Manus, *46:* 180,
    181, 182, 185, 188, 189, 190
Pinkwater, Manus, *8:* 156; *46:* 180
Pinto, Ralph, *10:* 131; *45:* 93
Pitz, Henry C., *4:* 168; *19:* 165;
    35: 128; *42:* 80; *YABC 2:* 95, 176
Pitzenberger, Lawrence J., *26:* 94
Plowden, David, *52:* 135, 136
Plummer, William, *32:* 31
Pogány, Willy, *15:* 46, 49; *19:* 222,
    256; *25:* 214; *44:* 142, 143, 144,
    145, 146, 147, 148
Poirson, V. A., *26:* 89
Polgreen, John, *21:* 44
Politi, Leo, *1:* 178; *4:* 53; *21:* 48;
    47: 173, 174, 176, 178, 179, 180,
    181
Polonsky, Arthur, *34:* 168
Polseno, Jo, *1:* 53; *3:* 117; *5:* 114;
    17: 154; *20:* 87; *32:* 49; *41:* 245
Ponter, James, *5:* 204
Poortvliet, Rien, *6:* 212
Portal, Colette, *6:* 186; *11:* 203
Porter, George, *7:* 181
Potter, Beatrix, *YABC 1:* 208-210,
    212, 213
Potter, Miriam Clark, *3:* 162
Powers, Richard M., *1:* 230; *3:* 218;
    7: 194; *26:* 186
Powledge, Fred, *37:* 154
Pratt, Charles, *23:* 29
Price, Christine, *2:* 247; *3:* 163, 253;
    8: 166
Price, Edward, *33:* 34
Price, Garrett, *1:* 76; *2:* 42
Price, Hattie Longstreet, *17:* 13
Price, Norman, *YABC 1:* 129
Price, Willard, *48:* 184
Primavera, Elise, *26:* 95
Primrose, Jean, *36:* 109
Prince, Leonora E., *7:* 170
Prittie, Edwin J., *YABC 1:* 120
Provensen, Alice, *37:* 204, 215, 222
Provensen, Martin, *37:* 204, 215, 222
Pucci, Albert John, *44:* 154
Pudlo, *8:* 59

Purdy, Susan, *8:* 162
Pursell, Weimer, *55:* 18
Puskas, James, *5:* 141
Pyk, Jan, *7:* 26; *38:* 123
Pyle, Howard, *16:* 225-228, 230-232,
    235; *24:* 27; *34:* 124, 125, 127,
    128

Quackenbush, Robert, *4:* 190; *6:* 166;
    7: 175, 178; *9:* 86; *11:* 65, 221;
    41: 154; *43:* 157
Quennell, Marjorie (Courtney),
    29: 163, 164
Quidor, John, *19:* 82
Quirk, Thomas, *12:* 81

Rackham, Arthur, *15:* 32, 78, 214-227;
    17: 105, 115; *18:* 233; *19:* 254;
    20: 151; *22:* 129, 131, 132, 133;
    23: 175; *24:* 161, 181; *26:* 91;
    32: 118; *YABC 1:* 25, 45, 55, 147;
    YABC 2: 103, 142, 173, 210
Rafilson, Sidney, *11:* 172
Raible, Alton, *1:* 202-203; *28:* 193;
    35: 181
Ramsey, James, *16:* 41
Ramus, Michael, *51:* 171
Rand, Paul, *6:* 188
Randell, William, *55:* 54
Ransome, Arthur, *22:* 201
Rao, Anthony, *28:* 126
Raphael, Elaine, *23:* 192
Rappaport, Eva, *6:* 190
Raskin, Ellen, *2:* 208-209; *4:* 142;
    13: 183; *22:* 68; *29:* 139; *36:* 134;
    38: 173, 174, 175, 176, 177, 178,
    179, 180, 181
Ratzkin, Lawrence, *40:* 143
Rau, Margaret, *9:* 157
Raverat, Gwen, *YABC 1:* 152
Ravielli, Anthony, *1:* 198; *3:* 168;
    11: 143
Ray, Deborah. *See* Kogan, Deborah
    Ray.
Ray, Ralph, *2:* 239; *5:* 73
Raymond, Larry, *31:* 108
Rayner, Mary, *22:* 207; *47:* 140
Raynor, Dorka, *28:* 168
Raynor, Paul, *24:* 73
Razzi, James, *10:* 127
Read, Alexander D. "Sandy," *20:* 45
Reasoner, Charles, *53:* 33, 36, 37
Reed, Tom, *34:* 171
Reid, Stephen, *19:* 213; *22:* 89
Reinertson, Barbara, *44:* 150
Reiniger, Lotte, *40:* 185
Reiss, John J., *23:* 193
Relf, Douglas, *3:* 63
Relyea, C. M., *16:* 29; *31:* 153
Rémi, Georges, *13:* 184
Remington, Frederic, *19:* 188; *41:* 178,
    179, 180, 181, 183, 184, 185,
    186, 187, 188
Renlie, Frank, *11:* 200
Reschofsky, Jean, *7:* 118

Réthi, Lili, *2:* 153; *36:* 156
Reusswig, William, *3:* 267
Rey, H. A., *1:* 182; *26:* 163, 164, 166, 167, 169; *YABC 2:* 17
Reynolds, Doris, *5:* 71; *31:* 77
Rhead, Louis, *31:* 91
Rhodes, Andrew, *38:* 204; *50:* 163; *54:* 76
Ribbons, Ian, *3:* 10; *37:* 161; *40:* 76
Rice, Elizabeth, *2:* 53, 214
Rice, James, *22:* 210
Rice, Eve, *34:* 174, 175
Richards, George, *40:* 116, 119, 121; *44:* 179
Richards, Henry, *YABC 1:* 228, 231
Richardson, Ernest, *2:* 144
Richardson, Frederick, *18:* 27, 31
Richman, Hilda, *26:* 132
Richmond, George, *24:* 179
Rieniets, Judy King, *14:* 28
Riger, Bob, *2:* 166
Riley, Kenneth, *22:* 230
Ringi, Kjell, *12:* 171
Rios, Tere. *See* Versace, Marie
Ripper, Charles L., *3:* 175
Ritz, Karen, *41:* 117
Rivkin, Jay, *15:* 230
Rivoche, Paul, *45:* 125
Roach, Marilynne, *9:* 158
Robbin, Jodi, *44:* 156, 159
Robbins, Frank, *42:* 167
Robbins, Ruth, *52:* 102
Roberts, Cliff, *4:* 126
Roberts, Doreen, *4:* 230; *28:* 105
Roberts, Jim, *22:* 166; *23:* 69; *31:* 110
Roberts, W., *22:* 2, 3
Robinson, Charles, *3:* 53; *5:* 14; *6:* 193; *7:* 150; *7:* 183; *8:* 38; *9:* 81; *13:* 188; *14:* 248-249; *23:* 149; *26:* 115; *27:* 48; *28:* 191; *32:* 28; *35:* 210; *36:* 37; *48:* 96; *52:* 33; *53:* 157
Robinson, Charles [1870-1937], *17:* 157, 171-173, 175-176; *24:* 207; *25:* 204; *YABC 2:* 308-310, 331
Robinson, Jerry, *3:* 262
Robinson, Joan G., *7:* 184
Robinson, T. H., *17:* 179, 181-183; *29:* 254
Robinson, W. Heath, *17:* 185, 187, 189, 191, 193, 195, 197, 199, 202; *23:* 167; *25:* 194; *29:* 150; *YABC 1:* 44; *YABC 2:* 183
Roche, Christine, *41:* 98
Rocker, Fermin, *7:* 34; *13:* 21; *31:* 40; *40:* 190, 191
Rockwell, Anne, *5:* 147; *33:* 171, 173
Rockwell, Gail, *7:* 186
Rockwell, Harlow, *33:* 171, 173, 175
Rockwell, Norman, *23:* 39, 196, 197, 199, 200, 203, 204, 207; *41:* 140, 143; *YABC 2:* 60
Rodegast, Roland, *43:* 100
Rodriguez, Joel, *16:* 65
Roever, J. M., *4:* 119; *26:* 170
Roffey, Maureen, *33:* 142, 176, 177
Rogasky, Barbara, *46:* 90
Rogers, Carol, *2:* 262; *6:* 164; *26:* 129

Rogers, Frances, *10:* 130
Rogers, Walter S., *31:* 135, 138
Rogers, William A., *15:* 151, 153-154; *33:* 35
Rojankovsky, Feodor, *6:* 134, 136; *10:* 183; *21:* 128, 129, 130; *25:* 110; *28:* 42
Rorer, Abigail, *43:* 222
Rosamilia, Patricia, *36:* 120
Rose, Carl, *5:* 62
Rose, David S., *29:* 109
Rosenbaum, Jonathan, *50:* 46
Rosenblum, Richard, *11:* 202; *18:* 18
Rosier, Lydia, *16:* 236; *20:* 104; *21:* 109; *22:* 125; *30:* 151, 158; *42:* 128; *45:* 214
Ross. *See* Thomson, Ross
Ross, Clare Romano, *3:* 123; *21:* 45; *48:* 199
Ross, Dave, *32:* 152
Ross, Herbert, *37:* 78
Ross, John, *3:* 123; *21:* 45
Ross, Johnny, *32:* 190
Ross, Larry, *47:* 168
Ross, Tony, *17:* 204
Rossetti, Dante Gabriel, *20:* 151, 153
Roth, Arnold, *4:* 238; *21:* 133
Rotondo, Pat, *32:* 158
Roughsey, Dick, *35:* 186
Rouille, M., *11:* 96
Rounds, Glen, *8:* 173; *9:* 171; *12:* 56; *32:* 194; *40:* 230; *51:* 161, 162, 166; *YABC 1:* 1-3
Rowan, Evadne, *52:* 51
Rowe, Gavin, *27:* 144
Rowell, Kenneth, *40:* 72
Rowen, Amy, *52:* 143
Roy, Jeroo, *27:* 229; *36:* 110
Rubel, Nicole, *18:* 255; *20:* 59
Rubel, Reina, *33:* 217
Rud, Borghild, *6:* 15
Rudolph, Norman Guthrie, *17:* 13
Rue, Leonard Lee III, *37:* 164
Ruff, Donna, *50:* 173
Ruffins, Reynold, *10:* 134-135; *41:* 191, 192-193, 194-195, 196
Ruhlin, Roger, *34:* 44
Ruse, Margaret, *24:* 155
Rush, Peter, *42:* 75
Russell, E. B., *18:* 177, 182
Russell, Jim, *53:* 134
Russo, Susan, *30:* 182; *36:* 144
Ruth, Rod, *9:* 161
Rutherford, Meg, *25:* 174; *34:* 178, 179
Rutland, Jonathan, *31:* 126
Ryden, Hope, *8:* 176
Rymer, Alta M., *34:* 181
Rystedt, Rex, *49:* 80

Saaf, Chuck, *49:* 179
Sabaka, Donna R., *21:* 172
Sabin, Robert, *45:* 35
Sacker, Amy, *16:* 100
Saffioti, Lino, *36:* 176; *48:* 60
Sagsoorian, Paul, *12:* 183; *22:* 154; *33:* 106

Saint Exupéry, Antoine de, *20:* 157
St. John, J. Allen, *41:* 62
Saldutti, Denise, *39:* 186
Sale, Morton, *YABC 2:* 31
Sambourne, Linley, *YABC 2:* 181
Sampson, Katherine, *9:* 197
Samson, Anne S., *2:* 216
Sancha, Sheila, *38:* 185
Sand, George X., *45:* 182
Sandberg, Lasse, *15:* 239, 241
Sanders, Beryl, *39:* 173
Sanderson, Ruth, *21:* 126; *24:* 53; *28:* 63; *33:* 67; *41:* 48, 198, 199, 200, 201, 202, 203; *43:* 79; *46:* 36, 44; *47:* 102; *49:* 58
Sandin, Joan, *4:* 36; *6:* 194; *7:* 177; *12:* 145, 185; *20:* 43; *21:* 74; *26:* 144; *27:* 142; *28:* 224, 225; *38:* 86; *41:* 46; *42:* 35
Sandland, Reg, *39:* 215
Sandoz, Edouard, *26:* 45, 47
San Souci, Daniel, *40:* 200
Santore, Charles, *54:* 139
Sapieha, Christine, *1:* 180
Sarg, Tony, *YABC 2:* 236
Sargent, Robert, *2:* 217
Saris, *1:* 33
Sarony, *YABC 2:* 170
Sasek, Miroslav, *16:* 239-242
Sassman, David, *9:* 79
Sätty, *29:* 203, 205
Sauber, Rob, *40:* 183
Savage, Steele, *10:* 203; *20:* 77; *35:* 28
Savitt, Sam, *8:* 66, 182; *15:* 278; *20:* 96; *24:* 192; *28:* 98
Say, Allen, *28:* 178
Scabrini, Janet, *13:* 191; *44:* 128
Scarry, Huck, *35:* 204-205
Scarry, Richard, *2:* 220-221; *18:* 20; *35:* 193, 194-195, 196, 197, 198, 199, 200-201, 202
Schaeffer, Mead, *18:* 81, 94; *21:* 137, 138, 139; *47:* 128
Scharl, Josef, *20:* 132; *22:* 128
Scheel, Lita, *11:* 230
Scheib, Ida, *29:* 28
Schermer, Judith, *30:* 184
Schick, Joel, *16:* 160; *17:* 167; *22:* 12; *27:* 176; *31:* 147, 148; *36:* 23; *38:* 64; *45:* 116, 117; *52:* 5, 85
Schindelman, Joseph, *1:* 74; *4:* 101; *12:* 49; *26:* 51; *40:* 146
Schindler, Edith, *7:* 22
Schindler, S. D., *38:* 107; *46:* 196
Schlesinger, Bret, *7:* 77
Schmid, Eleanore, *12:* 188
Schmiderer, Dorothy, *19:* 224
Schmidt, Elizabeth, *15:* 242
Schmidt, Karen, *54:* 12
Schneider, Rex, *29:* 64; *44:* 171
Schoenherr, Ian, *32:* 83
Schoenherr, John, *1:* 146-147, 173; *3:* 39, 139; *17:* 75; *29:* 72; *32:* 83; *37:* 168, 169, 170; *43:* 164, 165; *45:* 160, 162; *51:* 127
Schomburg, Alex, *13:* 23
Schongut, Emanuel, *4:* 102; *15:* 186; *47:* 218, 219; *52:* 147, 148, 149, 150

Schoonover, Frank, *17:* 107; *19:* 81, 190, 233; *22:* 88, 129; *24:* 189; *31:* 88; *41:* 69; *YABC 2:* 282, 316

Schottland, Miriam, *22:* 172

Schramm, Ulrik, *2:* 16; *14:* 112

Schreiber, Elizabeth Anne, *13:* 193

Schreiber, Ralph W., *13:* 193

Schreiter, Rick, *14:* 97; *23:* 171; *41:* 247; *49:* 131

Schroeder, E. Peter, *12:* 112

Schroeder, Ted, *11:* 160; *15:* 189; *30:* 91; *34:* 43

Schrotter, Gustav, *22:* 212; *30:* 225

Schucker, James, *31:* 163

Schulz, Charles M., *10:* 137-142

Schwark, Mary Beth, *51:* 155

Schwartz, Amy, *47:* 191

Schwartz, Charles, *8:* 184

Schwartz, Daniel, *46:* 37

Schwartzberg, Joan, *3:* 208

Schweitzer, Iris, *2:* 137; *6:* 207

Schweninger, Ann, *29:* 172

Scott, Anita Walker, *7:* 38

Scott, Art, *39:* 41

Scott, Frances Gruse, *38:* 43

Scott, Julian, *34:* 126

Scott, Roszel, *33:* 238

Scott, Trudy, *27:* 172

Scribner, Joanne, *14:* 236; *29:* 78; *33:* 185; *34:* 208

Scrofani, Joseph, *31:* 65

Seaman, Mary Lott, *34:* 64

Searle, Ronald, *24:* 98; *42:* 172, 173, 174, 176, 177, 179

Searle, Townley, *36:* 85

Sebree, Charles, *18:* 65

Sedacca, Joseph M., *11:* 25; *22:* 36

Ségur, Adrienne, *27:* 121

Seignobosc, Francoise, *21:* 145, 146

Sejima, Yoshimasa, *8:* 187

Selig, Sylvie, *13:* 199

Seltzer, Isadore, *6:* 18

Seltzer, Meyer, *17:* 214

Sempé, Jean-Jacques, *47:* 92; *YABC 2:* 109

Sendak, Maurice, *1:* 135, 190; *3:* 204; *7:* 142; *15:* 199; *17:* 210; *27:* 181, 182, 183, 185, 186, 187, 189, 190-191, 192, 193, 194, 195, 197, 198, 199, 203; *28:* 181, 182; *32:* 108; *33:* 148, 149; *35:* 238; *44:* 180, 181; *45:* 97, 99; *46:* 174; *YABC 1:* 167

Sengler, Johanna, *18:* 256

Seredy, Kate, *1:* 192; *14:* 20-21; *17:* 210

Sergeant, John, *6:* 74

Servello, Joe, *10:* 144; *24:* 139; *40:* 91

Seton, Ernest Thompson, *18:* 260-269, 271

Seuss, Dr. *See* Geisel, Theodor

Severin, John Powers, *7:* 62

Sewall, Marcia, *15:* 8; *22:* 170; *37:* 171, 172, 173; *39:* 73; *45:* 209

Seward, Prudence, *16:* 243

Sewell, Helen, *3:* 186; *15:* 308; *33:* 102; *38:* 189, 190, 191, 192

Seymour, Stephen, *54:* 21

Shahn, Ben, *39:* 178; *46:* 193

Shalansky, Len, *38:* 167

Shanks, Anne Zane, *10:* 149

Sharp, Paul, *52:* 60

Sharp, William, *6:* 131; *19:* 241; *20:* 112; *25:* 141

Shaw, Charles, *21:* 135; *38:* 187; *47:* 124

Shaw, Charles G., *13:* 200

Shearer, Ted, *43:* 193, 194, 195, 196

Shecter, Ben, *16:* 244; *25:* 109; *33:* 188, 191; *41:* 77

Shefcik, James, *48:* 221, 222

Shefts, Joelle, *48:* 210

Shekerjian, Haig, *16:* 245

Shekerjian, Regina, *16:* 245; *25:* 73

Shenton, Edward, *45:* 187, 188, 189; *YABC 1:* 218-219, 221

Shepard, Ernest H., *3:* 193; *4:* 74; *16:* 101; *17:* 109; *25:* 148; *33:* 152, 199, 200, 201, 202, 203, 204, 205, 206, 207; *46:* 194; *YABC 1:* 148, 153, 174, 176, 180-181

Shepard, Mary, *4:* 210; *22:* 205; *30:* 132, 133; *54:* 150, 152, 153, 157, 158

Sherman, Theresa, *27:* 167

Sherwan, Earl, *3:* 196

Shields, Charles, *10:* 150; *36:* 63

Shields, Leonard, *13:* 83, 85, 87

Shillabeer, Mary, *35:* 74

Shilston, Arthur, *49:* 61

Shimin, Symeon, *1:* 93; *2:* 128-129; *3:* 202; *7:* 85; *11:* 177; *12:* 139; *13:* 202-203; *27:* 138; *28:* 65; *35:* 129; *36:* 130; *48:* 151; *49:* 59

Shinn, Everett, *16:* 148; *18:* 229; *21:* 149, 150, 151; *24:* 218

Shore, Robert, *27:* 54; *39:* 192, 193; *YABC 2:* 200

Shortall, Leonard, *4:* 144; *8:* 196; *10:* 166; *19:* 227, 228-229, 230; *25:* 78; *28:* 66, 167; *33:* 127; *52:* 125

Shortt, T. M., *27:* 36

Shtainments, Leon, *32:* 161

Shulevitz, Uri, *3:* 198-199; *17:* 85; *22:* 204; *27:* 212; *28:* 184; *50:* 190, 191, 192, 193, 194-195, 196, 197, 198, 199, 201

Shute, Linda, *46:* 59

Siberell, Anne, *29:* 193

Sibley, Don, *1:* 39; *12:* 196; *31:* 47

Sidjakov, Nicolas, *18:* 274

Siebel, Fritz, *3:* 120; *17:* 145

Siegl, Helen, *12:* 166; *23:* 216; *34:* 185, 186

Sills, Joyce, *5:* 199

Silverstein, Alvin, *8:* 189

Silverstein, Shel, *33:* 211

Silverstein, Virginia, *8:* 189

Simon, Eric M., *7:* 82

Simon, Hilda, *28:* 189

Simon, Howard, *2:* 175; *5:* 132; *19:* 199; *32:* 163, 164, 165

Simont, Marc, *2:* 119; *4:* 213; *9:* 168; *13:* 238, 240; *14:* 262; *16:* 179; *18:* 221; *26:* 210; *33:* 189, 194; *44:* 132

Sims, Agnes, *54:* 152

Sims, Blanche, *44:* 116

Singer, Edith G., *2:* 30

Singer, Gloria, *34:* 56; *36:* 43

Singer, Julia, *28:* 190

Sivard, Robert, *26:* 124

Skardinski, Stanley, *23:* 144; *32:* 84

Slackman, Charles B., *12:* 201

Slater, Rod, *25:* 167

Sloan, Joseph, *16:* 68

Sloane, Eric, *21:* 3; *52:* 153, 154, 155, 156, 157, 158, 160

Slobodkin, Louis, *1:* 200; *3:* 232; *5:* 168; *13:* 251; *15:* 13, 88; *26:* 173, 174, 175, 176, 178, 179

Slobodkina, Esphyr, *1:* 201

Small, David, *50:* 204-205

Small, W., *33:* 113

Smalley, Janet, *1:* 154

Smedley, William T., *34:* 129

Smee, David, *14:* 78

Smith, A. G., Jr., *35:* 182

Smith, Alvin, *1:* 31, 229; *13:* 187; *27:* 216; *28:* 226; *48:* 149; *49:* 60

Smith, Anne Warren, *41:* 212

Smith, Carl, *36:* 41

Smith, Doris Susan, *41:* 139

Smith, E. Boyd, *19:* 70; *22:* 89; *26:* 63; *YABC 1:* 4-5, 240, 248-249

Smith, Edward J., *4:* 224

Smith, Eunice Young, *5:* 170

Smith, Howard, *19:* 196

Smith, Jacqueline Bardner, *27:* 108; *39:* 197

Smith, Jessie Willcox, *15:* 91; *16:* 95; *18:* 231; *19:* 57, 242; *21:* 29, 156, 157, 158, 159, 160, 161; *34:* 65; *YABC 1:* 6; *YABC 2:* 180, 185, 191, 311, 325

Smith, Joseph A., *52:* 131

Smith, Kenneth R., *47:* 182

Smith, L. H., *35:* 174

Smith, Lee, *29:* 32

Smith, Linell Nash, *2:* 195

Smith, Maggie Kaufman, *13:* 205; *35:* 191

Smith, Moishe, *33:* 155

Smith, Philip, *44:* 134; *46:* 203

Smith, Ralph Crosby, *2:* 267; *49:* 203

Smith, Robert D., *5:* 63

Smith, Susan Carlton, *12:* 208

Smith, Terry, *12:* 106; *33:* 158

Smith, Virginia, *3:* 157; *33:* 72

Smith, William A., *1:* 36; *10:* 154; *25:* 65

Smollin, Mike, *39:* 203

Smyth, M. Jane, *12:* 15

Snyder, Andrew A., *30:* 212

Snyder, Jerome, *13:* 207; *30:* 173

Snyder, Joel, *28:* 163

Sofia, *1:* 62; *5:* 90; *32:* 166

Sokol, Bill, *37:* 178; *49:* 23

Sokolov, Kirill, *34:* 188

Solbert, Ronni, *1:* 159; *2:* 232; *5:* 121; *6:* 34; *17:* 249

Solonevich, George, *15:* 246; *17:* 47

Sommer, Robert, *12:* 211
Sorel, Edward, *4:* 61; *36:* 82
Sotomayor, Antonio, *11:* 215
Soyer, Moses, *20:* 177
Spaenkuch, August, *16:* 28
Spanfeller, James, *1:* 72, 149; *2:* 183;
   19: 230, 231, 232; *22:* 66;
   36: 160, 161; *40:* 75; *52:* 166
Sparks, Mary Walker, *15:* 247
Spence, Geraldine, *21:* 163; *47:* 196
Spence, Jim, *38:* 89; *50:* 102
Spiegel, Doris, *29:* 111
Spier, Jo, *10:* 30
Spier, Peter, *3:* 155; *4:* 200; *7:* 61;
   11: 78; *38:* 106; *54:* 120, 121,
   122-123, 124-125, 126, 127, 128-
   129, 130, 131, 132-133, 134
Spilka, Arnold, *5:* 120; *6:* 204; *8:* 131
Spivak, I. Howard, *8:* 10
Spollen, Christopher J., *12:* 214
Spooner, Malcolm, *40:* 142
Sprattler, Rob, *12:* 176
Spring, Bob, *5:* 60
Spring, Ira, *5:* 60
Springer, Harriet, *31:* 92
Spurrier, Steven, *28:* 198
Spy. *See* Ward, Leslie
Staffan, Alvin E., *11:* 56; *12:* 187
Stahl, Ben, *5:* 181; *12:* 91; *49:* 122
Stair, Gobin, *35:* 214
Stamaty, Mark Alan, *12:* 215
Stampnick, Ken, *51:* 142
Stanley, Diane, *3:* 45; *37:* 180
Stasiak, Krystyna, *49:* 181
Stead, L., *55:* 51, 56
Steadman, Ralph, *32:* 180
Steichen, Edward, *30:* 79
Steig, William, *18:* 275-276
Stein, Harve, *1:* 109
Steinberg, Saul, *47:* 193
Steinel, William, *23:* 146
Steiner, Charlotte, *45:* 196
Stephens, Charles H., *YABC 2:* 279
Stephens, William M., *21:* 165
Steptoe, John, *8:* 197
Stern, Simon, *15:* 249-250; *17:* 58;
   34: 192-193
Sterret, Jane, *53:* 27
Stevens, Janet, *40:* 126
Stevens, Mary, *11:* 193; *13:* 129;
   43: 95
Stevenson, James, *42:* 182, 183;
   51: 163
Stewart, Arvis, *33:* 98; *36:* 69
Stewart, Charles, *2:* 205
Stiles, Fran, *26:* 85
Stillman, Susan, *44:* 130
Stimpson, Tom, *49:* 171
Stinemetz, Morgan, *40:* 151
Stirnweis, Shannon, *10:* 164
Stobbs, William, *1:* 48-49; *3:* 68;
   6: 20; *17:* 117, 217; *24:* 150;
   29: 250
Stock, Catherine, *37:* 55
Stoerrle, Tom, *55:* 147
Stolp, Jaap, *49:* 98
Stone, David, *9:* 173
Stone, David K., *4:* 38; *6:* 124;
   9: 180; *43:* 182

Stone, Helen, *44:* 121, 122, 126
Stone, Helen V., *6:* 209
Stratton, Helen, *33:* 151
Stratton-Porter, Gene, *15:* 254, 259,
   263-264, 268-269
Streano, Vince, *20:* 173
Strodl, Daniel, *47:* 95
Strong, Joseph D., Jr., *YABC 2:* 330
Ströyer, Poul, *13:* 221
Strugnell, Ann, *27:* 38
Stubis, Talivaldis, *5:* 182, 183; *10:* 45;
   11: 9; *18:* 304; *20:* 127
Stubley, Trevor, *14:* 43; *22:* 219;
   23: 37; *28:* 61
Stuecklen, Karl W., *8:* 34, 65; *23:* 103
Stull, Betty, *11:* 46
Suba, Susanne, *4:* 202-203; *14:* 261;
   23: 134; *29:* 222; *32:* 30
Sugarman, Tracy, *3:* 76; *8:* 199;
   37: 181, 182
Sugita, Yutaka, *36:* 180-181
Sullivan, Edmund J., *31:* 86
Sullivan, James F., *19:* 280; *20:* 192
Sumichrast, Józef, *14:* 253; *29:* 168,
   213
Sumiko, *46:* 57
Summers, Leo, *1:* 177; *2:* 273; *13:* 22
Svolinsky, Karel, *17:* 104
Swain, Su Zan Noguchi, *21:* 170
Swan, Susan, *22:* 220-221; *37:* 66
Swayne, Sam, *53:* 143, 145
Swayne, Zoa, *53:* 143, 145
Sweat, Lynn, *25:* 206
Sweet, Darryl, *1:* 163; *4:* 136
Sweet, Ozzie, *31:* 149, 151, 152
Sweetland, Robert, *12:* 194
Swope, Martha, *43:* 160
Sylvester, Natalie G., *22:* 222
Szafran, Gene, *24:* 144
Szasz, Susanne, *13:* 55, 226; *14:* 48
Szekeres, Cyndy, *2:* 218; *5:* 185;
   8: 85; *11:* 166; *14:* 19; *16:* 57,
   159; *26:* 49, 214; *34:* 205

Taback, Simms, *40:* 207; *52:* 120
Tafuri, Nancy, *39:* 210
Tait, Douglas, *12:* 220
Takakjian, Portia, *15:* 274
Takashima, Shizuye, *13:* 228
Talarczyk, June, *4:* 173
Tallon, Robert, *2:* 228; *43:* 200, 201,
   202, 203, 204, 205, 206, 207, 209
Tamas, Szecskó, *29:* 135
Tamburine, Jean, *12:* 222
Tandy, H. R., *13:* 69
Tannenbaum, Robert, *48:* 181
Tanobe, Miyuki, *23:* 221
Tarkington, Booth, *17:* 224-225
Taylor, Ann, *41:* 226
Taylor, Isaac, *41:* 228
Teale, Edwin Way, *7:* 196
Teason, James, *1:* 14
Teeple, Lyn, *33:* 147
Tee-Van, Helen Damrosch, *10:* 176;
   11: 182
Teicher, Dick, *50:* 211
Tempest, Margaret, *3:* 237, 238

Temple, Herbert, *45:* 201
Templeton, Owen, *11:* 77
Tenggren, Gustaf, *18:* 277-279; *19:* 15;
   28: 86; *YABC 2:* 145
Tenney, Gordon, *24:* 204
Tenniel, John, *YABC 2:* 99
Thacher, Mary M., *30:* 72
Thackeray, William Makepeace,
   23: 224, 228
Thamer, Katie, *42:* 187
Thelwell, Norman, *14:* 201
Theobalds, Prue, *40:* 23
Theurer, Marilyn Churchill, *39:* 195
Thistlethwaite, Miles, *12:* 224
Thollander, Earl, *11:* 47; *18:* 112;
   22: 224
Thomas, Allan, *22:* 13
Thomas, Art, *48:* 217
Thomas, Eric, *28:* 49
Thomas, Harold, *20:* 98
Thomas, Mark, *42:* 136
Thomas, Martin, *14:* 255
Thompson, Arthur, *34:* 107
Thompson, Ellen, *51:* 88, 151
Thompson, George, *22:* 18; *28:* 150;
   33: 135
Thompson, George, W., *33:* 135
Thompson, Julie, *44:* 158
Thomson, Arline K., *3:* 264
Thomson, Hugh, *26:* 88
Thomson, Ross, *36:* 179
Thorne, Diana, *25:* 212
Thorvall, Kerstin, *13:* 235
Thurber, James, *13:* 239, 242-245,
   248-249
Tibbles, Paul, *45:* 23
Tichenor, Tom, *14:* 207
Tiegreen, Alan, *36:* 143; *43:* 55, 56,
   58
Tilney, F. C., *22:* 231
Timbs, Gloria, *36:* 90
Timmins, Harry, *2:* 171
Tinkelman, Murray, *12:* 225; *35:* 44
Titherington, Jeanne, *39:* 90
Tolford, Joshua, *1:* 221
Tolkien, J. R. R., *2:* 243; *32:* 215
Tolmie, Ken, *15:* 292
Tomei, Lorna, *47:* 168, 171
Tomes, Jacqueline, *2:* 117; *12:* 139
Tomes, Margot, *1:* 224; *2:* 120-121;
   16: 207; *18:* 250; *20:* 7; *25:* 62;
   27: 78, 79; *29:* 81, 199; *33:* 82;
   36: 186, 187, 188, 189, 190;
   46: 129
Toner, Raymond John, *10:* 179
Toothill, Harry, *6:* 54; *7:* 49; *25:* 219;
   42: 192
Toothill, Ilse, *6:* 54
Topolski, Feliks, *44:* 48
Torbert, Floyd James, *22:* 226
Torgersen, Don, *55:* 157
Torrey, Marjorie, *34:* 105
Toschik, Larry, *6:* 102
Totten, Bob, *13:* 93
Trail, Lee, *55:* 157
Travers, Bob, *49:* 100
Tremain, Ruthven, *17:* 238
Tresilian, Stuart, *25:* 53; *40:* 212
Trez, Alain, *17:* 236

Trier, Walter, *14:* 96
Trimby, Elisa, *47:* 199
Trinkle, Sally, *53:* 27
Tripp, F. J., *24:* 167
Tripp, Wallace, *2:* 48; *7:* 28; *8:* 94; *10:* 54, 76; *11:* 92; *31:* 170, 171; *34:* 203; *42:* 57
Trivas, Irene, *53:* 4; *54:* 168
Trnka, Jiri, *22:* 151; *43:* 212, 213, 214, 215; *YABC 1:* 30-31
Troughton, Joanna, *37:* 186; *48:* 72
Troyer, Johannes, *3:* 16; *7:* 18
Trudeau, G. B., *35:* 220, 221, 222; *48:* 119, 123, 126, 127, 128-129, 133
Truesdell, Sue, *55:* 142
Tsinajinie, Andy, *2:* 62
Tsugami, Kyuzo, *18:* 198-199
Tuckwell, Jennifer, *17:* 205
Tudor, Bethany, *7:* 103
Tudor, Tasha, *18:* 227; *20:* 185, 186, 187; *36:* 111; *YABC 2:* 46, 314
Tulloch, Maurice, *24:* 79
Tunis, Edwin, *1:* 218-219; *28:* 209, 210, 211, 212
Turkle, Brinton, *1:* 211, 213; *2:* 249; *3:* 226; *11:* 3; *16:* 209; *20:* 22; *50:* 23; *YABC 1:* 79
Turska, Krystyna, *12:* 103; *31:* 173, 174-175
Tusan, Stan, *6:* 58; *22:* 236-237
Tworkov, Jack, *47:* 207
Tzimoulis, Paul, *12:* 104

Uchida, Yoshiko, *1:* 220
Uderzo, *47:* 88
Ulm, Robert, *17:* 238
Unada. *See* Gliewe, Unada
Underhill, Liz, *53:* 159
Underwood, Clarence, *40:* 166
Ungerer, Tomi, *5:* 188; *9:* 40; *18:* 188; *29:* 175; *33:* 221, 222-223, 225
Unwin, Nora S., *3:* 65, 234-235; *4:* 237; *44:* 173, 174; *YABC 1:* 59; *YABC 2:* 301
Uris, Jill, *49:* 188, 197
Ursell, Martin, *50:* 51
Utpatel, Frank, *18:* 114
Utz, Lois, *5:* 190

Van Abbé, S., *16:* 142; *18:* 282; *31:* 90; *YABC 2:* 157, 161
Van Allsburg, Chris, *37:* 205, 206; *53:* 161, 162, 163, 165, 166, 167, 168, 169, 170-171
Vandivert, William, *21:* 175
Van Everen, Jay, *13:* 160; *YABC 1:* 121
Van Horn, William, *43:* 218
Van Loon, Hendrik Willem, *18:* 285, 289, 291
Van Sciver, Ruth, *37:* 162
Ilvan Stockum, Hilda, *5:* 193
Van Wely, Babs, *16:* 50
Varga, Judy, *29:* 196

Vasiliu, Mircea, *2:* 166, 253; *9:* 166; *13:* 58
Vaughn, Frank, *34:* 157
Vavra, Robert, *8:* 206
Vawter, Will, *17:* 163
Veeder, Larry, *18:* 4
Velasquez, Eric, *45:* 217
Vendrell, Carme Solé, *42:* 205
Venezia, Mike, *54:* 17
Ver Beck, Frank, *18:* 16-17
Verney, John, *14:* 225
Verrier, Suzanne, *5:* 20; *23:* 212
Versace, Marie, *2:* 255
Vestal, H. B., *9:* 134; *11:* 101; *27:* 25; *34:* 158
Vickrey, Robert, *45:* 59, 64
Victor, Joan Berg, *30:* 193
Viereck, Ellen, *3:* 242; *14:* 229
Vigna, Judith, *15:* 293
Vilato, Gaspar E., *5:* 41
Villiard, Paul, *51:* 178
Vimnèra, A., *23:* 154
Vincent, Eric, *34:* 98
Vincent, Félix, *41:* 237
Vip, *45:* 164
Vivas, Julie, *51:* 67, 69
Vo-Dinh, Mai, *16:* 272
Vogel, Ilse-Margret, *14:* 230
Voigt, Erna, *35:* 228
Vojtech, Anna, *42:* 190
von Schmidt, Eric, *8:* 62; *50:* 209, 210
von Schmidt, Harold, *30:* 80
Vosburgh, Leonard, *1:* 161; *7:* 32; *15:* 295-296; *23:* 110; *30:* 214; *43:* 181
Voter, Thomas W., *19:* 3, 9
Vroman, Tom, *10:* 29

Waber, Bernard, *47:* 209, 210, 211, 212, 213, 214
Wagner, John, *8:* 200; *52:* 104
Wagner, Ken, *2:* 59
Waide, Jan, *29:* 225; *36:* 139
Wainwright, Jerry, *14:* 85
Wakeen, Sandra, *47:* 97
Waldman, Bruce, *15:* 297; *43:* 178
Waldman, Neil, *35:* 141; *50:* 163; *51:* 180; *54:* 78
Walker, Charles, *1:* 46; *4:* 59; *5:* 177; *11:* 115; *19:* 45; *34:* 74
Walker, Dugald Stewart, *15:* 47; *32:* 202; *33:* 112
Walker, Gil, *8:* 49; *23:* 132; *34:* 42
Walker, Jeff, *55:* 154
Walker, Jim, *10:* 94
Walker, Mort, *8:* 213
Walker, Norman, *41:* 37; *45:* 58
Walker, Stephen, *12:* 229; *21:* 174
Wallace, Beverly Dobrin, *19:* 259
Wallace, Ian, *53:* 176, 177
Waller, S. E., *24:* 36
Wallner, Alexandra, *15:* 120
Wallner, John C., *9:* 77; *10:* 188; *11:* 28; *14:* 209; *31:* 56, 118; *37:* 64; *51:* 186, 187, 188-189, 190-191, 192-193, 194, 195; *52:* 96; *53:* 23, 26

Wallower, Lucille, *11:* 226
Walters, Audrey, *18:* 294
Walther, Tom, *31:* 179
Walton, Tony, *11:* 164; *24:* 209
Waltrip, Lela, *9:* 195
Waltrip, Mildred, *3:* 209; *37:* 211
Waltrip, Rufus, *9:* 195
Wan, *12:* 76
Ward, Fred, *52:* 19
Ward, John, *42:* 191
Ward, Keith, *2:* 107
Ward, Leslie, *34:* 126; *36:* 87
Ward, Lynd, *1:* 99, 132, 133, 150; *2:* 108, 158, 196, 259; *18:* 86; *27:* 56; *29:* 79, 187, 253, 255; *36:* 199, 200, 201, 202, 203, 204, 205, 206, 207, 209; *43:* 34
Ward, Peter, *37:* 116
Warner, Peter, *14:* 87
Warren, Betsy, *2:* 101
Warren, Marion Cray, *14:* 215
Warshaw, Jerry, *30:* 197, 198; *42:* 165
Washington, Nevin, *20:* 123
Washington, Phyllis, *20:* 123
Waterman, Stan, *11:* 76
Watkins-Pitchford, D. J., *6:* 215, 217
Watson, Aldren A., *2:* 267; *5:* 94; *13:* 71; *19:* 253; *32:* 220; *42:* 193, 194, 195, 196, 197, 198, 199, 200, 201; *YABC 2:* 202
Watson, Gary, *19:* 147; *36:* 68; *41:* 122; *47:* 139
Watson, J. D., *22:* 86
Watson, Karen, *11:* 26
Watson, Wendy, *5:* 197; *13:* 101; *33:* 116; *46:* 163
Watts, Bernadette, *4:* 227
Watts, John, *37:* 149
Webber, Helen, *3:* 141
Webber, Irma E., *14:* 238
Weber, Florence, *40:* 153
Weber, William J., *14:* 239
Webster, Jean, *17:* 241
Wegner, Fritz, *14:* 250; *20:* 189; *44:* 165
Weidenear, Reynold H., *21:* 122
Weihs, Erika, *4:* 21; *15:* 299
Weil, Lisl, *7:* 203; *10:* 58; *21:* 95; *22:* 188, 217; *33:* 193
Weiman, Jon, *50:* 162, 165; *52:* 103; *54:* 78, 79, 81
Weiner, Sandra, *14:* 240
Weiner, Scott, *55:* 27
Weinhaus, Karen Ann, *53:* 90
Weisgard, Leonard, *1:* 65; *2:* 191, 197, 204, 264-265; *5:* 108; *21:* 42; *30:* 200, 201, 203, 204; *41:* 47; *44:* 125; *53:* 25; *YABC 2:* 13
Weiss, Ellen, *44:* 202
Weiss, Emil, *1:* 168; *7:* 60
Weiss, Harvey, *1:* 145, 223; *27:* 224, 227
Weiss, Nicki, *33:* 229
Weissman, Bari, *49:* 72
Wells, Frances, *1:* 183
Wells, H. G., *20:* 194, 200
Wells, Haru, *53:* 120, 121
Wells, Rosemary, *6:* 49; *18:* 297
Wells, Susan, *22:* 43

Wendelin, Rudolph, *23:* 234
Wengenroth, Stow, *37:* 47
Werenskiold, Erik, *15:* 6
Werner, Honi, *24:* 110; *33:* 41
Werth, Kurt, *7:* 122; *14:* 157; *20:* 214;
   39: 128
Westerberg, Christine, *29:* 226
Weston, Martha, *29:* 116; *30:* 213;
   33: 85, 100; *53:* 181, 182, 183,
   184
Wetherbee, Margaret, *5:* 3
Wexler, Jerome, *49:* 73
Whalley, Peter, *50:* 49
Wheatley, Arabelle, *11:* 231; *16:* 276
Wheeler, Cindy, *49:* 205
Wheeler, Dora, *44:* 179
Wheelright, Rowland, *15:* 81;
   YABC 2: 286
Whistler, Rex, *16:* 75; *30:* 207, 208
White, David Omar, *5:* 56; *18:* 6
White, Martin, *51:* 197
Whitear, *32:* 26
Whithorne, H. S., *7:* 49
Whitney, George Gillett, *3:* 24
Whittam, Geoffrey, *30:* 191
Wiberg, Harald, *38:* 127
Wiese, Kurt, *3:* 255; *4:* 206; *14:* 17;
   17: 18-19; *19:* 47; *24:* 152;
   25: 212; *32:* 184; *36:* 211, 213,
   214, 215, 216, 217, 218; *45:* 161
Wiesner, David, *33:* 47; *51:* 106
Wiesner, William, *4:* 100; *5:* 200, 201;
   14: 262
Wiggins, George, *6:* 133
Wikkelsoe, Otto, *45:* 25, 26
Wikland, Ilon, *5:* 113; *8:* 150;
   38: 124, 125, 130
Wilbur, C. Keith, M.D., *27:* 228
Wilburn, Kathy, *53:* 102
Wilcox, J.A.J., *34:* 122
Wilcox, R. Turner, *36:* 219
Wild, Jocelyn, *46:* 220-221, 222
Wilde, George, *7:* 139
Wildsmith, Brian, *16:* 281-282;
   18: 170-171
Wilkin, Eloise, *36:* 173; *49:* 208, 209,
   210
Wilkinson, Barry, *50:* 213
Wilkinson, Gerald, *3:* 40
Wilkoń, Józef, *31:* 183, 184
Wilks, Mike, *34:* 24; *44:* 203
Williams, Ferelith Eccles, *22:* 238
Williams, Garth, *1:* 197; *2:* 49, 270;
   4: 205; *15:* 198, 302-304, 307;
   16: 34; *18:* 283, 298-301;
   29: 177, 178, 179, 232-233,
   241-245, 248; *40:* 106;
   YABC 2: 15-16, 19
Williams, J. Scott, *48:* 28
Williams, Kit, *44:* 206-207, 208, 209,
   211, 212
Williams, Maureen, *12:* 238
Williams, Patrick, *14:* 218

Williams, Richard, *44:* 93
Williams, Vera B., *53:* 186, 187, 188,
   189
Willmore, J. T., *54:* 113, 114
Wilson, Charles Banks, *17:* 92; *43:* 73
Wilson, Dagmar, *10:* 47
Wilson, Edward A., *6:* 24; *16:* 149;
   20: 220-221; *22:* 87; *26:* 67;
   38: 212, 214, 215, 216, 217
Wilson, Forrest, *27:* 231
Wilson, Gahan, *35:* 234; *41:* 136
Wilson, Jack, *17:* 139
Wilson, John, *22:* 240
Wilson, Maurice, *46:* 224
Wilson, Patten, *35:* 61
Wilson, Peggy, *15:* 4
Wilson, Rowland B., *30:* 170
Wilson, Sarah, *50:* 215
Wilson, Tom, *33:* 232
Wilson, W. N., *22:* 26
Wilwerding, Walter J., *9:* 202
Winchester, Linda, *13:* 231
Wind, Betty, *28:* 158
Windham, Kathryn Tucker, *14:* 260
Wing, Ron, *50:* 85
Winslow, Will, *21:* 124
Winsten, Melanie Willa, *41:* 41
Winter, Milo, *15:* 97; *19:* 221;
   21: 181, 203, 204, 205;
   YABC 2: 144
Winter, Paula, *48:* 227
Wise, Louis, *13:* 68
Wiseman, Ann, *31:* 187
Wiseman, B., *4:* 233
Wishnefsky, Phillip, *3:* 14
Wiskur, Darrell, *5:* 72; *10:* 50; *18:* 246
Wittman, Sally, *30:* 219
Woehr, Lois, *12:* 5
Wohlberg, Meg, *12:* 100; *14:* 197;
   41: 255
Woldin, Beth Weiner, *34:* 211
Wolf, J., *16:* 91
Wolf, Linda, *33:* 163
Wolff, Ashley, *50:* 217
Wondriska, William, *6:* 220
Wonsetler, John C., *5:* 168
Wood, Audrey, *50:* 221, 222, 223
Wood, Don, *50:* 220, 225, 226, 228-
   229
Wood, Grant, *19:* 198
Wood, Muriel, *36:* 119
Wood, Myron, *6:* 220
Wood, Owen, *18:* 187
Wood, Ruth, *8:* 11
Woodson, Jack, *10:* 201
Woodward, Alice, *26:* 89; *36:* 81
Wool, David, *26:* 27
Wooten, Vernon, *23:* 70; *51:* 170
Worboys, Evelyn, *1:* 166-167
Worth, Jo, *34:* 143
Worth, Wendy, *4:* 133
Wosmek, Frances, *29:* 251

Wrenn, Charles L., *38:* 96;
   YABC 1: 20, 21
Wright, Dare, *21:* 206
Wright, George, *YABC 1:* 268
Wright, Joseph, *30:* 160
Wronker, Lili Cassel, *3:* 247; *10:* 204;
   21: 10
Wyatt, Stanley, *46:* 210
Wyeth, Andrew, *13:* 40;
   YABC 1: 133-134
Wyeth, Jamie, *41:* 257
Wyeth, N. C., *13:* 41; *17:* 252-259,
   264-268; *18:* 181; *19:* 80, 191,
   200; *21:* 57, 183; *22:* 91; *23:* 152;
   24: 28, 99; *35:* 61; *41:* 65;
   YABC 1: 133, 223; *YABC 2:* 53,
   75, 171, 187, 317

Yang, Jay, *1:* 8; *12:* 239
Yap, Weda, *6:* 176
Yaroslava. *See* Mills, Yaroslava
   Surmach
Yashima, Taro, *14:* 84
Ylla. *See* Koffler, Camilla
Yohn, F. C., *23:* 128; *YABC 1:* 269
Young, Ed, *7:* 205; *10:* 206; *40:* 124;
   YABC 2: 242
Young, Noela, *8:* 221

Zacks, Lewis, *10:* 161
Zadig, *50:* 58
Zaffo, George, *42:* 208
Zaid, Barry, *50:* 127; *51:* 201
Zaidenberg, Arthur, *34:* 218, 219, 220
Zalben, Jane Breskin, *7:* 211
Zallinger, Jean, *4:* 192; *8:* 8, 129;
   14: 273
Zallinger, Rudolph F., *3:* 245
Zeck, Gerry, *40:* 232
Zeiring, Bob, *42:* 130
Zeldich, Arieh, *49:* 124
Zelinsky, Paul O., *14:* 269; *43:* 56;
   49: 218, 219, 220, 221, 222-223;
   53: 111
Zemach, Margot, *3:* 270; *8:* 201;
   21: 210-211; *27:* 204, 205, 210;
   28: 185; *49:* 22, 183, 224;
   53: 151
Zemsky, Jessica, *10:* 62
Zepelinsky, Paul, *35:* 93
Zimmer, Dirk, *38:* 195; *49:* 71
Zimnik, Reiner, *36:* 224
Zinkeisen, Anna, *13:* 106
Zoellick, Scott, *33:* 231
Zonia, Dhimitri, *20:* 234-235
Zweifel, Francis, *14:* 274; *28:* 187
Zwerger, Lisbeth, *54:* 176, 178
Zwinger, Herman H., *46:* 227

Author Index

The following index gives the number of the volume in which an author's biographical sketch, Brief Entry, or Obituary appears.

This index includes references to all entries in the following series, which are also published by Gale Research Company.

YABC—*Yesterday's Authors of Books for Children: Facts and Pictures about Authors and Illustrators of Books for Young People from Early Times to 1960*, Volumes 1-2
CLR—*Children's Literature Review: Excerpts from Reviews, Criticism, and Commentary on Books for Children*, Volumes 1-15
SAAS—*Something about the Author Autobiography Series*, Volumes 1-7

A

Aardema, Verna 1911- *4*
Aaron, Chester 1923- *9*
Aaseng, Nate
  See Aaseng, Nathan
Aaseng, Nathan 1938- *51*
  Brief Entry *38*
Abbott, Alice
  See Borland, Kathryn Kilby
Abbott, Alice
  See Speicher, Helen Ross (Smith)
Abbott, Jacob 1803-1879 .... *22*
Abbott, Manager Henry
  See Stratemeyer, Edward L.
Abbott, Sarah
  See Zolotow, Charlotte S.
Abdul, Raoul 1929- *12*
Abel, Raymond 1911- *12*
Abell, Kathleen 1938- *9*
Abels, Harriette S(heffer)
  1926- *50*
Abercrombie, Barbara (Mattes)
  1939- *16*
Abernethy, Robert G. 1935- *5*
Abisch, Roslyn Kroop 1927- *9*
Abisch, Roz
  See Abisch, Roslyn Kroop
Abodaher, David J. (Naiph)
  1919- *17*
Abolafia, Yossi
  Brief Entry *46*
Abrahall, C. H.
  See Hoskyns-Abrahall, Clare
Abrahall, Clare Hoskyns
  See Hoskyns-Abrahall, Clare
Abrahams, Hilary (Ruth)
  1938- *29*
Abrahams, Robert D(avid)
  1905- *4*
Abrams, Joy 1941- *16*
Abrams, Lawrence F.
  Brief Entry *47*
Abrashkin, Raymond
  1911-1960 .... *50*
Achebe, Chinua 1930- *40*
  Brief Entry *38*
Ackerman, Eugene 1888-1974 .... *10*
Acs, Laszlo (Bela) 1931- *42*
  Brief Entry *32*
Acuff, Selma Boyd 1924- *45*
Ada, Alma Flor 1938- *43*

Adair, Ian 1942- *53*
Adair, Margaret Weeks
  (?)-1971 .... *10*
Adam, Cornel
  See Lengyel, Cornel Adam
Adams, Adrienne 1906- *8*
Adams, Andy
  1859-1935 .... *YABC 1*
Adams, Dale
  See Quinn, Elisabeth
Adams, Harriet S(tratemeyer)
  1893(?)-1982 .... *1*
  Obituary *29*
Adams, Harrison
  See Stratemeyer, Edward L.
Adams, Hazard 1926- *6*
Adams, Laurie 1941- *33*
Adams, Lowell
  See Joseph, James (Herz)
Adams, Richard 1920- *7*
Adams, Ruth Joyce *14*
Adams, William Taylor
  1822-1897 .... *28*
Adamson, Gareth 1925-1982 ...... *46*
  Obituary *30*
Adamson, George Worsley
  1913- *30*
Adamson, Graham
  See Groom, Arthur William
Adamson, Joy 1910-1980 .... *11*
  Obituary *22*
Adamson, Wendy Wriston
  1942- *22*
Addams, Charles (Samuel)
  1912-1988 .... *55*
Addona, Angelo F. 1925- *14*
Addy, Ted
  See Winterbotham, R(ussell)
  R(obert)
Adelberg, Doris
  See Orgel, Doris
Adelson, Leone 1908- *11*
Adkins, Jan 1944- *8*
  See also CLR 7
Adler, C(arole) S(chwerdtfeger)
  1932- *26*
Adler, David A. 1947- *14*
Adler, Irene
  See Penzler, Otto
  See Storr, Catherine (Cole)
Adler, Irving 1913- *29*
  Earlier sketch in SATA 1

Adler, Larry 1939- *36*
Adler, Peggy *22*
Adler, Ruth 1915-1968 .... *1*
Adoff, Arnold 1935- *5*
  See also CLR 7
Adorjan, Carol 1934- *10*
Adrian, Mary
  See Jorgensen, Mary Venn
Adshead, Gladys L. 1896- *3*
Aesop 620(?)-564(?)B.C.
  See CLR 14
Aesop, Abraham
  See Newbery, John
Agapida, Fray Antonio
  See Irving, Washington
Agard, Nadema 1948- *18*
Agle, Nan Hayden 1905- *3*
Agnew, Edith J(osephine)
  1897- *11*
Ahern, Margaret McCrohan
  1921- *10*
Ahl, Anna Maria 1926- *32*
Ahlberg, Allan
  Brief Entry *35*
Ahlberg, Janet
  Brief Entry *32*
Aichinger, Helga 1937- *4*
Aiken, Clarissa (Lorenz)
  1899- *12*
Aiken, Conrad (Potter)
  1889-1973 .... *30*
  Earlier sketch in SATA 3
Aiken, Joan 1924- *30*
  Earlier sketch in SATA 2
  See also CLR 1
  See also SAAS 1
Ainsworth, Norma *9*
Ainsworth, Ruth 1908- *7*
Ainsworth, William Harrison
  1805-1882 .... *24*
Aistrop, Jack 1916- *14*
Aitken, Amy 1952- *54*
  Brief Entry *40*
Aitken, Dorothy 1916- *10*
Akaba, Suekichi 1910- *46*
Akers, Floyd
  See Baum, L(yman) Frank
Alain
  See Brustlein, Daniel
Alajalov, Constantin 1900-1987
  Obituary *53*
Albert, Burton, Jr. 1936- *22*

Alberts, Frances Jacobs 1907- *14*
Albion, Lee Smith *29*
Albrecht, Lillie (Vanderveer)
1894- *12*
Alcock, Gudrun
Brief Entry *33*
Alcock, Vivien 1924- *45*
Brief Entry *38*
Alcorn, John 1935- *31*
Brief Entry *30*
Alcott, Louisa May
1832-1888 ....*YABC 1*
See also CLR 1
Alda, Arlene 1933- *44*
Brief Entry *36*
Alden, Isabella (Macdonald)
1841-1930 ....*YABC 2*
Alderman, Clifford Lindsey
1902- *3*
Alderson, Sue Ann 1940-
Brief Entry *48*
Aldis, Dorothy (Keeley)
1896-1966 .... *2*
Aldiss, Brian W(ilson) 1925- *34*
Aldon, Adair
See Meigs, Cornelia
Aldous, Allan (Charles) 1911- *27*
Aldrich, Ann
See Meaker, Marijane
Aldrich, Thomas Bailey
1836-1907 .... *17*
Aldridge, Alan 1943(?)-
Brief Entry *33*
Aldridge, Josephine Haskell *14*
Alegria, Ricardo E. 1921- *6*
Aleksin, Anatolii (Georgievich)
1924- *36*
Alex, Ben [a pseudonym]
1946- *45*
Alex, Marlee [a pseudonym]
1948- *45*
Alexander, Anna Cooke 1913- *1*
Alexander, Frances 1888- *4*
Alexander, Jocelyn (Anne) Arundel
1930- *22*
Alexander, Linda 1935- *2*
Alexander, Lloyd 1924- *49*
Earlier sketch in SATA 3
See also CLR 1, 5
Alexander, Martha 1920- *11*
Alexander, Rae Pace
See Alexander, Raymond Pace
Alexander, Raymond Pace
1898-1974 .... *22*
Alexander, Sue 1933- *12*
Alexander, Vincent Arthur 1925-1980
Obituary *23*
Alexeieff, Alexandre A.
1901- *14*
Alger, Horatio, Jr. 1832-1899 ..... *16*
Alger, Leclaire (Gowans)
1898-1969 .... *15*
Aliki
See Brandenberg, Aliki
See also CLR 9
Alkema, Chester Jay 1932- *12*
Allamand, Pascale 1942- *12*
Allan, Mabel Esther 1915- *32*
Earlier sketch in SATA 5

Allard, Harry
See Allard, Harry G(rover), Jr.
Allard, Harry G(rover), Jr.
1928- *42*
Allee, Marjorie Hill
1890-1945 .... *17*
Allen, Adam [Joint pseudonym]
See Epstein, Beryl and Epstein,
Samuel
Allen, Alex B.
See Heide, Florence Parry
Allen, Allyn
See Eberle, Irmengarde
Allen, Betsy
See Cavanna, Betty
Allen, Gertrude E(lizabeth)
1888- *9*
Allen, Jack 1899-
Brief Entry *29*
Allen, Jeffrey (Yale) 1948- *42*
Allen, Laura Jean
Brief Entry *53*
Allen, Leroy 1912- *11*
Allen, Linda 1925- *33*
Allen, Marjorie 1931- *22*
Allen, Maury 1932- *26*
Allen, Merritt Parmelee
1892-1954 .... *22*
Allen, Nina (Strömgren)
1935- *22*
Allen, Pamela 1934- *50*
Allen, Rodney F. 1938- *27*
Allen, Ruth
See Peterson, Esther (Allen)
Allen, Samuel (Washington)
1917- *9*
Allen, T. D. [Joint pseudonym]
See Allen, Terril Diener
Allen, Terril Diener 1908- *35*
Allen, Terry D.
See Allen, Terril Diener
Allen, Thomas B(enton)
1929- *45*
Allen, Tom
See Allen, Thomas B(enton)
Allerton, Mary
See Govan, Christine Noble
Alleyn, Ellen
See Rossetti, Christina (Georgina)
Allington, Richard L(loyd)
1947- *39*
Brief Entry *35*
Allison, Bob *14*
Allison, Linda 1948- *43*
Allmendinger, David F(rederick), Jr.
1938- *35*
Allred, Gordon T. 1930- *10*
Allsop, Kenneth 1920-1973 .... *17*
Almedingen, E. M.
1898-1971 .... *3*
Almedingen, Martha Edith von
See Almedingen, E. M.
Almond, Linda Stevens 1881(?)-1987
Obituary *50*
Almquist, Don 1929- *11*
Alsop, Mary O'Hara
1885-1980 .... *34*
Obituary *24*
Earlier sketch in SATA 5

Alter, Judith (MacBain) 1938- *52*
Alter, Judy
See Alter, Judith (MacBain)
Alter, Robert Edmond
1925-1965 .... *9*
Althea
See Braithwaite, Althea *23*
Altschuler, Franz 1923- *45*
Altsheler, Joseph A(lexander)
1862-1919 ....*YABC 1*
Alvarez, Joseph A. 1930- *18*
Alzada, Juan Sanchez
See Joseph, James (Herz)
Ambler, C(hristopher) Gifford 1886-
Brief Entry *29*
Ambrose, Stephen E(dward)
1936- *40*
Ambrus, Gyozo (Laszlo)
1935- *41*
Earlier sketch in SATA 1
Ambrus, Victor G.
See Ambrus, Gyozo (Laszlo)
See also SAAS 4
Amerman, Lockhart
1911-1969 .... *3*
Ames, Evelyn 1908- *13*
Ames, Gerald 1906- *11*
Ames, Lee J. 1921- *3*
Ames, Mildred 1919- *22*
Amon, Aline 1928- *9*
Amoss, Berthe 1925- *5*
Anastasio, Dina 1941- *37*
Brief Entry *30*
Anckarsvard, Karin
1915-1969 .... *6*
Ancona, George 1929- *12*
Andersdatter, Karla M(argaret)
1938- *34*
Andersen, Hans Christian
1805-1875 ....*YABC 1*
See also CLR 6
Andersen, Ted
See Boyd, Waldo T.
Andersen, Yvonne 1932- *27*
Anderson, Bernice G(oudy)
1894- *33*
Anderson, Brad(ley Jay)
1924- *33*
Brief Entry *31*
Anderson, C(larence) W(illiam)
1891-1971 .... *11*
Anderson, Clifford [Joint pseudonym]
See Gardner, Richard
Anderson, Ella
See MacLeod, Ellen Jane (Anderson)
Anderson, Eloise Adell 1927- *9*
Anderson, George
See Groom, Arthur William
Anderson, Grace Fox 1932- *43*
Anderson, J(ohn) R(ichard) L(ane)
1911-1981 .... *15*
Obituary *27*
Anderson, Joy 1928- *1*
Anderson, LaVere (Francis Shoenfelt)
1907- *27*
Anderson, Leone Castell
1923- *53*
Brief Entry *49*

Anderson, (John) Lonzo
1905- 2
Anderson, Lucia (Lewis)
1922- 10
Anderson, Madelyn Klein 28
Anderson, Margaret J(ean)
1931- 27
Anderson, Mary 1939- 7
Anderson, Mona 1910- 40
Anderson, Norman D(ean)
1928- 22
Anderson, Poul (William) 1926-
Brief Entry 39
Anderson, Rachel 1943- 34
Andre, Evelyn M(arie) 1924- 27
Andree, Louise
See Coury, Louise Andree
Andrews, Benny 1930- 31
Andrews, F(rank) Emerson
1902-1978 22
Andrews, J(ames) S(ydney)
1934- 4
Andrews, Jan 1942-
Brief Entry 49
Andrews, Julie 1935- 7
Andrews, Laura
See Coury, Louise Andree
Andrews, Roy Chapman
1884-1960 19
Andrews, V(irginia) C(leo) (?)-1986
Obituary 50
Andrézel, Pierre
See Blixen, Karen (Christentze
Dinesen)
Andriola, Alfred J. 1912-1983
Obituary 34
Andrist, Ralph K. 1914- 45
Anfousse, Ginette 1944-
Brief Entry 48
Angel, Marie (Felicity) 1923- 47
Angeles, Peter A. 1931- 40
Angell, Judie 1937- 22
Angell, Madeline 1919- 18
Angelo, Valenti 1897- 14
Angelou, Maya 1928- 49
Angier, Bradford 12
Angle, Paul M(cClelland) 1900-1975
Obituary 20
Anglund, Joan Walsh 1926- 2
See also CLR 1
Angrist, Stanley W(olff)
1933- 4
Anita
See Daniel, Anita
Annett, Cora
See Scott, Cora Annett
Annixter, Jane
See Sturtzel, Jane Levington
Annixter, Paul
See Sturtzel, Howard A.
Anno, Mitsumasa 1926- 38
Earlier sketch in SATA 5
See also CLR 2, 14
Anrooy, Frans van
See Van Anrooy, Francine
Antell, Will D. 1935- 31
Anthony, Barbara 1932- 29
Anthony, C. L.
See Smith, Dodie

Anthony, Edward 1895-1971 21
Anticaglia, Elizabeth 1939- 12
Antolini, Margaret Fishback
1904-1985
Obituary 45
Anton, Michael (James) 1940- 12
Antonacci, Robert J(oseph)
1916- 45
Brief Entry 37
Aoki, Hisako 1942- 45
Apfel, Necia H(alpern) 1930- 51
Brief Entry 41
Aphrodite, J.
See Livingston, Carole
Appel, Benjamin 1907-1977 39
Obituary 21
Appel, Martin E(liot) 1948- 45
Appel, Marty
See Appel, Martin E(liot)
Appiah, Peggy 1921- 15
Apple, Margot
Brief Entry 42
Applebaum, Stan 1929- 45
Appleton, Victor [Collective
pseudonym] 1
Appleton, Victor II [Collective
pseudonym] 1
See also Adams, Harriet
S(tratemeyer)
Apsler, Alfred 1907- 10
Aquillo, Don
See Prince, J(ack) H(arvey)
Aragonés, Sergio 1937- 48
Brief Entry 39
Arbuckle, Dorothy Fry 1910-1982
Obituary 33
Arbuthnot, May Hill
1884-1969 2
Archer, Frank
See O'Connor, Richard
Archer, Jules 1915- 4
See also SAAS 5
Archer, Marion Fuller 1917- 11
Archibald, Joe
See Archibald, Joseph S(topford)
Archibald, Joseph S(topford)
1898-1986 3
Obituary 47
Arden, Barbie
See Stoutenburg, Adrien
Arden, William
See Lynds, Dennis
Ardizzone, Edward 1900-1979 28
Obituary 21
Earlier sketch in SATA 1
See also CLR 3
Ardley, Neil (Richard) 1937- 43
Arehart-Treichel, Joan 1942- 22
Arenella, Roy 1939- 14
Arkin, Alan (Wolf) 1934-
Brief Entry 32
Armer, Alberta (Roller) 1904- 9
Armer, Laura Adams
1874-1963 13
Armitage, David 1943-
Brief Entry 38
Armitage, Ronda (Jacqueline)
1943- 47
Brief Entry 38

Armour, Richard 1906- 14
Armstrong, George D. 1927- 10
Armstrong, Gerry (Breen)
1929- 10
Armstrong, Louise 43
Brief Entry 33
Armstrong, Richard 1903- 11
Armstrong, William H. 1914- 4
See also CLR 1
See also SAAS 7
Arndt, Ursula (Martha H.)
Brief Entry 39
Arneson, D(on) J(on) 1935- 37
Arnett, Carolyn
See Cole, Lois Dwight
Arno, Enrico 1913-1981 43
Obituary 28
Arnold, Caroline 1944- 36
Brief Entry 34
Arnold, Elliott 1912-1980 5
Obituary 22
Arnold, Emily 1939- 50
Arnold, Oren 1900- 4
Arnoldy, Julie
See Bischoff, Julia Bristol
Arnosky, Jim 1946- 22
See also CLR 15
Arnott, Kathleen 1914- 20
Arnov, Boris, Jr. 1926- 12
Arnow, Harriette (Louisa Simpson)
1908-1986 42
Obituary 47
Arnstein, Helene S(olomon)
1915- 12
Arntson, Herbert E(dward)
1911- 12
Aronin, Ben 1904-1980
Obituary 25
Arora, Shirley (Lease) 1930- 2
Arquette, Lois S(teinmetz)
1934- 1
See also Duncan, Lois S(teinmetz)
Arrowood, (McKendrick Lee) Clinton
1939- 19
Arthur, Robert
See Feder, Robert Arthur
Arthur, Ruth M(abel)
1905-1979 7
Obituary 26
Artis, Vicki Kimmel 1945- 12
Artzybasheff, Boris (Miklailovich)
1899-1965 14
Aruego, Ariane
See Dewey, Ariane
Aruego, Jose 1932- 6
See also CLR 5
Arundel, Honor (Morfydd)
1919-1973 4
Obituary 24
Arundel, Jocelyn
See Alexander, Jocelyn (Anne)
Arundel
Asbjörnsen, Peter Christen
1812-1885 15
Asch, Frank 1946- 5
Ash, Jutta 1942- 38
Ashabranner, Brent (Kenneth)
1921- 1
Ashby, Gwynneth 1922- 44

Ashe, Geoffrey (Thomas)
1923- *17*
Asher, Sandy (Fenichel)
1942- *36*
  Brief Entry *34*
Ashey, Bella
  See Breinburg, Petronella
Ashford, Daisy
  See Ashford, Margaret Mary
Ashford, Margaret Mary
1881-1972 .... *10*
Ashley, Bernard 1935- *47*
  Brief Entry *39*
  See also CLR 4
Ashley, Elizabeth
  See Salmon, Annie Elizabeth
Ashley, Ray
  See Abrashkin, Raymond
Ashton, Warren T.
  See Adams, William Taylor
Asimov, Isaac 1920- *26*
  Earlier sketch in SATA 1
  See also CLR 12
Asimov, Janet (Jeppson)
1926- *54*
Asinof, Eliot 1919- *6*
Astley, Juliet
  See Lofts, Nora (Robinson)
Aston, James
  See White, T(erence) H(anbury)
Atene, Ann
  See Atene, (Rita) Anna
Atene, (Rita) Anna 1922- *12*
Atkinson, Allen G. 1953(?)-1987
  Obituary *55*
  Brief Entry *46*
Atkinson, M. E.
  See Frankau, Mary Evelyn
Atkinson, Margaret Fleming *14*
Atticus
  See Davies, (Edward) Hunter
  See Fleming, Ian (Lancaster)
Atwater, Florence (Hasseltine
  Carroll) *16*
Atwater, Montgomery Meigs
1904- *15*
Atwater, Richard Tupper
1892-1948 .... *54*
  Brief Entry *27*
Atwood, Ann 1913- *7*
Atwood, Margaret (Eleanor)
1939- *50*
Aubry, Claude B. 1914-1984 ..... *29*
  Obituary *40*
Augarde, Steve 1950- *25*
Augelli, John P(at) 1921- *46*
Ault, Phillip H. 1914- *23*
Ault, Rosalie Sain 1942- *38*
Ault, Roz
  See Ault, Rosalie Sain
Aung, (Maung) Htin 1910- *21*
Aung, U. Htin
  See Aung, (Maung) Htin
Auntie Deb
  See Coury, Louise Andree
Auntie Louise
  See Coury, Louise Andree
Austin, Elizabeth S. 1907- *5*
Austin, Margot *11*

Austin, Oliver L., Jr. 1903- *7*
Austin, R. G.
  See Gelman, Rita Golden
Austin, Tom
  See Jacobs, Linda C.
Auth, Tony
  See Auth, William Anthony, Jr.
Auth, William Anthony, Jr.
1942- *51*
Averill, Esther 1902- *28*
  Earlier sketch in SATA 1
Avery, Al
  See Montgomery, Rutherford
Avery, Gillian 1926- *7*
  See also SAAS 6
Avery, Kay 1908- *5*
Avery, Lynn
  See Cole, Lois Dwight
Avi
  See Wortis, Avi
Ayars, James S(terling) 1898- *4*
Ayer, Jacqueline 1930- *13*
Ayer, Margaret *15*
Aylesworth, Jim 1943- *38*
Aylesworth, Thomas G(ibbons)
1927- *4*
  See also CLR 6
Aymar, Brandt 1911- *22*
Ayres, Carole Briggs
  See Briggs, Carole S(uzanne)
Ayres, Patricia Miller 1923-1985
  Obituary *46*
Azaid
  See Zaidenberg, Arthur

B

B
  See Gilbert, W(illiam) S(chwenk)
B., Tania
  See Blixen, Karen (Christentze
  Dinesen)
BB
  See Watkins-Pitchford, D. J.
Baastad, Babbis Friis
  See Friis-Baastad, Babbis
Bab
  See Gilbert, W(illiam) S(chwenk)
Babbis, Eleanor
  See Friis-Baastad, Babbis
Babbitt, Natalie 1932- *6*
  See also CLR 2
  See also SAAS 5
Babcock, Dennis Arthur
1948- *22*
Bach, Alice (Hendricks)
1942- *30*
  Brief Entry *27*
Bach, Richard David 1936- *13*
Bachman, Fred 1949- *12*
Bachman, Richard
  See King, Stephen (Edwin)
Bacmeister, Rhoda W(arner)
1893- *11*
Bacon, Elizabeth 1914- *3*
Bacon, Joan Chase
  See Bowden, Joan Chase

Bacon, Josephine Dodge (Daskam)
1876-1961 .... *48*
Bacon, Margaret Frances 1895-1987
  Obituary *50*
Bacon, Margaret Hope 1921- *6*
Bacon, Martha Sherman
1917-1981 .... *18*
  Obituary *27*
  See also CLR 3
Bacon, Peggy 1895- *2*
  See also Bacon, Margaret Frances
Bacon, R(onald) L(eonard)
1924- *26*
Baden-Powell, Robert (Stephenson
  Smyth) 1857-1941 .... *16*
Baerg, Harry J(ohn) 1909- *12*
Bagnold, Enid 1889-1981 .... *25*
  Earlier sketch in SATA 1
Bahr, Robert 1940- *38*
Bahti, Tom
  Brief Entry *31*
Bailey, Alice Cooper 1890- *12*
Bailey, Bernadine Freeman *14*
Bailey, Carolyn Sherwin
1875-1961 .... *14*
Bailey, Jane H(orton) 1916- *12*
Bailey, John (Robert) 1940- *52*
Bailey, Maralyn Collins (Harrison)
1941- *12*
Bailey, Matilda
  See Radford, Ruby L.
Bailey, Maurice Charles
1932- *12*
Bailey, Ralph Edgar 1893- *11*
Baird, Bil 1904-1987 .... *30*
  Obituary *52*
Baird, Thomas P. 1923- *45*
  Brief Entry *39*
Baity, Elizabeth Chesley
1907- *1*
Bakeless, John (Edwin) 1894- *9*
Bakeless, Katherine Little
1895- *9*
Baker, Alan 1951- *22*
Baker, Augusta 1911- *3*
Baker, Betty (Lou) 1928-1987 .... *5*
  Obituary *54*
Baker, Charlotte 1910- *2*
Baker, Elizabeth 1923- *7*
Baker, Eugene H.
  Brief Entry *50*
Baker, Gayle C(unningham)
1950- *39*
Baker, James W. 1924- *22*
Baker, Janice E(dla) 1941- *22*
Baker, Jeannie 1950- *23*
Baker, Jeffrey J(ohn) W(heeler)
1931- *5*
Baker, Jim
  See Baker, James W.
Baker, Laura Nelson 1911- *3*
Baker, Margaret 1890- *4*
Baker, Margaret J(oyce)
1918- *12*
Baker, Mary Gladys Steel
1892-1974 .... *12*
Baker, (Robert) Michael
1938- *4*

Baker, Nina (Brown)
1888-1957 .... *15*
Baker, Rachel 1904-1978 .... *2*
Obituary *26*
Baker, Samm Sinclair 1909- *12*
Baker, Susan (Catherine)
1942- *29*
Balaam
See Lamb, G(eoffrey) F(rederick)
Balch, Glenn 1902- *3*
Baldridge, Cyrus LeRoy 1889-
Brief Entry *29*
Balducci, Carolyn Feleppa
1946- *5*
Baldwin, Anne Norris 1938- *5*
Baldwin, Clara *11*
Baldwin, Gordo
See Baldwin, Gordon C.
Baldwin, Gordon C. 1908- *12*
Baldwin, James 1841-1925 .... *24*
Baldwin, James (Arthur)
1924-1987 .... *9*
Obituary *54*
Baldwin, Margaret
See Weis, Margaret (Edith)
Baldwin, Stan(ley C.) 1929-
Brief Entry *28*
Bales, Carol Ann 1940-
Brief Entry *29*
Balet, Jan (Bernard) 1913- *11*
Balian, Lorna 1929- *9*
Ball, Zachary
See Masters, Kelly R.
Ballantine, Lesley Frost
See Frost, Lesley
Ballantyne, R(obert) M(ichael)
1825-1894 .... *24*
Ballard, Lowell Clyne
1904-1986 .... *12*
Obituary *49*
Ballard, (Charles) Martin
1929- *1*
Ballard, Mignon Franklin 1934-
Brief Entry *49*
Balogh, Penelope 1916-1975 ...... *1*
Obituary *34*
Balow, Tom 1931- *12*
Baltzer, Hans (Adolf) 1900- *40*
Bamfylde, Walter
See Bevan, Tom
Bamman, Henry A. 1918- *12*
Bancroft, Griffing 1907- *6*
Bancroft, Laura
See Baum, L(yman) Frank
Bandel, Betty 1912- *47*
Baner, Skulda V(anadis)
1897-1964 .... *10*
Bang, Betsy (Garrett) 1912- *48*
Brief Entry *37*
Bang, Garrett
See Bang, Molly Garrett
Bang, Molly Garrett 1943- *24*
See also CLR 8
Banks, Laura Stockton Voorhees
1908(?)-1980
Obituary *23*
Banks, Sara (Jeanne Gordon Harrell)
1937- *26*

Banner, Angela
See Maddison, Angela Mary
Bannerman, Helen (Brodie Cowan
Watson) 1863(?)-1946 .... *19*
Banning, Evelyn I. 1903- *36*
Bannon, Laura (?)-1963 .... *6*
Barbary, James
See Baumann, Amy (Brown)
Barbary, James
See Beeching, Jack
Barbe, Walter Burke 1926- *45*
Barber, Antonia
See Anthony, Barbara
Barber, Linda
See Graham-Barber, Lynda
Barber, Richard (William)
1941- *35*
Barbera, Joe
See Barbera, Joseph Roland
Barbera, Joseph Roland 1911- *51*
Barbour, Ralph Henry
1870-1944 .... *16*
Barclay, Isabel
See Dobell, I.M.B.
Bare, Arnold Edwin 1920- *16*
Bare, Colleen Stanley *32*
Barish, Matthew 1907- *12*
Barker, Albert W. 1900- *8*
Barker, Carol (Minturn) 1938- *31*
Barker, Cicely Mary
1895-1973 .... *49*
Brief Entry *39*
Barker, Melvern 1907- *11*
Barker, S. Omar 1894- *10*
Barker, Will 1908- *8*
Barkhouse, Joyce 1913-
Brief Entry *48*
Barkin, Carol 1944- *52*
Barkley, James Edward 1941- *6*
Barks, Carl 1901- *37*
Barnaby, Ralph S(tanton)
1893- *9*
Barner, Bob 1947- *29*
Barnes, (Frank) Eric Wollencott
1907-1962 .... *22*
Barnes, Malcolm 1909(?)-1984
Obituary *41*
Barnes, Michael 1934- *55*
Barnett, Lincoln (Kinnear)
1909-1979 .... *36*
Barnett, Moneta 1922-1976 .... *33*
Barnett, Naomi 1927- *40*
Barney, Maginel Wright
1881-1966 .... *39*
Brief Entry *32*
Barnhart, Clarence L(ewis)
1900- *48*
Barnouw, Adriaan Jacob 1877-1968
Obituary *27*
Barnouw, Victor 1915- *43*
Brief Entry *28*
Barnstone, Willis 1927- *20*
Barnum, Jay Hyde
1888(?)-1962 .... *20*
Barnum, Richard [Collective
pseudonym] *1*
Baron, Virginia Olsen 1931- *46*
Brief Entry *28*
Barr, Donald 1921- *20*

Barr, George 1907- *2*
Barr, Jene 1900-1985 .... *16*
Obituary *42*
Barrer, Gertrude
See Barrer-Russell, Gertrude
Barrer-Russell, Gertrude
1921- *27*
Barrett, Ethel
Brief Entry *44*
Barrett, Judith 1941- *26*
Barrett, Ron 1937- *14*
Barrett, William E(dmund) 1900-1986
Obituary *49*
Barrie, J(ames) M(atthew)
1860-1937 .... *YABC 1*
Barris, George 1925- *47*
Barrol, Grady
See Bograd, Larry
Barry, James P(otvin) 1918- *14*
Barry, Katharina (Watjen)
1936- *4*
Barry, Robert 1931- *6*
Barry, Scott 1952- *32*
Bartenbach, Jean 1918- *40*
Barth, Edna 1914-1980 .... *7*
Obituary *24*
Barthelme, Donald 1931- *7*
Bartholomew, Barbara 1941-
Brief Entry *42*
Bartlett, Philip A. [Collective
pseudonym] *1*
Bartlett, Robert Merrill 1899- *12*
Barton, Byron 1930- *9*
Barton, Harriett
Brief Entry *43*
Barton, May Hollis [Collective
pseudonym] *1*
See also Adams, Harriet
S(tratemeyer)
Bartos-Hoeppner, Barbara
1923- *5*
Bartsch, Jochen 1906- *39*
Baruch, Dorothy W(alter)
1899-1962 .... *21*
Bas, Rutger
See Rutgers van der Loeff, An(na)
Basenau
Bashevis, Isaac
See Singer, Isaac Bashevis
Baskin, Leonard 1922- *30*
Brief Entry *27*
Bason, Lillian 1913- *20*
Bassett, Jeni 1960(?)-
Brief Entry *43*
Bassett, John Keith
See Keating, Lawrence A.
Batchelor, Joy 1914-
Brief Entry *29*
Bate, Lucy 1939- *18*
Bate, Norman 1916- *5*
Bates, Barbara S(nedeker)
1919- *12*
Bates, Betty 1921- *19*
Batey, Tom 1946- *52*
Brief Entry *41*
Batherman, Muriel
See Sheldon, Muriel
Batiuk, Thomas M(artin) 1947-
Brief Entry *40*

Batson, Larry 1930- *35*
Battaglia, Aurelius 1910- *50*
  Brief Entry *33*
Batten, H(arry) Mortimer
  1888-1958 .... *25*
Batten, Mary 1937- *5*
Batterberry, Ariane Ruskin
  1935- *13*
Batterberry, Michael (Carver)
  1932- *32*
Battles, Edith 1921- *7*
Baudouy, Michel-Aime 1909- *7*
Bauer, Caroline Feller 1935- *52*
  Brief Entry *46*
Bauer, Fred 1934- *36*
Bauer, Helen 1900- *2*
Bauer, Marion Dane 1938- *20*
Bauernschmidt, Marjorie
  1926- *15*
Baum, Allyn Z(elton) 1924- *20*
Baum, L(yman) Frank
  1856-1919 .... *18*
  See also CLR 15
Baum, Louis 1948-
  Brief Entry *52*
Baum, Willi 1931- *4*
Baumann, Amy (Brown)
  1922- *10*
Baumann, Elwood D.
  Brief Entry *33*
Baumann, Hans 1914- *2*
Baumann, Kurt 1935- *21*
Bawden, Nina
  See Kark, Nina Mary
  See also CLR 2
Bayer, Jane E. (?)-1985
  Obituary *44*
Bayley, Nicola 1949- *41*
Baylor, Byrd 1924- *16*
  See also CLR 3
Baynes, Pauline (Diana)
  1922- *19*
Beach, Charles
  See Reid, (Thomas) Mayne
Beach, Charles Amory [Collective
  pseudonym] *1*
Beach, Edward L(atimer)
  1918- *12*
Beach, Stewart Taft 1899- *23*
Beachcroft, Nina 1931- *18*
Bealer, Alex W(inkler III)
  1921-1980 .... *8*
  Obituary *22*
Beals, Carleton 1893- *12*
Beals, Frank Lee 1881-1972
  Obituary *26*
Beame, Rona 1934- *12*
Beamer, (G.) Charles, (Jr.)
  1942- *43*
Beaney, Jan
  See Udall, Jan Beaney
Beard, Charles Austin
  1874-1948 .... *18*
Beard, Dan(iel Carter)
  1850-1941 .... *22*
Bearden, Romare (Howard)
  1914- *22*
Beardmore, Cedric
  See Beardmore, George

Beardmore, George
  1908-1979 .... *20*
Bearman, Jane (Ruth) 1917- *29*
Beatty, Elizabeth
  See Holloway, Teresa (Bragunier)
Beatty, Hetty Burlingame
  1907-1971 .... *5*
Beatty, Jerome, Jr. 1918- *5*
Beatty, John (Louis)
  1922-1975 .... *6*
  Obituary *25*
Beatty, Patricia (Robbins)
  1922- *30*
  Earlier sketch in SATA 1
  See also SAAS 4
Bechtel, Louise Seaman
  1894-1985 .... *4*
  Obituary *43*
Beck, Barbara L. 1927- *12*
Becker, Beril 1901- *11*
Becker, John (Leonard) 1901- *12*
Becker, Joyce 1936- *39*
Becker, May Lamberton
  1873-1958 .... *33*
Beckett, Sheilah 1913- *33*
Beckman, Delores 1914- *51*
Beckman, Gunnel 1910- *6*
Beckman, Kaj
  See Beckman, Karin
Beckman, Karin 1913- *45*
Beckman, Per (Frithiof) 1913- *45*
Bedford, A. N.
  See Watson, Jane Werner
Bedford, Annie North
  See Watson, Jane Werner
Bedoukian, Kerop 1907-1981 ..... *53*
Beebe, B(urdetta) F(aye)
  1920- *1*
Beebe, (Charles) William
  1877-1962 .... *19*
Beeby, Betty 1923- *25*
Beech, Webb
  See Butterworth, W. E.
Beeching, Jack 1922- *14*
Beeler, Nelson F(rederick)
  1910- *13*
Beers, Dorothy Sands 1917- *9*
Beers, Lorna 1897- *14*
Beers, V(ictor) Gilbert 1928- *9*
Begley, Kathleen A(nne)
  1948- *21*
Behn, Harry 1898-1973 .... *2*
  Obituary *34*
Behnke, Frances L. *8*
Behr, Joyce 1929- *15*
Behrens, June York 1925- *19*
Behrman, Carol H(elen) 1925- *14*
Beiser, Arthur 1931- *22*
Beiser, Germaine 1931- *11*
Belair, Richard L. 1934- *45*
Belaney, Archibald Stansfeld
  1888-1938 .... *24*
Belknap, B. H.
  See Ellis, Edward S(ylvester)
Bell, Corydon 1894- *3*
Bell, Emily Mary
  See Cason, Mabel Earp
Bell, Gertrude (Wood) 1911- *12*

Bell, Gina
  See Iannone, Jeanne
Bell, Janet
  See Clymer, Eleanor
Bell, Margaret E(lizabeth)
  1898- *2*
Bell, Neill 1946-
  Brief Entry *50*
Bell, Norman (Edward) 1899- *11*
Bell, Raymond Martin 1907- *13*
Bell, Robert S(tanley) W(arren)
  1871-1921
  Brief Entry *27*
Bell, Thelma Harrington
  1896- *3*
Bellairs, John 1938- *2*
Bellingham, Brenda 1931-
  Brief Entry *51*
Belloc, (Joseph) Hilaire (Pierre)
  1870-1953 ....*YABC 1*
Bellville, Cheryl Walsh 1944- *54*
  Brief Entry *49*
Bell-Zano, Gina
  See Iannone, Jeanne
Belpré, Pura 1899-1982 .... *16*
  Obituary *30*
Belting, Natalie Maree 1915- *6*
Belton, John Raynor 1931- *22*
Beltran, Alberto 1923- *43*
Belvedere, Lee
  See Grayland, Valerie
Bemelmans, Ludwig
  1898-1962 .... *15*
  See also CLR 6
Benary, Margot
  See Benary-Isbert, Margot
Benary-Isbert, Margot
  1889-1979 .... *2*
  Obituary *21*
  See also CLR 12
Benasutti, Marion 1908- *6*
Benchley, Nathaniel (Goddard)
  1915-1981 .... *25*
  Obituary *28*
  Earlier sketch in SATA 3
Benchley, Peter 1940- *3*
Bender, Lucy Ellen 1942- *22*
Bendick, Jeanne 1919- *2*
  See also CLR 5
  See also SAAS 4
Bendick, Robert L(ouis)
  1917- *11*
Benedict, Dorothy Potter
  1889-1979 .... *11*
  Obituary *23*
Benedict, Lois Trimble
  1902-1967 .... *12*
Benedict, Rex 1920- *8*
Benedict, Stewart H(urd)
  1924- *26*
Benét, Laura 1884-1979 .... *3*
  Obituary *23*
Benét, Stephen Vincent
  1898-1943 ....*YABC 1*
Benet, Sula 1903(?)-1982 .... *21*
  Obituary *33*
Benezra, Barbara 1921- • *10*
Benham, Leslie 1922- *48*
Benham, Lois (Dakin) 1924- *48*

Benham, Mary Lile 1914- 55
Benjamin, Nora
  See Kubie, Nora (Gottheil) Benjamin
Bennett, Dorothea
  See Young, Dorothea Bennett
Bennett, Jay 1912- 41
  Brief Entry 27
  See also SAAS 4
Bennett, Jill (Crawford) 1934- 41
Bennett, John 1865-1956 ..... *YABC 1*
Bennett, Rachel
  See Hill, Margaret (Ohler)
Bennett, Rainey 1907- 15
Bennett, Richard 1899- 21
Bennett, Russell H(oradley)
  1896- 25
Benson, Sally 1900-1972 35
  Obituary 27
  Earlier sketch in SATA 1
Bentley, Judith (McBride)
  1945- 40
Bentley, Nicolas Clerihew 1907-1978
  Obituary 24
Bentley, Phyllis (Eleanor)
  1894-1977 6
  Obituary 25
Bentley, Roy 1947- 46
Berelson, Howard 1940- 5
Berends, Polly B(errien)
  1939- 50
  Brief Entry 38
Berenstain, Janice 12
Berenstain, Michael 1951-
  Brief Entry 45
Berenstain, Stan(ley) 1923- 12
Beresford, Elisabeth 25
Berg, Björn 1923-
  Brief Entry 47
Berg, Dave
  See Berg, David
Berg, David 1920- 27
Berg, Jean Horton 1913- 6
Berg, Joan
  See Victor, Joan Berg
Berg, Ron 1952- 48
Bergaust, Erik 1925-1978 20
Berger, Gilda
  Brief Entry 42
Berger, Josef 1903-1971 36
Berger, Melvin H. 1927- 5
  See also SAAS 2
Berger, Terry 1933- 8
Bergey, Alyce (Mae) 1934- 45
Berkebile, Fred D(onovan) 1900-1978
  Obituary 26
Berkey, Barry Robert 1935- 24
Berkowitz, Freda Pastor 1910- 12
Berliner, Don 1930- 33
Berliner, Franz 1930- 13
Berlitz, Charles L. (Frambach)
  1913- 32
Berman, Linda 1948- 38
Berna, Paul 1910- 15
Bernadette
  See Watts, Bernadette
Bernard, George I. 1949- 39
Bernard, Jacqueline (de Sieyes)
  1921-1983 8
  Obituary 45

Bernays, Anne
  See Kaplan, Anne Bernays
Bernstein, Joanne E(ckstein)
  1943- 15
Bernstein, Theodore M(enline)
  1904-1979 12
  Obituary 27
Berrien, Edith Heal
  See Heal, Edith
Berrill, Jacquelyn (Batsel)
  1905- 12
Berrington, John
  See Brownjohn, Alan
Berry, B. J.
  See Berry, Barbara J.
Berry, Barbara J. 1937- 7
Berry, Erick
  See Best, Allena Champlin
Berry, Jane Cobb 1915(?)-1979
  Obituary 22
Berry, Joy Wilt
  Brief Entry 46
Berry, William D(avid) 1926- 14
Berson, Harold 1926- 4
Berwick, Jean
  See Meyer, Jean Shepherd
Beskow, Elsa (Maartman)
  1874-1953 20
Best, (Evangel) Allena Champlin
  1892-1974 2
  Obituary 25
Best, (Oswald) Herbert 1894- 2
Bestall, Alfred (Edmeades) 1892-1986
  Obituary 48
Betancourt, Jeanne 1941- 55
  Brief Entry 43
Beth, Mary
  See Miller, Mary Beth
Bethancourt, T. Ernesto 1932- 11
  See also CLR 3
Bethel, Dell 1929- 52
Bethell, Jean (Frankenberry)
  1922- 8
Bethers, Ray 1902- 6
Bethune, J. G.
  See Ellis, Edward S(ylvester)
Betteridge, Anne
  See Potter, Margaret (Newman)
Bettina
  See Ehrlich, Bettina
Bettmann, Otto Ludwig 1903- 46
Betts, James [Joint pseudonym]
  See Haynes, Betsy
Betz, Eva Kelly 1897-1968 10
Bevan, Tom
  1868-1930(?) .... *YABC 2*
Bewick, Thomas 1753-1828 16
Beyer, Audrey White 1916- 9
Bezencon, Jacqueline (Buxcel)
  1924- 48
Bhatia, June
  See Forrester, Helen
Bialk, Elisa 1
Bianco, Margery (Williams)
  1881-1944 15
Bianco, Pamela 1906- 28
Bibby, Violet 1908- 24
Bible, Charles 1937- 13
Bice, Clare 1909-1976 22

Bickerstaff, Isaac
  See Swift, Jonathan
Biegel, Paul 1925- 16
Biemiller, Carl L(udwig)
  1912-1979 40
  Obituary 21
Bienenfeld, Florence L(ucille)
  1929- 39
Bierhorst, John 1936- 6
Bileck, Marvin 1920- 40
Bill, Alfred Hoyt 1879-1964 44
Billings, Charlene W(interer)
  1941- 41
Billington, Elizabeth T(hain) 50
  Brief Entry 43
Billout, Guy René 1941- 10
Binkley, Anne
  See Rand, Ann (Binkley)
Binzen, Bill 24
Binzen, William
  See Binzen, Bill
Birch, Reginald B(athurst)
  1856-1943 19
Birmingham, Lloyd 1924- 12
Biro, Val 1921- 1
Bischoff, Julia Bristol
  1909-1970 12
Bishop, Bonnie 1943- 37
Bishop, Claire (Huchet) 14
Bishop, Curtis 1912-1967 6
Bishop, Elizabeth 1911-1979
  Obituary 24
Bisset, Donald 1910- 7
Bitter, Gary G(len) 1940- 22
Bixby, William (Courtney)
  1920-1986 6
  Obituary 47
Bjerregaard-Jensen, Vilhelm Hans
  See Hillcourt, William
Bjorklund, Lorence F.
  1913-1978 35
  Brief Entry 32
Black, Algernon David 1900- 12
Black, Irma S(imonton)
  1906-1972 2
  Obituary 25
Black, Mansell
  See Trevor, Elleston
Black, Susan Adams 1953- 40
Blackburn, Claire
  See Jacobs, Linda C.
Blackburn, John(ny) Brewton
  1952- 15
Blackburn, Joyce Knight
  1920- 29
Blackett, Veronica Heath
  1927- 12
Blackton, Peter
  See Wilson, Lionel
Blades, Ann 1947- 16
  See also CLR 15
Bladow, Suzanne Wilson
  1937- 14
Blaine, John
  See Goodwin, Harold Leland
Blaine, John
  See Harkins, Philip
Blaine, Margery Kay 1937- 11
Blair, Anne Denton 1914- 46

Blair, Eric Arthur 1903-1950 29
Blair, Helen 1910-
  Brief Entry 29
Blair, Jay 1953- 45
Blair, Ruth Van Ness 1912- 12
Blair, Walter 1900- 12
Blake, Olive
  See Supraner, Robyn
Blake, Quentin 1932- 52
Blake, Robert 1949- 42
Blake, Walker E.
  See Butterworth, W. E.
Blake, William 1757-1827 30
Bland, Edith Nesbit
  See Nesbit, E(dith)
Bland, Fabian [Joint pseudonym]
  See Nesbit, E(dith)
Blane, Gertrude
  See Blumenthal, Gertrude
Blassingame, Wyatt Rainey
  1909-1985 34
  Obituary 41
  Earlier sketch in SATA 1
Blauer, Ettagale 1940- 49
Bleeker, Sonia 1909-1971 2
  Obituary 26
Blegvad, Erik 1923- 14
Blegvad, Lenore 1926- 14
Blishen, Edward 1920- 8
Bliss, Corinne D(emas) 1947- 37
Bliss, Reginald
  See Wells, H(erbert) G(eorge)
Bliss, Ronald G(ene) 1942- 12
Bliven, Bruce, Jr. 1916- 2
Blixen, Karen (Christentze Dinesen)
  1885-1962 44
Bloch, Lucienne 1909- 10
Bloch, Marie Halun 1910- 6
Bloch, Robert 1917- 12
Blochman, Lawrence G(oldtree)
  1900-1975 22
Block, Irvin 1917- 12
Blocksma, Mary
  Brief Entry 44
Blood, Charles Lewis 1929- 28
Bloom, Freddy 1914- 37
Bloom, Lloyd
  Brief Entry 43
Blos, Joan W(insor) 1928- 33
  Brief Entry 27
Blough, Glenn O(rlando)
  1907- 1
Blue, Rose 1931- 5
Blumberg, Rhoda 1917- 35
Blume, Judy (Sussman) 1938- 31
  Earlier sketch in SATA 2
  See also CLR 2, 15
Blumenthal, Gertrude 1907-1971
  Obituary 27
Blumenthal, Shirley 1943- 46
Blutig, Eduard
  See Gorey, Edward St. John
Bly, Janet Chester 1945- 43
Bly, Robert W(ayne) 1957-
  Brief Entry 48
Bly, Stephen A(rthur) 1944- 43
Blyton, Carey 1932- 9
Blyton, Enid (Mary)
  1897-1968 25

Boardman, Fon Wyman, Jr.
  1911- 6
Boardman, Gwenn R. 1924- 12
Boase, Wendy 1944- 28
Boatner, Mark Mayo III
  1921- 29
Bobbe, Dorothie 1905-1975 1
  Obituary 25
Bobri
  See Bobritsky, Vladimir
Bobri, Vladimir
  See Bobritsky, Vladimir
Bobritsky, Vladimir 1898- 47
  Brief Entry 32
Bock, Hal
  See Bock, Harold I.
Bock, Harold I. 1939- 10
Bock, William Sauts
  Netamux'we 14
Bodecker, N(iels) M(ogens)
  1922-1988 8
  Obituary 54
Boden, Hilda
  See Bodenham, Hilda Esther
Bodenham, Hilda Esther
  1901- 13
Bodie, Idella F(allaw) 1925- 12
Bodker, Cecil 1927- 14
Bodsworth, (Charles) Fred(erick)
  1918- 27
Boeckman, Charles 1920- 12
Boegehold, Betty (Doyle) 1913-1985
  Obituary 42
Boesch, Mark J(oseph) 1917- 12
Boesen, Victor 1908- 16
Boggs, Ralph Steele 1901- 7
Bograd, Larry 1953- 33
Bohdal, Susi 1951- 22
Boles, Paul Darcy 1916-1984 9
  Obituary 38
Bolian, Polly 1925- 4
Bollen, Roger 1941(?)-
  Brief Entry 29
Bolliger, Max 1929- 7
Bolognese, Don(ald Alan)
  1934- 24
Bolton, Carole 1926- 6
Bolton, Elizabeth
  See Johnston, Norma
Bolton, Evelyn
  See Bunting, Anne Evelyn
Bond, B. J.
  See Heneghan, James
Bond, Felicia 1954- 49
Bond, Gladys Baker 1912- 14
Bond, J. Harvey
  See Winterbotham, R(ussell)
  R(obert)
Bond, Michael 1926- 6
  See also CLR 1
  See also SAAS 3
Bond, Nancy (Barbara) 1945- 22
  See also CLR 11
Bond, Ruskin 1934- 14
Bonehill, Captain Ralph
  See Stratemeyer, Edward L.
Bonestell, Chesley 1888-1986
  Obituary 48
Bonham, Barbara 1926- 7

Bonham, Frank 1914- 49
  Earlier sketch in SATA 1
  See also SAAS 3
Bonn, Pat
  See Bonn, Patricia Carolyn
Bonn, Patricia Carolyn 1948- 43
Bonner, Mary Graham
  1890-1974 19
Bonners, Susan
  Brief Entry 48
Bonsall, Crosby (Barbara Newell)
  1921- 23
Bontemps, Arna 1902-1973 44
  Obituary 24
  Earlier sketch in SATA 2
  See also CLR 6
Bonzon, Paul-Jacques 1908- 22
Booher, Dianna Daniels 1948- 33
Bookman, Charlotte
  See Zolotow, Charlotte S.
Boone, Pat 1934- 7
Boorman, Linda (Kay) 1940- 46
Boorstin, Daniel J(oseph)
  1914- 52
Booth, Ernest Sheldon
  1915-1984 43
Booth, Graham (Charles)
  1935- 37
Bordier, Georgette 1924- 16
Boring, Mel 1939- 35
Borja, Corinne 1929- 22
Borja, Robert 1923- 22
Borland, Hal 1900-1978 5
  Obituary 24
Borland, Harold Glen
  See Borland, Hal
Borland, Kathryn Kilby 1916- 16
Born, Adolf 1930- 49
Bornstein, Ruth 1927- 14
Borski, Lucia Merecka 18
Borten, Helen Jacobson 1930- 5
Borton, Elizabeth
  See Treviño, Elizabeth B. de
Bortstein, Larry 1942- 16
Bosco, Jack
  See Holliday, Joseph
Boshell, Gordon 1908- 15
Boshinski, Blanche 1922- 10
Bosse, Malcolm J(oseph)
  1926- 35
Bossom, Naomi 1933- 35
Boston, Lucy Maria (Wood)
  1892- 19
  See also CLR 3
Bosworth, J. Allan 1925- 19
Bothwell, Jean 2
Botkin, B(enjamin) A(lbert)
  1901-1975 40
Botting, Douglas (Scott)
  1934- 43
Bottner, Barbara 1943- 14
Boulet, Susan Seddon 1941- 50
Boulle, Pierre (Francois Marie-Louis)
  1912- 22
Bourdon, David 1934- 46
Bourne, Leslie
  See Marshall, Evelyn
Bourne, Miriam Anne 1931- 16

Boutet De Monvel, (Louis) M(aurice)
  1850(?)-1913 30
Bova, Ben 1932- 6
  See also CLR 3
Bowden, Joan Chase 1925- 51
  Brief Entry 38
Bowen, Betty Morgan
  See West, Betty
Bowen, Catherine Drinker
  1897-1973 7
Bowen, David
  See Bowen, Joshua David
Bowen, Joshua David 1930- 22
Bowen, R(obert) Sidney
  1900(?)-1977 52
  Obituary 21
Bowie, Jim
  See Stratemeyer, Edward L.
Bowler, Jan Brett
  See Brett, Jan
Bowman, James Cloyd
  1880-1961 23
Bowman, John S(tewart)
  1931- 16
Bowman, Kathleen (Gill)
  1942- 52
  Brief Entry 40
Boyce, George A(rthur) 1898- 19
Boyd, Pauline
  See Schock, Pauline
Boyd, Selma
  See Acuff, Selma Boyd
Boyd, Waldo T. 1918- 18
Boyer, Robert E(rnst) 1929- 22
Boyle, Ann (Peters) 1916- 10
Boyle, Eleanor Vere (Gordon)
  1825-1916 28
Boylston, Helen (Dore)
  1895-1984 23
  Obituary 39
Boynton, Sandra 1953-
  Brief Entry 38
Boz
  See Dickens, Charles
Bradbury, Bianca 1908- 3
Bradbury, Ray (Douglas)
  1920- 11
Bradford, Ann (Liddell) 1917-
  Brief Entry 38
Bradford, Karleen 1936- 48
Bradford, Lois J(ean) 1936- 36
Bradley, Duane
  See Sanborn, Duane
Bradley, Virginia 1912- 23
Brady, Esther Wood
  1905-1987 31
  Obituary 53
Brady, Irene 1943- 4
Brady, Lillian 1902- 28
Bragdon, Elspeth 1897- 6
Bragdon, Lillian (Jacot) 24
Bragg, Mabel Caroline
  1870-1945 24
Bragg, Michael 1948- 46
Braithwaite, Althea 1940- 23
Bram, Elizabeth 1948- 30
Brancato, Robin F(idler)
  1936- 23

Brandenberg, Aliki (Liacouras)
  1929- 35
  Earlier sketch in SATA 2
Brandenberg, Franz 1932- 35
  Earlier sketch in SATA 8
Brandhorst, Carl T(heodore)
  1898- 23
Brandon, Brumsic, Jr. 1927- 9
Brandon, Curt
  See Bishop, Curtis
Brandreth, Gyles 1948- 28
Brandt, Catharine 1905- 40
Brandt, Keith
  See Sabin, Louis
Branfield, John (Charles)
  1931- 11
Branley, Franklyn M(ansfield)
  1915- 4
  See also CLR 13
Branscum, Robbie 1937- 23
Bransom, (John) Paul
  1885-1979 43
Bratton, Helen 1899- 4
Braude, Michael 1936- 23
Braymer, Marjorie 1911- 6
Brecht, Edith 1895-1975 6
  Obituary 25
Breck, Vivian
  See Breckenfeld, Vivian Gurney
Breckenfeld, Vivian Gurney
  1895- 1
Breda, Tjalmar
  See DeJong, David C(ornel)
Breinburg, Petronella 1927- 11
Breisky, William J(ohn) 1928- 22
Brennan, Gale Patrick 1927-
  Brief Entry 53
Brennan, Joseph L. 1903- 6
Brennan, Tim
  See Conroy, Jack (Wesley)
Brenner, Barbara (Johnes)
  1925- 42
  Earlier sketch in SATA 4
Brenner, Fred 1920- 36
  Brief Entry 34
Brent, Hope 1935(?)-1984
  Obituary 39
Brent, Stuart 14
Brett, Bernard 1925- 22
Brett, Grace N(eff) 1900-1975 23
Brett, Hawksley
  See Bell, Robert S(tanley) W(arren)
Brett, Jan 1949- 42
Brewer, Sally King 1947- 33
Brewster, Benjamin
  See Folsom, Franklin
Brewster, Patience 1952- 51
Brewton, John E(dmund)
  1898- 5
Brick, John 1922-1973 10
Bridgers, Sue Ellen 1942- 22
  See also SAAS 1
Bridges, Laurie
  See Bruck, Lorraine
Bridges, William (Andrew)
  1901- 5
Bridwell, Norman 1928- 4
Brier, Howard M(axwell)
  1903-1969 8

Briggs, Carole S(uzanne) 1950-
  Brief Entry 47
Briggs, Katharine Mary 1898-1980
  Obituary 25
Briggs, Peter 1921-1975 39
  Obituary 31
Briggs, Raymond (Redvers)
  1934- 23
  See also CLR 10
Bright, Robert 1902- 24
Brightfield, Richard 1927-
  Brief Entry 53
Brightfield, Rick
  See Brightfield, Richard
Brightwell, L(eonard) R(obert) 1889-
  Brief Entry 29
Brimberg, Stanlee 1947- 9
Brin, Ruth F(irestone) 1921- 22
Brinckloe, Julie (Lorraine)
  1950- 13
Brindel, June (Rachuy) 1919- 7
Brindze, Ruth 1903- 23
Brink, Carol Ryrie 1895-1981 31
  Obituary 27
  Earlier sketch in SATA 1
Brinsmead, H(esba) F(ay)
  1922- 18
  See also SAAS 5
Briquebec, John
  See Rowland-Entwistle, (Arthur)
  Theodore (Henry)
Brisco, Pat A.
  See Matthews, Patricia
Brisco, Patty
  See Matthews, Patricia
Briscoe, Jill (Pauline) 1935-
  Brief Entry 47
Brisley, Joyce Lankester
  1896- 22
Britt, Albert 1874-1969
  Obituary 28
Britt, Dell 1934- 1
Brittain, Bill
  See Brittain, William
  See also SAAS 7
Brittain, William 1930- 36
Britton, Kate
  See Stegeman, Janet Allais
Britton, Louisa
  See McGuire, Leslie (Sarah)
Bro, Marguerite (Harmon)
  1894-1977 19
  Obituary 27
Broadhead, Helen Cross
  1913- 25
Brochmann, Elizabeth (Anne)
  1938- 41
Brock, Betty 1923- 7
Brock, C(harles) E(dmund)
  1870-1938 42
  Brief Entry 32
Brock, Delia
  See Ephron, Delia
Brock, Emma L(illian)
  1886-1974 8
Brock, H(enry) M(atthew)
  1875-1960 42
Brockett, Eleanor Hall
  1913-1967 10

Brockman, C(hristian) Frank
1902- 26
Broderick, Dorothy M. 1929- 5
Brodie, Sally
See Cavin, Ruth (Brodie)
Broekel, Rainer Lothar 1923- 38
Broekel, Ray
See Broekel, Rainer Lothar
Bröger, Achim 1944- 31
Brokamp, Marilyn 1920- 10
Bromhall, Winifred 26
Bromley, Dudley 1948-
Brief Entry 51
Brommer, Gerald F(rederick)
1927- 28
Brondfield, Jerome 1913- 22
Brondfield, Jerry
See Brondfield, Jerome
Bronowski, Jacob 1908-1974 55
Bronson, Lynn
See Lampman, Evelyn Sibley
Bronson, Wilfrid Swancourt
1894-1985
Obituary 43
Brook, Judith Penelope 1926-
Brief Entry 51
Brook, Judy
See Brook, Judith Penelope
Brooke, L(eonard) Leslie
1862-1940 17
Brooke-Haven, P.
See Wodehouse, P(elham)
G(renville)
Brookins, Dana 1931- 28
Brooks, Anita 1914- 5
Brooks, Barbara
See Simons, Barbara B(rooks)
Brooks, Bruce
Brief Entry 53
Brooks, Charlotte K. 24
Brooks, Gwendolyn 1917- 6
Brooks, Jerome 1931- 23
Brooks, Lester 1924- 7
Brooks, Maurice (Graham)
1900- 45
Brooks, Polly Schoyer 1912- 12
Brooks, Ron(ald George) 1948-
Brief Entry 33
Brooks, Walter R(ollin)
1886-1958 17
Brosnan, James Patrick 1929- 14
Brosnan, Jim
See Brosnan, James Patrick
Brothers Hildebrandt, The
See Hildebrandt, Greg
See also Hildebrandt, Tim(othy)
Broun, Emily
See Sterne, Emma Gelders
Brower, Millicent 8
Brower, Pauline (York) 1929- 22
Browin, Frances Williams
1898- 5
Brown, Alexis
See Baumann, Amy (Brown)
Brown, Bill
See Brown, William L.
Brown, Billye Walker
See Cutchen, Billye Walker

Brown, Bob
See Brown, Robert Joseph
Brown, Buck 1936- 45
Brown, Cassie 1919-1986 55
Brown, Conrad 1922- 31
Brown, David
See Myller, Rolf
Brown, Dee (Alexander)
1908- 5
Brown, Drollene P. 1939- 53
Brown, Eleanor Frances 1908- 3
Brown, Elizabeth M(yers)
1915- 43
Brown, Fern G. 1918- 34
Brown, (Robert) Fletch 1923- 42
Brown, George Earl
1883-1964 11
Brown, George Mackay 1921- 35
Brown, Irene Bennett 1932- 3
Brown, Irving
See Adams, William Taylor
Brown, Ivor (John Carnegie)
1891-1974 5
Obituary 26
Brown, Joe David 1915-1976 44
Brown, Joseph E(dward) 1929-
Brief Entry 51
Brown, Judith Gwyn 1933- 20
Brown, Laurene Krasny 1945- 54
Brown, Lloyd Arnold
1907-1966 36
Brown, Marc Tolon 1946- 53
Earlier sketch in SATA 10
Brown, Marcia 1918- 47
Earlier sketch in SATA 7
See also CLR 12
Brown, Margaret Wise
1910-1952 ....YABC 2
See also CLR 10
Brown, Margery 5
Brown, Marion Marsh 1908- 6
Brown, Myra Berry 1918- 6
Brown, Palmer 1919- 36
Brown, Pamela 1924- 5
Brown, Robert Joseph 1907- 14
Brown, Rosalie (Gertrude) Moore
1910- 9
Brown, Roswell
See Webb, Jean Francis (III)
Brown, Roy (Frederick)
1921-1982 51
Obituary 39
Brown, Vinson 1912- 19
Brown, Walter R(eed) 1929- 19
Brown, Will
See Ainsworth, William Harrison
Brown, William L(ouis)
1910-1964 5
Browne, Anthony (Edward Tudor)
1946- 45
Brief Entry 44
Browne, Dik
See Browne, Richard
Browne, Hablot Knight
1815-1882 21
Browne, Matthew
See Rands, William Brighty
Browne, Richard 1917-
Brief Entry 38

Browning, Robert
1812-1889 ....YABC 1
Brownjohn, Alan 1931- 6
Bruce, Dorita Fairlie 1885-1970
Obituary 27
Bruce, Mary 1927- 1
Bruchac, Joseph III 1942- 42
Bruck, Lorraine 1921- 55
Brief Entry 46
Bruemmer, Fred 1929- 47
Bruna, Dick 1927- 43
Brief Entry 30
See also CLR 7
Brunhoff, Jean de 1899-1937 24
See also CLR 4
Brunhoff, Laurent de 1925- 24
See also CLR 4
Brustlein, Daniel 1904- 40
Brustlein, Janice Tworkov 40
Bryan, Ashley F. 1923- 31
Bryan, Dorothy (Marie) 1896(?)-1984
Obituary 39
Bryant, Bernice (Morgan)
1908- 11
Brychta, Alex 1956- 21
Bryson, Bernarda 1905- 9
Buba, Joy Flinsch 1904- 44
Buchan, Bryan 1945- 36
Buchan, John 1875-1940 .....YABC 2
Buchan, Stuart 1942-1987
Obituary 54
Buchheimer, Naomi Barnett
See Barnett, Naomi
Buchwald, Art(hur) 1925- 10
Buchwald, Emilie 1935- 7
Buck, Lewis 1925- 18
Buck, Margaret Waring 1910- 3
Buck, Pearl S(ydenstricker)
1892-1973 25
Earlier sketch in SATA 1
Buckeridge, Anthony 1912- 6
Buckholtz, Eileen (Garber)
1949- 54
Brief Entry 47
Buckler, Ernest 1908-1984 47
Buckley, Helen E(lizabeth)
1918- 2
Buckmaster, Henrietta 6
Budd, Lillian 1897- 7
Buehr, Walter 1897-1971 3
Buff, Conrad 1886-1975 19
Buff, Mary Marsh 1890-1970 19
Bugbee, Emma 1888(?)-1981
Obituary 29
Bulfinch, Thomas 1796-1867 35
Bull, Angela (Mary) 1936- 45
Bull, Norman John 1916- 41
Bull, Peter (Cecil) 1912-1984
Obituary 39
Bulla, Clyde Robert 1914- 41
Earlier sketch in SATA 2
See also SAAS 6
Bumstead, Kathleen (Mary)
1918-1987 53
Bunin, Catherine 1967- 30
Bunin, Sherry 1925- 30
Bunting, A. E.
See Bunting, Anne Evelyn
Bunting, Anne Evelyn 1928- 18

Bunting, Eve
  See Bunting, Anne Evelyn
Bunting, Glenn (Davison)
  1957- 22
Burack, Sylvia K. 1916- 35
Burbank, Addison (Buswell)
  1895-1961 37
Burch, Robert J(oseph) 1925- 1
Burchard, Peter D(uncan) 5
Burchard, Sue 1937- 22
Burchardt, Nellie 1921- 7
Burdick, Eugene (Leonard)
  1918-1965 22
Burford, Eleanor
  See Hibbert, Eleanor
Burger, Carl 1888-1967 9
Burgess, Anne Marie
  See Gerson, Noel B(ertram)
Burgess, Em
  See Burgess, Mary Wyche
Burgess, (Frank) Gelett
  1866-1951 32
  Brief Entry 30
Burgess, Mary Wyche 1916- 18
Burgess, Michael
  See Gerson, Noel B(ertram)
Burgess, Robert F(orrest)
  1927- 4
Burgess, Thornton W(aldo)
  1874-1965 17
Burgess, Trevor
  See Trevor, Elleston
Burgwyn, Mebane H. 1914- 7
Burke, David 1927- 46
Burke, John
  See O'Connor, Richard
Burkert, Nancy Ekholm 1933- 24
Burland, Brian (Berkeley)
  1931- 34
Burland, C. A.
  See Burland, Cottie A.
Burland, Cottie A. 1905- 5
Burleigh, Robert 1936- 55
Burlingame, (William) Roger
  1889-1967 2
Burman, Alice Caddy 1896(?)-1977
  Obituary 24
Burman, Ben Lucien
  1896-1984 6
  Obituary 40
Burn, Doris 1923- 1
Burnett, Constance Buel
  1893-1975 36
Burnett, Frances (Eliza) Hodgson
  1849-1924 ....*YABC* 2
Burnford, S. D.
  See Burnford, Sheila
Burnford, Sheila 1918-1984 3
  Obituary 38
  See also CLR 2
Burningham, John (Mackintosh)
  1936- 16
  See also CLR 9
Burns, Marilyn
  Brief Entry 33
Burns, Paul C. 5
Burns, Raymond (Howard)
  1924- 9
Burns, William A. 1909- 5

Burr, Lonnie 1943- 47
Burroughs, Edgar Rice
  1875-1950 41
Burroughs, Jean Mitchell
  1908- 28
Burroughs, Polly 1925- 2
Burroway, Janet (Gay) 1936- 23
Burstein, John 1949- 54
  Brief Entry 40
Burt, Jesse Clifton 1921-1976 46
  Obituary 20
Burt, Olive Woolley 1894- 4
Burton, Hester 1913- 7
  See also CLR 1
Burton, Leslie
  See McGuire, Leslie (Sarah)
Burton, Marilee Robin 1950- 46
Burton, Maurice 1898- 23
Burton, Robert (Wellesley)
  1941- 22
Burton, Virginia Lee
  1909-1968 2
  See also CLR 11
Burton, William H(enry)
  1890-1964 11
Busby, Edith (?)-1964
  Obituary 29
Busch, Phyllis S. 1909- 30
Bushmiller, Ernie 1905-1982
  Obituary 31
Busoni, Rafaello 1900-1962 16
Butler, Beverly 1932- 7
Butler, Suzanne
  See Perreard, Suzanne Louise Butler
Butters, Dorothy Gilman
  1923- 5
Butterworth, Emma Macalik
  1928- 43
Butterworth, Oliver 1915- 1
Butterworth, W(illiam) E(dmund III)
  1929- 5
Byars, Betsy (Cromer) 1928- 46
  Earlier sketch in SATA 4
  See also CLR 1
  See also SAAS 1
Byfield, Barbara Ninde 1930- 8
Byrd, Elizabeth 1912- 34
Byrd, Robert (John) 1942- 33

C

C.3.3.
  See Wilde, Oscar (Fingal O'Flahertie Wills)
Cable, Mary 1920- 9
Cabral, O. M.
  See Cabral, Olga
Cabral, Olga 1909- 46
Caddy, Alice
  See Burman, Alice Caddy
Cadwallader, Sharon 1936- 7
Cady, (Walter) Harrison
  1877-1970 19
Cagle, Malcolm W(infield)
  1918- 32
Cahn, Rhoda 1922- 37
Cahn, William 1912-1976 37
Cain, Arthur H. 1913- 3

Cain, Christopher
  See Fleming, Thomas J(ames)
Caines, Jeanette (Franklin)
  Brief Entry 43
Cairns, Trevor 1922- 14
Caldecott, Moyra 1927- 22
Caldecott, Randolph (J.)
  1846-1886 17
  See also CLR 14
Calder, Lyn
  See Calmenson, Stephanie
Caldwell, John C(ope) 1913- 7
Calhoun, Mary (Huiskamp)
  1926- 2
Calkins, Franklin
  See Stratemeyer, Edward L.
Call, Hughie Florence
  1890-1969 1
Callahan, Dorothy M. 1934- 39
  Brief Entry 35
Callahan, Philip S(erna) 1923- 25
Callaway, Bernice (Anne)
  1923- 48
Callaway, Kathy 1943- 36
Callen, Larry
  See Callen, Lawrence Willard, Jr.
Callen, Lawrence Willard, Jr.
  1927- 19
Calmenson, Stephanie 1952- 51
  Brief Entry 37
Calvert, John
  See Leaf, (Wilbur) Munro
Calvert, Patricia 1931- 45
Cameron, Ann 1943- 27
Cameron, Edna M. 1905- 3
Cameron, Eleanor (Butler)
  1912- 25
  Earlier sketch in SATA 1
  See also CLR 1
Cameron, Elizabeth
  See Nowell, Elizabeth Cameron
Cameron, Elizabeth Jane
  1910-1976 32
  Obituary 30
Cameron, Ian
  See Payne, Donald Gordon
Cameron, Polly 1928- 2
Camp, Charles Lewis 1893-1975
  Obituary 31
Camp, Walter (Chauncey)
  1859-1925 ....*YABC* 1
Campbell, (Elizabeth) Andréa
  1963- 50
Campbell, Ann R. 1925- 11
Campbell, Bruce
  See Epstein, Samuel
Campbell, Camilla 1905- 26
Campbell, Hope 20
Campbell, Jane
  See Edwards, Jane Campbell
Campbell, Patricia J(ean)
  1930- 45
Campbell, Patty
  See Campbell, Patricia J(ean)
Campbell, R. W.
  See Campbell, Rosemae Wells
Campbell, Rod 1945- 51
  Brief Entry 44

Campbell, Rosemae Wells
1909- *1*
Campion, Nardi Reeder 1917- 22
Campling, Elizabeth 1948- 53
Candell, Victor 1903-1977
Obituary 24
Canfield, Dorothy
See Fisher, Dorothy Canfield
Canfield, Jane White
1897-1984 32
Obituary 38
Cannon, Cornelia (James) 1876-1969
Brief Entry 28
Cannon, Ravenna
See Mayhar, Ardath
Canusi, Jose
See Barker, S. Omar
Caplin, Alfred Gerald 1909-1979
Obituary 21
Capp, Al
See Caplin, Alfred Gerald
Cappel, Constance 1936- 22
Capps, Benjamin (Franklin)
1922- 9
Captain Kangaroo
See Keeshan, Robert J.
Captain, W. E. Johns
See Johns, W(illiam) E(arl)
Carafoli, Marci
See Ridlon, Marci
Caras, Roger A(ndrew) 1928- 12
Carbonnier, Jeanne 1894-1974 3
Obituary 34
Care, Felicity
See Coury, Louise Andree
Carew, Jan (Rynveld) 1925- 51
Brief Entry 40
Carey, Bonnie 1941- 18
Carey, Ernestine Gilbreth
1908- 2
Carey, M. V.
See Carey, Mary (Virginia)
Carey, Mary (Virginia) 1925- 44
Brief Entry 39
Carigiet, Alois 1902-1985 24
Obituary 47
Carini, Edward 1923- 9
Carle, Eric 1929- 4
See also CLR 10
See also SAAS 6
Carleton, Captain L. C.
See Ellis, Edward S(ylvester)
Carley, V(an Ness) Royal 1906-1976
Obituary 20
Carlisle, Clark, Jr.
See Holding, James
Carlisle, Olga A(ndreyev)
1930- 35
Carlsen, G(eorge) Robert
1917- 30
Carlsen, Ruth C(hristoffer) 2
Carlson, Bernice Wells 1910- 8
Carlson, Dale Bick 1935- 1
Carlson, Daniel 1960- 27
Carlson, Nancy L(ee) 1953-
Brief Entry 45
Carlson, Natalie Savage 1906- ... 2
See also SAAS 4
Carlson, Vada F. 1897- 16

Carlstrom, Nancy White
1948- 53
Brief Entry 48
Carlyon, Richard 55
Carmer, Carl (Lamson)
1893-1976 37
Obituary 30
Carmer, Elizabeth Black
1904- 24
Carmichael, Carrie 40
Carmichael, Harriet
See Carmichael, Carrie
Carol, Bill J.
See Knott, William Cecil, Jr.
Caroselli, Remus F(rancis)
1916- 36
Carpelan, Bo (Gustaf Bertelsson)
1926- 8
Carpenter, Allan 1917- 3
Carpenter, Frances 1890-1972 3
Obituary 27
Carpenter, Patricia (Healy Evans)
1920- 11
Carr, Glyn
See Styles, Frank Showell
Carr, Harriett Helen 1899- 3
Carr, Mary Jane 1899-1988 2
Obituary 55
Carrick, Carol 1935- 7
Carrick, Donald 1929- 7
Carrick, Malcolm 1945- 28
Carrier, Lark 1947-
Brief Entry 50
Carrighar, Sally 24
Carris, Joan Davenport 1938- 44
Brief Entry 42
Carroll, Curt
See Bishop, Curtis
Carroll, Elizabeth
See Barkin, Carol
See James, Elizabeth
Carroll, Latrobe 7
Carroll, Laura
See Parr, Lucy
Carroll, Lewis
See Dodgson, Charles Lutwidge
See also CLR 2
Carroll, Raymond
Brief Entry 47
Carruth, Hayden 1921- 47
Carse, Robert 1902-1971 5
Carson, Captain James
See Stratemeyer, Edward L.
Carson, John F. 1920- 1
Carson, Rachel (Louise)
1907-1964 23
Carson, Rosalind
See Chittenden, Margaret
Carson, S. M.
See Gorsline, (Sally) Marie
Carter, Bruce
See Hough, Richard (Alexander)
Carter, Dorothy Sharp 1921- 8
Carter, Forrest 1927(?)-1979 32
Carter, Helene 1887-1960 15
Carter, (William) Hodding
1907-1972 2
Obituary 27

Carter, Katharine J(ones)
1905- 2
Carter, Nick
See Lynds, Dennis
Carter, Phyllis Ann
See Eberle, Irmengarde
Carter, Samuel III 1904- 37
Carter, William E. 1926-1983 1
Obituary 35
Cartlidge, Michelle 1950- 49
Brief Entry 37
Cartner, William Carruthers
1910- 11
Cartwright, Sally 1923- 9
Carver, John
See Gardner, Richard
Carwell, L'Ann
See McKissack, Patricia (L'Ann) C(arwell)
Cary
See Cary, Louis F(avreau)
Cary, Barbara Knapp 1912(?)-1975
Obituary 31
Cary, Louis F(avreau) 1915- 9
Caryl, Jean
See Kaplan, Jean Caryl Korn
Case, Marshal T(aylor) 1941- 9
Case, Michael
See Howard, Robert West
Caseley, Judith 1951-
Brief Entry 53
Casewit, Curtis 1922- 4
Casey, Brigid 1950- 9
Casey, Winifred Rosen
See Rosen, Winifred
Cason, Mabel Earp 1892-1965 10
Cass, Joan E(velyn) 1
Cassedy, Sylvia 1930- 27
Cassel, Lili
See Wronker, Lili Cassell
Cassel-Wronker, Lili
See Wronker, Lili Cassell
Castellanos, Jane Mollie (Robinson)
1913- 9
Castellon, Federico 1914-1971 48
Castillo, Edmund L. 1924- 1
Castle, Lee [Joint pseudonym]
See Ogan, George F. and Ogan, Margaret E. (Nettles)
Castle, Paul
See Howard, Vernon (Linwood)
Caswell, Helen (Rayburn)
1923- 12
Cate, Dick
See Cate, Richard (Edward Nelson)
Cate, Richard (Edward Nelson)
1932- 28
Cather, Willa (Sibert)
1873-1947 30
Catherall, Arthur 1906- 3
Cathon, Laura E(lizabeth)
1908- 27
Catlin, Wynelle 1930- 13
Catton, (Charles) Bruce
1899-1978 2
Obituary 24
Catz, Max
See Glaser, Milton
Caudell, Marian 1930- 52

Caudill, Rebecca 1899-1985 ...... *1*
　Obituary *44*
Caulfield, Peggy F. 1926-1987
　Obituary *53*
Cauley, Lorinda Bryan 1951- *46*
　Brief Entry *43*
Cauman, Samuel 1910-1971 ...... *48*
Causley, Charles 1917- *3*
Cavallo, Diana 1931- *7*
Cavanagh, Helen (Carol)
　1939- *48*
　Brief Entry *37*
Cavanah, Frances 1899-1982 ...... *31*
　Earlier sketch in SATA 1
Cavanna, Betty 1909- *30*
　Earlier sketch in SATA 1
　See also SAAS 4
Cavin, Ruth (Brodie) 1918- *38*
Cawley, Winifred 1915- *13*
Caxton, Pisistratus
　See Lytton, Edward G(eorge) E(arle)
　L(ytton) Bulwer-Lytton, Baron
Cazet, Denys 1938- *52*
　Brief Entry *41*
Cebulash, Mel 1937- *10*
Ceder, Georgiana Dorcas *10*
Celestino, Martha Laing
　1951- *39*
Cerf, Bennett 1898-1971 .... *7*
Cerf, Christopher (Bennett)
　1941- *2*
Cermak, Martin
　See Duchacek, Ivo D(uka)
Cervon, Jacqueline
　See Moussard, Jacqueline
Cetin, Frank (Stanley) 1921- *2*
Chadwick, Lester [Collective
　pseudonym] *1*
Chaffee, Allen *3*
Chaffin, Lillie D(orton) 1925- *4*
Chaikin, Miriam 1928- *24*
Challans, Mary 1905-1983 .... *23*
　Obituary *36*
Chalmers, Mary 1927- *6*
Chamberlain, Margaret 1954- *46*
Chambers, Aidan 1934- *1*
Chambers, Bradford 1922-1984
　Obituary *39*
Chambers, Catherine E.
　See Johnston, Norma
Chambers, John W. 1933-
　Brief Entry *46*
Chambers, Margaret Ada Eastwood
　1911- *2*
Chambers, Peggy
　See Chambers, Margaret Ada
　Eastwood
Chandler, Caroline A(ugusta)
　1906-1979 .... *22*
　Obituary *24*
Chandler, David Porter 1933- *28*
Chandler, Edna Walker
　1908-1982 .... *11*
　Obituary *31*
Chandler, Linda S(mith)
　1929- *39*
Chandler, Robert 1953- *40*

Chandler, Ruth Forbes
　1894-1978 .... *2*
　Obituary *26*
Channel, A. R.
　See Catherall, Arthur
Chapian, Marie 1938- *29*
Chapin, Alene Olsen Dalton
　1915(?)-1986
　Obituary *47*
Chapman, Allen [Collective
　pseudonym] *1*
Chapman, (Constance) Elizabeth
　(Mann) 1919- *10*
Chapman, Gaynor 1935- *32*
Chapman, Jean *34*
Chapman, John Stanton Higham
　1891-1972
　Obituary *27*
Chapman, Maristan [Joint pseudonym]
　See Chapman, John Stanton Higham
Chapman, Vera 1898- *33*
Chapman, Walker
　See Silverberg, Robert
Chappell, Warren 1904- *6*
Chardiet, Bernice (Kroll) *27*
Charles, Donald
　See Meighan, Donald Charles
Charles, Louis
　See Stratemeyer, Edward L.
Charlip, Remy 1929- *4*
　See also CLR 8
Charlot, Jean 1898-1979 .... *8*
　Obituary *31*
Charlton, Michael (Alan)
　1923- *34*
Charmatz, Bill 1925- *7*
Charosh, Mannis 1906- *5*
Chase, Alice
　See McHargue, Georgess
Chase, Emily
　See Sachs, Judith
Chase, Mary (Coyle)
　1907-1981 .... *17*
　Obituary *29*
Chase, Mary Ellen 1887-1973 ..... *10*
Chase, Samantha
　See Buckholtz, Eileen (Garber)
Chastain, Madye Lee 1908- *4*
Chauncy, Nan 1900-1970 .... *6*
　See also CLR 6
Chaundler, Christine
　1887-1972 .... *1*
　Obituary *25*
Chen, Tony 1929- *6*
Chenault, Nell
　See Smith, Linell Nash
Chenery, Janet (Dai) 1923- *25*
Cheney, Cora 1916- *3*
Cheney, Ted
　See Cheney, Theodore Albert
Cheney, Theodore Albert
　1928- *11*
Cheng, Judith 1955- *36*
Chermayeff, Ivan 1932- *47*
Chernoff, Dorothy A.
　See Ernst, (Lyman) John
Chernoff, Goldie Taub 1909- *10*
Cherry, Lynne 1952- *34*

Cherryholmes, Anne
　See Price, Olive
Chess, Victoria (Dickerson)
　1939- *33*
Chessare, Michele
　Brief Entry *42*
Chesterton, G(ilbert) K(eith)
　1874-1936 .... *27*
Chetin, Helen 1922- *6*
Chetwin, Grace
　Brief Entry *50*
Chevalier, Christa 1937- *35*
Chew, Ruth *7*
Chidsey, Donald Barr
　1902-1981 .... *3*
　Obituary *27*
Child, Philip 1898-1978 .... *47*
Childress, Alice 1920- *48*
　Earlier sketch in SATA 7
　See also CLR 14
Childs, (Halla) Fay (Cochrane)
　1890-1971 .... *1*
　Obituary *25*
Chimaera
　See Farjeon, Eleanor
Chin, Richard (M.) 1946- *52*
Chinery, Michael 1938- *26*
Chipperfield, Joseph E(ugene)
　1912- *2*
Chittenden, Elizabeth F.
　1903- *9*
Chittenden, Margaret 1933- *28*
Chittum, Ida 1918- *7*
Choate, Judith (Newkirk)
　1940- *30*
Chorao, (Ann Mc)Kay (Sproat)
　1936- *8*
Chorpenning, Charlotte (Lee Barrows)
　1872-1955
　Brief Entry *37*
Chrisman, Arthur Bowie
　1889-1953 .... *YABC 1*
Christelow, Eileen 1943- *38*
　Brief Entry *35*
Christensen, Gardell Dano
　1907- *1*
Christesen, Barbara 1940- *40*
Christgau, Alice Erickson
　1902- *13*
Christian, Mary Blount 1933- *9*
Christie, Agatha (Mary Clarissa)
　1890-1976 .... *36*
Christopher, John
　See Youd, (Christopher) Samuel
　See also CLR 2
Christopher, Louise
　See Hale, Arlene
Christopher, Matt(hew F.)
　1917- *47*
　Earlier sketch in SATA 2
Christopher, Milbourne
　1914(?)-1984 .... *46*
Christy, Howard Chandler
　1873-1952 .... *21*
Chu, Daniel 1933- *11*
Chukovsky, Kornei (Ivanovich)
　1882-1969 .... *34*
　Earlier sketch in SATA 5
Church, Richard 1893-1972 .... *3*

Churchill, E. Richard 1937- *11*
Chute, B(eatrice) J(oy)
    1913-1987 .... *2*
    Obituary 53
Chute, Marchette (Gaylord)
    1909- *1*
Chwast, Jacqueline 1932- *6*
Chwast, Seymour 1931- *18*
Ciardi, John (Anthony)
    1916-1986 .... *1*
    Obituary 46
Clair, Andrée *19*
Clampett, Bob
    Obituary 38
    See also Clampett, Robert
Clampett, Robert
    1914(?)-1984 44
Clapp, Patricia 1912- *4*
    See also SAAS 4
Clare, Helen
    See Hunter, Blair Pauline
Clark, Ann Nolan 1898- *4*
Clark, Champ 1923- 47
Clark, David
    See Hardcastle, Michael
Clark, David Allen
    See Ernst, (Lyman) John
Clark, Frank J(ames) 1922- *18*
Clark, Garel [Joint pseudonym]
    See Garelick, May
Clark, Leonard 1905-1981 30
    Obituary 29
Clark, Margaret Goff 1913- *8*
Clark, Mary Higgins 46
Clark, Mavis Thorpe *8*
    See also SAAS 5
Clark, Merle
    See Gessner, Lynne
Clark, Patricia (Finrow) 1929- *11*
Clark, Ronald William
    1916-1987 .... *2*
    Obituary 52
Clark, Van D(eusen) 1909- *2*
Clark, Virginia
    See Gray, Patricia
Clark, Walter Van Tilburg
    1909-1971 .... *8*
Clarke, Arthur C(harles)
    1917- *13*
Clarke, Clorinda 1917- *7*
Clarke, Joan 1921- 42
    Brief Entry 27
Clarke, John
    See Laklan, Carli
Clarke, Mary Stetson 1911- *5*
Clarke, Michael
    See Newlon, Clarke
Clarke, Pauline
    See Hunter Blair, Pauline
Clarkson, E(dith) Margaret
    1915- 37
Clarkson, Ewan 1929- *9*
Claverie, Jean 1946- 38
Clay, Patrice 1947- 47
Claypool, Jane
    See Miner, Jane Claypool
Cleary, Beverly (Bunn) 1916- 43
    Earlier sketch in SATA 2
    See also CLR 2, 8

Cleaver, Bill 1920-1981 22
    Obituary 27
    See also CLR 6
Cleaver, Carole 1934- *6*
Cleaver, Elizabeth (Mrazik)
    1939-1985 23
    Obituary 43
    See also CLR 13
Cleaver, Hylton (Reginald)
    1891-1961 49
Cleaver, Vera 22
    See also CLR 6
Cleishbotham, Jebediah
    See Scott, Sir Walter
Cleland, Mabel
    See Widdemer, Mabel Cleland
Clemens, Samuel Langhorne
    1835-1910 ....*YABC 2*
Clemens, Virginia Phelps
    1941- 35
Clements, Bruce 1931- 27
Clemons, Elizabeth
    See Nowell, Elizabeth Cameron
Clerk, N. W.
    See Lewis, C. S.
Cleveland, Bob
    See Cleveland, George
Cleveland, George 1903(?)-1985
    Obituary 43
Cleven, Cathrine
    See Cleven, Kathryn Seward
Cleven, Kathryn Seward *2*
Clevin, Jörgen 1920- *7*
Clewes, Dorothy (Mary)
    1907- *1*
Clifford, Eth
    See Rosenberg, Ethel
Clifford, Harold B. 1893- *10*
Clifford, Margaret Cort 1929- *1*
Clifford, Martin
    See Hamilton, Charles H. St. John
Clifford, Mary Louise (Beneway)
    1926- 23
Clifford, Peggy
    See Clifford, Margaret Cort
Clifton, Harry
    See Hamilton, Charles H. St. John
Clifton, Lucille 1936- 20
    See also CLR 5
Clifton, Martin
    See Hamilton, Charles H. St. John
Climo, Shirley 1928- 39
    Brief Entry 35
Clinton, Jon
    See Prince, J(ack) H(arvey)
Clish, (Lee) Marian 1946- 43
Clive, Clifford
    See Hamilton, Charles H. St. John
Cloudsley-Thompson, J(ohn) L(eonard)
    1921- *19*
Clymer, Eleanor 1906- *9*
Clyne, Patricia Edwards 31
Coalson, Glo 1946- 26
Coates, Belle 1896- *2*
Coates, Ruth Allison 1915- *11*
Coats, Alice M(argaret) 1905- *11*
Coatsworth, Elizabeth
    1893-1986 .... *2*
    Obituary 49
    See also CLR 2

Cobb, Jane
    See Berry, Jane Cobb
Cobb, Vicki 1938- *8*
    See also CLR 2
    See also SAAS 6
Cobbett, Richard
    See Pluckrose, Henry (Arthur)
Cober, Alan E. 1935- *7*
Cobham, Sir Alan
    See Hamilton, Charles H. St. John
Cocagnac, A(ugustin) M(aurice-Jean)
    1924- *7*
Cochran, Bobbye A. 1949- *11*
Cockett, Mary *3*
Coe, Douglas [Joint pseudonym]
    See Epstein, Beryl and Epstein,
    Samuel
Coe, Lloyd 1899-1976
    Obituary 30
Coen, Rena Neumann 1925- 20
Coerr, Eleanor 1922- *1*
Coffin, Geoffrey
    See Mason, F. van Wyck
Coffman, Ramon Peyton
    1896- *4*
Coggins, Jack (Banham)
    1911- *2*
Cohen, Barbara 1932- *10*
    See also SAAS 7
Cohen, Daniel 1936- *8*
    See also CLR 3
    See also SAAS 4
Cohen, Jene Barr
    See Barr, Jene
Cohen, Joan Lebold 1932- *4*
Cohen, Miriam 1926- 29
Cohen, Peter Zachary 1931- *4*
Cohen, Robert Carl 1930- *8*
Cohn, Angelo 1914- *19*
Coit, Margaret L(ouise) *2*
Colbert, Anthony 1934- *15*
Colby, C(arroll) B(urleigh)
    1904-1977 35
    Earlier sketch in SATA 3
Colby, Jean Poindexter 1909- 23
Cole, Annette
    See Steiner, Barbara A(nnette)
Cole, Davis
    See Elting, Mary
Cole, Jack
    See Stewart, John (William)
Cole, Jackson
    See Schisgall, Oscar
Cole, Jennifer
    See Zach, Cheryl (Byrd)
Cole, Joanna 1944- 49
    Brief Entry 37
    See also CLR 5
Cole, Lois Dwight
    1903(?)-1979 .... *10*
    Obituary 26
Cole, Sheila R(otenberg)
    1939- 24
Cole, William (Rossa) 1919- *9*
Coleman, William L(eRoy)
    1938- 49
    Brief Entry 34
Coles, Robert (Martin) 1929- 23

Colin, Ann
  See Ure, Jean
Collier, Christopher 1930- *16*
Collier, Ethel 1903- *22*
Collier, James Lincoln 1928- *8*
  See also CLR 3
Collier, Jane
  See Collier, Zena
Collier, Zena 1926- *23*
Collins, David 1940- *7*
Collins, Hunt
  See Hunter, Evan
Collins, Michael
  See Lynds, Dennis
Collins, Pat Lowery 1932- *31*
Collins, Ruth Philpott 1890-1975
  Obituary *30*
Collodi, Carlo
  See Lorenzini, Carlo
  See also CLR 5
Colloms, Brenda 1919- *40*
Colman, Hila *53*
  Earlier sketch in SATA 1
Colman, Morris 1899(?)-1981
  Obituary *25*
Colombo, John Robert 1936- *50*
Colonius, Lillian 1911- *3*
Colorado (Capella), Antonio J(ulio)
  1903- *23*
Colt, Martin [Joint pseudonym]
  See Epstein, Beryl and Epstein,
    Samuel
Colum, Padraic 1881-1972 .... *15*
Columella
  See Moore, Clement Clarke
Colver, Anne 1908- *7*
Colwell, Eileen (Hilda) 1904- *2*
Combs, Robert
  See Murray, John
Comfort, Jane Levington
  See Sturtzel, Jane Levington
Comfort, Mildred Houghton
  1886- *3*
Comins, Ethel M(ae) *11*
Comins, Jeremy 1933- *28*
Commager, Henry Steele
  1902- *23*
Comus
  See Ballantyne, R(obert) M(ichael)
Conan Doyle, Arthur
  See Doyle, Arthur Conan
Condit, Martha Olson 1913- *28*
Cone, Ferne Geller 1921- *39*
Cone, Molly (Lamken) 1918- *28*
  Earlier sketch in SATA 1
Conford, Ellen 1942- *6*
  See also CLR 10
Conger, Lesley
  See Suttles, Shirley (Smith)
Conklin, Gladys (Plemon)
  1903- *2*
Conklin, Paul S. *43*
  Brief Entry *33*
Conkling, Hilda 1910- *23*
Conly, Robert Leslie
  1918(?)-1973 .... *23*
Connell, Kirk [Joint pseudonym]
  See Chapman, John Stanton Higham

Connelly, Marc(us Cook) 1890-1980
  Obituary *25*
Connolly, Jerome P(atrick)
  1931- *8*
Connolly, Peter 1935- *47*
Conover, Chris 1950- *31*
Conquest, Owen
  See Hamilton, Charles H. St. John
Conrad, Joseph 1857-1924 .... *27*
Conrad, Pam(ela) 1947- *52*
  Brief Entry *49*
Conroy, Jack (Wesley) 1899- *19*
Conroy, John
  See Conroy, Jack (Wesley)
Constant, Alberta Wilson
  1908-1981 .... *22*
  Obituary *28*
Conway, Gordon
  See Hamilton, Charles H. St. John
Cook, Bernadine 1924- *11*
Cook, Fred J(ames) 1911- *2*
Cook, Joseph J(ay) 1924- *8*
Cook, Lyn
  See Waddell, Evelyn Margaret
Cooke, Ann
  See Cole, Joanna
Cooke, David Coxe 1917- *2*
Cooke, Donald Ewin
  1916-1985 .... *2*
  Obituary *45*
Cookson, Catherine (McMullen)
  1906- *9*
Coolidge, Olivia E(nsor)
  1908- *26*
  Earlier sketch in SATA 1
Coombs, Charles I(ra) 1914- *43*
  Earlier sketch in SATA 3
Coombs, Chick
  See Coombs, Charles I(ra)
Coombs, Patricia 1926- *51*
  Earlier sketch in SATA 3
Cooney, Barbara 1917- *6*
Cooney, Caroline B. 1947- *48*
  Brief Entry *41*
Cooney, Nancy Evans 1932- *42*
Coontz, Otto 1946- *33*
Cooper, Elizabeth Keyser *47*
Cooper, Gordon 1932- *23*
Cooper, James Fenimore
  1789-1851 .... *19*
Cooper, James R.
  See Stratemeyer, Edward L.
Cooper, John R. [Collective
  pseudonym] *1*
Cooper, Kay 1941- *11*
Cooper, Lee (Pelham) *5*
Cooper, Lester (Irving)
  1919-1985 .... *32*
  Obituary *43*
Cooper, Lettice (Ulpha) 1897- *35*
Cooper, Susan 1935- *4*
  See also CLR 4
  See also SAAS 6
Copeland, Helen 1920- *4*
Copeland, Paul W. *23*
Copley, (Diana) Heather Pickering
  1918- *45*
Coppard, A(lfred) E(dgar)
  1878-1957 .... *YABC 1*

Corbett, Grahame *43*
  Brief Entry *36*
Corbett, Scott 1913- *42*
  Earlier sketch in SATA 2
  See also CLR 1
  See also SAAS 2
Corbett, W(illiam) J(esse)
  1938- *50*
  Brief Entry *44*
Corbin, Sabra Lee
  See Malvern, Gladys
Corbin, William
  See McGraw, William Corbin
Corby, Dan
  See Catherall, Arthur
Corcoran, Barbara 1911- *3*
Corcos, Lucille 1908-1973 .... *10*
Cordell, Alexander
  See Graber, Alexander
Coren, Alan 1938- *32*
Corey, Dorothy *23*
Corfe, Thomas Howell 1928- *27*
Corfe, Tom
  See Corfe, Thomas Howell
Corlett, William 1938- *46*
  Brief Entry *39*
Cormack, M(argaret) Grant
  1913- *11*
Cormack, Maribelle B.
  1902-1984 .... *39*
Cormier, Robert (Edmund)
  1925- *45*
  Earlier sketch in SATA 10
  See also CLR 12
Cornelius, Carol 1942- *40*
Cornell, J.
  See Cornell, Jeffrey
Cornell, James (Clayton, Jr.)
  1938- *27*
Cornell, Jean Gay 1920- *23*
Cornell, Jeffrey 1945- *11*
Cornish, Samuel James 1935- *23*
Cornwall, Nellie
  See Sloggett, Nellie
Correy, Lee
  See Stine, G. Harry
Corrigan, (Helen) Adeline
  1909- *23*
Corrigan, Barbara 1922- *8*
Corrin, Sara 1918-
  Brief Entry *48*
Corrin, Stephen
  Brief Entry *48*
Cort, M. C.
  See Clifford, Margaret Cort
Corwin, Judith Hoffman
  1946- *10*
Cosgrave, John O'Hara II 1908-1968
  Obituary *21*
Cosgrove, Margaret (Leota)
  1926- *47*
Cosgrove, Stephen E(dward)
  1945- *53*
  Brief Entry *40*
Coskey, Evelyn 1932- *7*
Cosner, Shaaron 1940- *43*
Costabel, Eva Deutsch 1924- *45*
Costello, David F(rancis)
  1904- *23*

Cott, Jonathan 1942- 23
Cottam, Clarence 1899-1974 25
Cottler, Joseph 1899- 22
Cottrell, Leonard 1913-1974 24
The Countryman
  See Whitlock, Ralph
Courlander, Harold 1908- 6
Courtis, Stuart Appleton 1874-1969
  Obituary 29
Coury, Louise Andree 1895(?)-1983
  Obituary 34
Cousins, Margaret 1905- 2
Cousteau, Jacques-Yves 1910- 38
Coville, Bruce 1950- 32
Cowen, Eve
  See Werner, Herma
Cowie, Leonard W(allace)
  1919- 4
Cowles, Kathleen
  See Krull, Kathleen
Cowley, Joy 1936- 4
Cox, Donald William 1921- 23
Cox, Jack
  See Cox, John Roberts
Cox, John Roberts 1915- 9
Cox, Palmer 1840-1924 24
Cox, Victoria
  See Garretson, Victoria Diane
Cox, Wally 1924-1973 25
Cox, William R(obert) 1901- 46
  Brief Entry 31
Coy, Harold 1902- 3
Craft, Ruth
  Brief Entry 31
Craig, A. A.
  See Anderson, Poul (William)
Craig, Alisa
  See MacLeod, Charlotte (Matilda
  Hughes)
Craig, Helen 1934- 49
  Brief Entry 46
Craig, John Eland
  See Chipperfield, Joseph
Craig, John Ernest 1921- 23
Craig, M. Jean 17
Craig, Margaret Maze
  1911-1964 9
Craig, Mary Francis 1923- 6
  See also SAAS 7
Craik, Dinah Maria (Mulock)
  1826-1887 34
Crane, Barbara J. 1934- 31
Crane, Caroline 1930- 11
Crane, M. A.
  See Wartski, Maureen (Ann Crane)
Crane, Roy
  See Crane, Royston Campbell
Crane, Royston Campbell 1901-1977
  Obituary 22
Crane, Stephen (Townley)
  1871-1900 .... *YABC* 2
Crane, Walter 1845-1915 18
Crane, William D(wight)
  1892- 1
Crary, Elizabeth (Ann) 1942-
  Brief Entry 43
Crary, Margaret (Coleman)
  1906- 9
Craven, Thomas 1889-1969 22

Crawford, Charles P. 1945- 28
Crawford, Deborah 1922- 6
Crawford, John E. 1904-1971 3
Crawford, Mel 1925- 44
  Brief Entry 33
Crawford, Phyllis 1899- 3
Craz, Albert G. 1926- 24
Crayder, Dorothy 1906- 7
Crayder, Teresa
  See Colman, Hila
Crayon, Geoffrey
  See Irving, Washington
Crecy, Jeanne
  See Williams, Jeanne
Credle, Ellis 1902- 1
Cresswell, Helen 1934- 48
  Earlier sketch in SATA 1
Cretan, Gladys (Yessayan)
  1921- 2
Crew, Helen (Cecilia) Coale
  1866-1941 .... *YABC* 2
Crews, Donald 1938- 32
  Brief Entry 30
  See also CLR 7
Crichton, (J.) Michael 1942- 9
Crofut, Bill
  See Crofut, William E. III
Crofut, William E. III 1934- 23
Croll, Carolyn 1945-
  Brief Entry 52
Croman, Dorothy Young
  See Rosenberg, Dorothy
Cromie, Alice Hamilton 1914- 24
Cromie, William J(oseph)
  1930- 4
Crompton, Anne Eliot 1930- 23
Crompton, Richmal
  See Lamburn, Richmal Crompton
Cronbach, Abraham
  1882-1965 11
Crone, Ruth 1919- 4
Cronin, A(rchibald) J(oseph)
  1896-1981 47
  Obituary 25
Crook, Beverly Courtney 38
  Brief Entry 35
Cros, Earl
  See Rose, Carl
Crosby, Alexander L.
  1906-1980 2
  Obituary 23
Crosher, G(eoffry) R(obins)
  1911- 14
Cross, Gilbert B. 1939-
  Brief Entry 51
Cross, Gillian (Clare) 1945- 38
Cross, Helen Reeder
  See Broadhead, Helen Cross
Cross, Wilbur Lucius III
  1918- 2
Crossley-Holland, Kevin 5
Crouch, Marcus 1913- 4
Crout, George C(lement)
  1917- 11
Crow, Donna Fletcher 1941- 40
Crowe, Bettina Lum 1911- 6
Crowe, John
  See Lynds, Dennis

Crowell, Grace Noll
  1877-1969 34
Crowell, Pers 1910- 2
Crowfield, Christopher
  See Stowe, Harriet (Elizabeth)
  Beecher
Crowley, Arthur M(cBlair)
  1945- 38
Crownfield, Gertrude
  1867-1945 .... *YABC* 1
Crowther, James Gerald 1899- 14
Cruikshank, George
  1792-1878 22
Crump, Fred H., Jr. 1931- 11
Crump, J(ames) Irving 1887-1979
  Obituary 21
Crunden, Reginald
  See Cleaver, Hylton (Reginald)
Crutcher, Chris(topher C.)
  1946- 52
Cruz, Ray 1933- 6
Ctvrtek, Vaclav 1911-1976
  Obituary 27
Cuffari, Richard 1925-1978 6
  Obituary 25
Cullen, Countee 1903-1946 18
Culliford, Pierre 1928- 40
Culp, Louanna McNary
  1901-1965 2
Cumming, Primrose (Amy)
  1915- 24
Cummings, Betty Sue 1918- 15
Cummings, Parke 1902-1987 2
  Obituary 53
Cummings, Pat 1950- 42
Cummings, Richard
  See Gardner, Richard
Cummins, Maria Susanna
  1827-1866 .... *YABC* 1
Cunliffe, John Arthur 1933- 11
Cunliffe, Marcus (Falkner)
  1922- 37
Cunningham, Captain Frank
  See Glick, Carl (Cannon)
Cunningham, Cathy
  See Cunningham, Chet
Cunningham, Chet 1928- 23
Cunningham, Dale S(peers)
  1932- 11
Cunningham, E.V.
  See Fast, Howard
Cunningham, Julia W(oolfolk)
  1916- 26
  Earlier sketch in SATA 1
  See also SAAS 2
Cunningham, Virginia
  See Holmgren, Virginia
  C(unningham)
Curiae, Amicus
  See Fuller, Edmund (Maybank)
Curie, Eve 1904- 1
Curley, Daniel 1918- 23
Curry, Jane L(ouise) 1932- 52
  Earlier sketch in SATA 1
  See also SAAS 6
Curry, Peggy Simson
  1911-1987 8
  Obituary 50
Curtis, Bruce (Richard) 1944- 30

Curtis, Patricia 1921- 23
Curtis, Peter
   See Lofts, Norah (Robinson)
Curtis, Richard (Alan) 1937- 29
Curtis, Wade
   See Pournelle, Jerry (Eugene)
Cushman, Jerome 2
Cutchen, Billye Walker 1930- 15
Cutler, (May) Ebbitt 1923- 9
Cutler, Ivor 1923- 24
Cutler, Samuel
   See Folsom, Franklin
Cutt, W(illiam) Towrie 1898- 16
Cuyler, Margery Stuyvesant
   1948- 39
Cuyler, Stephen
   See Bates, Barbara S(nedeker)

D

Dabcovich, Lydia
   Brief Entry 47
Dahl, Borghild 1890-1984 7
   Obituary 37
Dahl, Roald 1916- 26
   Earlier sketch in SATA 1
   See also CLR 1; 7
Dahlstedt, Marden 1921- 8
Dain, Martin J. 1924- 35
Dale, Jack
   See Holliday, Joseph
Dale, Margaret J(essy) Miller
   1911- 39
Dale, Norman
   See Denny, Norman (George)
Dalgliesh, Alice 1893-1979 17
   Obituary 21
Dalton, Alene
   See Chapin, Alene Olsen Dalton
Dalton, Anne 1948- 40
Daly, Jim
   See Stratemeyer, Edward L.
Daly, Kathleen N(orah)
   Brief Entry 37
Daly, Maureen 2
   See also SAAS 1
Daly, Nicholas 1946- 37
Daly, Niki
   See Daly, Nicholas
D'Amato, Alex 1919- 20
D'Amato, Janet 1925- 9
Damrosch, Helen Therese
   See Tee-Van, Helen Damrosch
Dana, Barbara 1940- 22
Dana, Richard Henry, Jr.
   1815-1882 26
Danachair, Caoimhin O.
   See Danaher, Kevin
Danaher, Kevin 1913- 22
D'Andrea, Kate
   See Steiner, Barbara A(nnette)
Dangerfield, Balfour
   See McCloskey, Robert
Daniel, Alan 1939-
   Brief Entry 53
Daniel, Anita 1893(?)-1978 23
   Obituary 24

Daniel, Anne
   See Steiner, Barbara A(nnette)
Daniel, Hawthorne 1890- 8
Daniels, Guy 1919- 11
Dank, Gloria Rand 1955-
   Brief Entry 46
Dank, Leonard D(ewey)
   1929- 44
Dank, Milton 1920- 31
Danziger, Paula 1944- 36
   Brief Entry 30
Darby, J. N.
   See Govan, Christine Noble
Darby, Patricia (Paulsen) 14
Darby, Ray K. 1912- 7
Daringer, Helen Fern 1892- 1
Darke, Marjorie 1929- 16
Darley, F(elix) O(ctavius) C(arr)
   1822-1888 35
Darling, David J.
   Brief Entry 44
Darling, Kathy
   See Darling, Mary Kathleen
Darling, Lois M. 1917- 3
Darling, Louis, Jr. 1916-1970 3
   Obituary 23
Darling, Mary Kathleen 1943- 9
Darrow, Whitney, Jr. 1909- 13
Darwin, Len
   See Darwin, Leonard
Darwin, Leonard 1916- 24
Dasent, Sir George Webbe 1817-1896
   Brief Entry 29
Daskam, Josephine Dodge
   See Bacon, Josephine Dodge
   (Daskam)
Dauer, Rosamond 1934- 23
Daugherty, Charles Michael
   1914- 16
Daugherty, James (Henry)
   1889-1974 13
Daugherty, Richard D(eo)
   1922- 35
Daugherty, Sonia Medwedeff (?)-1971
   Obituary 27
d'Aulaire, Edgar Parin
   1898-1986 5
   Obituary 47
d'Aulaire, Ingri (Maartenson Parin)
   1904-1980 5
   Obituary 24
Daveluy, Paule Cloutier 1919- 11
Davenport, Spencer
   See Stratemeyer, Edward L.
Daves, Michael 1938- 40
David, Jonathan
   See Ames, Lee J.
Davidson, Alice Joyce 1932- 54
   Brief Entry 45
Davidson, Basil 1914- 13
Davidson, Jessica 1915- 5
Davidson, Judith 1953- 40
Davidson, Margaret 1936- 5
Davidson, Marion
   See Garis, Howard R(oger)
Davidson, Mary R.
   1885-1973 9
Davidson, R.
   See Davidson, Raymond

Davidson, Raymond 1926- 32
Davidson, Rosalie 1921- 23
Davies, Andrew (Wynford)
   1936- 27
Davies, Bettilu D(onna) 1942- 33
Davies, (Edward) Hunter
   1936- 55
   Brief Entry 45
Davies, Joan 1934- 50
   Brief Entry 47
Davies, Peter 1937- 52
Davies, Sumiko 1942- 46
Davis, Bette J. 1923- 15
Davis, Burke 1913- 4
Davis, Christopher 1928- 6
Davis, D(elbert) Dwight
   1908-1965 33
Davis, Daniel S(heldon) 1936- 12
Davis, Gibbs 1953- 46
   Brief Entry 41
Davis, Grania 1943-
   Brief Entry 50
Davis, Hubert J(ackson) 1904- 31
Davis, James Robert 1945- 32
Davis, Jim
   See Davis, James Robert
Davis, Julia 1904- 6
Davis, Louise Littleton 1921- 25
Davis, Marguerite 1889- 34
Davis, Mary L(ee) 1935- 9
Davis, Mary Octavia 1901- 6
Davis, Paxton 1925- 16
Davis, Robert
   1881-1949 ....YABC 1
Davis, Russell G. 1922- 3
Davis, Verne T. 1889-1973 6
Dawson, Elmer A. [Collective
   pseudonym] 1
Dawson, Mary 1919- 11
Day, Beth (Feagles) 1924- 33
Day, Maurice 1892-
   Brief Entry 30
Day, Thomas 1748-1789 .....YABC 1
Dazey, Agnes J(ohnston) 2
Dazey, Frank M. 2
Deacon, Eileen
   See Geipel, Eileen
Deacon, Richard
   See McCormick, (George) Donald
   (King)
Dean, Anabel 1915- 12
Dean, Karen Strickler 1923- 49
de Angeli, Marguerite
   1889-1987 27
   Obituary 51
   Earlier sketch in SATA 1
   See also CLR 1
DeArmand, Frances Ullmann
   1904(?)-1984 10
   Obituary 38
Deary, Terry 1946- 51
   Brief Entry 41
deBanke, Cecile 1889-1965 11
De Bruyn, Monica 1952- 13
de Camp, Catherine C(rook)
   1907- 12
DeCamp, L(yon) Sprague
   1907- 9
Decker, Duane 1910-1964 5

DeClements, Barthe 1920- 35
Deedy, John 1923- 24
Deegan, Paul Joseph 1937- 48
  Brief Entry 38
Defoe, Daniel 1660(?)-1731 22
deFrance, Anthony
  See Di Franco, Anthony (Mario)
Degen, Bruce
  Brief Entry 47
DeGering, Etta 1898- 7
De Grazia
  See De Grazia, Ted
De Grazia, Ted 1909-1982 39
De Grazia, Ettore
  See De Grazia, Ted
De Groat, Diane 1947- 31
deGros, J. H.
  See Villiard, Paul
de Grummond, Lena Young 6
Deiss, Joseph J. 1915- 12
DeJong, David C(ornel)
  1905-1967 10
de Jong, Dola 7
De Jong, Meindert 1906- 2
  See also CLR 1
de Kay, Ormonde, Jr. 1923- 7
de Kiriline, Louise
  See Lawrence, Louise de Kiriline
Dekker, Carl
  See Laffin, John (Alfred Charles)
Dekker, Carl
  See Lynds, Dennis
deKruif, Paul (Henry)
  1890-1971 50
  Earlier sketch in SATA 5
Delacre, Lulu 1957- 36
De Lage, Ida 1918- 11
de la Mare, Walter 1873-1956 16
Delaney, Harry 1932- 3
Delaney, Ned 1951- 28
Delano, Hugh 1933- 20
De La Ramée, (Marie) Louise
  1839-1908 20
Delaune, Lynne 7
DeLaurentis, Louise Budde
  1920- 12
Delderfield, Eric R(aymond)
  1909- 14
Delderfield, R(onald) F(rederick)
  1912-1972 20
De Leeuw, Adele Louise
  1899- 30
  Earlier sketch in SATA 1
Delessert, Etienne 1941- 46
  Brief Entry 27
Delmar, Roy
  See Wexler, Jerome (LeRoy)
Deloria, Vine (Victor), Jr.
  1933- 21
Del Rey, Lester 1915- 22
Delton, Judy 1931- 14
Delulio, John 1938- 15
Delving, Michael
  See Williams, Jay
Demarest, Chris(topher) L(ynn)
  1951- 45
  Brief Entry 44
Demarest, Doug
  See Barker, Will

Demas, Vida 1927- 9
De Mejo, Oscar 1911- 40
de Messières, Nicole 1930- 39
Demijohn, Thom
  See Disch, Thomas M(ichael)
Deming, Richard 1915- 24
Demuth, Patricia Brennan 1948-
  Brief Entry 51
Dengler, Sandy 1939- 54
  Brief Entry 40
Denmark, Harrison
  See Zelazny, Roger (Joseph
  Christopher)
Denney, Diana 1910- 25
Dennis, Morgan 1891(?)-1960 18
Dennis, Wesley 1903-1966 18
Denniston, Elinore 1900-1978
  Obituary 24
Denny, Norman (George)
  1901-1982 43
Denslow, W(illiam) W(allace)
  1856-1915 16
  See also CLR 15
Denzel, Justin F(rancis) 1917- 46
  Brief Entry 38
Denzer, Ann Wiseman
  See Wiseman, Ann (Sayre)
de Paola, Thomas Anthony
  1934- 11
de Paola, Tomie
  See de Paola, Thomas Anthony
  See also CLR 4
DePauw, Linda Grant 1940- 24
deRegniers, Beatrice Schenk
  (Freedman) 1914- 2
  See also SAAS 6
Derleth, August (William)
  1909-1971 5
Derman, Sarah Audrey 1915- 11
de Roo, Anne Louise 1931- 25
De Roussan, Jacques 1929-
  Brief Entry 31
Derry Down Derry
  See Lear, Edward
Derwent, Lavinia 14
Desbarats, Peter 1933- 39
De Selincourt, Aubrey
  1894-1962 14
Desmond, Adrian J(ohn)
  1947- 51
Desmond, Alice Curtis 1897- 8
Detine, Padre
  See Olsen, Ib Spang
Deutsch, Babette 1895-1982 1
  Obituary 33
De Valera, Sinead 1870(?)-1975
  Obituary 30
Devaney, John 1926- 12
Devereux, Frederick L(eonard), Jr.
  1914- 9
Devlin, Harry 1918- 11
Devlin, (Dorothy) Wende
  1918- 11
DeWaard, E. John 1935- 7
DeWeese, Gene
  See DeWeese, Thomas Eugene
DeWeese, Jean
  See DeWeese, Thomas Eugene

DeWeese, Thomas Eugene
  1934- 46
  Brief Entry 45
Dewey, Ariane 1937- 7
Dewey, Jennifer (Owings)
  Brief Entry 48
Dewey, Ken(neth Francis)
  1940- 39
DeWit, Dorothy (May Knowles)
  1916-1980 39
  Obituary 28
Deyneka, Anita 1943- 24
Deyrup, Astrith Johnson
  1923- 24
Diamond, Donna 1950- 35
  Brief Entry 30
Diamond, Petra
  See Sachs, Judith
Diamond, Rebecca
  See Sachs, Judith
Dias, Earl Joseph 1916- 41
Dick, Cappy
  See Cleveland, George
Dick, Trella Lamson
  1889-1974 9
Dickens, Charles 1812-1870 15
Dickens, Frank
  See Huline-Dickens, Frank William
Dickens, Monica 1915- 4
Dickerson, Roy Ernest 1886-1965
  Obituary 26
Dickinson, Emily (Elizabeth)
  1830-1886 29
Dickinson, Mary 1949- 48
  Brief Entry 41
Dickinson, Peter 1927- 5
Dickinson, Susan 1931- 8
Dickinson, William Croft
  1897-1973 13
Dickmeyer, Lowell A. 1939-
  Brief Entry 51
Dickson, Helen
  See Reynolds, Helen Mary
  Greenwood Campbell
Dickson, Naida 1916- 8
Dietz, David H(enry)
  1897-1984 10
  Obituary 41
Dietz, Lew 1907- 11
Di Franco, Anthony (Mario)
  1945- 42
Digges, Jeremiah
  See Berger, Josef
D'Ignazio, Fred 1949- 39
  Brief Entry 35
Di Grazia, Thomas (?)-1983 32
Dillard, Annie 1945- 10
Dillard, Polly (Hargis) 1916- 24
Dillon, Barbara 1927- 44
  Brief Entry 39
Dillon, Diane 1933- 51
  Earlier sketch in SATA 15
Dillon, Eilis 1920- 2
Dillon, Leo 1933- 51
  Earlier sketch in SATA 15
Dilson, Jesse 1914- 24
Dinan, Carolyn
  Brief Entry 47
Dines, Glen 1925- 7

Dinesen, Isak
  See Blixen, Karen (Christentze Dinesen)
Dinnerstein, Harvey 1928- *42*
Dinsdale, Tim 1924- *11*
Dirks, Rudolph 1877-1968
  Brief Entry *31*
Disch, Thomas M(ichael)
  1940- *54*
Disney, Walt(er Elias)
  1901-1966 .... *28*
  Brief Entry *27*
DiValentin, Maria 1911- *7*
Divine, Arthur Durham 1904-1987
  Obituary *52*
Divine, David
  See Divine, Arthur Durham
Dixon, Dougal 1947- *45*
Dixon, Franklin W. [Collective
  pseudonym] *1*
  See also Adams, Harriet
  S(tratemeyer); McFarlane, Leslie;
  Stratemeyer, Edward L.; Svenson,
  Andrew E.
Dixon, Jeanne 1936- *31*
Dixon, Peter L. 1931- *6*
Doane, Pelagie 1906-1966 .... *7*
Dobell, I(sabel) M(arian) B(arclay)
  1909- *11*
Dobie, J(ames) Frank
  1888-1964 .... *43*
Dobkin, Alexander 1908-1975
  Obituary *30*
Dobler, Lavinia G. 1910- *6*
Dobrin, Arnold 1928- *4*
Dobson, Julia 1941- *48*
Dockery, Wallene T. 1941- *27*
"Dr. A"
  See Silverstein, Alvin
Dr. X
  See Nourse, Alan E(dward)
Dodd, Ed(ward) Benton 1902- *4*
Dodd, Lynley (Stuart) 1941- *35*
Dodge, Bertha S(anford)
  1902- *8*
Dodge, Mary (Elizabeth) Mapes
  1831-1905 .... *21*
Dodgson, Charles Lutwidge
  1832-1898 .... *YABC 2*
Dodson, Kenneth M(acKenzie)
  1907- *11*
Dodson, Susan 1941- *50*
  Brief Entry *40*
Doerksen, Nan 1934-
  Brief Entry *50*
Doherty, C. H. 1913- *6*
Dolan, Edward F(rancis), Jr.
  1924- *45*
  Brief Entry *31*
Dolch, Edward William
  1889-1961 .... *50*
Dolch, Marguerite Pierce
  1891-1978 .... *50*
Dolson, Hildegarde 1908- *5*
Domanska, Janina *6*
Domino, John
  See Averill, Esther
Domjan, Joseph 1907- *25*

Donalds, Gordon
  See Shirreffs, Gordon D.
Donna, Natalie 1934- *9*
Donovan, Frank (Robert) 1906-1975
  Obituary *30*
Donovan, John 1928-
  Brief Entry *29*
  See also CLR 3
Donovan, William
  See Berkebile, Fred D(onovan)
Doob, Leonard W(illiam)
  1909- *8*
Dor, Ana
  See Ceder, Georgiana Dorcas
Doré, (Louis Christophe Paul) Gustave
  1832-1883 .... *19*
Doremus, Robert 1913- *30*
Dorian, Edith M(cEwen)
  1900- *5*
Dorian, Harry
  See Hamilton, Charles H. St. John
Dorian, Marguerite *7*
Dorin, Patrick C(arberry) 1939-
  Brief Entry *52*
Dorman, Michael 1932- *7*
Dorman, N. B. 1927- *39*
Dorson, Richard M(ercer)
  1916-1981 .... *30*
Doss, Helen (Grigsby) 1918- *20*
Doss, Margot Patterson *6*
dos Santos, Joyce Audy
  Brief Entry *42*
Dottig
  See Grider, Dorothy
Dotts, Maryann J. 1933- *35*
Doty, Jean Slaughter 1929- *28*
Doty, Roy 1922- *28*
Doubtfire, Dianne (Abrams)
  1918- *29*
Dougherty, Charles 1922- *18*
Douglas, James McM.
  See Butterworth, W. E.
Douglas, Kathryn
  See Ewing, Kathryn
Douglas, Marjory Stoneman
  1890- *10*
Douglass, Barbara 1930- *40*
Douglass, Frederick
  1817(?)-1895 .... *29*
Douty, Esther M(orris)
  1911-1978 .... *8*
  Obituary *23*
Dow, Emily R. 1904- *10*
Dowdell, Dorothy (Florence) Karns
  1910- *12*
Dowden, Anne Ophelia 1907- *7*
Dowdey, Landon Gerald
  1923- *11*
Dowdy, Mrs. Regera
  See Gorey, Edward St. John
Downer, Marion 1892(?)-1971 .... *25*
Downey, Fairfax 1893- *3*
Downie, Mary Alice 1934- *13*
Doyle, Arthur Conan
  1859-1930 .... *24*
Doyle, Donovan
  See Boegehold, Betty (Doyle)
Doyle, Richard 1824-1883 .... *21*
Drabble, Margaret 1939- *48*

Drackett, Phil(ip Arthur)
  1922- *53*
Draco, F.
  See Davis, Julia
Drager, Gary
  See Edens, Cooper
Dragonwagon, Crescent 1952- *41*
  Earlier sketch in SATA 11
Drake, Frank
  See Hamilton, Charles H. St. John
Drapier, M. B.
  See Swift, Jonathan
Drawson, Blair 1943- *17*
Dresang, Eliza (Carolyn Timberlake)
  1941- *19*
Drescher, Joan E(lizabeth)
  1939- *30*
Dreves, Veronica R. 1927-1986
  Obituary *50*
Drew, Patricia (Mary) 1938- *15*
Drewery, Mary 1918- *6*
Drial, J. E.
  See Laird, Jean E(louise)
Drucker, Malka 1945- *39*
  Brief Entry *29*
Drummond, V(iolet) H. 1911- *6*
Drummond, Walter
  See Silverberg, Robert
Drury, Roger W(olcott) 1914- *15*
Dryden, Pamela
  See Johnston, Norma
Duane, Diane (Elizabeth) 1952-
  Brief Entry *46*
du Blanc, Daphne
  See Groom, Arthur William
DuBois, Rochelle Holt
  See Holt, Rochelle Lynn
Du Bois, Shirley Graham
  1907-1977 .... *24*
Du Bois, W(illiam) E(dward)
  B(urghardt) 1868-1963 .... *42*
du Bois, William Pène 1916- *4*
  See also CLR 1
DuBose, LaRocque (Russ)
  1926- *2*
Duchacek, Ivo D(uka) 1913-1988
  Obituary *55*
Du Chaillu, Paul (Belloni)
  1831(?)-1903 .... *26*
Duchesne, Janet 1930-
  Brief Entry *32*
Ducornet, Erica 1943- *7*
Dudley, Martha Ward 1909(?)-1985
  Obituary *45*
Dudley, Nancy
  See Cole, Lois Dwight
Dudley, Robert
  See Baldwin, James
Dudley, Ruth H(ubbell) 1905- *11*
Dueland, Joy V(ivian) *27*
Duff, Annis (James) 1904(?)-1986
  Obituary *49*
Duff, Maggie
  See Duff, Margaret K.
Duff, Margaret K. *37*
Dugan, Michael (Gray) 1947- *15*
Duggan, Alfred Leo
  1903-1964 .... *25*

Duggan, Maurice (Noel)
  1922-1974 .... *40*
  Obituary *30*
du Jardin, Rosamond (Neal)
  1902-1963 .... *2*
Duka, Ivo
  See Duchacek, Ivo D(uka)
Dulac, Edmund 1882-1953 .... *19*
Dumas, Alexandre (the elder)
  1802-1870 .... *18*
Dumas, Jacqueline (Claudia)
  1946- *55*
Dumas, Philippe 1940- *52*
du Maurier, Daphne 1907- *27*
Dunbar, Paul Laurence
  1872-1906 .... *34*
Dunbar, Robert E(verett)
  1926- *32*
Duncan, Frances (Mary) 1942-
  Brief Entry *48*
Duncan, Gregory
  See McClintock, Marshall
Duncan, Jane
  See Cameron, Elizabeth Jane
Duncan, Julia K. [Collective
  pseudonym] *1*
Duncan, Lois S(teinmetz)
  1934- *36*
  Earlier sketch in SATA 1
  See also SAAS 2
Duncan, Norman
  1871-1916 .... *YABC 1*
Duncombe, Frances (Riker)
  1900- *25*
Dunlop, Agnes M.R. *3*
Dunlop, Eileen (Rhona) 1938- ... *24*
Dunn, Harvey T(homas)
  1884-1952 .... *34*
Dunn, Judy
  See Spangenberg, Judith Dunn
Dunn, Mary Lois 1930- *6*
Dunnahoo, Terry 1927- *7*
Dunne, Mary Collins 1914- *11*
Dunnett, Margaret (Rosalind)
  1909-1977 .... *42*
Dunrea, Olivier 1953-
  Brief Entry *46*
Dupuy, T(revor) N(evitt)
  1916- *4*
Durant, John 1902- *27*
Durrell, Gerald (Malcolm)
  1925- *8*
Du Soe, Robert C.
  1892-1958 .... *YABC 2*
Dutz
  See Davis, Mary Octavia
Duval, Katherine
  See James, Elizabeth
Duvall, Evelyn Millis 1906- *9*
Duvoisin, Roger (Antoine)
  1904-1980 .... *30*
  Obituary *23*
  Earlier sketch in SATA 2
Dwiggins, Don 1913- *4*
Dwight, Allan
  See Cole, Lois Dwight
Dyer, James (Frederick) 1934- ... *37*
Dygard, Thomas J. 1931- *24*
Dyke, John 1935- *35*

E

E.V.B.
  See Boyle, Eleanor Vere (Gordon)
Eagar, Frances (Elisabeth Stuart)
  1940-1978 .... *11*
  Obituary *55*
Eager, Edward (McMaken)
  1911-1964 .... *17*
Eagle, Mike 1942- *11*
Earle, Olive L. *7*
Earle, William
  See Johns, W(illiam) E(arl)
Early, Jon
  See Johns, W(illiam) E(arl)
Earnshaw, Brian 1929- *17*
Eastman, Charles A(lexander)
  1858-1939 ....*YABC 1*
Eastman, P(hilip) D(ey)
  1909-1986 .... *33*
  Obituary *46*
Eastwick, Ivy O. *3*
Eaton, Anne T(haxter)
  1881-1971 .... *32*
Eaton, George L.
  See Verral, Charles Spain
Eaton, Jeanette 1886-1968 .... *24*
Eaton, Tom 1940- *22*
Ebel, Alex 1927- *11*
Eber, Dorothy (Margaret) Harley
  1930- *27*
Eberle, Irmengarde 1898-1979 .... *2*
  Obituary *23*
Eccles
  See Williams, Ferelith Eccles
Eckblad, Edith Berven 1923- *23*
Ecke, Wolfgang 1927-1983
  Obituary *37*
Eckert, Allan W. 1931- *29*
  Brief Entry *27*
Eckert, Horst 1931- *8*
Ede, Janina 1937- *33*
Edell, Celeste *12*
Edelman, Elaine
  Brief Entry *50*
Edelman, Lily (Judith) 1915- *22*
Edelson, Edward 1932- *51*
Edens, Cooper 1945- *49*
Edens, (Bishop) David 1926- *39*
Edey, Maitland A(rmstrong)
  1910- *25*
Edgeworth, Maria 1767-1849 ..... *21*
Edmonds, I(vy) G(ordon)
  1917- *8*
Edmonds, Walter D(umaux)
  1903- *27*
  Earlier sketch in SATA 1
  See also SAAS 4
Edmund, Sean
  See Pringle, Laurence
Edsall, Marian S(tickney)
  1920- *8*
Edwards, Al
  See Nourse, Alan E(dward)
Edwards, Alexander
  See Fleischer, Leonore
Edwards, Anne 1927- *35*
Edwards, Audrey 1947- *52*
  Brief Entry *31*

Edwards, Bertram
  See Edwards, Herbert Charles
Edwards, Bronwen Elizabeth
  See Rose, Wendy
Edwards, Cecile (Pepin)
  1916- *25*
Edwards, Dorothy 1914-1982 ..... *4*
  Obituary *31*
Edwards, Gunvor *32*
Edwards, Harvey 1929- *5*
Edwards, Herbert Charles
  1912- *12*
Edwards, Jane Campbell
  1932- *10*
Edwards, Julie
  See Andrews, Julie
Edwards, Julie
  See Stratemeyer, Edward L.
Edwards, June
  See Forrester, Helen
Edwards, Linda Strauss 1948- *49*
  Brief Entry *42*
Edwards, Monica le Doux Newton
  1912- *12*
Edwards, Olwen
  See Gater, Dilys
Edwards, Sally 1929- *7*
Edwards, Samuel
  See Gerson, Noel B(ertram)
Egan, E(dward) W(elstead)
  1922- *35*
Eggenberger, David 1918- *6*
Eggleston, Edward 1837-1902 ..... *27*
Egielski, Richard 1952- *49*
  Earlier sketch in SATA 11
Egypt, Ophelia Settle
  1903-1984 .... *16*
  Obituary *38*
Ehlert, Lois (Jane) 1934- *35*
Ehrlich, Amy 1942- *25*
Ehrlich, Bettina (Bauer) 1903- *1*
Eichberg, James Bandman
  See Garfield, James B.
Eichenberg, Fritz 1901- *50*
  Earlier sketch in SATA 9
Eichler, Margrit 1942- *35*
Eichner, James A. 1927- *4*
Eifert, Virginia S(nider)
  1911-1966 .... *2*
Einsel, Naiad *10*
Einsel, Walter 1926- *10*
Einzig, Susan 1922- *43*
Eiseman, Alberta 1925- *15*
Eisenberg, Azriel 1903- *12*
Eisenberg, Lisa 1949-
  Brief Entry *50*
Eisenberg, Phyllis Rose 1924- *41*
Eisner, Vivienne
  See Margolis, Vivienne
Eisner, Will(iam Erwin) 1917- *31*
Eitzen, Allan 1928- *9*
Eitzen, Ruth (Carper) 1924- *9*
Elam, Richard M(ace, Jr.)
  1920- *9*
Elfman, Blossom 1925- *8*
Elgin, Kathleen 1923- *39*
Elia
  See Lamb, Charles

Eliot, Anne
 See Cole, Lois Dwight
Elisofon, Eliot 1911-1973
 Obituary *21*
Elkin, Benjamin 1911- *3*
Elkins, Dov Peretz 1937- *5*
Ellacott, S(amuel) E(rnest)
 1911- *19*
Elliott, Sarah M(cCarn) 1930- *14*
Ellis, Anyon
 See Rowland-Entwistle, (Arthur)
  Theodore (Henry)
Ellis, Edward S(ylvester)
 1840-1916 ....*YABC 1*
Ellis, Ella Thorp 1928- *7*
Ellis, Harry Bearse 1921- *9*
Ellis, Herbert
 See Wilson, Lionel
Ellis, Mel 1912-1984 .... *7*
 Obituary *39*
Ellison, Lucile Watkins
 1907(?)-1979 .... *50*
 Obituary *22*
Ellison, Virginia Howell
 1910- *4*
Ellsberg, Edward 1891- *7*
Elmore, (Carolyn) Patricia
 1933- *38*
 Brief Entry *35*
Elspeth
 See Bragdon, Elspeth
Elting, Mary 1906- *2*
Elwart, Joan Potter 1927- *2*
Elwood, Ann 1931- *55*
 Brief Entry *52*
Emberley, Barbara A(nne) *8*
 See also CLR 5
Emberley, Ed(ward Randolph)
 1931- *8*
 See also CLR 5
Emberley, Michael 1960- *34*
Embry, Margaret (Jacob)
 1919- *5*
Emerson, Alice B. [Collective
 pseudonym] *1*
Emerson, William K(eith)
 1925- *25*
Emery, Anne (McGuigan)
 1907- *33*
 Earlier sketch in SATA 1
Emmens, Carol Ann 1944- *39*
Emmons, Della (Florence) Gould
 1890-1983
 Obituary *39*
Emrich, Duncan (Black Macdonald)
 1908- *11*
Emslie, M. L.
 See Simpson, Myrtle L(illias)
Ende, Michael 1930(?)-
 Brief Entry *42*
 See also CLR 14
Enderle, Judith (Ann) 1941- *38*
Enfield, Carrie
 See Smith, Susan Vernon
Engdahl, Sylvia Louise 1933- *4*
 See also CLR 2
 See also SAAS 5
Engle, Eloise Katherine 1923- *9*
Englebert, Victor 1933- *8*

English, James W(ilson)
 1915- *37*
Enright, D(ennis) J(oseph)
 1920- *25*
Enright, Elizabeth 1909-1968 ..... *9*
 See also CLR 4
Enright, Maginel Wright
 See Barney, Maginel Wright
Enys, Sarah L.
 See Sloggett, Nellie
Ephron, Delia 1944-
 Brief Entry *50*
Epp, Margaret A(gnes) *20*
Eppenstein, Louise (Kohn) 1892-1987
 Obituary *54*
Epple, Anne Orth 1927- *20*
Epstein, Anne Merrick 1931- *20*
Epstein, Beryl (Williams)
 1910- *31*
 Earlier sketch in SATA 1
Epstein, Perle S(herry) 1938- *27*
Epstein, Samuel 1909- *31*
 Earlier sketch in SATA 1
Erdman, Loula Grace *1*
Erdoes, Richard 1912- *33*
 Brief Entry *28*
Erhard, Walter 1920-
 Brief Entry *30*
Erickson, Russell E(verett)
 1932- *27*
Erickson, Sabra R(ollins)
 1912- *35*
Ericson, Walter
 See Fast, Howard
Erikson, Mel 1937- *31*
Erlanger, Baba
 See Trahey, Jane
Erlanger, Ellen (Louise) 1950-
 Brief Entry *52*
Erlich, Lillian (Feldman)
 1910- *10*
Ernest, William
 See Berkebile, Fred D(onovan)
Ernst, (Lyman) John 1940- *39*
Ernst, Kathryn (Fitzgerald)
 1942- *25*
Ernst, Lisa Campbell 1957- *55*
 Brief Entry *44*
Ervin, Janet Halliday 1923- *4*
Erwin, Will
 See Eisner, Will(iam Erwin)
Esbensen, Barbara Juster
 Brief Entry *53*
Eshmeyer, R(einhart) E(rnst)
 1898- *29*
Espeland, Pamela (Lee) 1951- *52*
 Brief Entry *38*
Espriella, Don Manuel Alvarez
 See Southey, Robert
Espy, Willard R(ichardson)
 1910- *38*
Estep, Irene (Compton) *5*
Estes, Eleanor 1906- *7*
 See also CLR 2
Estoril, Jean
 See Allan, Mabel Esther
Etchemendy, Nancy 1952- *38*
Etchison, Birdie L(ee) 1937- *38*
Ets, Marie Hall *2*

Eunson, Dale 1904- *5*
Evans, Eva Knox 1905- *27*
Evans, Hubert Reginald 1892-1986
 Obituary *48*
Evans, Katherine (Floyd)
 1901-1964 .... *5*
Evans, Mari *10*
Evans, Mark *19*
Evans, Patricia Healy
 See Carpenter, Patricia
Evarts, Esther
 See Benson, Sally
Evarts, Hal G. (Jr.) 1915- *6*
Everett, Gail
 See Hale, Arlene
Evernden, Margery 1916- *5*
Evslin, Bernard 1922- *45*
 Brief Entry *28*
Ewen, David 1907-1985 .... *4*
 Obituary *47*
Ewing, Juliana (Horatia Gatty)
 1841-1885 .... *16*
Ewing, Kathryn 1921- *20*
Eyerly, Jeannette Hyde 1908- *4*
Eyre, Dorothy
 See McGuire, Leslie (Sarah)
Eyre, Katherine Wigmore
 1901-1970 .... *26*
Eyvindson, Peter (Knowles) 1946-
 Brief Entry *52*
Ezzell, Marilyn 1937- *42*
 Brief Entry *38*

F

Fabe, Maxene 1943- *15*
Faber, Doris 1924- *3*
Faber, Harold 1919- *5*
Fabre, Jean Henri (Casimir)
 1823-1915 .... *22*
Facklam, Margery Metz 1927- *20*
Fadiman, Clifton (Paul) 1904- *11*
Fair, Sylvia 1933- *13*
Fairfax-Lucy, Brian (Fulke Cameron-
 Ramsay) 1898-1974 .... *6*
 Obituary *26*
Fairlie, Gerard 1899-1983
 Obituary *34*
Fairman, Joan A(lexandra)
 1935- *10*
Faithfull, Gail 1936- *8*
Falconer, James
 See Kirkup, James
Falkner, Leonard 1900- *12*
Fall, Thomas
 See Snow, Donald Clifford
Falls, C(harles) B(uckles)
 1874-1960 .... *38*
 Brief Entry *27*
Falstein, Louis 1909- *37*
Fanning, Leonard M(ulliken)
 1888-1967 .... *5*
Faralla, Dana 1909- *9*
Faralla, Dorothy W.
 See Faralla, Dana
Farb, Peter 1929-1980 .... *12*
 Obituary *22*

Farber, Norma 1909-1984 25
    Obituary 38
Farge, Monique
    See Grée, Alain
Farjeon, (Eve) Annabel 1919- 11
Farjeon, Eleanor 1881-1965 2
Farley, Carol 1936- 4
Farley, Walter 1920- 43
    Earlier sketch in SATA 2
Farmer, Penelope (Jane)
    1939- 40
    Brief Entry 39
    See also CLR 8
Farmer, Peter 1950- 38
Farnham, Burt
    See Clifford, Harold B.
Farquhar, Margaret C(utting)
    1905- 13
Farquharson, Alexander 1944- 46
Farquharson, Martha
    See Finley, Martha
Farr, Finis (King) 1904- 10
Farrar, Susan Clement 1917- 33
Farrell, Ben
    See Cebulash, Mel
Farrington, Benjamin 1891-1974
    Obituary 20
Farrington, Selwyn Kip, Jr.
    1904- 20
Farthing, Alison 1936- 45
    Brief Entry 36
Fassler, Joan (Grace) 1931- 11
Fast, Howard 1914- 7
Fatchen, Max 1920- 20
Father Xavier
    See Hurwood, Bernhardt J.
Fatigati, (Frances) Evelyn de Buhr
    1948- 24
Fatio, Louise 6
Faulhaber, Martha 1926- 7
Faulkner, Anne Irvin 1906- 23
Faulkner, Nancy
    See Faulkner, Anne Irvin
Fax, Elton Clay 1909- 25
Feagles, Anita MacRae 9
Feagles, Elizabeth
    See Day, Beth (Feagles)
Feague, Mildred H. 1915- 14
Fecher, Constance 1911- 7
Feder, Paula (Kurzband)
    1935- 26
Feder, Robert Arthur 1909-1969
    Brief Entry 35
Feelings, Muriel (Grey) 1938- 16
    See also CLR 5
Feelings, Thomas 1933- 8
Feelings, Tom
    See Feelings, Thomas
    See also CLR 5
Fehrenbach, T(heodore) R(eed, Jr.)
    1925- 33
Feiffer, Jules 1929- 8
Feig, Barbara Krane 1937- 34
Feikema, Feike
    See Manfred, Frederick F(eikema)
Feil, Hila 1942- 12
Feilen, John
    See May, Julian

Feldman, Anne (Rodgers)
    1939- 19
Félix
    See Vincent, Félix
Fellows, Muriel H. 10
Felsen, Henry Gregor 1916- 1
    See also SAAS 2
Felton, Harold William 1902- 1
Felton, Ronald Oliver 1909- 3
Felts, Shirley 1934- 33
Fenderson, Lewis H.
    1907-1983 47
    Obituary 37
Fenner, Carol 1929- 7
Fenner, Phyllis R(eid)
    1899-1982 1
    Obituary 29
Fenten, Barbara D(oris) 1935- 26
Fenten, D. X. 1932- 4
Fenton, Carroll Lane
    1900-1969 5
Fenton, Edward 1917- 7
Fenton, Mildred Adams 1899- 21
Fenwick, Patti
    See Grider, Dorothy
Feravolo, Rocco Vincent
    1922- 10
Ferber, Edna 1887-1968 7
Ferguson, Bob
    See Ferguson, Robert Bruce
Ferguson, Cecil 1931- 45
Ferguson, Robert Bruce 1927- 13
Ferguson, Walter (W.) 1930- 34
Fergusson, Erna 1888-1964 5
Fermi, Laura (Capon)
    1907-1977 6
    Obituary 28
Fern, Eugene A. 1919-1987 10
    Obituary 54
Ferrier, Lucy
    See Penzler, Otto
Ferris, Helen Josephine
    1890-1969 21
Ferris, James Cody [Collective
    pseudonym] 1
    See also McFarlane, Leslie;
    Stratemeyer, Edward L.
Ferris, Jean 1939-
    Brief Entry 50
Ferry, Charles 1927- 43
Fetz, Ingrid 1915- 30
Feydy, Anne Lindbergh
    Brief Entry 32
    See Sapieyevski, Anne Lindbergh
Fiammenghi, Gioia 1929- 9
Fiarotta, Noel 1944- 15
Fiarotta, Phyllis 1942- 15
Fichter, George S. 1922- 7
Fidler, Kathleen (Annie)
    1899-1980 3
    Obituary 45
Fiedler, Jean 4
Field, Edward 1924- 8
Field, Elinor Whitney 1889-1980
    Obituary 28
Field, Eugene 1850-1895 16
Field, Gans T.
    See Wellman, Manly Wade

Field, Peter
    See Hobson, Laura Z(ametkin)
Field, Rachel (Lyman)
    1894-1942 15
Fife, Dale (Odile) 1901- 18
Fighter Pilot, A
    See Johnston, H(ugh) A(nthony)
    S(tephen)
Figueroa, Pablo 1938- 9
Fijan, Carol 1918- 12
Fillmore, Parker H(oysted)
    1878-1944 .... YABC 1
Filstrup, Chris
    See Filstrup, E(dward) Christian
Filstrup, E(dward) Christian
    1942- 43
Filstrup, Jane Merrill
    See Merrill, Jane
Filstrup, Janie
    See Merrill, Jane
Finder, Martin
    See Salzmann, Siegmund
Fine, Anne 1947- 29
Finger, Charles J(oseph)
    1869(?)-1941 42
Fink, William B(ertrand)
    1916- 22
Finke, Blythe F(oote) 1922- 26
Finkel, George (Irvine)
    1909-1975 8
Finlay, Winifred 1910- 23
Finlayson, Ann 1925- 8
Finley, Martha 1828-1909 43
Firmin, Charlotte 1954- 29
Firmin, Peter 1928- 15
Fischbach, Julius 1894- 10
Fischler, Stan(ley I.)
    Brief Entry 36
Fishback, Margaret
    See Antolini, Margaret Fishback
Fisher, Aileen (Lucia) 1906- 25
    Earlier sketch in SATA 1
Fisher, Barbara 1940- 44
    Brief Entry 34
Fisher, Clavin C(argill) 1912- ... 24
Fisher, Dorothy Canfield
    1879-1958 .... YABC 1
Fisher, John (Oswald Hamilton)
    1909- 15
Fisher, Laura Harrison 1934- 5
Fisher, Leonard Everett 1924- 34
    Earlier sketch in SATA 4
    See also SAAS 1
Fisher, Lois I. 1948- 38
    Brief Entry 35
Fisher, Margery (Turner)
    1913- 20
Fisher, Robert (Tempest)
    1943- 47
Fisk, Nicholas 1923- 25
Fitch, Clarke
    See Sinclair, Upton (Beall)
Fitch, John IV
    See Cormier, Robert (Edmund)
Fitschen, Dale 1937- 20
Fitzalan, Roger
    See Trevor, Elleston
Fitzgerald, Captain Hugh
    See Baum, L(yman) Frank

FitzGerald, Cathleen 1932-1987
  Obituary 50
Fitzgerald, Edward Earl 1919- 20
Fitzgerald, F(rancis) A(nthony)
  1940- 15
Fitzgerald, John D(ennis)
  1907- 20
  See also CLR 1
Fitzgerald, Merni I(ngrassia)
  1955- 53
Fitzhardinge, Joan Margaret
  1912- 2
Fitzhugh, Louise (Perkins)
  1928-1974 45
  Obituary 24
  Earlier sketch in SATA 1
  See also CLR 1
Fitz-Randolph, Jane (Currens)
  1915- 51
Flack, Marjorie
  1899-1958 .... YABC 2
Flack, Naomi John (White) 40
  Brief Entry 35
Flash Flood
  See Robinson, Jan M.
Fleischer, Leonore 1934(?)-
  Brief Entry 47
Fleischer, Max 1889-1972
  Brief Entry 30
Fleischhauer-Hardt, Helga
  1936- 30
Fleischman, Paul 1952- 39
  Brief Entry 32
Fleischman, (Albert) Sid(ney)
  1920- 8
  See also CLR 1, 15
Fleisher, Robbin 1951-1977 52
  Brief Entry 49
Fleishman, Seymour 1918-
  Brief Entry 32
Fleming, Alice Mulcahey
  1928- 9
Fleming, Elizabeth P. 1888-1985
  Obituary 48
Fleming, Ian (Lancaster)
  1908-1964 9
Fleming, Susan 1932- 32
Fleming, Thomas J(ames)
  1927- 8
Flesch, Yolande (Catarina)
  1950- 55
Fletcher, Charlie May 1897- 3
Fletcher, Colin 1922- 28
Fletcher, Helen Jill 1911- 13
Fletcher, Richard E. 1917(?)-1983
  Obituary 34
Fletcher, Rick
  See Fletcher, Richard E.
Fleur, Anne 1901-
  Brief Entry 31
Flexner, James Thomas 1908- 9
Flitner, David P. 1949- 7
Floethe, Louise Lee 1913- 4
Floethe, Richard 1901- 4
Floherty, John Joseph
  1882-1964 25
Flood, Flash
  See Robinson, Jan M.

Flora, James (Royer) 1914- 30
  Earlier sketch in SATA 1
  See also SAAS 6
Florian, Douglas 1950- 19
Flory, Jane Trescott 1917- 22
Flowerdew, Phyllis 33
Floyd, Gareth 1940-
  Brief Entry 31
Fluchère, Henri A(ndré) 1914- 40
Flynn, Barbara 1928- 9
Flynn, Jackson
  See Shirreffs, Gordon D.
Flynn, Mary
  See Welsh, Mary Flynn
Fodor, Ronald V(ictor) 1944- 25
Foley, (Anna) Bernice Williams
  1902- 28
Foley, June 1944- 44
Foley, (Mary) Louise Munro
  1933- 54
  Brief Entry 40
Foley, Rae
  See Denniston, Elinore
Folkard, Charles James 1878-1963
  Brief Entry 28
Follett, Helen (Thomas) 1884(?)-1970
  Obituary 27
Folsom, Franklin (Brewster)
  1907- 5
Folsom, Michael (Brewster)
  1938- 40
Fontenot, Mary Alice 1910- 34
Fooner, Michael 22
Foote, Timothy (Gilson)
  1926- 52
Forberg, Ati 1925- 22
Forbes, Bryan 1926- 37
Forbes, Cabot L.
  See Hoyt, Edwin P(almer), Jr.
Forbes, Esther 1891-1967 2
Forbes, Graham B. [Collective
  pseudonym] 1
Forbes, Kathryn
  See McLean, Kathryn (Anderson)
Ford, Albert Lee
  See Stratemeyer, Edward L.
Ford, Barbara
  Brief Entry 34
Ford, Brian J(ohn) 1939- 49
Ford, Elbur
  See Hibbert, Eleanor
Ford, George (Jr.) 31
Ford, Hilary
  See Youd, (Christopher) Samuel
Ford, Hildegarde
  See Morrison, Velma Ford
Ford, Marcia
  See Radford, Ruby L.
Ford, Nancy K(effer) 1906-1961
  Obituary 29
Foreman, Michael 1938- 2
Forest, Antonia 29
Forester, C(ecil) S(cott)
  1899-1966 13
Forman, Brenda 1936- 4
Forman, James Douglas 1932- 8
Forrest, Sybil
  See Markun, Patricia M(aloney)

Forrester, Frank H. 1919(?)-1986
  Obituary 52
Forrester, Helen 1919- 48
Forrester, Marian
  See Schachtel, Roger
Forrester, Victoria 1940- 40
  Brief Entry 35
Forsee, (Frances) Aylesa 1
Fort, Paul
  See Stockton, Francis Richard
Fortnum, Peggy 1919- 26
Fortune, Brad W. 1955- 34
Foster, Doris Van Liew 1899- 10
Foster, E(lizabeth) C(onnell)
  1902- 9
Foster, Elizabeth 1905-1963 10
Foster, Elizabeth Vincent
  1902- 12
Foster, F. Blanche 1919- 11
Foster, G(eorge) Allen
  1907-1969 26
Foster, Genevieve (Stump)
  1893-1979 2
  Obituary 23
  See also CLR 7
Foster, Hal
  See Foster, Harold Rudolf
Foster, Harold Rudolf 1892-1982
  Obituary 31
Foster, John T(homas) 1925- 8
Foster, Laura Louise 1918- 6
Foster, Margaret Lesser 1899-1979
  Obituary 21
Foster, Marian Curtis
  1909-1978 23
Foulds, Elfrida Vipont 1902- 52
Fourth Brother, The
  See Aung, (Maung) Htin
Fowke, Edith (Margaret)
  1913- 14
Fowles, John 1926- 22
Fox, Charles Philip 1913- 12
Fox, Eleanor
  See St. John, Wylly Folk
Fox, Fontaine Talbot, Jr. 1884-1964
  Obituary 23
Fox, Fred 1903(?)-1981
  Obituary 27
Fox, Freeman
  See Hamilton, Charles H. St. John
Fox, Grace
  See Anderson, Grace Fox
Fox, Larry 30
Fox, Lorraine 1922-1975 11
  Obituary 27
Fox, Mary Virginia 1919- 44
  Brief Entry 39
Fox, Mem
  See Fox, Merrion Frances
Fox, Merrion Frances 1946- 51
Fox, Michael Wilson 1937- 15
Fox, Paula 1923- 17
  See also CLR 1
Fox, Petronella
  See Balogh, Penelope
Fox, Robert J. 1927- 33
Fradin, Dennis Brindel 1945- 29
Frame, Paul 1913-
  Brief Entry 33

Franchere, Ruth *18*
Francis, Charles
  See Holme, Bryan
Francis, Dee
  See Haas, Dorothy F.
Francis, Dorothy Brenner
  1926- *10*
Francis, Pamela (Mary) 1926- *11*
Franco, Marjorie *38*
Francois, André 1915- *25*
Francoise
  See Seignobosc, Francoise
Frank, Anne 1929-1945(?)
  Brief Entry *42*
Frank, Daniel B. 1956- *55*
Frank, Hélène
  See Vautier, Ghislaine
Frank, Josette 1893- *10*
Frank, Mary 1933- *34*
Frank, R., Jr.
  See Ross, Frank (Xavier), Jr.
Frankau, Mary Evelyn 1899- *4*
Frankel, Bernice *9*
Frankel, Edward 1910- *44*
Frankel, Julie 1947- *40*
  Brief Entry *34*
Frankenberg, Robert 1911- *22*
Franklin, Harold 1920- *13*
Franklin, Max
  See Deming, Richard
Franklin, Steve
  See Stevens, Franklin
Franzén, Nils-Olof 1916- *10*
Frascino, Edward 1938- *48*
  Brief Entry *33*
Frasconi, Antonio 1919- *53*
  Earlier sketch in SATA 6
Fraser, Antonia (Pakenham) 1932-
  Brief Entry *32*
Fraser, Betty
  See Fraser, Elizabeth Marr
Fraser, Elizabeth Marr 1928- *31*
Fraser, Eric (George)
  1902-1983 .... *38*
Frazier, Neta Lohnes *7*
Freed, Alvyn M. 1913- *22*
Freedman, Benedict 1919- *27*
Freedman, Nancy 1920- *27*
Freedman, Russell (Bruce)
  1929- *16*
Freeman, Barbara C(onstance)
  1906- *28*
Freeman, Bill
  See Freeman, William Bradford
Freeman, Don 1908-1978 .... *17*
Freeman, Ira M(aximilian)
  1905- *21*
Freeman, Lucy (Greenbaum)
  1916- *24*
Freeman, Mae (Blacker)
  1907- *25*
Freeman, Peter J.
  See Calvert, Patricia
Freeman, Tony
  Brief Entry *44*
Freeman, William Bradford 1938-
  Brief Entry *48*
Fregosi, Claudia (Anne Marie)
  1946- *24*

French, Allen 1870-1946 ..... *YABC 1*
French, Dorothy Kayser 1926- *5*
French, Fiona 1944- *6*
French, Kathryn
  See Mosesson, Gloria R(ubin)
French, Michael 1944- *49*
  Brief Entry *38*
French, Paul
  See Asimov, Isaac
Freund, Rudolf 1915-1969
  Brief Entry *28*
Frewer, Glyn 1931- *11*
Frick, C. H.
  See Irwin, Constance Frick
Frick, Constance
  See Irwin, Constance Frick
Friedlander, Joanne K(ohn)
  1930- *9*
Friedman, Estelle 1920- *7*
Friedman, Frieda 1905- *43*
Friedman, Ina R(osen) 1926- *49*
  Brief Entry *41*
Friedman, Marvin 1930- *42*
  Brief Entry *33*
Friedrich, Otto (Alva) 1929- *33*
Friedrich, Priscilla 1927- *39*
Friendlich, Dick
  See Friendlich, Richard J.
Friendlich, Richard J. 1909- *11*
Friermood, Elisabeth Hamilton
  1903- *5*
Friis, Babbis
  See Friis-Baastad, Babbis
Friis-Baastad, Babbis
  1921-1970 .... *7*
Frimmer, Steven 1928- *31*
Friskey, Margaret Richards
  1901- *5*
Fritz, Jean (Guttery) 1915- *29*
  Earlier sketch in SATA 1
  See also CLR 2, 14
  See also SAAS 2
Froissart, Jean
  1338(?)-1410(?) *28*
Froman, Elizabeth Hull
  1920-1975 .... *10*
Froman, Robert (Winslow)
  1917- *8*
Fromm, Lilo 1928- *29*
Frommer, Harvey 1937- *41*
Frost, A(rthur) B(urdett)
  1851-1928 .... *19*
Frost, Erica
  See Supraner, Robyn
Frost, Lesley 1899(?)-1983 .... *14*
  Obituary *34*
Frost, Robert (Lee) 1874-1963 .... *14*
Fry, Edward Bernard 1925- *35*
Fry, Rosalie 1911- *3*
Fuchs, Erich 1916- *6*
Fuchs, Lucy 1935-
  Brief Entry *52*
Fuchshuber, Annegert 1940- *43*
Fujikawa, Gyo 1908- *39*
  Brief Entry *30*
Fujita, Tamao 1905- *7*
Fujiwara, Michiko 1946- *15*
Fuka, Vladimir 1926-1977
  Obituary *27*

Fuller, Catherine L(euthold)
  1916- *9*
Fuller, Edmund (Maybank)
  1914- *21*
Fuller, Iola
  See McCoy, Iola Fuller
Fuller, Lois Hamilton 1915- *11*
Fuller, Margaret
  See Ossoli, Sarah Margaret (Fuller)
  marchesa d'
Fults, John Lee 1932- *33*
Funai, Mamoru (Rolland) 1932-
  Brief Entry *46*
Funk, Thompson
  See Funk, Tom
Funk, Tom 1911- *7*
Funke, Lewis 1912- *11*
Furchgott, Terry 1948- *29*
Furniss, Tim 1948- *49*
Furukawa, Toshi 1924- *24*
Fyleman, Rose 1877-1957 .... *21*
Fyson, J(enny) G(race) 1904- *42*

G

Gackenbach, Dick *48*
  Brief Entry *30*
Gaddis, Vincent H. 1913- *35*
Gadler, Steve J. 1905- *36*
Gaeddert, Lou Ann (Bigge)
  1931- *20*
Gàg, Flavia 1907-1979
  Obituary *24*
Gàg, Wanda (Hazel)
  1893-1946 .... *YABC 1*
  See also CLR 4
Gage, Wilson
  See Steele, Mary Q(uintard Govan)
Gagliardo, Ruth Garver 1895(?)-1980
  Obituary *22*
Gál, László 1933- *52*
  Brief Entry *32*
Galdone, Paul 1914-1986 .... *17*
  Obituary *49*
Galinsky, Ellen 1942- *23*
Gallant, Roy (Arthur) 1924- *4*
Gallico, Paul 1897-1976 .... *13*
Galt, Thomas Franklin, Jr.
  1908- *5*
Galt, Tom
  See Galt, Thomas Franklin, Jr.
Gamerman, Martha 1941- *15*
Gammell, Stephen 1943- *53*
Gannett, Ruth Chrisman (Arens)
  1896-1979 .... *33*
Gannett, Ruth Stiles 1923- *3*
Gannon, Robert (Haines)
  1931- *8*
Gans, Roma 1894- *45*
Gantos, Jack
  See Gantos, John (Bryan), Jr.
Gantos, John (Bryan), Jr.
  1951- *20*
Ganz, Yaffa 1938-
  Brief Entry *52*
Garbutt, Bernard 1900-
  Brief Entry *31*

Gard, Joyce
  See Reeves, Joyce
Gard, Robert Edward 1910- *18*
Gard, (Sanford) Wayne 1899-1986
  Obituary *49*
Gardam, Jane 1928- *39*
  Brief Entry *28*
  See also CLR 12
Garden, Nancy 1938- *12*
Gardner, Beau
  Brief Entry *50*
Gardner, Dic
  See Gardner, Richard
Gardner, Hugh 1910-1986
  Obituary *49*
Gardner, Jeanne LeMonnier *5*
Gardner, John (Champlin, Jr.)
  1933-1982 .... *40*
  Obituary *31*
Gardner, Martin 1914- *16*
Gardner, Richard 1931- *24*
Gardner, Richard A. 1931- *13*
Gardner, Robert 1929-
  Brief Entry *43*
Gardner, Sheldon 1934- *33*
Garelick, May *19*
Garfield, James B. 1881-1984 ..... *6*
  Obituary *38*
Garfield, Leon 1921- *32*
  Earlier sketch in SATA 1
Garis, Howard R(oger)
  1873-1962 .... *13*
Garner, Alan 1934- *18*
Garnett, Eve C. R. *3*
Garraty, John A. 1920- *23*
Garret, Maxwell R. 1917- *39*
Garretson, Victoria Diane
  1945- *44*
Garrett, Helen 1895- *21*
Garrigue, Sheila 1931- *21*
Garrison, Barbara 1931- *19*
Garrison, Frederick
  See Sinclair, Upton (Beall)
Garrison, Webb B(lack) 1919- *25*
Garst, Doris Shannon 1894- *1*
Garst, Shannon
  See Garst, Doris Shannon
Garthwaite, Marion H. 1893- *7*
Garton, Malinda D(ean) (?)-1976
  Obituary *26*
Gasperini, Jim 1952- *54*
  Brief Entry *49*
Gater, Dilys 1944- *41*
Gates, Doris 1901-1987 .... *34*
  Obituary *54*
  Earlier sketch in SATA 1
  See also SAAS 1
Gates, Frieda 1933- *26*
Gathorne-Hardy, Jonathan G.
  1933- *26*
Gatty, Juliana Horatia
  See Ewing, Juliana (Horatia Gatty)
Gatty, Margaret Scott 1809-1873
  Brief Entry *27*
Gauch, Patricia Lee 1934- *26*
Gault, Clare S. 1925- *36*
Gault, Frank 1926-1982 .... *36*
  Brief Entry *30*

Gault, William Campbell
  1910- *8*
Gaver, Becky
  See Gaver, Rebecca
Gaver, Rebecca 1952- *20*
Gay, Francis
  See Gee, H(erbert) L(eslie)
Gay, Kathlyn 1930- *9*
Gay, Zhenya 1906-1978 .... *19*
Gee, H(erbert) L(eslie) 1901-1977
  Obituary *26*
Gee, Maurice (Gough) 1931- *46*
Geer, Charles 1922- *42*
  Brief Entry *32*
Gehr, Mary *32*
Geipel, Eileen 1932- *30*
Geis, Darlene *7*
Geisel, Helen 1898-1967 .... *26*
Geisel, Theodor Seuss 1904- *28*
  Earlier sketch in SATA 1
  See also CLR 1
Geisert, Arthur (Frederick) 1941-
  Brief Entry *52*
Geldart, William 1936- *15*
Gelinas, Paul J. 1911- *10*
Gelman, Rita Golden 1937-
  Brief Entry *51*
Gelman, Steve 1934- *3*
Gemming, Elizabeth 1932- *11*
Gendel, Evelyn W. 1916(?)-1977
  Obituary *27*
Gennaro, Joseph F(rancis), Jr.
  1924- *53*
Gentle, Mary 1956- *48*
Gentleman, David 1930- *7*
George, Jean Craighead 1919- *2*
  See also CLR 1
George, John L(othar) 1916- *2*
George, S(idney) C(harles)
  1898- *11*
George, W(illiam) Lloyd 1900(?)-1975
  Obituary *30*
Georgiou, Constantine 1927- *7*
Gérard, Jean Ignace Isidore
  1803-1847 .... *45*
Geras, Adele (Daphne) 1944- *23*
Gergely, Tibor 1900-1978 .... *54*
  Obituary *20*
Geringer, Laura 1948- *29*
Gerler, William R(obert)
  1917- *47*
Gerrard, Jean 1933- *51*
Gerrard, Roy 1935- *47*
  Brief Entry *45*
Gerson, Corinne *37*
Gerson, Noel B(ertram) 1914- *22*
Gerstein, Mordicai 1935- *47*
  Brief Entry *36*
Gesner, Clark 1938- *40*
Gessner, Lynne 1919- *16*
Gevirtz, Eliezer 1950- *49*
Gewe, Raddory
  See Gorey, Edward St. John
Gibbons, Gail 1944- *23*
  See also CLR 8
Gibbs, Alonzo (Lawrence)
  1915- *5*
Gibbs, (Cecilia) May 1877-1969
  Obituary *27*

Gibbs, Tony
  See Gibbs, Wolcott, Jr.
Gibbs, Wolcott, Jr. 1935- *40*
Giblin, James Cross 1933- *33*
Gibson, Josephine
  See Joslin, Sesyle
Gidal, Sonia 1922- *2*
Gidal, Tim N(ahum) 1909- *2*
Giegling, John A(llan) 1935- *17*
Giff, Patricia Reilly 1935- *33*
Gifford, Griselda 1931- *42*
Gilbert, Ann
  See Taylor, Ann
Gilbert, Harriett 1948- *30*
Gilbert, (Agnes) Joan (Sewell)
  1931- *10*
Gilbert, John (Raphael) 1926- *36*
Gilbert, Miriam
  See Presberg, Miriam Goldstein
Gilbert, Nan
  See Gilbertson, Mildred
Gilbert, Sara (Dulaney) 1943- *11*
Gilbert, W(illiam) S(chwenk)
  1836-1911 .... *36*
Gilbertson, Mildred Geiger
  1908- *2*
Gilbreath, Alice (Thompson)
  1921- *12*
Gilbreth, Frank B., Jr. 1911- *2*
Gilfond, Henry *2*
Gilge, Jeanette 1924- *22*
Gill, Derek L(ewis) T(heodore)
  1919- *9*
Gill, Margery Jean 1925- *22*
Gillett, Mary *7*
Gillette, Henry Sampson
  1915- *14*
Gillham, Bill
  See Gillham, William Edwin Charles
Gillham, William Edwin Charles
  1936- *42*
Gilliam, Stan 1946- *39*
  Brief Entry *35*
Gilman, Dorothy
  See Butters, Dorothy Gilman
Gilman, Esther 1925- *15*
Gilmore, Iris 1900- *22*
Gilmore, Mary (Jean Cameron)
  1865-1962 .... *49*
Gilson, Barbara
  See Gilson, Charles James Louis
Gilson, Charles James Louis
  1878-1943 .... *YABC 2*
Gilson, Jamie 1933- *37*
  Brief Entry *34*
Ginsburg, Mirra *6*
Giovanni, Nikki 1943- *24*
  See also CLR 6
Giovanopoulos, Paul 1939- *7*
Gipson, Frederick B.
  1908-1973 .... *2*
  Obituary *24*
Girard, Linda Walvoord 1942- *41*
Girion, Barbara 1937- *26*
Gittings, Jo Manton 1919- *3*
Gittings, Robert 1911- *6*
Gladstone, Eve
  See Werner, Herma
Gladstone, Gary 1935- *12*

Gladstone, M(yron) J. 1923- 37
Gladwin, William Zachary
    See Zollinger, Gulielma
Glanville, Brian (Lester)
    1931- 42
Glanzman, Louis S. 1922- 36
Glaser, Dianne E(lizabeth)
    1937- 50
    Brief Entry 31
Glaser, Milton 1929- 11
Glaspell, Susan
    1882-1948 ....YABC 2
Glass, Andrew
    Brief Entry 46
Glauber, Uta (Heil) 1936- 17
Glazer, Tom 1914- 9
Gleasner, Diana (Cottle)
    1936- 29
Gleason, Judith 1929- 24
Glendinning, Richard 1917- 24
Glendinning, Sally
    See Glendinning, Sara W(ilson)
Glendinning, Sara W(ilson)
    1913- 24
Glenn, Mel 1943- 51
    Brief Entry 45
Gles, Margaret Breitmaier
    1940- 22
Glick, Carl (Cannon)
    1890-1971 14
Glick, Virginia Kirkus 1893-1980
    Obituary 23
Gliewe, Unada 1927- 3
Glines, Carroll V(ane), Jr.
    1920- 19
Globe, Leah Ain 1900- 41
Glovach, Linda 1947- 7
Glubok, Shirley 6
    See also CLR 1
    See also SAAS 7
Gluck, Felix 1924(?)-1981
    Obituary 25
Glynne-Jones, William 1907- 11
Gobbato, Imero 1923- 39
Goble, Dorothy 26
Goble, Paul 1933- 25
Goble, Warwick (?)-1943 46
Godden, Rumer 1907- 36
    Earlier sketch in SATA 3
Gode, Alexander
    See Gode von Aesch, Alexander
        (Gottfried Friedrich)
Gode von Aesch, Alexander (Gottfried
    Friedrich) 1906-1970 14
Godfrey, Jane
    See Bowden, Joan Chase
Godfrey, William
    See Youd, (Christopher) Samuel
Goettel, Elinor 1930- 12
Goetz, Delia 1898- 22
Goffstein, M(arilyn) B(rooke)
    1940- 8
    See also CLR 3
Golann, Cecil Paige 1921- 11
Golbin, Andrée 1923- 15
Gold, Phyllis 1941- 21
Gold, Sharlya 9
Goldberg, Herbert S. 1926- 25
Goldberg, Stan J. 1939- 26

Goldfeder, Cheryl
    See Pahz, Cheryl Suzanne
Goldfeder, Jim
    See Pahz, James Alon
Goldfrank, Helen Colodny
    1912- 6
Goldin, Augusta 1906- 13
Goldsborough, June 1923- 19
Goldsmith, Howard 1943- 24
Goldsmith, John Herman Thorburn
    1903-1987
    Obituary 52
Goldsmith, Oliver 1728-1774 26
Goldstein, Ernest A. 1933-
    Brief Entry 52
Goldstein, Nathan 1927- 47
Goldstein, Philip 1910- 23
Goldston, Robert (Conroy)
    1927- 6
Goll, Reinhold W(eimar)
    1897- 26
Gonzalez, Gloria 1940- 23
Goodall, John S(trickland)
    1908- 4
Goodbody, Slim
    See Burstein, John
Goode, Diane 1949- 15
Goode, Stephen 1943- 55
    Brief Entry 40
Goodenow, Earle 1913- 40
Goodman, Deborah Lerme
    1956- 50
    Brief Entry 49
Goodman, Elaine 1930- 9
Goodman, Joan Elizabeth
    1950- 50
Goodman, Walter 1927- 9
Goodrich, Samuel Griswold
    1793-1860 23
Goodwin, Hal
    See Goodwin, Harold Leland
Goodwin, Harold Leland
    1914- 51
    Earlier sketch in SATA 13
Goor, Nancy (Ruth Miller)
    1944- 39
    Brief Entry 34
Goor, Ron(ald Stephen) 1940- 39
    Brief Entry 34
Goossen, Agnes
    See Epp, Margaret A(gnes)
Gordon, Bernard Ludwig
    1931- 27
Gordon, Colonel H. R.
    See Ellis, Edward S(ylvester)
Gordon, Donald
    See Payne, Donald Gordon
Gordon, Dorothy 1893-1970 20
Gordon, Esther S(aranga)
    1935- 10
Gordon, Frederick [Collective
    pseudonym] 1
Gordon, Hal
    See Goodwin, Harold Leland
Gordon, John 1925- 6
Gordon, John
    See Gesner, Clark
Gordon, Lew
    See Baldwin, Gordon C.

Gordon, Margaret (Anna)
    1939- 9
Gordon, Mildred 1912-1979
    Obituary 24
Gordon, Selma
    See Lanes, Selma G.
Gordon, Shirley 1921- 48
    Brief Entry 41
Gordon, Sol 1923- 11
Gordon, Stewart
    See Shirreffs, Gordon D.
Gordons, The [Joint pseudonym]
    See Gordon, Mildred
Gorelick, Molly C. 1920- 9
Gorey, Edward St. John
    1925- 29
    Brief Entry 27
Gorham, Charles Orson
    1911-1975 36
Gorham, Michael
    See Folsom, Franklin
Gormley, Beatrice 1942- 39
    Brief Entry 35
Gorog, Judith (Allen) 1938- 39
Gorsline, Douglas (Warner)
    1913-1985 11
    Obituary 43
Gorsline, (Sally) Marie 1928- 28
Gorsline, S. M.
    See Gorsline, (Sally) Marie
Goryan, Sirak
    See Saroyan, William
Goscinny, René 1926-1977 47
    Brief Entry 39
Gottlieb, Bill
    See Gottlieb, William P(aul)
Gottlieb, Gerald 1923- 7
Gottlieb, William P(aul) 24
Goudey, Alice E. 1898- 20
Goudge, Elizabeth 1900-1984 2
    Obituary 38
Gough, Catherine 1931- 24
Gough, Philip 1908- 45
Goulart, Ron 1933- 6
Gould, Chester 1900-1985 49
    Obituary 43
Gould, Jean R(osalind) 1919- 11
Gould, Lilian 1920- 6
Gould, Marilyn 1923- 15
Govan, Christine Noble 1898- 9
Govern, Elaine 1939- 26
Graaf, Peter
    See Youd, (Christopher) Samuel
Graber, Alexander 7
Graber, Richard (Fredrick)
    1927- 26
Grabiański, Janusz 1929-1976 39
    Obituary 30
Graboff, Abner 1919- 35
Grace, F(rances Jane) 45
Graeber, Charlotte Towner
    Brief Entry 44
Graff, Polly Anne
    See Colver, Anne
Graff, (S.) Stewart 1908- 9
Graham, Ada 1931- 11
Graham, Brenda Knight 1942- 32
Graham, Charlotte
    See Bowden, Joan Chase

Graham, Eleanor 1896-1984 ...... *18*
  Obituary *38*
Graham, Frank, Jr. 1925- *11*
Graham, John 1926- *11*
Graham, Kennon
  See Harrison, David Lee
Graham, Lorenz B(ell) 1902- *2*
  See also CLR 10
  See also SAAS 5
Graham, Margaret Bloy 1920- *11*
Graham, Robin Lee 1949- *7*
Graham, Shirley
  See Du Bois, Shirley Graham
Graham-Barber, Lynda 1944- *42*
Graham-Cameron, M.
  See Graham-Cameron, M(alcolm)
  G(ordon)
Graham-Cameron, M(alcolm) G(ordon)
  1931- *53*
  Brief Entry *45*
Graham-Cameron, Mike
  See Graham-Cameron, M(alcolm)
  G(ordon)
Grahame, Kenneth
  1859-1932 .... *YABC 1*
  See also CLR 5
Gramatky, Hardie 1907-1979 ..... *30*
  Obituary *23*
  Earlier sketch in SATA 1
Grand, Samuel 1912- *42*
Grandville, J. J.
  See Gérard, Jean Ignace Isidore
Grandville, Jean Ignace Isidore Gérard
  See Gérard, Jean Ignace Isidore
Grange, Peter
  See Nicole, Christopher Robin
Granger, Margaret Jane 1925(?)-1977
  Obituary *27*
Granger, Peggy
  See Granger, Margaret Jane
Granstaff, Bill 1925- *10*
Grant, Bruce 1893-1977 .... *5*
  Obituary *25*
Grant, Cynthia D. 1950- *33*
Grant, Eva 1907- *7*
Grant, Evva H. 1913-1977
  Obituary *27*
Grant, Gordon 1875-1962 .... *25*
Grant, Gwen(doline Ellen)
  1940- *47*
Grant, (Alice) Leigh 1947- *10*
Grant, Matthew C.
  See May, Julian
Grant, Maxwell
  See Lynds, Dennis
Grant, Myrna (Lois) 1934- *21*
Grant, Neil 1938- *14*
Gravel, Fern
  See Hall, James Norman
Graves, Charles Parlin
  1911-1972 .... *4*
Graves, Robert (von Ranke)
  1895-1985 .... *45*
Gray, Elizabeth Janet 1902- *6*
Gray, Genevieve S. 1920- *4*
Gray, Harold (Lincoln)
  1894-1968 .... *33*
  Brief Entry *32*

Gray, Jenny
  See Gray, Genevieve S.
Gray, Marian
  See Pierce, Edith Gray
Gray, Nicholas Stuart
  1922-1981 .... *4*
  Obituary *27*
Gray, Nigel 1941- *33*
Gray, (Lucy) Noel (Clervaux)
  1898-1983 .... *47*
Gray, Patricia *7*
Gray, Patsey
  See Gray, Patricia
Grayland, V. Merle
  See Grayland, Valerie
Grayland, Valerie *7*
Great Comte, The
  See Hawkesworth, Eric
Greaves, Margaret 1914- *7*
Grée, Alain 1936- *28*
Green, Adam
  See Weisgard, Leonard
Green, D.
  See Casewit, Curtis
Green, Hannah
  See Greenberg, Joanne (Goldenberg)
Green, Jane 1937- *9*
Green, Mary Moore 1906- *11*
Green, Morton 1937- *8*
Green, Norma B(erger) 1925- *11*
Green, Phyllis 1932- *20*
Green, Roger James 1944-
  Brief Entry *52*
Green, Roger (Gilbert) Lancelyn
  1918-1987 .... *2*
  Obituary *53*
Green, Sheila Ellen 1934- *8*
Greenaway, Kate
  1846-1901 .... *YABC 2*
  See also CLR 6
Greenbank, Anthony Hunt
  1933- *39*
Greenberg, Harvey R. 1935- *5*
Greenberg, Joanne (Goldenberg)
  1932- *25*
Greenberg, Polly 1932- *52*
  Brief Entry *43*
Greene, Bette 1934- *8*
  See also CLR 2
Greene, Carla 1916- *1*
Greene, Carol
  Brief Entry *44*
Greene, Constance C(larke)
  1924- *11*
Greene, Ellin 1927- *23*
Greene, Graham 1904- *20*
Greene, Laura 1935- *38*
Greene, Wade 1933- *11*
Greene, Yvonne
  See Flesch, Yolande (Catarina)
Greenfeld, Howard *19*
Greenfield, Eloise 1929- *19*
  See also CLR 4
Greenhaus, Thelma Nurenberg
  1903-1984 .... *45*
Greening, Hamilton
  See Hamilton, Charles H. St. John
Greenleaf, Barbara Kaye
  1942- *6*

Greenleaf, Peter 1910- *33*
Greenwald, Sheila
  See Green, Sheila Ellen
Gregg, Walter H(arold) 1919- *20*
Gregor, Arthur 1923- *36*
Gregori, Leon 1919- *15*
Gregorian, Joyce Ballou
  1946- *30*
Gregorowski, Christopher
  1940- *30*
Gregory, Diana (Jean) 1933- *49*
  Brief Entry *42*
Gregory, Jean
  See Ure, Jean
Gregory, Stephen
  See Penzler, Otto
Greisman, Joan Ruth 1937- *31*
Grendon, Stephen
  See Derleth, August (William)
Grenville, Pelham
  See Wodehouse, P(elham)
  G(renville)
Gretz, Susanna 1937- *7*
Gretzer, John *18*
Grey, Jerry 1926- *11*
Grey Owl
  See Belaney, Archibald Stansfeld
Gri
  See Denney, Diana
Grice, Frederick 1910- *6*
Grider, Dorothy 1915- *31*
Gridley, Marion E(leanor)
  1906-1974 .... *35*
  Obituary *26*
Grieder, Walter 1924- *9*
Griese, Arnold A(lfred) 1921- *9*
Grifalconi, Ann 1929- *2*
Griffin, Gillett Good 1928- *26*
Griffin, Judith Berry *34*
Griffith, Helen V(irginia)
  1934- *39*
Griffith, Jeannette
  See Eyerly, Jeanette
Griffiths, G(ordon) D(ouglas)
  1910-1973
  Obituary *20*
Griffiths, Helen 1939- *5*
  See also SAAS 5
Grimm, Cherry Barbara Lockett 1930-
  Brief Entry *43*
Grimm, Jacob Ludwig Karl
  1785-1863 .... *22*
Grimm, Wilhelm Karl
  1786-1859 .... *22*
Grimm, William C(arey)
  1907- *14*
Grimshaw, Nigel (Gilroy)
  1925- *23*
Grimsley, Gordon
  See Groom, Arthur William
Gringhuis, Dirk
  See Gringhuis, Richard H.
Gringhuis, Richard H.
  1918-1974 .... *6*
  Obituary *25*
Grinnell, George Bird
  1849-1938 .... *16*
Gripe, Maria (Kristina) 1923- *2*
  See also CLR 5

Groch, Judith (Goldstein)
  1929- 25
Grode, Redway
  See Gorey, Edward St. John
Grohskopf, Bernice 7
Grol, Lini Richards 1913- 9
Grollman, Earl A. 1925- 22
Groom, Arthur William
  1898-1964 10
Gross, Alan 1947- 54
  Brief Entry 43
Gross, Ruth Belov 1929- 33
Gross, Sarah Chokla
  1906-1976 9
  Obituary 26
Grossman, Nancy 1940- 29
Grossman, Robert 1940- 11
Groth, John 1908- 21
Groves, Georgina
  See Symons, (Dorothy) Geraldine
Gruelle, John (Barton)
  1880-1938 35
  Brief Entry 32
Gruelle, Johnny
  See Gruelle, John
Gruenberg, Sidonie M(atsner)
  1881-1974 2
  Obituary 27
Grummer, Arnold E(dward)
  1923- 49
Guay, Georgette (Marie Jeanne)
  1952- 54
Guck, Dorothy 1913- 27
Gugliotta, Bobette 1918- 7
Guillaume, Jeanette G. (Flierl)
  1899- 8
Guillot, Rene 1900-1969 7
Gundersheimer, Karen
  Brief Entry 44
Gundrey, Elizabeth 1924- 23
Gunn, James E(dwin) 1923- 35
Gunston, Bill
  See Gunston, William Tudor
Gunston, William Tudor
  1927- 9
Gunterman, Bertha Lisette
  1886(?)-1975
  Obituary 27
Gunther, John 1901-1970 2
Gurko, Leo 1914- 9
Gurko, Miriam 9
Gustafson, Anita 1942-
  Brief Entry 45
Gustafson, Sarah R.
  See Riedman, Sarah R.
Gustafson, Scott 1956- 34
Guthrie, Anne 1890-1979 28
Gutman, Bill
  Brief Entry 43
Gutman, Naham 1899(?)-1981
  Obituary 25
Guy, Rosa (Cuthbert) 1928- 14
  See also CLR 13
Guymer, (Wilhelmina) Mary
  1909- 50
Gwynne, Fred(erick Hubbard)
  1926- 41
  Brief Entry 27

H

Haar, Jaap ter 1922-
  See also CLR 15
Haas, Carolyn Buhai 1926- 43
Haas, Dorothy F. 46
  Brief Entry 43
Haas, Irene 1929- 17
Haas, James E(dward) 1943- 40
Haas, Merle S. 1896(?)-1985
  Obituary 41
Habenstreit, Barbara 1937- 5
Haber, Louis 1910- 12
Hader, Berta (Hoerner)
  1891(?)-1976 16
Hader, Elmer (Stanley)
  1889-1973 16
Hadley, Franklin
  See Winterbotham, R(ussell)
  R(obert)
Hadley, Lee 1934- 47
  Brief Entry 38
Hafner, Marylin 1925- 7
Hager, Alice Rogers 1894-1969
  Obituary 26
Haggard, H(enry) Rider
  1856-1925 16
Haggerty, James J(oseph)
  1920- 5
Hagon, Priscilla
  See Allan, Mabel Esther
Hague, (Susan) Kathleen
  1949- 49
  Brief Entry 45
Hague, Michael (Riley) 1948- 48
  Brief Entry 32
Hahn, Emily 1905- 3
Hahn, Hannelore 1926- 8
Hahn, James (Sage) 1947- 9
Hahn, (Mona) Lynn 1949- 9
Hahn, Mary Downing 1937- 50
  Brief Entry 44
Haig-Brown, Roderick (Langmere)
  1909-1976 12
Haight, Anne Lyon 1895-1977
  Obituary 30
Haines, Gail Kay 1943- 11
Haining, Peter 1940- 14
Halacy, D(aniel) S(tephen), Jr.
  1919- 36
Haldane, Roger John 1945- 13
Hale, Arlene 1924-1982 49
Hale, Edward Everett
  1822-1909 16
Hale, Helen
  See Mulcahy, Lucille Burnett
Hale, Irina 1932- 26
Hale, Kathleen 1898- 17
Hale, Linda 1929- 6
Hale, Lucretia Peabody
  1820-1900 26
Hale, Nancy 1908- 31
Haley, Gail E(inhart) 1939- 43
  Brief Entry 28
Haley, Neale 52
Hall, Adam
  See Trevor, Elleston
Hall, Adele 1910- 7

Hall, Anna Gertrude
  1882-1967 8
Hall, Borden
  See Yates, Raymond F(rancis)
Hall, Brian P(atrick) 1935- 31
Hall, Caryl
  See Hansen, Caryl (Hall)
Hall, Donald (Andrew, Jr.)
  1928- 23
Hall, Douglas 1931- 43
Hall, Elvajean 6
Hall, James Norman
  1887-1951 21
Hall, Jesse
  See Boesen, Victor
Hall, Katy
  See McMullan, Kate (Hall)
Hall, Lynn 1937- 47
  Earlier sketch in SATA 2
  See also SAAS 4
Hall, Malcolm 1945- 7
Hall, Marjory
  See Yeakley, Marjory Hall
Hall, Rosalys Haskell 1914- 7
Hallard, Peter
  See Catherall, Arthur
Hallas, Richard
  See Knight, Eric (Mowbray)
Hall-Clarke, James
  See Rowland-Entwistle, (Arthur)
  Theodore (Henry)
Haller, Dorcas Woodbury
  1946- 46
Halliburton, Warren J. 1924- 19
Halliday, William R(oss)
  1926- 52
Hallin, Emily Watson 1919- 6
Hallinan, P(atrick) K(enneth)
  1944- 39
  Brief Entry 37
Hallman, Ruth 1929- 43
  Brief Entry 28
Hall-Quest, (Edna) Olga W(ilbourne)
  1899-1986 11
  Obituary 47
Hallstead, William F(inn) III
  1924- 11
Hallward, Michael 1889- 12
Halsell, Grace 1923- 13
Halsted, Anna Roosevelt 1906-1975
  Obituary 30
Halter, Jon C(harles) 1941- 22
Hamalian, Leo 1920- 41
Hamberger, John 1934- 14
Hamblin, Dora Jane 1920- 36
Hamerstrom, Frances 1907- 24
Hamil, Thomas Arthur 1928- 14
Hamil, Tom
  See Hamil, Thomas Arthur
Hamill, Ethel
  See Webb, Jean Francis (III)
Hamilton, Alice
  See Cromie, Alice Hamilton
Hamilton, Charles Harold St. John
  1875-1961 13
Hamilton, Clive
  See Lewis, C. S.
Hamilton, Dorothy 1906-1983 12
  Obituary 35

Hamilton, Edith 1867-1963 20
Hamilton, Elizabeth 1906- 23
Hamilton, Mary (E.) 1927- 55
Hamilton, Morse 1943- 35
Hamilton, Robert W.
   See Stratemeyer, Edward L.
Hamilton, Virginia 1936- 4
   See also CLR 1, 11
Hamley, Dennis 1935- 39
Hammer, Richard 1928- 6
Hammerman, Gay M(orenus)
   1926- 9
Hammond, Winifred G(raham)
   1899- 29
Hammontree, Marie (Gertrude)
   1913- 13
Hampson, (Richard) Denman
   1929- 15
Hampson, Frank 1918(?)-1985
   Obituary 46
Hamre, Leif 1914- 5
Hamsa, Bobbie 1944- 52
   Brief Entry 38
Hancock, Mary A. 1923- 31
Hancock, Sibyl 1940- 9
Handforth, Thomas (Schofield)
   1897-1948 42
Handville, Robert (Tompkins)
   1924- 45
Hane, Roger 1940-1974
   Obituary 20
Haney, Lynn 1941- 23
Hanff, Helene 11
Hanlon, Emily 1945- 15
Hann, Jacquie 1951- 19
Hanna, Bill
   See Hanna, William
Hanna, Nell(ie L.) 1908- 55
Hanna, Paul R(obert) 1902- 9
Hanna, William 1910- 51
Hannam, Charles 1925- 50
Hano, Arnold 1922- 12
Hansen, Caryl (Hall) 1929- 39
Hansen, Joyce 1942- 46
   Brief Entry 39
Hanser, Richard (Frederick)
   1909- 13
Hanson, Joan 1938- 8
Hanson, Joseph E. 1894(?)-1971
   Obituary 27
Harald, Eric
   See Boesen, Victor
Harcourt, Ellen Knowles 1890(?)-1984
   Obituary 36
Hardcastle, Michael 1933- 47
   Brief Entry 38
Harding, Lee 1937- 32
   Brief Entry 31
Hardwick, Richard Holmes, Jr.
   1923- 12
Hardy, Alice Dale [Collective
   pseudonym] 1
Hardy, David A(ndrews)
   1936- 9
Hardy, Jon 1958- 53
Hardy, Stuart
   See Schisgall, Oscar
Hardy, Thomas 1840-1928 25

Hare, Norma Q(uarles) 1924- 46
   Brief Entry 41
Harford, Henry
   See Hudson, W(illiam) H(enry)
Hargrave, Leonie
   See Disch, Thomas M(ichael)
Hargrove, James 1947-
   Brief Entry 50
Hargrove, Jim
   See Hargrove, James
Hark, Mildred
   See McQueen, Mildred Hark
Harkaway, Hal
   See Stratemeyer, Edward L.
Harkins, Philip 1912- 6
Harlan, Elizabeth 1945- 41
   Brief Entry 35
Harlan, Glen
   See Cebulash, Mel
Harman, Fred 1902(?)-1982
   Obituary 30
Harman, Hugh 1903-1982
   Obituary 33
Harmelink, Barbara (Mary) 9
Harmer, Mabel 1894- 45
Harmon, Margaret 1906- 20
Harnan, Terry 1920- 12
Harnett, Cynthia (Mary)
   1893-1981 5
   Obituary 32
Harper, Anita 1943- 41
Harper, Mary Wood
   See Dixon, Jeanne
Harper, Wilhelmina
   1884-1973 4
   Obituary 26
Harrah, Michael 1940- 41
Harrell, Sara Gordon
   See Banks, Sara (Jeanne Gordon
   Harrell)
Harries, Joan 1922- 39
Harrington, Lyn 1911- 5
Harris, Aurand 1915- 37
Harris, Christie 1907- 6
Harris, Colver
   See Colver, Anne
Harris, Dorothy Joan 1931- 13
Harris, Geraldine (Rachel)
   1951- 54
Harris, Janet 1932-1979 4
   Obituary 23
Harris, Joel Chandler
   1848-1908 .... YABC 1
Harris, Jonathan 1921- 52
Harris, Lavinia
   See Johnston, Norma
Harris, Leon A., Jr. 1926- 4
Harris, Lorle K(empe) 1912- 22
Harris, Marilyn
   See Springer, Marilyn Harris
Harris, Mark Jonathan 1941- 32
Harris, Robie H.
   Brief Entry 53
Harris, Rosemary (Jeanne) 4
   See also SAAS 7
Harris, Sherwood 1932- 25
Harris, Steven Michael 1957- 55
Harrison, C. William 1913- 35
Harrison, David Lee 1937- 26

Harrison, Deloris 1938- 9
Harrison, Harry 1925- 4
Harrison, Molly 1909- 41
Harshaw, Ruth H(etzel)
   1890-1968 27
Hart, Bruce 1938-
   Brief Entry 39
Hart, Carole 1943-
   Brief Entry 39
Harte, (Francis) Bret(t)
   1836-1902 26
Hartley, Ellen (Raphael)
   1915- 23
Hartley, Fred Allan III 1953- 41
Hartley, William B(rown)
   1913- 23
Hartman, Evert 1937- 38
   Brief Entry 35
Hartman, Jane E(vangeline)
   1928- 47
Hartman, Louis F(rancis)
   1901-1970 22
Hartshorn, Ruth M. 1928- 11
Harvey, Edith 1908(?)-1972
   Obituary 27
Harwin, Brian
   See Henderson, LeGrand
Harwood, Pearl Augusta (Bragdon)
   1903- 9
Haseley, Dennis
   Brief Entry 44
Haskell, Arnold 1903- 6
Haskins, James 1941- 9
   See also CLR 3
Haskins, Jim
   See Haskins, James
   See also SAAS 4
Hasler, Joan 1931- 28
Hassall, Joan 1906- 43
Hassler, Jon (Francis) 1933- 19
Hastings, Beverly
   See Barkin, Carol
   See James, Elizabeth
Hatch, Mary Cottam 1912-1970
   Brief Entry 28
Hatlo, Jimmy 1898-1963
   Obituary 23
Haugaard, Erik Christian
   1923- 4
   See also CLR 11
Hauman, Doris 1898- 32
Hauman, George 1890-1961 32
Hauser, Margaret L(ouise)
   1909- 10
Hausman, Gerald 1945- 13
Hausman, Gerry
   See Hausman, Gerald
Hautzig, Deborah 1956- 31
Hautzig, Esther 1930- 4
Havenhand, John
   See Cox, John Roberts
Havighurst, Walter (Edwin)
   1901- 1
Haviland, Virginia 1911-1988 6
   Obituary 54
Hawes, Judy 1913- 4
Hawk, Virginia Driving
   See Sneve, Virginia Driving Hawk
Hawkesworth, Eric 1921- 13

Hawkins, Arthur 1903- *19*
Hawkins, Quail 1905- *6*
Hawkinson, John 1912- *4*
Hawkinson, Lucy (Ozone)
  1924-1971 .... *21*
Hawley, Mable C. [Collective
  pseudonym] *1*
Hawthorne, Captain R. M.
  See Ellis, Edward S(ylvester)
Hawthorne, Nathaniel
  1804-1864 ....*YABC 2*
Hay, John 1915- *13*
Hay, Timothy
  See Brown, Margaret Wise
Haycraft, Howard 1905- *6*
Haycraft, Molly Costain
  1911- *6*
Hayden, Gwendolen Lampshire
  1904- *35*
Hayden, Robert C(arter), Jr.
  1937- *47*
  Brief Entry *28*
Hayden, Robert E(arl)
  1913-1980 .... *19*
  Obituary *26*
Hayes, Carlton J. H.
  1882-1964 .... *11*
Hayes, Geoffrey 1947- *26*
Hayes, John F. 1904- *11*
Hayes, Sheila 1937- *51*
  Brief Entry *50*
Hayes, Will *7*
Hayes, William D(imitt)
  1913- *8*
Haynes, Betsy 1937- *48*
  Brief Entry *37*
Hays, H(offman) R(eynolds)
  1904-1980 .... *26*
Hays, Wilma Pitchford 1909- *28*
  Earlier sketch in SATA 1
  See also SAAS 3
Hayward, Linda 1943-
  Brief Entry *39*
Haywood, Carolyn 1898- *29*
  Earlier sketch in SATA 1
Hazen, Barbara Shook 1930- *27*
Head, Gay
  See Hauser, Margaret L(ouise)
Headley, Elizabeth
  See Cavanna, Betty
Headstrom, Richard 1902- *8*
Heady, Eleanor B(utler) 1917- *8*
Heal, Edith 1903- *7*
Healey, Brooks
  See Albert, Burton, Jr.
Healey, Larry 1927- *44*
  Brief Entry *42*
Heaps, Willard (Allison)
  1909- *26*
Hearn, Emily
  See Valleau, Emily
Hearne, Betsy Gould 1942- *38*
Heath, Charles D(ickinson)
  1941- *46*
Heath, Veronica
  See Blackett, Veronica Heath
Heaven, Constance
  See Fecher, Constance

Hecht, George J(oseph) 1895-1980
  Obituary *22*
Hecht, Henri Joseph 1922- *9*
Hechtkopf, Henryk 1910- *17*
Heck, Bessie Holland 1911- *26*
Hedderwick, Mairi 1939- *30*
Hedges, Sid(ney) G(eorge)
  1897-1974 .... *28*
Hefter, Richard 1942- *31*
Hegarty, Reginald Beaton
  1906-1973 .... *10*
Heide, Florence Parry 1919- *32*
  See also SAAS 6
Heiderstadt, Dorothy 1907- *6*
Heilbrun, Lois Hussey 1922(?)-1987
  Obituary *54*
Heilman, Joan Rattner *50*
Hein, Lucille Eleanor 1915- *20*
Heinemann, George Alfred 1918-
  Brief Entry *31*
Heinlein, Robert A(nson)
  1907- *9*
Heins, Paul 1909- *13*
Heintze, Carl 1922- *26*
Heinz, W(ilfred) C(harles)
  1915- *26*
Heinzen, Mildred
  See Masters, Mildred
Helfman, Elizabeth S(eaver)
  1911- *3*
Helfman, Harry 1910- *3*
Hellberg, Hans-Eric 1927- *38*
Heller, Linda 1944- *46*
  Brief Entry *40*
Hellman, Hal
  See Hellman, Harold
Hellman, Harold 1927- *4*
Helps, Racey 1913-1971 .... *2*
  Obituary *25*
Helweg, Hans H. 1917- *50*
  Brief Entry *33*
Hemming, Roy 1928- *11*
Hemphill, Martha Locke
  1904-1973 .... *37*
Henbest, Nigel 1951- *55*
  Brief Entry *52*
Henderley, Brooks [Collective
  pseudonym] *1*
Henderson, Gordon 1950- *53*
Henderson, Kathy 1949- *55*
  Brief Entry *53*
Henderson, LeGrand
  1901-1965 .... *9*
Henderson, Nancy Wallace
  1916- *22*
Henderson, Zenna (Chlarson)
  1917- *5*
Hendrickson, Walter Brookfield, Jr.
  1936- *9*
Heneghan, James 1930- *53*
Henkes, Kevin 1960- *43*
Henriod, Lorraine 1925- *26*
Henry, Joanne Landers 1927- *6*
Henry, Marguerite *11*
  See also CLR 4
  See also SAAS 7
Henry, O.
  See Porter, William Sydney

Henry, Oliver
  See Porter, William Sydney
Henry, T. E.
  See Rowland-Entwistle, (Arthur)
  Theodore (Henry)
Henson, James Maury 1936- *43*
Henson, Jim
  See Henson, James Maury
Henstra, Friso 1928- *8*
Hentoff, Nat(han Irving)
  1925- *42*
  Brief Entry *27*
  See also CLR 1
Herald, Kathleen
  See Peyton, Kathleen (Wendy)
Herbert, Cecil
  See Hamilton, Charles H. St. John
Herbert, Don 1917- *2*
Herbert, Frank (Patrick)
  1920-1986 .... *37*
  Obituary *47*
  Earlier sketch in SATA 9
Herbert, Wally
  See Herbert, Walter William
Herbert, Walter William
  1934- *23*
Hergé
  See Rémi, Georges
  See also CLR 6
Herkimer, L(awrence) R(ussell)
  1925- *42*
Herman, Charlotte 1937- *20*
Hermanson, Dennis (Everett)
  1947- *10*
Hermes, Patricia 1936- *31*
Herriot, James
  See Wight, James Alfred
Herrmanns, Ralph 1933- *11*
Herriot, James
  See Wight, James Alfred
Herron, Edward A(lbert)
  1912- *4*
Hersey, John (Richard) 1914- *25*
Hertz, Grete Janus 1915- *23*
Hess, Lilo 1916- *4*
Hesse, Hermann 1877-1962 ...... *50*
Hest, Amy 1950- *55*
Heuer, Kenneth John 1927- *44*
Heuman, William 1912-1971 ..... *21*
Hewes, Agnes Danforth
  1874-1963 .... *35*
Hewett, Anita 1918- *13*
Hext, Harrington
  See Phillpotts, Eden
Hey, Nigel S(tewart) 1936- *20*
Heyduck-Huth, Hilde 1929- *8*
Heyerdahl, Thor 1914- *52*
  Earlier sketch in SATA 2
Heyliger, William
  1884-1955 ....*YABC 1*
Heyman, Ken(neth Louis)
  1930- *34*
Heyward, Du Bose 1885-1940 .... *21*
Heywood, Karen 1946- *48*
Hibbert, Christopher 1924- *4*
Hibbert, Eleanor Burford
  1906- *2*
Hickman, Janet 1940- *12*

Hickman, Martha Whitmore
1925- 26
Hickok, Lorena A.
1892(?)-1968 20
Hickok, Will
See Harrison, C. William
Hicks, Clifford B. 1920- 50
Hicks, Eleanor B.
See Coerr, Eleanor
Hicks, Harvey
See Stratemeyer, Edward L.
Hieatt, Constance B(artlett)
1928- 4
Hiebert, Ray Eldon 1932- 13
Higdon, Hal 1931- 4
Higginbottom, J(effrey) Winslow
1945- 29
Higham, David (Michael)
1949- 50
Highet, Helen
See MacInnes, Helen
Hightower, Florence Cole
1916-1981 4
Obituary 27
Highwater, Jamake 1942- 32
Brief Entry 30
Hildebrandt, Greg 1939- 55
Brief Entry 33
Hildebrandt, Tim(othy) 1939- 55
Brief Entry 33
Hildebrandt, The Brothers
See Hildebrandt, Greg
See also Hildebrandt, Tim(othy)
Hildebrandts, The
See Hildebrandt, Greg
See also Hildebrandt, Tim(othy)
Hilder, Rowland 1905- 36
Hildick, E. W.
See Hildick, Wallace
See also SAAS 6
Hildick, (Edmund) Wallace
1925- 2
Hill, Donna (Marie) 24
Hill, Douglas (Arthur) 1935- 39
Hill, Elizabeth Starr 1925- 24
Hill, Eric 1927-
Brief Entry 53
See also CLR 13
Hill, Grace Brooks [Collective
pseudonym] 1
Hill, Grace Livingston
1865-1947 .... *YABC* 2
Hill, Helen M(orey) 1915- 27
Hill, Kathleen Louise 1917- 4
Hill, Kay
See Hill, Kathleen Louise
Hill, Lorna 1902- 12
Hill, Margaret (Ohler) 1915- 36
Hill, Meg
See Hill, Margaret (Ohler)
Hill, Monica
See Watson, Jane Werner
Hill, Robert W(hite)
1919-1982 12
Obituary 31
Hill, Ruth A.
See Viguers, Ruth Hill
Hill, Ruth Livingston
See Munce, Ruth Hill

Hillcourt, William 1900- 27
Hillerman, Tony 1925- 6
Hillert, Margaret 1920- 8
Hillman, Martin
See Hill, Douglas (Arthur)
Hillman, Priscilla 1940- 48
Brief Entry 39
Hills, C(harles) A(lbert) R(eis)
1955- 39
Hilton, Irene (P.) 1912- 7
Hilton, James 1900-1954 34
Hilton, Ralph 1907- 8
Hilton, Suzanne 1922- 4
Him, George 1900-1982
Obituary 30
Himler, Ann 1946- 8
Himler, Ronald 1937- 6
Himmelman, John (Carl)
1959- 47
Hinckley, Helen
See Jones, Helen Hinckley
Hind, Dolores (Ellen) 1931- 53
Brief Entry 49
Hines, Anna G(rossnickle)
1946- 51
Brief Entry 45
Hinton, S(usan) E(loise)
1950- 19
See also CLR 3
Hinton, Sam 1917- 43
Hintz, (Loren) Martin 1945- 47
Brief Entry 39
Hirsch, Phil 1926- 35
Hirsch, S. Carl 1913- 2
See also SAAS 7
Hirschmann, Linda (Ann)
1941- 40
Hirsh, Marilyn 1944- 7
Hirshberg, Al(bert Simon)
1909-1973 38
Hiser, Iona Seibert 1901- 4
Hitchcock, Alfred (Joseph)
1899-1980 27
Obituary 24
Hitte, Kathryn 1919- 16
Hitz, Demi 1942- 11
Hnizdovsky, Jacques 1915- 32
Ho, Minfong 1951- 15
Hoagland, Edward 1932- 51
Hoare, Robert J(ohn)
1921-1975 38
Hoban, Lillian 1925- 22
Hoban, Russell C(onwell)
1925- 40
Earlier sketch in SATA 1
See also CLR 3
Hoban, Tana 22
See also CLR 13
Hobart, Lois 7
Hoberman, Mary Ann 1930- 5
Hobson, Burton (Harold)
1933- 28
Hobson, Laura Z(ametkin)
1900-1986 52
Hochschild, Arlie Russell
1940- 11
Hockaby, Stephen
See Mitchell, Gladys (Maude
Winifred)

Hockenberry, Hope
See Newell, Hope (Hockenberry)
Hodge, P(aul) W(illiam)
1934- 12
Hodgell, P(atricia) C(hristine)
1951- 42
Hodges, C(yril) Walter 1909- 2
Hodges, Carl G. 1902-1964 10
Hodges, Elizabeth Jamison 1
Hodges, Margaret Moore
1911- 33
Earlier sketch in SATA 1
Hodgetts, Blake Christopher
1967- 43
Hoexter, Corinne K. 1927- 6
Hoff, Carol 1900- 11
Hoff, Syd(ney) 1912- 9
See also SAAS 4
Hoffman, Edwin D. 49
Hoffman, Phyllis M. 1944- 4
Hoffman, Rosekrans 1926- 15
Hoffmann, E(rnst) T(heodor)
A(madeus) 1776-1822 27
Hoffmann, Felix 1911-1975 9
Hoffmann, Margaret Jones
1910- 48
Hoffmann, Peggy
See Hoffmann, Margaret Jones
Hofsinde, Robert 1902-1973 21
Hogan, Bernice Harris 1929- 12
Hogan, Inez 1895- 2
Hogarth, Jr.
See Kent, Rockwell
Hogarth, Paul 1917- 41
Hogg, Garry 1902- 2
Hogner, Dorothy Childs 4
Hogner, Nils 1893-1970 25
Hogrogian, Nonny 1932- 7
See also CLR 2
See also SAAS 1
Hoh, Diane 1937- 52
Brief Entry 48
Hoke, Helen (L.) 1903- 15
Hoke, John 1925- 7
Holbeach, Henry
See Rands, William Brighty
Holberg, Ruth Langland
1889- 1
Holbrook, Peter
See Glick, Carl (Cannon)
Holbrook, Sabra
See Erickson, Sabra R(ollins)
Holbrook, Stewart Hall
1893-1964 2
Holden, Elizabeth Rhoda
See Lawrence, Louise
Holding, James 1907- 3
Holisher, Desider 1901-1972 6
Holl, Adelaide (Hinkle) 8
Holl, Kristi D(iane) 1951- 51
Holland, Isabelle 1920- 8
Holland, Janice 1913-1962 18
Holland, John L(ewis) 1919- 20
Holland, Lys
See Gater, Dilys
Holland, Marion 1908- 6
Hollander, John 1929- 13
Hollander, Phyllis 1928- 39
Holldobler, Turid 1939- 26

Holliday, Joe
See Holliday, Joseph
Holliday, Joseph 1910- 11
Holling, Holling C(lancy)
1900-1973 15
Obituary 26
Hollingsworth, Alvin C(arl)
1930- 39
Holloway, Teresa (Bragunier)
1906- 26
Holm, (Else) Anne (Lise)
1922- 1
See also SAAS 7
Holman, Felice 1919- 7
Holme, Bryan 1913- 26
Holmes, Marjorie 1910- 43
Holmes, Oliver Wendell
1809-1894 34
Holmes, Rick
See Hardwick, Richard Holmes, Jr.
Holmgren, George Ellen
See Holmgren, Helen Jean
Holmgren, Helen Jean 1930- 45
Holmgren, Virginia C(unningham)
1909- 26
Holmquist, Eve 1921- 11
Holt, Margaret 1937- 4
Holt, Margaret Van Vechten
(Saunders) 1899-1963 32
Holt, Michael (Paul) 1929- 13
Holt, Rackham
See Holt, Margaret Van Vechten
(Saunders)
Holt, Rochelle Lynn 1946- 41
Holt, Stephen
See Thompson, Harlan H.
Holt, Victoria
See Hibbert, Eleanor
Holton, Leonard
See Wibberley, Leonard (Patrick
O'Connor)
Holyer, Erna Maria 1925- 22
Holyer, Ernie
See Holyer, Erna Maria
Holz, Loretta (Marie) 1943- 17
Homze, Alma C. 1932- 17
Honig, Donald 1931- 18
Honness, Elizabeth H. 1904- 2
Hoobler, Dorothy 28
Hoobler, Thomas 28
Hood, Joseph F. 1925- 4
Hood, Robert E. 1926- 21
Hook, Frances 1912- 27
Hook, Martha 1936- 27
Hooker, Ruth 1920- 21
Hooks, William H(arris)
1921- 16
Hooper, Byrd
See St. Clair, Byrd Hooper
Hooper, Meredith (Jean)
1939- 28
Hoopes, Lyn L(ittlefield)
1953- 49
Brief Entry 44
Hoopes, Ned E(dward) 1932- 21
Hoopes, Roy 1922- 11
Hoople, Cheryl G.
Brief Entry 32

Hoover, H(elen) M(ary) 1935- 44
Brief Entry 33
Hoover, Helen (Drusilla Blackburn)
1910-1984 12
Obituary 39
Hope, Laura Lee [Collective
pseudonym] 1
See also Adams, Harriet
S(tratemeyer)
Hope Simpson, Jacynth 1930- 12
Hopf, Alice
See Hopf, Alice (Martha) L(ightner)
Hopf, Alice (Martha) L(ightner)
Obituary 55
Hopf, Alice L(ightner) 1904- 5
Hopkins, A. T.
See Turngren, Annette
Hopkins, Clark 1895-1976
Obituary 34
Hopkins, Joseph G(erard) E(dward)
1909- 11
Hopkins, Lee Bennett 1938- 3
See also SAAS 4
Hopkins, Lyman
See Folsom, Franklin
Hopkins, Marjorie 1911- 9
Hoppe, Joanne 1932- 42
Hopper, Nancy J. 1937- 38
Brief Entry 35
Horgan, Paul 1903- 13
Hornblow, Arthur (Jr.)
1893-1976 15
Hornblow, Leonora (Schinasi)
1920- 18
Horne, Richard Henry
1803-1884 29
Horner, Althea (Jane) 1926- 36
Horner, Dave 1934- 12
Hornos, Axel 1907- 20
Horvath, Betty 1927- 4
Horwich, Frances R(appaport)
1908- 11
Horwitz, Elinor Lander 45
Brief Entry 33
Hosford, Dorothy (Grant)
1900-1952 22
Hosford, Jessie 1892- 5
Hoskyns-Abrahall, Clare 13
Houck, Carter 1924- 22
Hough, (Helen) Charlotte
1924- 9
Hough, Judy Taylor 1932-
Brief Entry 51
Hough, Richard (Alexander)
1922- 17
Houghton, Eric 1930- 7
Houlehen, Robert J. 1918- 18
Household, Geoffrey (Edward West)
1900- 14
Houselander, (Frances) Caryll
1900-1954
Brief Entry 31
Housman, Laurence
1865-1959 25
Houston, James A(rchibald)
1921- 13
See also CLR 3
Houton, Kathleen
See Kilgore, Kathleen

Howard, Alan 1922- 45
Howard, Alyssa
See Buckholtz, Eileen (Garber)
Howard, Elizabeth
See Mizner, Elizabeth Howard
Howard, Prosper
See Hamilton, Charles H. St. John
Howard, Robert West 1908- 5
Howard, Vernon (Linwood)
1918- 40
Howarth, David 1912- 6
Howe, Deborah 1946-1978 29
Howe, Fanny 1940-
Brief Entry 52
Howe, James 1946- 29
See also CLR 9
Howell, Pat 1947- 15
Howell, S.
See Styles, Frank Showell
Howell, Virginia Tier
See Ellison, Virginia Howell
Howes, Barbara 1914- 5
Howker, Janni
Brief Entry 46
See also CLR 14
Hoy, Nina
See Roth, Arthur J(oseph)
Hoyle, Geoffrey 1942- 18
Hoyt, Edwin P(almer), Jr.
1923- 28
Hoyt, Olga (Gruhzit) 1922- 16
Hubbell, Patricia 1928- 8
Hubley, Faith (Elliot) 1924- 48
Hubley, John 1914-1977 48
Obituary 24
Hudson, Jeffrey
See Crichton, (J.) Michael
Hudson, (Margaret) Kirsty
1947- 32
Hudson, W(illiam) H(enry)
1841-1922 35
Huffaker, Sandy 1943- 10
Huffman, Tom 24
Hughes, Dean 1943- 33
Hughes, (James) Langston
1902-1967 33
Earlier sketch in SATA 4
Hughes, Matilda
See MacLeod, Charlotte (Matilda
Hughes)
Hughes, Monica 1925- 15
See also CLR 9
Hughes, Richard (Arthur Warren)
1900-1976 8
Obituary 25
Hughes, Sara
See Saunders, Susan
Hughes, Shirley 1929- 16
See also CLR 15
Hughes, Ted 1930- 49
Brief Entry 27
See also CLR 3
Hughes, Thomas 1822-1896 31
Hughes, Walter (Llewellyn)
1910- 26
Hugo, Victor (Marie)
1802-1885 47
Huline-Dickens, Frank William
1931- 34

Hull, Eleanor (Means) 1913- *21*
Hull, Eric Traviss
  See Harnan, Terry
Hull, H. Braxton
  See Jacobs, Helen Hull
Hull, Jesse Redding
  See Hull, Jessie Redding
Hull, Jessie Redding 1932- *51*
Hull, Katharine 1921-1977 .... *23*
Hülsmann, Eva 1928- *16*
Hults, Dorothy Niebrugge
  1898- *6*
Hume, Lotta Carswell *7*
Hume, Ruth (Fox) 1922-1980 ..... *26*
  Obituary *22*
Hummel, Berta 1909-1946 .... *43*
Hummel, Sister Maria Innocentia
  See Hummel, Berta
Humphrey, Henry (III) 1930- *16*
Humphreys, Graham 1945-
  Brief Entry *32*
Hungerford, Pixie
  See Brinsmead, H(esba) F(ay)
Hunkin, Tim(othy Mark Trelawney)
  1950- *53*
Hunt, Francis
  See Stratemeyer, Edward L.
Hunt, Irene 1907- *2*
  See also CLR 1
Hunt, Joyce 1927- *31*
Hunt, Linda Lawrence 1940- *39*
Hunt, Mabel Leigh 1892-1971 .... *1*
  Obituary *26*
Hunt, Morton 1920- *22*
Hunt, Nigel
  See Greenbank, Anthony Hunt
Hunter, Bernice Thurman 1922-
  Brief Entry *45*
Hunter, Clingham, M.D.
  See Adams, William Taylor
Hunter, Dawe
  See Downie, Mary Alice
Hunter, Edith Fisher 1919- *31*
Hunter, Evan 1926- *25*
Hunter, Hilda 1921- *7*
Hunter, Kristin (Eggleston)
  1931- *12*
  See also CLR 3
Hunter, Leigh
  See Etchison, Birdie L(ee)
Hunter, Mel 1927- *39*
Hunter, Mollie 1922- *54*
  See also SAAS 7
Hunter, Norman (George Lorimer)
  1899- *26*
Hunter Blair, Pauline 1921- *3*
Huntington, Harriet E(lizabeth)
  1909- *1*
Huntsberry, William E(mery)
  1916- *5*
Hurd, Clement (G) 1908-1988 .... *2*
  Obituary *54*
Hurd, Edith Thacher 1910- *2*
Hurd, Thacher 1949- *46*
  Brief Entry *45*
Hürlimann, Bettina 1909-1983 .... *39*
  Obituary *34*
Hürlimann, Ruth 1939- *32*
  Brief Entry *31*

Hurwitz, Johanna 1937- *20*
Hurwood, Bernhardt J.
  1926-1987 .... *12*
  Obituary *50*
Hutchens, Paul 1902-1977 .... *31*
Hutchins, Carleen Maley
  1911- *9*
Hutchins, Hazel J. 1952-
  Brief Entry *51*
Hutchins, Pat 1942- *15*
Hutchins, Ross E(lliott) 1906- *4*
Hutchmacher, J. Joseph 1929- *5*
Hutto, Nelson (Allen) 1904- *20*
Hutton, Warwick 1939- *20*
Hyde, Dayton O(gden) *9*
Hyde, Hawk
  See Hyde, Dayton O(gden)
Hyde, Margaret Oldroyd
  1917- *42*
  Earlier sketch in SATA 1
Hyde, Shelley
  See Reed, Kit
Hyde, Wayne F. 1922- *7*
Hylander, Clarence J.
  1897-1964 .... *7*
Hyman, Robin P(hilip) 1931- *12*
Hyman, Trina Schart 1939- *46*
  Earlier sketch in SATA 7
Hymes, Lucia M. 1907- *7*
Hyndman, Jane Andrews
  1912-1978 .... *46*
  Obituary *23*
  Earlier sketch in SATA 1
Hyndman, Robert Utley
  1906(?)-1973 .... *18*

I

I.W.
  See Watts, Isaac
Iannone, Jeanne *7*
Ibbotson, Eva 1925- *13*
Ibbotson, M. C(hristine)
  1930- *5*
Ichikawa, Satomi 1949- *47*
  Brief Entry *36*
Ilowite, Sheldon A. 1931- *27*
Ilsley, Dent [Joint pseudonym]
  See Chapman, John Stanton Higham
Ilsley, Velma (Elizabeth)
  1918- *12*
Immel, Mary Blair 1930- *28*
Ingelow, Jean 1820-1897 .... *33*
Ingham, Colonel Frederic
  See Hale, Edward Everett
Ingman, Nicholas 1948- *52*
Ingraham, Leonard W(illiam)
  1913- *4*
Ingrams, Doreen 1906- *20*
Inyart, Gene 1927- *6*
Ionesco, Eugene 1912- *7*
Ipcar, Dahlov (Zorach) 1917- *49*
  Earlier sketch in SATA 1
Irvin, Fred 1914- *15*
Irving, Alexander
  See Hume, Ruth (Fox)
Irving, Robert
  See Adler, Irving

Irving, Washington
  1783-1859 .... *YABC 2*
Irwin, Ann(abelle Bowen)
  1915- *44*
  Brief Entry *38*
Irwin, Constance Frick 1913- *6*
Irwin, Hadley [Joint pseudonym]
  See Hadley, Lee and Irwin, Ann
Irwin, Keith Gordon
  1885-1964 .... *11*
Isaac, Joanne 1934- *21*
Isaacs, Jacob
  See Kranzler, George G(ershon)
Isadora, Rachel 1953(?)- *54*
  Brief Entry *32*
  See also CLR 7
Isham, Charlotte H(ickox)
  1912- *21*
Ish-Kishor, Judith 1892-1972 ..... *11*
Ish-Kishor, Sulamith
  1896-1977 .... *17*
Ishmael, Woodi 1914- *31*
Israel, Elaine 1945- *12*
Israel, Marion Louise 1882-1973
  Obituary *26*
Iverson, Genie 1942-
  Brief Entry *52*
Iwamatsu, Jun Atsushi 1908- *14*

J

Jac, Lee
  See Morton, Lee Jack, Jr.
Jackson, Anne 1896(?)-1984
  Obituary *37*
Jackson, C. Paul 1902- *6*
Jackson, Caary
  See Jackson, C. Paul
Jackson, Geoffrey (Holt Seymour)
  1915-1987
  Obituary *53*
Jackson, Jesse 1908-1983 .... *29*
  Obituary *48*
  Earlier sketch in SATA 2
Jackson, O. B.
  See Jackson, C. Paul
Jackson, Robert B(lake) 1926- *8*
Jackson, Sally
  See Kellogg, Jean
Jackson, Shirley 1919-1965 .... *2*
Jacob, Helen Pierce 1927- *21*
Jacobi, Kathy
  Brief Entry *42*
Jacobs, Flora Gill 1918- *5*
Jacobs, Francine 1935- *43*
  Brief Entry *42*
Jacobs, Frank 1929- *30*
Jacobs, Helen Hull 1908- *12*
Jacobs, Joseph 1854-1916 .... *25*
Jacobs, Leland Blair 1907- *20*
Jacobs, Linda C. 1943- *21*
Jacobs, Lou(is), Jr. 1921- *2*
Jacobs, Susan 1940- *30*
Jacobs, William Jay 1933- *28*
Jacobson, Daniel 1923- *12*
Jacobson, Morris K(arl) 1906- *21*
Jacopetti, Alexandra 1939- *14*

Jacques, Robin 1920- *32*
  Brief Entry *30*
  See also SAAS 5
Jaffee, Al(lan) 1921-
  Brief Entry *37*
Jagendorf, Moritz (Adolf)
  1888-1981 .... *2*
  Obituary *24*
Jahn, (Joseph) Michael 1943- *28*
Jahn, Mike
  See Jahn, (Joseph) Michael
Jahsmann, Allan Hart 1916- *28*
James, Andrew
  See Kirkup, James
James, Dynely
  See Mayne, William
James, Edwin
  See Gunn, James E(dwin)
James, Elizabeth 1942- *52*
James, Harry Clebourne 1896- *11*
James, Josephine
  See Sterne, Emma Gelders
James, Robin (Irene) 1953- *50*
James, T. F.
  See Fleming, Thomas J(ames)
James, Will(iam Roderick)
  1892-1942 .... *19*
Jance, J. A.
  See Jance, Judith A(nn)
Jance, Judith A(nn) 1944-
  Brief Entry *50*
Jane, Mary Childs 1909- *6*
Janeczko, Paul B(ryan) 1945- *53*
Janes, Edward C. 1908- *25*
Janes, J(oseph) Robert 1935-
  Brief Entry *50*
Janeway, Elizabeth (Hall)
  1913- *19*
Janice
  See Brustlein, Janice Tworkov
Janosch
  See Eckert, Horst
Jansen, Jared
  See Cebulash, Mel
Janson, Dora Jane 1916- *31*
Janson, H(orst) W(oldemar)
  1913- *9*
Jansson, Tove (Marika) 1914- *41*
  Earlier sketch in SATA 3
  See also CLR 2
Janus, Grete
  See Hertz, Grete Janus
Jaques, Faith 1923- *21*
Jaques, Francis Lee 1887-1969
  Brief Entry *28*
Jaquith, Priscilla 1908- *51*
Jarman, Rosemary Hawley
  1935- *7*
Jarrell, Mary von Schrader
  1914- *35*
Jarrell, Randall 1914-1965 .... *7*
  See also CLR 6
Jarrett, Roxanne
  See Werner, Herma
Jasner, W. K.
  See Watson, Jane Werner
Jauss, Anne Marie 1907- *10*
Jayne, Lieutenant R. H.
  See Ellis, Edward S(ylvester)

Jaynes, Clare [Joint pseudonym]
  See Mayer, Jane Rothschild
Jeake, Samuel, Jr.
  See Aiken, Conrad
Jefferds, Vincent H(arris) 1916-
  Brief Entry *49*
Jefferies, (John) Richard
  1848-1887 .... *16*
Jeffers, Susan *17*
Jefferson, Sarah
  See Farjeon, Annabel
Jeffries, Roderic 1926- *4*
Jenkins, Marie M. 1909- *7*
Jenkins, William A(twell)
  1922- *9*
Jenkyns, Chris 1924- *51*
Jennings, Gary (Gayne) 1928- *9*
Jennings, Robert
  See Hamilton, Charles H. St. John
Jennings, S. M.
  See Meyer, Jerome Sydney
Jennison, C. S.
  See Starbird, Kaye
Jennison, Keith Warren 1911- *14*
Jensen, Niels 1927- *25*
Jensen, Virginia Allen 1927- *8*
Jeppson, J. O.
  See Asimov, Janet (Jeppson)
Jeschke, Susan *42*
  Brief Entry *27*
Jessel, Camilla (Ruth) 1937- *29*
Jewell, Nancy 1940-
  Brief Entry *41*
Jewett, Eleanore Myers
  1890-1967 .... *5*
Jewett, Sarah Orne 1849-1909 .... *15*
Jezard, Alison 1919-
  Brief Entry *34*
Jiler, John 1946- *42*
  Brief Entry *35*
Jobb, Jamie 1945- *29*
Joerns, Consuelo *44*
  Brief Entry *33*
John, Naomi
  See Flack, Naomi John (White)
Johns, Avery
  See Cousins, Margaret
Johns, W(illiam) E(arl)
  1893-1968 .... *55*
Johnson, A. E. [Joint pseudonym]
  See Johnson, Annabell and Johnson,
  Edgar
Johnson, Annabell Jones
  1921- *2*
Johnson, Benj. F., of Boone
  See Riley, James Whitcomb
Johnson, Charles R. 1925- *11*
Johnson, Charlotte Buel
  1918-1982 .... *46*
Johnson, Chuck
  See Johnson, Charles R.
Johnson, Crockett
  See Leisk, David (Johnson)
Johnson, D(ana) William
  1945- *23*
Johnson, Dorothy M(arie)
  1905-1984 .... *6*
  Obituary *40*
Johnson, E(ugene) Harper *44*

Johnson, Edgar Raymond
  1912- *2*
Johnson, Eleanor (Murdock)
  1892-1987
  Obituary *54*
Johnson, Elizabeth 1911-1984 ..... *7*
  Obituary *39*
Johnson, Eric W(arner) 1918- *8*
Johnson, Evelyne 1932- *20*
Johnson, Gaylord 1884- *7*
Johnson, Gerald White
  1890-1980 .... *19*
  Obituary *28*
Johnson, Harper
  See Johnson, E(ugene) Harper
Johnson, Harriett 1908-1987
  Obituary *53*
Johnson, James Ralph 1922- *1*
Johnson, James Weldon
  See Johnson, James William
Johnson, James William
  1871-1938 .... *31*
Johnson, Jane 1951- *48*
Johnson, John E(mil) 1929- *34*
Johnson, LaVerne B(ravo)
  1925- *13*
Johnson, Lois S(mith) *6*
Johnson, Lois W(alfrid) 1936- *22*
Johnson, Margaret S(weet)
  1893-1964 .... *35*
Johnson, Mary Frances K.
  1929(?)-1979
  Obituary *27*
Johnson, Maud Battle 1918(?)-1985
  Obituary *46*
Johnson, Milton 1932- *31*
Johnson, Natalie
  See Robison, Nancy L(ouise)
Johnson, (Walter) Ryerson
  1901- *10*
Johnson, Shirley K(ing) 1927- *10*
Johnson, Siddie Joe 1905-1977
  Obituary *20*
Johnson, Spencer 1938-
  Brief Entry *38*
Johnson, Sylvia A.
  Brief Entry *52*
Johnson, William R. *38*
Johnson, William Weber
  1909- *7*
Johnston, Agnes Christine
  See Dazey, Agnes J.
Johnston, Annie Fellows
  1863-1931 .... *37*
Johnston, Dorothy Grunbock
  1915-1979 .... *54*
Johnston, H(ugh) A(nthony) S(tephen)
  1913-1967 .... *14*
Johnston, Johanna
  1914(?)-1982 .... *12*
  Obituary *33*
Johnston, Norma *29*
Johnston, Portia
  See Takakjian, Portia
Johnston, Tony 1942- *8*
Jonas, Ann 1932- *50*
  Brief Entry *42*
  See also CLR 12
Jones, Adrienne 1915- *7*

Jones, Betty Millsaps 1940- *54*
Jones, Charles M(artin) 1912- *53*
Jones, Chuck
  See Jones, Charles M(artin)
Jones, Diana Wynne 1934- *9*
  See also SAAS 7
Jones, Douglas C(lyde) 1924- *52*
Jones, Elizabeth Orton 1910- *18*
Jones, Evan 1915- *3*
Jones, Geraldine 1951- *43*
Jones, Gillingham
  See Hamilton, Charles H. St. John
Jones, Harold 1904- *14*
Jones, Helen Hinckley 1903- *26*
Jones, Helen L. 1904(?)-1973
  Obituary *22*
Jones, Hettie 1934- *42*
  Brief Entry *27*
Jones, Hortense P. 1918- *9*
Jones, Jessie Mae Orton 1887(?)-1983
  Obituary *37*
Jones, Margaret Boone
  See Zarif, Margaret Min'imah
Jones, Mary Alice *6*
Jones, McClure *34*
Jones, Penelope 1938- *31*
Jones, Rebecca C(astaldi)
  1947- *33*
Jones, Terry 1942- *51*
Jones, Weyman 1928- *4*
Jonk, Clarence 1906- *10*
Joosse, Barbara M(onnot)
  1949- *52*
Jordan, Don
  See Howard, Vernon (Linwood)
Jordan, E(mil) L(eopold) 1900-
  Brief Entry *31*
Jordan, Hope (Dahle) 1905- *15*
Jordan, Jael (Michal) 1949- *30*
Jordan, June 1936- *4*
  See also CLR 10
Jordan, Mildred 1901- *5*
Jorgensen, Mary Venn *36*
Jorgenson, Ivar
  See Silverberg, Robert
Joseph, James (Herz) 1924- *53*
Joseph, Joan 1939- *34*
Joseph, Joseph M(aron)
  1903-1979 .... *22*
Joslin, Sesyle 1929- *2*
Joyce, J(ames) Avery
  1902-1987 .... *11*
  Obituary *50*
Joyce, William 1959(?)-
  Brief Entry *46*
Joyner, Jerry 1938- *34*
Jucker, Sita 1921- *5*
Judd, Denis (O'Nan) 1938- *33*
Judd, Frances K. [Collective
  pseudonym] *1*
Judson, Clara Ingram
  1879-1960 .... *38*
  Brief Entry *27*
Judy, Stephen
  See Tchudi, Stephen N.
Judy, Stephen N.
  See Tchudi, Stephen N.
Jukes, Mavis
  Brief Entry *43*

Jumpp, Hugo
  See MacPeek, Walter G.
Jupo, Frank J. 1904- *7*
Juster, Norton 1929- *3*
Justus, May 1898- *1*
Juvenilia
  See Taylor, Ann

K

Kabdebo, Tamas
  See Kabdebo, Thomas
Kabdebo, Thomas 1934- *10*
Kabibble, Osh
  See Jobb, Jamie
Kadesch, Robert R(udstone)
  1922- *31*
Kahl, M(arvin) P(hilip) 1934- *37*
Kahl, Virginia (Caroline)
  1919- *48*
  Brief Entry *38*
Kahn, Joan 1914- *48*
Kahn, Roger 1927- *37*
Kakimoto, Kozo 1915- *11*
Kalashnikoff, Nicholas
  1888-1961 .... *16*
Kalb, Jonah 1926- *23*
Kaler, James Otis 1848-1912 ...... *15*
Kalnay, Francis 1899- *7*
Kalow, Gisela 1946- *32*
Kamen, Gloria 1923- *9*
Kamerman, Sylvia E.
  See Burack, Sylvia K.
Kamm, Josephine (Hart)
  1905- *24*
Kandell, Alice S. 1938- *35*
Kane, Henry Bugbee
  1902-1971 .... *14*
Kane, Robert W. 1910- *18*
Kanetzke, Howard W(illiam)
  1932- *38*
Kanzawa, Toshiko
  See Furukawa, Toshi
Kaplan, Anne Bernays 1930- *32*
Kaplan, Bess 1927- *22*
Kaplan, Boche 1926- *24*
Kaplan, Irma 1900- *10*
Kaplan, Jean Caryl Korn
  1926- *10*
Karageorge, Michael
  See Anderson, Poul (William)
Karasz, Ilonka 1896-1981
  Obituary *29*
Karen, Ruth 1922-1987 .... *9*
  Obituary *54*
Kark, Nina Mary 1925- *4*
Karl, Jean E(dna) 1927- *34*
Karlin, Eugene 1918- *10*
Karp, Naomi J. 1926- *16*
Kashiwagi, Isami 1925- *10*
Kassem, Lou
  Brief Entry *51*
Kästner, Erich 1899-1974 .... *14*
  See also CLR 4
Kasuya, Masahiro 1937- *51*
Katchen, Carole 1944- *9*
Kathryn
  See Searle, Kathryn Adrienne

Katona, Robert 1949- *21*
Katsarakis, Joan Harries
  See Harries, Joan
Katz, Bobbi 1933- *12*
Katz, Fred 1938- *6*
Katz, Jane 1934- *33*
Katz, Marjorie P.
  See Weiser, Marjorie P(hillis) K(atz)
Katz, William Loren 1927- *13*
Kaufman, Joe 1911- *33*
Kaufman, Mervyn D. 1932- *4*
Kaufmann, Angelika 1935- *15*
Kaufmann, John 1931- *18*
Kaula, Edna Mason 1906- *13*
Kavaler, Lucy 1930- *23*
Kay, Helen
  See Goldfrank, Helen Colodny
Kay, Mara *13*
Kaye, Danny 1913-1987
  Obituary *50*
Kaye, Geraldine 1925- *10*
Keane, Bil 1922- *4*
Keating, Bern
  See Keating, Leo Bernard
Keating, Lawrence A.
  1903-1966 .... *23*
Keating, Leo Bernard 1915- *10*
Keats, Ezra Jack 1916-1983 .... *14*
  Obituary *34*
  See also CLR 1
Keegan, Marcia 1943- *9*
Keel, Frank
  See Keeler, Ronald F(ranklin)
Keeler, Ronald F(ranklin)
  1913-1983 .... *47*
Keen, Martin L. 1913- *4*
Keene, Carolyn [Collective
  pseudonym]
  See Adams, Harriet S.
Keeping, Charles (William James)
  1924- *9*
Keeshan, Robert J. 1927- *32*
Keir, Christine
  See Pullein-Thompson, Christine
Keith, Carlton
  See Robertson, Keith
Keith, Eros 1942- *52*
Keith, Hal 1934- *36*
Keith, Harold (Verne) 1903- *2*
Keith, Robert
  See Applebaum, Stan
Kelen, Emery 1896-1978 .... *13*
  Obituary *26*
Kelleam, Joseph E(veridge)
  1913-1975 .... *31*
Kelleher, Victor 1939-
  Brief Entry *52*
Keller, B(everly) L(ou) *13*
Keller, Charles 1942- *8*
Keller, Dick 1923- *36*
Keller, Gail Faithfull
  See Faithfull, Gail
Keller, Holly
  Brief Entry *42*
Keller, Irene (Barron) 1927- *36*
Keller, Mollie
  Brief Entry *50*
Kelley, Leo P(atrick) 1928- *32*
  Brief Entry *31*

Kelley, True Adelaide 1946- 41
  Brief Entry 39
Kellin, Sally Moffet 1932- 9
Kelling, Furn L. 1914- 37
Kellogg, Gene
  See Kellogg, Jean
Kellogg, Jean 1916- 10
Kellogg, Steven 1941- 8
  See also CLR 6
Kellow, Kathleen
  See Hibbert, Eleanor
Kelly, Eric P(hilbrook)
  1884-1960 .... YABC 1
Kelly, Martha Rose
  1914-1983 37
Kelly, Marty
  See Kelly, Martha Rose
Kelly, Ralph
  See Geis, Darlene
Kelly, Regina Z. 5
Kelly, Rosalie (Ruth) 43
Kelly, Walt(er Crawford)
  1913-1973 18
Kelsey, Alice Geer 1896- 1
Kemp, Gene 1926- 25
Kempner, Mary Jean
  1913-1969 10
Kempton, Jean Welch 1914- 10
Kendall, Carol (Seeger) 1917- 11
  See also SAAS 7
Kendall, Lace
  See Stoutenburg, Adrien
Kenealy, James P. 1927- 52
  Brief Entry 29
Kenealy, Jim
  See Kenealy, James P.
Kennedy, Dorothy M(intzlaff)
  1931- 53
Kennedy, John Fitzgerald
  1917-1963 11
Kennedy, Joseph 1929- 14
Kennedy, Paul E(dward)
  1929- 33
Kennedy, (Jerome) Richard
  1932- 22
Kennedy, T(eresa) A. 1953- 42
  Brief Entry 35
Kennedy, X. J.
  See Kennedy, Joseph
Kennell, Ruth E(pperson)
  1893-1977 6
  Obituary 25
Kenny, Ellsworth Newcomb
  1909-1971
  Obituary 26
Kenny, Herbert A(ndrew)
  1912- 13
Kenny, Kathryn
  See Bowden, Joan Chase
  See Krull, Kathleen
Kenny, Kevin
  See Krull, Kathleen
Kent, Alexander
  See Reeman, Douglas Edward
Kent, David
  See Lambert, David (Compton)
Kent, Deborah Ann 1948- 47
  Brief Entry 41

Kent, Jack
  See Kent, John Wellington
Kent, John Wellington
  1920-1985 24
  Obituary 45
Kent, Margaret 1894- 2
Kent, Rockwell 1882-1971 6
Kent, Sherman 1903-1986 20
  Obituary 47
Kenward, Jean 1920- 42
Kenworthy, Leonard S. 1912- 6
Kenyon, Kate
  See Ransom, Candice F.
Kenyon, Ley 1913- 6
Kepes, Juliet A(ppleby) 1919- 13
Kerigan, Florence 1896- 12
Kerman, Gertrude Lerner
  1909- 21
Kerr, Jessica 1901- 13
Kerr, (Anne) Judith 1923- 24
Kerr, M. E.
  See Meaker, Marijane
  See also SAAS 1
Kerry, Frances
  See Kerigan, Florence
Kerry, Lois
  See Duncan, Lois S(teinmetz)
Ker Wilson, Barbara 1929- 20
Kessel, Joyce Karen 1937- 41
Kessler, Ethel 1922- 44
  Brief Entry 37
Kessler, Leonard P. 1921- 14
Kesteven, G. R.
  See Crosher, G(eoffry) R(obins)
Ketcham, Hank
  See Ketcham, Henry King
Ketcham, Henry King 1920- 28
  Brief Entry 27
Kettelkamp, Larry 1933- 2
  See also SAAS 3
Kevles, Bettyann 1938- 23
Key, Alexander (Hill)
  1904-1979 8
  Obituary 23
Keyes, Daniel 1927- 37
Keyes, Fenton 1915- 34
Keyser, Marcia 1933- 42
Keyser, Sarah
  See McGuire, Leslie (Sarah)
Khanshendel, Chiron
  See Rose, Wendy
Kherdian, David 1931- 16
Kidd, Ronald 1948- 42
Kiddell, John 1922- 3
Kiddell-Monroe, Joan 1908- 55
Kidwell, Carl 1910- 43
Kiefer, Irene 1926- 21
Kiesel, Stanley 1925- 35
Kikukawa, Cecily H. 1919- 44
  Brief Entry 35
Kilgore, Kathleen 1946- 42
Kilian, Crawford 1941- 35
Killilea, Marie (Lyons) 1913- 2
Kilreon, Beth
  See Walker, Barbara K.
Kimball, Yeffe 1914-1978 37
Kimbrough, Emily 1899- 2
Kimmel, Eric A. 1946- 13

Kimmel, Margaret Mary
  1938- 43
  Brief Entry 33
Kindred, Wendy 1937- 7
Kines, Pat Decker 1937- 12
King, Adam
  See Hoare, Robert J(ohn)
King, Arthur
  See Cain, Arthur H.
King, Billie Jean 1943- 12
King, (David) Clive 1924- 28
King, Cynthia 1925- 7
King, Frank O. 1883-1969
  Obituary 22
King, Marian 1900(?)-1986 23
  Obituary 47
King, Martin
  See Marks, Stan(ley)
King, Martin Luther, Jr.
  1929-1968 14
King, Paul
  See Drackett, Phil(ip Arthur)
King, Reefe
  See Barker, Albert W.
King, Stephen (Edwin) 1947- 55
  Earlier sketch in SATA 9
King, Tony 1947- 39
Kingman, Dong (Moy Shu)
  1911- 44
Kingman, (Mary) Lee 1919- 1
  See also SAAS 3
Kingsland, Leslie William
  1912- 13
Kingsley, Charles
  1819-1875 .... YABC 2
Kingsley, Emily Perl 1940- 33
King-Smith, Dick 1922- 47
  Brief Entry 38
Kingston, Maxine (Ting Ting) Hong
  1940- 53
Kinney, C. Cle 1915- 6
Kinney, Harrison 1921- 13
Kinney, Jean Stout 1912- 12
Kinsey, Elizabeth
  See Clymer, Eleanor
Kipling, (Joseph) Rudyard
  1865-1936 .... YABC 2
Kirk, Ruth (Kratz) 1925- 5
Kirkland, Will
  See Hale, Arlene
Kirkup, James 1927- 12
Kirkus, Virginia
  See Glick, Virginia Kirkus
Kirtland, G. B.
  See Joslin, Sesyle
Kishida, Eriko 1929- 12
Kisinger, Grace Gelvin
  1913-1965 10
Kissin, Eva H. 1923- 10
Kjelgaard, James Arthur
  1910-1959 17
Kjelgaard, Jim
  See Kjelgaard, James Arthur
Klagsbrun, Francine (Lifton) 36
Klaits, Barrie 1944- 52
Klaperman, Gilbert 1921- 33
Klaperman, Libby Mindlin
  1921-1982 33
  Obituary 31

Klass, Morton 1927- *11*
Klass, Sheila Solomon 1927- *45*
Kleberger, Ilse 1921- *5*
Klein, Aaron E. 1930- *45*
  Brief Entry *28*
Klein, Gerda Weissmann
  1924- *44*
Klein, H. Arthur *8*
Klein, Leonore 1916- *6*
Klein, Mina C(ooper) *8*
Klein, Norma 1938- *7*
  See also CLR 2
  See also SAAS 1
Klein, Robin 1936- *55*
  Brief Entry *45*
Klemm, Edward G., Jr. 1910- *30*
Klemm, Roberta K(ohnhorst)
  1884- *30*
Klevin, Jill Ross 1935- *39*
  Brief Entry *38*
Kliban, B. 1935- *35*
Klimowicz, Barbara 1927- *10*
Kline, Suzy 1943-
  Brief Entry *48*
Klug, Ron(ald) 1939- *31*
Knapp, Ron 1952- *34*
Knebel, Fletcher 1911- *36*
Knickerbocker, Diedrich
  See Irving, Washington
Knifesmith
  See Cutler, Ivor
Knigge, Robert (R.) 1921(?)-1987
  Obituary *50*
Knight, Anne (Katherine)
  1946- *34*
Knight, Damon 1922- *9*
Knight, David C(arpenter) *14*
Knight, Eric (Mowbray)
  1897-1943 .... *18*
Knight, Francis Edgar *14*
Knight, Frank
  See Knight, Francis Edgar
Knight, Hilary 1926- *15*
Knight, Mallory T.
  See Hurwood, Bernhardt J.
Knight, Ruth Adams 1898-1974
  Obituary *20*
Knott, Bill
  See Knott, William Cecil, Jr.
Knott, William Cecil, Jr.
  1927- *3*
Knotts, Howard (Clayton, Jr.)
  1922- *25*
Knowles, Anne 1933- *37*
Knowles, John 1926- *8*
Knox, Calvin
  See Silverberg, Robert
Knox, (Mary) Eleanor Jessie
  1909- *30*
Knox, James
  See Brittain, William
Knudsen, James 1950- *42*
Knudson, Richard L(ewis)
  1930- *34*
Knudson, R. R.
  See Knudson, Rozanne
Knudson, Rozanne 1932- *7*
Knye, Cassandra
  See Disch, Thomas M(ichael)

Koch, Dorothy Clarke 1924- *6*
Kocsis, J. C.
  See Paul, James
Koehn, Ilse
  See Van Zwienen, Ilse (Charlotte
  Koehn)
Koerner, W(illiam) H(enry) D(avid)
  1878-1938 .... *21*
Koertge, Ronald 1940- *53*
Kogan, Deborah 1940- *50*
Kohl, Herbert 1937- *47*
Kohler, Julilly H(ouse) 1908-1976
  Obituary *20*
Kohn, Bernice (Herstein)
  1920- *4*
Kohner, Frederick 1905-1986 ... *10*
  Obituary *48*
Koide, Tan 1938-1986 .... *50*
Kolba, Tamara *22*
Komisar, Lucy 1942- *9*
Komoda, Beverly 1939- *25*
Komoda, Kiyo 1937- *9*
Komroff, Manuel 1890-1974 ..... *2*
  Obituary *20*
Konigsburg, E(laine) L(obl) *48*
  Earlier sketch in SATA 4
  See also CLR 1
Koning, Hans
  See Koningsberger, Hans
Koningsberger, Hans 1921- *5*
Konkle, Janet Everest 1917- *12*
Koob, Theodora (Johanna Foth)
  1918- *23*
Kooiker, Leonie
  See Kooyker-Romijn, Johanna Maria
Kooyker-Romijn, Johanna Maria
  1927- *48*
Kopper, Lisa (Esther) 1950-
  Brief Entry *51*
Korach, Mimi 1922- *9*
Koren, Edward 1935- *5*
Korinetz, Yuri (Iosifovich)
  1923- *9*
  See also CLR 4
Korman, Gordon 1963- *49*
  Brief Entry *41*
Korty, Carol 1937- *15*
Kossin, Sandy (Sanford)
  1926- *10*
Kotzwinkle, William 1938- *24*
  See also CLR 6
Kouhi, Elizabeth 1917- *54*
  Brief Entry *49*
Koutoukas, H. M.
  See Rivoli, Mario
Kouts, Anne 1945- *8*
Krahn, Fernando 1935- *49*
  Brief Entry *31*
  See also CLR 3
Kramer, Anthony
  Brief Entry *42*
Kramer, George
  See Heuman, William
Kramer, Nora 1896(?)-1984 ...... *26*
  Obituary *39*
Krantz, Hazel (Newman)
  1920- *12*
Kranzler, George G(ershon)
  1916- *28*

Kranzler, Gershon
  See Kranzler, George G(ershon)
Krasilovsky, Phyllis 1926- *38*
  Earlier sketch in SATA 1
  See also SAAS 5
Kraske, Robert
  Brief Entry *36*
Kraus, Robert 1925- *4*
Krauss, Ruth (Ida) 1911- *30*
  Earlier sketch in SATA 1
Krautter, Elisa
  See Bialk, Elisa
Krauze, Andrzej 1947-
  Brief Entry *46*
Kredel, Fritz 1900-1973 .... *17*
Krementz, Jill 1940- *17*
  See also CLR 5
Krensky, Stephen (Alan)
  1953- *47*
  Brief Entry *41*
Kripke, Dorothy Karp *30*
Kristof, Jane 1932- *8*
Kroeber, Theodora (Kracaw)
  1897- *1*
Kroll, Francis Lynde
  1904-1973 .... *10*
Kroll, Steven 1941- *19*
  See also SAAS 7
Kropp, Paul (Stephen) 1948- *38*
  Brief Entry *34*
Krull, Kathleen 1952- *52*
  Brief Entry *39*
Krumgold, Joseph 1908-1980 ..... *48*
  Obituary *23*
  Earlier sketch in SATA 1
Krupp, E(dwin) C(harles)
  1944- *53*
Krupp, Robin Rector 1946- *53*
Krush, Beth 1918- *18*
Krush, Joe 1918- *18*
Krüss, James 1926- *8*
  See also CLR 9
Kubie, Nora (Gottheil) Benjamin
  1899- *39*
Kubinyi, Laszlo 1937- *17*
Kuh, Charlotte 1892(?)-1985
  Obituary *43*
Kujoth, Jean Spealman 1935-1975
  Obituary *30*
Kullman, Harry 1919-1982 .... *35*
Kumin, Maxine (Winokur)
  1925- *12*
Kunhardt, Dorothy (Meserve)
  1901-1979 .... *53*
  Obituary *22*
Künstler, Morton 1927- *10*
Kunz, Roxane (Brown) 1932-
  Brief Entry *53*
Kupferberg, Herbert 1918- *19*
Kuratomi, Chizuko 1939- *12*
Kurelek, William 1927-1977 ...... *8*
  Obituary *27*
  See also CLR 2
Kurland, Gerald 1942- *13*
Kurland, Michael (Joseph)
  1938- *48*
Kushner, Donn 1927- *52*

Kuskin, Karla (Seidman)
  1932- 2
  See also CLR 4
  See also SAAS 3
Kuttner, Paul 1931- 18
Kuzma, Kay 1941- 39
Kvale, Velma R(uth) 1898- 8
Kyle, Elisabeth
  See Dunlop, Agnes M. R.
Kyte, Kathy S. 1946- 50
  Brief Entry 44

L

Lacy, Leslie Alexander 1937- 6
Ladd, Veronica
  See Miner, Jane Claypool
Lader, Lawrence 1919- 6
Lady, A
  See Taylor, Ann
Lady Mears
  See Tempest, Margaret Mary
Lady of Quality, A
  See Bagnold, Enid
La Farge, Oliver (Hazard Perry)
  1901-1963 19
La Farge, Phyllis 14
Laffin, John (Alfred Charles)
  1922- 31
La Fontaine, Jean de
  1621-1695 18
Lager, Marilyn 1939- 52
Lagercrantz, Rose (Elsa)
  1947- 39
Lagerlöf, Selma (Ottiliana Lovisa)
  1858-1940 15
  See also CLR 7
Laiken, Deirdre S(usan) 1948- 48
  Brief Entry 40
Laimgruber, Monika 1946- 11
Laing, Martha
  See Celestino, Martha Laing
Laird, Jean E(louise) 1930- 38
Laite, Gordon 1925- 31
Lake, Harriet
  See Taylor, Paula (Wright)
Laklan, Carli 1907- 5
la Mare, Walter de
  See de la Mare, Walter
Lamb, Beatrice Pitney 1904- 21
Lamb, Charles 1775-1834 17
Lamb, Elizabeth Searle 1917- 31
Lamb, G(eoffrey) F(rederick) 10
Lamb, Harold (Albert)
  1892-1962 53
Lamb, Lynton 1907- 10
Lamb, Mary Ann 1764-1847 17
Lamb, Robert (Boyden) 1941- 13
Lambert, David (Compton) 1932-
  Brief Entry 49
Lambert, Janet (Snyder)
  1894-1973 25
Lambert, Saul 1928- 23
Lamburn, Richmal Crompton
  1890-1969 5
Lamorisse, Albert (Emmanuel)
  1922-1970 23

Lampert, Emily 1951- 52
  Brief Entry 49
Lamplugh, Lois 1921- 17
Lampman, Evelyn Sibley
  1907-1980 4
  Obituary 23
Lamprey, Louise
  1869-1951 .... YABC 2
Lampton, Chris
  See Lampton, Christopher
Lampton, Christopher
  Brief Entry 47
Lancaster, Bruce 1896-1963 9
Lancaster, Matthew 1973(?)-1983
  Obituary 45
Land, Barbara (Neblett) 1923- 16
Land, Jane [Joint pseudonym]
  See Borland, Kathryn Kilby and
  Speicher, Helen Ross (Smith)
Land, Myrick (Ebben) 1922- 15
Land, Ross [Joint pseudonym]
  See Borland, Kathryn Kilby and
  Speicher, Helen Ross (Smith)
Landau, Elaine 1948- 10
Landau, Jacob 1917- 38
Landeck, Beatrice 1904- 15
Landin, Les(lie) 1923- 2
Landis, J(ames) D(avid) 1942-
  Brief Entry 52
Landon, Lucinda 1950-
  Brief Entry 51
Landon, Margaret (Dorothea
  Mortenson) 1903- 50
Landshoff, Ursula 1908- 13
Lane, Carolyn 1926- 10
Lane, Jerry
  See Martin, Patricia Miles
Lane, John 1932- 15
Lane, Margaret 1907-
  Brief Entry 38
Lane, Rose Wilder 1886-1968 29
  Brief Entry 28
Lanes, Selma G. 1929- 3
Lang, Andrew 1844-1912 16
Lange, John
  See Crichton, (J.) Michael
Lange, Suzanne 1945- 5
Langley, Noel 1911-1980
  Obituary 25
Langner, Nola 1930- 8
Langone, John (Michael)
  1929- 46
  Brief Entry 38
Langstaff, John 1920- 6
  See also CLR 3
Langstaff, Launcelot
  See Irving, Washington
Langton, Jane 1922- 3
  See also SAAS 5
Lanier, Sidney 1842-1881 18
Lansing, Alfred 1921-1975 35
Lantz, Paul 1908- 45
Lantz, Walter 1900- 37
Lappin, Peter 1911- 32
Larom, Henry V. 1903(?)-1975
  Obituary 30
Larrecq, John M(aurice)
  1926-1980 44
  Obituary 25

Larrick, Nancy G. 1910- 4
Larsen, Egon 1904- 14
Larsen, Rebecca 1944- 54
Larson, Eve
  See St. John, Wylly Folk
Larson, Norita D. 1944- 29
Larson, William H. 1938- 10
Larsson, Carl (Olof)
  1853-1919 35
Lasell, Elinor H. 1929- 19
Lasell, Fen H.
  See Lasell, Elinor H.
Lash, Joseph P. 1909- 43
Lasher, Faith B. 1921- 12
Lasker, David 1950- 38
Lasker, Joe 1919- 9
Laski, Marghanita 1915-1988 55
Lasky, Kathryn 1944- 13
  See also CLR 11
Lassalle, C. E.
  See Ellis, Edward S(ylvester)
Latham, Barbara 1896- 16
Latham, Frank B. 1910- 6
Latham, Jean Lee 1902- 2
Latham, Mavis
  See Clark, Mavis Thorpe
Latham, Philip
  See Richardson, Robert S(hirley)
Lathrop, Dorothy P(ulis)
  1891-1980 14
  Obituary 24
Lathrop, Francis
  See Leiber, Fritz
Lattimore, Eleanor Frances
  1904-1986 7
  Obituary 48
Lauber, Patricia (Grace) 1924- 33
  Earlier sketch in SATA 1
Laugesen, Mary E(akin)
  1906- 5
Laughbaum, Steve 1945- 12
Laughlin, Florence 1910- 3
Lauré, Ettagale
  See Blauer, Ettagale
Lauré, Jason 1940- 50
  Brief Entry 44
Laurence, Ester Hauser 1935- 7
Laurence, (Jean) Margaret (Wemyss)
  1926-1987
  Obituary 50
Laurie, Rona 1916- 55
Laurin, Anne
  See McLaurin, Anne
Lauritzen, Jonreed 1902- 13
Lauscher, Hermann
  See Hesse, Hermann
Laux, Dorothy 1920- 49
Lavine, David 1928- 31
Lavine, Sigmund A. 1908- 3
Laviolette, Emily A. 1923(?)-1975
  Brief Entry 49
Lawford, Paula Jane 1960-
  Brief Entry 53
Lawrence, Ann (Margaret)
  1942-1987 41
  Obituary 54
Lawrence, Isabelle (Wentworth)
  Brief Entry 29

Lawrence, J. T.
  See Rowland-Entwistle, (Arthur)
  Theodore (Henry)
Lawrence, John 1933- 30
Lawrence, Josephine 1890(?)-1978
  Obituary 24
Lawrence, Linda
  See Hunt, Linda Lawrence
Lawrence, Louise 1943- 38
Lawrence, Louise de Kiriline
  1894- 13
Lawrence, Mildred 1907- 3
Lawrence, R(onald) D(ouglas)
  1921- 55
Lawson, Carol (Antell) 1946- 42
Lawson, Don(ald Elmer)
  1917- 9
Lawson, Joan 1906- 55
Lawson, Marion Tubbs 1896- 22
Lawson, Robert
  1892-1957 .... YABC 2
  See also CLR 2
Laycock, George (Edwin)
  1921- 5
Lazare, Gerald John 1927- 44
Lazare, Jerry
  See Lazare, Gerald John
Lazarevich, Mila 1942- 17
Lazarus, Keo Felker 1913- 21
Lea, Alec 1907- 19
Lea, Richard
  See Lea, Alec
Leach, Maria 1892-1977 39
  Brief Entry 28
Leacroft, Helen 1919- 6
Leacroft, Richard 1914- 6
Leaf, Margaret P. 1909(?)-1988
  Obituary 55
Leaf, (Wilbur) Munro
  1905-1976 20
Leaf, VaDonna Jean 1929- 26
Leakey, Richard E(rskine Frere)
  1944- 42
Leander, Ed
  See Richelson, Geraldine
Lear, Edward 1812-1888 18
  See also CLR 1
Leasor, (Thomas) James
  1923- 54
Leavitt, Jerome E(dward)
  1916- 23
LeBar, Mary E(velyn)
  1910-1982 35
LeBlanc, L(ee) 1913- 54
LeCain, Errol 1941- 6
Leder, Jane Mersky 1945-
  Brief Entry 51
Lederer, Muriel 1929- 48
Lee, Amanda
  See Buckholtz, Eileen (Garber)
Lee, Benjamin 1921- 27
Lee, Betsy 1949- 37
Lee, Carol
  See Fletcher, Helen Jill
Lee, Dennis (Beynon) 1939- 14
  See also CLR 3
Lee, Doris (Emrick)
  1905-1983 44
  Obituary 35

Lee, (Nelle) Harper 1926- 11
Lee, John R(obert) 1923-1976 27
Lee, Manning de V(illeneuve)
  1894-1980 37
  Obituary 22
Lee, Marian
  See Clish, (Lee) Marian
Lee, Mary Price 1934- 8
Lee, Mildred 1908- 6
Lee, Robert C. 1931- 20
Lee, Robert J. 1921- 10
Lee, Roy
  See Hopkins, Clark
Lee, Tanith 1947- 8
Leedy, Loreen (Janelle) 1959- 54
  Brief Entry 50
Leekley, Thomas B(riggs)
  1910- 23
Leeming, Jo Ann
  See Leeming, Joseph
Leeming, Joseph 1897-1968 26
Leeson, Muriel 1920- 54
Leeson, R. A.
  See Leeson, Robert (Arthur)
Leeson, Robert (Arthur) 1928- 42
Lefler, Irene (Whitney) 1917- 12
Le Gallienne, Eva 1899- 9
Legg, Sarah Martha Ross Bruggeman
  (?)-1982
  Obituary 40
LeGrand
  See Henderson, LeGrand
Le Guin, Ursula K(roeber)
  1929- 52
  Earlier sketch in SATA 4
  See also CLR 3
Legum, Colin 1919- 10
Lehn, Cornelia 1920- 46
Lehr, Delores 1920- 10
Leiber, Fritz 1910- 45
Leibold, Jay 1957-
  Brief Entry 52
Leichman, Seymour 1933- 5
Leigh, Tom 1947- 46
Leigh-Pemberton, John 1911- 35
Leighton, Clare (Veronica Hope)
  1900(?)- 37
Leighton, Margaret 1896-1987 1
  Obituary 52
Leipold, L. Edmond 1902- 16
Leisk, David (Johnson)
  1906-1975 30
  Obituary 26
  Earlier sketch in SATA 1
Leister, Mary 1917- 29
Leitch, Patricia 1933- 11
LeMair, H(enriette) Willebeek
  1889-1966
  Brief Entry 29
Lemke, Horst 1922- 38
Lenanton, C.
  See Oman, Carola (Mary Anima)
Lenard, Alexander 1910-1972
  Obituary 21
L'Engle, Madeleine 1918- 27
  Earlier sketch in SATA 1
  See also CLR 1, 14
Lengyel, Cornel Adam 1915- 27

Lengyel, Emil 1895-1985 3
  Obituary 42
Lens, Sidney 1912-1986 13
  Obituary 48
Lenski, Lois 1893-1974 26
  Earlier sketch in SATA 1
Lent, Blair 1930- 2
Lent, Henry Bolles 1901-1973 17
Leodhas, Sorche Nic
  See Alger, Leclaire (Gowans)
Leokum, Arkady 1916(?)- 45
Leonard, Constance (Brink)
  1923- 42
  Brief Entry 40
Leonard, Jonathan N(orton)
  1903-1975 36
Leong Gor Yun
  See Ellison, Virginia Howell
Lerner, Aaron B(unsen) 1920- 35
Lerner, Carol 1927- 33
Lerner, Marguerite Rush
  1924-1987 11
  Obituary 51
Lerner, Sharon (Ruth)
  1938-1982 11
  Obituary 29
Leroe, Ellen W(hitney) 1949-
  Brief Entry 51
LeRoy, Gen 52
  Brief Entry 36
Lerrigo, Marion Olive 1898-1968
  Obituary 29
LeShan, Eda J(oan) 1922- 21
  See also CLR 6
LeSieg, Theo
  See Geisel, Theodor Seuss
Leslie, Robert Franklin 1911- 7
Leslie, Sarah
  See McGuire, Leslie (Sarah)
Lesser, Margaret 1899(?)-1979
  Obituary 22
Lesser, Rika 1953- 53
Lester, Alison 1952- 50
Lester, Helen 1936- 46
Lester, Julius B. 1939- 12
  See also CLR 2
Le Sueur, Meridel 1900- 6
Le Tord, Bijou 1945- 49
Leutscher, Alfred (George)
  1913- 23
Levai, Blaise 1919- 39
LeVert (William) John 1946- 55
Levin, Betty 1927- 19
Levin, Marcia Obrasky 1918- 13
Levin, Meyer 1905-1981 21
  Obituary 27
Levine, Abby 1943- 54
  Brief Entry 52
Levine, David 1926- 43
  Brief Entry 35
Levine, Edna S(imon) 35
Levine, I(srael) E. 1923- 12
Levine, Joan Goldman 11
Levine, Joseph 1910- 33
Levine, Rhoda 14
Levinson, Nancy Smiler
  1938- 33
Levinson, Riki 52
  Brief Entry 49

Levitin, Sonia 1934- *4*
 See also SAAS 2
Levoy, Myron *49*
 Brief Entry *37*
Levy, Elizabeth 1942- *31*
Lewees, John
 See Stockton, Francis Richard
Lewin, Betsy 1937- *32*
Lewin, Hugh (Francis) 1939-
 Brief Entry *40*
 See also CLR 9
Lewin, Ted 1935- *21*
Lewis, Alfred E. 1912-1968
 Brief Entry *32*
Lewis, Alice C. 1936- *46*
Lewis, Alice Hudson 1895(?)-1971
 Obituary *29*
Lewis, (Joseph) Anthony
 1927- *27*
Lewis, C(live) S(taples)
 1898-1963 .... *13*
 See also CLR 3
Lewis, Claudia (Louise) 1907- *5*
Lewis, E. M. *20*
Lewis, Elizabeth Foreman
 1892-1958 ....*YABC 2*
Lewis, Francine
 See Wells, Helen
Lewis, Hilda (Winifred) 1896-1974
 Obituary *20*
Lewis, Lucia Z.
 See Anderson, Lucia (Lewis)
Lewis, Marjorie 1929- *40*
 Brief Entry *35*
Lewis, Paul
 See Gerson, Noel B(ertram)
Lewis, Richard 1935- *3*
Lewis, Roger
 See Zarchy, Harry
Lewis, Shari 1934- *35*
 Brief Entry *30*
Lewis, Thomas P(arker) 1936- *27*
Lewiton, Mina 1904-1970 .... *2*
Lexau, Joan M. *36*
 Earlier sketch in SATA 1
Ley, Willy 1906-1969 .... *2*
Leydon, Rita (Flodén) 1949- *21*
Leyland, Eric (Arthur) 1911- *37*
L'Hommedieu, Dorothy K(easley)
 1885-1961
 Obituary *29*
Libby, Bill
 See Libby, William M.
Libby, William M. 1927-1984 .... *5*
 Obituary ..../......*39*
Liberty, Gene 1924- *3*
Liebers, Arthur 1913- *12*
Lieblich, Irene 1923- *22*
Liers, Emil E(rnest)
 1890-1975 .... *37*
Lietz, Gerald S. 1918- *11*
Lifton, Betty Jean *6*
Lightner, A. M.
 See Hopf, Alice (Martha) L(ightner)
Lightner, Alice
 See Hopf, Alice (Martha) L(ightner)
Lignell, Lois 1911- *37*
Lillington, Kenneth (James)
 1916- *39*

Lilly, Charles
 Brief Entry *33*
Lilly, Ray
 See Curtis, Richard (Alan)
Lim, John 1932- *43*
Liman, Ellen (Fogelson)
 1936- *22*
Limburg, Peter R(ichard)
 1929- *13*
Lincoln, C(harles) Eric 1924- *5*
Lindbergh, Anne
 See Sapieyevski, Anne Lindbergh
Lindbergh, Anne Morrow (Spencer)
 1906- *33*
Lindbergh, Charles A(ugustus, Jr.)
 1902-1974 .... *33*
Lindblom, Steven (Winther)
 1946- *42*
 Brief Entry *39*
Linde, Gunnel 1924- *5*
Lindgren, Astrid 1907- *38*
 Earlier sketch in SATA 2
 See also CLR 1
Lindgren, Barbro 1937-
 Brief Entry *46*
Lindman, Maj (Jan)
 1886-1972 .... *43*
Lindop, Edmund 1925- *5*
Lindquist, Jennie Dorothea
 1899-1977 .... *13*
Lindquist, Willis 1908- *20*
Lindsay, Norman (Alfred William)
 1879-1969
 See CLR 8
Lindsay, (Nicholas) Vachel
 1879-1931 .... *40*
Line, Les 1935- *27*
Linfield, Esther *40*
Lingard, Joan *8*
 See also SAAS 5
Link, Martin 1934- *28*
Lionni, Leo 1910- *8*
 See also CLR 7
Lipinsky de Orlov, Lino S.
 1908- *22*
Lipkind, William 1904-1974 ...... *15*
Lipman, David 1931- *21*
Lipman, Matthew 1923- *14*
Lippincott, Bertram 1898(?)-1985
 Obituary *42*
Lippincott, Joseph Wharton
 1887-1976 .... *17*
Lippincott, Sarah Lee 1920- *22*
Lippman, Peter J. 1936- *31*
Lipsyte, Robert 1938- *5*
Lisker, Sonia O. 1933- *44*
Lisle, Janet Taylor
 Brief Entry *47*
Lisle, Seward D.
 See Ellis, Edward S(ylvester)
Lisowski, Gabriel 1946- *47*
 Brief Entry *31*
Liss, Howard 1922- *4*
Lissim, Simon 1900-1981
 Brief Entry *28*
List, Ilka Katherine 1935- *6*
Liston, Robert A. 1927- *5*
Litchfield, Ada B(assett)
 1916- *5*

Litowinsky, Olga (Jean) 1936- *26*
Littke, Lael J. 1929- *51*
Little, A. Edward
 See Klein, Aaron E.
Little, (Flora) Jean 1932- *2*
 See also CLR 4
Little, Lessie Jones 1906-1986
 Obituary *50*
Little, Mary E. 1912- *28*
Littledale, Freya (Lota) *2*
Lively, Penelope 1933- *7*
 See also CLR 7
Liversidge, (Henry) Douglas
 1913- *8*
Livingston, Carole 1941- *42*
Livingston, Myra Cohn 1926- *5*
 See also CLR 7
 See also SAAS 1
Livingston, Richard R(oland)
 1922- *8*
Llerena-Aguirre, Carlos Antonio
 1952- *19*
Llewellyn, Richard
 See Llewellyn Lloyd, Richard
 Dafydd Vyvyan
Llewellyn, T. Harcourt
 See Hamilton, Charles H. St. John
Llewellyn Lloyd, Richard Dafydd
 Vyvyan 1906-1983 .... *11*
 Obituary *37*
Lloyd, E. James
 See James, Elizabeth
Lloyd, Errol 1943- *22*
Lloyd, James
 See James, Elizabeth
Lloyd, Norman 1909-1980
 Obituary *23*
Lloyd, (Mary) Norris 1908- *10*
Lobel, Anita (Kempler) 1934- *55*
 Earlier sketch in SATA 6
Lobel, Arnold (Stark)
 1933-1987 .... *55*
 Obituary *54*
 Earlier sketch in SATA 6
 See also CLR 5
Lobsenz, Amelia *12*
Lobsenz, Norman M. 1919- *6*
Lochak, Michèle 1936- *39*
Lochlons, Colin
 See Jackson, C. Paul
Locke, Clinton W. [Collective
 pseudonym] *1*
Locke, Lucie 1904- *10*
Locker, Thomas 1937-
 See CLR 14
Lockwood, Mary
 See Spelman, Mary
Lodge, Bernard 1933- *33*
Lodge, Maureen Roffey
 See Roffey, Maureen
Loeb, Robert H., Jr. 1917- *21*
Loeper, John J(oseph) 1929- *10*
Loescher, Ann Dull 1942- *20*
Loescher, Gil(burt Damian)
 1945- *20*
Loewenstein, Bernice
 Brief Entry *40*
Löfgren, Ulf 1931- *3*
Lofting, Hugh 1886-1947 .... *15*

Lofts, Norah (Robinson)
1904-1983 8
Obituary 36
Logue, Christopher 1926- 23
Loken, Newton (Clayton)
1919- 26
Lomas, Steve
See Brennan, Joseph L.
Lomask, Milton 1909- 20
London, Jack 1876-1916 18
London, Jane
See Geis, Darlene
London, John Griffith
See London, Jack
Lonergan, (Pauline) Joy (Maclean)
1909- 10
Lonette, Reisie (Dominee)
1924- 43
Long, Earlene (Roberta)
1938- 50
Long, Helen Beecher [Collective
pseudonym] 1
Long, Judith Elaine 1953- 20
Long, Judy
See Long, Judith Elaine
Long, Laura Mooney 1892-1967
Obituary 29
Longfellow, Henry Wadsworth
1807-1882 19
Longman, Harold S. 1919- 5
Longsworth, Polly 1933- 28
Longtemps, Kenneth 1933- 17
Longway, A. Hugh
See Lang, Andrew
Loomis, Robert D. 5
Lopshire, Robert 1927- 6
Lord, Athena V. 1932- 39
Lord, Beman 1924- 5
Lord, (Doreen Mildred) Douglas
1904- 12
Lord, John Vernon 1939- 21
Lord, Nancy
See Titus, Eve
Lord, Walter 1917- 3
Lorenz, Lee (Sharp) 1932(?)-
Brief Entry 39
Lorenzini, Carlo 1826-1890 29
Loring, Emilie (Baker)
1864(?)-1951 51
Lorraine, Walter (Henry)
1929- 16
Loss, Joan 1933- 11
Lot, Parson
See Kingsley, Charles
Lothrop, Harriet Mulford Stone
1844-1924 20
Louie, Ai-Ling 1949- 40
Brief Entry 34
Louisburgh, Sheila Burnford
See Burnford, Sheila
Lourie, Helen
See Storr, Catherine (Cole)
Love, Katherine 1907- 3
Love, Sandra (Weller) 1940- 26
Lovelace, Delos Wheeler
1894-1967 7
Lovelace, Maud Hart
1892-1980 2
Obituary 23

Lovell, Ingraham
See Bacon, Josephine Dodge
(Daskam)
Lovett, Margaret (Rose) 1915- 22
Low, Alice 1926- 11
Low, Elizabeth Hammond
1898- 5
Low, Joseph 1911- 14
Lowe, Jay, Jr.
See Loper, John J(oseph)
Lowenstein, Dyno 1914- 6
Lowitz, Anson C.
1901(?)-1978 18
Lowitz, Sadyebeth (Heath)
1901-1969 17
Lowrey, Janette Sebring
1892- 43
Lowry, Lois 1937- 23
See also CLR 6
See also SAAS 3
Lowry, Peter 1953- 7
Lowther, George F. 1913-1975
Obituary 30
Lozier, Herbert 1915- 26
Lubell, Cecil 1912- 6
Lubell, Winifred 1914- 6
Lubin, Leonard B. 1943- 45
Brief Entry 37
Lucas, E(dward) V(errall)
1868-1938 20
Lucas, Jerry 1940- 33
Luce, Celia (Geneva Larsen)
1914- 38
Luce, Willard (Ray) 1914- 38
Luckhardt, Mildred Corell
1898- 5
Ludden, Allen (Ellsworth)
1918(?)-1981
Obituary 27
Ludlam, Mabel Cleland
See Widdemer, Mabel Cleland
Ludwig, Helen 33
Lueders, Edward (George)
1923- 14
Luenn, Nancy 1954- 51
Lufkin, Raymond H. 1897- 38
Lugard, Flora Louisa Shaw
1852-1929 21
Luger, Harriett M(andelay)
1914- 23
Luhrmann, Winifred B(ruce)
1934- 11
Luis, Earlene W. 1929- 11
Lum, Peter
See Crowe, Bettina Lum
Lund, Doris (Herold) 1919- 12
Lunn, Janet 1928- 4
Lurie, Alison 1926- 46
Lustig, Loretta 1944- 46
Luther, Frank 1905-1980
Obituary 25
Luttrell, Guy L. 1938- 22
Luttrell, Ida (Alleene) 1934- 40
Brief Entry 35
Lutzker, Edythe 1904- 5
Luzzati, Emanuele 1912- 7
Luzzatto, Paola (Caboara)
1938- 38
Lydon, Michael 1942- 11

Lyfick, Warren
See Reeves, Lawrence F.
Lyle, Katie Letcher 1938- 8
Lynch, Lorenzo 1932- 7
Lynch, Marietta 1947- 29
Lynch, Patricia (Nora)
1898-1972 9
Lynds, Dennis 1924- 47
Brief Entry 37
Lyngseth, Joan
See Davies, Joan
Lynn, Mary
See Brokamp, Marilyn
Lynn, Patricia
See Watts, Mabel Pizzey
Lyon, Elinor 1921- 6
Lyon, Lyman R.
See De Camp, L(yon) Sprague
Lyons, Dorothy 1907- 3
Lyons, Grant 1941- 30
Lystad, Mary (Hanemann)
1928- 11
Lyttle, Richard B(ard) 1927- 23
Lytton, Edward G(eorge) E(arle)
L(ytton) Bulwer-Lytton, Baron
1803-1873 23

M

Maar, Leonard (F., Jr.) 1927- 30
Maas, Selve 14
Mabery, D. L. 1953-
Brief Entry 53
Mac
See MacManus, Seumas
Mac Aodhagáin, Eamon
See Egan, E(dward) W(elstead)
MacArthur-Onslow, Annette
(Rosemary) 1933- 26
Macaulay, David (Alexander)
1946- 46
Brief Entry 27
See also CLR 3, 14
MacBeth, George 1932- 4
MacClintock, Dorcas 1932- 8
MacDonald, Anson
See Heinlein, Robert A(nson)
MacDonald, Betty (Campbell Bard)
1908-1958 .... YABC 1
Macdonald, Blackie
See Emrich, Duncan
Macdonald, Dwight
1906-1982 29
Obituary 33
MacDonald, George
1824-1905 33
Mac Donald, Golden
See Brown, Margaret Wise
Macdonald, Marcia
See Hill, Grace Livingston
Macdonald, Mary
See Gifford, Griselda
Macdonald, Shelagh 1937- 25
MacDonald, Suse 1940- 54
Brief Entry 52
Macdonald, Zillah K(atherine)
1885- 11
Mace, Elisabeth 1933- 27

Author Index

Mace, Varian 1938- 49
MacEwen, Gwendolyn (Margaret)
  1941-1987 50
  Obituary 55
MacFarlan, Allan A.
  1892-1982 35
MacFarlane, Iris 1922- 11
MacGregor, Ellen 1906-1954 39
  Brief Entry 27
MacGregor-Hastie, Roy 1929- 3
Machetanz, Frederick 1908- 34
Machin Goodall, Daphne
  (Edith) 37
MacInnes, Helen 1907-1985 22
  Obituary 44
MacIntyre, Elisabeth 1916- 17
Mack, Stan(ley) 17
Mackay, Claire 1930- 40
MacKaye, Percy (Wallace)
  1875-1956 32
MacKellar, William 1914- 4
Macken, Walter 1915-1967 36
Mackenzie, Dr. Willard
  See Stratemeyer, Edward L.
MacKenzie, Garry 1921-
  Brief Entry 31
MacKinstry, Elizabeth
  1879-1956 42
MacLachlan, Patricia 1938-
  Brief Entry 42
  See also CLR 14
MacLean, Alistair (Stuart)
  1923-1987 23
  Obituary 50
MacLeod, Beatrice (Beach)
  1910- 10
MacLeod, Charlotte (Matilda Hughes)
  1922- 28
MacLeod, Ellen Jane (Anderson)
  1916- 14
MacManus, James
  See MacManus, Seumas
MacManus, Seumas
  1869-1960 25
MacMaster, Eve (Ruth) B(owers)
  1942- 46
MacMillan, Annabelle
  See Quick, Annabelle
MacPeek, Walter G.
  1902-1973 4
  Obituary 25
MacPherson, Margaret 1908- 9
  See also SAAS 4
MacPherson, Thomas George
  1915-1976
  Obituary 30
Macrae, Hawk
  See Barker, Albert W.
MacRae, Travi
  See Feagles, Anita (MacRae)
Macumber, Mari
  See Sandoz, Mari
Madden, Don 1927- 3
Maddison, Angela Mary
  1923- 10
Maddock, Reginald 1912- 15
Madian, Jon 1941- 9
Madison, Arnold 1937- 6
Madison, Winifred 5

Maestro, Betsy 1944-
  Brief Entry 30
Maestro, Giulio 1942- 8
Magorian, James 1942- 32
Maguire, Anne
  See Nearing, Penny
Maguire, Gregory 1954- 28
Maher, Ramona 1934- 13
Mählqvist, (Karl) Stefan
  1943- 30
Mahon, Julia C(unha) 1916- 11
Mahony, Elizabeth Winthrop
  1948- 8
Mahood, Kenneth 1930- 24
Mahy, Margaret 1936- 14
  See also CLR 7
Maiden, Cecil (Edward)
  1902-1981 52
Maidoff, Ilka List
  See List, Ilka Katherine
Maik, Henri
  See Hecht, Henri Joseph
Maiorano, Robert 1946- 43
Maitland, Antony (Jasper)
  1935- 25
Major, Kevin 1949- 32
  See also CLR 11
Makie, Pam 1943- 37
Malcolmson, Anne
  See Storch, Anne B. von
Malcolmson, David 1899- 6
Mali, Jane Lawrence 1937- 51
  Brief Entry 44
Mallowan, Agatha Christie
  See Christie, Agatha (Mary Clarissa)
Malmberg, Carl 1904- 9
Malo, John 1911- 4
Malory, (Sir) Thomas 1410(?)-1471(?)
  Brief Entry 33
Maltese, Michael 1908(?)-1981
  Obituary 24
Malvern, Corinne 1905-1956 34
Malvern, Gladys (?)-1962 23
Mama G.
  See Davis, Grania
Manchel, Frank 1935- 10
Manes, Stephen 1949- 42
  Brief Entry 40
Manfred, Frederick F(eikema)
  1912- 30
Mangione, Jerre 1909- 6
Mango, Karin N. 1936- 52
Mangurian, David 1938- 14
Maniscalco, Joseph 1926- 10
Manley, Deborah 1932- 28
Manley, Seon 15
  See also CLR 3
  See also SAAS 2
Mann, Peggy 6
Mannetti, Lisa 1953-
  Brief Entry 51
Mannheim, Grete (Salomon)
  1909- 10
Manniche, Lise 1943- 31
Manning, Rosemary 1911- 10
Manning-Sanders, Ruth 1895- 15
Manson, Beverlie 1945-
  Brief Entry 44

Manton, Jo
  See Gittings, Jo Manton
Manushkin, Fran(ces) 1942- 54
  Earlier sketch in SATA 7
Mapes, Mary A.
  See Ellison, Virginia Howell
Mara, Barney
  See Roth, Arthur J(oseph)
Mara, Jeanette
  See Cebulash, Mel
Marais, Josef 1905-1978
  Obituary 24
Marasmus, Seymour
  See Rivoli, Mario
Marcellino
  See Agnew, Edith J.
Marchant, Bessie
  1862-1941 .... YABC 2
Marchant, Catherine
  See Cookson, Catherine (McMulen)
Marcher, Marion Walden
  1890- 10
Marcus, Rebecca B(rian)
  1907- 9
Marek, Margot L. 1934(?)-1987
  Obituary 54
Margaret, Karla
  See Andersdatter, Karla M(argaret)
Margolis, Richard J(ules)
  1929- 4
Margolis, Vivienne 1922- 46
Mariana
  See Foster, Marian Curtis
Marino, Dorothy Bronson
  1912- 14
Maris, Ron
  Brief Entry 45
Mark, Jan 1943- 22
  See also CLR 11
Mark, Pauline (Dahlin) 1913- 14
Mark, Polly
  See Mark, Pauline (Dahlin)
Markins, W. S.
  See Jenkins, Marie M.
Markle, Sandra L(ee) 1946-
  Brief Entry 41
Marko, Katherine D(olores) 28
Marks, Burton 1930- 47
  Brief Entry 43
Marks, Hannah K.
  See Trivelpiece, Laurel
Marks, J
  See Highwater, Jamake
Marks, J(ames) M(acdonald)
  1921- 13
Marks, Margaret L. 1911(?)-1980
  Obituary 23
Marks, Mickey Klar 12
Marks, Peter
  See Smith, Robert Kimmel
Marks, Rita 1938- 47
Marks, Stan(ley) 1929- 14
Marks-Highwater, J
  See Highwater, Jamake
Markun, Patricia M(aloney)
  1924- 15
Marlowe, Amy Bell [Collective
  pseudonym] 1
Marokvia, Artur 1909- 31

Marokvia, Mireille (Journet)
  1918- 5
Marr, John S(tuart) 1940- 48
Marrin, Albert 1936- 53
  Brief Entry 43
Marriott, Alice Lee 1910- 31
Marriott, Pat(ricia) 1920- 35
Mars, W. T.
  See Mars, Witold Tadeusz J.
Mars, Witold Tadeusz J.
  1912- 3
Marsh, J. E.
  See Marshall, Evelyn
Marsh, Jean
  See Marshall, Evelyn
Marshall, Anthony D(ryden)
  1924- 18
Marshall, (Sarah) Catherine
  1914-1983 2
  Obituary 34
Marshall, Douglas
  See McClintock, Marshall
Marshall, Edward
  See Marshall, James (Edward)
Marshall, Evelyn 1897- 11
Marshall, James (Edward)
  1942- 51
  Earlier sketch in SATA 6
Marshall, James Vance
  See Payne, Donald Gordon
Marshall, Kim
  See Marshall, Michael (Kimbrough)
Marshall, Michael (Kimbrough)
  1948- 37
Marshall, Percy
  See Young, Percy M(arshall)
Marshall, S(amuel) L(yman) A(twood)
  1900-1977 21
Marsoli, Lisa Ann 1958-
  Brief Entry 53
Marsten, Richard
  See Hunter, Evan
Marston, Hope Irvin 1935- 31
Martchenko, Michael 1942- 50
Martignoni, Margaret E. 1908(?)-1974
  Obituary 27
Martin, Ann M(atthews)
  1955- 44
  Brief Entry 41
Martin, Bill, Jr.
  See Martin, William Ivan
Martin, David Stone 1913- 39
Martin, Dorothy 1921- 47
Martin, Eugene [Collective
  pseudonym] 1
Martin, Frances M(cEntee)
  1906- 36
Martin, Fredric
  See Christopher, Matt(hew F.)
Martin, J(ohn) P(ercival)
  1880(?)-1966 15
Martin, Jeremy
  See Levin, Marcia Obransky
Martin, Lynne 1923- 21
Martin, Marcia
  See Levin, Marcia Obransky
Martin, Nancy
  See Salmon, Annie Elizabeth

Martin, Patricia Miles
  1899-1986 43
  Obituary 48
  Earlier sketch in SATA 1
Martin, Peter
  See Chaundler, Christine
Martin, René 1891-1977 42
  Obituary 20
Martin, Rupert (Claude) 1905- 31
Martin, Stefan 1936- 32
Martin, Vicky
  See Storey, Victoria Carolyn
Martin, William Ivan 1916-
  Brief Entry 40
Martineau, Harriet
  1802-1876 .... YABC 2
Martini, Teri 1930- 3
Marx, Robert F(rank) 1936- 24
Marzani, Carl (Aldo) 1912- 12
Marzollo, Jean 1942- 29
Masefield, John 1878-1967 19
Mason, Edwin A. 1905-1979
  Obituary 32
Mason, F. van Wyck
  1901-1978 3
  Obituary 26
Mason, Frank W.
  See Mason, F. van Wyck
Mason, George Frederick
  1904- 14
Mason, Miriam (Evangeline)
  1900-1973 2
  Obituary 26
Mason, Tally
  See Derleth, August (William)
Mason, Van Wyck
  See Mason, F. van Wyck
Masselman, George
  1897-1971 19
Massie, Diane Redfield 16
Masters, Kelly R. 1897- 3
Masters, Mildred 1932- 42
Masters, William
  See Cousins, Margaret
Matchette, Katharine E. 1941- 38
Math, Irwin 1940- 42
Mathews, Janet 1914- 41
Mathews, Louise
  See Tooke, Louise Mathews
Mathiesen, Egon 1907-1976
  Obituary 28
Mathieu, Joe
  See Mathieu, Joseph P.
Mathieu, Joseph P. 1949- 43
  Brief Entry 36
Mathis, Sharon Bell 1937- 7
  See also CLR 3
  See also SAAS 3
Matson, Emerson N(els)
  1926- 12
Matsui, Tadashi 1926- 8
Matsuno, Masako 1935- 6
Matte, (Encarnacion) L'Enc
  1936- 22
Matthews, Ann
  See Martin, Ann M(atthews)
Matthews, Ellen 1950- 28
Matthews, Jacklyn Meek
  See Meek, Jacklyn O'Hanlon

Matthews, Patricia 1927- 28
Matthews, William Henry III
  1919- 45
  Brief Entry 28
Matthias, Catherine 1945-
  Brief Entry 41
Matthiessen, Peter 1927- 27
Mattingley, Christobel (Rosemary)
  1931- 37
Matulay, Laszlo 1912- 43
Matulka, Jan 1890-1972
  Brief Entry 28
Matus, Greta 1938- 12
Maugham, W(illiam) Somerset
  1874-1965 54
Mauser, Patricia Rhoads
  1943- 37
Maves, Mary Carolyn 1916- 10
Maves, Paul B(enjamin)
  1913- 10
Mawicke, Tran 1911- 15
Max, Peter 1939- 45
Maxon, Anne
  See Best, Allena Champlin
Maxwell, Arthur S.
  1896-1970 11
Maxwell, Edith 1923- 7
May, Charles Paul 1920- 4
May, Julian 1931- 11
May, Robert Lewis 1905-1976
  Obituary 27
May, Robert Stephen 1929- 46
May, Robin
  See May, Robert Stephen
Mayberry, Florence V(irginia
  Wilson) 10
Mayer, Albert Ignatius, Jr. 1906-1960
  Obituary 29
Mayer, Ann M(argaret) 1938- 14
Mayer, Jane Rothschild 1903- 38
Mayer, Marianna 1945- 32
Mayer, Mercer 1943- 32
  Earlier sketch in SATA 16
  See also CLR 11
Mayerson, Charlotte Leon 36
Mayerson, Evelyn Wilde
  1935- 55
Mayhar, Ardath 1930- 38
Maynard, Chris
  See Maynard, Christopher
Maynard, Christopher 1949-
  Brief Entry 43
Maynard, Olga 1920- 40
Mayne, William 1928- 6
Maynes, Dr. J. O. Rocky
  See Maynes, J. Oscar, Jr.
Maynes, J. O. Rocky, Jr.
  See Maynes, J. Oscar, Jr.
Maynes, J. Oscar, Jr. 1929- 38
Mayo, Margaret (Mary) 1935- 38
Mays, Lucinda L(a Bella)
  1924- 49
Mays, (Lewis) Victor, (Jr.)
  1927- 5
Mazer, Harry 1925- 31
Mazer, Norma Fox 1931- 24
  See also SAAS 1
Mazza, Adriana 1928- 19

McBain, Ed
  See Hunter, Evan
McCaffery, Janet 1936- 38
McCaffrey, Anne 1926- 8
McCaffrey, Mary
  See Szudek, Agnes S(usan)
    P(hilomena)
McCain, Murray (David, Jr.)
  1926-1981 7
  Obituary 29
McCall, Edith S. 1911- 6
McCall, Virginia Nielsen
  1909- 13
McCallum, Phyllis 1911- 10
McCann, Gerald 1916- 41
McCannon, Dindga Fatima
  1947- 41
McCarter, Neely Dixon 1929- 47
McCarthy, Agnes 1933- 4
McCarty, Rega Kramer 1904- 10
McCaslin, Nellie 1914- 12
McCaughrean, Geraldine
  See Jones, Geraldine
McCay, Winsor 1869-1934 41
McClintock, Marshall
  1906-1967 3
McClintock, Mike
  See McClintock, Marshall
McClintock, Theodore
  1902-1971 14
McClinton, Leon 1933- 11
McCloskey, (John) Robert
  1914- 39
  Earlier sketch in SATA 2
  See also CLR 7
McClung, Robert M. 1916- 2
  See also CLR 11
McClure, Gillian Mary 1948- 31
McConnell, James Douglas
  (Rutherford) 1915- 40
McCord, Anne 1942- 41
McCord, David (Thompson Watson)
  1897- 18
  See also CLR 9
McCord, Jean 1924- 34
McCormick, Brooks
  See Adams, William Taylor
McCormick, Dell J.
  1892-1949 19
McCormick, (George) Donald (King)
  1911- 14
McCormick, Edith (Joan)
  1934- 30
McCourt, Edward (Alexander)
  1907-1972
  Obituary 28
McCoy, Iola Fuller 3
McCoy, J(oseph) J(erome)
  1917- 8
McCoy, Lois (Rich) 1941- 38
McCrady, Lady 1951- 16
McCrea, James 1920- 3
McCrea, Ruth 1921- 3
McCullers, (Lula) Carson
  1917-1967 27
McCulloch, Derek (Ivor Breashur)
  1897-1967
  Obituary 29

McCulloch, Sarah
  See Ure, Jean
McCullough, Frances Monson
  1938- 8
McCully, Emily Arnold 1939- 5
  See also Arnold, Emily
  See also SAAS 7
McCurdy, Michael 1942- 13
McDearmon, Kay 20
McDermott, Beverly Brodsky
  1941- 11
McDermott, Gerald 1941- 16
  See also CLR 9
McDole, Carol
  See Farley, Carol
McDonald, Gerald D.
  1905-1970 3
McDonald, Jamie
  See Heide, Florence Parry
McDonald, Jill (Masefield)
  1927-1982 13
  Obituary 29
McDonald, Lucile Saunders
  1898- 10
McDonnell, Christine 1949- 34
McDonnell, Lois Eddy 1914- 10
McEntee, Dorothy (Layng)
  1902- 37
McEwen, Robert (Lindley) 1926-1980
  Obituary 23
McFall, Christie 1918- 12
McFarland, Kenton D(ean)
  1920- 11
McFarlane, Leslie 1902-1977 31
McGaw, Jessie Brewer 1913- 10
McGee, Barbara 1943- 6
McGiffin, (Lewis) Lee (Shaffer)
  1908- 1
McGill, Marci
  See Ridlon, Marci
McGinley, Phyllis 1905-1978 44
  Obituary 24
  Earlier sketch in SATA 2
McGinnis, Lila S(prague)
  1924- 44
McGough, Elizabeth (Hemmes)
  1934- 33
McGovern, Ann 8
McGowen, Thomas E. 1927- 2
McGowen, Tom
  See McGowen, Thomas E.
McGrady, Mike 1933- 6
McGrath, Thomas 1916- 41
McGraw, Eloise Jarvis 1915- 1
  See also SAAS 6
McGraw, William Corbin
  1916- 3
McGregor, Craig 1933- 8
McGregor, Iona 1929- 25
McGuire, Edna 1899- 13
McGuire, Leslie (Sarah)
  1945- 52
  Brief Entry 45
McGurk, Slater
  See Roth, Arthur J(oseph)
McHargue, Georgess 4
  See also CLR 2
  See also SAAS 5

McHugh, (Berit) Elisabet
  1941- 55
  Brief Entry 44
McIlwraith, Maureen 1922- 2
McIlwraith, Maureen Mollie Hunter
  See Hunter, Mollie
McInerney, Judith Whitelock
  1945- 49
  Brief Entry 46
McKay, Donald 1895- 45
McKay, Robert W. 1921- 15
McKeever, Marcia
  See Laird, Jean E(louise)
McKendrick, Melveena (Christine)
  1941- 55
McKenzie, Dorothy Clayton
  1910-1981
  Obituary 28
McKillip, Patricia A(nne)
  1948- 30
McKim, Audrey Margaret
  1909- 47
McKinley, (Jennifer Carolyn)
  Robin 50
  Brief Entry 32
  See also CLR 10
McKissack, Fredrick L(emuel) 1939-
  Brief Entry 53
McKissack, Patricia (L'Ann) C(arwell)
  1944-
  Brief Entry 51
McKown, Robin 6
McLaurin, Anne 1953- 27
McLean, Kathryn (Anderson)
  1909-1966 9
McLeish, Kenneth 1940- 35
McLenighan, Valjean 1947- 46
  Brief Entry 40
McLeod, Emilie Warren
  1926-1982 23
  Obituary 31
McLeod, Kirsty
  See Hudson, (Margaret) Kirsty
McLeod, Margaret Vail
  See Holloway, Teresa (Bragunier)
McLoughlin, John C. 1949- 47
McMahan, Ian
  Brief Entry 45
McManus, Patrick (Francis)
  1933- 46
McMeekin, Clark
  See McMeekin, Isabel McLennan
McMeekin, Isabel McLennan
  1895- 3
McMillan, Bruce 1947- 22
McMullan, Kate (Hall) 1947- 52
  Brief Entry 48
McMullan, Katy Hall
  See McMullan, Kate (Hall)
McMullen, Catherine
  See Cookson, Catherine (McMullen)
McMurtrey, Martin A(loysius)
  1921- 21
McNair, Kate 3
McNamara, Margaret C(raig)
  1915-1981
  Obituary 24
McNaught, Harry 32
McNaughton, Colin 1951- 39

McNeely, Jeannette 1918- 25
McNeer, May 1
McNeill, Janet 1907- 1
McNickle, (William) D'Arcy
  1904-1977
  Obituary 22
McNulty, Faith 1918- 12
McPhail, David M(ichael)
  1940- 47
  Brief Entry 32
McPharlin, Paul 1903-1948
  Brief Entry 31
McPhee, Richard B(yron)
  1934- 41
McPherson, James M. 1936- 16
McQueen, Lucinda
  Brief Entry 48
McQueen, Mildred Hark
  1908- 12
McShean, Gordon 1936- 41
McSwigan, Marie 1907-1962 24
McVicker, Charles (Taggart)
  1930- 39
McVicker, Chuck
  See McVicker, Charles (Taggart)
McWhirter, Norris (Dewar)
  1925- 37
McWhirter, (Alan) Ross
  1925-1975 37
  Obituary 31
Mead, Margaret 1901-1978
  Obituary 20
Mead, Russell (M., Jr.) 1935- 10
Mead, Stella (?)-1981
  Obituary 27
Meade, Ellen (Roddick) 1936- 5
Meade, Marion 1934- 23
Meader, Stephen W(arren)
  1892- 1
Meadmore, Susan
  See Sallis, Susan (Diana)
Meadow, Charles T(roub)
  1929- 23
Meadowcroft, Enid LaMonte
  See Wright, Enid Meadowcroft
Meaker, M. J.
  See Meaker, Marijane
Meaker, Marijane 1927- 20
Means, Florence Crannell
  1891-1980 1
  Obituary 25
Mearian, Judy Frank 1936- 49
Medary, Marjorie 1890- 14
Meddaugh, Susan 1944- 29
Medearis, Mary 1915- 5
Mee, Charles L., Jr. 1938- 8
Meek, Jacklyn O'Hanlon
  1933- 51
  Brief Entry 34
Meek, S(terner St.) P(aul) 1894-1972
  Obituary 28
Meeker, Oden 1918(?)-1976 14
Meeks, Esther MacBain 1
Meggendorfer, Lothar 1847-1925
  Brief Entry 36
Mehdevi, Alexander 1947- 7
Mehdevi, Anne (Marie)
  Sinclair 8

Meighan, Donald Charles
  1929- 30
Meigs, Cornelia Lynde
  1884-1973 6
Meier, Minta 1906- 55
Meilach, Dona Z(weigoron)
  1926- 34
Melady, John 1938-
  Brief Entry 49
Melcher, Daniel 1912-1985
  Obituary 43
Melcher, Frederic Gershom 1879-1963
  Obituary 22
Melcher, Marguerite Fellows
  1879-1969 10
Melin, Grace Hathaway
  1892-1973 10
Mellersh, H(arold) E(dward) L(eslie)
  1897- 10
Meltzer, Milton 1915- 50
  Earlier sketch in SATA 1
  See also SAAS 1
  See also CLR 13
Melville, Anne
  See Potter, Margaret (Newman)
Melwood, Mary
  See Lewis, E. M.
Melzack, Ronald 1929- 5
Memling, Carl 1918-1969 6
Mendel, Jo [House pseudonym]
  See Bond, Gladys Baker
Mendonca, Susan
  Brief Entry 49
  See also Smith, Susan Vernon
Mendoza, George 1934- 41
  Brief Entry 39
  See also SAAS 7
Meng, Heinz (Karl) 1924- 13
Menotti, Gian Carlo 1911- 29
Menuhin, Yehudi 1916- 40
Mercer, Charles (Edward)
  1917- 16
Meredith, David William
  See Miers, Earl Schenck
Meringoff, Laurene Krasny
  See Brown, Laurene Krasny
Meriwether, Louise 1923- 52
  Brief Entry 31
Merriam, Eve 1916- 40
  Earlier sketch in SATA 3
  See also CLR 14
Merrill, Jane 1946- 42
Merrill, Jean (Fairbanks)
  1923- 1
Merrill, Phil
  See Merrill, Jane
Mertz, Barbara (Gross) 1927- ... 49
Merwin, Decie 1894-1961
  Brief Entry 32
Messick, Dale 1906-
  Brief Entry 48
Messmer, Otto 1892(?)-1983 37
Metcalf, Suzanne
  See Baum, L(yman) Frank
Metos, Thomas H(arry) 1932- ... 37
Meyer, Carolyn 1935- 9
Meyer, Edith Patterson 1895- ... 5
Meyer, F(ranklyn) E(dward)
  1932- 9

Meyer, Jean Shepherd 1929- 11
Meyer, Jerome Sydney
  1895-1975 3
  Obituary 25
Meyer, June
  See Jordan, June
Meyer, Kathleen Allan 1918- 51
  Brief Entry 46
Meyer, Louis A(lbert) 1942- 12
Meyer, Renate 1930- 6
Meyers, Susan 1942- 19
Meynier, Yvonne (Pollet)
  1908- 14
Mezey, Robert 1935- 33
Mian, Mary (Lawrence Shipman)
  1902-
  Brief Entry 47
Micale, Albert 1913- 22
Michael, Manfred
  See Winterfeld, Henry
Michaels, Barbara
  See Mertz, Barbara (Gross)
Michaels, Ski
  See Pellowski, Michael J(oseph)
Michel, Anna 1943- 49
  Brief Entry 40
Micklish, Rita 1931- 12
Miers, Earl Schenck
  1910-1972 1
  Obituary 26
Miklowitz, Gloria D. 1927- 4
Mikolaycak, Charles 1937- 9
  See also SAAS 4
Mild, Warren (Paul) 1922- 41
Miles, Betty 1928- 8
Miles, Miska
  See Martin, Patricia Miles
Miles, (Mary) Patricia 1930- 29
Miles, Patricia A.
  See Martin, Patricia Miles
Milgrom, Harry 1912- 25
Milhous, Katherine 1894-1977 15
Militant
  See Sandburg, Carl (August)
Millar, Barbara F. 1924- 12
Miller, Albert G(riffith)
  1905-1982 12
  Obituary 31
Miller, Alice P(atricia
  McCarthy) 22
Miller, Don 1923- 15
Miller, Doris R.
  See Mosesson, Gloria R(ubin)
Miller, Eddie
  See Miller, Edward
Miller, Edna (Anita) 1920- 29
Miller, Edward 1905-1974 8
Miller, Elizabeth 1933- 41
Miller, Eugene 1925- 33
Miller, Frances A. 1937- 52
  Brief Entry 46
Miller, Helen M(arkley) 5
Miller, Helen Topping 1884-1960
  Obituary 29
Miller, Jane (Judith) 1925- 15
Miller, John
  See Samachson, Joseph
Miller, Margaret J.
  See Dale, Margaret J(essy) Miller

Miller, Marilyn (Jean) 1925- 33
Miller, Mary
    See Northcott, (William) Cecil
Miller, Mary Beth 1942- 9
Miller, Natalie 1917-1976 35
Miller, Ruth White
    See White, Ruth C.
Miller, Sandy (Peden) 1948- 41
    Brief Entry 35
Milligan, Spike
    See Milligan, Terence Alan
Milligan, Terence Alan 1918- 29
Mills, Claudia 1954- 44
    Brief Entry 41
Mills, Yaroslava Surmach
    1925- 35
Millstead, Thomas Edward 30
Milne, A(lan) A(lexander)
    1882-1956 ....YABC 1
    See also CLR 1
Milne, Lorus J. 5
Milne, Margery 5
Milonas, Rolf
    See Myller, Rolf
Milotte, Alfred G(eorge)
    1904- 11
Milton, Hilary (Herbert)
    1920- 23
Milton, John R(onald) 1924- 24
Milton, Joyce 1946- 52
    Brief Entry 41
Milverton, Charles A.
    See Penzler, Otto
Minarik, Else Holmelund
    1920- 15
Miner, Jane Claypool 1933- 38
    Brief Entry 37
Miner, Lewis S. 1909- 11
Minier, Nelson
    See Stoutenburg, Adrien
Mintonye, Grace 4
Mirsky, Jeannette 1903-1987 8
    Obituary 51
Mirsky, Reba Paeff
    1902-1966 1
Miskovits, Christine 1939- 10
Miss Francis
    See Horwich, Frances R.
Miss Read
    See Saint, Dora Jessie
Mister Rogers
    See Rogers, Fred (McFeely)
Mitchell, Cynthia 1922- 29
Mitchell, (Sibyl) Elyne (Keith)
    1913- 10
Mitchell, Gladys (Maude Winifred)
    1901-1983 46
    Obituary 35
Mitchell, Joyce Slayton 1933- 46
    Brief Entry 43
Mitchell, Yvonne 1925-1979
    Obituary 24
Mitchison, Naomi Margaret (Haldane)
    1897- 24
Mitchnik, Helen 1901- 41
    Brief Entry 35
Mitsuhashi, Yoko 45
    Brief Entry 33

Mizner, Elizabeth Howard
    1907- 27
Mizumura, Kazue 18
Moché, Dinah (Rachel) L(evine)
    1936- 44
    Brief Entry 40
Mochi, Ugo (A.) 1889-1977 38
Modell, Frank B. 1917- 39
    Brief Entry 36
Moe, Barbara 1937- 20
Moeri, Louise 1924- 24
Moffett, Martha (Leatherwood)
    1934- 8
Mofsie, Louis B. 1936-
    Brief Entry 33
Mohn, Peter B(urnet) 1934- 28
Mohn, Viola Kohl 1914- 8
Mohr, Nicholasa 1935- 8
Molarsky, Osmond 1909- 16
Moldon, Peter L(eonard)
    1937- 49
Mole, John 1941- 36
Molloy, Anne Baker 1907- 32
Molloy, Paul 1920- 5
Momaday, N(avarre) Scott
    1934- 48
    Brief Entry 30
Moncure, Jane Belk 23
Monjo, F(erdinand) N.
    1924-1978 16
    See also CLR 2
Monroe, Lyle
    See Heinlein, Robert A(nson)
Monroe, Marion 1898-1983
    Obituary 34
Monsell, Helen (Albee)
    1895-1971 24
Montana, Bob 1920-1975
    Obituary 21
Montgomerie, Norah Mary
    1913- 26
Montgomery, Constance
    See Cappell, Constance
Montgomery, Elizabeth Rider
    1902-1985 34
    Obituary 41
    Earlier sketch in SATA 3
Montgomery, L(ucy) M(aud)
    1874-1942 ....YABC 1
    See also CLR 8
Montgomery, R(aymond) A., (Jr.)
    1936- 39
Montgomery, Rutherford George
    1894- 3
Montgomery, Vivian 36
Montresor, Beni 1926- 38
    Earlier sketch in SATA 3
    See also SAAS 4
Moody, Ralph Owen 1898- 1
Moon, Carl 1879-1948 25
Moon, Grace 1877(?)-1947 25
Moon, Sheila (Elizabeth)
    1910- 5
Mooney, Elizabeth C(omstock)
    1918-1986
    Obituary 48
Moor, Emily
    See Deming, Richard

Moore, Anne Carroll
    1871-1961 13
Moore, Clement Clarke
    1779-1863 18
Moore, Don W. 1905(?)-1986
    Obituary 48
Moore, Eva 1942- 20
Moore, Fenworth
    See Stratemeyer, Edward L.
Moore, Jack (William) 1941- 46
    Brief Entry 32
Moore, Janet Gaylord 1905- 18
Moore, Jim 1946- 42
Moore, John Travers 1908- 12
Moore, Lamont 1909-
    Brief Entry 29
Moore, Lilian 1909- 52
    See also CLR 15
Moore, Margaret Rumberger
    1903- 12
Moore, Marianne (Craig)
    1887-1972 20
Moore, Patrick (Alfred) 1923- 49
    Brief Entry 39
Moore, Ray (S.) 1905(?)-1984
    Obituary 37
Moore, Regina
    See Dunne, Mary Collins
Moore, Rosalie
    See Brown, Rosalie (Gertrude)
    Moore
Moore, Ruth 23
Moore, Ruth Nulton 1923- 38
Moore, S. E. 23
Moores, Dick
    See Moores, Richard (Arnold)
Moores, Richard (Arnold) 1909-1986
    Obituary 48
Mooser, Stephen 1941- 28
Mordvinoff, Nicolas
    1911-1973 17
More, Caroline [Joint pseudonym]
    See Cone, Molly Lamken and
    Strachan, Margaret Pitcairn
Morey, Charles
    See Fletcher, Helen Jill
Morey, Walt 1907- 51
    Earlier sketch in SATA 3
Morgan, Alfred P(owell)
    1889-1972 33
Morgan, Alison Mary 1930- 30
Morgan, Ellen
    See Bumstead, Kathleen (Mary)
Morgan, Geoffrey 1916- 46
Morgan, Helen (Gertrude Louise)
    1921- 29
Morgan, Helen Tudor
    See Morgan, Helen (Gertrude
    Louise)
Morgan, Jane
    See Cooper, James Fenimore
Morgan, Lenore 1908- 8
Morgan, Louise
    See Morgan, Helen (Gertrude
    Louise)
Morgan, Shirley 1933- 10
Morgan, Tom 1942- 42
Morgenroth, Barbara
    Brief Entry 36

Morrah, Dave
  See Morrah, David Wardlaw, Jr.
Morrah, David Wardlaw, Jr.
  1914- *10*
Morressy, John 1930- *23*
Morrill, Leslie H(olt) 1934- *48*
  Brief Entry *33*
Morris, Desmond (John)
  1928- *14*
Morris, Robert A. 1933- *7*
Morris, William 1913- *29*
Morrison, Bill 1935-
  Brief Entry *37*
Morrison, Dorothy Nafus *29*
Morrison, Gert W.
  See Stratemeyer, Edward L.
Morrison, Lillian 1917- *3*
Morrison, Lucile Phillips
  1896- *17*
Morrison, Roberta
  See Webb, Jean Francis (III)
Morrison, Velma Ford 1909- *21*
Morrison, William
  See Samachson, Joseph
Morriss, James E(dward)
  1932- *8*
Morrow, Betty
  See Bacon, Elizabeth
Morse, Carol
  See Yeakley, Marjory Hall
Morse, Dorothy B(ayley) 1906-1979
  Obituary *24*
Morse, Flo 1921- *30*
Mort, Vivian
  See Cromie, Alice Hamilton
Mortimer, Mary H.
  See Coury, Louise Andree
Morton, (Eva) Jane 1931- *50*
Morton, Lee Jack, Jr. 1928- *32*
Morton, Miriam 1918(?)-1985 ..... *9*
  Obituary *46*
Moscow, Alvin 1925- *3*
Mosel, Arlene 1921- *7*
Moser, Don
  See Moser, Donald Bruce
Moser, Donald Bruce 1932- *31*
Mosesson, Gloria R(ubin) *24*
Moskin, Marietta D(unston)
  1928- *23*
Moskof, Martin Stephen
  1930- *27*
Moss, Don(ald) 1920- *11*
Moss, Elaine Dora 1924-
  Brief Entry *31*
Most, Bernard 1937- *48*
  Brief Entry *40*
Motz, Lloyd *20*
Mountain, Robert
  See Montgomery, R(aymond) A.,
  (Jr.)
Mountfield, David
  See Grant, Neil
Moussard, Jacqueline 1924- *24*
Mowat, Farley (McGill) 1921- *55*
  Earlier sketch in SATA 3
Moyler, Alan (Frank Powell)
  1926- *36*
Mozley, Charles 1915- *43*
  Brief Entry *32*

Mrs. Fairstar
  See Horne, Richard Henry
Mueller, Virginia 1924- *28*
Muir, Frank 1920- *30*
Mukerji, Dhan Gopal
  1890-1936 .... *40*
  See also CLR 10
Mulcahy, Lucille Burnett *12*
Mulford, Philippa Greene
  1948- *43*
Mulgan, Catherine
  See Gough, Catherine
Muller, Billex
  See Ellis, Edward S(ylvester)
Mullins, Edward S(wift)
  1922- *10*
Mulock, Dinah Maria
  See Craik, Dinah Maria (Mulock)
Mulvihill, William Patrick
  1923- *8*
Mun
  See Leaf, (Wilbur) Munro
Munari, Bruno 1907- *15*
  See also CLR 9
Munce, Ruth Hill 1898- *12*
Munowitz, Ken 1935-1977 .... *14*
Muñoz, William 1949- *42*
Munro, Alice 1931- *29*
Munro, Eleanor 1928- *37*
Munsch, Robert N. 1945- *50*
  Brief Entry *48*
Munsinger, Lynn 1951- *33*
Munson(-Benson), Tunie
  1946- *15*
Munthe, Nelly 1947- *53*
Munves, James (Albert) 1922- *30*
Munzer, Martha E. 1899- *4*
Murch, Mel and Starr, Ward [Joint
  double pseudonym]
  See Manes, Stephen
Murphy, Barbara Beasley
  1933- *5*
Murphy, E(mmett) Jefferson
  1926- *4*
Murphy, Jill 1949- *37*
Murphy, Jim 1947- *37*
  Brief Entry *32*
Murphy, Pat
  See Murphy, E(mmett) Jefferson
Murphy, Robert (William)
  1902-1971 .... *10*
Murphy, Shirley Rousseau
  1928- *36*
Murray, John 1923- *39*
Murray, Marian *5*
Murray, Michele 1933-1974 .... *7*
Murray, Ossie 1938- *43*
Musgrave, Florence 1902- *3*
Musgrove, Margaret W(ynkoop)
  1943- *26*
Mussey, Virginia T. H.
  See Ellison, Virginia Howell
Mutz
  See Kunstler, Morton
Myers, Arthur 1917- *35*
Myers, Bernice *9*
Myers, Caroline Elizabeth (Clark)
  1887-1980 .... *28*

Myers, Elisabeth P(erkins)
  1918- *36*
Myers, Hortense (Powner)
  1913- *10*
Myers, Walter Dean 1937- *41*
  Brief Entry *27*
  See also CLR 4
  See also SAAS 2
Myller, Rolf 1926- *27*
Myra, Harold L(awrence)
  1939- *46*
  Brief Entry *42*
Myrus, Donald (Richard)
  1927- *23*

N

Nakatani, Chiyoko 1930-1981 ..... *55*
  Brief Entry *40*
Namioka, Lensey 1929- *27*
Napier, Mark
  See Laffin, John (Alfred Charles)
Nash, Bruce M(itchell) 1947- *34*
Nash, Linell
  See Smith, Linell Nash
Nash, Mary (Hughes) 1925- *41*
Nash, (Frederic) Ogden
  1902-1971 .... *46*
  Earlier sketch in SATA 2
Nast, Elsa Ruth
  See Watson, Jane Werner
Nast, Thomas 1840-1902 .... *51*
  Brief Entry *33*
Nastick, Sharon 1954- *41*
Nathan, Adele (Gutman) 1900(?)-1986
  Obituary *48*
Nathan, Dorothy (Goldeen)
  (?)-1966 .... *15*
Nathan, Robert (Gruntal)
  1894-1985 .... *6*
  Obituary *43*
Natti, Susanna 1948- *32*
Navarra, John Gabriel 1927- *8*
Naylor, Penelope 1941- *10*
Naylor, Phyllis Reynolds
  1933- *12*
Nazaroff, Alexander I. 1898- *4*
Neal, Harry Edward 1906- *5*
Nearing, Penny 1916- *47*
  Brief Entry *42*
Nebel, Gustave E. *45*
  Brief Entry *33*
Nebel, Mimouca
  See Nebel, Gustave E.
Nee, Kay Bonner *10*
Needle, Jan 1943- *30*
Needleman, Jacob 1934- *6*
Negri, Rocco 1932- *12*
Neigoff, Anne *13*
Neigoff, Mike 1920- *13*
Neilson, Frances Fullerton (Jones)
  1910- *14*
Neimark, Anne E. 1935- *4*
Neimark, Paul G. 1934-
  Brief Entry *37*
Nell
  See Hanna, Nell(ie L.)

Nelson, Cordner (Bruce)
1918- 54
Brief Entry 29
Nelson, Esther L. 1928- 13
Nelson, Lawrence E(rnest) 1928-1977
Obituary 28
Nelson, Mary Carroll 1929- 23
Nerlove, Miriam 1959- 53
Brief Entry 49
Nesbit, E(dith)
1858-1924 .... YABC 1
See also CLR 3
Nesbit, Troy
See Folsom, Franklin
Nespojohn, Katherine V.
1912- 7
Ness, Evaline (Michelow)
1911-1986 26
Obituary 49
Earlier sketch in SATA 1
See also CLR 6
See also SAAS 1
Nestor, William P(rodromos)
1947- 49
Neufeld, John 1938- 6
See also SAAS 3
Neumeyer, Peter F(lorian)
1929- 13
Neurath, Marie (Reidemeister)
1898- 1
Neusner, Jacob 1932- 38
Neville, Emily Cheney 1919- 1
See also SAAS 2
Neville, Mary
See Woodrich, Mary Neville
Nevins, Albert J. 1915- 20
Newberry, Clare Turlay
1903-1970 1
Obituary 26
Newbery, John 1713-1767 20
Newcomb, Ellsworth
See Kenny, Ellsworth Newcomb
Newcombe, Jack 45
Brief Entry 33
Newell, Crosby
See Bonsall, Crosby (Barbara
Newell)
Newell, Edythe W. 1910- 11
Newell, Hope (Hockenberry)
1896-1965 24
Newfeld, Frank 1928- 26
Newlon, (Frank) Clarke
1905(?)-1982 6
Obituary 33
Newman, Daisy 1904- 27
Newman, Gerald 1939- 46
Brief Entry 42
Newman, Robert (Howard)
1909- 4
Newman, Shirlee Petkin
1924- 10
Newsom, Carol 1948- 40
Newton, James R(obert)
1935- 23
Newton, Suzanne 1936- 5
Ney, John 1923- 43
Brief Entry 33
Nic Leodhas, Sorche
See Alger, Leclaire (Gowans)

Nichols, Cecilia Fawn 1906- 12
Nichols, Peter
See Youd, (Christopher) Samuel
Nichols, (Joanna) Ruth 1948- 15
Nicholson, Joyce Thorpe
1919- 35
Nickelsburg, Janet 1893- 11
Nickerson, Betty
See Nickerson, Elizabeth
Nickerson, Elizabeth 1922- 14
Nicklaus, Carol
Brief Entry 33
Nicol, Ann
See Turnbull, Ann (Christine)
Nicolas
See Mordvinoff, Nicolas
Nicolay, Helen
1866-1954 .... YABC 1
Nicole, Christopher Robin
1930- 5
Nielsen, Kay (Rasmus)
1886-1957 16
Nielsen, Virginia
See McCall, Virginia Nielsen
Niland, Deborah 1951- 27
Nixon, Hershell Howard
1923- 42
Nixon, Joan Lowery 1927- 44
Earlier sketch in SATA 8
Nixon, K.
See Nixon, Kathleen Irene (Blundell)
Nixon, Kathleen Irene
(Blundell) 14
Noble, Iris 1922-1986 5
Obituary 49
Noble, Trinka Hakes
Brief Entry 37
Nodset, Joan L.
See Lexau, Joan M.
Noguere, Suzanne 1947- 34
Nolan, Dennis 1945- 42
Brief Entry 34
Nolan, Jeannette Covert
1897-1974 2
Obituary 27
Nolan, Paul T(homas) 1919- 48
Nolan, William F(rancis) 1928-
Brief Entry 28
Noonan, Julia 1946- 4
Norcross, John
See Conroy, Jack (Wesley)
Nordhoff, Charles (Bernard)
1887-1947 23
Nordlicht, Lillian 29
Nordstrom, Ursula 3
Norman, Charles 1904- 38
Norman, James
See Schmidt, James Norman
Norman, Mary 1931- 36
Norman, Steve
See Pashko, Stanley
Norris, Gunilla B(rodde)
1939- 20
North, Andrew
See Norton, Alice Mary
North, Captain George
See Stevenson, Robert Louis
North, Joan 1920- 16

North, Robert
See Withers, Carl A.
North, Sterling 1906-1974 45
Obituary 26
Earlier sketch in SATA 1
Northcott, (William) Cecil 1902-1987
Obituary 55
Norton, Alice Mary 1912- 43
Earlier sketch in SATA 1
Norton, André
See Norton, Alice Mary
Norton, Browning
See Norton, Frank R(owland)
B(rowning)
Norton, Frank R(owland) B(rowning)
1909- 10
Norton, Mary 1903- 18
See also CLR 6
Nöstlinger, Christine 1936-
Brief Entry 37
See also CLR 12
Nourse, Alan E(dward) 1928- 48
Novak, Matt 1962-
Brief Entry 52
Nowell, Elizabeth Cameron 12
Numeroff, Laura Joffe 1953- 28
Nurenberg, Thelma
See Greenhaus, Thelma Nurenberg
Nurnberg, Maxwell
1897-1984 27
Obituary 41
Nussbaumer, Paul (Edmond)
1934- 16
Nyce, (Nellie) Helene von Strecker
1885-1969 19
Nyce, Vera 1862-1925 19
Nye, Harold G.
See Harding, Lee
Nye, Robert 1939- 6

O

Oakes, Vanya 1909-1983 6
Obituary 37
Oakley, Don(ald G.) 1927- 8
Oakley, Graham 1929- 30
See also CLR 7
Oakley, Helen 1906- 10
Oana, Katherine D. 1929- 53
Brief Entry 37
Oana, Kay D.
See Oana, Katherine D.
Obligado, Lilian (Isabel) 1931-
Brief Entry 45
Obrant, Susan 1946- 11
O'Brien, Anne Sibley 1952- 53
Brief Entry 48
O'Brien, Esse Forrester 1895(?)-1975
Obituary 30
O'Brien, Robert C.
See Conly, Robert Leslie
See also CLR 2
O'Brien, Thomas C(lement)
1938- 29
O'Carroll, Ryan
See Markun, Patricia M(aloney)

O'Connell, Margaret F(orster)
1935-1977 .... *49*
   Obituary *30*
O'Connell, Peg
   See Ahern, Margaret McCrohan
O'Connor, Jane 1947-
   Brief Entry *47*
O'Connor, Karen 1938- *34*
O'Connor, Patrick
   See Wibberley, Leonard (Patrick
   O'Connor)
O'Connor, Richard 1915-1975
   Obituary *21*
O'Daniel, Janet 1921- *24*
O'Dell, Scott 1903- *12*
   See also CLR 1
Odenwald, Robert P(aul)
1899-1965 .... *11*
Odor, Ruth Shannon 1926-
   Brief Entry *44*
Oechsli, Kelly 1918- *5*
Ofek, Uriel 1926- *36*
Offit, Sidney 1928- *10*
Ofosu-Appiah, L(awrence) H(enry)
1920- *13*
Ogan, George F. 1912- *13*
Ogan, M. G. [Joint pseudonym]
   See Ogan, George F. and Ogan,
   Margaret E. (Nettles)
Ogan, Margaret E. (Nettles)
1923- *13*
Ogburn, Charlton, Jr. 1911- *3*
Ogilvie, Elisabeth May 1917- *40*
   Brief Entry *29*
O'Hagan, Caroline 1946- *38*
O'Hanlon, Jacklyn
   See Meek, Jacklyn O'Hanlon
O'Hara, Mary
   See Alsop, Mary O'Hara
Ohlsson, Ib 1935- *7*
Ohtomo, Yasuo 1946- *37*
O'Kelley, Mattie Lou 1908- *36*
Okimoto, Jean Davies 1942- *34*
Olcott, Frances Jenkins
1872(?)-1963 .... *19*
Old Boy
   See Hughes, Thomas
Old Fag
   See Bell, Robert S(tanley) W(arren)
Oldenburg, E(gbert) William
1936-1974 .... *35*
Olds, Elizabeth 1896- *3*
Olds, Helen Diehl 1895-1981 ..... *9*
   Obituary *25*
Oldstyle, Jonathan
   See Irving, Washington
O'Leary, Brian 1940- *6*
Oleksy, Walter 1930- *33*
Olesky, Walter
   See Oleksy, Walter
Oliver, John Edward 1933- *21*
Olmstead, Lorena Ann 1890- *13*
Olney, Ross R. 1929- *13*
Olschewski, Alfred 1920- *7*
Olsen, Ib Spang 1921- *6*
Olson, Gene 1922- *32*
Olson, Helen Kronberg *48*
Olugebefola, Ademole 1941- *15*

Oman, Carola (Mary Anima)
1897-1978 .... *35*
Ommanney, F(rancis) D(ownes)
1903-1980 .... *23*
O Mude
   See Gorey, Edward St. John
Oneal, Elizabeth 1934- *30*
Oneal, Zibby
   See Oneal, Elizabeth
   See also CLR 13
O'Neill, Judith (Beatrice)
1930- *34*
O'Neill, Mary L(e Duc) 1908- *2*
Onslow, John 1906-1985
   Obituary *47*
Opgenoorth, Winfried 1939-
   Brief Entry *50*
Opie, Iona 1923- *3*
   See also SAAS 6
Opie, Peter (Mason)
1918-1982 .... *3*
   Obituary *28*
Oppenheim, Joanne 1934- *5*
Oppenheimer, Joan L(etson)
1925- *28*
Optic, Oliver
   See Adams, William Taylor
Orbach, Ruth Gary 1941- *21*
Orczy, Emmuska, Baroness
1865-1947 .... *40*
O'Reilly, Sean
   See Deegan, Paul Joseph
Orgel, Doris 1929- *7*
Oriolo, Joe
   See Oriolo, Joseph
Oriolo, Joseph 1913-1985
   Obituary *46*
Orleans, Ilo 1897-1962 .... *10*
Ormai, Stella
   Brief Entry *48*
Ormerod, Jan(ette Louise)
1946- *55*
   Brief Entry *44*
Ormes, Jackie
   See Ormes, Zelda J.
Ormes, Zelda J. 1914-1986
   Obituary *47*
Ormondroyd, Edward 1925- *14*
Ormsby, Virginia H(aire) *11*
Orris
   See Ingelow, Jean
Orth, Richard
   See Gardner, Richard
Orwell, George
   See Blair, Eric Arthur
Osborne, Chester G. 1915- *11*
Osborne, David
   See Silverberg, Robert
Osborne, Leone Neal 1914- *2*
Osborne, Mary Pope 1949- *55*
   Brief Entry *41*
Osceola
   See Blixen, Karen (Christentze
   Dinesen)
Osgood, William E(dward)
1926- *37*
Osmond, Edward 1900- *10*
Ossoli, Sarah Margaret (Fuller)
   marchesa d' 1810-1850 .... *25*

Otis, James
   See Kaler, James Otis
O'Trigger, Sir Lucius
   See Horne, Richard Henry
Ottley, Reginald (Leslie) *26*
Otto, Margaret Glover 1909-1976
   Obituary *30*
Ouida
   See De La Ramée, (Marie) Louise
Ousley, Odille 1896- *10*
Overton, Jenny (Margaret Mary)
1942- *52*
   Brief Entry *36*
Owen, Caroline Dale
   See Snedecker, Caroline Dale
   (Parke)
Owen, Clifford
   See Hamilton, Charles H. St. John
Owen, Dilys
   See Gater, Dilys
Owen, (Benjamin) Evan
1918-1984 .... *38*
Owens, Gail 1939- *54*
Oxenbury, Helen 1938- *3*

P

Pace, Mildred Mastin 1907- *46*
   Brief Entry *29*
Packard, Edward 1931- *47*
Packer, Vin
   See Meaker, Marijane
Page, Eileen
   See Heal, Edith
Page, Eleanor
   See Coerr, Eleanor
Page, Lou Williams 1912- *38*
Paget-Fredericks, Joseph E. P. Rous-
Marten 1903-1963
   Brief Entry *30*
Pahz, (Anne) Cheryl Suzanne
1949- *11*
Pahz, James Alon 1943- *11*
Paice, Margaret 1920- *10*
Paige, Harry W. 1922- *41*
   Brief Entry *35*
Paine, Roberta M. 1925- *13*
Paisley, Tom
   See Bethancourt, T. Ernesto
Palazzo, Anthony D.
1905-1970 .... *3*
Palazzo, Tony
   See Palazzo, Anthony D.
Palder, Edward L. 1922- *5*
Palladini, David (Mario)
1946- *40*
   Brief Entry *32*
Pallas, Norvin 1918- *23*
Pallister, John C(lare) 1891-1980
   Obituary *26*
Palmer, Bernard 1914- *26*
Palmer, C(yril) Everard 1930- *14*
Palmer, (Ruth) Candida 1926- *11*
Palmer, Heidi 1948- *15*
Palmer, Helen Marion
   See Geisel, Helen
Palmer, Juliette 1930- *15*
Palmer, Robin 1911- *43*

Paltrowitz, Donna (Milman) 1950-
  Brief Entry 50
Paltrowitz, Stuart 1946-
  Brief Entry 50
Panetta, George 1915-1969 15
Panowski, Eileen Thompson
  1920- 49
Pansy
  See Alden, Isabella (Macdonald)
Pantell, Dora (Fuchs) 1915- 39
Panter, Carol 1936- 9
Papas, William 1927- 50
Papashvily, George
  1898-1978 17
Papashvily, Helen (Waite)
  1906- 17
Pape, D(onna) L(ugg) 1930- 2
Paperny, Myra (Green) 1932- 51
  Brief Entry 33
Paradis, Adrian A(lexis)
  1912- 1
Paradis, Marjorie (Bartholomew)
  1886(?)-1970 17
Parenteau, Shirley (Laurolyn)
  1935- 47
  Brief Entry 40
Parish, Peggy 1927- 17
Park, Barbara 1947- 40
  Brief Entry 35
Park, Bill
  See Park, W(illiam) B(ryan)
Park, Ruth 25
Park, W(illiam) B(ryan) 1936- 22
Parker, Elinor 1906- 3
Parker, Lois M(ay) 1912- 30
Parker, Margot M. 1937- 52
Parker, Nancy Winslow 1930- 10
Parker, Richard 1915- 14
Parker, Robert
  See Boyd, Waldo T.
Parkinson, Ethelyn M(inerva)
  1906- 11
Parks, Edd Winfield
  1906-1968 10
Parks, Gordon (Alexander Buchanan)
  1912- 8
Parley, Peter
  See Goodrich, Samuel Griswold
Parlin, John
  See Graves, Charles Parlin
Parnall, Peter 1936- 16
Parr, Letitia (Evelyn) 1906- 37
Parr, Lucy 1924- 10
Parrish, Anne 1888-1957 27
Parrish, Mary
  See Cousins, Margaret
Parrish, (Frederick) Maxfield
  1870-1966 14
Parry, Marian 1924- 13
Parsons, Tom
  See MacPherson, Thomas George
Partch, Virgil Franklin II
  1916-1984 45
  Obituary 39
Partridge, Benjamin W(aring), Jr.
  1915- 28
Partridge, Jenny (Lilian)
  1947- 52
  Brief Entry 37

Pascal, David 1918- 14
Pascal, Francine 1938- 51
  Brief Entry 37
Paschal, Nancy
  See Trotter, Grace V(iolet)
Pashko, Stanley 1913- 29
Patent, Dorothy Hinshaw
  1940- 22
Paterson, Diane (R. Cole) 1946-
  Brief Entry 33
Paterson, Katherine (Womeldorf)
  1932- 53
  Earlier sketch in SATA 13
  See also CLR 7
Paton, Alan (Stewart) 1903- 11
Paton, Jane (Elizabeth) 1934- 35
Paton Walsh, Gillian 1939- 4
  See also SAAS 3
Patten, Brian 1946- 29
Patterson, Geoffrey 1943- 54
  Brief Entry 44
Patterson, Lillie G. 14
Paul, Aileen 1917- 12
Paul, Elizabeth
  See Crow, Donna Fletcher
Paul, James 1936- 23
Paul, Robert
  See Roberts, John G(aither)
Pauli, Hertha (Ernestine)
  1909-1973 3
  Obituary 26
Paull, Grace A. 1898- 24
Paulsen, Gary 1939- 54
  Earlier sketch in SATA 22
Paulson, Jack
  See Jackson, C. Paul
Pavel, Frances 1907- 10
Payne, Donald Gordon 1924- 37
Payne, Emmy
  See West, Emily G(ovan)
Payson, Dale 1943- 9
Payzant, Charles 18
Payzant, Jessie Mercer Knechtel
  See Shannon, Terry
Paz, A.
  See Pahz, James Alon
Paz, Zan
  See Pahz, Cheryl Suzanne
Peake, Mervyn 1911-1968 23
Peale, Norman Vincent 1898- 20
Pearce, (Ann) Philippa 1920- 1
  See also CLR 9
Peare, Catherine Owens 1911- 9
Pears, Charles 1873-1958
  Brief Entry 30
Pearson, Gayle 1947- 53
Pearson, Susan 1946- 39
  Brief Entry 27
Pease, Howard 1894-1974 2
  Obituary 25
Peavy, Linda 1943- 54
Peck, Anne Merriman 1884- 18
Peck, Richard 1934- 55
  Earlier sketch in SATA 18
  See also SAAS 2
  See also CLR 15
Peck, Robert Newton III
  1928- 21
  See also SAAS 1

Peek, Merle 1938- 39
Peel, Norman Lemon
  See Hirsch, Phil
Peeples, Edwin A. 1915- 6
Peet, Bill
  See Peet, William Bartlett
  See also CLR 12
Peet, Creighton B. 1899-1977 30
Peet, William Bartlett 1915- 41
  Earlier sketch in SATA 2
Peirce, Waldo 1884-1970
  Brief Entry 28
Pelaez, Jill 1924- 12
Pellowski, Anne 1933- 20
Pellowski, Michael J(oseph) 1949-
  Brief Entry 48
Pelta, Kathy 1928- 18
Peltier, Leslie C(opus) 1900- 13
Pembury, Bill
  See Groner, Arthur William
Pemsteen, Hans
  See Manes, Stephen
Pendennis, Arthur, Esquire
  See Thackeray, William Makepeace
Pender, Lydia 1907- 3
Pendery, Rosemary 7
Pendle, Alexy 1943- 29
Pendle, George 1906-1977
  Obituary 28
Penn, Ruth Bonn
  See Rosenberg, Ethel
Pennage, E. M.
  See Finkel, George (Irvine)
Penney, Grace Jackson 1904- 35
Pennington, Eunice 1923- 27
Pennington, Lillian Boyer
  1904- 45
Penrose, Margaret
  See Stratemeyer, Edward L.
Penzler, Otto 1942- 38
Pepe, Phil(ip) 1935- 20
Peppe, Rodney 1934- 4
Percy, Charles Henry
  See Smith, Dodie
Perera, Thomas Biddle 1938- 13
Perez, Walter
  See Joseph, James (Herz)
Perkins, Al(bert Rogers)
  1904-1975 30
Perkins, Marlin 1905-1986 21
  Obituary 48
Perl, Lila 6
Perl, Susan 1922-1983 22
  Obituary 34
Perlmutter, O(scar) William
  1920-1975 8
Perrault, Charles 1628-1703 25
Perreard, Suzanne Louise Butler 1919-
  Brief Entry 29
Perrine, Mary 1913- 2
Perry, Barbara Fisher
  See Fisher, Barbara
Perry, Patricia 1949- 30
Perry, Roger 1933- 27
Pershing, Marie
  See Schultz, Pearle Henriksen
Peters, Caroline
  See Betz, Eva Kelly

Peters, Elizabeth
 See Mertz, Barbara (Gross)
Peters, S. H.
 See Porter, William Sydney
Petersen, P(eter) J(ames)
 1941- *48*
 Brief Entry *43*
Petersham, Maud (Fuller)
 1890-1971 .... *17*
Petersham, Miska 1888-1960 ...... *17*
Peterson, Esther (Allen) 1934- *35*
Peterson, Hans 1922- *8*
Peterson, Harold L(eslie)
 1922- *8*
Peterson, Helen Stone 1910- *8*
Peterson, Jeanne Whitehouse
 See Whitehouse, Jeanne
Peterson, Lorraine 1940-
 Brief Entry *44*
Petie, Haris 1915- *10*
Petrides, Heidrun 1944- *19*
Petrie, Catherine 1947- *52*
 Brief Entry *41*
Petroski, Catherine (Ann Groom)
 1939- *48*
Petrovich, Michael B(oro)
 1922- *40*
Petrovskaya, Kyra
 See Wayne, Kyra Petrovskaya
Petry, Ann (Lane) 1908- *5*
 See also CLR 12
Pevsner, Stella *8*
Peyo
 See Culliford, Pierre
Peyton, K. M.
 See Peyton, Kathleen (Wendy)
 See also CLR 3
Peyton, Kathleen (Wendy)
 1929- *15*
Pfeffer, Susan Beth 1948- *4*
 See also CLR 11
Phelan, Josephine 1905-
 Brief Entry *30*
Phelan, Mary Kay 1914- *3*
Phelps, Ethel Johnston 1914- *35*
Philbrook, Clem(ent E.) 1917- *24*
Phillips, Betty Lou
 See Phillips, Elizabeth Louise
Phillips, Elizabeth Louise
 Brief Entry *48*
Phillips, Irv
 See Phillips, Irving W.
Phillips, Irving W. 1908- *11*
Phillips, Jack
 See Sandburg, Carl (August)
Phillips, Leon
 See Gerson, Noel B(ertram)
Phillips, Loretta (Hosey)
 1893- *10*
Phillips, Louis 1942- *8*
Phillips, Mary Geisler
 1881-1964 .... *10*
Phillips, Prentice 1894- *10*
Phillpotts, Eden 1862-1960 .... *24*
Phipson, Joan
 See Fitzhardinge, Joan M.
 See also CLR 5
 See also SAAS 3

Phiz
 See Browne, Hablot Knight
Phleger, Fred B. 1909- *34*
Phleger, Marjorie Temple
 1908(?)-1986 .... *1*
 Obituary *47*
Phypps, Hyacinthe
 See Gorey, Edward St. John
Piaget, Jean 1896-1980
 Obituary *23*
Piatti, Celestino 1922- *16*
Picard, Barbara Leonie 1917- *2*
Pickard, Charles 1932- *36*
Pickering, James Sayre
 1897-1969 .... *36*
 Obituary *28*
Pienkowski, Jan 1936- *6*
 See also CLR 6
Pierce, Edith Gray 1893-1977 ..... *45*
Pierce, Katherine
 See St. John, Wylly Folk
Pierce, Meredith Ann 1958-
 Brief Entry *48*
Pierce, Ruth (Ireland) 1936- *5*
Pierce, Tamora 1954- *51*
 Brief Entry *49*
Pierik, Robert 1921- *13*
Pig, Edward
 See Gorey, Edward St. John
Pike, E(dgar) Royston 1896- *22*
Pilarski, Laura 1926- *13*
Pilgrim, Anne
 See Allan, Mabel Esther
Pilkington, Francis Meredyth
 1907- *4*
Pilkington, Roger (Windle)
 1915- *10*
Pinchot, David 1914(?)-1983
 Obituary *34*
Pincus, Harriet 1938- *27*
Pine, Tillie S(chloss) 1897- *13*
Pinkerton, Kathrene Sutherland
 (Gedney) 1887-1967
 Obituary *26*
Pinkney, Jerry 1939- *41*
 Brief Entry *32*
Pinkwater, Daniel Manus
 1941- *46*
 Earlier sketch in SATA 8
 See also CLR 4
 See also SAAS 3
Pinner, Joma
 See Werner, Herma
Pioneer
 See Yates, Raymond F(rancis)
Piowaty, Kim Kennelly 1957- *49*
Piper, Roger
 See Fisher, John (Oswald Hamilton)
Piper, Watty
 See Bragg, Mabel Caroline
Piro, Richard 1934- *7*
Pirsig, Robert M(aynard)
 1928- *39*
Pitman, (Isaac) James 1901-1985
 Obituary *46*
Pitrone, Jean Maddern 1920- *4*
Pitz, Henry C(larence)
 1895-1976 .... *4*
 Obituary *24*

Pizer, Vernon 1918- *21*
Place, Marian T. 1910- *3*
Plaidy, Jean
 See Hibbert, Eleanor
Plaine, Alfred R. 1898(?)-1981
 Obituary *29*
Platt, Kin 1911- *21*
Plimpton, George (Ames)
 1927- *10*
Plomer, William (Charles Franklin)
 1903-1973 .... *24*
Plotz, Helen (Ratnoff) 1913- *38*
Plowden, David 1932- *52*
Plowhead, Ruth Gipson
 1877-1967 .... *43*
Plowman, Stephanie 1922- *6*
Pluckrose, Henry (Arthur)
 1931- *13*
Plum, J.
 See Wodehouse, P(elham)
 G(renville)
Plum, Jennifer
 See Kurland, Michael (Joseph)
Plumb, Charles P. 1900(?)-1982
 Obituary *29*
Plume, Ilse
 Brief Entry *43*
Plummer, Margaret 1911- *2*
Podendorf, Illa E.
 1903(?)-1983 .... *18*
 Obituary *35*
Poe, Edgar Allan 1809-1849 ...... *23*
Pogány, William Andrew
 1882-1955 .... *44*
Pogány, Willy
 Brief Entry *30*
 See Pogány, William Andrew
Pohl, Frederik 1919- *24*
Pohlmann, Lillian (Grenfell)
 1902- *11*
Pointon, Robert
 See Rooke, Daphne (Marie)
Pola
 See Watson, Pauline
Polatnick, Florence T. 1923- *5*
Polder, Markus
 See Krüss, James
Polette, Nancy (Jane) 1930- *42*
Polhamus, Jean Burt 1928- *21*
Politi, Leo 1908- *47*
 Earlier sketch in SATA 1
Polking, Kirk 1925- *5*
Pollack, Merrill S. 1924-1988
 Obituary *55*
Polland, Barbara K(ay) 1939- *44*
Polland, Madeleine A. 1918- *6*
Pollock, Bruce 1945- *46*
Pollock, Mary
 See Blyton, Enid (Mary)
Pollock, Penny 1935- *44*
 Brief Entry *42*
Pollowitz, Melinda (Kilborn)
 1944- *26*
Polonsky, Arthur 1925- *34*
Polseno, Jo *17*
Pomerantz, Charlotte *20*
Pomeroy, Pete
 See Roth, Arthur J(oseph)
Pond, Alonzo W(illiam) 1894- *5*

Pontiflet, Ted 1932- 32
Poole, Gray Johnson 1906- 1
Poole, Josephine 1933- 5
    See also SAAS 2
Poole, Lynn 1910-1969 1
Poole, Peggy 1925- 39
Poortvliet, Marien
    See Poortvliet, Rien
Poortvliet, Rien 1933(?)-
    Brief Entry 37
Pope, Elizabeth Marie 1917- 38
    Brief Entry 36
Portal, Colette 1936- 6
Porte, Barbara Ann
    Brief Entry 45
Porter, Katherine Anne
    1890-1980 39
    Obituary 23
Porter, Sheena 1935- 24
Porter, William Sydney
    1862-1910 .... YABC 2
Portteus, Eleanora Marie Manthei
    (?)-1983
    Obituary 36
Posell, Elsa Z. 3
Posten, Margaret L(ois) 1915- 10
Potok, Chaim 1929- 33
Potter, (Helen) Beatrix
    1866-1943 .... YABC 1
    See also CLR 1
Potter, Margaret (Newman)
    1926- 21
Potter, Marian 1915- 9
Potter, Miriam Clark
    1886-1965 3
Pournelle, Jerry (Eugene)
    1933- 26
Powell, A. M.
    See Morgan, Alfred P(owell)
Powell, Ann 1951-
    Brief Entry 51
Powell, Richard Stillman
    See Barbour, Ralph Henry
Powers, Anne
    See Schwartz, Anne Powers
Powers, Bill 1931- 52
    Brief Entry 31
Powers, Margaret
    See Heal, Edith
Powledge, Fred 1935- 37
Poynter, Margaret 1927- 27
Prager, Arthur 44
Preiss, Byron (Cary) 47
    Brief Entry 42
Prelutsky, Jack 22
    See also CLR 13
Presberg, Miriam Goldstein 1919-1978
    Brief Entry 38
Preston, Edna Mitchell 40
Preston, Lillian Elvira 1918- 47
Preussler, Otfried 1923- 24
Prevert, Jacques (Henri Marie)
    1900-1977
    Obituary 30
Price, Christine 1928-1980 3
    Obituary 23
Price, Garrett 1896-1979
    Obituary 22

Price, Jennifer
    See Hoover, Helen (Drusilla
    Blackburn)
Price, Jonathan (Reeve) 1941- 46
Price, Lucie Locke
    See Locke, Lucie
Price, Margaret (Evans) 1888-1973
    Brief Entry 28
Price, Olive 1903- 8
Price, Susan 1955- 25
Price, Willard 1887-1983 48
    Brief Entry 38
Prideaux, Tom 1908- 37
Priestley, Lee (Shore) 1904- 27
Prieto, Mariana B(eeching)
    1912- 8
Primavera, Elise 1954-
    Brief Entry 48
Prime, Derek (James) 1931- 34
Prince, Alison 1931- 28
Prince, J(ack) H(arvey) 1908- 17
Pringle, Laurence 1935- 4
    See also SAAS 6
    See also CLR 4
Pritchett, Elaine H(illyer)
    1920- 36
Proctor, Everitt
    See Montgomery, Rutherford
Professor Zingara
    See Leeming, Joseph
Provensen, Alice 1918- 9
    See also CLR 11
Provensen, Martin 1916-1987 9
    Obituary 51
    See also CLR 11
Pryor, Helen Brenton
    1897-1972 4
Pucci, Albert John 1920- 44
Pudney, John (Sleigh)
    1909-1977 24
Pugh, Ellen T. 1920- 7
Pullein-Thompson, Christine
    1930- 3
Pullein-Thompson, Diana 3
Pullein-Thompson, Josephine 3
Puner, Helen W(alker) 1915- 37
Purdy, Susan Gold 1939- 8
Purscell, Phyllis 1934- 7
Purtill, Richard L. 1931- 53
Putnam, Arthur Lee
    See Alger, Horatio, Jr.
Putnam, Peter B(rock) 1920- 30
Pyle, Howard 1853-1911 16
Pyne, Mable Mandeville
    1903-1969 9
Python, Monty
    See Jones, Terry

Q

Quackenbush, Robert M.
    1929- 7
    See also SAAS 7
Quammen, David 1948- 7
Quarles, Benjamin 1904- 12
Queen, Ellery, Jr.
    See Holding, James

Quennell, Marjorie (Courtney)
    1884-1972 29
Quick, Annabelle 1922- 2
Quigg, Jane (Hulda) (?)-1986
    Obituary 49
Quin-Harkin, Janet 1941- 18
Quinn, Elisabeth 1881-1962 22
Quinn, Susan
    See Jacobs, Susan
Quinn, Vernon
    See Quinn, Elisabeth

R

Rabe, Berniece 1928- 7
Rabe, Olive H(anson)
    1887-1968 13
Rabinowich, Ellen 1946- 29
Rabinowitz, Sandy 1954- 52
    Brief Entry 39
Raboff, Ernest Lloyd
    Brief Entry 37
Rachlin, Harvey (Brant) 1951- 47
Rachlis, Eugene (Jacob) 1920-1986
    Obituary 50
Rackham, Arthur 1867-1939 15
Radford, Ruby L(orraine)
    1891-1971 6
Radin, Ruth Yaffe 1938-
    Brief Entry 52
Radlauer, David 1952- 28
Radlauer, Edward 1921- 15
Radlauer, Ruth (Shaw) 1926- 15
Radley, Gail 1951- 25
Rae, Gwynedd 1892-1977 37
Raebeck, Lois 1921- 5
Raftery, Gerald (Bransfield)
    1905- 11
Rahn, Joan Elma 1929- 27
Raible, Alton (Robert) 1918- 35
Raiff, Stan 1930- 11
Rainey, W. B.
    See Blassingame, Wyatt Rainey
Ralston, Jan
    See Dunlop, Agnes M. R.
Ramal, Walter
    See de la Mare, Walter
Rame, David
    See Divine, Arthur Durham
Rana, J.
    See Forrester, Helen
Ranadive, Gail 1944- 10
Rand, Ann (Binkley) 30
Rand, Paul 1914- 6
Randall, Florence Engel 1917- 5
Randall, Janet [Joint pseudonym]
    See Young, Janet Randall and
    Young, Robert W.
Randall, Robert
    See Silverberg, Robert
Randall, Ruth Painter
    1892-1971 3
Randolph, Lieutenant J. H.
    See Ellis, Edward S(ylvester)
Rands, William Brighty
    1823-1882 17
Ranney, Agnes V. 1916- 6

Ransom, Candice F. 1952- 52
  Brief Entry 49
Ransome, Arthur (Michell)
  1884-1967 22
  See also CLR 8
Rapaport, Stella F(read) 10
Raphael, Elaine (Chionchio)
  1933- 23
Rappaport, Eva 1924- 6
Rarick, Carrie 1911- 41
Raskin, Edith (Lefkowitz)
  1908- 9
Raskin, Ellen 1928-1984 38
  Earlier sketch in SATA 2
  See also CLR 1, 12
Raskin, Joseph 1897-1982 12
  Obituary 29
Rasmussen, Knud Johan Victor
  1879-1933
  Brief Entry 34
Rathjen, Carl H(enry) 1909- 11
Rattray, Simon
  See Trevor, Elleston
Rau, Margaret 1913- 9
  See also CLR 8
Rauch, Mabel Thompson 1888-1972
  Obituary 26
Raucher, Herman 1928- 8
Ravielli, Anthony 1916- 3
Rawding, F(rederick) W(illiam)
  1930- 55
Rawlings, Marjorie Kinnan
  1896-1953 .... YABC 1
Rawls, (Woodrow) Wilson
  1913- 22
Ray, Deborah
  See Kogan, Deborah
Ray, Deborah Kogan
  See Kogan, Deborah
Ray, Irene
  See Sutton, Margaret Beebe
Ray, JoAnne 1935- 9
Ray, Mary (Eva Pedder)
  1932- 2
Raymond, James Crossley 1917-1981
  Obituary 29
Raymond, Robert
  See Alter, Robert Edmond
Rayner, Mary 1933- 22
Rayner, William 1929- 55
  Brief Entry 36
Raynor, Dorka 28
Rayson, Steven 1932- 30
Razzell, Arthur (George)
  1925- 11
Razzi, James 1931- 10
Read, Elfreida 1920- 2
Read, Piers Paul 1941- 21
Ready, Kirk L. 1943- 39
Reaney, James 1926- 43
Reck, Franklin Mering 1896-1965
  Brief Entry 30
Redding, Robert Hull 1919- 2
Redway, Ralph
  See Hamilton, Charles H. St. John
Redway, Ridley
  See Hamilton, Charles H. St. John
Reed, Betty Jane 1921- 4

Reed, Gwendolyn E(lizabeth)
  1932- 21
Reed, Kit 1932- 34
Reed, Philip G. 1908-
  Brief Entry 29
Reed, Thomas (James) 1947- 34
Reed, William Maxwell
  1871-1962 15
Reeder, Colonel Red
  See Reeder, Russell P., Jr.
Reeder, Russell P., Jr. 1902- 4
Reeman, Douglas Edward 1924-
  Brief Entry 28
Rees, David Bartlett 1936- 36
  See also SAAS 5
Rees, Ennis 1925- 3
Reese, Bob
  See Reese, Robert A.
Reese, Robert A. 1938-
  Brief Entry 53
Reeve, Joel
  See Cox, William R(obert)
Reeves, James 1909- 15
Reeves, Joyce 1911- 17
Reeves, Lawrence F. 1926- 29
Reeves, Ruth Ellen
  See Ranney, Agnes V.
Regehr, Lydia 1903- 37
Reggiani, Renée 18
Reid, Alastair 1926- 46
Reid, Barbara 1922- 21
Reid, Dorothy M(arion) (?)-1974
  Brief Entry 29
Reid, Eugenie Chazal 1924- 12
Reid, John Calvin 21
Reid, (Thomas) Mayne
  1818-1883 24
Reid, Meta Mayne 1905-
  Brief Entry 36
Reid Banks, Lynne 1929- 22
Reiff, Stephanie Ann 1948- 47
  Brief Entry 28
Reig, June 1933- 30
Reigot, Betty Polisar 1924- 55
  Brief Entry 41
Reinach, Jacquelyn (Krasne)
  1930- 28
Reiner, William B(uck)
  1910-1976 46
  Obituary 30
Reinfeld, Fred 1910-1964 3
Reiniger, Lotte 1899-1981 40
  Obituary 33
Reiss, Johanna de Leeuw
  1932- 18
Reiss, John J. 23
Reit, Seymour 21
Reit, Sy
  See Reit, Seymour
Rémi, Georges 1907-1983 13
  Obituary 32
Remington, Frederic (Sackrider)
  1861-1909 41
Renault, Mary
  See Challans, Mary
Rendell, Joan 28
Rendina, Laura Cooper 1902- 10
Renick, Marion (Lewis) 1905- 1
Renken, Aleda 1907- 27

Renlie, Frank H. 1936- 11
Rensie, Willis
  See Eisner, Will(iam Erwin)
Renvoize, Jean 1930- 5
Resnick, Michael D(iamond)
  1942- 38
Resnick, Mike
  See Resnick, Michael D(iamond)
Resnick, Seymour 1920- 23
Retla, Robert
  See Alter, Robert Edmond
Reuter, Carol (Joan) 1931- 2
Revena
  See Wright, Betty Ren
Rey, H(ans) A(ugusto)
  1898-1977 26
  Earlier sketch in SATA 1
  See also CLR 5
Rey, Margret (Elizabeth)
  1906- 26
  See also CLR 5
Reyher, Becky
  See Reyher, Rebecca Hourwich
Reyher, Rebecca Hourwich
  1897-1987 18
  Obituary 50
Reynolds, Dickson
  See Reynolds, Helen Mary
  Greenwood Campbell
Reynolds, Helen Mary Greenwood
  Campbell 1884-1969
  Obituary 26
Reynolds, John
  See Whitlock, Ralph
Reynolds, Madge
  See Whitlock, Ralph
Reynolds, Malvina 1900-1978 44
  Obituary 24
Reynolds, Pamela 1923- 34
Rhodes, Bennie (Loran) 1927- ... 35
Rhodes, Frank H(arold Trevor)
  1926- 37
Rhue, Morton
  See Strasser, Todd
Rhys, Megan
  See Williams, Jeanne
Ribbons, Ian 1924- 37
  Brief Entry 30
  See also SAAS 3
Ricciuti, Edward R(aphael)
  1938- 10
Rice, Charles D(uane) 1910-1971
  Obituary 27
Rice, Dale R(ichard) 1948- 42
Rice, Edward 1918- 47
  Brief Entry 42
Rice, Elizabeth 1913- 2
Rice, Eve (Hart) 1951- 34
Rice, Inez 1907- 13
Rice, James 1934- 22
Rich, Elaine Sommers 1926- 6
Rich, Josephine 1912- 10
Rich, Louise Dickinson 1903- 54
Rich, Mark J. 1948-
  Brief Entry 53
Richard, Adrienne 1921- 5
Richard, James Robert
  See Bowen, R(obert) Sydney

Richards, Curtis
See Curtis, Richard (Alan)
Richards, Frank
See Hamilton, Charles H. St. John
Richards, Hilda
See Hamilton, Charles H. St. John
Richards, Kay
See Baker, Susan (Catherine)
Richards, Laura E(lizabeth Howe)
1850-1943 ....*YABC 1*
Richards, Norman 1932- *48*
Richards, R(onald) C(harles) W(illiam)
1923-
Brief Entry *43*
Richardson, Frank Howard 1882-1970
Obituary *27*
Richardson, Grace Lee
See Dickson, Naida
Richardson, Robert S(hirley)
1902- *8*
Richelson, Geraldine 1922- *29*
Richler, Mordecai 1931- *44*
Brief Entry *27*
Richoux, Pat 1927- *7*
Richter, Alice 1941- *30*
Richter, Conrad 1890-1968 ......*3*
Richter, Hans Peter 1925- *6*
Rico, Don(ato) 1917-1985
Obituary *43*
Ridge, Antonia (Florence)
(?)-1981 ....*7*
Obituary *27*
Ridge, Martin 1923- *43*
Ridley, Nat, Jr.
See Stratemeyer, Edward L.
Ridlon, Marci 1942- *22*
Riedman, Sarah R(egal) 1902- *1*
Riesenberg, Felix, Jr.
1913-1962 ....*23*
Rieu, E(mile) V(ictor)
1887-1972 ....*46*
Obituary *26*
Riggs, Sidney Noyes 1892-1975
Obituary *28*
Rikhoff, Jean 1928- *9*
Riley, James Whitcomb
1849-1916 ....*17*
Riley, Jocelyn (Carol) 1949-
Brief Entry *50*
Rinaldi, Ann 1934- *51*
Brief Entry *50*
Rinard, Judith E(llen) 1947- *44*
Ringi, Kjell Arne Sörensen
1939- *12*
Rinkoff, Barbara (Jean)
1923-1975 ....*4*
Obituary *27*
Riordan, James 1936- *28*
Rios, Tere
See Versace, Marie Teresa
Ripley, Elizabeth Blake
1906-1969 ....*5*
Ripper, Charles L. 1929- *3*
Riq
See Atwater, Richard (Tupper)
Rissman, Art
See Sussman, Susan
Rissman, Susan
See Sussman, Susan

Ritchie, Barbara (Gibbons) *14*
Ritts, Paul 1920(?)-1980
Obituary *25*
Rivera, Geraldo (Miguel)
1943- *54*
Brief Entry *28*
Riverside, John
See Heinlein, Robert A(nson)
Rivkin, Ann 1920- *41*
Rivoli, Mario 1943- *10*
Roach, Marilynne K(athleen)
1946- *9*
Roach, Portia
See Takakjian, Portia
Robbins, Frank 1917- *42*
Brief Entry *32*
Robbins, Ken
Brief Entry *53*
Robbins, Raleigh
See Hamilton, Charles H. St. John
Robbins, Ruth 1917(?)- *14*
Robbins, Tony
See Pashko, Stanley
Roberson, John R(oyster)
1930- *53*
Roberts, Bruce (Stuart) 1930- *47*
Brief Entry *39*
Roberts, Charles G(eorge) D(ouglas)
1860-1943
Brief Entry *29*
Roberts, David
See Cox, John Roberts
Roberts, Elizabeth Madox
1886-1941 ....*33*
Brief Entry *27*
Roberts, Jim
See Bates, Barbara S(nedeker)
Roberts, John G(aither) 1913- *27*
Roberts, Nancy Correll 1924- *52*
Brief Entry *28*
Roberts, Terence
See Sanderson, Ivan T.
Roberts, Willo Davis 1928- *21*
Robertson, Barbara (Anne)
1931- *12*
Robertson, Don 1929- *8*
Robertson, Dorothy Lewis
1912- *12*
Robertson, Jennifer (Sinclair)
1942- *12*
Robertson, Keith 1914- *1*
Robinet, Harriette Gillem
1931- *27*
Robins, Seelin
See Ellis, Edward S(ylvester)
Robinson, Adjai 1932- *8*
Robinson, Barbara (Webb)
1927- *8*
Robinson, C(harles) A(lexander), Jr.
1900-1965 ....*36*
Robinson, Charles 1870-1937 .....*17*
Robinson, Charles 1931- *6*
Robinson, Dorothy W. 1929- *54*
Robinson, Jan M. 1933- *6*
Robinson, Jean O. 1934- *7*
Robinson, Jerry 1922-
Brief Entry *34*
Robinson, Joan (Mary) G(ale Thomas)
1910- *7*

Robinson, Marileta 1942- *32*
Robinson, Maudie (Millian Oller)
1914- *11*
Robinson, Maurice R. 1895-1982
Obituary *29*
Robinson, Nancy K(onheim)
1942- *32*
Brief Entry *31*
Robinson, Ray(mond Kenneth)
1920- *23*
Robinson, Shari
See McGuire, Leslie (Sarah)
Robinson, T(homas) H(eath)
1869-1950 ....*17*
Robinson, (Wanda) Veronica
1926- *30*
Robinson, W(illiam) Heath
1872-1944 ....*17*
Robison, Bonnie 1924- *12*
Robison, Nancy L(ouise)
1934- *32*
Robottom, John 1934- *7*
Roche, A. K. [Joint pseudonym]
See Abisch, Roslyn Kroop and
Kaplan, Boche
Roche, P(atricia) K.
Brief Entry *34*
Roche, Terry
See Poole, Peggy
Rock, Gail
Brief Entry *32*
Rocker, Fermin 1907- *40*
Rockwell, Anne F. 1934- *33*
Rockwell, Gail
Brief Entry *36*
Rockwell, Harlow *33*
Rockwell, Norman (Percevel)
1894-1978 ....*23*
Rockwell, Thomas 1933- *7*
See also CLR 6
Rockwood, Joyce 1947- *39*
Rockwood, Roy [Collective
pseudonym] *1*
See also McFarlane, Leslie;
Stratemeyer, Edward L.
Rodd, Kathleen Tennant
1912-1988 ....*6*
Obituary *55*
Roddenberry, Eugene Wesley
1921- *45*
Roddenberry, Gene
See Roddenberry, Eugene Wesley
Rodgers, Mary 1931- *8*
Rodman, Emerson
See Ellis, Edward S(ylvester)
Rodman, Maia
See Wojciechowska, Maia
Rodman, Selden 1909- *9*
Rodowsky, Colby 1932- *21*
Roe, Harry Mason
See Stratemeyer, Edward L.
Roever, J(oan) M(arilyn)
1935- *26*
Rofes, Eric Edward 1954- *52*
Roffey, Maureen 1936- *33*
Rogers, (Thomas) Alan (Stinchcombe)
1937- *2*
Rogers, Frances 1888-1974 ....*10*
Rogers, Fred (McFeely) 1928- *33*

Rogers, Jean 1919- 55
   Brief Entry 47
Rogers, Matilda 1894-1976 5
   Obituary 34
Rogers, Pamela 1927- 9
Rogers, Paul 1950- 54
Rogers, Robert
   See Hamilton, Charles H. St. John
Rogers, W(illiam) G(arland)
   1896-1978 23
Rojan
   See Rojankovsky, Feodor
   (Stepanovich)
Rojankovsky, Feodor (Stepanovich)
   1891-1970 21
Rokeby-Thomas, Anna E(lma)
   1911- 15
Roland, Albert 1925- 11
Rolerson, Darrell A(llen)
   1946- 8
Roll, Winifred 1909- 6
Rollins, Charlemae Hill
   1897-1979 3
   Obituary 26
Romano, Clare
   See Ross, Clare (Romano)
Romano, Louis 1921- 35
Rongen, Björn 1906- 10
Rood, Ronald (N.) 1920- 12
Rooke, Daphne (Marie) 1914- 12
Roop, Connie
   See Roop, Constance Betzer
Roop, Constance Betzer 1951- 54
   Brief Entry 49
Roop, Peter (G.) 1951- 54
   Brief Entry 49
Roos, Stephen (Kelley) 1945- 47
   Brief Entry 41
Roosevelt, (Anna) Eleanor
   1884-1962 50
Root, Phyllis 1949- 55
   Brief Entry 48
Root, Shelton L., Jr. 1923-1986
   Obituary 51
Roote, Mike
   See Fleischer, Leonore
Roper, Laura Wood 1911- 34
Roscoe, D(onald) T(homas)
   1934- 42
Rose, Anna Perrot
   See Wright, Anna (Maria Louisa
   Perrot) Rose
Rose, Anne 8
Rose, Carl 1903-1971
   Brief Entry 31
Rose, Elizabeth Jane (Pretty) 1933-
   Brief Entry 28
Rose, Florella
   See Carlson, Vada F.
Rose, Gerald (Hembdon Seymour)
   1935-
   Brief Entry 30
Rose, Nancy A.
   See Sweetland, Nancy A(nn)
Rose, Wendy 1948- 12
Roseman, Kenneth David 1939-
   Brief Entry 52

Rosen, Michael (Wayne)
   1946- 48
   Brief Entry 40
Rosen, Sidney 1916- 1
Rosen, Winifred 1943- 8
Rosenbaum, Maurice 1907- 6
Rosenberg, Dorothy 1906- 40
Rosenberg, Ethel 3
Rosenberg, Maxine B(erta)
   1939- 55
   Brief Entry 47
Rosenberg, Nancy Sherman
   1931- 4
Rosenberg, Sharon 1942- 8
Rosenblatt, Arthur S. 1938-
   Brief Entry 45
Rosenbloom, Joseph 1928- 21
Rosenblum, Richard 1928- 11
Rosenburg, John M. 1918- 6
Rosenthal, Harold 1914- 35
Ross, Alan
   See Warwick, Alan R(oss)
Ross, Alex(ander) 1909-
   Brief Entry 29
Ross, Clare (Romano) 1922- 48
Ross, Dave 1949- 32
Ross, David 1896-1975 49
   Obituary 20
Ross, Diana
   See Denney, Diana
Ross, Frank (Xavier), Jr.
   1914- 28
Ross, John 1921- 45
Ross, Judy 1942- 54
Ross, Pat(ricia Kienzle) 1943- 53
   Brief Entry 48
Ross, Tony 1938- 17
Ross, Wilda 1915- 51
   Brief Entry 39
Rossel, Seymour 1945- 28
Rössel-Waugh, C. C. [Joint
   pseudonym]
   See Waugh, Carol-Lynn Rössel
Rossetti, Christiana (Georgina)
   1830-1894 20
Roth, Arnold 1929- 21
Roth, Arthur J(oseph) 1925- 43
   Brief Entry 28
Roth, David 1940- 36
Roth, Harold
   Brief Entry 49
Rothkopf, Carol Z. 1929- 4
Rothman, Joel 1938- 7
Roueché, Berton 1911- 28
Roughsey, Dick 1921(?)- 35
Rounds, Glen (Harold) 1906- 8
Rourke, Constance (Mayfield)
   1885-1941 ....*YABC 1*
Rowe, Viola Carson 1903-1969
   Obituary 26
Rowland, Florence Wightman
   1900- 8
Rowland-Entwistle, (Arthur) Theodore
   (Henry) 1925- 31
Rowsome, Frank (Howard), Jr.
   1914-1983 36
Roy, Jessie Hailstalk 1895-1986
   Obituary 51

Roy, Liam
   See Scarry, Patricia
Roy, Ron(ald) 1940- 40
   Brief Entry 35
Royds, Caroline 1953- 55
Rubel, Nicole 1953- 18
Rubin, Eva Johanna 1925- 38
Rubinstein, Robert E(dward)
   1943- 49
Ruby, Lois 1942- 35
   Brief Entry 34
Ruchlis, Hy 1913- 3
Ruckman, Ivy 1931- 37
Ruck-Pauquèt, Gina 1931- 40
   Brief Entry 37
Rudeen, Kenneth
   Brief Entry 36
Rudley, Stephen 1946- 30
Rudolph, Marguerita 1908- 21
Rudomin, Esther
   See Hautzig, Esther
Rue, Leonard Lee III 1926- 37
Ruedi, Norma Paul
   See Ainsworth, Norma
Ruffell, Ann 1941- 30
Ruffins, Reynold 1930- 41
Rugoff, Milton 1913- 30
Ruhen, Olaf 1911- 17
Rukeyser, Muriel 1913-1980
   Obituary 22
Rumsey, Marian (Barritt)
   1928- 16
Runyan, John
   See Palmer, Bernard
Rush, Alison 1951- 41
Rush, Peter 1937- 32
Rushmore, Helen 1898- 3
Rushmore, Robert (William)
   1926-1986 8
   Obituary 49
Ruskin, Ariane
   See Batterberry, Ariane Ruskin
Ruskin, John 1819-1900 24
Russell, Charlotte
   See Rathjen, Carl H(enry)
Russell, Don(ald Bert) 1899-1986
   Obituary 47
Russell, Franklin 1926- 11
Russell, Helen Ross 1915- 8
Russell, James 1933- 53
Russell, Jim
   See Russell, James
Russell, Patrick
   See Sammis, John
Russell, Sarah
   See Laski, Marghanita
Russell, Solveig Paulson
   1904- 3
Russo, Susan 1947- 30
Rutgers van der Loeff, An(na) Basenau
   1910- 22
Ruth, Rod 1912- 9
Rutherford, Douglas
   See McConnell, James Douglas
   (Rutherford)
Rutherford, Meg 1932- 34
Ruthin, Margaret 4
Rutz, Viola Larkin 1932- 12

Ruzicka, Rudolph 1883-1978
  Obituary 24
Ryan, Betsy
  See Ryan, Elizabeth (Anne)
Ryan, Cheli Durán 20
Ryan, Elizabeth (Anne) 1943- 30
Ryan, John (Gerald Christopher)
  1921- 22
Ryan, Peter (Charles) 1939- 15
Rydberg, Ernest E(mil) 1901- 21
Rydberg, Lou(isa Hampton)
  1908- 27
Rydell, Wendell
  See Rydell, Wendy
Rydell, Wendy 4
Ryden, Hope 8
Ryder, Joanne
  Brief Entry 34
Rye, Anthony
  See Youd, (Christopher) Samuel
Rylant, Cynthia 1954- 50
  Brief Entry 44
  See also CLR 15
Rymer, Alta May 1925- 34

S

Saal, Jocelyn
  See Sachs, Judith
Saberhagen, Fred (Thomas)
  1930- 37
Sabin, Edwin Legrand
  1870-1952 .... *YABC 2*
Sabin, Francene 27
Sabin, Louis 1930- 27
Sabre, Dirk
  See Laffin, John (Alfred Charles)
Sabuso
  See Phillips, Irving W.
Sachar, Louis 1954-
  Brief Entry 50
Sachs, Elizabeth-Ann 1946- 48
Sachs, Judith 1947- 52
  Brief Entry 51
Sachs, Marilyn 1927- 52
  Earlier sketch in SATA 3
  See also CLR 2
  See also SAAS 2
Sackett, S(amuel) J(ohn)
  1928- 12
Sackson, Sid 1920- 16
Saddler, Allen
  See Richards, R(onald) C(harles)
    W(illiam)
Saddler, K. Allen
  See Richards, R(onald) C(harles)
    W(illiam)
Sadie, Stanley (John) 1930- 14
Sadler, Catherine Edwards
  Brief Entry 45
Sadler, Mark
  See Lynds, Dennis
Sage, Juniper [Joint pseudonym]
  See Brown, Margaret Wise and
    Hurd, Edith
Sagsoorian, Paul 1923- 12
Saida
  See LeMair, H(enriette) Willebeek

Saint, Dora Jessie 1913- 10
St. Briavels, James
  See Wood, James Playsted
St. Clair, Byrd Hooper 1905-1976
  Obituary 28
Saint Exupéry, Antoine de
  1900-1944 20
  See also CLR 10
St. George, Judith 1931- 13
St. John, Nicole
  See Johnston, Norma
  See also SAAS 7
St. John, Philip
  See Del Rey, Lester
St. John, Wylly Folk
  1908-1985 10
  Obituary 45
St. Meyer, Ned
  See Stratemeyer, Edward L.
St. Tamara
  See Kolba, Tamara
Saito, Michiko
  See Fujiwara, Michiko
Salassi, Otto R(ussell) 1939- 38
Saldutti, Denise 1953- 39
Salkey, (Felix) Andrew (Alexander)
  1928- 35
Sallis, Susan (Diana) 1929- 55
Salmon, Annie Elizabeth
  1899- 13
Salten, Felix
  See Salzmann, Siegmund
Salter, Cedric
  See Knight, Francis Edgar
Salvadori, Mario (George)
  1907- 40
Salzer, L. E.
  See Wilson, Lionel
Salzman, Yuri
  Brief Entry 42
Salzmann, Siegmund
  1869-1945 25
Samachson, Dorothy 1914- 3
Samachson, Joseph 1906-1980 3
  Obituary 52
Sammis, John 1942- 4
Sampson, Fay (Elizabeth)
  1935- 42
  Brief Entry 40
Samson, Anne S(tringer)
  1933- 2
Samson, Joan 1937-1976 13
Samuels, Charles 1902- 12
Samuels, Gertrude 17
Sanborn, Duane 1914- 38
Sancha, Sheila 1924- 38
Sanchez Alzada, Juan
  See Joseph, James (Herz)
Sanchez, Sonia 1934- 22
Sánchez-Silva, José María
  1911- 16
  See also CLR 12
Sand, George X. 45
Sandak, Cass R(obert) 1950- 51
  Brief Entry 37
Sandberg, (Karin) Inger 1930- ... 15
Sandberg, Karl C. 1931- 35
Sandberg, Lasse (E. M.)
  1924- 15

Sandburg, Carl (August)
  1878-1967 8
Sandburg, Charles A.
  See Sandburg, Carl (August)
Sandburg, Helga 1918- 3
Sanderlin, George 1915- 4
Sanderlin, Owenita (Harrah)
  1916- 11
Sanders, Winston P.
  See Anderson, Poul (William)
Sanderson, Ivan T. 1911-1973 6
Sanderson, Ruth (L.) 1951- 41
Sandin, Joan 1942- 12
Sandison, Janet
  See Cameron, Elizabeth Jane
Sandoz, Mari (Susette)
  1901-1966 5
Sanger, Marjory Bartlett
  1920- 8
Sankey, Alice (Ann-Susan)
  1910- 27
San Souci, Robert D. 1946- 40
Santesson, Hans Stefan 1914(?)-1975
  Obituary 30
Sapieyevski, Anne Lindbergh
  1940- 35
Sarac, Roger
  See Caras, Roger A(ndrew)
Sarasin, Jennifer
  See Sachs, Judith
Sarg, Anthony Fredrick
  See Sarg, Tony
Sarg, Tony 1880-1942 .... *YABC 1*
Sargent, Pamela 29
Sargent, Robert 1933- 2
Sargent, Sarah 1937- 44
  Brief Entry 41
Sargent, Shirley 1927- 11
Sari
  See Fleur, Anne
Sarnoff, Jane 1937- 10
Saroyan, William 1908-1981 23
  Obituary 24
Sarton, Eleanore Marie
  See Sarton, (Eleanor) May
Sarton, (Eleanor) May 1912- 36
Sasek, Miroslav 1916-1980 16
  Obituary 23
  See also CLR 4
Satchwell, John
  Brief Entry 49
Sattler, Helen Roney 1921- 4
Sauer, Julia (Lina) 1891-1983 32
  Obituary 36
Saul, (E.) Wendy 1946- 42
Saunders, Caleb
  See Heinlein, Robert A(nson)
Saunders, Keith 1910- 12
Saunders, Rubie (Agnes)
  1929- 21
Saunders, Susan 1945- 46
  Brief Entry 41
Savage, Blake
  See Goodwin, Harold Leland
Savery, Constance (Winifred)
  1897- 1
Saville, (Leonard) Malcolm
  1901-1982 23
  Obituary 31

Saviozzi, Adriana
  See Mazza, Adriana
Savitt, Sam 8
Savitz, Harriet May 1933- 5
Sawyer, Ruth 1880-1970 17
Saxon, Antonia
  See Sachs, Judith
Say, Allen 1937- 28
Sayers, Frances Clarke 1897- 3
Sazer, Nina 1949- 13
Scabrini, Janet 1953- 13
Scagnetti, Jack 1924- 7
Scanlon, Marion Stephany 11
Scarf, Maggi
  See Scarf, Maggie
Scarf, Maggie 1932- 5
Scarlett, Susan
  See Streatfeild, (Mary) Noel
Scarry, Huck
  See Scarry, Richard, Jr.
Scarry, Patricia (Murphy)
  1924- 2
Scarry, Patsy
  See Scarry, Patricia
Scarry, Richard (McClure)
  1919- 35
  Earlier sketch in SATA 2
  See also CLR 3
Scarry, Richard, Jr. 1953- 35
Schachtel, Roger (Bernard)
  1949- 38
Schaefer, Jack 1907- 3
Schaeffer, Mead 1898- 21
Schaller, George B(eals)
  1933- 30
Schatell, Brian
  Brief Entry 47
Schatzki, Walter 1899-
  Brief Entry 31
Schechter, Betty (Goodstein)
  1921- 5
Scheer, Julian (Weisel) 1926- 8
Scheffer, Victor B. 1906- 6
Scheier, Michael 1943- 40
  Brief Entry 36
Schell, Mildred 1922- 41
Schell, Orville H. 1940- 10
Schellie, Don 1932- 29
Schemm, Mildred Walker
  1905- 21
Scher, Paula 1948- 47
Scherf, Margaret 1908- 10
Schermer, Judith (Denise)
  1941- 30
Schertle, Alice 1941- 36
Schick, Alice 1946- 27
Schick, Eleanor 1942- 9
Schick, Joel 1945- 31
  Brief Entry 30
Schiff, Ken 1942- 7
Schiller, Andrew 1919- 21
Schiller, Barbara (Heyman)
  1928- 21
Schiller, Justin G. 1943-
  Brief Entry 31
Schindelman, Joseph 1923-
  Brief Entry 32
Schindler, S(tephen) D.
  Brief Entry 50

Schisgall, Oscar 1901-1984 12
  Obituary 38
Schlee, Ann 1934- 44
  Brief Entry 36
Schlein, Miriam 1926- 2
Schloat, G. Warren, Jr. 1914- 4
Schmid, Eleonore 1939- 12
Schmiderer, Dorothy 1940- 19
Schmidt, Elizabeth 1915- 15
Schmidt, James Norman
  1912- 21
Schneider, Herman 1905- 7
Schneider, Laurie
  See Adams, Laurie
Schneider, Nina 1913- 2
Schneider, Rex 1937- 44
Schnirel, James R(einhold)
  1931- 14
Schock, Pauline 1928- 45
Schoen, Barbara 1924- 13
Schoenherr, John (Carl) 1935- 37
Scholastica, Sister Mary
  See Jenkins, Marie M.
Scholefield, Edmund O.
  See Butterworth, W. E.
Scholey, Arthur 1932- 28
Scholz, Jackson (Volney) 1897-1986
  Obituary 49
Schone, Virginia 22
Schongut, Emanuel 52
  Brief Entry 36
Schoonover, Frank (Earle)
  1877-1972 24
Schoor, Gene 1921- 3
Schraff, Anne E(laine) 1939- 27
Schrank, Joseph 1900-1984
  Obituary 38
Schreiber, Elizabeth Anne (Ferguson)
  1947- 13
Schreiber, Georges 1904-1977
  Brief Entry 29
Schreiber, Ralph W(alter)
  1942- 13
Schroeder, Ted 1931(?)-1973
  Obituary 20
Schulman, Janet 1933- 22
Schulman, L(ester) M(artin)
  1934- 13
Schulte, Elaine L(ouise) 1934- .. 36
Schultz, Gwendolyn 21
Schultz, James Willard
  1859-1947 .... YABC 1
Schultz, Pearle Henriksen
  1918- 21
Schulz, Charles M(onroe)
  1922- 10
Schur, Maxine 1948- 53
  Brief Entry 49
Schurfranz, Vivian 1925- 13
Schutzer, A. I. 1922- 13
Schuyler, Pamela R(icka)
  1948- 30
Schwark, Mary Beth 1954- 51
Schwartz, Alvin 1927- 4
  See also CLR 3
Schwartz, Amy 1954- 47
  Brief Entry 41
Schwartz, Ann Powers 1913- 10

Schwartz, Charles W(alsh)
  1914- 8
Schwartz, Daniel (Bennet) 1929-
  Brief Entry 29
Schwartz, Elizabeth Reeder
  1912- 8
Schwartz, Joel L. 1940- 54
  Brief Entry 51
Schwartz, Julius 1907- 45
Schwartz, Sheila (Ruth) 1929- ... 27
Schwartz, Stephen (Lawrence)
  1948- 19
Schweitzer, Iris
  Brief Entry 36
Schweninger, Ann 1951- 29
Scoggin, Margaret C.
  1905-1968 47
  Brief Entry 28
Scoppettone, Sandra 1936- 9
Scott, Ann Herbert 1926-
  Brief Entry 29
Scott, Bill 1902(?)-1985
  Obituary 46
Scott, Cora Annett (Pipitone)
  1931- 11
Scott, Dan [House pseudonym]
  See Barker, S. Omar; Stratemeyer,
  Edward L.
Scott, Elaine 1940- 36
Scott, Jack Denton 1915- 31
Scott, Jane (Harrington) 1931- ... 55
Scott, John 1912-1976 14
Scott, John Anthony 1916- 23
Scott, John M(artin) 1913- 12
Scott, Sally (Elisabeth) 1948- .. 44
Scott, Sally Fisher 1909-1978 ... 43
Scott, Tony
  See Scott, John Anthony
Scott, Sir Walter
  1771-1832 .... YABC 2
Scott, Warwick
  See Trevor, Elleston
Scribner, Charles, Jr. 1921- 13
Scribner, Joanne L. 1949- 33
Scrimsher, Lila Gravatt 1897-1974
  Obituary 28
Scuro, Vincent 1951- 21
Seabrooke, Brenda 1941- 30
Seaman, Augusta Huiell
  1879-1950 31
Seamands, Ruth (Childers)
  1916- 9
Searcy, Margaret Z(ehmer)
  1926- 54
  Brief Entry 39
Searight, Mary W(illiams)
  1918- 17
Searle, Kathryn Adrienne
  1942- 10
Searle, Ronald (William Fordham)
  1920- 42
Sears, Stephen W. 1932- 4
Sebastian, Lee
  See Silverberg, Robert
Sebestyen, Igen
  See Sebestyen, Ouida
Sebestyen, Ouida 1924- 39
Sechrist, Elizabeth Hough
  1903- 2

Author Index

Sedges, John
  See Buck, Pearl S.
Seed, Jenny 1930- *8*
Seed, Sheila Turner 1937(?)-1979
  Obituary *23*
Seeger, Elizabeth 1889-1973
  Obituary *20*
Seeger, Pete(r) 1919- *13*
Seever, R.
  See Reeves, Lawrence F.
Sefton, Catherine
  See Waddell, Martin
Segal, Joyce 1940- *35*
Segal, Lore 1928- *4*
Segovia, Andrés 1893(?)-1987
  Obituary *52*
Seidelman, James Edward
  1926- *6*
Seiden, Art(hur)
  Brief Entry *42*
Seidler, Tor 1952- *52*
  Brief Entry *46*
Seidman, Laurence (Ivan)
  1925- *15*
Seigel, Kalman 1917- *12*
Seignobosc, Francoise
  1897-1961 .... *21*
Seitz, Jacqueline 1931- *50*
Seixas, Judith S. 1922- *17*
Sejima, Yoshimasa 1913- *8*
Selden, George
  See Thompson, George Selden
  See also CLR 8
Self, Margaret Cabell 1902- *24*
Selig, Sylvie 1942- *13*
Selkirk, Jane [Joint pseudonym]
  See Chapman, John Stanton
    Higham
Sellers, Naomi John
  See Flack, Naomi John (White)
Selman, LaRue W. 1927- *55*
Selsam, Millicent E(llis)
  1912- *29*
  Earlier sketch in SATA 1
  See also CLR 1
Seltzer, Meyer 1932- *17*
Seltzer, Richard (Warren, Jr.)
  1946- *41*
Sendak, Jack *28*
Sendak, Maurice (Bernard)
  1928- *27*
  Earlier sketch in SATA 1
  See also CLR 1
Sengler, Johanna 1924- *18*
Senn, Steve 1950-
  Brief Entry *48*
Serage, Nancy 1924- *10*
Seredy, Kate 1899-1975 .... *1*
  Obituary *24*
  See also CLR 10
Seroff, Victor I(lyitch)
  1902-1979 .... *12*
  Obituary *26*
Serraillier, Ian (Lucien) 1912- *1*
  See also CLR 2
  See also SAAS 3
Servello, Joe 1932- *10*
Service, Robert W(illiam)
  1874(?)-1958 .... *20*

Serwadda, William Moses
  1931- *27*
Serwer, Blanche L. 1910- *10*
Seth, Marie
  See Lexau, Joan M.
Seton, Anya *3*
Seton, Ernest Thompson
  1860-1946 .... *18*
Seuling, Barbara 1937- *10*
Seuss, Dr.
  See Geisel, Theodor Seuss
  See also CLR 9
Severn, Bill
  See Severn, William Irving
Severn, David
  See Unwin, David S(torr)
Severn, William Irving 1914- *1*
Sewall, Marcia 1935- *37*
Seward, Prudence 1926- *16*
Sewell, Anna 1820-1878 .... *24*
Sewell, Helen (Moore)
  1896-1957 .... *38*
Sexton, Anne (Harvey)
  1928-1974 .... *10*
Seymour, Alta Halverson *10*
Shachtman, Tom 1942- *49*
Shackleton, C. C.
  See Aldiss, Brian W(ilson)
Shafer, Robert E(ugene)
  1925- *9*
Shahn, Ben(jamin) 1898-1969
  Obituary *21*
Shahn, Bernarda Bryson
  See Bryson, Bernarda
Shane, Harold Gray 1914- *36*
Shanks, Ann Zane (Kushner) *10*
Shannon, George (William Bones)
  1952- *35*
Shannon, Monica (?)-1965 .... *28*
Shannon, Terry *21*
Shapiro, Irwin 1911-1981 .... *32*
Shapiro, Milton J. 1926- *32*
Shapp, Martha 1910- *3*
Sharfman, Amalie *14*
Sharma, Partap 1939- *15*
Sharmat, Marjorie Weinman
  1928- *33*
  Earlier sketch in SATA 4
Sharmat, Mitchell 1927- *33*
Sharp, Margery 1905- *29*
  Earlier sketch in SATA 1
Sharp, Zerna A. 1889-1981
  Obituary *27*
Sharpe, Mitchell R(aymond)
  1924- *12*
Shaw, Arnold 1909- *4*
Shaw, Charles (Green)
  1892-1974 .... *13*
Shaw, Evelyn 1927- *28*
Shaw, Flora Louisa
  See Lugard, Flora Louisa Shaw
Shaw, Ray *7*
Shaw, Richard 1923- *12*
Shay, Arthur 1922- *4*
Shay, Lacey
  See Shebar, Sharon Sigmond
Shea, George 1940- *54*
  Brief Entry *42*

Shearer, John 1947- *43*
  Brief Entry *27*
Shearer, Ted 1919- *43*
Shebar, Sharon Sigmond
  1945- *36*
Shecter, Ben 1935- *16*
Sheedy, Alexandra (Elizabeth)
  1962- *39*
  Earlier sketch in SATA 19
Sheedy, Ally
  See Sheedy, Alexandra (Elizabeth)
Sheehan, Ethna 1908- *9*
Sheffer, H. R.
  See Abels, Harriette S(heffer)
Sheffield, Janet N. 1926- *26*
Shefts, Joelle
  Brief Entry *49*
Shekerjian, Regina Tor *16*
Sheldon, Ann [Collective
  pseudonym] *1*
Sheldon, Aure 1917-1976 .... *12*
Sheldon, Muriel 1926- *45*
  Brief Entry *39*
Shelley, Mary Wollstonecraft
  (Godwin) 1797-1851 .... *29*
Shelton, William Roy 1919- *5*
Shemin, Margaretha 1928- *4*
Shenton, Edward 1895-1977 ...... *45*
Shepard, Ernest Howard
  1879-1976 .... *33*
  Obituary *24*
  Earlier sketch in SATA 3
Shepard, Mary
  See Knox, (Mary) Eleanor Jessie
Shephard, Esther 1891-1975 ...... *5*
  Obituary *26*
Shepherd, Elizabeth *4*
Sherburne, Zoa 1912- *3*
Sherman, D(enis) R(onald)
  1934- *48*
  Brief Entry *29*
Sherman, Diane (Finn) 1928- *12*
Sherman, Elizabeth
  See Friskey, Margaret Richards
Sherman, Harold (Morrow)
  1898- *37*
Sherman, Nancy
  See Rosenberg, Nancy Sherman
Sherrod, Jane
  See Singer, Jane Sherrod
Sherry, (Dulcie) Sylvia 1932- *8*
Sherwan, Earl 1917- *3*
Shiefman, Vicky *22*
Shields, Brenda Desmond (Armstrong)
  1914- *37*
Shields, Charles 1944- *10*
Shimin, Symeon 1902- *13*
Shinn, Everett 1876-1953 .... *21*
Shippen, Katherine B(inney)
  1892-1980 .... *1*
  Obituary *23*
Shipton, Eric 1907- *10*
Shirer, William L(awrence)
  1904- *45*
Shirreffs, Gordon D(onald)
  1914- *11*
Sholokhov, Mikhail A. 1905-1984
  Obituary *36*
Shore, June Lewis *30*

Shore, Robert 1924- *39*
Shortall, Leonard W. *19*
Shotwell, Louisa R. 1902- *3*
Showalter, Jean B(reckinridge) *12*
Showell, Ellen Harvey 1934- *33*
Showers, Paul C. 1910- *21*
  See also CLR 6
  See also SAAS 7
Shreve, Susan Richards 1939- *46*
  Brief Entry *41*
Shtainmets, Leon *32*
Shub, Elizabeth *5*
Shulevitz, Uri 1935- *50*
  Earlier sketch in SATA 3
  See also CLR 5
Shulman, Alix Kates 1932- *7*
Shulman, Irving 1913- *13*
Shumsky, Zena
  See Collier, Zena
Shura, Mary Francis
  See Craig, Mary Francis
Shuttlesworth, Dorothy *3*
Shyer, Marlene Fanta *13*
Siberell, Anne *29*
Sibley, Don 1922- *12*
Siculan, Daniel 1922- *12*
Sidjakov, Nicolas 1924- *18*
Sidney, Frank [Joint pseudonym]
  See Warwick, Alan R(oss)
Sidney, Margaret
  See Lothrop, Harriet Mulford Stone
Siebel, Fritz (Frederick) 1913-
  Brief Entry *44*
Siegal, Aranka 1930-
  Brief Entry *37*
Siegel, Beatrice *36*
Siegel, Helen
  See Siegl, Helen
Siegel, Robert (Harold) 1939- *39*
Siegl, Helen 1924- *34*
Silas
  See McCay, Winsor
Silcock, Sara Lesley 1947- *12*
Silver, Ruth
  See Chew, Ruth
Silverberg, Robert *13*
Silverman, Mel(vin Frank)
  1931-1966 .... *9*
Silverstein, Alvin 1933- *8*
Silverstein, Shel(by) 1932- *33*
  Brief Entry *27*
  See also CLR 5
Silverstein, Virginia B(arbara
  Opshelor) 1937- *8*
Silverthorne, Elizabeth 1930- *35*
Simon, Charlie May
  See Fletcher, Charlie May
Simon, Hilda (Rita) 1921- *28*
Simon, Howard 1903-1979 .... *32*
  Obituary *21*
Simon, Joe
  See Simon, Joseph H.
Simon, Joseph H. 1913- *7*
Simon, Martin P(aul William)
  1903-1969 .... *12*
Simon, Mina Lewiton
  See Lewiton, Mina
Simon, Norma 1927- *3*

Simon, Seymour 1931- *4*
  See also CLR 9
Simon, Shirley (Schwartz)
  1921- *11*
Simon, Solomon 1895-1970 .... *40*
Simonetta, Linda 1948- *14*
Simonetta, Sam 1936- *14*
Simons, Barbara B(rooks)
  1934- *41*
Simont, Marc 1915- *9*
Simpson, Colin 1908- *14*
Simpson, Harriette
  See Arnow, Harriette (Louisa)
  Simpson
Simpson, Myrtle L(illias)
  1931- *14*
Sinclair, Clover
  See Gater, Dilys
Sinclair, Emil
  See Hesse, Hermann
Sinclair, Upton (Beall)
  1878-1968 .... *9*
Singer, Isaac Bashevis 1904- *27*
  Earlier sketch in SATA 3
  See also CLR 1
Singer, Jane Sherrod
  1917-1985 .... *4*
  Obituary *42*
Singer, Julia 1917- *28*
Singer, Kurt D(eutsch) 1911- *38*
Singer, Marilyn 1948- *48*
  Brief Entry *38*
Singer, Susan (Mahler) 1941- *9*
Sirof, Harriet 1930- *37*
Sisson, Rosemary Anne 1923- *11*
Sitomer, Harry 1903- *31*
Sitomer, Mindel 1903- *31*
Sive, Helen R. 1951- *30*
Sivulich, Sandra (Jeanne) Stroner
  1941- *9*
Skelly, James R(ichard) 1927- *17*
Skinner, Constance Lindsay
  1882-1939 .... *YABC 1*
Skinner, Cornelia Otis 1901- *2*
Skipper, G. C. 1939- *46*
  Brief Entry *38*
Skofield, James
  Brief Entry *44*
Skold, Betty Westrom 1923- *41*
Skorpen, Liesel Moak 1935- *3*
Skurzynski, Gloria (Joan)
  1930- *8*
Slackman, Charles B. 1934- *12*
Slade, Richard 1910-1971 .... *9*
Slate, Joseph (Frank) 1928- *38*
Slater, Jim 1929-
  Brief Entry *34*
Slaughter, Jean
  See Doty, Jean Slaughter
Sleator, William 1945- *3*
Sleigh, Barbara 1906-1982 .... *3*
  Obituary *30*
Slepian, Jan(ice B.) 1921- *51*
  Brief Entry *45*
Slicer, Margaret O. 1920- *4*
Sloane, Eric 1910(?)-1985 .... *52*
  Obituary *42*
Slobodkin, Florence (Gersh)
  1905- *5*

Slobodkin, Louis 1903-1975 ...... *26*
  Earlier sketch in SATA 1
Slobodkina, Esphyr 1909- *1*
Sloggett, Nellie 1851-1923 .... *44*
Slote, Alfred 1926- *8*
  See also CLR 4
Small, David 1945- *50*
  Brief Entry *46*
Small, Ernest
  See Lent, Blair
Smallwood, Norah (Evelyn)
  1910(?)-1984
  Obituary *41*
Smaridge, Norah 1903- *6*
Smiley, Virginia Kester 1923- *2*
Smith, Anne Warren 1938- *41*
  Brief Entry *34*
Smith, Beatrice S(chillinger) *12*
Smith, Betsy Covington 1937- *55*
  Brief Entry *43*
Smith, Betty 1896-1972 .... *6*
Smith, Bradford 1909-1964 .... *5*
Smith, Caesar
  See Trevor, Elleston
Smith, Datus C(lifford), Jr.
  1907- *13*
Smith, Dodie *4*
Smith, Doris Buchanan 1934- *28*
Smith, Dorothy Stafford
  1905- *6*
Smith, E(lmer) Boyd
  1860-1943 .... *YABC 1*
Smith, E(dric) Brooks 1917- *40*
Smith, Elva S(ophronia) 1871-1965
  Brief Entry *31*
Smith, Emma 1923- *52*
  Brief Entry *36*
Smith, Eunice Young 1902- *5*
Smith, Frances C. 1904- *3*
Smith, Fredrika Shumway 1877-1968
  Brief Entry *30*
Smith, Gary R(ichard) 1932- *14*
Smith, George Harmon 1920- *5*
Smith, H(arry) Allen 1907-1976
  Obituary *20*
Smith, Howard Everett, Jr.
  1927- *12*
Smith, Hugh L(etcher)
  1921-1968 .... *5*
Smith, Imogene Henderson
  1922- *12*
Smith, Jacqueline B. 1937- *39*
Smith, Janice Lee 1949- *54*
Smith, Jean
  See Smith, Frances C.
Smith, Jean Pajot 1945- *10*
Smith, Jessie Willcox
  1863-1935 .... *21*
Smith, Jim 1920-
  Brief Entry *36*
Smith, Joan (Mary) 1933- *54*
  Brief Entry *46*
Smith, Johnston
  See Crane, Stephen (Townley)
Smith, Lafayette
  See Higdon, Hal
Smith, Lee
  See Albion, Lee Smith

Smith, Lillian H(elena) 1887-1983
  Obituary 32
Smith, Linell Nash 1932- 2
Smith, Lucia B. 1943- 30
Smith, Marion Hagens 1913- 12
Smith, Marion Jaques 1899- 13
Smith, Mary Ellen 10
Smith, Mike
  See Smith, Mary Ellen
Smith, Nancy Covert 1935- 12
Smith, Norman F. 1920- 5
Smith, Pauline C(oggeshall)
  1908- 27
Smith, Philip Warren 1936- 46
Smith, Robert Kimmel 1930- 12
Smith, Robert Paul 1915-1977 52
  Obituary 30
Smith, Ruth Leslie 1902- 2
Smith, Samantha 1972-1985
  Obituary 45
Smith, Sarah Stafford
  See Smith, Dorothy Stafford
Smith, Susan Carlton 1923- 12
Smith, Susan Mathias 1950- 43
  Brief Entry 35
Smith, Susan Vernon 1950- 48
Smith, Ursula 1934- 54
Smith, Vian (Crocker)
  1919-1969 11
Smith, Ward
  See Goldsmith, Howard
Smith, William A. 10
Smith, William Jay 1918- 2
Smith, Winsome 1935- 45
Smith, Z. Z.
  See Westheimer, David
Smits, Teo
  See Smits, Theodore R(ichard)
Smits, Theodore R(ichard)
  1905- 45
  Brief Entry 28
Smucker, Barbara (Claassen)
  1915- 29
  See also CLR 10
Snedeker, Caroline Dale (Parke)
  1871-1956 .... YABC 2
Snell, Nigel (Edward Creagh) 1936-
  Brief Entry 40
Snellgrove, L(aurence) E(rnest)
  1928- 53
Sneve, Virginia Driving Hawk
  1933- 8
  See also CLR 2
Sniff, Mr.
  See Abisch, Roslyn Kroop
Snodgrass, Thomas Jefferson
  See Clemens, Samuel Langhorne
Snook, Barbara (Lillian)
  1913-1976 34
Snow, Donald Clifford 1917- 16
Snow, Dorothea J(ohnston)
  1909- 9
Snow, Richard F(olger) 1947- 52
  Brief Entry 37
Snyder, Anne 1922- 4
Snyder, Carol 1941- 35
Snyder, Gerald S(eymour)
  1933- 48
  Brief Entry 34

Snyder, Jerome 1916-1976
  Obituary 20
Snyder, Zilpha Keatley 1927- 28
  Earlier sketch in SATA 1
  See also SAAS 2
Snyderman, Reuven K. 1922- 5
Soble, Jennie
  See Cavin, Ruth (Brodie)
Sobol, Donald J. 1924- 31
  Earlier sketch in SATA 1
  See also CLR 4
Sobol, Harriet Langsam 1936- 47
  Brief Entry 34
Soderlind, Arthur E(dwin)
  1920- 14
Softly, Barbara (Frewin)
  1924- 12
Soglow, Otto 1900-1975
  Obituary 30
Sohl, Frederic J(ohn) 1916- 10
Sokol, Bill
  See Sokol, William
Sokol, William 1923- 37
Sokolov, Kirill 1930- 34
Solbert, Romaine G. 1925- 2
Solbert, Ronni
  See Solbert, Romaine G.
Solomon, Joan 1930(?)- 51
  Brief Entry 40
Solomons, Ikey, Esquire, Jr.
  See Thackeray, William Makepeace
Solonevich, George 1915- 15
Solot, Mary Lynn 1939- 12
Sommer, Elyse 1929- 7
Sommer, Robert 1929- 12
Sommerfelt, Aimee 1892- 5
Sonneborn, Ruth (Cantor) A.
  1899-1974 4
  Obituary 27
Sorche, Nic Leodhas
  See Alger, Leclaire (Gowans)
Sorel, Edward 1929-
  Brief Entry 37
Sorensen, Virginia 1912- 2
Sorley Walker, Kathrine 41
Sorrentino, Joseph N. 6
Sortor, June Elizabeth 1939- 12
Sortor, Toni
  See Sortor, June Elizabeth
Soskin, V. H.
  See Ellison, Virginia Howell
Sotomayor, Antonio 1902- 11
Soudley, Henry
  See Wood, James Playsted
Soule, Gardner (Bosworth)
  1913- 14
Soule, Jean Conder 1919- 10
Southall, Ivan 1921- 3
  See also CLR 2
  See also SAAS 3
Southey, Robert 1774-1843 54
Southgate, Vera 54
Spanfeller, James J(ohn)
  1930- 19
Spangenberg, Judith Dunn
  1942- 5
Spar, Jerome 1918- 10

Sparks, Beatrice Mathews
  1918- 44
  Brief Entry 28
Sparks, Mary W. 1920- 15
Spaulding, Leonard
  See Bradbury, Ray
Speare, Elizabeth George
  1908- 5
  See also CLR 8
Spearing, Judith (Mary Harlow)
  1922- 9
Specking, Inez 1890-196(?) 11
Speicher, Helen Ross (Smith)
  1915- 8
Spellman, John W(illard)
  1934- 14
Spelman, Mary 1934- 28
Spence, Eleanor (Rachel)
  1927- 21
Spence, Geraldine 1931- 47
Spencer, Ann 1918- 10
Spencer, Cornelia
  See Yaukey, Grace S.
Spencer, Donald D(ean) 1931- 41
Spencer, Elizabeth 1921- 14
Spencer, William 1922- 9
Spencer, Zane A(nn) 1935- 35
Sperry, Armstrong W.
  1897-1976 1
  Obituary 27
Sperry, Raymond, Jr. [Collective
  pseudonym] 1
Spicer, Dorothy (Gladys)
  (?)-1975 32
Spiegelman, Judith M. 5
Spielberg, Steven 1947- 32
Spier, Peter (Edward) 1927- 54
  Earlier sketch in SATA 4
  See also CLR 5
Spilhaus, Athelstan 1911- 13
Spilka, Arnold 1917- 6
Spinelli, Eileen 1942- 38
Spinelli, Jerry 1941- 39
Spink, Reginald (William)
  1905- 11
Spinner, Stephanie 1943- 38
Spinossimus
  See White, William
Splaver, Sarah 1921-
  Brief Entry 28
Spollen, Christopher 1952- 12
Sprague, Gretchen (Burnham)
  1926- 27
Sprigge, Elizabeth 1900-1974 10
Spring, (Robert) Howard
  1889-1965 28
Springer, Marilyn Harris
  1931- 47
Springstubb, Tricia 1950- 46
  Brief Entry 40
Spykman, E(lizabeth) C.
  19(?)-1965 10
Spyri, Johanna (Heusser)
  1827-1901 19
  See also CLR 13
Squire, Miriam
  See Sprigge, Elizabeth
Squires, Phil
  See Barker, S. Omar

S-Ringi, Kjell
  See Ringi, Kjell
Srivastava, Jane Jonas
  Brief Entry 37
Stadtler, Bea 1921- 17
Stafford, Jean 1915-1979
  Obituary 22
Stahl, Ben(jamin Albert)
  1910-1987 5
  Obituary 54
Stahl, Hilda 1938- 48
Stair, Gobin (John) 1912- 35
Stalder, Valerie 27
Stamaty, Mark Alan 1947- 12
Stambler, Irwin 1924- 5
Stanek, Muriel (Novella) 1915-
  Brief Entry 34
Stang, Judit 1921-1977 29
Stang, Judy
  See Stang, Judit
Stanhope, Eric
  See Hamilton, Charles H. St. John
Stankevich, Boris 1928- 2
Stanley, Diana 1909-
  Brief Entry 30
Stanley, Diane 1943- 37
  Brief Entry 32
Stanley, George Edward
  1942- 53
Stanley, Robert
  See Hamilton, Charles H. St. John
Stanli, Sue
  See Meilach, Dona Z(weigoron)
Stanovich, Betty Jo 1954-
  Brief Entry 51
Stanstead, John
  See Groom, Arthur William
Stapleton, Marjorie (Winifred)
  1932- 28
Stapp, Arthur D(onald)
  1906-1972 4
Starbird, Kaye 1916- 6
Stark, James
  See Goldston, Robert
Starkey, Marion L. 1901- 13
Starr, Ward and Murch, Mel [Joint
  double pseudonym]
  See Manes, Stephen
Starret, William
  See McClintock, Marshall
Stasiak, Krystyna 49
Stauffer, Don
  See Berkebile, Fred D(onovan)
Staunton, Schuyler
  See Baum, L(yman) Frank
Steadman, Ralph (Idris) 1936- 32
Stearns, Monroe (Mather)
  1913-1987 5
  Obituary 55
Steele, Chester K.
  See Stratemeyer, Edward L.
Steele, Mary Q(uintard Govan)
  1922- 51
  Earlier sketch in SATA 3
Steele, (Henry) Max(well)
  1922- 10
Steele, William O(wen)
  1917-1979 51
  Obituary 27
  Earlier sketch in SATA 1

Stefanik, Alfred T. 1939- 55
Stegeman, Janet Allais 1923- 53
  Brief Entry 49
Steig, William 1907- 18
  See also CLR 2, 15
Stein, Harvé 1904-
  Brief Entry 30
Stein, M(eyer) L(ewis) 6
Stein, Mini 2
Stein, R(ichard) Conrad 1937- 31
Stein, Sara Bonnett
  Brief Entry 34
Steinbeck, John (Ernst)
  1902-1968 9
Steinberg, Alfred 1917- 9
Steinberg, Fannie 1899- 43
Steinberg, Fred J. 1933- 4
Steinberg, Phillip Orso 1921- 34
Steinberg, Rafael (Mark)
  1927- 45
Steiner, Barbara A(nnette)
  1934- 13
Steiner, Charlotte 1900-1981 45
Steiner, Jörg 1930- 35
Steiner, Stan(ley) 1925-1987 14
  Obituary 50
Steiner-Prag, Hugo 1880-1945
  Brief Entry 32
Stephens, Mary Jo 1935- 8
Stephens, William M(cLain)
  1925- 21
Stephensen, A. M.
  See Manes, Stephen
Stepp, Ann 1935- 29
Steptoe, John (Lewis) 1950- 8
  See also CLR 2, 12
Sterling, Brett
  See Samachson, Joseph
Sterling, Dorothy 1913- 1
  See also CLR 1
  See also SAAS 2
Sterling, Helen
  See Hoke, Helen (L.)
Sterling, Philip 1907- 8
Stern, Ellen N(orman) 1927- 26
Stern, Madeleine B(ettina)
  1912- 14
Stern, Philip Van Doren
  1900-1984 13
  Obituary 39
Stern, Simon 1943- 15
Sterne, Emma Gelders
  1894-1971 6
Steurt, Marjorie Rankin 1888- 10
Stevens, Carla M(cBride)
  1928- 13
Stevens, Franklin 1933- 6
Stevens, Gwendolyn 1944- 33
Stevens, Kathleen 1936- 49
Stevens, Patricia Bunning
  1931- 27
Stevens, Peter
  See Geis, Darlene
Stevenson, Anna (M.) 1905- 12
Stevenson, Augusta
  1869(?)-1976 2
  Obituary 26
Stevenson, Burton E(gbert)
  1872-1962 25

Stevenson, James 1929- 42
  Brief Entry 34
Stevenson, Janet 1913- 8
Stevenson, Robert Louis
  1850-1894 ....YABC 2
  See also CLR 10, 11
Stewart, A(gnes) C(harlotte) 15
Stewart, Charles
  See Zurhorst, Charles (Stewart, Jr.)
Stewart, Elizabeth Laing
  1907- 6
Stewart, George Rippey
  1895-1980 3
  Obituary 23
Stewart, John (William) 1920- 14
Stewart, Mary (Florence Elinor)
  1916- 12
Stewart, Robert Neil
  1891-1972 7
Stewart, Scott
  See Zaffo, George J.
Stewart, W(alter) P. 1924- 53
Stewig, John Warren 1937- 26
Stiles, Martha Bennett 6
Stiles, Norman B. 1942-
  Brief Entry 36
Still, James 1906- 29
Stillerman, Robbie 1947- 12
Stilley, Frank 1918- 29
Stine, G(eorge) Harry 1928- 10
Stine, Jovial Bob
  See Stine, Robert Lawrence
Stine, Robert Lawrence 1943- 31
Stinetorf, Louise 1900- 10
Stirling, Arthur
  See Sinclair, Upton (Beall)
Stirling, Nora B. 3
Stirnweis, Shannon 1931- 10
Stobbs, William 1914- 17
Stockton, Francis Richard
  1834-1902 44
Stockton, Frank R(ichard)
  Brief Entry 32
  See Stockton, Francis Richard
Stoddard, Edward G. 1923- 10
Stoddard, Hope 1900- 6
Stoddard, Sandol
  See Warburg, Sandol Stoddard
Stoiko, Michael 1919- 14
Stoker, Abraham 1847-1912 29
Stoker, Bram
  See Stoker, Abraham
Stokes, Cedric
  See Beardmore, George
Stokes, Jack (Tilden) 1923- 13
Stokes, Olivia Pearl 1916- 32
Stolz, Mary (Slattery) 1920- 10
  See also SAAS 3
Stone, Alan [Collective
  pseudonym] 1
  See also Svenson, Andrew E.
Stone, D(avid) K(arl) 1922- 9
Stone, Eugenia 1879-1971 7
Stone, Gene
  See Stone, Eugenia
Stone, Helen V. 6
Stone, Irving 1903- 3
Stone, Jon 1931- 39

Author Index

Stone, Josephine Rector
  See Dixon, Jeanne
Stone, Raymond [Collective
  pseudonym] *1*
Stone, Richard A.
  See Stratemeyer, Edward L.
Stonehouse, Bernard 1926- *13*
Stong, Phil(ip Duffield)
  1899-1957 .... *32*
Storch, Anne B. von
  See von Storch, Anne B.
Storey, (Elizabeth) Margaret (Carlton)
  1926- *9*
Storey, Victoria Carolyn
  1945- *16*
Storme, Peter
  See Stern, Philip Van Doren
Storr, Catherine (Cole) 1913- *9*
Story, Josephine
  See Loring, Emilie (Baker)
Stoutenburg, Adrien 1916- *3*
Stover, Allan C(arl) 1938- *14*
Stover, Marjorie Filley 1914- *9*
Stowe, Harriet (Elizabeth) Beecher
  1811-1896 .... *YABC 1*
Strachan, Margaret Pitcairn
  1908- *14*
Strait, Treva Adams 1909- *35*
Strand, Mark 1934- *41*
Strange, Philippa
  See Coury, Louise Andree
Stranger, Joyce
  See Wilson, Joyce M(uriel Judson)
Strasser, Todd 1950- *45*
  See also CLR 11
Stratemeyer, Edward L.
  1862-1930 .... *1*
Stratford, Philip 1927- *47*
Stratton, Thomas [Joint pseudonym]
  See DeWeese, Thomas Eugene
Stratton-Porter, Gene
  1863-1924 .... *15*
Strauss, Joyce 1936- *53*
Strayer, E. Ward
  See Stratemeyer, Edward L.
Streano, Vince(nt Catello)
  1945- *20*
Streatfeild, Noel 1897-1985 .... *20*
  Obituary *48*
Street, Julia Montgomery
  1898- *11*
Stren, Patti 1949-
  Brief Entry *41*
  See also CLR 5
Strete, Craig Kee 1950- *44*
Stretton, Barbara (Humphrey)
  1936- *43*
  Brief Entry *35*
Strong, Charles [Joint pseudonym]
  See Epstein, Beryl and Epstein,
  Samuel
Strong, David
  See McGuire, Leslie (Sarah)
Strong, J. J.
  See Strong, Jeremy
Strong, Jeremy 1949- *36*
Ströyer, Poul 1923- *13*
Stuart, David
  See Hoyt, Edwin P(almer), Jr.

Stuart, Forbes 1924- *13*
Stuart, Ian
  See MacLean, Alistair (Stuart)
Stuart, (Hilton) Jesse
  1907-1984 .... *2*
  Obituary *36*
Stuart, Sheila
  See Baker, Mary Gladys Steel
Stuart-Clark, Christopher
  1940- *32*
Stubbs, Joanna 1940-
  Brief Entry *53*
Stubis, Talivaldis 1926- *5*
Stubley, Trevor (Hugh) 1932- *22*
Stultifer, Morton
  See Curtis, Richard (Alan)
Sture-Vasa, Mary
  See Alsop, Mary O'Hara
Sturton, Hugh
  See Johnston, H(ugh) A(nthony)
  S(tephen)
Sturtzel, Howard A(llison)
  1894- *1*
Sturtzel, Jane Levington
  1903- *1*
Styles, Frank Showell 1908- *10*
Suba, Susanne *4*
Subond, Valerie
  See Grayland, Valerie
Sudbery, Rodie 1943- *42*
Sugarman, Tracy 1921- *37*
Sugita, Yutaka 1930- *36*
Suhl, Yuri 1908-1986 .... *8*
  Obituary *50*
  See also CLR 2
  See also SAAS 1
Suid, Murray 1942- *27*
Sullivan, George E(dward)
  1927- *4*
Sullivan, Mary W(ilson)
  1907- *13*
Sullivan, Thomas Joseph, Jr.
  1947- *16*
Sullivan, Tom
  See Sullivan, Thomas Joseph, Jr.
Sumichrast, Józef 1948- *29*
Sumiko
  See Davies, Sumiko
Summers, James L(evingston) 1910-
  Brief Entry *28*
Sunderlin, Sylvia 1911- *28*
Sung, Betty Lee *26*
Supraner, Robyn 1930- *20*
Surge, Frank 1931- *13*
Susac, Andrew 1929- *5*
Sussman, Susan 1942- *48*
Sutcliff, Rosemary 1920- *44*
  Earlier sketch in SATA 6
  See also CLR 1
Sutherland, Efua (Theodora Morgue)
  1924- *25*
Sutherland, Margaret 1941- *15*
Sutherland, Zena B(ailey)
  1915- *37*
Suttles, Shirley (Smith) 1922- *21*
Sutton, Ann (Livesay) 1923- *31*
Sutton, Eve(lyn Mary) 1906- *26*
Sutton, Felix 1910(?)- *31*

Sutton, Jane 1950- *52*
  Brief Entry *43*
Sutton, Larry M(atthew)
  1931- *29*
Sutton, Margaret (Beebe)
  1903- *1*
Sutton, Myron Daniel 1925- *31*
Svenson, Andrew E.
  1910-1975 .... *2*
  Obituary *26*
Swain, Su Zan (Noguchi)
  1916- *21*
Swan, Susan 1944- *22*
Swarthout, Glendon (Fred)
  1918- *26*
Swarthout, Kathryn 1919- *7*
Swayne, Sam(uel F.) 1907- *53*
Swayne, Zoa (Lourana) 1905- *53*
Sweeney, James B(artholomew)
  1910- *21*
Sweeney, Karen O'Connor
  See O'Connor, Karen
Sweetland, Nancy A(nn)
  1934- *48*
Swenson, Allan A(rmstrong)
  1933- *21*
Swenson, May 1919- *15*
Swift, David
  See Kaufmann, John
Swift, Hildegarde Hoyt 1890(?)-1977
  Obituary *20*
Swift, Jonathan 1667-1745 .... *19*
Swift, Merlin
  See Leeming, Joseph
Swiger, Elinor Porter 1927- *8*
Swinburne, Laurence 1924- *9*
Swindells, Robert E(dward)
  1939- *50*
  Brief Entry *34*
Switzer, Ellen 1923- *48*
Sydney, Frank [Joint pseudonym]
  See Warwick, Alan R(oss)
Sylvester, Natalie G(abry)
  1922- *22*
Syme, (Neville) Ronald 1913- *2*
Symons, (Dorothy) Geraldine
  1909- *33*
Symons, Stuart
  See Stanley, George Edward
Synge, (Phyllis) Ursula 1930- *9*
Sypher, Lucy Johnston 1907- *7*
Szasz, Suzanne Shorr 1919- *13*
Szekeres, Cyndy 1933- *5*
Szudek, Agnes S(usan) P(hilomena)
  Brief Entry *49*
Szulc, Tad 1926- *26*

T

Taback, Simms 1932- *40*
  Brief Entry *36*
Taber, Gladys (Bagg) 1899-1980
  Obituary *22*
Tabrah, Ruth Milander 1921- *14*
Tafuri, Nancy 1946- *39*
Tait, Douglas 1944- *12*
Takakjian, Portia 1930- *15*
Takashima, Shizuye 1928- *13*

Talbot, Charlene Joy 1928- *10*
Talbot, Toby 1928- *14*
Talker, T.
  See Rands, William Brighty
Tallcott, Emogene *10*
Tallon, Robert 1939- *43*
  Brief Entry *28*
Talmadge, Marian *14*
Tamarin, Alfred *13*
Tamburine, Jean 1930- *12*
Tang, You-Shan 1946- *53*
Tannen, Mary 1943- *37*
Tannenbaum, Beulah 1916- *3*
Tannenbaum, D(onald) Leb
  1948- *42*
Tanner, Louise S(tickney)
  1922- *9*
Tanobe, Miyuki 1937- *23*
Tapio, Pat Decker
  See Kines, Pat Decker
Tapp, Kathy Kennedy 1949-
  Brief Entry *50*
Tarkington, (Newton) Booth
  1869-1946 .... *17*
Tarry, Ellen 1906- *16*
Tarshis, Jerome 1936- *9*
Tarsky, Sue 1946- *41*
Tashjian, Virginia A. 1921- *3*
Tasker, James *9*
Tate, Eleanora E(laine) 1948- *38*
Tate, Ellalice
  See Hibbert, Eleanor
Tate, Joan 1922- *9*
Tate, Mary Anne
  See Hale, Arlene
Tatham, Campbell
  See Elting, Mary
Taves, Isabella 1915- *27*
Taylor, Ann 1782-1866 .... *41*
  Brief Entry *35*
Taylor, Barbara J. 1927- *10*
Taylor, Carl 1937- *14*
Taylor, David 1900-1965 .... *10*
Taylor, Elizabeth 1912-1975 ...... *13*
Taylor, Florence Walton *9*
Taylor, Florence M(arion Tompkins)
  1892- *9*
Taylor, Herb(ert Norman, Jr.)
  1942-1987 .... *22*
  Obituary *54*
Taylor, Jane 1783-1824 .... *41*
  Brief Entry *35*
Taylor, Jerry Duncan 1938- *47*
Taylor, Judy
  See Hough, Judy Taylor
Taylor, Kenneth N(athaniel)
  1917- *26*
Taylor, L(ester) B(arbour), Jr.
  1932- *27*
Taylor, Louise Todd 1939- *47*
Taylor, Mark 1927- *32*
  Brief Entry *28*
Taylor, Mildred D. *15*
  See also CLR 9
  See also SAAS 5
Taylor, Paula (Wright) 1942- *48*
  Brief Entry *33*
Taylor, Robert Lewis 1912- *10*

Taylor, Sydney (Brenner)
  1904(?)-1978 .... *28*
  Obituary *26*
  Earlier sketch in SATA 1
Taylor, Theodore 1921- *54*
  Earlier sketch in SATA 5
  See also SAAS 4
Tchudi, Stephen N. 1942- *55*
Teague, Bob
  See Teague, Robert
Teague, Robert 1929- *32*
  Brief Entry *31*
Teal, Val 1903- *10*
Teale, Edwin Way 1899-1980 ..... *7*
  Obituary *25*
Teasdale, Sara 1884-1933 .... *32*
Tebbel, John (William) 1912- *26*
Tee-Van, Helen Damrosch
  1893-1976 .... *10*
  Obituary *27*
Teleki, Geza 1943- *45*
Telemaque, Eleanor Wong
  1934- *43*
Telescope, Tom
  See Newbery, John
Temkin, Sara Anne (Schlossberg)
  1913- *26*
Temko, Florence *13*
Tempest, Margaret Mary 1892-1982
  Obituary *33*
Templar, Maurice
  See Groom, Arthur William
Temple, Arthur
  See Northcott, (William) Cecil
Temple, Herbert 1919- *45*
Temple, Paul [Joint pseudonym]
  See McConnell, James Douglas
  (Rutherford)
Tenggren, Gustaf 1896-1970 ...... *18*
  Obituary *26*
Tennant, Kylie
  See Rodd, Kathleen Tennant
Tennant, Veronica 1946- *36*
Tenniel, Sir John 1820-1914
  Brief Entry *27*
Terban, Marvin 1940- *54*
  Brief Entry *45*
ter Haar, Jaap 1922- *6*
Terhune, Albert Payson
  1872-1942 .... *15*
Terlouw, Jan (Cornelis) 1931- *30*
Terris, Susan 1937- *3*
Terry, Luther L(eonidas)
  1911-1985 .... *11*
  Obituary *42*
Terry, Walter 1913- *14*
Terzian, James P. 1915- *14*
Tester, Sylvia Root 1939-
  Brief Entry *37*
Tether, (Cynthia) Graham
  1950- *46*
  Brief Entry *36*
Thacher, Mary McGrath
  1933- *9*
Thackeray, William Makepeace
  1811-1863 .... *23*
Thaler, Michael C. 1936-
  Brief Entry *47*

Thaler, Mike
  See Thaler, Michael C.
Thamer, Katie 1955- *42*
Thane, Elswyth 1900- *32*
Tharp, Louise Hall 1898- *3*
Thayer, Jane
  See Woolley, Catherine
Thayer, Marjorie
  Brief Entry *37*
Thayer, Peter
  See Wyler, Rose
Thelwell, Norman 1923- *14*
Theroux, Paul 1941- *44*
Thieda, Shirley Ann 1943- *13*
Thiele, Colin (Milton) 1920- *14*
  See also SAAS 2
Thiry, Joan (Marie) 1926- *45*
Thistlethwaite, Miles 1945- *12*
Thollander, Earl 1922- *22*
Thomas, Allison
  See Fleischer, Leonore
Thomas, Andrea
  See Hill, Margaret (Ohler)
Thomas, Art(hur Lawrence)
  1952- *48*
  Brief Entry *38*
Thomas, Estelle Webb 1899- *26*
Thomas, H. C.
  See Keating, Lawrence A.
Thomas, Ianthe 1951-
  Brief Entry *42*
  See also CLR 8
Thomas, J. F.
  See Fleming, Thomas J(ames)
Thomas, Jane Resh 1936- *38*
Thomas, Joan Gale
  See Robinson, Joan G.
Thomas, Joyce Carol 1938- *40*
  See also SAAS 7
Thomas, Lowell (Jackson), Jr.
  1923- *15*
Thomas, Patricia J. 1934- *51*
Thomas, Victoria [Joint pseudonym]
  See DeWeese, Thomas Eugene
Thompson, Brenda 1935- *34*
Thompson, Christine Pullein
  See Pullein-Thompson, Christine
Thompson, David H(ugh)
  1941- *17*
Thompson, Diana Pullein
  See Pullein-Thompson, Diana
Thompson, Eileen
  See Panowski, Eileen Thompson
Thompson, George Selden
  1929- *4*
Thompson, Harlan H.
  1894-1987 .... *10*
  Obituary *53*
Thompson, Hilary 1943-
  Brief Entry *49*
Thompson, Josephine
  See Pullein-Thompson, Josephine
Thompson, Julian F(rancis)
  1927- *55*
  Brief Entry *40*
Thompson, Kay 1912- *16*
Thompson, Stith 1885-1976
  Obituary *20*
Thompson, Vivian L. 1911- *3*

Thomson, David (Robert Alexander)
1914-1988 .... *40*
  Obituary *55*
Thomson, Peggy 1922- *31*
Thorburn, John
  See Goldsmith, John Herman
  Thorburn
Thorndyke, Helen Louise
  [Collective pseudonym] *1*
Thorne, Ian
  See May, Julian
Thornton, W. B.
  See Burgess, Thornton Waldo
Thorpe, E(ustace) G(eorge)
1916- *21*
Thorvall, Kerstin 1925- *13*
Thrasher, Crystal (Faye)
1921- *27*
Thum, Gladys 1920- *26*
Thum, Marcella *28*
  Earlier sketch in SATA 3
Thundercloud, Katherine
  See Witt, Shirley Hill
Thurber, James (Grover)
1894-1961 .... *13*
Thurman, Judith 1946- *33*
Thwaite, Ann (Barbara Harrop)
1932- *14*
Ticheburn, Cheviot
  See Ainsworth, William Harrison
Tichenor, Tom 1923- *14*
Tichy, William 1924- *31*
Tiegreen, Alan F. 1935-
  Brief Entry *36*
Tierney, Frank M. 1930- *54*
Tilton, Madonna Elaine 1929- *41*
Tilton, Rafael
  See Tilton, Madonna Elaine
Timmins, William F. *10*
Tiner, John Hudson 1944- *32*
Tinkelman, Murray 1933- *12*
Tinkle, (Julien) Lon
1906-1980 .... *36*
Titler, Dale M(ilton) 1926- *35*
  Brief Entry *28*
Titmarsh, Michael Angelo
  See Thackeray, William Makepeace
Titus, Eve 1922- *2*
Tobias, Tobi 1938- *5*
  See also CLR 4
Todd, Anne Ophelia
  See Dowden, Anne Ophelia
Todd, Barbara K. 1917- *10*
Todd, H(erbert) E(atton)
1908- *11*
Todd, Loreto 1942- *30*
Tolan, Stephanie S. 1942- *38*
Toland, John (Willard) 1912- *38*
Tolkien, J(ohn) R(onald) R(euel)
1892-1973 .... *32*
  Obituary *24*
  Earlier sketch in SATA 2
Tolles, Martha 1921- *8*
Tolliver, Ruby C(hangos)
1922- *55*
  Brief Entry *41*
Tolmie, Ken(neth Donald)
1941- *15*

Tolstoi, Leo (Nikolaevich)
1828-1910 26
Tomalin, Ruth 29
Tomes, Margot (Ladd) 1917- 36
  Brief Entry 27
Tomfool
  See Farjeon, Eleanor
Tomkins, Jasper
  See Batey, Tom
Tomline, F. Latour
  See Gilbert, W(illiam) S(chwenk)
Tomlinson, Jill 1931-1976 3
  Obituary 24
Tomlinson, Reginald R(obert)
1885-1979(?)
  Obituary 27
Tompert, Ann 1918- 14
Toner, Raymond John 1908- 10
Took, Belladonna
  See Chapman, Vera
Tooke, Louise Mathews 1950- 38
Toonder, Martin
  See Groom, Arthur William
Toothaker, Roy Eugene 1928- 18
Tooze, Ruth 1892-1972 4
Topping, Audrey R(onning)
1928- 14
Tor, Regina
  See Shekerjian, Regina Tor
Torbert, Floyd James 1922- 22
Torgersen, Don Arthur 1934- 55
  Brief Entry 41
Torrie, Malcolm
  See Mitchell, Gladys (Maude
  Winifred)
Totham, Mary
  See Breinburg, Petronella
Tournier, Michel 1924- 23
Towne, Mary
  See Spelman, Mary
Townsend, John Rowe 1922- 4
  See also CLR 2
  See also SAAS 2
Townsend, Sue 1946- 55
  Brief Entry 48
Toye, Clive 1933(?)-
  Brief Entry 30
Toye, William E(ldred) 1926- 8
Traherne, Michael
  See Watkins-Pitchford, D. J.
Trahey, Jane 1923- 36
Trapp, Maria (Augusta) von
1905- 16
Travers, P(amela) L(yndon)
1906- 54
  Earlier sketch in SATA 4
  See also CLR 2
  See also SAAS 2
Treadgold, Mary 1910- 49
Trease, (Robert) Geoffrey
1909- 2
  See also SAAS 6
Tredez, Alain 1926- 17
Tredez, Denise (Laugier)
1930- 50
Treece, Henry 1911-1966 2
  See also CLR 2
Tregarthen, Enys
  See Sloggett, Nellie

Tregaskis, Richard 1916-1973 ..... *3*
  Obituary *26*
Trell, Max 1900- *14*
Tremain, Ruthven 1922- *17*
Trent, Robbie 1894- *26*
Trent, Timothy
  See Malmberg, Carl
Tresilian, (Cecil) Stuart
1891-19(?) *40*
Tresselt, Alvin 1916- *7*
Treviño, Elizabeth B(orton) de
1904- *29*
  Earlier sketch in SATA 1
  See also SAAS 5
Trevor, Elleston 1920- *28*
Trevor, Glen
  See Hilton, James
Trevor, (Lucy) Meriol 1919- *10*
Trez, Alain
  See Tredez, Alain
Trez, Denise
  See Tredez, Denise (Laugier)
Trimby, Elisa 1948- *47*
  Brief Entry *40*
Tripp, Eleanor B. 1936- *4*
Tripp, Paul *8*
Tripp, Wallace (Whitney)
1940- *31*
Trivelpiece, Laurel 1926-
  Brief Entry *46*
Trivett, Daphne (Harwood)
1940- *22*
Trnka, Jiri 1912-1969 .... *43*
  Brief Entry *32*
Trollope, Anthony 1815-1882 .... *22*
Trost, Lucille Wood 1938- *12*
Trotter, Grace V(iolet) 1900- *10*
Troughton, Joanna (Margaret)
1947- *37*
Troyer, Johannes 1902-1969
  Brief Entry *40*
Trudeau, G(arretson) B(eekman)
1948- *35*
Trudeau, Garry B.
  See Trudeau, G(arretson) B(eekman)
Truesdell, Sue
  See Truesdell, Susan G.
Truesdell, Susan G.
  Brief Entry *45*
Truss, Jan 1925- *35*
Tucker, Caroline
  See Nolan, Jeannette
Tudor, Tasha *20*
  See also CLR 13
Tully, John (Kimberley)
1923- *14*
Tunis, Edwin (Burdett)
1897-1973 .... *28*
  Obituary *24*
  Earlier sketch in SATA 1
  See also CLR 2
Tunis, John R(oberts)
1889-1975 .... *37*
  Brief Entry *30*
Turkle, Brinton 1915- *2*
Turlington, Bayly 1919-1977 ..... *5*
  Obituary *52*
Turnbull, Agnes Sligh *14*

Turnbull, Ann (Christine)
  1943- *18*
Turner, Alice K. 1940- *10*
Turner, Ann W(arren) 1945- *14*
Turner, Elizabeth
  1774-1846 .... *YABC 2*
Turner, Josie
  See Crawford, Phyllis
Turner, Philip 1925- *11*
  See also SAAS 6
Turner, Sheila R.
  See Seed, Sheila Turner
Turngren, Annette 1902(?)-1980
  Obituary *23*
Turngren, Ellen (?)-1964 .... *3*
Turska, Krystyna Zofia 1933- *31*
  Brief Entry *27*
Tusan, Stan 1936- *22*
Tusiani, Joseph 1924- *45*
Twain, Mark
  See Clemens, Samuel Langhorne
Tweedsmuir, Baron
  See Buchan, John
Tweton, D. Jerome 1933- *48*
Tworkov, Jack 1900-1982 .... *47*
  Obituary *31*
Tyler, Anne 1941- *7*

U

Ubell, Earl 1926- *4*
Uchida, Yoshiko 1921- *53*
  Earlier sketch in SATA 1
  See also CLR 6
  See also SAAS 1
Udall, Jan Beaney 1938- *10*
Uden, (Bernard Gilbert) Grant
  1910- *26*
Udry, Janice May 1928- *4*
Ulam, S(tanislaw) M(arcin)
  1909-1984 .... *51*
Ullman, James Ramsey
  1907-1971 .... *7*
Ulm, Robert 1934-1977 .... *17*
Ulmer, Louise 1943- *53*
Ulyatt, Kenneth 1920- *14*
Unada
  See Gliewe, Unada
Uncle Gus
  See Rey, H. A.
Uncle Mac
  See McCulloch, Derek (Ivor
  Breashur)
Uncle Ray
  See Coffman, Ramon Peyton
Uncle Shelby
  See Silverstein, Shel(by)
Underhill, Alice Mertie 1900-1971
Underhill, Liz 1948- *53*
  Brief Entry *49*
Ungerer, (Jean) Thomas 1931- *33*
  Earlier sketch in SATA 5
Ungerer, Tomi
  See Ungerer, (Jean) Thomas
  See also CLR 3
Unkelbach, Kurt 1913- *4*
Unnerstad, Edith 1900- *3*
Unrau, Ruth 1922- *9*

Unstead, R(obert) J(ohn)
  1915- *12*
Unsworth, Walt 1928- *4*
Untermeyer, Louis 1885-1977 .... *37*
  Obituary *26*
  Earlier sketch in SATA 2
Unwin, David S(torr) 1918- *14*
Unwin, Nora S. 1907-1982 .... *3*
  Obituary *49*
Ure, Jean *48*
Uris, Leon (Marcus) 1924- *49*
Usher, Margo Scegge
  See McHargue, Georgess
Uttley, Alice Jane (Taylor)
  1884-1976 .... *3*
  Obituary *26*
Uttley, Alison
  See Uttley, Alice Jane (Taylor)
Utz, Lois 1932-1986 .... *5*
  Obituary *50*
Uzair, Salem ben
  See Horne, Richard Henry

V

Vaeth, J(oseph) Gordon 1921- *17*
Valen, Nanine 1950- *21*
Valencak, Hannelore 1929- *42*
Valens, Evans G., Jr. 1920- *1*
Valleau, Emily 1925- *51*
Van Abbé, Salaman
  1883-1955 .... *18*
Van Allsburg, Chris 1949- *53*
  Earlier sketch in SATA 37
  See also CLR 5
  See also CLR 13
Van Anrooy, Francine 1924- *2*
Van Anrooy, Frans
  See Van Anrooy, Francine
Vance, Eleanor Graham 1908- *11*
Vance, Marguerite 1889-1965 ..... *29*
Vandenburg, Mary Lou 1943- *17*
Vander Boom, Mae M. *14*
Van der Veer, Judy
  1912-1982 .... *4*
  Obituary *33*
Vandivert, Rita (Andre) 1905- *21*
Van Duyn, Janet 1910- *18*
Van Dyne, Edith
  See Baum, L(yman) Frank
Van Horn, William 1939- *43*
Van Iterson, S(iny) R(ose) *26*
Van Kampen, Vlasta 1943- *54*
Van Leeuwen, Jean 1937- *6*
Van Lhin, Erik
  See Del Rey, Lester
Van Loon, Hendrik Willem
  1882-1944 .... *18*
Van Orden, M(erton) D(ick)
  1921- *4*
Van Rensselaer, Alexander (Taylor
  Mason) 1892-1962 .... *14*
Van Riper, Guernsey, Jr.
  1909- *3*
Van Steenwyk, Elizabeth Ann
  1928- *34*
Van Stockum, Hilda 1908- *5*
Van Tuyl, Barbara 1940- *11*

Van Vogt, A(lfred) E(lton)
  1912- *14*
Van Woerkom, Dorothy (O'Brien)
  1924- *21*
Van Wormer, Joe
  See Van Wormer, Joseph Edward
Van Wormer, Joseph Edward
  1913- *35*
Van-Wyck Mason, F.
  See Mason, F. van Wyck
Van Zwienen, Ilse (Charlotte Koehn)
  1929- *34*
  Brief Entry *28*
Varga, Judy
  See Stang, Judit
Varley, Dimity V. 1906- *10*
Vasiliu, Mircea 1920- *2*
Vass, George 1927-
  Brief Entry *31*
Vaughan, Carter A.
  See Gerson, Noel B(ertram)
Vaughan, Harold Cecil 1923- *14*
Vaughan, Sam(uel) S. 1928- *14*
Vaughn, Ruth 1935- *14*
Vautier, Ghislaine 1932- *53*
Vavra, Robert James 1944- *8*
Vecsey, George 1939- *9*
Veglahn, Nancy (Crary) 1937- *5*
Velthuijs, Max 1923- *53*
Venable, Alan (Hudson)
  1944- *8*
Venn, Mary Eleanor
  See Jorgensen, Mary Venn
Ventura, Piero (Luigi) 1937-
  Brief Entry *43*
Vequin, Capini
  See Quinn, Elisabeth
Verne, Jules 1828-1905 .... *21*
Verner, Gerald 1897(?)-1980
  Obituary *25*
Verney, John 1913- *14*
Vernon, (Elda) Louise A(nderson)
  1914- *14*
Vernon, Rosemary
  See Smith, Susan Vernon
Vernor, D.
  See Casewit, Curtis
Verral, Charles Spain 1904- *11*
Verrone, Robert J. 1935(?)-1984
  Obituary *39*
Versace, Marie Teresa Rios
  1917- *2*
Vesey, Paul
  See Allen, Samuel (Washington)
Vestly, Anne-Cath(arina)
  1920- *14*
Vevers, (Henry) Gwynne
  1916- *45*
Viator, Vacuus
  See Hughes, Thomas
Vicarion, Count Palmiro
  See Logue, Christopher
Vicker, Angus
  See Felsen, Henry Gregor
Vickery, Kate
  See Kennedy, T(eresa) A.
Victor, Edward 1914- *3*
Victor, Joan Berg 1937- *30*
Viereck, Ellen K. 1928- *14*

Viereck, Phillip 1925- 3
Viertel, Janet 1915- 10
Vigna, Judith 1936- 15
Viguers, Ruth Hill 1903-1971 6
Villiard, Paul 1910-1974 51
  Obituary 20
Villiers, Alan (John) 1903- 10
Vincent, Eric Douglas 1953- 40
Vincent, Félix 1946- 41
Vincent, Gabrielle
  See CLR 13
Vincent, Mary Keith
  See St. John, Wylly Folk
Vinge, Joan D(ennison) 1948- 36
Vining, Elizabeth Gray
  See Gray, Elizabeth Janet
Vinson, Kathryn 1911- 21
Vinton, Iris 1906(?)-1988 24
  Obituary 55
Viorst, Judith 7
  See also CLR 3
Vip
  See Partch, Virgil Franklin II
Vipont, Charles
  See Foulds, Elfrida Vipont
Vipont, Elfrida
  See Foulds, Elfrida Vipont
Visser, W(illiam) F(rederick)
  H(endrik) 1900-1968 10
Vlahos, Olivia 1924- 31
Vlasic, Bob
  See Hirsch, Phil
Vo-Dinh, Mai 1933- 16
Vogel, Ilse-Margret 1914- 14
Vogel, John H(ollister), Jr.
  1950- 18
Vogt, Esther Loewen 1915- 14
Vogt, Gregory
  Brief Entry 45
Vogt, Marie Bollinger 1921- 45
Voight, Virginia Frances
  1909- 8
Voigt, Cynthia 1942- 48
  Brief Entry 33
  See also CLR 13
Voigt, Erna 1925- 35
Voigt-Rother, Erna
  See Voigt, Erna
Vojtech, Anna 1946- 42
von Almedingen, Martha Edith
  See Almedingen, E. M.
Von Hagen, Victor Wolfgang
  1908- 29
von Klopp, Vahrah
  See Malvern, Gladys
von Schmidt, Eric 1931- 50
  Brief Entry 36
von Storch, Anne B. 1910- 1
Vosburgh, Leonard (W.)
  1912- 15
Voyle, Mary
  See Manning, Rosemary

W

Waber, Bernard 1924- 47
  Brief Entry 40

Wachter, Oralee Roberts 1935-
  Brief Entry 51
Waddell, Evelyn Margaret
  1918- 10
Waddell, Martin 1941- 43
Wade, Theodore E., Jr. 1936- 37
Wagenheim, Kal 1935- 21
Wagner, Jane 33
Wagner, Sharon B. 1936- 4
Wagoner, David (Russell)
  1926- 14
Wahl, Jan 1933- 34
  Earlier sketch in SATA 2
  See also SAAS 3
Waide, Jan 1952- 29
Wainscott, John Milton
  1910-1981 53
Waitley, Douglas 1927- 30
Wakefield, Jean L.
  See Laird, Jean E(louise)
Wakin, Edward 1927- 37
Walck, Henry Z(eigler) 1908-1984
  Obituary 40
Walden, Amelia Elizabeth 3
Waldman, Bruce 1949- 15
Waldman, Neil 1947- 51
Waldron, Ann Wood 1924- 16
Walker, Alice 1944- 31
Walker, Barbara K. 1921- 4
Walker, (James) Braz(elton)
  1934-1983 45
Walker, David Harry 1911- 8
Walker, Diana 1925- 9
Walker, Frank 1930- 36
Walker, Holly Beth
  See Bond, Gladys Baker
Walker, Lou Ann 1952-
  Brief Entry 53
Walker, Louise Jean 1891-1976
  Obituary 35
Walker, Mildred
  See Schemm, Mildred Walker
Walker, (Addison) Mort
  1923- 8
Walker, Pamela 1948- 24
Walker, Stephen J. 1951- 12
Wallace, Barbara Brooks 4
Wallace, Beverly Dobrin
  1921- 19
Wallace, Bill 1947-
  See Wallace, William Keith
  Brief Entry 47
Wallace, Daisy
  See Cuyler, Margery Stuyvesant
Wallace, Ian 1950- 53
Wallace, John A. 1915- 3
Wallace, Nigel
  See Hamilton, Charles H. St. John
Wallace, Robert 1932- 47
  Brief Entry 37
Wallace, William Keith 1947- 53
Wallace-Brodeur, Ruth 1941- 51
  Brief Entry 41
Waller, Leslie 1923- 20
Wallis, G. McDonald
  See Campbell, Hope
Wallner, Alexandra 1946- 51
  Brief Entry 41

Wallner, John C. 1945- 51
  Earlier sketch in SATA 10
Wallower, Lucille 11
Walsh, Ellen Stoll 1942- 49
Walsh, George Johnston
  1889-1981 53
Walsh, Jill Paton
  See Paton Walsh, Gillian
  See also CLR 2
Walter, Mildred Pitts
  Brief Entry 45
  See also CLR 15
Walter, Villiam Christian
  See Andersen, Hans Christian
Walters, Audrey 1929- 18
Walters, Helen B. (?)-1987
  Obituary 50
Walters, Hugh
  See Hughes, Walter (Llewellyn)
Walther, Thomas A. 1950- 31
Walther, Tom
  See Walther, Thomas A.
Waltner, Elma 1912- 40
Waltner, Willard H. 1909- 40
Walton, Richard J. 1928- 4
Waltrip, Lela (Kingston)
  1904- 9
Waltrip, Mildred 1911- 37
Waltrip, Rufus (Charles)
  1898- 9
Walworth, Nancy Zinsser
  1917- 14
Wangerin, Walter, Jr. 1944- 45
  Brief Entry 37
Wannamaker, Bruce
  See Moncure, Jane Belk
Warbler, J. M.
  See Cocagnac, A. M.
Warburg, Sandol Stoddard
  1927- 14
Ward, John (Stanton) 1917- 42
Ward, Lynd (Kendall)
  1905-1985 36
  Obituary 42
  Earlier sketch in SATA 2
Ward, Martha (Eads) 1921- 5
Ward, Melanie
  See Curtis, Richard (Alan)
Wardell, Dean
  See Prince, J(ack) H(arvey)
Ware, Leon (Vernon) 1909- 4
Warner, Frank A. [Collective
  pseudonym] 1
Warner, Gertrude Chandler
  1890- 9
Warner, Lucille Schulberg 30
Warner, Oliver 1903-1976 29
Warren, Betsy
  See Warren, Elizabeth Avery
Warren, Billy
  See Warren, William Stephen
Warren, Cathy
  Brief Entry 46
Warren, Elizabeth
  See Supraner, Robyn
Warren, Elizabeth Avery
  1916- 46
  Brief Entry 38

Warren, Joyce W(illiams) 1935- 18
Warren, Mary Phraner 1929- 10
Warren, Robert Penn 1905- 46
Warren, William Stephen 1882-1968 9
Warrick, Patricia Scott 1925- 35
Warriner, John 1907(?)-1987 Obituary 53
Warsh See Warshaw, Jerry
Warshaw, Jerry 1929- 30
Warshofsky, Fred 1931- 24
Warshofsky, Isaac See Singer, Isaac Bashevis
Wartski, Maureen (Ann Crane) 1940- 50
Brief Entry 37
Warwick, Alan R(oss) 1900-1973 42
Wa-sha-quon-asin See Belaney, Archibald Stansfeld
Washburn, (Henry) Bradford (Jr.) 1910- 38
Washburne, Heluiz Chandler 1892-1970 10
Obituary 26
Washington, Booker T(aliaferro) 1858(?)-1915 28
Watanabe, Shigeo 1928- 39
Brief Entry 32
See also CLR 8
Waters, John F(rederick) 1930- 4
Waterton, Betty (Marie) 1923- 37
Brief Entry 34
Watkins-Pitchford, D. J. 1905- 6
See also SAAS 4
Watson, Aldren A(uld) 1917- 42
Brief Entry 36
Watson, Clyde 1947- 5
See also CLR 3
Watson, Helen Orr 1892-1978 Obituary 24
Watson, James 1936- 10
Watson, Jane Werner 1915- 54
Earlier sketch in SATA 3
Watson, Nancy Dingman 32
Watson, Pauline 1925- 14
Watson, Sally 1924- 3
Watson, Wendy (McLeod) 1942- 5
Watson Taylor, Elizabeth 1915- 41
Watt, Thomas 1935- 4
Watts, Bernadette 1942- 4
Watts, Ephraim See Horne, Richard Henry
Watts, Franklin (Mowry) 1904-1978 46
Obituary 21
Watts, Isaac 1674-1748 52
Watts, Mabel Pizzey 1906- 11
Waugh, Carol-Lynn Rössel 1947- 41
Waugh, Dorothy 11
Wayland, Patrick See O'Connor, Richard

Wayne, (Anne) Jenifer 1917-1982 32
Wayne, Kyra Petrovskaya 1918- 8
Wayne, Richard See Decker, Duane
Waystaff, Simon See Swift, Jonathan
Weales, Gerald (Clifford) 1925- 11
Weary, Ogdred See Gorey, Edward St. John
Weaver, John L. 1949- 42
Weaver, Ward See Mason, F. van Wyck
Webb, Christopher See Wibberley, Leonard (Patrick O'Connor)
Webb, Jean Francis (III) 1910- 35
Webb, Sharon 1936- 41
Webber, Irma E(leanor Schmidt) 1904- 14
Weber, Alfons 1921- 8
Weber, Lenora Mattingly 1895-1971 2
Obituary 26
Weber, William John 1927- 14
Webster, Alice (Jane Chandler) 1876-1916 17
Webster, David 1930- 11
Webster, Frank V. [Collective pseudonym] 1
Webster, Gary See Garrison, Webb B(lack)
Webster, James 1925-1981 17
Obituary 27
Webster, Jean See Webster, Alice (Jane Chandler)
Wechsler, Herman 1904-1976 Obituary 20
Weddle, Ethel H(arshbarger) 1897- 11
Wegen, Ron(ald) Brief Entry 44
Wegner, Fritz 1924- 20
Weihs, Erika 1917- 15
Weik, Mary Hays 1898(?)-1979 3
Obituary 23
Weil, Ann Yezner 1908-1969 9
Weil, Lisl 7
Weilerstein, Sadie Rose 1894- 3
Weinberg, Larry See Weinberg, Lawrence (E.)
Weinberg, Lawrence (E.) Brief Entry 48
Weiner, Sandra 1922- 14
Weingarten, Violet (Brown) 1915-1976 3
Obituary 27
Weingartner, Charles 1922- 5
Weir, LaVada 2
Weir, Rosemary (Green) 1905- 21
Weis, Margaret (Edith) 1948- 38
Weisberger, Bernard A(llen) 1922- 21

Weiser, Marjorie P(hillis) K(atz) 1934- 33
Weisgard, Leonard (Joseph) 1916- 30
Earlier sketch in SATA 2
Weiss, Adelle 1920- 18
Weiss, Ann E(dwards) 1943- 30
Weiss, Ellen 1953- 44
Weiss, Harvey 1922- 27
Earlier sketch in SATA 1
See also CLR 4
Weiss, Leatie 1928- Brief Entry 50
Weiss, Malcolm E. 1928- 3
Weiss, Miriam See Schlein, Miriam
Weiss, Nicki 1954- 33
Weiss, Renee Karol 1923- 5
Weissenborn, Hellmuth 1898-1982 Obituary 31
Welber, Robert 26
Welch, D'Alte Aldridge 1907-1970 Obituary 27
Welch, Jean-Louise See Kempton, Jean Welch
Welch, Martha McKeen 1914- Brief Entry 45
Welch, Pauline See Bodenham, Hilda Esther
Welch, Ronald See Felton, Ronald Oliver
Weller, George (Anthony) 1907- 31
Welles, Winifred 1893-1939 Brief Entry 27
Wellman, Alice 1900-1984 51
Brief Entry 36
Wellman, Manly Wade 1903-1986 6
Obituary 47
Wellman, Paul I. 1898-1966 3
Wells, H(erbert) G(eorge) 1866-1946 20
Wells, Helen 1910-1986 49
Earlier sketch in SATA 2
Wells, J. Wellington See DeCamp, L(yon) Sprague
Wells, Rosemary 18
See also SAAS 1
Wels, Byron G(erald) 1924- 9
Welsh, Mary Flynn 1910(?)-1984 Obituary 38
Weltner, Linda R(iverly) 1938- 38
Welty, S. F. See Welty, Susan F.
Welty, Susan F. 1905- 9
Wendelin, Rudolph 1910- 23
Werner, Elsa Jane See Watson, Jane Werner
Werner, Herma 1926- 47
Brief Entry 41
Werner, Jane See Watson, Jane Werner
Werner, K. See Casewit, Curtis
Wersba, Barbara 1932- 1
See also CLR 3
See also SAAS 2

Author Index

Werstein, Irving 1914-1971 14
Werth, Kurt 1896- 20
Wesley, Alison
  See Barnes, Michael
West, Anna 1938- 40
West, Barbara
  See Price, Olive
West, Betty 1921- 11
West, C. P.
  See Wodehouse, P(elham)
  G(renville)
West, Emily G(ovan) 1919- 38
West, Emmy
  See West, Emily G(ovan)
West, James
  See Withers, Carl A.
West, Jerry
  See Stratemeyer, Edward L.
West, Jerry
  See Svenson, Andrew E.
West, (Mary) Jessamyn 1902(?)-1984
  Obituary 37
West, Ward
  See Borland, Hal
Westall, Robert (Atkinson)
  1929- 23
  See also SAAS 2
  See also CLR 13
Westerberg, Christine 1950- 29
Westervelt, Virginia (Veeder)
  1914- 10
Westheimer, David 1917- 14
Westmacott, Mary
  See Christie, Agatha (Mary Clarissa)
Westman, Paul (Wendell)
  1956- 39
Weston, Allen [Joint pseudonym]
  See Norton, Alice Mary
Weston, John (Harrison)
  1932- 21
Weston, Martha 1947- 53
Westwood, Jennifer 1940- 10
Wexler, Jerome (LeRoy)
  1923- 14
Wharf, Michael
  See Weller, George (Anthony)
Wheatley, Arabelle 1921- 16
Wheeler, Captain
  See Ellis, Edward S(ylvester)
Wheeler, Cindy 1955- 49
  Brief Entry 40
Wheeler, Janet D. [Collective
  pseudonym] 1
Wheeler, Opal 1898- 23
Whelan, Elizabeth M(urphy)
  1943- 14
Whistler, Reginald John
  1905-1944 30
Whistler, Rex
  See Whistler, Reginald John
Whitcomb, Jon 1906- 10
White, Anne Hitchcock 1902-1970
  Brief Entry 33
White, Anne Terry 1896- 2
White, Bessie (Felstiner) 1892(?)-1986
  Obituary 50
White, Dale
  See Place, Marian T.

White, Dori 1919- 10
White, E(lwyn) B(rooks)
  1899-1985 29
  Obituary 44
  Earlier sketch in SATA 2
  See also CLR 1
White, Eliza Orne
  1856-1947 .... YABC 2
White, Florence M(eiman)
  1910- 14
White, Laurence B., Jr. 1935- 10
White, Martin 1943- 51
White, Ramy Allison [Collective
  pseudonym] 1
White, Robb 1909- 1
  See also CLR 3
  See also SAAS 1
White, Ruth C. 1942- 39
White, T(erence) H(anbury)
  1906-1964 12
White, William, Jr. 1934- 16
Whitehead, Don(ald) F. 1908- 4
Whitehouse, Arch
  See Whitehouse, Arthur George
Whitehouse, Arthur George
  1895-1979 14
  Obituary 23
Whitehouse, Elizabeth S(cott)
  1893-1968 35
Whitehouse, Jeanne 1939- 29
Whitinger, R. D.
  See Place, Marian T.
Whitlock, Pamela 1921(?)-1982
  Obituary 31
Whitlock, Ralph 1914- 35
Whitman, Walt(er) 1819-1892 20
Whitney, Alex(andra) 1922- 14
Whitney, David C(harles)
  1921- 48
  Brief Entry 29
Whitney, Phyllis A(yame)
  1903- 30
  Earlier sketch in SATA 1
Whitney, Thomas P(orter)
  1917- 25
Wibberley, Leonard (Patrick
  O'Connor) 1915-1983 45
  Obituary 36
  Earlier sketch in SATA 2
  See also CLR 3
Wiberg, Harald (Albin) 1908-
  Brief Entry 40
Wicker, Ireene 1905(?)-1987
  Obituary 55
Widdemer, Mabel Cleland
  1902-1964 5
Widenberg, Siv 1931- 10
Wier, Ester 1910- 3
Wiese, Kurt 1887-1974 36
  Obituary 24
  Earlier sketch in SATA 3
Wiesner, Portia
  See Takakjian, Portia
Wiesner, William 1899- 5
Wiggin, Kate Douglas (Smith)
  1856-1923 .... YABC 1
Wight, James Alfred 1916- 55
  Brief Entry 44

Wikland, Ilon 1930-
  Brief Entry 32
Wilber, Donald N(ewton)
  1907- 35
Wilbur, C. Keith 1923- 27
Wilbur, Richard (Purdy)
  1921- 9
Wilcox, R(uth) Turner
  1888-1970 36
Wild, Jocelyn 1941- 46
Wild, Robin (Evans) 1936- 46
Wilde, D. Gunther
  See Hurwood, Bernhardt J.
Wilde, Oscar (Fingal O'Flahertie
  Wills) 1854-1900 24
Wilder, Cherry
  See Grimm, Cherry Barbara Lockett
Wilder, Laura Ingalls
  1867-1957 29
  See also CLR 2
Wildsmith, Brian 1930- 16
  See also CLR 2
  See also SAAS 5
Wilkie, Katharine E(lliott)
  1904-1980 31
Wilkin, Eloise (Burns)
  1904-1987 49
  Obituary 54
Wilkins, Frances 1923- 14
Wilkins, Marilyn (Ruth)
  1926- 30
Wilkins, Marne
  See Wilkins, Marilyn (Ruth)
Wilkinson, (Thomas) Barry
  1923- 50
  Brief Entry 32
Wilkinson, Brenda 1946- 14
Wilkinson, Burke 1913- 4
Wilkinson, Sylvia (J.) 1940-
  Brief Entry 39
Wilkoń, Józef 1930- 31
Wilks, Michael Thomas 1947- 44
Wilks, Mike
  See Wilks, Michael Thomas
Will
  See Lipkind, William
Willard, Barbara (Mary)
  1909- 17
  See also CLR 2
  See also SAAS 5
Willard, Mildred Wilds 1911- 14
Willard, Nancy 1936- 37
  Brief Entry 30
  See also CLR 5
Willcox, Isobel 1907- 42
Willey, Robert
  See Ley, Willy
William, Earle
  See Johns, W(illiam) E(arl)
Williams, Barbara 1925- 11
Williams, Beryl
  See Epstein, Beryl
Williams, Brian (Peter) 1943- 54
Williams, Charles
  See Collier, James Lincoln
Williams, Clyde C.
  1881-1974 8
  Obituary 27

Williams, Coe
  See Harrison, C. William
Williams, Eric (Ernest)
  1911-1983 .... *14*
  Obituary *38*
Williams, Ferelith Eccles
  1920- *22*
Williams, Frances B.
  See Browin, Frances Williams
Williams, Garth (Montgomery)
  1912- *18*
  See also SAAS 7
Williams, Guy R. 1920- *11*
Williams, Hawley
  See Heyliger, William
Williams, J. R.
  See Williams, Jeanne
Williams, J. Walker
  See Wodehouse, P(elham)
  G(renville)
Williams, Jay 1914-1978 .... *41*
  Obituary *24*
  Earlier sketch in SATA 3
  See also CLR 8
Williams, Jeanne 1930- *5*
Williams, Kit 1946(?)- *44*
  See also CLR 4
Williams, Leslie 1941- *42*
Williams, Louise Bonino 1904(?)-1984
  Obituary *39*
Williams, Lynn
  See Hale, Arlene
Williams, Maureen 1951- *12*
Williams, Michael
  See St. John, Wylly Folk
Williams, Patrick J.
  See Butterworth, W. E.
Williams, Selma R(uth) 1925- *14*
Williams, Slim
  See Williams, Clyde C.
Williams, Ursula Moray
  1911- *3*
Williams, Vera B. 1927- *53*
  Brief Entry *33*
  See also CLR 9
Williams-Ellis, (Mary) Amabel
  (Nassau) 1894-1984 .... *29*
  Obituary *41*
Williamson, Henry 1895-1977 .... *37*
  Obituary *30*
Williamson, Joanne Small
  1926- *3*
Willson, Robina Beckles (Ballard)
  1930- *27*
Wilma, Dana
  See Faralla, Dana
Wilson, Beth P(ierre) *8*
Wilson, Budge 1927- *55*
Wilson, Marjorie
  See Wilson, Budge
Wilson, Carter 1941- *6*
Wilson, Charles Morrow
  1905-1977 .... *30*
Wilson, Christopher B. 1910(?)-1985
  Obituary *46*
Wilson, Dagmar 1916-
  Brief Entry *31*
Wilson, Dorothy Clarke 1904- *16*

Wilson, Edward A(rthur)
  1886-1970 .... *38*
Wilson, Ellen (Janet Cameron)
  (?)-1976 .... *9*
  Obituary *26*
Wilson, Eric H. 1940- *34*
  Brief Entry *32*
Wilson, Erica *51*
Wilson, Forrest 1918- *27*
Wilson, Gahan 1930- *35*
  Brief Entry *27*
Wilson, Gina 1943- *36*
  Brief Entry *34*
Wilson, (Leslie) Granville
  1912- *14*
Wilson, Hazel 1898- *3*
Wilson, Jacqueline 1945-
  Brief Entry *52*
Wilson, John 1922- *22*
Wilson, Joyce M(uriel Judson) *21*
Wilson, Lionel 1924- *33*
  Brief Entry *31*
Wilson, Marjorie 1927-
  Brief Entry *51*
Wilson, Maurice (Charles John)
  1914- *46*
Wilson, Ron(ald William) *38*
Wilson, Sarah 1934- *50*
Wilson, Tom 1931- *33*
  Brief Entry *30*
Wilson, Walt(er N.) 1939- *14*
Wilton, Elizabeth 1937- *14*
Wilwerding, Walter Joseph
  1891-1966 .... *9*
Winchester, James H(ugh)
  1917-1985 .... *30*
  Obituary *45*
Winders, Gertrude Hecker *3*
Windham, Basil
  See Wodehouse, P(elham)
  G(renville)
Windham, Kathryn T(ucker)
  1918- *14*
Windsor, Claire
  See Hamerstrom, Frances
Windsor, Patricia 1938- *30*
Winfield, Arthur M.
  See Stratemeyer, Edward L.
Winfield, Edna
  See Stratemeyer, Edward L.
Winn, Chris 1952- *42*
Winn, Janet Bruce 1928- *43*
Winn, Marie 1936- *38*
Winnick, Karen B(eth) B(inkoff)
  1946- *51*
Winston, Clara 1921-1983 .... *54*
  Obituary *39*
Winston, Richard 1917-1979 ...... *54*
Winter, Milo (Kendall)
  1888-1956 .... *21*
Winter, Paula Cecelia 1929- *48*
Winter, R. R.
  See Winterbotham, R(ussell)
  R(obert)
Winterbotham, R(ussell) R(obert)
  1904-1971 .... *10*
Winterfeld, Henry *55*

Winters, Jon
  See Cross, Gilbert B.
Winterton, Gayle
  See Adams, William Taylor
Winthrop, Elizabeth
  See Mahony, Elizabeth Winthrop
Wirtenberg, Patricia Z. 1932- *10*
Wise, William 1923- *4*
Wise, Winifred E. *2*
Wiseman, Ann (Sayre) 1926- *31*
Wiseman, B(ernard) 1922- *4*
Wiseman, David 1916- *43*
  Brief Entry *40*
Wisler, G(ary) Clifton 1950-
  Brief Entry *46*
Wisner, Bill
  See Wisner, William L.
Wisner, William L.
  1914(?)-1983 .... *42*
Witham, (Phillip) Ross 1917- *37*
Withers, Carl A. 1900-1970 .... *14*
Witt, Shirley Hill 1934- *17*
Wittanen, Etolin 1907- *55*
Wittels, Harriet Joan 1938- *31*
Wittman, Sally (Anne Christensen)
  1941- *30*
Witty, Paul A(ndrew)
  1898-1976 .... *50*
  Obituary *30*
Wizard, Mr.
  See Herbert, Don
Wodehouse, P(elham) G(renville)
  1881-1975 .... *22*
Wodge, Dreary
  See Gorey, Edward St. John
Wohlberg, Meg 1905- *41*
Wohlrabe, Raymond A. 1900- *4*
Wojciechowska, Maia 1927- *28*
  Earlier sketch in SATA 1
  See also CLR 1
  See also SAAS 1
Wolcott, Patty 1929- *14*
Wold, Jo Anne 1938- *30*
Woldin, Beth Weiner 1955- *34*
Wolf, Bernard 1930-
  Brief Entry *37*
Wolfe, Burton H. 1932- *5*
Wolfe, Louis 1905- *8*
Wolfe, Rinna (Evelyn) 1925- *38*
Wolfenden, George
  See Beardmore, George
Wolff, (Jenifer) Ashley 1956- *50*
Wolff, Diane 1945- *27*
Wolff, Robert Jay 1905- *10*
Wolitzer, Hilma 1930- *31*
Wolkoff, Judie (Edwards)
  Brief Entry *37*
Wolkstein, Diane 1942- *7*
Wolny, P.
  See Janeczko, Paul B(ryan)
Wolters, Richard A. 1920- *35*
Wondriska, William 1931- *6*
Wood, Audrey *50*
  Brief Entry *44*
Wood, Catherine
  See Etchison, Birdie L(ee)
Wood, Don 1945- *50*
  Brief Entry *44*

Wood, Edgar A(llardyce)
1907- *14*
Wood, Esther
See Brady, Esther Wood
Wood, Frances Elizabeth *34*
Wood, James Playsted 1905- *1*
Wood, Kerry
See Wood, Edgar A(llardyce)
Wood, Laura N.
See Roper, Laura Wood
Wood, Nancy 1936- *6*
Wood, Phyllis Anderson
1923- *33*
Brief Entry *30*
Wood, Wallace 1927-1981
Obituary *33*
Woodard, Carol 1929- *14*
Woodburn, John Henry 1914- *11*
Woodford, Peggy 1937- *25*
Woodrich, Mary Neville
1915- *2*
Woods, George A(llan) 1926- *30*
Woods, Geraldine 1948-
Brief Entry *42*
Woods, Harold 1945-
Brief Entry *42*
Woods, Margaret 1921- *2*
Woods, Nat
See Stratemeyer, Edward L.
Woodson, Jack
See Woodson, John Waddie, Jr.
Woodson, John Waddie, Jr. *10*
Woodward, Cleveland
1900-1986 .... *10*
Obituary *48*
Woody, Regina Jones 1894- *3*
Wooldridge, Rhoda 1906- *22*
Woolley, Catherine 1904- *3*
Woolsey, Janette 1904- *3*
Worcester, Donald Emmet
1915- *18*
Work, Virginia 1946-
Brief Entry *45*
Worline, Bonnie Bess 1914- *14*
Wormser, Sophie 1896- *22*
Worth, Richard
Brief Entry *46*
Worth, Valerie 1933- *8*
Worthington, Phoebe 1910-
Brief Entry *52*
Wortis, Avi 1937- *14*
Wosmek, Frances 1917- *29*
Wriggins, Sally Hovey 1922 ...... *17*
Wright, Anna (Maria Louisa Perrot)
Rose 1890-1968
Brief Entry *35*
Wright, Betty Ren
Brief Entry *48*
Wright, Dare 1926(?)- *21*
Wright, Enid Meadowcroft
1898-1966 .... *3*
Wright, Esmond 1915- *10*
Wright, Frances Fitzpatrick
1897- *10*
Wright, Judith 1915- *14*
Wright, Katrina
See Gater, Dilys

Wright, Kenneth
See Del Rey, Lester
Wright, Nancy Means *38*
Wright, R(obert) H. 1906- *6*
Wrightson, Patricia 1921- *8*
See also CLR 4, 14
See also SAAS 4
Wronker, Lili Cassel 1924- *10*
Wulffson, Don L. 1943- *32*
Wuorio, Eva-Lis 1918- *34*
Brief Entry *28*
Wyeth, Betsy James 1921- *41*
Wyeth, N(ewell) C(onvers)
1882-1945 .... *17*
Wyler, Rose 1909- *18*
Wylie, Betty Jane *48*
Wylie, Laura
See Matthews, Patricia
Wymer, Norman George
1911- *25*
Wynants, Miche 1934-
Brief Entry *31*
Wyndham, Lee
See Hyndman, Jane Andrews
Wyndham, Robert
See Hyndman, Robert Utley
Wynter, Edward (John) 1914- *14*
Wynyard, Talbot
See Hamilton, Charles H. St. John
Wyss, Johann David Von
1743-1818 .... *29*
Brief Entry *27*
Wyss, Thelma Hatch 1934- *10*

Y

Yadin, Yigael 1917-1984 .... *55*
Yaffe, Alan
See Yorinks, Arthur
Yamaguchi, Marianne 1936- *7*
Yang, Jay 1941- *12*
Yarbrough, Ira 1910(?)-1983
Obituary *35*
Yaroslava
See Mills, Yaroslava Surmach
Yashima, Taro
See Iwamatsu, Jun Atsushi
See also CLR 4
Yates, Elizabeth 1905- *4*
See also SAAS 6
Yates, Raymond F(rancis)
1895-1966 .... *31*
Yaukey, Grace S(ydenstricker)
1899- *5*
Yeakley, Marjory Hall 1908- *21*
Yeatman, Linda 1938- *42*
Yensid, Retlaw
See Disney, Walt(er Elias)
Yeo, Wilma (Lethem) 1918- *24*
Yeoman, John (Brian) 1934- *28*
Yep, Laurence M. 1948- *7*
See also CLR 3
Yerian, Cameron John *21*
Yerian, Margaret A. *21*

Yolen, Jane H. 1939- *40*
Earlier sketch in SATA 4
See also CLR 4
See also SAAS 1
Yonge, Charlotte Mary
1823-1901 .... *17*
Yorinks, Arthur 1953- *49*
Earlier sketch in SATA 33
York, Andrew
See Nicole, Christopher Robin
York, Carol Beach 1928- *6*
York, Rebecca
See Buckholtz, Eileen (Garber)
Yost, Edna 1889-1971
Obituary *26*
Youd, C. S. 1922-
See SAAS 6
Youd, (Christopher) Samuel
1922- *47*
Brief Entry *30*
See also SAAS 6
Young, Bob
See Young, Robert W.
Young, Clarence [Collective
pseudonym] *1*
Young, Dorothea Bennett
1924- *31*
Young, Ed 1931- *10*
Young, Edward
See Reinfeld, Fred
Young, Elaine L.
See Schulte, Elaine L(ouise)
Young, Jan
See Young, Janet Randall
Young, Janet Randall 1919- *3*
Young, Lois Horton
1911-1981 .... *26*
Young, Margaret B(uckner)
1922- *2*
Young, Miriam 1913-1934 .... *7*
Young, (Rodney Lee) Patrick (Jr.)
1937- *22*
Young, Percy M(arshall)
1912- *31*
Young, Robert W. 1916-1969 ..... *3*
Young, Scott A(lexander)
1918- *5*
Young, Vivien
See Gater, Dilys
Youngs, Betty 1934-1985 .... *53*
Obituary *42*

Z

Zach, Cheryl (Byrd) 1947-
Brief Entry *51*
Zaffo, George J. (?)-1984 .... *42*
Zaid, Barry 1938- *51*
Zaidenberg, Arthur 1908(?)- *34*
Zalben, Jane Breskin 1950- *7*
Zallinger, Jean (Day) 1918- *14*
Zallinger, Peter Franz 1943- *49*
Zappler, Lisbeth 1930- *10*
Zarchy, Harry 1912- *34*
Zarif, Margaret Min'imah
(?)-1983 .... *33*
Zaring, Jane (Thomas) 1936- *51*
Brief Entry *40*

Zaslavsky, Claudia 1917- *36*
Zeck, Gerald Anthony 1939- *40*
Zeck, Gerry
  See Zeck, Gerald Anthony
Zei, Alki *24*
  See also CLR 6
Zelazny, Roger (Joseph Christopher)
  1937-
  Brief Entry *39*
Zelinsky, Paul O. 1953- *49*
  Brief Entry *33*
Zellan, Audrey Penn 1950- *22*
Zemach, Harve 1933- *3*
Zemach, Kaethe 1958- *49*
  Brief Entry *39*
Zemach, Margot 1931- *21*
Zens, Patricia Martin 1926-1972
  Brief Entry *50*

Zerman, Melvyn Bernard
  1930- *46*
Ziemienski, Dennis 1947- *10*
Zillah
  See Macdonald, Zillah K.
Zim, Herbert S(pencer) 1909- *30*
  Earlier sketch in SATA 1
  See also CLR 2
  See also SAAS 2
Zim, Sonia Bleeker
  See Bleeker, Sonia
Zimelman, Nathan
  Brief Entry *37*
Zimmerman, Naoma 1914- *10*
Zimnik, Reiner 1930- *36*
  See also CLR 3
Zindel, Bonnie 1943- *34*
Zindel, Paul 1936- *16*
  See also CLR 3

Ziner, (Florence) Feenie
  1921- *5*
Zion, (Eu)Gene 1913-1975 .... *18*
Zollinger, Gulielma 1856-1917
  Brief Entry *27*
Zolotow, Charlotte S. 1915- *35*
  Earlier sketch in SATA 1
  See also CLR 2
Zonia, Dhimitri 1921- *20*
Zubrowski, Bernard 1939- *35*
Zupa, G. Anthony
  See Zeck, Gerald Anthony
Zurhorst, Charles (Stewart, Jr.)
  1913- *12*
Zuromskis, Diane
  See Stanley, Diane
Zweifel, Frances 1931- *14*
Zwinger, Ann 1925- *46*